JUDICIAL CREATIVITY AT THE INTERNATIONAL CRIMINAL TRIBUNALS

Judicial Creativity at the International Criminal Tribunals

Edited by
SHANE DARCY
JOSEPH POWDERLY

This publication was grant-aided by the Publications Fund of National University of Ireland, Galway

OXFORD
UNIVERSITY PRESS

OXFORD
UNIVERSITY PRESS

Great Clarendon Street, Oxford OX2 6DP

Oxford University Press is a department of the University of Oxford.
It furthers the University's objective of excellence in research, scholarship,
and education by publishing worldwide in

Oxford New York

Auckland Cape Town Dar es Salaam Hong Kong Karachi
Kuala Lumpur Madrid Melbourne Mexico City Nairobi
New Delhi Shanghai Taipei Toronto

With offices in

Argentina Austria Brazil Chile Czech Republic France Greece
Guatemala Hungary Italy Japan Poland Portugal Singapore
South Korea Switzerland Thailand Turkey Ukraine Vietnam

Oxford is a registered trade mark of Oxford University Press
in the UK and in certain other countries

Published in the United States
by Oxford University Press Inc., New York

First published 2010

British Library Cataloguing in Publication Data
Data available

Library of Congress Cataloging-in-Publication Data
Judicial creativity at the international criminal tribunals / edited by
Shane Darcy and Joseph Powderly.
p. cm.
Includes bibliographical references and index.
ISBN 978–0–19–959146–6 (hardback: alk. paper)
1. International criminal courts. 2. International offences.
3. Criminal procedure (International law). 4. Judicial process.
I. Darcy, Shane. II. Powderly, Joseph.
KZ6304.J83 2010
345′.01—dc22 2010036769

Typeset by Newgen Imaging Systems (P) Ltd., Chennai, India
Printed in Great Britain
on acid-free paper by
CPI Antony Rowe, Chippenham, Wiltshire

ISBN 978–0–19–959146–6

3 5 7 9 10 8 6 4 2

Acknowledgements

This collection is the continuation of a conversation that began between the two editors a couple of years back on the subject of the judiciary's role in the development of international law. Struck by the rapid development of international criminal law and the part played by judges in that process, we decided to undertake further exploration of the subject and to bring together scholars, judges, and practitioners who could add more substance to the conversation. This took the form of the *Judges as Lawmakers? Lecture Series*, held at the Irish Centre for Human Rights, National University of Ireland, Galway during the academic year 2008/2009. From the outset of the project, enthusiastic support and participation was given by the Centre's Director, Professor William A Schabas, for which we are most grateful. Many of the participants in the *Lecture Series* also contributed chapters to this collection; we would like to thank them for their willingness to engage with the subject and their openness to our editorial suggestions. At Oxford University Press we would like to thank John Louth and Merel Alstein for the keen interest they showed in this venture and their assistance in seeing it to fruition, and that of Jodi Towler. We would also like to acknowledge the funding provided by the National University of Ireland, Galway for this publication and the support provided by the editors' respective institutions, the Irish Centre for Human Rights and the TMC Asser Institute. Various other individuals contributed in different ways during the life of the project and we would like to thank Abou Abass, Roger Clark, Niamh Hayes, Fergal Gaynor, Wolfgang Schomburg, and Mohamed Shahabuddeen. Particular thanks are owed to John Reynolds, Rachel Sanchez and Helen McDermott for their invaluable assistance.

Shane Darcy
Galway

Joseph Powderly
The Hague
May 2010

Contents—Summary

Contents

III. FORMS OF CRIMINAL LIABILITY

List of Contributors

Gideon Boas is a Senior Lecturer in the Law Faculty of Monash University, Australia, and a former Senior Legal Officer at the International Criminal Tribunal for the former Yugoslavia. He is widely published in the field of international criminal law, and is the author of *The Milošević Trial: Lessons for the Conduct of International Criminal Proceedings* (Cambridge University Press, 2007) and co-author of the three-volume International Criminal Law Practitioner Library Series (Cambridge University Press, 2007, 2008, Volume III in press). Dr Boas has worked for the Red Cross and has extensive experience as a consultant to governments, the United Nations, and non-governmental organizations in international, humanitarian, and criminal law.

John Coughlan is a legal consultant at the Cambodian Center for Human Rights and holds a BCL from University College Cork and an LLM from Queens University Belfast and the Irish Centre for Human Rights. He has previously worked on the appeal brief for Issa Hassan Sesay at the Special Court for Sierra Leone and for the Office of the Co-Prosecutor at the Extraordinary Chambers in the Courts of Cambodia.

Robert Cryer is Professor of International and Criminal Law at the University of Birmingham. In addition to a large number of articles and book chapters he is the author of several monographs including *The Tokyo International Military Tribunal: A Reappraisal* (Oxford University Press, 2008) with Neil Boister; *Introduction to International Criminal Law and Procedure* (Cambridge University Press, 2nd edn, 2010) with Elizabeth Wilmshurst, Håkan Friman, and Darryl Robinson; and *Prosecuting International Crimes: Selectivity in the International Criminal Regime* (Cambridge University Press, 2005). He is co-editor of the *Journal of Conflict and Security Law*.

Shane Darcy is a Lecturer at the Irish Centre for Human Rights, National University of Ireland, Galway. He has published several academic articles in the fields of international humanitarian law, criminal law, and human rights and is the author of the monograph *Collective Responsibility and Accountability under International Law* (Transnational, 2007). He also edited *Truth Commission and Courts: The Tension Between Criminal Prosecutions and the Search for Truth* (Kluwer, 2005) with William A Schabas. He is an associate editor of *Criminal Law Forum*.

Fidelma Donlon is the Deputy Registrar of the Special Court for Sierra Leone. She was formerly the Deputy Registrar of the Bosnian War Crimes Chamber, the Head of the Criminal Institutions and Prosecutorial Reform Unit in the Office of the High Representative, and an adviser to the Special Court for Sierra Leone on residual issues and its residual mechanism. She is a doctoral candidate at the Irish Centre for Human Rights, National University of Ireland, Galway.

Caroline Fournet is a Senior Lecturer in Law at the University of Exeter and a Fellow of the Higher Education Academy. She is the author of a number of articles and book chapters in the area of public international and international criminal law. She is the author of the books *International Crimes—Theories, Practice and Evolution* (Cameron May, 2006) and *The Crime of Destruction and The Law of Genocide: Their Impact on Collective Memory* (Ashgate, 2007).

Håkan Friman is Deputy Director-General of the Swedish Ministry of Justice Division for Criminal Cases and International Judicial Cooperation, Visiting Professor of Law at University College London, and a former Associate Judge of Appeals of Svea Court of Appeals, Sweden. He has served as a member of the Swedish International Criminal Court delegation since 1996, notably at the Rome Conference. He is the author of numerous publications in international criminal law, including the recent collaboration *An Introduction to International Criminal Law and Procedure* (Cambridge University Press, 2nd edn, 2010) with Elizabeth Wilmshurst, Gideon Boas, and Darryl Robinson. He is a member of the editorial board of the *Nordic Journal of Human Rights.*

Niamh Hayes is a PhD candidate at the Irish Centre for Human Rights, at the National University of Ireland, Galway, and the holder of a Government of Ireland Postgraduate Scholarship. She has lectured in International Criminal Law at Trinity College Dublin, is a case reporter in international criminal law for the *Oxford Reports on International Law*, and worked as a defence intern in the trial of Radovan Karadžić at the International Criminal Tribunal for the former Yugoslavia.

Larissa van den Herik is Associate Professor of Public International Law at Leiden University. She is editor-in-chief of the *Leiden Journal of International Law.* Her PhD thesis, *The Contribution of the Rwanda Tribunal to the Development of International Law*, was published by Martinus Nijhoff in 2005. She has published extensively on UN sanctions and international criminal law, and is co-editor of *Future Perspectives on International Criminal Justice* (Cambridge University Press, 2010) and *Diversification and Fragmentation in International Criminal Law* (Cambridge University Press, forthcoming in 2011), both with Carsten Stahn.

Gillian Higgins is a barrister at 25 Bedford Row, London and lectures in criminal defence and international criminal law. She has represented several individuals charged with genocide, crimes against humanity, and war crimes, including a former head of state before the Yugoslavia and Rwanda Tribunals. She has lectured extensively on fair trial rights and provided consultancy advice for NGOs and institutions, including the Kurdish Human Rights Project, the State Court of Bosnia and Herzegovina in Sarajevo, and the Extraordinary Chambers in the Courts of Cambodia. She is a founding member of the International Criminal Law Bureau <http://www.internationalcriminallawbureau.com>.

Wayne Jordash is a barrister at Doughty Street Chambers, London specializing in criminal defence and human rights law. He has represented clients in the United Kingdom, at the Yugoslavia and Rwanda Tribunals, and at the Special Court for Sierra Leone. He has been employed as a consultant to the Defence Support Service at the Extraordinary Chambers in the Courts of Cambodia and is a Counsellor at the Cambodian Center for Human Rights.

Joseph Powderly is a Researcher in international criminal law and humanitarian law at the TMC Asser Institute in the Netherlands. He is a PhD candidate and Government of

Ireland Postgraduate Scholar at the Irish Centre for Human Rights, researching theories of judicial interpretation and the development of international criminal and international humanitarian law. He holds an LLM in International Human Rights Law, BA and LLB from the National University of Ireland, Galway. He is the author of over 80 case reports of decisions from the major international criminal tribunals in the peer-reviewed *Oxford Reports on International Criminal Law* for Oxford University Press. He is Managing Editor of *Criminal Law Forum*.

Fabián Raimondo is Assistant Professor at the Department of International and European Law, Maastricht University and a Member of the List of Counsel before the International Criminal Court. He has published extensively in the area of public international and international criminal law. His book, *General Principles of Law in the Decisions of International Courts and Tribunals* was published by Martinus Nijhoff in 2008.

William A Schabas is Director of the Irish Centre for Human Rights at the National University of Ireland, Galway, where he holds the chair in human rights law. Professor Schabas was named an Officer of the Order of Canada in 2006 and was elected a member of the Royal Irish Academy in 2007. He is the author of numerous articles in academic journals and several monographs on human rights and international criminal law, including *The International Criminal Court:* A *Commentary on the Rome Statute* (Oxford University Press, 2010) and *Genocide in International Law* (Cambridge University Press, 2nd edn, 2009). He is editor-in-chief of *Criminal Law Forum*. He is also Global Legal Scholar at University of Warwick School of Law.

Mohamed Shahabuddeen served as a judge at the International Court of Justice (1988–1997) and in the Appeals Chamber of International Criminal Tribunals for Rwanda and the former Yugoslavia (1997–2009). Judge Shahabuddeen had been elected as a judge to the International Criminal Court in 2009 but resigned prior to taking up the position for personal reasons. He is the author of the monograph *Precedent in the World Court* (Cambridge University Press, 1996) and numerous academic articles and book chapters. He is a member of the Institut de Droit International and of the Société Française de Droit International.

Göran Sluiter is Professor of International Criminal Law at the University of Amsterdam and a judge at the district courts of Utrecht and The Hague. He has published a number of monographs in the area of international criminal law, including *International Criminal Law: A Critical Introduction* (Oxford University Press, 2007) with Alexander Zahar; and *The Emerging Practice of the International Criminal Court* (Brill, 2008) with Carsten Stahn. He is also co-editor (with André Klip) of the series entitled *Annotated Leading Cases of the International Criminal Tribunals* published by Intersentia.

Patricia M Wald served as a judge at the International Criminal Tribunal for the former Yugoslavia (1999–2001), after having served for 20 years on the United States Court of Appeals for the District of Columbia (1979–1999). She has served as vice president of the American Law Institute and is an adviser to the Model Penal Code Sentencing Project. Judge Wald serves on the Open Society Institute's Justice Initiative Board and was a member of the President's Commission on the Intelligence Capabilities of the United States Regarding Weapons of Mass Destruction. She is the author of *Tyrants on Trial; Keeping Order in the Courtroom* (Open Society Institute, 2009).

Table of Cases

INTERNATIONAL CRIMINAL TRIBUNAL FOR THE FORMER YUGOSLAVIA

INTERNATIONAL CRIMINAL TRIBUNAL FOR RWANDA

INTERNATIONAL CRIMINAL COURT

EXTRAORDINARY CHAMBERS IN THE COURTS OF CAMBODIA

SPECIAL COURT FOR SIERRA LEONE

INTERNATIONAL COURT OF JUSTICE

EUROPEAN COURT OF HUMAN RIGHTS

AFRICAN COMMISSION ON HUMAN AND PEOPLES' RIGHTS

NATIONAL COURTS

MILITARY TRIBUNALS

Note from the Bench

Doing justice in individual cases is hard enough. Creating a system for doing justice across international boundaries is of a different dimension entirely. That was, however, what the United Nations Security Council, with no experience at all in running a court, set out to do in 1993 as the means to prosecute and try the worst perpetrators of war crimes, crimes against humanity, and genocide against civilian victims in the still raging conflict in the former Yugoslavia. United Nations Security Council Resolution 808, accompanied by a relatively barebones statute and a Report by the Secretary-General, provided the provenance of the newborn International Criminal Tribunal for the former Yugoslavia (ICTY). Fourteen judges were to be selected by the General Assembly, a Prosecutor picked by the Security Council, and some basic trial rights guaranteed for accused persons—that was it. Unanchored in any cohesive system of governance such as surrounds most courts, wanting any unified code of laws except for the loose collection of treaties, treatises, and national precedents that make up 'customary law', without ancestry except for the Nuremberg and Tokyo post-Second World War tribunals established under Allied military auspices a half century before, the ICTY was launched onto an unpredictable geopolitical sea. What made its task even more awesome was the knowledge that its decisions and the consequences emanating therefrom would be final; no disgruntled legislature could change the law its judges pronounced and no higher court could reverse or revise its rulings. The Court's funding was subject to the volatile winds of United Nations budgeting and it had no process to compel the presence of witnesses or defendants. Even its supporters wondered if it would survive. The International Criminal Tribunal for Rwanda (ICTR), created by Security Council Resolution 955 in the following year, faced many of the same challenges.

And indeed the early years were lean; suspects did not voluntarily surrender in any numbers to the Tribunal nor did states hand them over willingly despite Article 9 of the ICTY Statute which accorded the Court jurisdictional priority over national judiciaries in cases which fell within its temporal and geographical jurisdiction. In 1994, the ICTY obtained custody of its first defendant by claiming priority over a low-level war crimes suspect in German custody. With the trial of Dŭsko Tadić began one of the twentieth century's most daring jurisprudential adventures, one which eventually morphed into a cluster of international and hybrid courts and the establishment of the world's first permanent international criminal tribunal, the International Criminal Court (ICC). Throughout their one-and-a-half-decade history, the finances of the ICTY and ICTR have never been secure, the sources of their 'law' never entirely clear-cut, the press often critical, and states whose nationals became suspects sometimes outright hostile. But over time the ICTY and ICTR have built a brand new justice institution which has impacted the way national leaders behave in wartime with respect to civilian populations and the way they are treated by other states when they resist the Court's jurisdiction. They have instilled the perception for atrocity victims that some accountability is attainable. The international court option has become an inevitable ingredient of the global dialogue during and in the aftermath of international and civil wars. Most critically, the ICTY and ICTR experience has demonstrated that a fair trial in accord with international standards may be had with judges from different legal cultures and judicial systems. It is fair to say that, had it failed on this critical criterion, the international court movement might well have been stillborn.

But make no mistake: creativity was the mantra of the new Courts. It had to be. Any court, no matter what its origins or its placement in a wider justice system, confronts daily myriad questions for which there is no ready answer in its statute or in precedent: the power relationship between the judges and the Prosecutor; the treatment of the defendant outside the courtroom; the protection of key witnesses; the selection and instruction of crucial court personnel, such as clerks, translators, and archivists—all of these day-to-day operational problems are negotiated with different results in different courts. In brand new courts they must be invented from scratch. Even the ethical 'dos and don'ts' for judges; the way in which their verdicts and rulings are written and delivered; the speed which they demand of one another in doing their work—all of these must come together early on and are subject to continual reappraisal thereafter. At the apex of the court's persona is the consuming question of where does the law come from? For if a court is to claim roots in a global rule of law community, it must make a persuasive case for the legitimacy of its authority to transcend national law and send men (and women) to prison with the infamous brand of war criminal or *génocidaire*.

The role of judicial creativity at the ICTY with which I am most familiar because of my service as a judge there, in identifying and articulating its law, was indisputable but it had to be performed in a cautious and carefully crafted way. The ICTY's baptismal papers—its Statute and the Secretary-General's Report—sought to reassure states and sceptics that this new court would not make up its own law, but rather administer that elusive body of 'customary international law' that has been described as the practices that civilized states follow from a sense of obligation. Customary law assuredly was 'out there' but not to be found in any single or set of books or opinions; its components lie quiescent in national court opinions, treatises, treaties, conventions, and declarations of international bodies. Inevitably judges and experts in the field will not agree as to what it is and where it is. Yet, acceptance of the concept of customary law and its discoverability was an essential umbrella for the Court. As one of the essays in this collection points out, that assumption was even more critical in criminal law than in civil law, given that under the universally recognized doctrine of *nullum crimen sine lege* no one must be convicted of a crime that was not recognized as such at the time of its commission. Yet, as Larissa van den Herik notes, when it comes to customary international law, 'a perceived vagueness regarding its content sits uneasily with the criminal law requirements of certainty and specificity of offences'.

Judges in all higher echelon courts, national or international, recognize early on that whatever the compulsory assurances they gave when appointed that they would only apply the law and not create it, drawing that line is not so simple in practice. First, the unique imperative that courts work under is that, unlike their political counterparts, the Executive and Legislature, they must decide the cases before them, one way or another, and decide them promptly. Other officials can on occasion kick them over to another branch or even bring them to popular vote; that choice is not open to criminal court judges. Just as higher court judges in democratic countries must find answers to the most controversial political and cultural, even moral questions of their day in cryptic phrases in their Constitutions, and just as different judges on the same court frequently construe the same phrases with vastly different outcomes, so the newly minted judges of the ICTY and their successors even to this day must hunt not only in their Statute, but in legal documents, general principles, and practices around the globe for their touchstones on what constitutes a fair and reasonably efficient process to try defendants for violations of international law. Not surprisingly for both national and international judges, the hunt seldom climaxes in a 'Eureka! I have found it' moment; it is rather a journey of exploration horizontally across courts and countries and vertically, through experience with different cases in the same court over time. The first search does not always produce the prize; a dialogue is often indispensable between judges from different backgrounds and even from different courts in order to arrive at an articulation of customary international law that is acceptable to a global audience. Even then the process does not stop. Debates ensue as to whether the customary law principle identified in one case can be extended to new situations or is frozen in its prior applications. Professor van den Herik's fascinating piece on the development of crimes against humanity, a jurisdictional growth stock at the ICTY, traces its path from the 'cacophony' of definitions inherited by the Court from a variety of sources, through a succession of refinements and reformulations that is still a work in progress. As she points out, customary law is theoretically based on accepted practices among states but, in the area of human rights, which in its very essence involves human beings in conflict with states rather than states in dispute with one another, relevant state practices may be scant or even non-existent, and creative resort to general principles and secondary sources must be made. Robert Cryer's chapter ventures into the law of command responsibility, a key to criminal liability for the highest rank of war criminals, and chronicles how the Court agonized over whether it could proceed 'creatively' from past applications of command responsibility for acts of subordinates committed while the defendant was in command to responsibility for acts committed before he took command, an interpretive process which underwent mid-term corrections from case to case and even in the rulings of individual judges. Future courts like the ICC may veer still further from the ICTY's latest ruling on the subject, but were it otherwise the path of international criminal law would be dead-ended.

Yes, of course the ICTY and the ICTR have and will be accused of 'creating' their own customary law. One can hope, however, that the criticism will not give way to a superficial and non-instructive debate about judicial activism or restraint such as our United States judges have had to endure. Law can progress and adapt nationally and internationally only through a creative process, taking what there is, be it customary international law, general principles, or statutory language and supplementing them (though not contradicting clear directives where they exist) by the common sense, experience, and logic that is required to make fair rulings in the cases at hand and to provide a base for future cases to build on. One particularly successful example of this approach is the evolution in the ICTY and the ICTR of the war crime of rape which had no definition in international criminal law and widely varying ones in national laws. There was no question it was and had to be a prosecutable war crime but there the consensus stopped. The *ad hoc* Tribunals were left to plunge ahead and come up with their consensual best in order to proceed with prosecutions of what had become a major instrument of abuse and torture used massively in the Bosnian and Rwandan conflicts. By using a combination of general principles, selecting among national decisions, and consulting scholarly writings, the Tribunals came up with workable definitions, though not identical ones, and dramatic advances were made for innocent women victims in the laws of war. If that be creativity, blessed be its name.

Judges universally acknowledge how important procedure is in determining outcomes: court rules govern the sequence of the proceedings, the admissibility of evidence, the consequences of parties' failures to follow rules. The ICTY was given unique powers not ordinarily accorded to national courts—its judges could make and amend their own rules in plenary session. In fifteen years the ICTY amended its rules 44 times, and much creativity was displayed. Interestingly, the Rome Statute took a different route for the ICC, giving its convenor Assembly of State Parties the ultimate rulemaking authority. Allowing judges to make their own rules, which in many cases turn out to be substantive in impact, and then letting the same judges interpret those rules and even amend them when they are unhappy with the results is somewhat problematic, as is persuasively argued in this collection. But to be fair, the ICTY judges have accomplished important and often necessary changes in the Court's operation through rulemaking: specifically the introduction of a pre-trial process nowhere to be found in its Statute whereby a pre-trial judge sorts out evidence disputes, works to cut down duplicative charges, and limits the number of witnesses or crime sites. In other procedural rulings the ICTY judges have accentuated their managerial role by radically altering their early tolerance of broad and vaguely worded indictments and insisting in later cases that charges be set out in detail, including material facts, precise modes of liability, and legal theories of the prosecution. One writer in this collection refers to the ICTY jurists as 'extremely powerful judges', and I would support that assessment. For both Tribunals.

Creativity in sum is necessary, proper, and desirable in a court, national or international. But it must have its own internal controls and it needs external critics and informed observers to call foul when it goes too far. International courts who have no partners in governance and who can function effectively only so long as they have credibility with those they exercise power over (and with donor governments who support them) are especially in need of responsible watchers. The former ICTY Chief Prosecutor, Carla Del Ponte, worries that the *ad hoc* courts have suffered from a lack of careful scrutiny and consequently vital 'course corrections' have not always occurred. In my own observation, internationalist and human rights sympathizers were so anxious for these courts to succeed that, in the early days, they were hesitant to apply the same critical yardsticks they regularly apply to national courts. However the pace and tenor of their criticism has quickened of late and not surprisingly it often comes from former Court staffers who have moved on to academia. And if the *ad hoc* Tribunals were spared biting critiques from the Academy in their infancy, that certainly is not true for the ICC which has become the focus of a great deal of popular, regional, and academic criticism (not all warranted in my view). Nonetheless, I believe that the ICTY would stand up against any attacks on the impartiality and independence of the judges from illegitimate homeland pressures, and given the difficulty of their task in finding the right legal principles to guide their decisions in the complex fact scenarios set before them, I suggest the appropriate standard by which they should be judged is adherence to a rule of law the sources of which they explain in a transparent and rational way so as to defuse any notion that they are acting out of personal preferences or whims. This in the main they have done, and as time goes by a larger body of precedent accumulates for them and other courts to draw upon.

Such a standard, however, puts great emphasis on the selection of judges of impeccable integrity and high intelligence. Candour compels an admission that the *ad hoc* Tribunals' process for picking judges has not always been geared to individual merit. In the beginning some countries nominated judges for their political loyalties or past national service, rather than for judicial or criminal law experience. Many had to learn on the job, and mistakes were made. Over the years it appears that countries have appreciated more the significance of an international court appointment but it is still not clear if selections by the United Nations or, in the case of the ICC, the Assembly of State Parties are made on an individual merits basis rather than in regional trade-offs. These are powerful men and women and they exercise extraordinary discretion in their judgments over the lives of accused persons and indeed over the future of international courts. They are our main guarantee that this new breed of international court will contribute its creative potential to world justice. The ICTY and the ICTR's intense and immense experience portrayed in a scholarly yet absorbing way in this compilation deserves a close reading by those who work in and around these courts and by those who should care about their future.

Patricia M Wald
Washington, DC
April 2010

Introduction

The International Criminal Tribunals and the Judicial Development of International Criminal Law

Shane Darcy and Joseph Powderly

> [I]n view of the difficulties surrounding the codification of international law, international tribunals will in the future fulfil, inconspicuously but efficiently, a large part of the task of developing international law.[1]

I. Introduction

After more than 15 years in operation, the International Criminal Tribunals for the former Yugoslavia (ICTY) and Rwanda (ICTR) are in the process of bringing their principal activities to an end. It is therefore an appropriate time to reflect upon the legacy of these ground-breaking institutions. Presently, much attention is being focused on the broader contributions that the Tribunals may have made to addressing issues such as impunity for international crimes, the restoration and maintenance of peace in war-torn countries, the delivery of justice for victims, the rebuilding and strengthening of domestic legal systems, and even the promotion of reconciliation among former parties to a conflict.[2] One of the most significant and more tangible achievements of the *ad hoc* Tribunals has

[1] RY Jennings and A Watts (eds), *Oppenheim's International Law: Volume I: Peace* (London/New York: Longmans, 9th edn, 1996) 41.

[2] 'Report of the President on the Conference Assessing the Legacy of the ICTY' (27 April 2010) availableat: <http://www.icty.org/x/file/Press/Events/100427_legacyconference_pdt_report.pdf>; F Pocar, 'Completion or Continuation Strategy? Appraising Problems and Possible Developments in Building the Legacy of the ICTY' (2008) 6(4) JICJ 655; T Abdulhak, 'Building Sustainable Capacities—From an International Tribunal to a Domestic War Crimes Chamber for Bosnia and Herzegovina' (2009) 9 ICLR 333; R Byrne, 'Promises of Peace and Reconciliation: Previewing the Legacy of the International Criminal Tribunal for Rwanda' (2006) 14 European Review 485; D Orentlicher, *Shrinking the Space for Denial: The Impact of the ICTY in Serbia* (London: Open Society Institute, 2008); JN Clark, 'International War Crimes Tribunals and the Challenge of Outreach' (2009) 9 ICLR 99.

been their progressive development of the rules, scope, and content of substantive and procedural international criminal law. The International Criminal Tribunals were the first international judicial bodies since Nuremberg and Tokyo tasked with trying individuals for crimes against humanity and war crimes; and for the crime of genocide they were the very first, as no international precedent existed for trying the 'crime of crimes'. In the prosecution of these crimes, the judges of the Tribunals have dutifully applied the laws and rules as set out in the Statutes, clarifying and elucidating legal concepts and principles in the nascent field of international criminal law. The *ad hoc* Tribunals have often gone beyond the mere application of the existing law, however, and have at times adopted highly creative interpretative approaches which have pushed the development of international criminal law. It is this judicial creativity at the International Criminal Tribunals that is the focus of this collection.

II. Context and Rationale

International criminal law is at a crossroads. The *ad hoc* Tribunals for Rwanda and the former Yugoslavia, the standard-bearers for the flourishing international criminal justice project for so many years, are edging towards the completion of their mandates. The permanent International Criminal Court (ICC), on the other hand, is now fully operational with a burgeoning caseload and is likely to eclipse if not replace other *ad hoc* international criminal justice efforts in the future. This reorientation requires an assessment of the contribution of the *ad hoc* Tribunals to the development of international criminal law thus far, the judicial role in that process, and the extent to which their approach has and may continue to influence the ICC. Taking stock of the achievements of the Tribunals at this juncture thus presents an opportunity for considering the present state of international criminal law as applied by international courts and tribunals. This collection explores the judicial creativity of the benches of the *ad hoc* Tribunals and seeks to establish and critique how their practice and jurisprudence has contributed to the development of international criminal law.

The collection focuses on the two seminal *ad hoc* international criminal courts established by the United Nations Security Council, the ICTY and the ICTR. They have been collectively responsible for the revival of international criminal law and represent the renewed commitment of the international community to the eradication of impunity for violations of international humanitarian law. One cannot be mentioned without the other; they are inextricably and deliberately linked not only in terms of their subject matter jurisdiction and the circumstances of their creation, but more significantly from the perspective of this collection, in terms of their shared judicial composition. They have benefited from a collective personality and their creative jurisprudential legacy must be considered in unison. As will be seen in the various chapters, the ICTY has often paved the way in this judicial enterprise, a reality that is partly explained as a matter of chronology. Although the collection's focus is ultimately on the ICTY and the ICTR, reference is also made to the practice and jurisprudence of other international and hybridized criminal tribunals, including the ICC, the Special Court for Sierra Leone (SCSL), and the Extraordinary Chambers in the Courts of Cambodia (ECCC). The focus on the ICTY and ICTR should not be considered as an affront to the jurisprudential contribution of these other important institutions.

III. Scope and Content

Judicial creativity at the International Criminal Tribunals for Rwanda and the former Yugoslavia and the challenges which it presents are addressed in this collection within five subject areas, each comprising a section of the book. The subjects are: sources of law and methods of judicial interpretation (Part I); definitions of substantive crimes (Part II); forms of criminal liability (Part III); fair trial rights and defences (Part IV); and procedure (Part V). The chapters within each section address a particular topic related to the subject area and consider the role that the judiciary has played in the evolution of that discrete aspect of criminal law at the international level. There are, however, clearly overlapping and recurring themes which are thoughtfully addressed by the authors throughout the collection. These include the role of judges in the creation of international law, the differing conceptions of this role in light of domestic traditions, and the compatibility of judicial creativity with the principle of legality.

In bringing these subjects and themes together, this collection seeks to address a *lacuna* in international criminal law scholarship within the specific context of the *ad hoc* Tribunals for the former Yugoslavia and Rwanda. The public international law canon contains notable studies on the nature of the international judicial function and the contribution of the judges to progressive legal development,[3] and international criminal law scholars have addressed this subject but often only with regard to specific issues.[4] This collection seeks to complement existing

[3] See eg H Lauterpacht, *The Development of International Law by the International Court* (London: Stevens & Sons, 1958); M Shahabuddeen, *Precedent in the World Court* (Cambridge: CUP, 1996); E McWhinney, *Judicial Settlement of International Disputes: Jurisdiction, Justiciability and Judicial Law-Making of the Contemporary International Court* (Boston: Martinus Nijhoff, 1991).

[4] See eg T Meron, 'War Crimes in Yugoslavia and the Development of International Law' (1994) 88 AJIL 78; A Cassese, 'Black Letter Lawyering v. Constructive Interpretation' (2004) 2 JICJ 265; L Sadat, 'The Legacy of the ICTY: The International Criminal Court' (2003) 37 *New England Law Review* 1073; WA Schabas, 'Interpreting the Statutes of the *ad hoc* Tribunals' in L Chand

studies which have focused on the emergence of the institutions of international criminal justice and the evolution of international criminal law,[5] by specifically considering judicial creativity at the *ad hoc* Tribunals across a range of substantive and procedural topics. The book brings together scholars, judges, and practitioners, seeking to provide a range of viewpoints in its comprehensive, although not exhaustive, analysis of the role of judges of the *ad hoc* Tribunals in the development of international criminal law.

A. Sources of law and judicial interpretation

The approach of the *ad hoc* Tribunals with respect to the treatment of the traditional sources of international law, as derived from Article 38(1) of the Statute of the International Court of Justice, has given rise to significant comment throughout the literature on the relevant jurisprudence. Of particular and persistent concern has been the manner in which the bench has gone about the task of identifying those legal norms that are 'beyond doubt' part of customary international law.[6] As emphasized in the Report of the Secretary-General on the establishment of the Yugoslavia Tribunal, the legitimacy of international criminal justice is fundamentally dependent on its interlinked conformity with customary international law and the principle of legality.[7] This theme is addressed in several of the contributions in this collection, notably in the chapters by Joseph Powderly and Larissa van den Herik. In his chapter, Joseph Powderly aptly lays the foundations for later discussions of the use of custom at the *ad hoc* Tribunals, as well as for the broader interpretational issues germane to the subject of judicial creativity in international criminal law. His chapter demonstrates how the absence of a provision explicitly setting down the methodology to be applied by the bench in the interpretation of the Statutes of the *ad hoc* Tribunals ensured that the only barriers to judicial creativity were the principle of legality (*nullum crimen sine lege*) and fidelity to customary international law. These were in essence the 'golden rules' guiding the bench. While the laconic nature of the Statutes may have weakened the traditional shackles on judicial lawmaking, this also gave rise to an element of interpretational uncertainty. Powderly shows, however, that attempts

Vohrah *et al* (eds), *Man's Inhumanity to Man: Essays on International Law in Honour of Antonio Cassese* (The Hague: Kluwer Law International, 2003) 847–88; AM Danner and JS Martinez, 'Guilty Associations: Joint Criminal Enterprise, Command Responsibility, and the Development of International Criminal Law' (2005) 93 *California Law Review* 75.

[5] WA Schabas, *The UN International Criminal Tribunals* (Cambridge: CUP, 2006); G Mettraux, *International Crimes and the Ad Hoc Tribunals* (Oxford: OUP, 2005); R May *et al* (eds), *Essays on ICTY Procedure and Evidence: In Honour of Gabrielle Kirk McDonald* (The Hague: Kluwer Law International, 2001); G Sluiter and A Zahar, *International Criminal Law: A Critical Introduction* (Oxford: OUP, 2007).

[6] 'Report of the Secretary-General Pursuant to Paragraph 2 of Security Council Resolution 808 (1993)', UN Doc S/25704 (3 May 1993) para 34. [7] ibid.

to remain within the confines of these golden rules, particularly with respect to customary international law, have proved difficult at times. This chapter also includes an examination of the manner in which the *ad hoc* Tribunals have applied the rules of interpretation which appear to have been available by analogy—namely the rules enumerated in Articles 31 to 33 of the Vienna Convention on the Law of Treaties. The discussion demonstrates that, although the resort to these rules was for the most part justified, their application was frequently chaotic and unsystematic. However, the results arrived at were undoubtedly responsible for the progressive development of international criminal law by the *ad hoc* Tribunals.

While Powderly focuses on issues relevant to conventional and customary sources of international law, Fabián Raimondo explores the manner in which the *ad hoc* Tribunals have had recourse to general principles of law. Although they are generally recognized as a secondary or subsidiary source of law, the chapter shows how general principles have proved to be a valuable and legitimate springboard for judicial creativity. Raimondo provides an important insight into the crucial role they have played both as gap-filling tools in the interpretation of the Statutes and as useful reinforcements of Tribunal findings vis-à-vis conventional treaty and customary law. These opening chapters give a sense of the significant interpretational hurdles facing the judges at the *ad hoc* Tribunals in the practical and legitimate implementation of their basic constituent statutes, while also examining the methodological options available in order to surmount these difficulties. The remainder of the chapters in the collection analyse the fruits of this judicially creative labour.

B. Definition of crimes

Even the most cursory consideration of international criminal law will reveal the considerable divergence that has existed among states as regards those activities that should be criminalized at the international level and how such crimes should then be defined. Terrorism, aggression, and drug-trafficking are particular examples of this continued debate. The subject-matter jurisdiction of the *ad hoc* Tribunals was clear in terms of the categories of crimes for which individuals could be tried: genocide, crimes against humanity, and war crimes. However, the Statute did not provide detailed definitions of these crimes and the Tribunals have had to grapple with the scope of the overarching categories and the definition of various elements of specific crimes. For Judge Abi-Saab of the Appeals Chamber of the ICTY, the pursuit of greater legal coherence in this context was 'a worthwhile judicial pursuit':

> The International Criminal Tribunal for the former Yugoslavia, together with the International Tribunal for Rwanda, are thus afforded a unique opportunity to assume the responsibility for the further rationalisation of these categories [of international crimes] at

some distance from the historical and psychological conditions from which they emerged and from the perspective of the evolving international legal order.[8]

Genocide was one of the first international crimes to be prohibited by an international treaty, the 1948 Convention on the Prevention and Punishment of the Crime of Genocide.[9] William Schabas considers judicial activism in the context of the crime of genocide and notes from the outset that, in contrast to crimes against humanity and war crimes, the definition of this crime has not evolved significantly since 1948. As international criminal judges broadened and expanded the scope of the former, they retained a strict and narrow construction of genocide. That being said, judicial creativity has not been absent when it comes to genocide, as was witnessed in the *Eichmann* case where the District Court of Jerusalem (with the subsequent approval of the Supreme Court, sitting as a Court of Criminal Appeal) determined that, despite the provisions of Article VI of the Genocide Convention, genocide was undoubtedly a crime to which universal jurisdiction was attached. In the context of the *ad hoc* Tribunals, Schabas explores the less successful attempts at judicial activism in the *Akayesu* and *Krstić* cases. The ICTR's attempt to extend the scope of genocide to any 'stable and permanent groups' in the *Akayesu* case, in particular, highlights the shortcomings of judicial creativity in the absence of a convincing legal analysis. That said, even the presence of sound analysis is no guarantee of development, as evidenced in the ICTY's failure to adopt the reasoning of Judge Shahabuddeen expressed in his dissenting opinion in the *Krstić* case to the effect that the crime of genocide included 'cultural genocide' and 'ethnic cleansing'. The expansive development of crimes against humanity, Schabas observes, explains the continued reliance on the definition of genocide as adopted in 1948.

The 'reconceptualization' of crimes against humanity by the *ad hoc* Tribunals is the subject of Larissa van den Herik's chapter. She looks at the use of customary international law in the context of crimes against humanity, a category of crimes which was largely uncodified prior to the adoption of the Rome Statute of the International Criminal Court. In addressing the various general requirements or *chapeau* elements of crimes against humanity—particularly in relation to the armed conflict nexus, the policy requirement, and the civilian population aspect—the judges were at times inconsistent in the means used for the identification of evidence of customary international law. This is especially evident in the selective use of national case law, from which questionable deductions were often made. Observing the trend towards a more modern formation of customary international law, the author recognizes the potential for judicial creativity based on this source but queries its overall suitability in the context of international criminal law. The pertinent question is posed as to whether the contribution of

[8] *Prosecutor v Tadić* (Appeals Chamber Decision on the Defence Motion for Interlocutory Appeal on Jurisdiction, Separate Opinion of Judge Abi-Saab) IT-94-1-AR72 (2 October 1995).

[9] (1951) 78 UNTS 277.

the *ad hoc* Tribunals to this renewed conception of crimes against humanity is 'sustainable beyond the particular field of operation of each tribunal'.

A similar question in the context of war crimes received an affirmative response from the drafters of the Rome Statute of the International Criminal Court, when they followed the ICTY finding in *Tadić* that war crimes could be committed in non-international armed conflicts. Shane Darcy looks at how judicial creativity at the *ad hoc* Tribunals has led to a reinvention of the law of war crimes, arguably the most far-reaching jurisprudential contribution of the Tribunals. Darcy carefully considers the *Tadić* jurisprudence relating to grave breaches and 'violations of the laws and customs of war' and explores how the formulation for war crimes devised by the Appeals Chamber has been followed with regard to specific offences. The potential downside of such expansive conceptions of the law is whether they compromise the rights of accused persons in possibly violating the principle of *nullum crimen sine lege*. In exploring this question, Darcy asserts that the culmination of the work of the *ad hoc* Tribunals may mark the end of an era of judicial creativity in the context of the international law of war crimes.

The crime of rape is one which has historically evaded both prosecution and definition in international criminal law. However, the jurisprudence of the *ad hoc* Tribunals fundamentally altered this shameful status quo. Rounding off this Part, Niamh Hayes argues that the efforts of the judges of the *ad hoc* Tribunals to identify and develop a definition of rape as an international crime are 'a classic illustration of judicial interpretation in action'. A contrast is drawn between the expansive, conceptual reasoning of the ICTR Trial Chamber in the *Akayesu* case and the mechanistic definition of the elements of the crime of rape derived from domestic criminal law in the *Kunarac* case. Hayes critically but constructively assesses various aspects of the reasoning of the *ad hoc* Tribunals and strongly questions the legitimacy of reading notions of consent into the *mens rea* of the offence. It is clear from the survey of the case law that judicial creativity has been the driving force behind the renewed impetus for the removal of impunity for gross acts of rape and sexual violence in contemporary armed conflicts. The pivotal role played by female judges such as Navanethem Pillay, Elizabeth Odio-Benito, and Florence Mumba is highlighted by Hayes in this regard.

C. Forms of criminal liability

The noteworthy contribution of the *ad hoc* Tribunals to substantive international criminal law has covered both the actual offences for which an accused may be prosecuted and the various modes of liability that may be used to connect an individual to the crimes perpetrated. The Statutes of the Tribunals adopt a broad approach, stating that individual criminal responsibility could arise for persons who 'planned, instigated, ordered, committed or otherwise aided and abetted in the planning, preparation or execution' of crimes within the Tribunals' jurisdiction.[10] Superior responsibility was also expressly included in the Statutes as a form of criminal liability,[11] although its statutory basis did not preclude creative judicial interpretation of its contours. The other forms of criminal liability explored in Part III, joint criminal enterprise and omission liability for aiding and abetting, have become somewhat synonymous in the literature, not with acceptable creative judicial interpretation, but rather with out-and-out excessive lawmaking from the bench of the *ad hoc* Tribunals.

In his chapter on command responsibility, Robert Cryer considers that 'many, if not the majority of the developments' relating to this form of criminal liability have been the result of creative judicial activity. In exploring the application and development of command responsibility at the *ad hoc* Tribunals, he evaluates the extent to which the ICTY in particular has crystallized the law or, in fact, judicially created it. Cryer also questions whether the judges at the *ad hoc* Tribunals have fundamentally altered the basis of this form of liability. The chapter provides a fascinating recounting of the interplay between the majority and dissenting judges regarding the nature of command responsibility. It testifies to the validity of the remark made by Judge Gabrielle Kirk McDonald, then President of the ICTY, at the Rome Conference in 1998: 'The Tribunal's rules allowing for separate and dissenting opinions had proved highly beneficial to the development of international criminal law, and the availability of differing interpretations of that embryonic body of law had contributed to its maturation.'[12]

The judicial development of the doctrine of joint criminal enterprise as a form of criminal liability has arguably provoked the most debate and controversy throughout the lifetime of the *ad hoc* Tribunals as to the nature of the judicial function in an international criminal law context. Mohamed Shahabuddeen, former member of the Appeals Chamber of the ICTY and ICTR, as well as the International Court of Justice, tackles this thorny subject, and provides a fascinating comparative analysis of the competing doctrines of joint criminal enterprise and co-perpetratorship. He takes the view that neither form of criminal liability 'can claim the status of customary international law', a view echoed by the Pre-Trial Chamber of the Extraordinary Chambers in the Courts of Cambodia.[13] Shahabuddeen considers the mental element required for the third category of

[10] Statute of the International Criminal Tribunal for the Prosecution of Persons Responsible for Genocide and Other Serious Violations of International Humanitarian Law Committed in the Territory of Rwanda, UN Doc S/Res/955 (1994), Art 6(1); Statute of the International Tribunal for the Prosecution of Persons Responsible for Serious Violations of International Humanitarian Law Committed in the Territory of the Former Yugoslavia since 1991, UN Doc S/25704 (1993) 36, Annex and S/25704/Add.1 (1993), UN Doc S/RES/827, Art 7(1).

[11] ibid Arts 6(3) and 7(3) respectively.

[12] *United Nations Diplomatic Conference of Plenipotentiaries on the Establishment of an International Criminal Court*, Rome, June 1998, *Official Records*, Vol II, *Summary records of the plenary meetings*, 3rd Plenary Meeting, 16 June 1998, A/CONF.183/SR.2, para 108, p 79.

[13] Pre-Trial Chamber Decision on the Appeals Against the Co-Investigating Judge's Order on Joint Criminal Enterprise (JCE), Criminal Case File No 002/19-09-2007/OCIJ (PTC38) (20 May 2010).

joint criminal enterprise, problematic in the context of specific intent crimes, although he finds that in such circumstances 'knowledge amounts to intent'. He justifies the *ad hoc* Tribunals' reliance on the creativity of the bench, whereby new law is fashioned 'on the basis of the policy of the law as it can be extracted from the roots of the law'. This is to be contrasted with 'judicial activism', whereby such law is created on the basis of the 'personal predilections of the judges not anchored in existing law'. Shahabuddeen finds that judicial creativity can be used if there is a gap in the law which would prevent a court from dispensing justice under its constituent instrument.

Of these various heads of liability available to the *ad hoc* Tribunals, command responsibility has a clear statutory basis, while joint criminal enterprise was derived from customary international law, albeit unconvincingly so. The form of liability examined by Gideon Boas, aiding and abetting by omission, falls somewhere between the two, as aiding and a betting is a form of liability expressly included in the *ad hoc* Tribunals' Statutes, whereas the omission aspect is the product of judicial creativity with a debatable basis in custom. Boas critically analyses the existing case law on aiding and abetting by omission and questions whether this form of liability has a clear or coherent place in international criminal law. Highlighting the perceived weakness of the reasoning of the ICTY and ICTR in specific instances, Boas notes the inconsistent methodology used in the identification of customary international norms and in this respect addresses a recurring theme of the collection. Using Radovan Karadžić's motion challenging the customary foundations of omission liability as a template, Boas queries the reliance of the Tribunal on domestic case law to establish custom. He persuasively argues that evidence of state practice and *opinio juris* is not provided by simply stating a line of authority, 'unless somewhere along that line of authority is an articulation of such evidence'.

D. Fair trial rights and defences

The at times questionable customary international law status of certain elements of crimes and modes of criminal liability has been used on numerous occasions by defendants who seek to challenge the legitimacy of the jurisdiction of the Tribunals on the basis of a violation of the principle of legality. Caroline Fournet briefly considers *nullum crimen sine lege,* in her chapter on defences, given that counsel before the Tribunals have treated the principle as a defence 'of sorts'.[14] She explores how the law relating to permissible defences has yet to be definitively codified, despite the terms of Article 31 of the Rome Statute, and its primary importance in the efficacy and legitimacy of international criminal justice. Given that the Statutes of the ICTY and ICTR are ambiguous as to the defences that may be raised, such questions being left to the discretion of the bench, Fournet

[14] Sluiter and Zahar (n 5 above) 397.

looks at the manner in which the *ad hoc* Tribunals have approached the law of defences in the international criminal context. Taking into consideration defences such as superior orders, self-defence, and *tu quoque*, she draws interesting comparisons with the post-Second World War jurisprudence and the Rome Statute and highlights instances of significant creative judicial interpretation at the *ad hoc* Tribunals in this regard. The treatment of duress in the *Erdemović* case is a unique example in this context.

Unlike the International Military Tribunals at Nuremberg and Tokyo, the *ad hoc* Tribunals operate within the concrete parameters of international human rights law. Naturally this body of law is of particular relevance given the panoply of fair trial rights accruing to accused persons, as set out in numerous international human rights instruments such as the International Covenant on Civil and Political Rights and the European Convention on Human Rights.[15] Two particular fair trial rights are addressed in this Part: the right to self-representation and the right of an accused to be informed in detail of the charges against them. Gillian Higgins provides a practitioner's perspective on the development of the right to self-representation at the *ad hoc* Tribunals. She traces the manner in which the bench at the *ad hoc* Tribunals has dealt with—or perhaps more accurately, managed—those accused who have sought to represent themselves in proceedings and considers in particular examples of individuals suffering from ill-health or deliberately engaging in obstructionist behaviour. Self-representation has been an extremely controversial issue at the international criminal tribunals, in no small part due the invocation of the right by both Slobodan Milošević and Radovan Karadžić. Higgins criticizes the approach taken by the judiciary in dealing with the issue and explains the rationale behind the inherent creativity demonstrated in the process.

The question of the specificity required in indictments and the evolution of judicial thinking in this regard at the *ad hoc* Tribunals is explored in the contribution by Wayne Jordash and John Coughlan. It is an issue at the very heart of fairness in international criminal justice and the chapter provides an important perspective on the Tribunals' commitment to issues pertaining to the fundamental rights of accused persons to the presumption of innocence, fair trial, and due process. It is evident from the early jurisprudence of the ICTY that significant latitude was afforded to the Prosecutor in designating both the nature of the charges against those accused and the factual parameters upon which the charges were based. The authors highlight the shift away from less specific indictments, which in themselves were below the standard required in the majority of domestic jurisdictions, towards a more comprehensive indictments regime in which the

[15] International Covenant on Civil and Political Rights (1966), entered into force 23 March 1976, 999 UNTS 171, Arts 14 and 15; European Convention for the Protection of Human Rights and Fundamental Freedoms (1950), entered into force 3 September 1953, 213 UNTS 221, ETS 5, Arts 6 and 7. See W Schomburg, 'The Role of International Criminal Tribunals in Promoting Respect for Fair Trial Rights' (2009) 8:1 Nw JIHR 1.

rights of the accused were more robustly taken into consideration. In so doing, it is clear that the bench was acutely aware of the clear standards established by international human rights law and the early practice of the ICC appears to suggest that the approach adopted at the *ad hoc* Tribunals has translated into best practice.

E. Procedure

The proper role of the judiciary in the creation and elucidation of international law has been addressed in many of the chapters outlined above, with the authors very often concluding that judges do not generally possess expressly accepted lawmaking capabilities. In his report on the creation of the ICTY, the Secretary-General observed:

> It should be pointed out that, in assigning to the International Tribunal the task of prosecuting persons responsible for serious violations of international humanitarian law, the Security Council would not be creating or purporting to 'legislate' that law. Rather, the International Tribunal would have the task of applying existing international humanitarian law.[16]

Of course, this comment was directed at the substantive law to be applied by the *ad hoc* Tribunals, and when it comes to matters of procedural law the judges were directly given the power to create this law. Göran Sluiter examines the role played by the judges in creating the procedural rules which govern the functioning of the *ad hoc* Tribunals. He describes the judges as 'zealous legislators', while accepting the need for a dynamic procedural system. Sluiter queries whether this aspect of judicial lawmaking at the Tribunals has proven effective on the whole, and highlights the lack of transparency regarding the process of amending the rules of procedure and evidence and the possibility that this lawmaking power undermines judicial independence and conceptions of the separation of powers. In considering possible lessons to be learned, he asks whether the *ad hoc* Tribunals may themselves have contravened international human rights law, most notably in relation to the mechanism allowing for provisional release.

The conclusions of Göran Sluiter's chapter may be usefully compared with those of Håkan Friman, who finds that the judicial treatment of procedural rules has been defensible and satisfactory on the whole. He explains that the divergent approach of lawyers from different legal traditions is central to questions relating to the legitimacy of procedural lawmaking by judges. Using *in absentia* trials and the substitute Rule 61 procedure developed by the *ad hoc* Tribunals, he investigates how judges have addressed their role as procedural lawmakers. Friman observes that the judges have treated this role with due diligence and have acted responsibly by avoiding any controversial mechanisms and seeking

16 'Report of the Secretary-General' (n 6 above) para 29.

widely acceptable solutions as issues arise. In particular, various safeguards relating to *in absentia* trials were observed, as shown by an examination of the various approaches in national law and the findings of human rights bodies. In evaluating the practice of the ICTY on this matter, he finds that this requires an assessment which considers not only legal aspects, but also systemic and political factors: 'clearly a task of a legislator, but not necessarily one that sits comfortably with the role of a judge'.

The final chapter of the collection appropriately considers the role played by the bench of the *ad hoc* Tribunals, and in particular the Office of the President, in developing and implementing a procedural mechanism for the completion of the mandates of the tribunals. As Fidelma Donlon points out, the tribunals by their very nature were not intended to be permanent institutions, but neither the establishing resolutions of the Security Council, nor the Statutes contain guidance as to how or when their mandates would be deemed to be completed. Donlon shows how the impetus behind this scheme was provided not by the Security Council, but primarily by the judges themselves. In the judicial development of Rule 11*bis* and Rule 28(A) the bench brought into existence a method of domestic case referral based on a number of strict criteria cognizant of fundamental concepts of justice and human rights. She explores a host of issues surrounding these rules and inquires into the appropriateness and efficacy of the judicial development of such a mechanism and whether it compromised the discretion and policy of the Office of the Prosecutor.

IV. Parting Remarks

During the drafting of the London Charter of the International Military Tribunal at Nuremberg, General Iona Nikitchenko, later the primary Soviet Judge during the trial of the Major War Criminals, remarked that:

> [t]he judges who will be trying the case will be special, and they will not be bound by the ordinary rules and principles of British, American, French, or Soviet judges. They will certainly be able to draw conclusions. Although a national judge might not, the international judge should find his way through this.[17]

Like their predecessors at Nuremberg and Tokyo, the judges at the *ad hoc* Tribunals for the former Yugoslavia and Rwanda were left with no option but to find their way through the countless jurisprudential challenges placed before them. Armed with their reason, they have responded admirably to the task and have given life to a body of international law which had been largely dormant

[17] *Report of Robert H Jackson, United States Representative to the International Conference on Military Trials*, Department of State Publication 3080, International Organization and Conference Series II, European and British Commonwealth (February 1949) 249.

for the best part of a half-century. In order to make the law effective, creative interpretation within the confines of customary international law and the principle of legality was the route forward. In this regard, it is worth reiterating that, if implicit permission was given to exercise judicial creativity, boundaries were also imposed. In the words of Hersh Lauterpacht: 'However extensive the scope of law-creating judicial interpretation may be, it is always limited, although not totally determined, by existing legal materials. The undeniable freedom of judicial decision is one within the law.'[18] The chapters in this collection consider whether that has been the case at the *ad hoc* Tribunals for Rwanda and the former Yugoslavia.

[18] H Lauterpacht, *The Function of Law in the International Community* (Oxford: OUP, 1933) 103.

PART I

SOURCES OF LAW AND JUDICIAL INTERPRETATION

1

Judicial Interpretation at the *Ad Hoc* Tribunals: Method From Chaos?

Joseph Powderly[*]

I. Introduction

The original cohort of judges, comprising nine men and two women, elected to the bench of the International Criminal Tribunal for the former Yugoslavia (ICTY) in the autumn of 1993 found themselves in what could quite justifiably be described as a state of acute existential uncertainty. Theirs, purportedly, was an *ad hoc* international criminal tribunal established pursuant to the dictates of a Security Council Resolution passed under the authority of Chapter VII of the United Nations Charter.[1] However, despite the revolutionary tenor of its creation, at the moment of their swearing-in on 17 November 1993, they had neither premises, prosecutors, accused, rules of criminal procedure, nor indeed robes to call their own.[2] In the absence of any accused, the first eighteen months of existence were, in the words of the Tribunal's first President, Antonio Cassese, 'marked by alternating periods of nerve-racking longing to succeed and excruciating fear of total failure'.[3] Given the substantively undernourished state of the constituent Statute of the Tribunal and the fact that, at that point, there existed no Rules of Procedure and Evidence, it is not unreasonable that any prospective judge would experience some serious

* The author wishes to thank Niamh Hayes for her comments on previous drafts.

[1] UN Doc S/RES/808 (22 February 1993).

[2] A Cassese, 'The ICTY: A Living and Vital Reality' (2004) 2 JICJ 585, 585: 'When we Judges met on 17 November 1993 to be sworn in, we donned gowns borrowed from The Hague Bar Association…Our borrowed robes symbolized the total lack of infrastructures or facilities at our disposal. We had no seat, no courtroom, no prison, no budget, no computers, no law clerks, no secretaries and no set rules governing the criminal procedure.' See MP Scharf, *Balkan Justice: The Story Behind the First International War Crimes Trial Since Nuremberg* (North Carolina: Carolina Academic Press, 1997) 66; and LC Vohrah, 'Introduction' in LC Vohrah *et al* (eds), *Man's Inhumanity to Man: Essays On International Law in Honour of Antonio Cassese* (The Hague: Kluwer Law International, 2003) xx.

[3] Cassese (n 2 above) 585.

fear of failure.[4] The laconic Statute, drafted by the United Nations Office of Legal Affairs (headed by Carl August Fleischauer), could reasonably frustrate even the most creative judicial voices.

In a similar vein to the judges at Nuremberg and Tokyo before them (not to mention those involved in the various domestic prosecutions of international crimes, most notably in the seminal *Eichmann* case), to sit on the bench of the ICTY was implicitly to acknowledge the acceptability of at least a modicum of judicial creativity. This was certainly not the best venue for the expression of a heartfelt belief in the fundamental applicability of legal positivism. As Judge David Hunt eloquently put it: 'There was no Moses to produce on slabs of stone a code of commandments which were intended to be all-encompassing for all time.'[5] Indeed, it is far from an exaggeration to claim that judicial creativity, the sculpting of the relatively featureless granite of existing law in order to give it form, effect, and reason, is the life blood of international criminal law. This proclamation was effectively acknowledged in the judgment of the International Military Tribunal at Nuremberg where it stated that the 'law of war' enumerated under the London Charter was 'not static, but by continual adaptation follows the needs of a changing world'.[6] This comment was subsequently developed further in the *Justice* case (a Control Council No 10 proceeding) where the Tribunal stated *obiter* that:

> [i]nternational law is not the product of a statute. Its content is not static. The absence from the world of any governmental body authorized to enact substantive rules of international law has not prevented the progressive development of the law. After the manner of the English common law, it has grown to meet the exigencies of changing conditions.[7]

International law, or international criminal law in the specific context of this chapter, requires kinetic energy if it is to survive and be continuously effective. On taking office in the Hague, President Cassese and his colleagues were confronted with a body of law which had lain largely motionless, but for the

[4] Given that '[t]he practical problems facing the Tribunal at its inception seemed endless', the temptation was there for the judges to adjourn the work of the Tribunal until the General Assembly had set about solving these issues. However, under Cassese's leadership they immediately got to work on the drafting of the Rules of Procedure and Evidence. In this sense the very first task undertaken by the bench was a clear exercise in judicial lawmaking (even if it was secondary legislation). See 'Report of the International Tribunal for the Prosecution of Persons Responsible for Serious Violations of International Law Committed in the Territory of the former Yugoslavia Since 1991', A/49/342, S/1994/1007 (29 August 1994) paras 30–33, 52–7.

[5] D Hunt, 'The International Criminal Court: High Hopes, "Creative Ambiguity" and an Unfortunate Mistrust in International Judges' (2004) 2 JICJ 56, 58.

[6] *Trials of the Major War Criminals before the International Military Tribunal, Nuremberg, 14 November 1945–1 October 1946* Vol 1, Judgment (International Military Tribunal, Nuremberg 1947–1949) 221.

[7] *United States of America v Alstötter et al* ('the *Justice* case') Judgment (4 December 1947), in *Trials of War Criminals before the Nuremberg Military Tribunals under Control Council Law No. 10*, Vol III, 974–5. Quoted approvingly by Hunt (n 5 above) 58.

occasional domestic jolt, since the heady days of Nuremberg. Part of their task then can be simply put: restore energy and life to international criminal law.

In approaching such a task—logically, in the absence of the right to expressly 'make' substantive law—there was only one acceptable or appropriate means available to the bench, namely the interpretation of the applicable law. It is of course trite to remark that all law is in need of interpretation, in the sense that the identification of legal meaning is the primary task of the bench.[8] However, it is important to get a sense in itself of the understanding to be given to the term 'judicial interpretation'—no apologies are made for the palpable circularity of such a question. At a theoretical level the debate as to the meaning and scope of concepts of legal interpretation continues to rage in the work of a number of renowned scholars from Dworkin to Raz and Marmour to MacCormick (to name but a few),[9] and it is neither the time nor the place to comment on the possible applicability of these exchanges in the context of international criminal law.[10] However, in a broad sense, legal interpretation describes the active apprehension of the authoritative meaning of norms of applicable law (including the principal sources of law). Professor Neil MacCormick succinctly describes it thus:

> The place of interpretation is an inevitable corollary of the place accorded to authority reasons in legal arguments. For the norm posed in an authoritative source of law has to be understood before it can be applied. Accordingly, in a wide sense of the term 'interpretation', every application of an authority reason requires some act of interpretation, since one has to form an understanding of what the authoritative text requires in order to apply it, and any act of apprehension of meaning can be said to involve interpretation.[11]

In the alternative, as pointed out in the Joint Separate Opinion of Judge Tieya and Judge Nieto-Navia in the *Kanyabashi* Interlocutory Appeals Decision before the ICTR, '[the] interpretation of a provision of any legal instrument is to establish the meaning which is intended by the parties making it'.[12] Further removing

[8] This is nicely put by Matthias Klatt in the following manner: 'Every application of law requires some act of interpretation. In its wide sense "interpretation", which refers to the simple necessity of some form of understanding, is a ubiquitous and unavoidable feature of every law applying activity.' M Klatt, *Making the Law Explicit: The Normativity of Legal Argumentation* (Oxford: Hart Publishing, 2008) 4.

[9] See most obviously in this regard R Dworkin, *Law's Empire* (Boston: Harvard University Press, 1986); J Raz, *Between Authority and Interpretation* (Oxford: OUP, 2009) 223, where Raz euphemistically declares that '[w]e—legal theorists—write a lot about interpretation'; A Marmor, *Interpretation and Legal Theory* (Oxford: Hart Publishing, 2005); and N MacCormick, 'Arguing About Interpretation' in N MacCormick (ed), *Rhetoric and the Rule of Law: A Theory of Legal Reasoning* (Oxford: OUP, 2005).

[10] See the contribution of Robert Cryer (Ch 7 below) for some remarks on the Dworkinian approach to the judicial function in an international criminal context.

[11] N MacCormick, 'Argumentation and Interpretation in Law' (1995) 9 *Argumentation* 467, 470.

[12] *Prosecutor v Kanyabashi* (Appeals Chamber Decision on the Defence Motion for Interlocutory Appeal on the Jurisdiction of Trial Chamber I, Separate and Concurring Opinion of Judge Wang Tieya and Rafael Nieto-Navia) ICTR-96-15-A (3 June 1999) para 11.

notions relating to the meaning of interpretation from the tight theoretical moorings expressed by MacCormick and harnessing its core meaning instead to the endeavour of the judges of the *ad hoc* Tribunals, we can say that, in giving life to the law through legal interpretation, they were fundamentally involved in understanding and applying norms derived from authoritative sources of law.[13] Of course a statement proclaiming an expressive creative function is unlikely to be made from the bench acting in unison. However, on occasion separate opinions have revealed that the judges were not unaware of the task confronting them. One obvious and frequently quoted example in this regard is the statement of Judge Abi-Saab in his Separate Opinion in the *Tadić* Jurisdiction Decision, where he opined that the *ad hoc* Tribunals were 'afforded a unique opportunity to assume responsibility for the further rationalization of these categories [of international crimes] at some distance from the historical and psychological conditions from which they emerged and from the perspective of the evolving international legal order'.[14]

However, such rationalization of the law is impossible in the absence of a recognizable interpretational method. The primary objective of this chapter is to look at a number of the legal interpretational methods, or canons in domestic legal parlance, employed by the ICTY and ICTR in the enforcement of their constituent Statutes which resulted, either consciously or unconsciously, in the progressive development of core aspects of international criminal law. The domestic aids to construction utilized in statutory and constitutional interpretation (literal, teleological, contextual, etc) are well known, especially in common law jurisdictions, as are the interpretational rules laid down in Articles 31 to 33 of the Vienna Convention on the Law of Treaties.[15] However, the manner in which they have interacted in the context of the judicial development of international criminal law remains a worthy avenue of inquiry.[16] It is essential to bear in mind the *sui generis* nature of the Statutes, that they are neither treaties favouring contextual and purposive interpretation nor straightforward penal statutes demanding strict construction.[17] In the notable absence of an express provision setting down the

[13] However, in this respect it is worth referring to the prescience of Judge Benjamin Cardozo: 'The judge, even when he is free, is not wholly free. He is not to innovate at pleasure. He is not a knight-errant roaming at will in pursuit of his own ideal of beauty or of goodness. He is to draw his inspiration from consecrated principles. He is not to yield to spasmodic sentiment, to vague and unregulated benevolence. He is to exercise a discretion informed by tradition, methodized by analogy, disciplined by system, and subordinated to "primordial necessity or order in the social life". Wide enough in all conscience is the field of discretion that remains.' BN Cardozo, *The Nature of the Judicial Process* (Delhi: Universal Law Publishing, 2006) 141.

[14] *Prosecutor v Tadić* (Appeals Chamber Decision on the Defence Motion for Interlocutory Appeal on Jurisdiction, Separate Opinion of Judge Abi-Saab) IT-94-1-AR72 (2 October 1995) 2.

[15] Vienna Convention on the Law of Treaties (1979) 1155 UNTS 331, Arts 31–3.

[16] William Schabas is among the only scholars to specifically tackle this issue: see WA Schabas, 'Interpreting the Statutes of the *ad hoc* Tribunals' in Vohrah (n 2 above) 847.

[17] The ICTR Appeals Chamber said as much in *Prosecutor v Kanyabashi et al* (Appeals Chamber, Joint and Separate Opinion of Judge McDonald and Judge Vohrah) ICTR-96-15-A (3 June 1999)

interpretational approach to be taken, the interaction of interpretational methods is not as simple as it may at first appear and has given rise to a somewhat chaotic mass of practice.

The purpose of this collection as a whole is to identify the progressive, creative means of interpretation applied by the *ad hoc* Tribunals in relation to various discrete areas of international criminal law. The aim of this chapter in itself is not to provide an exhaustive overview of every method of interpretation employed in the decisions and judgments of the ICTY and ICTR—such an undertaking would demand a dedicated volume—but to place the enormity of the task faced by the judges of those tribunals in context, and to highlight the differing judicial purposes which were served by means of recourse to each broad category of interpretational method. At the conclusion it is hoped not only that a sense of the creative interpretational schemes of the *ad hoc* Tribunals is apparent, but also that it is clear that such approaches were necessary in the interests of justice and effectiveness. The chapter begins in section II by giving a sense of the frenzied circumstances in which the Statutes of the *ad hoc* Tribunals were drafted and the ambiguous nature of the text that was eventually decided upon. From this survey it is clear that, in the struggle to countenance any challenges to the legitimacy of the institutions, the Secretary-General, with the express support of the Security Council, charged the Tribunals with the application of customary norms of international humanitarian law, via which it was believed the principle of legality or *nullum crimen sine lege* would be preserved. Section II(B) briefly examines the methodological approach the Tribunals have taken in the identification of customary norms of international humanitarian law. Its conclusion reinforces the frequently expressed view that the Tribunals' determination of custom has been inconsistent and at times fundamentally unsatisfying from a legal reasoning perspective. Section III turns to more concrete notions of interpretation and looks at the fractured manner in which the interpretational rules laid down in the Vienna Convention on the Law of Treaties have been utilized by the Tribunals as a means of buttressing their often creative enterprises. Section IV offers some conclusions and asks whether any method is descernible from the chaos.

II. The Rules of the Game: The Laconic Statutes and Fidelity to Customary International Law

A. The drafting of the Statutes and the challenge facing the bench

Before becoming embroiled in interpretational matters, it is necessary first to get a sense of some of the unique features of the constituent Statutes at the centre

para 15: 'Although the Statute is not a treaty, it is a *sui generis* international legal instrument resembling a treaty.'

of the story. It is common knowledge by now that the drafting of the Statutes was not the result of a wide-ranging multilateral consultative process, couched in concession and the political trading so characteristic of traditional notions of treaty drafting processes. The Statutes were rather the product of the United Nations Office of Legal Affairs. Looking at the Statute of the ICTY, it is fair to say that it is illustrative of the frenzied efforts of several individuals.[18] When placed before the Security Council on 3 May 1993, the Statute was appended to the Report of the Secretary-General (Boutros Boutros-Ghali) on the establishment of the Tribunal,[19] which was requested under paragraph 2 of Security Council Resolution 808.[20] As a key preparatory document or element of the *travaux préparatoires*, the Secretary-General's Report would come to be utilized as an important interpretational aid by the Tribunal.[21] The Report noted that the establishment of an international criminal tribunal by means of a Chapter VII decision was necessary given the urgency with which the United Nations was obliged to act. The approach adopted 'would have the advantage of being expeditious and of being immediately effective as all States would be under a binding obligation to take whatever action is required to carry out a decision taken as an enforcement measure under Chapter VII'.[22] As subsequently noted by one of the chief drafters, Ralph Zacklin:

> Although this proposal was sure to be controversial, it was felt that it was legally justified and sufficiently framed by the particular circumstances of the conflict in the former Yugoslavia, so as not to establish a broad precedent and, clearly, one which would fulfil the criteria of expeditiousness and effectiveness.[23]

It is beyond doubt that the alternative of resorting to the creation of a similar mechanism by way of a formal treaty requiring ratification by the relevant players in the conflict would have been a doomed undertaking. As William Schabas has noted, 'it was out of the question at the time that the warring States would accept a tribunal, as their subsequent lack of cooperation with it only confirms'.[24]

[18] See V Morris and MP Scharf, *An Insider's Guide to the International Criminal Tribunal for the former Yugoslavia: A Documentary History and Analysis* (New York: Transnational, 1995).

[19] 'Report of the Secretary-General Pursuant to Paragraph 2 of Security Council Resolution 808 (1993)', UN Doc S/25704 (3 May 1993).

[20] UNSC Res 808 (1993), UN Doc S/RES/808 (22 February 1993).

[21] See eg *Prosecutor v Delalić et al* (Appeals Chamber Judgment) IT-96-21-A (20 February 2001) para 131 discussing the inclusion of violations of common Art 3 to the Geneva Conventions of 1949 under Art 3 of the Statute; and *Prosecutor v Brđanin* (Trial Chamber Judgment) IT-99-36-T (1 September 2004) para 720, fn 1753 discussing superior responsibility under Art 7(3) of the Statute. This issue will be returned to later in the chapter during discussions relating to Art 32 of the Vienna Convention and the *ad hoc* Tribunal's recourse to supplementary means of interpretation.

[22] 'Report of the Secretary-General' (n 19 above) para 23.

[23] R Zacklin, 'Some Major Problems in the Drafting of the ICTY Statute' (2004) 2 JICJ 361, 363.

[24] WA Schabas, *The UN International Criminal Tribunals: The former Yugoslavia, Rwanda and Sierra Leone* (Cambridge: CUP, 2006) 49.

Nevertheless, the speed with which the ICTY was brought into existence was quite extraordinary.[25]

Turning to the substantive law to be enforced by the Tribunal, the drafters had to restrain themselves from the temptation of legislating for the Tribunal. As commented by Zacklin:

> However justifiable in theory, this would have been a dangerous course to take. To use Chapter VII in order to legislate for Member States would have constituted a highly controversial extension of the Security Council's competence and one which might very well have called into question the fundamental legal basis of the Tribunal itself. This injunction led to a further important conclusion: legislation was unnecessary.[26]

Rather than venture down the road of highly questionable 'legislative' practices potentially in violation of the principle of legality or *nullum crimen sine lege*, the Report of the Secretary-General provided that 'the international tribunal should apply rules of international humanitarian law which are beyond doubt part of customary law'.[27] The conventional international humanitarian law deemed to be 'beyond doubt' part of customary international law by the Secretary-General encompassed: the Geneva Conventions of 1949 for the Protection of War Victims; the Hague Convention (IV) Respecting the Laws and Customs of War on Land and the Regulations annexed thereto of 18 October 1907; the Genocide Convention of 1948; and the Charter of the International Military Tribunal (IMT) of 8 August 1945.[28] Articles 2 to 5 of the Statute, which set out the subject-matter jurisdiction of the Tribunal, reflect the principles arising from these instruments which the Secretary-General deemed to have customary status—grave breaches of the Geneva Conventions of 1948 (Article 2), violations of the laws and customs of war (Article 3), genocide (Article 4), and crimes against humanity (Article 5).[29] The Secretary-General's designation of these instruments and provisions as customary international law is relatively uncontroversial (even if few relevant authorities were cited in designating this status), with the exception of the wholesale inclusion of the Charter of the IMT, presumably including Article 6(a) on crimes against peace, the express definition of which remains subject to significant discussion.[30] This was not picked up on during the Security

[25] As summed-up by Zacklin: 'The task of the Secretary-General was to provide to the Security Council a report on all aspects of the matter and this was accomplished within 60 days. At the same time, the Secretary-General was determined to present the Council not only with a report, but also a complete Statute. The fact that the ICTY Statute was approved and adopted without change by the Security Council was quite remarkable. This could be achieved because the Statute was perceived as being legally sound.' Zacklin (n 23 above) 367.

[26] ibid, 363.

[27] 'Report of the Secretary-General' (n 19 above) para 34.

[28] ibid, para 35.

[29] Statute of the International Tribunal for the Prosecution of Persons Responsible for Serious Violations of International Humanitarian Law Committed in the Territory of the former Yugoslavia since 1991, UN Doc S/25704 at 36, Annex (1993) and S/25704/Add.1, (1993) UN Doc S/RES/827, Arts 2–5.

[30] Agreement for the Prosecution and Punishment of the Major War Criminals of the European Axis, and Charter of the International Military Tribunal. London, 8 August 1945, in *Trial of the*

Council debate on the Report, and in reality is likely to have been the consequence of sloppiness rather than some clandestine effort on the part of the Office of Legal Affairs to shoehorn the crime of aggression into the Statute.

At a fundamental level, however, it is evident that the Secretary-General intended the Tribunal to only have competence to try accused persons for violations of customary norms of international humanitarian law to which individual criminal responsibility was unquestionably attached. Fidelity to the principle of legality linked to the identification of customary norms were thus positioned by the Secretary-General's Report as the 'golden rules' of the bench, to the extent that they were to be adopted both as presumptions (ie the Security Council did not intend to create new law), and as interpretational tools.[31] This sentiment found significant support in the interpretative statements of a number of delegations during the Security Council debate on the Report. For example, the Venezuela delegate, Mr Arria, stated: 'as a subsidiary organ of the Council, [the Tribunal] would not be empowered with—nor would the Council be assuming—the ability to set down norms of international law or to legislate with respect to those rights. It simply applies existing international humanitarian law';[32] while the United Kingdom representative David Hannay simply declared '[t]he Statute does not, of course, create new law, but reflects existing international law in this field.'[33]

However, some twenty months later in May 1995, the Report of the Secretary-General on the establishment of the ICTR submitted to the Security Council pursuant to Resolution 955 (1994) appeared seriously to question this marriage of custom and legality.[34] Given the essentially non-international nature of the conflict in Rwanda, and the attendant difficulties in the identification of clear customary norms in this respect, it is not surprising that the Security Council felt compelled, no doubt by fear of a potential *non liquet* scenario, to provide for the application of conventional humanitarian law instruments addressing non-international armed conflict which were not beyond doubt customary in nature. The Secretary-General's Report provides:

> ... the Security Council has elected to take a more expansive approach to the choice of the applicable law than the one underlying the Statute of the Yugoslav Tribunal, and

Major War Criminals Before the International Military Tribunal, Nuremberg, 14 November 1945-1 October 1946, Vol 1 (International Military Tribunal, Nuremberg 1947–1949), Art 6(a): 'Crimes against Peace: namely, planning, preparation, initiation or waging of a war of aggression, or a war in violation of international treaties, agreements or assurances, or participation in a common plan or conspiracy for the accomplishment of any of the foregoing.' This point is excellently made in A Zahar and G Sluiter, *International Criminal Law: A Critical Introduction* (Oxford: OUP, 2008) 85.

31 Schabas (n 24 above) 63.

32 *Provisional Verbatim Record of the Three Thousand Two Hundred and Seventeenth Meeting*, UN Doc S/PV.3217 (25 May 1993) 7.

33 ibid, 19.

34 The Statute of the ICTR was appended directly to establishing Resolution 955 of 8 November 1994, as opposed to being annexed to the Report of the Secretary-General as was the case for the ICTY. The Statute of the ICTR was therefore in place some four months prior to the Secretary-General's interpretative report.

> included within the subject-matter jurisdiction of the Rwanda Tribunal international instruments *regardless of whether they were considered part of customary international law or whether they have customarily entailed the individual criminal responsibility of the perpetrator of the crime.* Article 4 of the statute, accordingly, includes violations of Additional Protocol II, which, as a whole, has not yet been universally recognized as part of customary international law, and *for the first time criminalizes common Article 3 of the four Geneva Conventions.*[35]

The Security Council was therefore prepared to bend the rules. Whereas in establishing the Yugoslav Tribunal, the Secretary-General, with the tacit support of the Security Council, was only too conscious of limiting as much as possible the scope of challenges to the legality of the Tribunal's subject-matter jurisdiction, the particular circumstances of the Rwanda conflict demanded that the existing law be seen to be flexible in order to be effective. In making the existing law effective—which in this instance took the form of Additional Protocol II to the Geneva Conventions of 1977—the Security Council was building on the increasing acceptance among states of the need to ensure that the object and purpose of international criminal justice be fulfilled: that individuals be held accountable for violations of humanitarian law.[36]

It is worth noting that, in approving Resolution 955 to which the ICTR Statute was appended, members of the Council did not feel compelled to make any interpretational statements along the lines of those entered into the record when it considered the Secretary-General's Report and the Statute of the ICTY. The French delegate was the exception, stating that the comments he had made with respect to the interpretation of the ICTY Statute—relating to the meaning attaching to the expression 'laws and customs of war', the definition of crimes against humanity, and the issue of the primacy of the Tribunal over domestic proceedings—equally applied to the Statute of the ICTR.[37] However, given the fact that the ICTR Statute is substantively and in places definitionally distinct from the ICTY Statute—the inclusion of violations of common Article 3 and Additional Protocol II under Article 4, and the insertion of a discriminatory intent requirement coupled with the removal of an armed conflict nexus for crimes against humanity under Article 3 are two very obvious examples—it would appear that the French delegate was either voicing polite criticism of the subject-matter jurisdiction of the Tribunal or was mistaken as to the content of the Statute. Irrespective of the fact that Rwanda was a

[35] 'Report of the Secretary-General Pursuant to Paragraph 5 of Security Council Resolution 955 (1994)', UN Doc S/1995/134 (13 February 1995) para 12 (emphasis added).

[36] *Provisional Verbatim Record of the Three Thousand Four Hundred and Fifty-Third Meeting of the United Nations Security Council*, UN Doc S/PV.3453 (8 November 1994) 18—Madeleine Albright, United States: 'The investigation of genocide is indeed very grim work, but we have a responsibility to see that the International Tribunal for Rwanda can accomplish its objective—one that this Council increasingly recognizes: to hold individuals accountable for their violations of international humanitarian law.'

[37] ibid, 4.

party to the Geneva Conventions and Additional Protocols of 1977, the ICTR Statute was expansive and appears to have broken the golden rule of fidelity to customary international law.

The benches of the ICTY and the ICTR were therefore left to ruminate on the polar opposite approaches that had been taken in the drafting of their constituent Statutes—one which hammered home the message of conformity with customary international law and the principle of legality, the other which was prepared to stretch these principles in order to promote the effectiveness of the existing law. It is worth noting in particular the mental gymnastics required of the shared Appeals Chamber, which had to attempt to provide consistent appellate review over the decisions of Trial Chambers acting within apparently contradictory interpretational paradigms. These divergent, fluid, and at times ambiguous statutory foundations provided the bench with significant interpretational scope and the opportunity to exploit notions pertaining to the drafters' intent. The essential fact of the matter is that there were no clear interpretational guidelines, either expressly within the Statutes themselves, in the reports of the Secretary-General, or in the discussions of the Security Council. For the prospective judge, all that could be gleaned was the fundamental need for creativity broadly within the confines of the principle of legality and identifiable customary international law. Indeed, it is the operation of the bench within these express confines that has given rise to the greatest controversy with respect to the development of international criminal law.

B. Recourse to customary law: sculpture from the bench of the *ad hoc* Tribunals

The approach of both the ICTY and the ICTR to the identification of the customary international law parameters of their subject-matter jurisdiction, as well as the attendant scope of modes of individual criminal responsibility, has been described as at best 'inconsistent and incoherent'.[38] However, it pervades the entirety of the case law history of both institutions. It is evident from several of the chapters in this collection that recourse to purportedly established norms of customary international law has at times been at the heart of the creative interpretative enterprises of the *ad hoc* Tribunals, be it with respect to the prevailing definition of war crimes, crimes against humanity and genocide, or issues relating to liability, the rights of the accused, and applicable rules of procedure and evidence. Rather than comment further on what will be discussed later in the collection, the modest objective here is merely to highlight the somewhat inconsistent approach (not necessarily always in the

[38] I Bantekas, 'Reflections on Some Sources and Methods of International Criminal and Humanitarian Law' (2006) 6 ICLR 121, 121.

negative sense) that has been had with respect to the identification of what is both a source of law and an interpretational aid, as well as the mainstay of the legitimacy of international criminal law.[39] As Theodor Meron has commented, 'the centrality of customary law... result[s] from the [Yugoslavia] Tribunal's obligation, as a criminal court, to respect the fundamental principle of *nullum crimen sine lege*'.[40] In this sense, recourse to customary international law is viewed alongside general principles of law as legitimate gap-filling tools.[41]

It is axiomatic that customary international law is traditionally identified on the basis of state practice and *opinio juris*.[42] Reference to 'modern' approaches to customary international law identification, however, tend to first look to *opinio juris* and then seek supporting state practice. In addition, such modern, *a priori* approaches take into account issues including treaty ratification and support of soft law sources, such as General Assembly resolutions.[43] International tribunals have had something of a chequered past, in terms of consistency and rigour, when it comes to the designation of customary norms.[44] The most obvious relevant example in this regard is the International Court of Justice's (ICJ) assertion in the *Nicaragua* case that Articles 1 and 3 common to the Geneva Conventions of 1949 constituted customary international law, without making any reference in support to either state practice or *opinio juris*.[45] A similarly lax application of the rule is recognizable in the judgment in the *Yerodia* case where the Court referred to the customary norms relating to immunities without any recourse to the regular formulation.[46] So, while the ICJ may have established the rule for

[39] *Prosecutor v Milutinović et al* (Appeals Chamber Decision on Dragoljub Ojdanic's Motion Challenging Jurisdiction—Joint Criminal Enterprise) IT-99-37-AR72 (21 May 2003) para 9; T Meron, 'The Revival of Customary Humanitarian Law' (2005) 99 AJIL 817, 821.

[40] Meron (n 39 above) ibid.

[41] The utilization of general principles of law in the progressive development of international criminal law is explored in the contribution of Fabián Raimondo (Ch 2 below). See also eg B Cheng, *General Principles of Law as Applied by International Courts and Tribunals* (Cambridge: CUP, 2006); MC Bassiouni, 'A Functional Approach to "General Principles of International Law"' (1989–1990) 11 Mich JIL 768.

[42] *North Sea Continental Shelf Cases (Federal Republic of Germany/Denmark; Federal Republic of Germany/Netherlands)* [1969] ICJ Rep, paras 73–81; see also *Continental Shelf (Libyan Arab Jamahiriya/Malta)* [1985] ICJ Rep, para 27. See I Brownlie, *Principles of Public International Law* (Oxford: OUP, 7th edn, 2008) 6–12.

[43] *Continental Shelf (Libyan Arab Jamahiriya/Malta)* (n 42 above) para 27. See AE Roberts, 'Traditional and Modern Approaches to Customary International Law: A Reconciliation' (2001) 95 AJIL 757.

[44] See B Simma and P Alston, 'The Sources of Human Rights Law: Custom, *Jus Cogens*, and General Principles' (1988–1989) 12 Aus YBIL 84.

[45] *Case Concerning Military and Paramilitary Activities in and against Nicaragua (Nicaragua v United States)* [1986] ICJ Rep, para 218.

[46] *Case Concerning the Arrest Warrant of 11 April 2000 (Democratic Republic of the Congo v Belgium)* [2002] ICJ Rep, paras 52–5.

the identification of customary international law, its formal application has left something to be desired.[47]

While from the outset the *ad hoc* Tribunals have made it clear that they will seek to have recourse to state practice and *opinio juris*, it has on many occasions been difficult to predict the relative weight that is to be attached to each limb of the customary law formulation.[48] For instance, in determining the customary status of Additional Protocol II to the Geneva Conventions of 1949, the Appeals Chamber in the *Tadić* jurisdiction decision referred almost exclusively to examples of *opinio juris* (in the form of statements of state plenipotentiaries, resolutions of the General Assembly, etc),[49] whereas in the *Erdemović* judgment, the Appeals Chamber—in particular Judge Antonio Cassese—in deciding on the applicability of the defence of duress, placed overwhelming weight on a deluge of state practice (taking the form of domestic decisions, statutory provisions, etc).[50] Indeed, in his scholarly writings Cassese has championed the value of recourse to domestic jurisprudence, stating that 'both customary rules and principles may normally be drawn or inferred from judicial decisions'.[51]

The ICTY has frequently placed significant weight on the provisions of conventional international treaties as evidence of the crystallization of a customary norm; this is especially true of instances in which the impugned law falls clearly within one of the conventional humanitarian law instruments identified as customary in the Secretary-General's Report.[52] In this regard, Schabas has commented that it is something of a paradox 'that the search for evidence of customary law seems to lead, inexorably, to treaties'.[53] However, André Nollkaemper has questioned the reliance on treaty law in the identification of custom: 'one cannot simply use behaviour that is treaty-governed as indicative of practice or take the ratification of a treaty as a sign of *opinio juris* and on that basis alone conclude

[47] O Schachter, 'New Custom: Power, *Opinio Juris* and Contrary Practice' in J Makarcyzk (ed), *Theory of International Law at the Threshold of the 21st Century: Essays in Honour of Krzysztof Skubiszewski* (The Hague: Kluwer Law International, 1996) 531.

[48] A Nollkaemper, 'The Legitimacy of International Law in the Case Law of the International Criminal Tribunal for the former Yugoslavia' in T Vandamme and J Reestman (eds), *Ambiguity in the Rule of Law: The Interface Between National and International Legal Systems* (Groningen: Europa Law Publishing, 2001) 16.

[49] *Tadić* (Appeals Chamber Jurisdiction Decision) (n 14 above) para 117.

[50] *Prosecutor v Erdemović* (Appeals Chamber Sentencing Judgment) IT-96-22-A (7 October 1997). This was particularly apparent in Judge Cassese's Separate Opinion. A similar approach was taken by the Trial and Appeals Chamber in deciding on the definition of rape for the purposes of the Statute in the *Furundžija* case—for more on this see the contribution of Niamh Hayes (Ch 6 below).

[51] A Cassese, *International Criminal Law* (Oxford: OUP, 2nd edn, 2008) 17. See also *Prosecutor v Tadić* (Appeals Chamber Judgment) IT-94-1-A (15 July 1999) para 15.

[52] See *Prosecutor v Furundžija* (Trial Chamber Judgment) IT-95-17/1-T (10 December 1998) para 137. There has been a particular fondness for designating certain provisions of the Additional Protocols to the Geneva Conventions as representative of emerging customary standards. See *Prosecutor v Kordić et al* (Appeals Chamber Judgment) IT-95-14/2-A (17 December 2004) paras 62–6; *Prosecutor v Kayeshima et al* (Appeals Chamber Judgment) ICTR-95-1-A (1 June 2001) para 51.

[53] Schabas (n 24 above) 98.

that custom exists. Such a view would sanction majoritarian law-making in the international legal order.'[54] It is nonetheless a facet of modern approaches to customary law identification.[55]

A curious example of recourse to an international treaty as evidence of a customary norm can be found in the Yugoslavia Tribunal's references to the Rome Statute of the International Criminal Court. Prior to its entry into force, the Rome Statute was considered as evidence of customary international law in a number of decisions on the basis that it constituted evidence of state practice and *opinio juris*. The *Furundžija* Trial Chamber acknowledged that the Statute could be taken as 'constituting an authoritative expression of the legal views of a great number of States',[56] while the *Tadić* appeal judgment noted that the Rome Statute had been adopted by an 'overwhelming majority' of states at the Rome Diplomatic Conference and endorsed by the UN General Assembly, which it took as evidence that 'the text is supported by a great number of States and may be taken to express the legal position, ie *opinio juris* of those States'.[57] Somewhat counter-intuitively, the work of the Preparatory Commission for the International Criminal Court in producing the draft Elements of Crimes was referred to in the *Krstić* trial judgment to support that Chamber's own assessment of the state of customary international law at the time relevant to the indictment.[58] It could be argued that this approach is disingenuous at best, as it ignores the vast differences in the landscape of international criminal law at the time of the work of the Preparatory Commission on the Elements of Crimes, given the drafting and adoption of the Rome Statute and the extraordinary impact the jurisprudence

[54] Nollkaemper (n 48 above) 16.

[55] For a closer examination of the debate surrounding the so-called 'modern approach' to customary international law identification, see H Meijers, 'How is International Law Made?—Stages of Growth of International Law and the Use of Its Customary Rules' (1978) 9 Neths YBIL 3; CM Chinkin, 'The Challenge of Soft Law: Development and Change in International Law' (1989) 38 ICLQ 850; K Wolfe, 'Some Persistent Controversies Regarding Customary International Law' (1993) 24 Neths YBIL 1; M Byers, 'Custom, Power, and the Power of Rules' (1995–1996) 17 Mich JIL 109; AE Roberts, 'Traditional and Modern Approaches to Customary Law: A Reconciliation' (2001) 95 AJIL 757; RB Baker, 'Customary International Law in the 21st Century: Old Challenges and New Debates' (2010) 21 EJIL 173.

[56] *Furundžija* (Trial Chamber Judgment) (n 52 above) para 227. The Chamber recognized that the Statute in its entirety could not be considered customary law: 'Depending on the matter at issue, the Rome Statute may be taken to restate, reflect or clarify customary rules or crystallise them, whereas in some areas it creates new law or modifies existing law.'

[57] *Prosecutor v Tadić* (Appeals Chamber Judgment) IT-94-1-A (15 July 1999) para 223. See also *Prosecutor v Milošević* (Decision on Preliminary Motions) IT-99-37-PT (8 November 2001) para 31.

[58] *Prosecutor v Krstić* (Trial Chamber Judgment) IT-98-33-T (2 August 2001) para 541. The Chamber noted that '[a]lthough that document post-dates the acts involved here, it has proved helpful in assessing the state of customary international law which the Chamber itself derived from other sources.' See also *Prosecutor v Kordić and Cerkez* (Appeals Chamber Judgment) IT-95-14/2-A (17 December 2004) fn 73, where the Appeals Chamber referred to controversial negotiations within the Working Group on the Elements of Crimes in 1999 as '[f]urther evidence of the unsettled nature of State *opinio juris* and practice' regarding the requirement of a result element for the crime of unlawful attack on civilians and civilian objects 'at the time the crimes were committed in this case'.

of the *ad hoc* Tribunals had on that process. To suggest that the statements of state parties in such a changed landscape could be retrospectively applied to shed light on the content of customary international law in the early to mid-1990s is both legally unsound and logically unsettling. Nollkaemper has gone as far as to suggest that such reliance 'tends to transform the process of law making' in the international legal context.[59]

An additional common feature of the ascertainment of customary rules by both *ad hoc* Tribunals has been the tendency to revert selectively to the *ratio* of post-Second World War case law, irrespective of the fact that the vast majority of such cases were in no sense international proceedings. Given the questions that may remain, for instance regarding the due process guarantees to defendants, it is uncertain what degree of relevance they have to contemporary international criminal law. This is a point well made by Alexander Zahar and Göran Sluiter who posit that, in citing such case law: 'It is not a matter of *following* a norm articulated in the courts of the Allies but merely of demonstrating that a given norm favoured today is not without historical support.'[60] On other occasions, and particularly with respect to the ICTR, the *Nicaragua* method of baldly declaring the existence of customary law has been adopted. On this point, Larissa van den Herik has commented:

> ...on many occasions the ICTR based its argument on the existence of a customary rule. However, the finding of a customary rule was not supported on all occasions by clear evidence of *opinio juris*, and, even less, of state practice. With regard to defining the physical acts that can constitute a crime against humanity or a war crime, the reference to customary international law was often confined to the mere statement that the finding was supported by customary international law, without any examination of State practice or indications of an existing *opinio juris* on the matter.[61]

The frequent neglect of recourse to state practice and *opinio juris* by the ICTR may be linked to the 'expansive approach' to law identified by the Secretary-General. It is evident from the case law that the ICTY has a much stronger record with respect to the reasoned pronouncement of customary norms.[62] However, whether legitimized or not by the usual channels, both Tribunals have used recourse to customary international law as their primary creative or developmental legal tool.

As discussed above, the Report of the Secretary-General regarding the Statute of the Yugoslavia Tribunal contained an explicit requirement that the Tribunal

[59] Nollkaemper (n 48 above) 17.

[60] Zahar and Sluiter (n 30 above) 98.

[61] L van den Herik, *The Contribution of the Rwanda Tribunal to the Development of International Law* (The Hague: Martinus Nijhoff, 2005) 275.

[62] A textbook example of use of the traditional formulation is evident in the approach of the Trial Chamber in the *Kupreškić* case in determining the customary legal parameters of the crime against humanity of persecution—*Prosecutor v Kupreškić et al* (Trial Chamber Judgment) IT-95-16-T (14 January 2000) paras 567–626. So textbook in fact, that it is cited by Cassese: Cassese (n 51 above) 19.

should only apply rules of international humanitarian law which were 'beyond any doubt part of customary international law' in order to comport with the principle of legality.[63] The judges of the ICTY have often made obedient reference to this requirement, and appear to take great pains to discuss (if not establish) the customary nature of crimes within their jurisdiction at the time relevant to the indictment.[64] The *Vasiljević* Trial Chamber cast this requirement more as a question of fairness to an accused than as solely the satisfaction of a legal doctrine.[65] In reality, however, regardless of the sometimes questionable methods used in its identification, this express fidelity to customary international law has been used as a springboard for judicial creativity at the *ad hoc* Tribunals.[66] It is of course not the only means used: resort to the identification of general principles of law has also been an important creative tool,[67] as have the other sources of law traditionally identified in Article 38 of the Statute of the ICJ.[68] As will be discussed in depth elsewhere in this collection, resort to customary international law has resulted in a fundamental recasting of the law of war crimes, the perfunctory removal of the requirement of a nexus with armed conflict for crimes against humanity, the development of an ever-more expansive doctrine of individual criminal responsibility under the rubrics of joint criminal enterprise and aiding and abetting, and the progressive restatement of the law on numerous other issues. However, in many of those cases the end result, although novel,

[63] See *Tadić* (Appeals Chamber Jurisdiction Decision) (n 14 above) para 143: 'the only reason behind the stated purpose of the drafters that the International Tribunal should apply customary international law was to avoid violating the principle of *nullum crimen sine lege* in the event that a party to the conflict did not adhere to a specific treaty'.

[64] See eg *Prosecutor v Galić* (Appeals Chamber Judgment) IT-98-29-A (30 November 2006) para 83: 'an analysis of the jurisprudence of the International Tribunal demonstrates that the Judges have consistently endeavoured to satisfy themselves that the crimes charged in the indictments before them were crimes under customary international law at the time of their commission and were sufficiently defined under that body of law'.

[65] *Prosecutor v Vasiljević* (Trial Chamber Judgment) IT-98-32-T (29 November 2002) para 193: 'From the perspective of the *nullum crimen sine lege* principle, it would be wholly unacceptable for a Trial Chamber to convict an accused person on the basis of a prohibition which, taking into account the specificity of customary international law and allowing for the gradual clarification of the rules of criminal law, is either insufficiently precise to determine conduct and distinguish the criminal from the permissible, or was not sufficiently accessible at the relevant time.' For further comment on this case, see A Cassese, 'Black Letter Lawyering v. Constructive Interpretation: The *Vasiljević* Case' (2004) 2 JICJ 265.

[66] Alison Marsten Danner has pointed out that the judges of the ICTY have never been censured for venturing beyond the constraints contained in the Secretary-General's Report, and questions whether, despite repeated statements from states to the contrary, the ICTY was in fact intended to update existing international criminal and international humanitarian law. See AM Danner, 'When Courts Make Law: How the International Criminal Tribunals Recast the Laws of War' (2006) 59 *Vanderbilt Law Review* 1, 47–51.

[67] This is explored in detail in the contribution of Fabián Raimondo (Ch 2 below).

[68] Art 38(1) of the ICJ Statute identifies four sources of international law (in order of hierarchy)—conventional treaty law, international custom, general principles of law recognized by civilized nations, and judicial decisions and the teachings of the most highly qualified publicists (which is naturally treated as a subsidiary source). See Statute of the International Court of Justice, Art 38.

was justified on the basis that it merely amounted to the application of an existing customary international law principle to facts which had not previously been addressed. As Judge Hunt has noted, 'the application of an existing principle accepted as customary international law to a new situation where that situation reasonably falls within its application is hardly a novel proposition', given that exactly such a process was the basis for the London Charter of the International Military Tribunal at Nuremberg.[69]

The objective of this section has not been to document the results of recourse to customary international law before the *ad hoc* Tribunals exhaustively, but rather to highlight the reality that the means and methods used in its identification as a source of law and interpretational gap-filling aid have at times been inconsistent, flawed, and potentially cast a significant pall over the legitimacy of the law 'produced' by the Tribunals. The following section will seek to apply a similar analysis to the utilization by the *ad hoc* Tribunals of the interpretational methods outlined in Articles 31 to 33 of the Vienna Convention on the Law of Treaties and the problems arising from the failure expressly to include a specific interpretational framework in the Tribunals' Statutes.

III. Methods of Interpretation: Piecemeal Identification and Fractured Application

A. A sound interpretational foundation: the Vienna Convention on the Law of Treaties

As proclaimed by Jan Klabbers: 'One among many curious things about interpretation of treaties is that the rules on interpretation of treaties are themselves laid down in a treaty.'[70] Credit for the drafting and development of the interpretational clauses of the Vienna Convention on the Law of Treaties rests with the International Law Commission (ILC). In arriving at a reasonable consensus-driven definition of the rules of treaty interpretation, the ILC stated frankly that:

> [m]ost cases submitted to international adjudication involve the interpretation of treaties and the jurisprudence of international tribunals is rich in reference to principles and maxims of interpretation. In fact, statements can be found in the decisions of international tribunals to support the use of almost every principle or maxim of which use is made in national systems of law in the interpretation of statutes and contracts.[71]

[69] *Prosecutor v Hadžihasanović et al* (Trial Chamber Decision on Interlocutory Appeal Challenging Jurisdiction in Relation to Command Responsibility, Separate and Partially Dissenting Opinion of Judge David Hunt) IT-01-47-AR72 (16 July 2003) para 4.

[70] J Klabbers, 'International Legal Histories: The Declining Importance of *Travaux Préparatoires* in Treaty Interpretation?' (2003) 50 Neth ILR 267, 270.

[71] ILC, 'Report of the Commission on the Work of its Eighteenth Session' (1966) *ILC Yearbook*, Vol II, 172, 218.

Faced with this situation, the ILC determined to limit itself 'to trying to isolate and codify the comparatively few general principles which appear to constitute general rules for the interpretation of treaties'.[72] This enterprise ultimately resulted in the interpretative provisions of the Vienna Convention, which provide a 'General rule of interpretation' (Article 31), 'Supplementary means of interpretation' (Article 32), and rules for the 'Interpretation of treaties authenticated in two or more languages' (Article 33).[73]

As noted above, the *ad hoc* Tribunals in a number of relatively early decisions acknowledged the *sui generis* nature of their respective Statutes, as neither treaties nor strictly penal statutes. However, it was nonetheless reasonable in their view that the general rules of interpretation codified in the Vienna Convention be applied *mutatis mutandis* to the Statutes:

> Although the Statute of the International Tribunal is a *sui generis* legal instrument and not a treaty, in interpreting its provisions and the drafter's conception of the applicability of the jurisprudence of other courts, the rules of treaty interpretation contained in the Vienna Convention on the Law of Treaties appear relevant.[74]

In fact, given that the Convention itself contains no express indication that the rules contained therein could conceivably be applied to a non-treaty text, coupled with the reality that a good number of the provisions pertain directly to inter-state disputes, there is quite a lot in the Convention that is entirely irrelevant to the interpretation of the Statutes.[75] That said, since the subject matter of the *ad hoc* Tribunals is derived from treaty law and the rules themselves are recognizable in their domestic legal origins, there can be few sustainable complaints with respect to their application.[76] This point was eloquently expressed by Judge Shahabuddeen in his Dissenting Opinion in the *Kanyabeshi* case:

> A Chamber of the Tribunal, seeking to apply the Statute, may obviously be faced with the task of interpreting it. The Statute prescribes no principles of interpretation. It may therefore be understood as authorising the Tribunal to interpret it in accordance with reason.

[72] ibid.

[73] For critical comment on the work of the ILC in this regard, see MS McDougal, 'Editorial Comment: "Law of Treaties" Issue of the Journal' (1967) 61 AJIL 990. See also generally, RD Kearney and RE Dalton, 'The Treaty on Treaties' (1970) 64 AJIL 495; FG Jacobs, 'Interpretation: With Special Reference to the Draft Convention on the Law of Treaties Before the Vienna Diplomatic Conference' (1969) 18 ICLQ 318; and DJ Bederman, *Classical Canons: Rhetoric, Classicism and Treaty Interpretation* (Aldershot: Ashgate Publishing, 2001).

[74] *Prosecutor v Tadić* (Trial Chamber Decision on the Prosecutor's Motion Requesting Protective Measures for Victims and Witnesses) IT-94-1-T (10 August 1995) para 18. See also *Prosecutor v Bagasora et al* (Appeals Chamber Decision on the Admissibility of the Prosecutor's Appeal from the Decision of a Confirming Judge Dismissing an Indictment against Théoneste Bagasora and 28 Others) ICTR-98-37-A (8 June 1998) para 28.

[75] A point well made in Schabas (n 16 above) 850.

[76] It should be noted at this point that reference to the 'rules' of interpretation enumerated in the Convention is merely a common, convenient label and should not be considered 'a precise signifier of the character of the provisions or how they are to be used'—R Gardiner, *Treaty Interpretation* (Oxford: OUP, 2008) 37.

But reason, which could sometimes be understood differently by each party concerned, suggests that some known body of principles of interpretation should be sought. In deciding what these should be, the Tribunal will naturally have regard to the character of the Statute…The Statute is not municipal legislation. And notwithstanding the treaty character of the Charter under which it was made, there could be difficulty in the argument that it is a 'treaty' within the meaning of the definition of that term as set out in Article 2(1)(a) of the Vienna Convention on the Law of Treaties 1969. It is, however, an international document proximate in nature to a treaty, having been promulgated by the Security Council acting on behalf of the member States of the United Nations. That proximity to a treaty will justify recourse being had, on an analogical basis, to principles of treaty interpretation. These will include, as has been held in the jurisprudence both of the International Criminal Tribunal for the former Yugoslavia and the International Criminal Tribunal for Rwanda, the principles set out in that Convention.[77]

On a number of occasions, however, the ICTY has sought to move significantly beyond the application by analogy of the Vienna Convention rules to the Statute, going as far as to declare that the Statute in its entirety—not just its subject-matter jurisdiction—was to be 'interpreted as a treaty'.[78] This is certainly a highly questionable conclusion, which at best is a misinterpretation of the previous statements of the Tribunal and at worst amounts to a fundamental miscategorization of the Statute as a conventional treaty text.[79]

The customary international law status of the Vienna rules is beyond doubt, having been confirmed by a host of international tribunals.[80] The general rule of treaty interpretation set out in Article 31(1) of the Convention states: 'A treaty shall be interpreted in good faith in accordance with the ordinary meaning to be given to the terms of the treaty in their context and in light of its object and

[77] *Prosecutor v Kanyabashi* (Appeals Chamber Decision on the Defence Motion for Interlocutory Appeal on the Jurisdiction of Trial Chamber I; Dissenting Opinion of Judge Shahabuddeen) ICTR-96-15-A (3 June 1999) 21.

[78] *Prosecutor v Milošević* (Decision on Preliminary Motions) IT-99-37-PT (8 November 2001) para 47; *Prosecutor v Milošević* (Reasons for Decision on Assignment of Defence Counsel) IT-99-37-T (22 September 2004). See also, C Lister, 'What's in a Name? Labels and the Statute of the International Criminal Tribunal for the former Yugoslavia' (2005) 18 LJIL 77, 78: 'The net result of all this is that, without any articulated analysis, the Tribunal has moved from an acknowledgement that the Statute is "legally very different" from a treaty to a perception that the Statute has been regarded as a treaty from the Tribunal's "earliest days".'

[79] See Lister (n 78 above) 91: 'treating the Statute as a treaty is unhelpful and potentially misleading. The characterization does not accurately reflect the actual manner of, or the intended basis for, the Statute's adoption…The trial chamber's characterization of the Statute caused it to search for the right rule in the wrong place.' Cassese avoids semantic arguments of this kind by boldly stating that 'in many respects these resolutions, and their annexed Statutes, may be equated with international treaties' Cassese (n 51 above) 16.

[80] See eg *Case Concerning Certain Questions of Mutual Assistance in Criminal Matters (Djibouti v France)* Judgment (4 June 2008) para 153; *Case Concerning Oil Platforms (Islamic Republic of Iran v United States of America)* Preliminary Objection, Judgment (12 December 1996) para 23; *Golder v UK* (Series A No 18) ECHR Judgment 21 February 1975, para 29. Even though the Convention had not yet entered into force, Arts 31–3 were nevertheless considered to 'enunciate in essence generally accepted principles of international law to which the Court has already referred on occasion'.

purpose'.[81] On the face of it, the rule expresses a broad teleological or purposive approach to the interpretation of treaty texts. It necessitates three steps to be taken collectively in good faith: (1) the identification of the ordinary meaning of the terms, (2) in their context, and (3) the shaping of this ordinary contextual meaning in light of the object and purpose of the treaty. As to the parameters of 'context', Article 31(2)(a) and (b) provides that it includes elements of the treaty such as the preamble, annexes, subsequent agreements, and related instruments, ie essentially other relevant textual material.[82] The provision is thus exceptionally broad and attempts to marry what would be considered at the domestic level to be four distinct approaches to statutory interpretation, namely good faith, textual interpretation (ie ordinary meaning), logical interpretation (context), and teleological interpretation (object and purpose), which in itself takes in a whole range of issues relating to the intentions of the framers of the text.

If after the application of this general rule the meaning of the text remains unclear, Article 32 provides that:

> [r]ecourse may be had to supplementary means of interpretation, including the preparatory work of the treaty and the circumstances of its conclusion, in order to confirm the meaning resulting from the application of article 31, or to determine the meaning when the interpretation according to article 31: (a) leaves the meaning ambiguous or obscure; or (b) leads to a result which is manifestly absurd or unreasonable.[83]

The purpose of Article 32 is to inquire into the intentions of the drafters of the instrument, via recourse to the *travaux préparatoires*, as a means of throwing light on the ordinary meaning of the text understood in accordance with its context and object and purpose. However, in all circumstances it is only to be reverted to where the application of Article 31 leaves the meaning unclear or gives rise to an absurdity. It is not intended to be utilized as a matter of course but rather only as a supplementary, secondary means not forming the sole basis of any one interpretative enterprise. The reasoning behind this obvious interpretational hierarchy was simply a belief, expressed by the ILC, that the text 'must be presumed to be the authentic expression of the intentions of the parties'.[84] However, such a contention constitutes a significant bone of contention, with commentators such as Klabbers arguing that the *travaux préparatoires* 'constitute merely evidence' and 'do not have a particularly strong relationship to the treaty'.[85]

[81] Vienna Convention (n 15 above) Art 31(1). [82] ibid Art 31(2)(a) and (b).

[83] ibid Art 32.

[84] H Waldock, 'Third Report on the Law of Treaties' (1964) *ILC Yearbook*, Vol II, 56.

[85] Klabbers (n 70 above) 276. Hersch Lauterpacht would doubtless strongly oppose this statement: 'An international judge who would interpret the provisions of important political treaties without reference to the prolonged correspondence which preceded them and which throws abundant light upon every expression and nuance of expression, upon what is included and what is omitted, would run the risk of reducing his work to the point of devastating barrenness': H Lauterpacht,

Aside from the worth to be attached to *travaux*, there has been some debate surrounding where the boundaries for the inclusion of material under this heading should be set.[86] With respect to the *ad hoc* Tribunals, the preparatory materials of the Statutes would appear to be readily identifiable: the Reports of the Secretary-General, the discussions of the Security Council including the individual interpretative statements of states, and the establishing resolutions. Unsurprisingly, however, this is far from the end of the story. Given the fact that the Tribunals purport, for the most part, to be applying customary rules of international humanitarian law, in interpretational terms the Tribunals are not grappling with a single instrument but with an entire raft of international instruments with individual—and potentially contradictory—drafting histories and intentions. The scope of applicable material falling under the heading of *travaux* is therefore vast and offers ample opportunity for selective readings for either restrictive or expansive and creative purposes.

Article 33 referring to the interpretation of treaty texts authenticated in two or more languages is of a distinctly different order but of relevance to the *ad hoc* Statutes, which exist in six language versions with the English and French versions (corresponding to the working languages of the Tribunals) having supposed authority. The most relevant provision of Article 33 for our purposes is paragraph 4, which states that 'when a comparison of the authentic texts discloses a difference of meaning which the application of articles 31 and 32 does not remove, the meaning which best reconciles the texts, having regard to the object and purpose of the treaty, shall be adopted'.[87] As with Articles 31 and 32, the interpretation given to a term rests with the understanding given to the object and purpose of the instrument.[88] While contradictory linguistic issues have not been an enormous stumbling block for the Tribunals, they have on more than one occasion thrown up some interesting constructions.[89]

'Some Observations on Preparatory Work in the Interpretation of Treaties' (1934–1935) 48 Harvard Law Review 549, 575.

[86] See R Gardiner, 'Treaties and Treaty Materials: Role, Relevance and Accessibility' (1997) 46 ICLQ 643.

[87] Vienna Convention (n 15 above) Art 33(4).

[88] For examples of the application of a literal or purposive approach to solve an apparent inconsistency between the French and English versions of a text, see *Prosecutor v Akayesu* (Appeals Chamber Judgment) ICTR-96-4-A (1 June 2001) paras 477–82; and *Prosecutor v Milosević* (Reasons for Decision on Prosecution Interlocutory Appeal from Refusal to Order Joiner) IT-01-51-AR73 (18 April 2002) paras 13–16.

[89] See eg the discussion in the *Kayishema* trial judgment of the distinction between '*assassinat*' and 'murder' used in the French and English versions of the ICTR Statute and the associated implications for the *mens rea* standard to be applied. This example is particularly noteworthy in that the Trial Chamber resorted to the principle of *in dubio pro reo* rather than a literal or purposive interpretation to resolve the discrepancy. *Prosecutor v Kayishema and Ruzindana* (Trial Chamber Judgment) ICTR-95-1-T (21 May 1999) paras 137–9.

B. The utilization of Articles 31 and 32 of the Vienna Convention: buttressing the creative enterprise

One of the major hurdles to be overcome in getting at the full extent to which the ICTY and the ICTR have had recourse to the Vienna rules is the simple fact that often, and in particular in the early years of their existence, they were implemented without express reference to their origin. For example, looking at the *Tadić* jurisdiction decision it is obvious that the question of the applicability of the Statute to non-international armed conflict was resolved via recourse to the Vienna rules.[90] In assessing the application of the grave breaches regime under Article 2 of the Statute, the Appeals Chamber clearly and systematically engaged in the three-step process for the implementation of the general rule of interpretation set out in Article 31.

The Chamber first looked at the 'literal' meaning attached to Article 2. While Article 31 refers to the 'ordinary' meaning attaching to a term, literal interpretation is simply a synonym for this approach.[91] As posited by Rupert Cross, ordinary or literal meaning 'is the meaning which results from giving to each word an ordinary meaning without much reference to the context and applying the provision to a particular situation without any regard to its purpose'.[92] This is precisely how this canon was used by the Appeals Chamber: 'A literal reading of this provision standing alone may lead one to believe that it applies to both kinds of conflict.'[93]

The Chamber acknowledged that the ordinary meaning cannot stand alone as an authoritative interpretation and must be better understood in light of the object and purpose of the Statute.[94] To this end, the Appeals Chamber then engaged in what it described as a teleological interpretation of the impugned provisions, which of course equates to recourse to the object and purpose behind the Statutes and necessarily involved recourse to the *travaux préparatoires*.[95] The result of this inquiry was the conclusion that:

> the Security Council's object in enacting the Statute—to prosecute and punish persons responsible for certain condemned acts being committed in a conflict understood to contain both internal and international aspects—suggests that the Security Council intended that, to the extent possible, the subject-matter jurisdiction of the International Tribunal should extend to both internal and international armed conflicts.[96]

[90] It is curious that in his separate opinion Judge Sidhwa uses language almost identical to Arts 31 and 32 without explicitly referring to them. *Tadić* (Appeals Chamber Jurisdiction Decision, Separate Opinion of Judge Sidhwa) (n 14 above) para 109.

[91] J Bell and G Engle (eds), *Cross-Statutory Interpretation* (Oxford: OUP, 3rd edn, 2005) 66.

[92] ibid.

[93] *Tadić* (Appeals Chamber Jurisdiction Decision) (n 14 above) para 71.

[94] ibid para 71: 'In order better to ascertain the meaning and scope of these provisions, the Appeals Chamber will therefore consider the object and purpose behind the enactment of the Statute.'

[95] ibid paras 72–8.

[96] ibid para 78.

The interpretation of the applicability of the Statute to the non-international armed conflicts was rounded off via recourse to a 'logical and systematic interpretation' of the provision, or (in Vienna terms) a contextual interpretation. Contextual interpretation dictates that no one provision should be looked at in isolation but must be logically interpreted in light of the entirety of the instrument. The Appeals Chamber determined that the relevant context of grave breaches under Article 2 logically required an examination of both the Statute and the Geneva Conventions of 1949. The result confirmed the meaning derived from the ordinary meaning and the object and purpose of the Statute, ie the grave breaches regime applied to non-international as well as international armed conflicts.[97] However, having implicitly and carefully followed the interpretational scheme of Article 31, the Chamber had to acknowledge that this interpretation was contrary to the current state of customary international law on the subject.[98] While appearing to remain faithful to customary international law, it was nonetheless concluded that there was evidence to suggest that international law was developing in this direction but had not yet fully crystallized.[99] This therefore is a perfect example of the Tribunal applying the Vienna rules and arriving at a non-creative conclusion. It is interesting to note that, in his Dissenting Opinion in the *Aleksovski* case, Presiding Judge Rodrigues followed exactly the same interpretational approach as the Appeals Chamber to the question but arrived at the conclusion that evolving state practice supported a changing of the rule to extend the grave breaches regime to internal armed conflicts.[100] In the course of his opinion, Judge Rodrigues stressed: 'These interpretations do not amount to an analogy or the creation of new law. Rather, they are merely a method of ascertaining law.'[101]

The apparent reluctance of the Appeals Chamber to refer explicitly to Vienna rules is perhaps illustrative of the relative confusion surrounding the *sui generis* characterization of the Statutes. In referring to literal, teleological, and logical interpretations, the Chamber was drawing implicitly on the Vienna rules, but more explicitly on canons of interpretation drawn from domestic practice. The outcome is identical, but the methodological label is different. On occasion there has been explicit reference to issues of 'statutory interpretation' in the domestic sense, as opposed to designating them as issues of treaty interpretation. For example, in the *Šešelj* case, the Appeals Chamber addressed a challenge to the jurisdictional basis of crimes against humanity under Article 5 of the Statute, and agreed that the issue was 'one of statutory interpretation'.[102] It is argued that this is more than a semantic point, and reveals the relative inconsistency of the interpretational methodology applied by the ICTY and ICTR.

[97] ibid para 83. [98] ibid para 84.

[99] For further comment on this see the contribution of Shane Darcy (Ch 5 below).

[100] *Prosecutor v Aleksovski* (Trial Chamber Judgment, Dissenting Opinion of Judge Rodrigues) IT-95-14/1-T (25 June 1999) paras 40–44. [101] ibid para 40.

[102] *Prosecutor v Šešelj* (Appeals Chamber Decision on the Interlocutory Appeal Concerning Jurisdiction) IT-03-67-AR72.1 (31 August 2004) para 12.

A clear example of the inconsistency of approach is revealed in circumstances where a chamber or individual judge professes to rely on Article 31 but then proceeds to fundamentally misapply it. For instance, in their Joint Separate Opinion in the *Kanyabashi* case, Judges Tieya and Nieto-Navia identify the general rule in Article 31 and yet declare that:

> ...the interpreter cannot abandon the plain textual meaning of a word or phrase, although the object and purpose of a treaty and the context of its terms are, of course, aids to interpretation...The general rule of interpretation of treaties thus require that the interpreters must give words, which are clear, plain and unambiguous their normal meaning, disregarding the literal meaning only in very exceptional circumstances.[103]

This quite clearly is not the approach enumerated in Article 31: in fact it is antithetical to its teleological ambit. Object and purpose and context are not mere aids to interpretation—in the sense of supplementary means—but rather are core principles. Judge Nieto-Navia took the same approach again in the *Aleksovski* case, where along with Judge Vohrah he exclusively referred to the literal meaning of the phrase 'protected persons'.[104] Absolute reliance on the ordinary or literal meaning of a provision is done for the express purpose of limiting the creative capacity of the adjudicator. In such circumstances it acts as an absolute rule rather than as part of a broader interpretational scheme.[105] It is rare indeed that a literal conception will progressively develop the law; on the contrary, it is much more likely to limit its effectiveness.[106] Judge Shahabuddeen memorably summed up the misapplication of priorities which would result from favouring a literal interpretation over a purposive one in the *Stakić* appeal judgment: 'Even more than domestic law, international law is concerned with substance; it is not willing to be mesmerised by sacramental words.'[107]

In the *Tadić* jurisdiction decision, the Appeals Chamber did not fall into the trap of applying the individual elements of the general rule contained in Article 31 of the Vienna Convention in isolation. However, it is worth noting that, as in the

[103] *Prosecutor v Kanyabashi* (Appeals Chamber Decision on the Defence Motion for Interlocutory Appeal on the Jurisdiction of Trial Chamber I; Separate and Concurring Opinion of Judge Wang Tieya and Rafael Nieto-Navia) ICTR-96-15-A (3 June 1999) para 13.

[104] *Prosecutor v Aleksovski* (Trial Chamber Judgment, Joint Concurring Opinion of Judge Vohrah and Judge Nieto-Navia) IT-95-14/1-T (25 June 1999) para 35.

[105] Schabas (n 16 above) 857, commenting on the difference between literal interpretation and the 'literal rule'. See also *Hadžihasanović et al* (Hunt Partial Dissent) (n 69 above) para 42, where Judge Hunt approvingly quoted from the *Nuclear Weapons* case at the ICJ: 'there is no reason why the interpretation of rules of international law should be limited to literal interpretation, any more than the interpretation of municipal law'.

[106] See eg *Prosecutor v Krajišnik and Plavsić* (Decision on Prosecution Motion for Clarification in Respect of Application of Rules 65*ter*, 66(B) and 67(C)) IT-00-39-PT & IT-00-40-PT (1 August 2001) para 9, where the Trial Chamber rejected a narrow literal interpretation of the Rules of Procedure and Evidence on disclosure, on the grounds that such an interpretation would undermine the guarantee of fair and expeditious proceedings.

[107] *Prosecutor v Stakić* (Appeals Chamber Judgment, Partly Dissenting Opinion of Judge Shahabuddeen) IT-97-24-A (22 March 2006) para 69.

case of literal interpretation discussed above, both Trial and Appeals Chambers have frequently referenced and applied teleological and contextual rules in isolation without making any reference to the ostensible source of such interpretative methods.[108] More often, reference to Article 31 is used as a trigger or justification for interpretational recourse to the nebulous and often expansive notion of the 'object and purpose' of a provision.[109] In other cases, the relevant provisions of both Articles 31 and 32 are quoted approvingly and applied in concert.[110] Some judgments and decisions, however, show a more nuanced understanding of Article 31 and have correctly identified the four interpretational methods contained within its provisions.[111]

Of course this discussion of whether the Vienna Convention rules could in fact be applied by analogy to the Statutes negates the elephant in the room, namely the fact that at their very core the Statutes are penal instruments which, applying an analysis based on domestic practice, should be subject to strict construction.[112] Some judgments of the *ad hoc* Tribunals, to their credit, have addressed the issue of whether the Vienna Convention can appropriately be applied by analogy to the Statute.[113] It is unfortunate that the same degree of introspection and caution about the appropriateness and applicability of the Vienna Convention to the *ad hoc* Tribunals was not more widespread. In some circumstances, the Vienna Convention was explicitly referenced as a guide to the interpretation of the Rules of Procedure and Evidence.[114] Given that the Vienna Convention was intended to apply to the interpretation of treaties, painstakingly drafted in the course of complex political negotiations between states, it seems entirely inappropriate to invoke its terms in relation to the Rules of Procedure and Evidence drawn up and habitually amended by the Tribunal's own judges. Although the interpretational methods referred to in the Vienna Convention may well be useful in the implementation of the Rules, it is an unnecessary application of the Convention and a corruption of its intended purpose to cite it in support of the use of such methods under those circumstances.

108 See eg *Prosecutor v Nikolić* (Decision on Defence Motion Challenging the Jurisdiction of the Tribunal) IT-94-2-PT (9 October 2002) para 55.

109 See eg *Prosecutor v Milutinović et al* (Decision on Request of the North Atlantic Treaty Organisation for Review) IT-05-87-AR108*bis*.1 (15 May 2006) paras 8–10; *Prosecutor v Krajišnik* (Appeals Chamber Decision on Krajišnik's Appeal Against the Trial Chamber's Decision Dismissing the Defence Motion for a Ruling that Judge Canivell is Unable to Continue Sitting in this Case) IT-00-39-AR73.2 (15 September 2006) paras 11–18.

110 See eg *Galić* (Appeals Chamber Judgment) (n 64 above) para 103.

111 See eg *Delalić* (Appeals Chamber Judgment) (n 21 above) para 68; and *Prosecutor v Milosević* (Reasons for Decision on Assignment of Defence Counsel) IT-02-54-T (22 September 2004) para 31.

112 Schabas (n 16 above) 852–5.

113 See eg *Krstić* (Trial Chamber Judgment) (n 58 above) para 541; *Prosecutor v Kanyabashi et al* (Appeals Chamber, Joint and Separate Opinion of Judge McDonald and Judge Vohrah) ICTR-96-15-A (3 June 1999) para 15.

114 See eg *Prosecutor v Milošević* (Decision on Motion for Judgment of Acquittal, Separate Opinion of Judge Patrick Robinson) IT-02-54-T (16 June 2004) para 6, quoting the Vienna Convention to justify applying a contextual and purposive interpretation to Rule 98*bis*.

It is clear from the analysis contained in the other chapters in this collection that recourse to the 'object and purpose' of the Statute or one of its provisions has frequently been used as a gateway to the expansion of existing law, despite the admonition of Judge Shahabuddeen that 'interpretation cannot camouflage expansion'.[115] Obviously, when attempting to identify the object and purpose of a provision, the Tribunals have frequently consulted the supplementary sources of interpretation identified in Article 32 of the Convention, namely recourse to the *travaux préparatoires*.[116] It is logical and unsurprising that the Tribunals have made such frequent reference to the *travaux préparatoires* of the various international instruments of relevance to their subject-matter jurisdiction as an aid in their interpretation. However, as noted by William Schabas in his contribution, the results of such an enquiry can often be distorted in order to reflect the desired interpretational outcome of the bench. In referring to *travaux préparatoires*, the objective is naturally to get at the intentions of the drafters of the instrument; however, the identification of intent can often appear to be a greater challenge than the determination of object and purpose. In the *Tadić* appeal judgment, the presumed purpose of the drafters of the ICTY Statute (to make all crimes against humanity punishable by the Tribunal) was invoked in order to trump explicit references in the Report of the Secretary-General and the Security Council debates which appeared to require evidence of discriminatory intent.[117] Another bizarre example can be found in the *Akayesu* trial judgment, where the Chamber suggested that, in order to ensure fidelity to the intentions of the drafters, the enumerated list of protected groups in the Genocide Convention could be expanded to include any stable and permanent group, despite extensive reference in the Convention's *travaux* to a deliberate reluctance on the part of states to extend the ambit of protected groups.[118]

The *travaux* have, on occasion, been treated as a primary, rather than merely supplementary, means of interpretation. For example, in the *Delalić* trial judgment, the Chamber held that violations of common Article 3 of the Geneva Conventions should be included within the subject-matter jurisdiction of the Tribunal despite the lack of explicit reference to them in the Statute. In support of this, the Chamber cited a statement by the United States delegate in the Security Council debates on Resolution 827, which it held to be authoritative on the basis that it had not been contradicted by other delegates.[119] It sets a somewhat reckless precedent to hold a single statement from the drafting history to be authoritative

[115] *Stakić* (Shahabuddeen Partial Dissent) (n 107 above) para 34.

[116] The Tribunals have examined the Report of the Secretary-General and Security Council debates as evidence of the drafting history of their own constituent Statutes. In relation to other international instruments, the Tribunals have made use of debates during the drafting process, the work of preparatory committees, and related material.

[117] *Prosecutor v Tadić* (Appeals Chamber Judgment) (n 57 above) paras 282–8.

[118] This issue is explored in greater detail in the contribution of William Schabas (Ch 3 below).

[119] *Prosecutor v Delalić* (Trial Chamber Judgment) IT-96-21-T (16 November 1998) paras 305–6.

merely because it did not give rise to explicit contradiction. It would be all too easy to conceive of a situation within the political crucible of the United Nations where a state would seek to limit the scope of applicable law where its own self-interest could be affected. Inadvertently creating a precedent whereby a statement made on the basis of such motivations could be taken as evidence of the intentions of all the drafters in the absence of express disagreement only highlights the inherent perils of insufficiently scrupulous use of the *travaux*.[120] In the words of Sir Eric Beckett, 'to hark back to the *travaux préparatoires* for the purposes of interpretation may operate like bringing a dead hand back from the grave, or subjecting a grown man to the paternal injunctions of his boyhood'.[121]

It is clear from the above discussion that the *ad hoc* Tribunals have utilized an overwhelming variety of interpretational methods, either individually or in concert, but have frequently neglected to exercise an appropriate degree of caution in relation to the source and scope of such methods. While it is true that the ICTY and ICTR Statutes were *sui generis* legal instruments, it was logical for the Tribunals to conclude that the principles contained in the Vienna Convention could be applied to them *mutatis mutandis*. The teleological tenor of the Vienna rules provides ample scope for judicial creativity; it is only regrettable that the *ad hoc* Tribunals did not make use of them in a more systematic and coherent manner. Ultimately, any mistakes made in the somewhat scattergun attempts of the judges of both Tribunals to identify, create, and apply their own rules of judicial interpretation are forgivable in light of the undernourished state of the law they sought to make effective and the void in the Statutes where a sensible interpretational mandate should have been. This section has, of course, been in no sense exhaustive in terms of adducing the entire expanse of the interpretational schemes undertaken by the *ad hoc* Tribunals. For instance, it has not commented on the use of rules and principles which are not recognizable by analogy in the Vienna Convention but which have played a role in the progressive development of the law. Most significant in this respect is recourse to conceptions of the inherent powers of the Tribunal[122] and the principle of effectiveness of law (*effet utile*).[123] Moreover, no comment has been made on the role *stare decisis* has played in the concretization of the creative enterprises of the Tribunals, giving rise to a quasi

[120] However, with the debunking of the interpretative weight of the Security Council debates by the Appeals Chamber in the *Tadić* Appeal Judgment, it appears that little will come of such fears.

[121] Quoted in J Stone, 'Fictional Elements in Treaty Interpretation: A Study in the International Judicial Process' (1953–1955) 1 *Sydney Law Review* 344, 351.

[122] For a discussion on the role of inherent powers, see the contribution of Fabián Raimondo (Ch 2 below). See also, generally, L Symons, 'The Inherent Powers of the ICTY and ICTR' (2003) 3 ICLR 369; G Sluiter, 'The ICTY and Offences Against the Administration of Justice' (2004) 2 JICJ 631; P Gaeta, 'Inherent Powers of International Courts and Tribunals' in Vohrah (n 2 above) 353; and C Brown, *A Common Law of International Adjudication* (Oxford: OUP, 2007) 55–82.

[123] Brown (n 122 above) 43–53.

common law model of international criminal law.[124] These approaches are perhaps the focus of another day's work.

IV. Conclusion

The failure of the drafters of the Statutes to include an express interpretational provision constitutes a major design flaw in their construction. It does nevertheless appear to have been deliberate. It is a truism to proclaim the revolutionary effects the establishment of the *ad hoc* Tribunals have had on the system of international criminal justice as it then existed. Looking at the circumstances of their establishment, it is clear that, in order to ensure that this new international criminal mechanism would be effective, it was necessary to place as few formal interpretational constraints as possible on those judges trusted with its implementation. The law was not sufficiently certain to allow a strict construction of its terms. All that could be said was that the system must be fair, it must not be in flagrant violation of the principle of legality, and it must be effective. Alexander Zahar and Göran Sluiter summarized this well:

> Compared with state jurisdictions, where the whole of the criminal law is found in Acts of Parliament and in judicial decisions that have interpreted and applied the legislature's provisions, the *ad hoc* tribunals, and in particular the ICTY and ICTR, have lived the life of hunter-gatherers in a legal wilderness. They have had to track down and synthesise for themselves the law to apply to the facts.[125]

It should be noted that some judges showed a particular awareness of the vacuum created by the absence of comprehensive rules of interpretation, and attempted to make their own contribution to the identification of a coherent interpretational model. Most notable in this regard are the efforts of Judge Karibi-Whyte, Judge Odio-Benito, and Judge Jan sitting as the Trial Chamber in the *Delalić* case,[126] Judge Robinson for his Declaration in the *Furundžija* appeal judgment,[127] and Judge Shahabuddeen in the *Stakić* appeal judgment.[128] In relation to the enormity of the interpretational task facing the Tribunals, former President of the ICTY Antonio Cassese has commented that:

> [t]his need [for developmental statements through *obiter dicta*] is all the more notable in the area of international criminal law—a corpus of rules that is unclear and underdeveloped. There, a set of judicial findings plus some appropriate *obiter dicta* on a few

[124] See C Harris, 'Precedent in the Practice of the ICTY' in R May *et al* (eds) *Essays on ICTY Procedure and Evidence: In Honour of Gabrielle Kirk McDonald* (The Hague: Kluwer Law International, 2001) 341.

[125] Zahar and Sluiter (n 30 above) 80.

[126] See *Delalić* (Trial Chamber Judgment) (n 119 above) paras 158–71.

[127] See *Prosecutor v Furundžija* (Appeals Chamber Judgment, Declaration of Judge Patrick Robinson) IT-95-17/1-A (21 July 2000) paras 1–12.

[128] See *Stakić* (Shahabuddeen Partial Dissent) (n 107 above) paras 34–9, 67–9.

important legal side-issues may contribute to the determination of applicable customary international law rules and principles, as well as to the proper construction of treaties and other written international rules. As long as the rights of the accused are respected and the *nullum crimen sine lege* principle is complied with, international judges may contribute to the gradual clarification of existing law. Of course, one should not be oblivious to the possible flaws or abuses. Courts may indulge in legal discussions that not only are peripheral to the *ratio decidendi*, but may also prove simply academic and sometimes also misleading for future courts pronouncing on the same matters.[129]

This chapter has endeavoured to place the interpretational efforts of the judges of the *ad hoc* Tribunals in context by examining the drafting of the Statutes, recourse to customary international law, the available methods of interpretation for international law, and the application of some of those methods in practice. Although there were clearly some missteps in this process, it would be churlish not to acknowledge that (as is evidenced throughout this collection) the end result was the progressive development of international criminal and international humanitarian law and a triumph of law over impunity. If in the view of strict legal positivists the creative interpretational enterprise of the *ad hoc* Tribunals was the epitome of judicial madness, they must surely admit that, in light of the unique challenges facing the judges of those institutions, there was undoubtedly some method in it. In this respect, it should always be borne in mind that 'nothing stands against lunacy in the law but the reasoning judge'.[130]

129 Cassese (n 2 above) 590.
130 RJ Traynor, 'The Limits of Judicial Creativity' (1977–1978) 63 *Iowa Law Review* 1, 6.

2

General Principles of Law, Judicial Creativity, and the Development of International Criminal Law

Fabián O Raimondo

I. Introduction

The International Criminal Tribunals have often invoked Article 38 of the International Court of Justice Statute and the 'usual sources of international law' in order to identify the law applicable to their operations.[1] As is well known, the principal sources of international law are international treaties, custom, and general principles of law.[2] In international criminal law, the expression 'general principles of law' is by and large used to mean legal principles generally recognized in national law. This understanding is present in the case law of the International Criminal Tribunal for the former Yugoslavia (ICTY) and the International Criminal Tribunal for Rwanda (ICTR),[3] as well as in the text of Article 21(1)(c) of the Rome Statute of the International Criminal Court (ICC).[4]

Classically, general principles of law as a source of international law are deemed to be subsidiary in nature; subsidiary, in the sense that if there exists an applicable

[1] See eg *Prosecutor v Delalić et al* (Trial Chamber Judgment) IT-96-21-T (16 November 1998) para 414; and *Prosecutor v Tadić* (Appeals Chamber Judgment on Allegation of Contempt against Prior Counsel, Milan Vujin) IT-94-1-A-AR77 (31 January 2000) para 13.

[2] cf the Statute of the International Court of Justice (ICJ), Art 38. According to Pellet and Daillier, international lawyers agree that that legal provision reflects general international law. See A Pellet and P Daillier, *Droit international public* (Paris: Librairie Générale de Droit et Jurisprudence, 7th edn, 2002) 114, para 59.

[3] For an examination of the case law of the *ad hoc* Tribunals on general principles of law, see generally F Raimondo, *General Principles of Law in the Decisions of International Criminal Courts and Tribunals* (The Hague: Brill/Martinus Nijhoff, 2008).

[4] Also, in general international law it promotes the conception of general principles of law as being those generally recognized *in foro domestico*: see Raimondo (n 3 above) 41–2. For an opposite conception, ie that general principles of law encompass principles generally recognized in national law and principles generally recognized in international law, see *Case concerning Pulp Mills (Argentina v Uruguay)* (Separate Opinion of Judge Cançado Trindade) ICJ 20 April 2010, paras 26–51.

conventional or customary rule, this shall prevail.[5] The *ad hoc* Tribunals have resorted to general principles of law in their decisions in order to fill legal gaps, to interpret unclear legal rules, and to reinforce their legal reasoning by applying a conventional or a customary rule of international law and a general principle of law simultaneously.[6] In contrast with the International Court of Justice (ICJ) for instance, the *ad hoc* Tribunals have frequently had recourse to general principles of law in order to address legal gaps. This may be largely due to the fact that international criminal law at the time of the creation of the Tribunals was a fairly new field of international law and was thus considerably under-developed.[7] It is worth observing that the gap-filling function of general principles of law has been particularly important in the practice of the *ad hoc* Tribunals, and for international criminal law more generally, because it has helped to identify those areas of the field in need of further regulation.

General principles of law are abstractions of legal rules from national legal orders. Given the malleability of their legal content, the *ad hoc* Tribunals have at times been tempted to pinpoint a general principle that best suited their needs in the case at hand. In doing so, the question has been prompted as to whether international courts or tribunals can make law. The classical view is that judicial bodies do not create law, but rather that they assist in identifying those rules of international law which do exist.[8] However, in modern times that view has been challenged by a number of international lawyers, such as Rosalyn Higgins, Alan Boyle, and Christine Chinkin.[9] This chapter explores issues of judicial creativity by the *ad hoc* Tribunals in the context of their application of general principles of law. It demonstrates that some of those instances led to the development of international criminal law, perhaps to the point of judicial lawmaking. It submits that it will be rather more difficult for the ICC to be as creative as the *ad hoc* Tribunals have been with regard to the application of general principles of law, as the legal regime of the ICC is much more detailed than those pertaining to the latter judicial bodies.

This chapter considers the treatment of general principles of law by the *ad hoc* Tribunals in the context of their inherent powers and in relation to the applicable substantive law. Section II considers the role that they have played in the practice and jurisprudence of the *ad hoc* Tribunals against the background

5 See Article 5 of the draft resolution by the *Institut de Droit International*, *Annuaire de l'Institut de Droit International*, Vol 37 (Paris: Pedone, 1932) 324–5, 328.

6 See Raimondo (n 3 above) 171–3.

7 For an explanation of the then rudimentary character of international criminal law, see A Cassese, *International Criminal Law* (Oxford: OUP, 2nd edn, 2008) 3–13.

8 Permanent Court of International Justice, Advisory Committee of Jurists, *Procès-Verbaux* of the Proceedings of the Committee, 16 June–24 July 1920, intervention by Baron Descamps, 336.

9 See R Higgins, *Problems and Process: International Law and How We Use It* (New York: OUP, 1995) 3 *et seq*; A Boyle and C Chinkin, *The Making of International Law* (New York: OUP, 2007) Ch 6.

of their perceived inherent powers. It shows how the ICTY adjusted the meaning of the principle that courts must be 'established by law' to the specific circumstances of international criminal justice. The discussion of the ICTR's application of the *iura novit curia* principle in appellate proceedings considers how this led to the enactment of a precise provision on this matter in the Tribunal's regulations. This section also considers whether the *ad hoc* Tribunals have the inherent power to deal with contempt under general principles of law. Section III explores the use of general principles of law in the context of the substantive law of defences and crimes. It shows the influence of the discussion of duress as a complete defence under general principles of law on the Rome Statute of the ICC and considers how the ICTY crafted a definition of the crime of rape via recourse to general principles of law. By way of a contrast, section IV outlines the emerging case law of the ICC on general principles of law and, in doing so, anticipates a more restricted role for this source in the future in international criminal law than that which has been seen to date. The conclusion is drawn in section V that the *ad hoc* Tribunals have identified areas of international criminal law in need of regulation and have determined the existence and content of some 'general principles of law' to the point of judicial lawmaking.

II. General Principles of Law and the Inherent Powers of the *Ad Hoc* Tribunals

International courts and tribunals apply general principles of law by analogy,[10] ie to the extent that there is an appropriate similarity between the national law institution from which the legal principle derives (the source of the analogy) and the parallel international law institution in which the legal principle would apply (the target of the analogy).[11] Once the existence of an appropriate analogy is established, the application of general principles of law by international courts and tribunals requires the previous transposition of those principles from national legal systems into international law. During the transposition, general principles of law may require 'adaptation' to their new setting—international law—given the different approaches between international law and national legal systems regarding sources, subjects, and enforcement mechanisms. Otherwise, they may be applied in international law without prior adaptation.[12]

[10] See H Lauterpacht, *Private Law Sources and Analogies of International Law (With Special Reference to International Arbitration)* (London: Longman, Green and Co, 1927) 81–7; D Anzilotti, *Corso di Diritto Internazionale* (Rome: Atheneum, 3rd edn, 1928) 106–9.

[11] This terminology follows L Weinreb, *Legal Reason: The Use of Analogy in Legal Argument* (Cambridge: CUP, 2005) 20–1.

[12] See Raimondo (n 3 above) 58 *et seq.*

Judge Cassese has vigorously opposed mechanical transpositions of national law concepts, such as general principles of law, into international criminal law.[13] In his view, the reasons for this are threefold. First, international criminal courts and tribunals should look at all the means available at the international level before resorting to national law. Secondly, international criminal law results from the combination of civil law and common law systems;[14] it is thus unique, in that it possesses a legal logic that is significantly different from that of each of those two legal families. Thirdly, international criminal proceedings are rather different from national criminal proceedings.[15] Judge Cassesse was right in affirming that national law concepts, including general principles of law, should not be mechanically applied at the international level. But his other two arguments are not necessarily compelling. Thus, it is right to avow that one should examine international law before having recourse to national law; after all, it is understood that international courts and tribunals apply first and foremost international law. The initial examination should cover the principal sources of international law, ie international treaties and customary law, and for the *ad hoc* Tribunals, the binding resolutions of the United Nations Security Council which contained the Statutes of the ICTY and the ICTR.

However, it is worth recalling that the combination of civil law and common law systems is not limited to international criminal law and international trials. National criminal procedures are to differing extents always hybrid; 'pure' inquisitorial or adversarial criminal procedures probably do not exist.[16] In addition, the combination of civil law and common law elements would not unavoidably thwart the application of general principles of law, because, by definition, these are legal principles common to the main legal families of the world.[17]

Furthermore, it should be noted that the quintessence of national and international trials is the same, ie establishing whether a criminal offence has been perpetrated, and, in the affirmative, determining the quantum and modality of the penalty to be imposed on the convicted person.[18] The basic analogies between domestic and international criminal law make possible the transposition of

[13] *Prosecutor v Erdemović* (Appeals Chamber Judgment, Separate and Dissenting Opinion of Judge Cassese) IT-96-22-A (7 October 1997).

[14] As explained elsewhere (see Raimondo (n 3 above) 55), there is a preference for the term 'Romano-Germanic' to the term 'civil law' because it acknowledges the efforts made by universities of Latin and German countries to develop legal studies after the 12th century. However, in this chapter, the term 'civil law' is used for the sake of consistency with the other chapters of this collection.

[15] *Erdemović* (Cassese Dissenting Opinion) (n 13 above) paras 2–5.

[16] D Pastor, 'El sistema penal internacional del Estatuto de Roma. Aproximaciones jurídicas críticas' in D Baigún *et al*, *Estudios sobre justicia penal. Homenaje al Profesor Julio BJ Maier* (Buenos Aires: Editores del Puerto, 2005) 701–2.

[17] eg see the definition of general principles of law in the Rome Statute of the ICC, Art 21(1)(c), especially the French version, as it is more telling in that regard.

[18] See A Gil Gil, *Derecho penal internacional: especial consideración del delito de genocidio* (Madrid: Tecnos, 1999) 20.

general principles of law into international criminal law and their ensuing application to the case in hand.

Accordingly, although it is acceptable to argue that the transposition of general principles of law into the international arena must not be mechanical, it is also right to assert that the *ad hoc* Tribunals have in fact never rejected the application of general principles of law to international criminal law just because of their inconsistency with the structure of the latter. Furthermore, the practice of the *ad hoc* Tribunals reveals that in those exceptional junctures at which some incongruity arose, the Tribunal concerned has adjusted the contents of the general principle of law at stake to the features of international law and applied it to the case. A clear example of this is the application by the ICTY in the *Tadić* case of the general principle of law that courts must be established by law.[19]

According to the defence in *Tadić*, the establishment of the ICTY was illegal because it was not established by law. To be duly established by law, in its view, the ICTY should have been created by treaty or by an amendment of the United Nations Charter.[20] The International Covenant on Civil and Political Rights, the European Convention on Human Rights and Fundamental Freedoms, and the American Convention on Human Rights insist on the right to a fair trial by a competent, independent, and impartial tribunal established by law.[21] In the defence's view, this right is a general principle of law because of its fundamental nature and since it is a minimum condition for the administration of international criminal justice.[22]

The Appeals Chamber held that the principle whereby courts must be established by law imposes an international obligation that applies only to domestic systems of criminal justice.[23] It went on to explain that the principle cannot mean the same at both the national and international levels, as the legislative, executive, and judicial division of powers which prevails in the generality of national legal systems does not apply to the international setting nor to the United Nations. Hence, the separation of powers element of the condition that a tribunal be 'established by law' does not apply in the international context.[24]

In spite of these considerations, the Appeals Chamber did not refuse to apply the principle that courts must be established by law, but it interpreted the principle in a way different from the typical interpretation at the national level. According to the Appeals Chamber, an international court or tribunal is deemed

[19] *Prosecutor v Tadić* (Appeals Chamber Decision on the Defence Motion for Interlocutory Appeal on Jurisdiction) IT-94-1-AR72 (2 October 1995) para 42. [20] ibid paras 26–7.

[21] ICCPR, Art 14(1) reads as follows: 'In the determination of any criminal charge against him, or of his rights and obligations in a suit at law, everyone shall be entitled to a fair and public hearing by a competent, independent and impartial tribunal established by law.' This right is also provided in the ECHR (Art 6(1)) and the ACHR (Art 8(1)). For a commentary on that legal provision of the ICCPR, see S Joseph *et al*, *The International Covenant on Civil and Political Rights: Cases, Materials, and Commentary* (Oxford: OUP, 2005) 391–426.

[22] *Tadić* (Appeals Chamber Jurisdiction Decision) (n 19 above) para 41.

[23] ibid para 42. [24] ibid para 43.

to be established by law if it provides for all guarantees of fairness in full conformity with internationally recognized human rights standards.[25] In its view, this interpretation is the 'most sensible' and the 'most likely meaning' in international law.[26] Given that the ICTY is 'established by law', because the Statute and Rules of Procedure and Evidence of the Tribunal guarantee a fair trial as well as the impartiality and independence of the judges,[27] the Appeals Chamber dismissed the defence's appeal on this ground.[28]

It is true that the meaning of the principle that a court must be established by law cannot be the same at the international level as at the level of national legal systems. The reason is that in national legal systems the word 'law' in the term 'established by law' means the law of the parliament or congress and,[29] as the Appeals Chamber declared, there is no such thing in international society. The Appeals Chamber did not, however, reject the application of the principle but rather adjusted the meaning of the principle to the special characteristics of the international setting. Following the adjustment, the principle meant for the Appeals Chamber that an international criminal court or tribunal is 'to be rooted in the rule of law and offer all guarantees embodied in the relevant international instruments'.[30]

It would appear that the adjustment added little or nothing to the meaning of the principle given that the ICTY, as well as any other international criminal court or tribunal, is already bound to comply with the rule of law and to ensure a fair trial for accused persons. The obligation to ensure a fair trial was also laid down in the Statutes of the *ad hoc* Tribunals and in customary law.[31] What is more, the ICTY Appeals Chamber deemed that this due process obligation was part of *ius cogens*, that Article 14 of the International Covenant on Civil and Political Rights 'reflects an imperative norm of international law to which the Tribunal must adhere'.[32] In short, the ICTY was already bound to comply with the rule of law regardless of the applicability of the principle that courts must be established by law.

Consequently, if one takes for granted that the ICTY should be rooted in the rule of law pursuant to its regulatory instruments and to customary law, then the best interpretation of the principle 'courts must be established by law' is the second possible interpretation mentioned by the Appeals Chamber. It considered that 'established by law' means the establishment of international courts and tribunals by an organ with the power to take compulsory decisions, such as the UN

[25] ibid para 45. [26] ibid. [27] ibid paras 45–46. [28] ibid para 47.
[29] ibid para 43. [30] ibid para 42.
[31] *Prosecutor v Kayishema and Ruzindana* (Appeals Chamber Judgment (Reasons)) ICTR-95-1-A (1 June 2001) para 51.
[32] *Prosecutor v Tadić* (Appeals Chamber Judgment on Allegations of Contempt against Prior Counsel, Milan Vujin) IT-94-1-A-AR77 (27 February 2001) 3. See also E Lambert-Abdelgawad, 'Les Tribunaux pénaux pour l'ex-Yougoslavie et le Rwanda et l'appel aux sources du droit international des droits de l'homme', in M Delmas-Marty *et al* (eds), *Les sources du droit international pénal* (Paris: Société de législation comparée, 2004) 105.

Security Council when acting under Chapter VII of the UN Charter.[33] Yet the Appeals Chamber rejected this interpretation as, in its view, the 'most sensible and most likely meaning of the term in the context of international law' is that 'established by law' means that the ICTY must be rooted in the rule of law.[34] Be this as it may, this example also shows the flexibility of the legal content of general principles of law, an adaptability that has allowed for the crafting of general principles of law to best suit the interests of the *ad hoc* Tribunals.

The *Tadić* approach to general principles of law paved the way for further reliance on this source of international law and also for the adoption of a flexible approach in its interpretation. General principles of law were used to fill perceived gaps in the law by the ICTR Appeals Chamber in the *Kambanda* case.[35] In its judgment, the Appeals Chamber applied the *iura novit curia* principle, as Kambanda had put forward on appeal that, if the Appeals Chamber were to dismiss his chief request to reverse the guilty verdict and order a retrial, it should also revise the whole sentence on five legal grounds. However, he failed to submit any legal ground and the prosecution argued, in its turn, that the appellant's failure to put forward any legal arguments was enough reason at the outset to dismiss Kambanda's submissions.[36] Against this background, the Appeals Chamber held that, in the case of errors of law, the arguments of the parties do not exhaust the subject. In other words: *iura novit curia*. In this vein, it considered the issue raised on appeal even in the absence of substantial argument presented by the appellant.[37]

This example illustrates that legal problems adjudicated by international criminal courts and tribunals on the basis of general principles of law may result in the enactment of suitable legal rules to address such problems. In fact, two years after the *Kambanda* case the President of the ICTR Appeals Chamber enacted the Practice Direction on Formal Requirements for Appeal from Judgments.[38] One of those requirements is that legal reasons are submitted with regard to the grounds of appeal.[39] If a party to the appellate proceedings does not comply with the requirements stipulated in the Practice Direction, a pre-trial judge or the Appeals Chamber may, 'within its discretion, decide upon an appropriate sanction, which can include an order for clarification or re-filing. The Appeals Chamber may also reject a filing or dismiss submissions therein.'[40]

The use of general principles of law has been particularly prominent at the *ad hoc* Tribunals in the context of the inherent power, or otherwise, to deal with the matter of contempt. It has revealed an at times questionable method for

[33] *Tadić* (Appeals Chamber Jurisdiction Decision) (n 19 above) para 44.

[34] ibid para 45.

[35] *Kambanda v The Prosecutor* (Appeals Chamber Judgment) ICTR-97-23-A (19 October 2000).

[36] ibid para 96.

[37] ibid para 98.

[38] Text at <http://69.94.11.53/ENGLISH/basicdocs/pracdirections/formalreqe.htm>.

[39] ibid Art 4(a).

[40] ibid Art 13.

determining the existence of general principles of law. The *ad hoc* Tribunals have usually determined the existence and content of general principles of law by relying on their own or other international decisions, or by comparative law.[41] The comparison with national legal systems typically consists of two distinct actions, which can be termed the 'vertical move' and the 'horizontal move'.[42] The 'vertical move' is the process of abstraction of domestic legal rules aimed at distilling an underlying legal principle.[43] The *ad hoc* Tribunals have derived general principles of law chiefly from national constitutions, statutes, and court decisions. Such a methodology is acceptable because in general domestic criminal law is to be found in those legal sources.[44] The 'horizontal move' is the corroboration that the generality of nations in fact acknowledges the legal principle obtained as a result of the vertical move.[45]

It would appear that the *ad hoc* Tribunals have at times manipulated the process of abstraction of legal rules from national legal systems, so as to create a legal principle apt for settling the legal issue at hand rather than to identify an existing legal principle. In the judgment on allegations of contempt against the previous counsel of Dŭsko Tadić, this matter came to the fore. In its judgment, the ICTY Appeals Chamber asserted the existence of a general principle of law whereby courts have an inherent power to deal with contempt.[46] The accused submitted that the changes made to Rule 77 of the ICTY Rules of Procedure and Evidence during the relevant period expanded the ambit of conduct that amounted to contempt of the Tribunal, thereby jeopardizing his due process rights.[47] Rule 77 describes the conduct that amounts to contempt.[48] Prior to the last amendment of Rule 77, it had stated in paragraph (E) that nothing in the rule affected the inherent power of the ICTY to hold in contempt persons who knowingly and wilfully interfered with its administration of justice. Since that amendment, Rule 77 no longer refers to such an inherent power.

In its treatment of the issue, the Appeals Chamber held that as a preliminary point it was necessary to examine the general question of the ICTY's power to deal with contempt. It found that the ICTY has this power as it is necessary for an international criminal tribunal to take action against interferences in the administration of justice. As for the content of the power, that could be determined in light of the 'usual sources of international law'.[49] Customary law did not regulate the matter, in the Tribunal's view.[50] Thus the Appeals Chamber proceeded to examine the 'general principles of law common to the major legal

[41] See Raimondo (n 3 above) 173 *et seq.*

[42] cf O Elias and C Lim, '"General Principles of Law", "Soft" Law and the Identification of International Law' (1997) 28 Neths YBIL 3.

[43] Raimondo (n 3 above) 46–50.

[44] ibid.

[45] ibid 51–7.

[46] *Tadić* (Appeals Chamber Contempt Judgment) (n 1 above).

[47] ibid para 12.

[48] Rule 77 was adopted on 11 February 1994, revised on 30 January 1995, amended on 25 July 1997, revised again on 12 November 1997, and amended again on 13 December 2001: <http://www.un.org/icty/legaldoc-e/index.htm> accessed 25 May 2010.

[49] *Tadić* (Appeals Chamber Contempt Judgment) (n 1 above) para 13.

[50] ibid para 14.

systems of the world, as developed and refined (where applicable) in international jurisprudence':[51] in short, the general principles of law.

Despite the fact that the law of contempt originated in the context of the common law, many civil law legal systems have passed legislation with parallel results.[52] While the power to deal with contempt in common law legal systems is part of the inherent jurisdiction of the courts, in the civil law legal family the power comes into existence only if enacted by legislation.[53] In spite of those findings, the Appeals Chamber concluded that the ICTY's inherent power to deal with contempt had existed since the establishment of the ICTY and it was not contingent on the existence of a specific provision of the Rules of Procedure and Evidence.[54] It is not certain whether there is a general principle of law giving courts the inherent power to deal with contempt, contrary to the Appeals Chamber's contention. The reason is that, as the Appeals Chamber showed, in the national legal systems of civil law countries the power to deal with contempt is only granted by a legislative act. There is thus no legal principle common to the main legal families of the world in that particular regard.

Scholarly writings on this judgment have disapproved of the Appeals Chamber's conclusion. According to Cockayne, the conclusion is disconcerting because the evidence presented by the Appeals Chamber can also be interpreted in the sense that civil law legal systems do not consider it vital for criminal courts to have the power to deal with contempt, and that, where the power is deemed essential, it must be granted by legislation. Had the ICTY followed that approach, it would have been able to exercise such power only if the United Nations Security Council had invested it with such.[55] The 'identification' of a general principle of law that courts have the inherent power to deal with contempt has amounted to judicial lawmaking, as the ICTY expanded the scope of jurisdiction attributed to it by the Security Council by relying on and applying a principle whose very existence is in fact doubtful. Beyond such procedural matters, the *ad hoc* Tribunals have also used general principles of law as a means of allowing judicial creativity in the field of substantive criminal law.

[51] ibid para 15. [52] ibid. [53] ibid para 17.

[54] 'The inherent power of the Tribunal to deal with contempt has necessarily existed ever since its creation, and the existence of that power does not depend upon a reference being made to it in the Rules of Procedure and Evidence. As the Appeals Chamber is satisfied that the current formulation of Rules 77(A) to (D) falls within that inherent power, the amendments made in December 1998 did not increase the nature of the conduct which amounts to contempt to the prejudice of the Respondent's rights' (ibid para 28). The finding was reaffirmed in a subsequent decision: *Prosecutor v Aleksovski* (Appeals Chamber Judgment on Appeal by Anto Nobilo against Finding of Contempt) IT-95-14/1-AR77 (30 May 2001) para 38.

[55] J Cockayne, 'Commentary', in A Klip and G Sluiter (eds), *Annotated Leading Cases of International Criminal Tribunals: The International Criminal Tribunal for the Former Yugoslavia 1999–2000*, Vol 4 (Antwerp: Intersentia, 2002) 193.

III. General Principles and the Substantive Law

The *ad hoc* Tribunals have resorted to general principles of law across a spectrum of legal issues that have arisen in the course of their acitivities. In the context of the substantive international criminal law, general principles of law have been relied upon by the Tribunals in establishing the scope of permissible defences and in defining the elements of specific crimes. The judgment of the ICTY Appeals Chamber in the *Erdemović* case provides one of the most prominent examples of the crucial importance that general principles of law may play as a source of international criminal law. The same tribunal relied upon the principle of human dignity in the *Furundžija* proceedings in order to advance a definition of the crime of rape under international criminal law.

In the *Erdemović* Appeals Chamber judgment,[56] the bench had to deal with particularly contentious legal problems, as is evidenced in part by the appending of five separate opinions to the judgment by the members of the Appeals Chamber. As far as general principles of law are concerned, the majority of the Appeals Chamber denied the existence of a principle whereby duress is a complete defence to a charge of crimes against humanity or war crimes involving the killing of innocent persons.[57] Moreover, it determined the existence of the general principle of law whereby duress is a mitigating factor in sentencing.

Erdemović was charged with one count of a crime against humanity, or alternatively with one count of a violation of the laws or customs of war. He had pleaded guilty to the crime against humanity charge and the Trial Chamber had upheld the plea and sentenced him to ten years' imprisonment.[58] Following this, the defence mounted an appeal requesting the Appeals Chamber to revise the sentence, for the reason that the crime had been committed under duress. The Appeals Chamber, by three votes to two, held that duress is not a complete defence in international law to a charge of crimes against humanity or war crimes involving the killing of innocent human beings.[59] According to Judges McDonald and Vohrah, the law to be applied was to be derived from the sources listed in Article 38 of the Statute of the International Court of Justice. After finding no applicable customary rule on the issue at hand, they compared a broad spectrum of national legal systems in order to extract, if possible, a general principle of law. In so doing they found the principle that duress is a mitigating factor in sentencing, but not a complete defence against a charge involving the killing of innocent human

[56] *Prosecutor v Erdemović* (Appeals Chamber Judgment) IT-96-22-A (7 October 1997).

[57] For a general discussion of that issue, see K Ambos, 'Other Grounds for Excluding Criminal Responsibility' in A Cassese *et al* (eds), *The Rome Statute of the International Criminal Court: A Commentary*, Vol I (New York: OUP, 2002) 1003–48.

[58] *Erdemović* (Appeals Chamber Judgment) (n 56 above) paras 1–10.

[59] ibid para 19.

beings.[60] Judge Li was of the same opinion in that regard.[61] It is worth observing that the comparative law analysis undertaken by Judges McDonald and Vohrah was comprehensive. It encompassed 30 national legal systems which covered civil law systems, common law systems, and a hybrid category which they called 'criminal law of other states' (China, Ethiopia, Japan, Morocco, and Somalia).

The judgment reveals that, notwithstanding the subsidiary nature of general principles of law as a source of international law, these principles may have a decisive role to play in international criminal law. Had the Appeals Chamber held that duress was a complete defence under general principles of law, the defendant would have been declared not guilty and released since he had been charged with only one count. Given that the majority of the Appeals Chamber did not find that such a general principle existed, Erdemović was sentenced to five years' imprisonment.[62] As far as personal defences are concerned, it may be the case that an individual's liberty may depend on the existence of a pertinent general principle of law.

In a more general sense, this treatment of the issue of duress as a complete defence in international law to a charge of murder as a crime against humanity or war crime has been the first divisive ICTY decision with respect to general principles of law. The decision has led to the progressive development of international criminal law, albeit with the reverse result: the ICC Statute acknowledges duress as a defence to such crimes, meaning that the state parties to this treaty have not followed the precedent of the Appeals Chamber.[63] The judicial creativity of the Appeals Chamber was not favoured by the drafter of the Rome Statute.

In the application of substantive international criminal law, the *ad hoc* Tribunals have sometimes interpreted legal rules in light of value-oriented general principles such as the principle of human dignity. Such a course of action has arguably resulted in judicial lawmaking from the bench. One such example is the resort to the principle of human dignity by the ICTY in the *Furundžija* judgment in order to define the crime of rape under international criminal law. The prosecutor charged the defendant with a count of violations of the laws and customs of war (outrages upon personal dignity including rape under Article 3 of the Statute). The alleged act of rape consisted of forced oral penetration. The Trial Chamber was unable to find a definition of the crime of rape under the ICTY Statute or customary international law. Moreover it could not ascertain the elements of the crime of rape under general principles of international criminal law and general principles of international law. As a result, in order to interpret Article 3 of the

[60] *Prosecutor v Erdemović* (Appeals Chamber Judgment, Joint Separate Opinion of Judge McDonald and Judge Vohrah) IT-96-22-A (7 October 1997) paras 40, 55–72.

[61] *Prosecutor v Erdemović* (Appeals Chamber Judgment, Separate and Dissenting Opinion of Judge Li) IT-96-22-A (7 October 1997) para 3.

[62] See *Prosecutor v Erdemović* (Sentencing Judgment) IT-96-22-T (5 March 1998) disposition.

[63] W Schabas, *An Introduction to the International Criminal Court* (Cambridge: CUP, 2001) 90–1. See also, ICC Statute, Art 31, para 1(d). See also Ambos (n 57 above) 1010 *et seq.*

Statute, it deemed it crucial 'to look for principles of criminal law common to the major legal systems of the world',[64] ie general principles of law.

The Trial Chamber first found that the majority of national legal systems, from both the civil law and the common law families, do not consider forced oral penetration to be rape.[65] It would follow that under general principles of law the definition of the crime of rape does not cover forced oral penetration. However, the Trial Chamber adopted the following legal reasoning in confirming the act amounted to rape. First, forced oral penetration is a humiliating and degrading attack on human dignity. Secondly, the quintessence of international humanitarian law and human rights law lies in the safeguarding of human dignity. Thirdly, given the preceding reasons, forced oral penetration should be qualified as rape.[66] In the end the Trial Chamber defined the *actus reus* of the crime of rape as follows: (1) the sexual penetration, however slight: (a) of the vagina or anus of the victim by the penis of the perpetrator or any other object used by the perpetrator; or (b) of the mouth of the victim by the penis of the perpetrator; (2) by coercion or force or threat of force against the victim or a third person.[67] The material element (*actus reus*) of the crime of rape as stated by the Trial Chamber is clearly wider than that under general principles of law, by including forced oral penetration. Regrettably, the majority of national legal systems still consider such misconduct as sexual assault and not rape.

By relying on the value-oriented general principle of human dignity, the Trial Chamber put forward a highly influential argument. Yet, it is worth observing that the definition of the crime of rape by the Trial Chamber amounted to the creation of law because it involved the formulation for the first time of a precise and detailed definition of the objective and subjective elements of the crime of rape, rather than to the identification of existing law.[68] This approach confirms how general principles of law have acted as a useful source for the judicial creativity exercised by the *ad hoc* Tribunals. More generally, it is worth observing that this Trial Chamber's decision also led to the progressive development of international criminal law: the Elements of Crimes of the ICC contain a very similar definition of the *actus reus* of the crime of rape as a crime against humanity and as a war crime.[69]

[64] *Prosecutor v Furundžija* (Trial Chamber Judgment) IT-95-17/1-T (10 December 1998) para 177. [65] ibid para 181.

[66] ibid para 183. [67] ibid para 185.

[68] See further the contribution of Niamh Hayes (Ch 6 below).

[69] See Elements of Crimes pertaining to Arts 7(1)(g)-1 and 8(2)(b)(xxii)-1. Paras 1 and 2 common to both provisions read as follows: '1. The perpetrator invaded the body of a person by conduct resulting in penetration, however slight, of any part of the body of the victim or of the perpetrator with a sexual organ, or of the anal or genital opening of the victim with any object or any other part of the body. 2. The invasion was commited by force, or by threat of force or coercion, such as that caused by fear of violence, duress, detention, psychological oppression or abuse of power, against such person or another person, or by taking advantage of a coercive environment, or the invasion was committed against a person incapable of giving genuine consent…' The Elements of Crimes of the ICC were adopted on 9 September 2002 and entered into force on the same

IV. General Principles of Law at the ICC: Limiting Judicial Creativity?

The starting point for an analysis of the legal regime of general principles of law in the context of the ICC is Article 21 of the Rome Statute, which states the applicable law of the Court. This article sets out the specific law of the ICC, its Statute, the Elements of Crimes, and the Rules of Procedure and Evidence,[70] and the more general sources of international law, including conventions, custom, and general principles of law.[71] It specifies:

> ...general principles of law derived by the Court from national laws of legal systems of the world including, as appropriate, the national laws of States that would normally exercise jurisdiction over the crime, provided that those principles are not inconsistent with this Statute and with international law and internationally recognized norms and standards.[72]

The formulation of this provision suggests that the ICC is to apply general principles of law if no applicable rules can be identified in the special law of the court or in conventional or customary law. The purpose, therefore, is to fill legal gaps.

Unlike the Statutes and Rules of Procedure and Evidence of the *ad hoc* Tribunals, the law of the ICC is almost all-encompassing and very detailed. It provides for legal rules and regulates aspects of the proceedings that were not legislated for at the *ad hoc* Tribunals, such as the functions and powers of the Pre-Trial Chamber, the elements of the crimes, and victims' participation in the process. This, together with the fact that the *ad hoc* Tribunals have determined many customary rules of international criminal law (and, in so doing, made them accessible to the ICC for their application pursuant to Article 21(1)(b)), limits the possibility for the ICC to resort to general principles of law in order to fill gaps. It is thus not surprising that there have been just a few instances in which a chamber of the Court has thus far dealt with such principles.

The first instance of such reliance on general principles related to an application by the prosecutor for extraordinary review of a decision denying leave to appeal.[73] The Statute and the Rules of procedure and Evidence do not provide for any extraordinary review,[74] but the prosecutor submitted that such a review could be granted on the basis of general principles of law.[75] However, the Appeals Chamber noted that, in all the civil law and common law legal systems referred

date, available at: <http://www.icc-cpi.int/Menus/ICC/Legal+Texts+and+Tools/Official+Journal/Elements+of+Crimes.htm>.

70 Rome Statute, Art 21(1)(a). 71 ibid Art 21(1)(b)–(c). 72 ibid Art 21(1)(c).

73 *Situation in the Democratic Republic of the Congo* (Appeals Chamber Judgment on the Prosecutor's Application for Extraordinary Review of Pre-Trial Chamber I's 31 March 2006 Decision Denying Leave to Appeal) ICC-01/04 (13 July 2006). 74 ibid para 3.

75 ibid paras 5, 22.

to by the prosecutor, the right to review decisions of lower courts is granted by legislation, and it accordingly dismissed the motion. Concerning the practice of witness proofing, ie measures intended to help testifying witnesses in the process of recollection, the Pre-Trial Chamber found a great divergence in the various national legal systems examined,[76] and concluded that there was no general principle of law permitting witness proofing.[77]

The ICC has also resorted to general principles in the context of the burden of proof with regard to the evidence submitted in support of victims' applications for participation in the proceedings and the admissibility of evidence, an issue that is not covered by the Rome Statute or the Rules of Procedure and Evidence. The Pre-Trial Chamber applied the general principle of law that the burden of proof is on the claimant. It also accepted, based on ICJ case law,[78] the general principle of law that proof may be administered by means of circumstantial evidence.[79] The Pre-Trial Chamber's later decision to revoke the prohibition of contact and communication between two defendants was a dismissal of the prosecutor's application, because the analysis of case law made in the application was limited to merely two national jurisdictions. In the Pre-Trial Chamber's view, the sample was too limited to evidence the existence of a relevant general principle of law.[80] These examples are few and far between, and highlight the fact that the specialized law of the ICC is quite detailed in comparison with that of the *ad hoc* Tribunals. The existence of an important corpus of customary international criminal law will also reduce the likelihood of identifiable legal gaps and thus remove the necessity for resort to general principles of law in the future.

V. Conclusion

General principles of law have on occasion proved to be the 'magic wand' with which the *ad hoc* Tribunals have been able to express their judicial creativity. By identifying gaps in their statutes and rules of procedure and evidence, as well as in customary law, the *ad hoc* Tribunals turned to these principles to address areas of international criminal law that were in need of further regulation, such as the inherent powers of an international criminal tribunal, grounds for excluding

[76] *The Case of the Prosecutor v Thomas Lubanga Dyilo* (Pre-Trial Chamber Decision on the Practices of Witnesses' Familiarization and Witness Proofing) ICC-01/04–01/06 (8 November 2006) para 36. [77] ibid para 42.

[78] See Raimondo (n 3 above) 28.

[79] *The Case of the Prosecutor v Joseph Kony, Vincent Otti, Okot Odhiambo, Dominic Ongwen* (Pre-Trial Chamber Decision on Victims' Applications for Participation a/0010/06, a/0064/06 to a/0070/06, a/0081/06 to a/0104/06, and a/0111/06 to a/0127/06) ICC-02/04–01/05 (10 August 2007) paras 13, 15.

[80] *The Case of the Prosecutor v Germain Katanga and Mathieu Ngudjolo Chui* (Pre-Trial Chamber Decision Revoking the Prohibition of Contact and Communication between Germain Katanga and Mathieu Ngudjolo Chui) ICC-01/04–01/07 (13 March 2008) 12.

criminal responsibility, and the definition of crimes. In interpreting legal rules with the help of general principles of law, the *ad hoc* Tribunals have often crafted precise and detailed legal rules, as was the case with the crime of rape. The practice of the Tribunals thus challenges the fiction that judges do not make law but rather that they simply identify and apply it.

The jurisprudence demonstrates that, as far as the application of general principles of law is concerned, the *ad hoc* Tribunals have at times been extraordinarily creative. Their position as forerunners allowed them to be so. In addition, the era in which the Tribunals started operating—the 1990s—was marked by goodwill, enthusiasm, and great expectations, while international criminal law was underdeveloped. This scene and spirit may have encouraged the *ad hoc* Tribunals to read beyond the black letter of the law and to fill the book of international criminal law with newly found and created rules. It is remarkable to contrast this approach with that of the ICC, a treaty-based institution with an elaborate Statute that began operating in a new millennium. The ICC is much more cautious in its use of general principles of law. So far, it has mainly turned to this source of law to elaborate on procedural principles and it has done so mainly at the instigation of the prosecutor. The contrast between the *ad hoc* Tribunals' use of general principles of law and the more cautious approach of the ICC is illustrative of general principles of law as a subsidiary source of law. It demonstrates that, particularly in nascent areas and new domains of international law, this source of law can play a powerful role. The *ad hoc* Tribunals are to be praised for their functional and creative use of this source of law for the advancement of the project of international criminal justice.

PART II
DEFINITION OF CRIMES

3

Judicial Activism and the Crime of Genocide

William A Schabas

I. Introduction

Genocide has been called 'the crime of crimes'. It was applied and interpreted, as a legal concept, by post-Second World War tribunals even before the United Nations General Assembly had formulated what has become the authoritative definition.[1] Provisions of the Convention itself were interpreted by the International Court of Justice (ICJ) in an early advisory opinion.[2] But until the 1990s, there was really only one serious criminal prosecution for the crime, that of Adolf Eichmann by the Israeli courts. For its first 45 years or so, interpretation of the term genocide was mainly the preserve of social scientists, historians, and human rights activists. Then, as the socialist empires were fracturing and new states were becoming sovereign, international criminal law re-emerged onto the stage as an important feature in the protection and promotion of human rights, and in the quest for international peace and security. Over the next 15 years or so the law of genocide became enriched by unprecedented judicial and scholarly activity.

In rather startling contrast with the other two primary categories of international atrocity crimes, namely crimes against humanity and war crimes, the definition of the crime of genocide has not evolved in any significant fashion. For decades, activists and academics had grumbled about the narrow conception set out in the 1948 Convention on the Prevention and Punishment of the Crime of Genocide,[3] calling for its enlargement either by amendment or judicial interpretation. But, in the result, this did not take place. Despite frequent opportunities to modify the text adopted by the General Assembly in 1948, it has

[1] eg *Poland v Goeth* (1946) 7 LRTWC 4 (Supreme National Tribunal of Poland); *Poland v Greiser* (1948) 13 LRTWC 70, 112–14, [1946] ILR 389 (Supreme National Tribunal of Poland); *United States of America v Greifelt et al* ('the RuSHA Case') (1951) 5 LRTWC 88, 253 (United States Military Tribunal); *United States of America v Alstötter et al* ('the Justice Case') (1951) 3 TWC 954, 963 (United States Military Tribunal).

[2] *Reservations to the Convention on Genocide* (Advisory Opinion) [1951] ICJ Rep 14.

[3] (1951) 78 UNTS 277.

remained essentially untouched. By comparison, the definitions of crimes against humanity and war crimes underwent significant judicial development, followed by important developments in terms of codification.[4] In other words, the resistance to judicial modification of the definition of genocide cannot be dismissed as the result of some innate conservative culture among the international judiciary. Quite the contrary. Just as international criminal judges were broadening and expanding the scope of war crimes and crimes against humanity, they were also holding to a rather strict and narrow construction of the crime of genocide.

II. The *Eichmann* Trial: Customary Law and Universal Jurisdiction

Adolf Eichmann was prosecuted in Israel under provisions of the Nazi and Nazi Collaborators (Punishment) Law.[5] Enacted in the aftermath of the adoption of the 1948 Genocide Convention, it was only retroactive in its application. It did not apply generally to the protected groups listed in Article 2 of the Genocide Convention, but only to 'crimes against the Jewish people'. Otherwise, the definition in the Israeli law was identical to that of the Convention. At the same time, Israel adopted legislation to provide for prospective application of the Genocide Convention, this time with respect to all protected groups enumerated in the Convention.

To great international excitement, Eichmann was kidnapped in Argentina and brought to Israel illegally for trial. There, he invoked a range of arguments to resist the authority of the Israeli courts. None met with any success. In particular, he argued that it would be contrary to international law for Israel to exercise jurisdiction given that the alleged crimes had not taken place on its territory. Eichmann supported his argument with reference to Article 6 of the 1948 Convention: 'Persons charged with genocide or any of the other acts enumerated in Article 3 shall be tried by a competent tribunal of the State in the territory of which the act was committed, or by such international penal tribunal as may have jurisdiction with respect to those Contracting Parties which shall have accepted its jurisdiction.'[6] Indeed, the *travaux préparatoires* of the Convention confirmed that Article 6 had been drafted in such a way as to manifest the intent of the drafters to exclude universal jurisdiction over the crime of genocide.

The jurisdictional argument had figured in the codification of genocide from the word's first appearance, in the November 1944 book *Axis Rule in Occupied Europe*. Its celebrated author, Raphael Lemkin, argued that genocide should be punishable under universal jurisdiction. Lemkin made the analogy with other

[4] See the contributions of Larissa van den Herik and Shane Darcy (Chs 4 and 5 below).

[5] Nazi and Nazi Collaborators (Punishment) Law 1950 (Law 5710/1950), s I(a).

[6] *A-G Israel v Eichmann* (1968) 36 ILR 5 (District Court, Jerusalem) para 20.

offences that were *delicta juris gentium* such as 'white slavery', trade in children, and piracy, saying genocide should be added to the list of such crimes.[7] This viewpoint is reflected in the first draft of General Assembly Resolution 96(I), which was allegedly prepared by Lemkin himself:

> Whereas the punishment of the very serious crime of genocide when committed in time of peace lies within the exclusive territorial jurisdiction of the judiciary of every State concerned, while crimes of a relatively lesser importance such as piracy, trade in women, children, drugs, obscene publications are declared as international crimes and have been made matters of international concern . . .[8]

One of the primary purposes of those who proposed the 1946 General Assembly Resolution, and of Lemkin himself, was to recognize genocide as an international crime that would be subject to universal jurisdiction. At the same session of the General Assembly, a draft genocide convention was proposed by Saudi Arabia. Article 4 of the draft contemplated the exercise of universal jurisdiction: 'Acts of genocide shall be prosecuted and punished by any State regardless of the place of the commission of the offence or of the nationality of the offender, in conformity with the laws of the country prosecuting.'[9] These materials were reworked in a sub-committee. What emerged was a substantially revised text in which the fairly explicit reference to universal jurisdiction was toned down substantially, leaving only the following: 'The punishment of the crime of genocide is a matter of international concern.'[10]

The following year, in 1947, Raphael Lemkin and two other experts consulted by the Secretariat, Vaspasian Pella and Henri Donnedieu de Vabres, considered that Resolution 96(I) was consistent with recognition of universal jurisdiction, despite the changes in the final version from the original draft. They advanced the following provision:

> [Universal Enforcement of Municipal Criminal Law] The High Contracting Parties pledge themselves to punish any offender under this Convention within any territory under their jurisdiction, irrespective of the nationality of the offender or of the place where the offence has been committed.[11]

But as the Secretariat draft of Lemkin and the other experts made its way through the negotiations, the opposition to universal jurisdiction became quite manifest. In the *Ad Hoc* Committee, which studied the draft prior to debate in the General Assembly itself, the Soviet Union,[12] France,[13] and the United States[14]

[7] R Lemkin, *Axis Rule in Occupied Europe: Laws of Occupation, Analysis of Government, Proposals for Redress* (Washington: Carnegie Endowment for World Peace, 1944) 93–4.
[8] UN Doc A/BUR/50. [9] UN Doc A/C.6/86. [10] UNGA Res 96(I).
[11] UN Doc E/447, pp 5–13, Art VII. See also UN Doc E/AC.25/8.
[12] 'Basic Principles of a Convention on Genocide', UN Doc E/AC.25/7, Principle IX.
[13] UN Doc E/AC.25/SR.7, p 9. [14] UN Doc E/AC.25/SR.8, p 11.

were all opposed to the idea. It was rejected by four votes to two, with China abstaining.[15]

Universal jurisdiction fared no better in the General Assembly, in the final negotiations in late 1948. During the debates, Iran submitted an amendment authorizing universal jurisdiction subject to the failure by the territorial state to seek extradition.[16] Brazil was supportive, noting that the principle of universal punishment had been accepted since the Middle Ages, and was reflected in nineteenth-century legislation.[17] But India argued that analogies with other universal jurisdiction crimes, such as piracy, were not helpful. India said that universal repression of piracy was recognized because it was committed on the high seas and not on the territory of a state.[18] Similarly, the Soviet Union explained that universal punishment 'was justified in the cases of traffic in women or piracy by the fact that it was often extremely hard, if not impossible, to determine the place where the crime had been committed', something that was not the case with genocide.[19] According to Egypt, universal jurisdiction was not yet generally accepted. Contrasting genocide with piracy, Egypt said: 'It would be very dangerous if statesmen could be tried by the courts of countries with a political ideology different from that of their own country.'[20] For the delegate of the United States: 'The principle of universal punishment was one of the most dangerous and unacceptable of principles, and he hoped, consequently, that the Committee would reject it.'[21] Its provocative example was prosecution of an individual 'for having uttered certain opinions in his own country where the Press was free'.[22] The United Kingdom opposed universal jurisdiction because its criminal law was based on the territorial principle.[23] Others, while not questioning the principle of universal jurisdiction, felt its incorporation was inopportune. Jean Spiropoulos of Greece said that 'jurisprudence would have taken a great step forward if the principle of universal punishment would be applied to the crime of genocide'. He said it was 'questionable' to include the notion if it would make it impossible for three of the great powers to ratify the Convention. The real remedy was not to adopt the principle of universal punishment but rather to create the international tribunal, said Spiropoulos.[24]

Iran's proposal was decisively defeated, with only six in favour and twenty-nine votes against.[25] Subsequent debates suggested that despite the silence of the text of Article 6 on the issue, it did not exclude a state exercising extra-territorial

[15] ibid 12.

[16] UN Doc A/C.6/218. 'Add a paragraph: They may also be tried by tribunals other than those of the States in the territories of which the act was committed, if they have been arrested by the authorities of such States, and provided no request has been made for their extradition.'

[17] UN Doc A/C.6/SR.100 (Amado, Brazil). See also ibid (Pérez-Perozo, Venezuela).

[18] ibid (Sundaram, India).

[19] ibid (Morozov, Soviet Union).

[20] ibid (Raafat, Egypt). See also ibid (Manini y Rios, Uruguay).

[21] ibid (Maktos, USA).

[22] ibid.

[23] ibid (Fitzmaurice, UK).

[24] ibid (Spiropoulos, Greece).

[25] UN Doc A/C.6/SR.100.

jurisdiction over its own nationals.[26] However, an attempt to broaden this still further, so as to include jurisdiction where a state's nationals were the victims, did not meet with the same success. The United States and the United Kingdom were opposed,[27] with Fitzmaurice stating it was dangerous to go beyond 'the two universally recognized principles according to which the jurisdiction of courts was based on the territoriality or the nationality of the perpetrators of a crime'.[28] Belgium observed that passive personality jurisdiction was 'not generally accepted and was embodied only in some of the various national legal systems'.[29] Eventually the chair proposed that the following language be included in the report: 'The first part of Article VI contemplates the obligation of the State in whose territory acts of genocide have been committed. Thus, in particular, it does not affect the right of any State to bring to trial before its own tribunals any of its nationals for acts committed outside the State.'[30]

Article 6 of the Genocide Convention states:

> Persons charged with genocide or any of the other acts enumerated in Article 3 shall be tried by a competent tribunal of the State in the territory of which the act was committed, or by such international penal tribunal as may have jurisdiction with respect to those Contracting Parties which shall have accepted its jurisdiction.

No literal reading of the text supports the suggestion that universal jurisdiction is authorized. Moreover, no reasonable reading of the drafting of Article 6 of the Genocide Convention can permit the conclusion that universal jurisdiction over genocide was acceptable to a significant number of states at the time of its adoption. Certainly, in light of the preparatory work, it is legitimate to view the provision as not excluding other traditional forms of jurisdiction, in particular active personality jurisdiction. Passive personality jurisdiction is more doubtful. But the discussion in the General Assembly after Article 6 was adopted by which active personality jurisdiction was admitted, although this does not appear in the text, only confirms the resistance of the drafters to the notion of universal jurisdiction.

So when Eichmann raised the objection before the Israeli courts that they were exceeding international law, which did not allow for prosecution of genocide or 'crimes against the Jewish people', he had a good argument:

> If the United Nations has failed to support universal jurisdiction for each country to try a crime of genocide committed outside its boundaries, but has expressly provided that, in the absence of an international criminal tribunal, those accused of this crime shall be tried by 'a competent tribunal of the State in the territory of which the act was committed', how, it is asked, may Israel try the accused for a crime that constitutes 'genocide'?[31]

26 UN Doc A/C.6/SR.130 (Abdoh, Iran). 27 UN Doc A/C.6/SR.131 (Maktos, USA).
28 ibid (Fitzmaurice, UK). 29 UN Doc A/C.6/SR.132 (Kaeckenbeeck, Belgium).
30 Ibid. 31 *A-G Israel v Eichmann* (n 6 above) para 20.

The 'activist' judges of the District Court of Jerusalem dismissed Eichmann's objection. They began by recalling the words of the ICJ which, in its 1951 Advisory Opinion, declared that 'the principles underlying the Convention are principles which are recognized by civilized nations as binding on States, even without any conventional obligation'.[32] For the District Court, there was an important distinction between such principles, which applied even prior to the adoption of Resolution 96(I) in 1946, and Article 6 of the Convention, 'which comprises a special provision undertaken by the contracting parties with regard to the trial of crimes that may be committed in the future'.[33] Speaking to the debates in the General Assembly in 1948, the District Court explained that the drafters of Article 6 did not intend to confine prosecution of genocide to the territorial state. The Court cited the statement in the report of the Sixth Committee, stating that Article 6 was not meant to limit the right of states to try their own nationals for acts committed outside the state. Referring to commentaries on the Convention,[34] the Court said that Article 6 imposed a duty of punishment, but did not impinge upon jurisdictional rules in criminal matters applicable within different states. According to the Court, territorial jurisdiction was nothing more than a 'compulsory minimum', a conservative compromise that could be contrasted with the more exigent provisions of the Geneva Conventions, which imposed a rule of compulsory universal jurisdiction:[35]

> It is the consensus of opinion that the absence from this Convention of a provision establishing the principle of universality (together with the failure to constitute an international criminal tribunal) is a grave defect in the Convention, which is likely to weaken the joint effort for the prevention of the commission of this abhorrent crime and punishment therefor, but there is nothing in this defect to lead us to deduce any rule against the principle of universality of jurisdiction with respect to the crime in question. It is clear that the reference in Article VI to territorial jurisdiction, apart from the jurisdiction of the non-existent international tribunal, is not exhaustive.[36]

The Israeli Court also took the view that it was entitled to exercise jurisdiction under the 'protective principle', 'which gives the victim nation the right to try any who assault its existence'.[37] The Court cited Hugo Grotius and other authorities:

> All this applies to the crime of genocide (including the 'crime against the Jewish people') which, although committed by the killing of individuals, was intended to exterminate the Nation as a group... The State of Israel, the sovereign State of the Jewish people, performs through its legislation the task of carrying into effect the right of the Jewish people to punish the criminals who killed its sons with intent to put an end to the survival

[32] *Reservations to the Convention on Genocide* (Advisory Opinion) (n 2 above) 23.

[33] *A-G Israel v Eichmann* (n 6 above) para 22.

[34] N Robinson, *The Genocide Convention: A Commentary* (New York: Institute of Jewish Affairs, 1960) 84; PN Drost, *Genocide, United Nations Legislation on International Criminal Law* (Leiden: AW Sythoff, 1959) 101–2.

[35] *A-G Israel v Eichmann* (n 6 above) paras 24–5.

[36] ibid para 25.

[37] ibid para 30.

of this people. We are convinced that this power conforms to the subsisting principles of nations.[38]

On appeal, the Supreme Court of Israel, while noting full agreement with the District Court on the protective principle of jurisdiction, insisted upon the universal jurisdiction argument, as this applied not only to Jews, in whose name Israel claimed to exercise protective jurisdiction, but also to Poles, Slovenes, Czechs, and Gypsies.[39]

That Eichmann should have escaped prosecution is, of course, an outrageous idea. Hannah Arendt believed that the interests of justice required he be tried in Germany or in Poland, where the crimes took place.[40] But there is no evidence of any serious attempt by those states to obtain custody. Be that as it may, the position taken by the Israeli judges amounts to saying that there was a rule of customary law in existence prior to the adoption of the Genocide Convention in 1948, authorizing universal jurisdiction over genocide. But any honest reading of the debates makes clear that a large majority of states was opposed to the principle of universal jurisdiction over genocide. The draft resolution prepared by Raphael Lemkin himself, in 1946, implicitly acknowledged that there was no pre-existing universal jurisdiction over genocide. Lemkin had said as much in his book, in which he lamented the lack of universal jurisdiction over genocide. The purpose of General Assembly Resolution 96(I) was to rectify this situation, something that it failed to accomplish. If universal jurisdiction over genocide already existed under international law, why did so many states resist its codification?

Even assuming that there was a basis for prosecution of genocide prior to 1948, rooted in customary law or in general principles of law, as the ICJ indicated in its 1951 Advisory Opinion, to dismiss the relevance of the debates surrounding adoption of Article 6 to a determination of jurisdictional rules is a significant expression of judicial activism. But a successful one. For, since the final ruling of the Supreme Court of Israel in the *Eichmann* case, the universality principle for genocide has been endorsed by a range of other judicial bodies. For example, in a recent decision, a Chamber of the European Court of Human Rights invoked *Eichmann* to support its conclusion that universal jurisdiction over genocide is compatible with international law.[41] According to the European Court of Human Rights:

In determining whether the domestic courts' interpretation of the applicable rules and provisions of public international law on jurisdiction was reasonable, the Court is in particular required to examine their interpretation of Article VI of the Genocide Convention. It observes, as was also noted by the domestic courts (see, in particular, paragraph 20 above), that the Contracting Parties to the Genocide Convention, despite

[38] ibid para 38.

[39] *A-G Israel v Eichmann* (1968) 36 ILR 277 (Israel Supreme Court) para 12 *in fine*.

[40] H Arendt, *Eichmann in Jerusalem, A Report on the Banality of Evil* (New York: Penguin Books, 1994).

[41] *Jorgić v Germany* (App No 74613/01) ECHR 12 July 2007, para 51.

proposals in earlier drafts to that effect, had not agreed to codify the principle of universal jurisdiction over genocide for the domestic courts of all Contracting States in that Article (compare paragraphs 20 and 54 above). However, pursuant to Article I of the Genocide Convention, the Contracting Parties were under an *erga omnes* obligation to prevent and punish genocide, the prohibition of which forms part of the *jus cogens*. In view of this, the national courts' reasoning that the purpose of the Genocide Convention, as expressed notably in that Article, did not exclude jurisdiction for the punishment of genocide by States whose laws establish extraterritoriality in this respect must be considered as reasonable (and indeed convincing). Having thus reached a reasonable and unequivocal interpretation of Article VI of the Genocide Convention in accordance with the aim of that Convention, there was no need, in interpreting the said Convention, to have recourse to the preparatory documents, which play only a subsidiary role in the interpretation of public international law.[42]

The reasoning of the European Court was inspired by *Eichmann*. Like the Israeli judges, the Strasbourg court shows a similar disregard for the *travaux préparatoires* of the Convention.

Yet since *Eichmann* there have only been a handful of prosecutions for genocide based upon universal jurisdiction. Aside from *Eichmann*, we may count the extradition proceedings against John Demjanjuk from the United States to Israel,[43] the *Jorgić* case in Germany,[44] *Munyaneza* in Canada,[45] and a few Rwandan nuns in Belgium. The opposition to universal jurisdiction in 1948 was driven by fears of abusive prosecution that were obviously exaggerated, given subsequent practice. But probably most states still remain wary of universal jurisdiction, as they did in 1948. Were the issue to come to a vote in an amending protocol to the Genocide Convention, as some have proposed, the result might not be so different from what it was when the Convention itself was adopted. However, the infrequent (and prudent) use of universal jurisdiction for genocide has meant that it is not particularly threatening. States seem to have chosen to leave well enough alone, and this may have contributed to a fertile environment propitious for judicial activism.

III. *Akayesu*: 'Permanent and Stable Groups'

In the early years of the International Criminal Tribunal for Rwanda (ICTR), some judges were uncertain about where to classify the Tutsi among the victim

[42] ibid para 68.

[43] *In the Matter of the Extradition of John Demjanjuk* 612 F Supp 544 (DC Ohio 1985); *Demjanjuk v Petrovsky* 776 F 2d 571 (6th Cir 1985).

[44] *Public Prosecutor v Djajic* No 20/96, Supreme Court of Bavaria, 3rd Strafsenat (23 May 1997) excerpted in (1998) *Neue Juristische Wochenschrift* 392; *Public Prosecutor v Jorgić* Federal Constitutional Court, 2BvR 1290/99 (12 December 2000).

[45] *R v Munyaneza* [2009] QCCS 2201; *R v Munyaneza* [2009] QCCS 4865; *Munyaneza v R* [2009] QCCA 1279.

groups protected by the 1948 Convention. The reference in Article 2 to 'national, racial, ethnical and religious groups' had been reproduced without any change in the Statute of the International Criminal Tribunal, adopted in November 1994 by the United Nations Security Council.[46] Earlier authority, and notably the *Eichmann* judgments of the Israeli courts, which dealt with 'crimes against the Jewish people' and did not therefore consider the scope of the protected groups, provided little assistance on this issue.

The Rwandan Tutsi were certainly not a religious group, nor could they be distinguished from the majority Hutu on the basis of nationality, something that both groups shared. They might have been described as an 'ethnical group', although here too the main features of ethnic identification—language and culture—were no different than those of the Hutu. 'Racial group' might have seemed the best choice, but some of the judges were probably uncomfortable with the notion itself and its whiff of racism.

With no shortage of judicial activists, the Trial Chamber that sat in the first trial at the Tribunal proposed a radical interpretation of the expression 'national, racial, ethnical, and religious groups':

> On reading through the *travaux préparatoires* of the Genocide Convention, it appears that the crime of genocide was allegedly perceived as targeting only 'stable' groups, constituted in a permanent fashion and membership of which is determined by birth, with the exclusion of the more 'mobile' groups which one joins through individual voluntary commitment, such as political and economic groups. Therefore, a common criterion in the four types of groups protected by the Genocide Convention is that membership in such groups would seem to be normally not challengeable by its members, who belong to it automatically, by birth, in a continuous and often irremediable manner.[47]
>
> Moreover, the Chamber considered whether the groups protected by the Genocide Convention, echoed in Article 2 of the Statute, should be limited to only the four groups expressly mentioned and whether they should not also include any group which is stable and permanent like the said four groups. In other words, the question that arises is whether it would be impossible to punish the physical destruction of a group as such under the Genocide Convention, if the said group, although stable and membership is by birth, does not meet the definition of any one of the four groups expressly protected by the Genocide Convention. In the opinion of the Chamber, it is particularly important to respect the intention of the drafters of the Genocide Convention, which according to the *travaux préparatoires,* was patently to ensure the protection of any stable and permanent group.[48]

The Trial Chamber noted that the Tutsi had been officially classified in Rwanda as an 'ethnic group'. Nevertheless, 'in any case, at the time of the alleged events,

[46] UN Doc S/RES/955 (1994), Annex, Art 2.

[47] *Prosecutor v Akayesu* (Trial Chamber Judgment) ICTR-96-4-T (2 September 1998) para 510 (reference omitted).

[48] ibid para 515. Also para 699.

the Tutsi did indeed constitute a stable and permanent group and were identified as such by all.'[49]

The importance of the references to 'stable and permanent groups' in the *travaux préparatoires* was certainly overstated by the Trial Chamber. There were a few such comments, to be sure, and it is likely that some delegations considered that groups protected by the Convention should be confined to those that were 'stable and permanent'. The argument was used in order to exclude political groups from the scope of the Convention. It was never used in the expansive way suggested by the Trial Chamber. When the *Akayesu* judgment was released, this aspect of the ruling was welcomed as evincing 'the kind of flexibility that drafts of the Convention had, in fact endorsed'.[50] But Guénaël Mettraux wrote that '[a]lthough the meritorious agenda behind such a position is obvious, this proposition would appear to be, unfortunately, unsupported in law and at the time of its exposition in fact constituted purely judicial law-making.'[51] The Trial Chamber's novel interpretation was not unsurprisingly repeated in two of its subsequent decisions, although in a rather more guarded fashion:

> It appears from a reading of the *travaux préparatoires* of the Genocide Convention that certain groups, such as political and economic groups have been excluded from the protected groups, because they are considered to be 'mobile groups' which one joins through individual, political commitment. That would seem to suggest *a contrario* that the Convention was presumably intended to cover relatively stable and permanent groups.[52]

However, the 'stable and permanent' theory was never endorsed or otherwise espoused by any of the other Chambers at either of the two *ad hoc* Tribunals. Rather, they adopted an essentially subjective approach to the groups protected under the Convention. In *Kayishema and Ruzindana*, another Trial Chamber of the ICTR held that an ethnic group could be 'a group identified as such by others, including perpetrators of the crimes'.[53] It concluded that the Tutsi were an ethnic group based on the existence of government-issued official identity cards describing them as such.[54] A similar approach was taken by a Trial Chamber of the International Criminal Tribunal for the former Yugoslavia (ICTY). In the *Jelisić* case it said: 'It is the stigmatization of a group as a distinct national, ethnical or racial unit by the community which allows it to be determined whether a targeted population constitutes a national, ethnical or racial group in the eyes of the alleged perpetrators.'[55] In the *Brđanin* case a Trial Chamber said:

> ... the relevant protected group may be identified by means of the subjective criterion of the stigmatisation of the group, notably by the perpetrators of the crime, on the basis of

[49] ibid para 700. [50] D Amann, '*Prosecutor v Akayesu*' (1999) 93 AJIL 195, 198.

[51] G Mettraux, *International Crimes and the* ad hoc *Tribunals* (Oxford: OUP, 2005) 230.

[52] *Prosecutor v Rutaganda* (Trial Chamber Judgment and Sentence) ICTR-96-3-T (6 December 1999) para 57; *Prosecutor v Musema* (Trial Chamber Judgment) ICTR-96-13-T (27 January 2000) para 162 (reference omitted).

[53] *Prosecutor v Kayishema et al* (Trial Chamber Judgment) ICTR-95-1-T (21 May 1999) para 98.

[54] ibid paras 522–30.

[55] *Prosecutor v Jelisić* (Trial Chamber Judgment) IT-95-10-T (14 December 1999) para 70.

its perceived national, ethnical, racial or religious characteristics. In some instances, the victim may perceive himself or herself to belong to the aforesaid group.[56]

The 'stable and permanent' hypothesis had been effectively forgotten until the Darfur Commission of Inquiry set up at the request of the United Nations Security Council revived the matter in its January 2005 report. According to the Commission, the 'interpretative expansion' effected by the Trial Chamber in the *Akayesu* case was 'in line with the object and scope of the rules on genocide (to protect from deliberate annihilation essentially stable and permanent human groups, which can be differentiated on one of the grounds contemplated by the Convention and the corresponding customary rules)'. It discussed this under the heading '*The question of genocidal acts against groups that do not perfectly match the definitions of the four above mentioned groups*'. The Commission suggested that the 'stable and permanent' theory had been generally accepted by both of the *ad hoc* Tribunals, adding that 'perhaps more importantly, this broad interpretation has not been challenged by States'. Consequently: 'It may therefore be safely held that that interpretation and expansion has become part and parcel of international customary law.'[57]

It was inaccurate for the Darfur Commission to imply that the 'stable and permanent' approach had been well accepted by the *ad hoc* Tribunals. The result of this error is to render rather meaningless the suggestion that states have accepted this broadened interpretation by their failure to object. States do not normally object to isolated judicial findings that appear to be generally rejected in favour of an alternative approach. Their silence is therefore of no assistance in identifying a customary norm, contrary to the suggestion of the Darfur Commission. Trial Chambers of the Yugoslavia Tribunal have noted that the crime of genocide in many respects fits within the historical framework of the international legal protection of national minorities, and that the concept of 'national, racial, ethnical, or religious' groups should be interpreted in this context.[58] This approach indicates a quite different view of the philosophical basis for the crime of genocide than the 'stable and permanent groups' theory initially advanced in the *Akayesu* ruling. The Darfur Commission went too far in suggesting that the interpretative expansion of the four groups enumerated in the Genocide Convention 'has become part and parcel of international customary law'. The Commission said this could be 'safely held', but the opposite is the better view.

Only time will tell whether the 'stable and permanent' approach of the *Akayesu* Trial Chamber will survive and prosper. In 2004, the leading genocide ruling of the Appeals Chamber of the ICTY discussed the nature of protected groups but

[56] *Prosecutor v Brđanin* (Trial Chamber Judgment) IT-99-36-T (1 September 2004) para 683 (references omitted).

[57] 'Report of the International Commission of Inquiry on violations of international humanitarian law and human rights law in Darfur', UN Doc S/2005/60, para 501.

[58] *Prosecutor v Krstić* (Trial Chamber Judgment) IT-98-33-T (2 August 2001) paras 555–6. Also: *Brđanin* (Trial Chamber Judgment) (n 56 above) para 682.

made no mention of the theory.[59] The ICJ, in its important ruling on genocide in the *Bosnia* case, cited *Akayesu* with respect to gender crimes but did not in any way consider the 'stable and permanent' issue. But it cannot be ruled out that the rather isolated finding of one Trial Chamber of the Rwanda Tribunal, energized by the conclusion of the prestigious Darfur Commission stating that it may be 'safely held' that such 'interpretative expansion ... has become part and parcel of international customary law', will not return.

IV. The *Krstić* Dissent: Cultural Genocide and Ethnic Cleansing

One of the most vexing issues in the interpretation and application of the Genocide Convention in recent years has been tracing the boundaries of the crime with respect to acts of persecution of protected groups falling short of outright physical destruction. The Convention itself is not without ambiguity. The introductory sentence of the definition refers to 'intent to destroy', but without qualifying whether the destruction must be physical or whether it may also be cultural in nature. The list of punishable acts that follows comprises physical, biological, and cultural destruction. The latter is covered by the act of forcibly transferring children from one group to another. In other words, the victims are not murdered, but they are deprived of their ethnic identity through assimilation.

The *travaux préparatoires* provide much illumination, however. The initial menu of options proposed in the Secretariat draft of the Convention contained distinct lists of acts of physical, biological, and cultural genocide. According to the Secretariat (Raphael Lemkin was one of the consultants), physical genocide involved acts intended to cause the death of members of a human group; biological genocide consisted in placing restrictions upon births; cultural genocide was the destruction 'by brutal means of the specific characteristics of a human group, that is to say, its moral and sociological characteristics'.[60] Cultural genocide was extremely controversial. In the General Assembly, a resolution was adopted to exclude cultural genocide from the ambit of the Convention.[61] The Soviet Union and Venezuela returned to the point in the General Assembly debate on 9 December 1948 with amendments aimed at incorporating cultural genocide in the Convention. Venezuela quickly withdrew its proposal after realizing

[59] *Brđanin* (Trial Chamber Judgment) (n 56 above). There are three references to the *Akayesu* trial chamber decision in the *Krstić* Appeals Chamber ruling, none of them bearing on the 'stable and permanent' issue.

[60] UN Doc E/447, p 27.

[61] UN Doc A/C.6/SR.83 (25 in favour, 16 against, with 4 abstentions).

that there was no chance of success. The Soviet proposal was defeated on a roll-call vote.[62]

The provision in Article 2(e) on forcible transfer of children is thus an anomaly. Indeed, it was presented as such. The act had been listed under the rubric of cultural genocide in the early drafts. In the Sixth Committee, after the notion of cultural genocide had been definitively rejected, Greece proposed adding 'Forced transfer of children to another human group' to the list of punishable acts, noting that states opposed to cultural genocide did not necessarily contest 'forced transfer'.[63] Thus, with the exception of forcible transfer of children, the *travaux préparatoires* of the Convention point to an interpretation that excludes all but physical and biological extermination of a protected group.

The phenomenon of ethnic cleansing is related to this debate. The ICJ has described ethnic cleansing as 'rendering an area ethnically homogeneous by using force or intimidation to remove persons of given groups from the area'.[64] Although the term was unknown in 1948, this concept was specifically addressed in a Syrian proposal in the Sixth Committee. Syria proposed an amendment to the definition of genocide corresponding closely to the contemporary notion of 'ethnic cleansing'. The Syrian amendment read: 'Imposing measures intended to oblige members of a group to abandon their homes in order to escape the threat of subsequent ill-treatment.'[65] The Syrian representative said: 'The problem of refugees and displaced persons to which his delegation's proposal referred had arisen at the end of the Second World War and remained extremely acute.'[66] The Syrian amendment was resoundingly defeated, by twenty-nine votes to five, with eight abstentions.[67] There has been reference in the case law to the rejection of the Syrian amendment as evidence of the exclusion of 'ethnic cleansing' from the scope of the Convention.[68]

The relationship between 'ethnic cleansing' and genocide has never arisen in any significant way before the ICTR. The 1994 massacres were clearly aimed at physical destruction, rather than displacement, of the Rwandan Tutsi. Not so, however, with respect to the former Yugoslavia, where debate has raged about the relevance of the term genocide to the entire conflict since it broke out in 1991. Similar disputes have emerged more recently with respect to Darfur where, once again, the evidence of physical extermination has never been very clear.

The most significant attempt at judicial activism aimed at enlarging the scope of genocide is the partially dissenting opinion of Judge Shahabuddeen in the Appeals Chamber ruling in the *Krstić* case. According to Judge Shahabuddeen,

62 UN Doc A/PV.179 (14 in favour, 31 against, with 10 abstentions).

63 UN Doc A/C.6/SR.82 (Vallindas, Greece).

64 *Case Concerning the Application of the Convention on the Prevention and Punishment of the Crime of Genocide (Bosnia and Herzegovina v Serbia and Montenegro)* (Judgment) (26 February 2007) para 190.

65 UN Doc A/C.6/234.

66 UN Doc A/C.6/SR.82 (Tarazi, Syria).

67 UN Doc A/C.6/SR.82.

68 *Prosecutor v Stakić* (Trial Chamber Judgment) IT-97-24-T (31 July 2003) para 519; *Bosnia and Herzegovina v Serbia and Montenegro* (n 64 above) para 190.

the proposition that the intended destruction must always be physical or biological 'overlooks a distinction between the nature of the listed "acts" and the "intent" with which they are done'.[69] Adopting an essentially literal approach to interpretation, Judge Shahabuddeen noted that the act of 'deliberately inflicting on the group conditions of life calculated to bring about its physical destruction' specifically addressed the issue of physical destruction. Similarly, the fourth act, of imposing 'measures intended to prevent births within the group' indicated biological destruction. He continued: 'However, *a contrario*, it would seem that, in other cases, the Statute itself does not require an intent to cause physical or biological destruction of the group in whole or in part.'[70] 'It is not apparent why an intent to destroy a group in a non-physical or non-biological way should be outside the ordinary reach of the Convention on which the Statute is based, provided that that intent attached to a listed act, this being of a physical or biological nature', he continued.[71] Aware of the difficulty that the preparatory work creates for such a literal argument, Judge Shahabuddeen said:

> The *travaux préparatoires* relating to the Genocide Convention are of course valuable; they have been and will be consulted with profit. But I am not satisfied that there is anything in them which is inconsistent with this interpretation of the Convention. However, if there is an inconsistency, the interpretation of the final text of the Convention is too clear to be set aside by the *travaux préparatoires*. On settled principles of construction, there is no need to consult this material, however interesting it may be.[72]

He concluded that 'the intent to destroy the group as a group is capable of being proved by evidence of an intent to cause the non-physical destruction of the group in whole or in part, except in particular cases in which physical destruction is required by the Statute.'[73]

The *Krstić* Appeals Chamber ruling seems to have left judges at the Tribunal's Trial Chambers unsettled, and in the months that followed there were some apparently contradictory rulings. In September 2004, a Trial Chamber in the *Brđanin* case followed the approach of the majority in *Krstić*, to which it made abundant reference, and dismissed genocide charges.[74] Probably conscious of the fragility of *Krstić*, and a concern that a subsequent ruling might narrow still further its interpretation of the scope of the crime of genocide, the Prosecutor did not appeal the genocide acquittals. Then, in January 2005, another Trial Chamber, in the *Blagojević* case, endorsed the partially dissenting opinion of Judge Shahabudden.[75] The Chamber argued for a 'broader notion' of genocide so as to encompass acts falling short of physical extermination:

> The Trial Chamber finds in this respect that the physical or biological destruction of a group is not necessarily the death of the group members. While killing large numbers of a

[69] *Prosecutor v Krstić* (Partially Dissenting Opinion of Judge Shahabuddeen) IT-98-33-A (19 April 2004) para 48. [70] ibid.

[71] ibid para 49. [72] ibid para 52 (reference omitted). [73] ibid para 54.

[74] *Brđanin* (Trial Chamber Judgment) (n 56 above).

[75] *Prosecutor v Blagojević* (Trial Chamber Judgment) IT-02-60-T (17 January 2005) para 659.

group may be the most direct means of destroying a group, other acts or series of acts, can also lead to the destruction of the group.[76]

The genocide conviction of Colonel Blagojević was overturned by a unanimous Appeals Chamber (including Judge Shahabuddeen), which confirmed the rejection of Judge Shahabuddeen's innovative approach in *Krstić*. According to the Appeals Chamber ruling: 'It follows from the *Krstić* Appeal Judgment that the existence of the mass killings which followed the take-over of Srebrenica was key to the finding that genocide had been committed.'[77] Judge Shahabuddeen dissented, but on unrelated grounds.[78]

V. Conclusion

This chapter has considered three examples of attempts by judges to enlarge the scope of the term 'genocide'. The applicable definition appears in Article 2 of the 1948 Convention. In contrast with the other two cognate international crimes, crimes against humanity and war crimes, for which the definitions have changed and evolved over the years, that of genocide has remained untouched. The 1948 text reappears in the Statutes of the *ad hoc* Tribunals for the former Yugoslavia and Rwanda, and of the International Criminal Court (ICC), and in most national implementing legislation. It is, therefore, a definition that has stood the test of time. But it was adopted at an early stage in the development of international criminal law, and there can be no doubt that the drafters were very concerned about defining it too broadly, or imposing radical norms such as universal jurisdiction for which many of them were unprepared.

The definition has nevertheless been a source of much frustration because of its narrow scope. Over the decades, there have been many proposals to broaden the definition, primarily by extending the list of protected groups or by adding to the enumeration of prohibited acts. In the Sub-Commission on Prevention of Discrimination and Protection of Minorities, Benjamin Whitaker argued for a broader 'lay' concept of genocide, applied by sociologists and historians, which includes political groups.[79] Occasionally, national legislators have attempted some reforms in response to such critiques. For example, the French *Code pénal* defines genocide as the destruction of any group whose identification is based on arbitrary criteria.[80] The Canadian implementing legislation for the Rome Statute states that ' "genocide" means an act or omission committed with intent to destroy, in whole or in part, an identifiable group of persons, as such, that, at

[76] ibid para 666.

[77] *Prosecutor v Blagojević* (Appeals Chamber Judgment) IT-02-60-A (9 May 2007) para 122.

[78] *Prosecutor v Blagojević* (Partly Dissenting Opinion of Judge Shahabuddeen) IT-02-60-A (9 May 2007), para 122.

[79] B Whitaker, 'Revised and Updated Report on the Question of the Prevention and Punishment of the Crime of Genocide', UN Doc E/CN.4/Sub.2/1985/6, p 20.

[80] Penal Code (France), *Journal officiel*, 23 July 1992, art 211–1.

the time and in the place of its commission, constitutes genocide according to customary international law'.[81] But at the international level, more than 60 years after its adoption by the General Assembly, the definition remains unchanged. As Herman von Hebel and Daryl Robinson have observed: 'At the Rome Conference, the definition of the crime of genocide was not discussed in substance...'[82] Only one state, Cuba, sought to seize the occasion and modify the definition. But the response was virtually unanimous opposition to any change.[83]

This resistance to amendment of the definition may seem hard to explain, given the general spirit of the Rome Conference, which was to broaden and enlarge definitions of the core crimes. The other two crimes over which the ICC can exercise jurisdiction, crimes against humanity and war crimes, underwent dramatic revision. For the first time, international law contained a widely accepted formulation of crimes against humanity with no nexus to armed conflict. Similarly, the definition of war crimes was set out to encompass non-international armed conflict. Genocide, on the other hand, was left unchanged, probably because no serious argument could any longer be made that such amendment was necessary in order to close a gap in the law. Any *lacunae* have been filled by the new texts covering crimes against humanity and war crimes.

This can helpfully be understood with reference to the origins of the codification of genocide. General Assembly Resolution 96(I), and subsequently the Genocide Convention itself, emerged out of disappointment with the narrow conception of crimes against humanity confirmed in the Nuremberg judgment. Essentially, Nuremberg excluded peacetime atrocities, even those involving the intentional destruction of groups. For this reason, Article 1 of the Genocide Convention confirms that the crime may be committed 'in time of peace or in time of war'. By 1998, the nexus between crimes against humanity and armed conflict had clearly disappeared. Henceforth, the physical destruction of a political group, or the ethnic cleansing of an ethnic group, perpetrated in peacetime, was adequately covered by international law. Thus, there was no need to change the definition of genocide. This same approach, it is suggested, has characterized judicial 'lawmaking'. For these reasons, the attempts at broadened judicial interpretation of the definition of genocide have not generally been successful. Indeed,

[81] Crimes Against Humanity and War Crimes Act, 48–49 Elizabeth II, 1999–2000, C-19, s 4.

[82] H von Hebel and D Robinson, 'Crimes Within the Jurisdiction of the Court' in R Lee (ed), *The International Criminal Court, the Making of the Rome Statute, Issues, Negotiations, Results* (Ardsley, New York: Transnational, 1999) 89.

[83] UN Doc A/CONF.183/C.1/SR.3, paras 2, 18, 20, (Germany) 22, (Syria) 24, (United Arab Emirates) 26, (Bahrain) 28, (Jordan) 29, (Lebanon) 30, (Belgium) 31, (Saudi Arabia) 33, (Tunisia) 35, (Czech Republic) 38, (Morocco) 40, (Malta) 41, (Algeria) 44, (India) 49, (Brazil) 54, (Denmark) 57, (Lesotho) 59, (Greece) 64, (Malawi) 67, (Sudan) 72, (China) 76, (Republic of Korea) 80, (Poland) 84, (Trinidad and Tobago) 85, (Iraq) 107, (Thailand) 111, (Norway) 113, (Côte d'Ivoire) 116, (South Africa) 119, (Egypt) 122, (Pakistan) 123, (Mexico) 127, (Libya) 132, (Colombia) 135, (Iran) 137, (United States) 141, (Djibouti) 143, (Indonesia) 145, (Spain) 150, (Romania) 151, (Senegal) 153, (Sri Lanka) 157, (Venezuela) 161, (Italy) 166, (Ireland) 172, (Turkey) 174.

if this analysis of the evolution of the core international crimes is correct, it would seem unlikely that the definition of genocide will change in the future along the lines suggested by the Trial Chamber in *Akayesu* or by Judge Shahabuddeen in *Krstić*.

All three examples discussed in this essay turn to the *travaux préparatoires* in the interpretative debate. In two, *Eichmann* and the *Krstić* dissent, the preparatory work presented an obstacle to judicial innovation. The judges responded by recalling the subsidiary role of the *travaux* in interpretation. The *Akayesu* case stands as a curious exception, in that the Trial Chamber purported to support its argument with reference to the debates in the General Assembly. There is more smoke than fire in these citations, however. Isolated remarks by delegates, rather than decisive votes or declarations, are transformed by the judges into general expressions of legislative intent. The approach is a hazardous one. Not only should the *travaux* be used judiciously, their significance should not be distorted. But the real issue here is not the classic debate between respect for legislative intent and the need for dynamic construction of treaties in order to keep pace with evolution in law and values. Rather, as explained above, the uniqueness of a narrowly-defined concept of genocide seems almost more relevant than ever. A robust modern vision of crimes against humanity, which fills the gaps in international law that so many had hoped would be addressed in an expanded notion of genocide, has solved the problem. The integrity of genocide remains as 'the crime of crimes'.

4

Using Custom to Reconceptualize Crimes Against Humanity

Larissa van den Herik

I. Introduction

For a considerable length of time, crimes against humanity were the uncodified category of international crimes. As a consequence and in sharp contrast to the crime of genocide, the definition of which has remained unchanged since the adoption of the 1948 Genocide Convention,[1] the definition of crimes against humanity has differed in various statutes and International Law Commission (ILC) draft codes.[2] Legal ingredients, such as the requirements of a nexus to an armed conflict, a widespread and/or systematic attack against any civilian population, or discriminatory grounds, have been swapped back and forth in a cacophony of definitions. In this context, it may not be surprising that the *ad hoc* Tribunals for the former Yugoslavia and Rwanda have gone beyond their statutes in picking and choosing relevant legal ingredients. The legal basis for overlooking certain statutory elements of crimes and for bringing into play unmentioned requirements has been customary international law. In terms of legacy, the question arises as to what extent the vast contribution of the *ad hoc* Tribunals to a renewed conception of crimes against humanity is sustainable beyond the particular field of operation of each tribunal. The fact that the Rome Statute of the International Criminal Court (ICC) appears to deviate from tribunal jurisprudence in relation to some elements renders this question even more pertinent.

The concept of crimes against humanity as it has emerged over the years is succinctly set out in section II of this chapter, following which the case law of the *ad hoc* Tribunals is scrutinized with regard to three *chapeau* elements that have at some point been deemed critical for the conceptualization of the crime. The

[1] See the contribution of WA Schabas (Ch 3 above).

[2] For an overview and analysis of the different definitions, see Y Dinstein, 'Crimes against humanity after *Tadić*' (2000) 13 LJIL 373–93.

analysis focuses specifically on the evidence adduced to determine the existence of a given customary norm relating to these three elements. The three *chapeau* requirements are: the armed conflict requirement (section III); the policy requirement (section IV); and the requirement that the act be part of an attack against a civilian population (section V). The impact of the *ad hoc* Tribunals' statutes and jurisprudence relating to these elements on the definition adopted by the Rome Statute has been varied. The ICTR statutory definition and the ICTY case law on the first element, the armed conflict requirement, or rather the absence of such a requirement, have been reaffirmed in the Rome Statute. In contrast, the Rome Statute apparently deviates from the tribunals' case law on the second chosen element, the policy requirement. Whereas this element is not required pursuant to the Tribunals' approach, the Rome Statute ostensibly reintroduces it. In relation to the third element, the attack on a civilian population, and in particular the interpretation of the word 'civilian', it is not yet clear whether the ICC will adopt the same approach that the *ad hoc* Tribunals have taken.

Although the tribunals articulated that all their findings were grounded in customary international law, it remains the case that, whereas some findings have been reaffirmed in the Rome Statute, others have not. It may well be that the Rome Statute deviates from customary international law,[3] or alternatively, that the tribunals were too expansive in their articulations that certain findings were merely in line with customary international law. In this overview, the assertions of the tribunals in relation to customary international law are examined and in particular some insights are provided into the nature and contents of the evidence relating to custom that underlies some of their crucial rulings on crimes against humanity. The *ad hoc* Tribunals' identification of customary international law and their overall contribution to reshaping crimes against humanity as an international crime are appraised finally in section VI.

II. The Concept of Crimes Against Humanity

The term 'crimes against humanity' was first used in relation to the Armenian massacres in 1915.[4] The notion entered the scene of positive international law with the promulgation of the Nuremberg Charter in 1945. It was Sir Hersch Lauterpacht who had suggested the term in this context to Justice Robert

[3] As has been argued in relation to crimes against humanity specifically by A Cassese, *International Criminal Law* (Oxford: OUP, 2nd edn, 2008) 123–6. More generally on the relationship between the Rome Statute and customary international law and in particular Art 10 of the Rome Statute, L Sadat, 'Custom, Codification and Some Thoughts about the Relationship between the Two: Article 10 of the ICC Statute' (2000) 49 *DePaul Law Review* 909.

[4] In a Declaration issued by the French, British, and Russian governments of 28 May 1915: see Cassese (n 3 above) 101–2. Cassese explains that the Russians had originally proposed the term crimes against Christianity, but the French put forward the term crimes against humanity in order not to offend the Muslim populations under its colonial domination.

Jackson, the United States representative at the London conference and subsequently chief United States Prosecutor at Nuremberg.[5] In the context of the Nuremberg Tribunal, the notion of crimes against humanity was used to complement existing laws of war and in particular to cover crimes committed by the German Nazi state against its own Jewish citizens. In order to limit its scope, the definition of crimes against humanity required a connection with one of the other two crimes in the Statute, ie crimes against peace or war crimes.[6] The Charter of the Tokyo Military Tribunal copied the definition from the Nuremberg Charter, albeit with a number of differences. Notably, the Tokyo definition did not include the term 'any civilian population'.[7] Furthermore, racial and religious grounds were omitted as discriminatory grounds for persecution as these grounds were irrelevant in the field of operation of the Tokyo Tribunal. Eventually, no individual was charged with crimes against humanity before the Tokyo Tribunal, with the focus remaining on war crimes and aggression. There were no prosecutions of crimes committed by Japan against their own nationals or nationals of satellite territories.[8]

Despite the birth of crimes against humanity in the context of post-war prosecutions by international military tribunals, crimes against humanity gradually began to evolve into a crime also applicable in peacetime, although this process might have been slower than some scholars suggest.[9] Notably, in the 1954 ILC draft codes, emphasis was placed on the passive or active involvement of state authorities rather than on the linkage to war.[10] Although some scholars maintain that the involvement of state authorities was already implicit in the linkage to war,[11] others describe the ILC vision emanating from the 1954 Draft Code as

[5] M Koskenniemi, 'Hersch Lauterpacht and the Development of International Criminal Law' (2004) 2 JICJ 810, 810–11.

[6] Charter of the International Military Tribunal, Nuremberg Rules, in Agreement for the Prosecution and Punishment of the Major War Criminals of the European Axis (entered into force 8 August 1945) 82 UNTS 279, Art 6(c). The provision reads: 'CRIMES AGAINST HUMANITY: namely, murder, extermination, enslavement, deportation, and other inhumane acts committed against any civilian population, before or during the war; or persecutions on political, racial or religious grounds in execution of or in connection with any crime within the jurisdiction of the Tribunal, whether or not in violation of the domestic law of the country where perpetrated.'

[7] Apparently, this phrase was deleted from the definition at the request of the Prosecutor, just before the trial began. N Boister and R Cryer, *The Tokyo International Military Tribunal* (Oxford: OUP, 2008) 156–7.

[8] ibid 64–5.

[9] Some scholars even argue that the nexus requirement never was a substantive element of crimes against humanity, but rather a jurisdictional requirement particular to the IMTs and possibly the subsequent Control Council Law No 10 proceedings: E Schwelb, 'Crimes against humanity' (1946) 23 BYBIL 178, 206; and R Clark, 'Crimes against humanity at Nuremberg' in G Ginsburgs and VN Kudriavtsev (eds), *The Nuremberg trial and international law* (Dordrecht: Nijhoff, 1990) 195–6.

[10] Ford shows that this proposal was not the result of a clear and general consensus that the armed conflict linkage was no longer required under customary international law, but rather the contrary. See S Ford, 'Crimes against Humanity at the Extraordinary Chambers in the Courts of Cambodia' (2007) 24 *UCLA Pacific Basin Law Journal* 125, 153–8.

[11] D Luban, 'A theory of crimes against humanity' (2004) 29 Yale JIL 85, 95–6.

a 'new approach', resembling the architecture of human rights law in which the relationship between the state and the individual plays a central role.[12]

The Statutes of the ICTY and the ICTR reveal the definitional and conceptual confusion that existed in relation to crimes against humanity since they came into being, as well as the tendency to tailor definitions to particular situations, as had also been done in the context of the Tokyo Tribunal.[13] Hence, in the definition of crimes against humanity in Article 5 of the ICTY Statute, the *chapeau* reads: 'The International Tribunal shall have the power to prosecute persons responsible for the following crimes when committed in armed conflict, whether international or internal in character, and directed against any civilian population.' The requirement that the crimes had to be committed during an armed conflict, either international or internal, is in keeping with the fact that an armed conflict was ongoing in the former Yugoslavia at the time the Statute was adopted.

Deviating from the ICTY precedent, the *chapeau* of crimes against humanity in Article 3 of the ICTR Statute reads:

> The International Tribunal for Rwanda shall have the power to prosecute persons responsible for the following crimes when committed as part of a widespread or systematic attack against any civilian population on national, political, ethnic, racial or religious grounds.

The omission of an armed conflict requirement may be explained by the confusion which existed at the time regarding the relationship between the genocide and the armed conflict.[14] Instead of the armed conflict requirement, the ICTR definition enshrined a requirement of discriminatory intent for all crimes against humanity. This requirement mirrored the inherently discriminatory nature of the genocidal acts committed in Rwanda in 1994.

In the context of the Rome negotiations, a more universal definition had to be composed that was unrelated to any specific conflict or situation. Inspired by the jurisprudence of the *ad hoc* Tribunals, the following *chapeau* was eventually adopted as part of the definition of crimes against humanity in Article 7(1) of the Rome Statute: 'For the purpose of this Statute, "crime against humanity" means any of the following acts when committed as part of a widespread or systematic attack directed against any civilian population, with knowledge of the attack.' This *chapeau* was complemented by the explanation in Article 7(2)(a):

> 'Attack directed against any civilian population' means a course of conduct involving the multiple commission of acts referred to in paragraph 1 against any civilian

[12] K Ambos and S Wirth, 'The current law of crimes against humanity; an analysis of UNTAET Regulation 15/2000' (2002) 13 *Criminal Law Forum* 1, 7.

[13] cf Larry Johnson, who was involved in the drafting of the Statutes for both *ad hoc* Tribunals, sets out that the intention was to draft Statutes that were meant to address a given threat to peace and thus to tailor the definition of crimes against humanity to that situation rather than to present a general definition, LD Johnson, 'Ten Years Later: Reflections on the Drafting' (2004) 2 JICJ 368, 372.

[14] A Des Forges, *Leave None to Tell the Story* (Human Rights Watch, 1999) 22.

population, pursuant to or in furtherance of a State or organizational policy to commit such attack.

This was further explained in the Elements of Crimes with regard to crimes against humanity:

'Attack directed against a civilian population' in these context elements is understood to mean a course of conduct involving the multiple commission of acts referred to in article 7, paragraph 1, of the Statute against any civilian population, pursuant to or in furtherance of a State or organizational policy to commit such attack. The acts need not constitute a military attack. It is understood that 'policy to commit such attack' requires that the State or organization actively promote or encourage such an attack against a civilian population.[15]

The explanation was footnoted as follows:

A policy which has a civilian population as the object of the attack would be implemented by State or organizational action. Such a policy may, in exceptional circumstances, be implemented by a deliberate failure to take action, which is consciously aimed at encouraging such attack. The existence of such a policy cannot be inferred solely from the absence of governmental or organizational action.[16]

The ICC *chapeau* was evidently informed by jurisprudence of the *ad hoc* Tribunals and took on board some major developments that the Tribunals had already effected. In turn, after the adoption of the Rome Statute, the *ad hoc* Tribunals relied in many instances on the Rome Statute as an instrument indicative of customary international law.[17] The interplay between the *ad hoc* Tribunals and the Rome Statute on specific aspects of crimes against humanity is explored in the following sections.

[15] Elements of Crimes, Art 7, Introduction, para 3, UN Doc PCNICC/2000/INF/3/Add.2 (6 July 2000) 9.

[16] UN Doc PCNICC/2000/INF/3/Add.2 (6 July 2000) 9, fn 6.

[17] In the *Furundžija* judgment, the Trial Chamber stated that: 'As for the Rome Statute, at present it is still a non-binding international treaty (it has not yet entered into force). It was adopted by an overwhelming majority of the States attending the Rome Diplomatic Conference and was substantially endorsed by the General Assembly's Sixth Committee on 26 November 1998. In many areas the Statute may be regarded as indicative of the legal views, ie *opinio juris* of a great number of States. Notwithstanding article 10 of the Statute, the purpose of which is to ensure that existing or developing law is not "limited" or "prejudiced" by the Statute's provisions, resort may be had *cum grano salis* to these provisions to help elucidate customary international law. Depending on the matter at issue, the Rome Statute may be taken to restate, reflect or clarify customary rules or crystallise them, whereas in some areas it creates new law or modifies existing law. At any event, the Rome Statute by and large may be taken as constituting an authoritative expression of the legal views of a great number of States', *Prosecutor v Furundžija* (Trial Chamber Judgment) IT-95-17/1-T (10 December 1998) para 227, as endorsed by the Appeals Chamber in *Prosecutor v Tadić* (Appeals Chamber Judgment) IT-94-1-A (15 July 1999) para 223. In contrast, in the *Blaškić* case, the Appeals Chamber specifically observed that institutions like the Rome Statute for the International Criminal Court were not indicative of the state of customary international law in 1993: *Prosecutor v Blaškić* (Appeals Chamber Judgment) IT-95-14-A (29 July 2004) fn 1366.

III. The Absence of the Armed Conflict Requirement

Among the modern international criminal tribunals, the armed conflict requirement was peculiar only to the ICTY Statute and was not repeated in the ICTR Statute. Officials involved in the drafting of the Statute have indicated that the requirement was meant to emphasize the irrelevance of whether the armed conflict was international or non-international in character, rather than to make a statement on whether the existence of an armed conflict was a requirement of crimes against humanity under customary international law.[18] It may well have been that the drafters believed that the armed conflict requirement was still part of the customary law definition of crimes against humanity,[19] or at best that the existence of the requirement under customary international law was subject to debate.[20]

In the 1995 *Tadić* appeal decision, the ICTY determined that the nexus requirement to other crimes as formulated in the Charter of the Nuremberg Tribunal was unique to that Tribunal. In relation to the armed conflict requirement more generally, it observed that:

> . . . it is by now a settled rule of customary international law that crimes against humanity do not require a connection to an international armed conflict. Indeed, as the Prosecutor points out, customary international law may not require a connection between crimes against humanity and any conflict at all.[21]

The Appeals Chamber held that Article II(1)(c) of Control Council Law No 10 was an instance of state practice that supported the elimination of the armed conflict requirement.[22] The Chamber also referred to the 1948 Genocide Convention and the 1973 Apartheid Convention as further evidence of this evolution.[23] Although these conventions only concern two specific types of crime against humanity, the logic behind the reference may be that the two conventions evince a certain trend that also has implications for the broader concept of crimes against humanity.

[18] Johnson (n 13 above) 372.

[19] WA Schabas, *The UN International Criminal Tribunals; the former Yugoslavia, Rwanda and Sierra Leone* (Cambridge: CUP, 2006) 188.

[20] D Shraga and R Zacklin, 'The International Criminal Tribunal for the former Yugoslavia' (2004) 5 EJIL 360, 367–8.

[21] *Prosecutor v Tadić* (Appeals Chamber Jurisdiction Decision) IT-94-1 (2 October 1995) para 141.

[22] ibid para 140.

[23] ibid.

In the *Kupreškić* trial judgment more references were provided for the view that customary international law no longer required a link between crimes against humanity and war crimes.[24] These references were:

(1) Control Council Law No 10;
(2) national legislation, with Canada and France as the only two precise examples mentioned;
(3) case law, specifically *Ohlendorf et al* (the *Einsatzgruppen* case) and *Alstötter et al* (the *Justice* case), with the *Flick et al* (the *Industrialist* case) mentioned as giving a contrary view;
(4) treaties, particularly the 1948 Genocide Convention, the 1973 Apartheid Convention, and the Convention on the Non-Applicability of Statutory Limitations to War Crimes and Crimes Against Humanity of 1968; and
(5) past jurisprudence of the Tribunal, referring back to the *Tadić* appeal decision.[25]

In the *Tadić* trial judgment, further reference was made to the 1996 ILC Report,[26] the report of the Secretary-General,[27] and the absence of the requirement from the definition as included in the ICTR Statute. In the *Mrkšić* trial judgment, reference was also made to Statutes of subsequent international criminal courts which did not include the armed conflict requirement, such as the Rome Statute and the Statute of the Special Court for Sierra Leone.[28]

The question as to whether Control Council Law No 10 is evidence of a conception of crimes against humanity not requiring a link to an armed conflict gives rise to mixed answers, and particularly so when read in conjunction with the jurisprudence emanating from that law. The United States Military Tribunal III in the *Alstötter* case stated that the Nuremberg requirement that crimes against humanity are committed 'in execution of, or in connection with, any crime within the jurisdiction of the tribunal' was deliberately omitted from Control Council Law No 10.[29] Similarly, in the *Ohlendorf* case, the United States Military Tribunal II-A further explained that this omission 'recognizes that crimes against humanity are, in international law, completely independent of either crimes against peace or war crimes.

[24] This was done in the context of defence arguments that a nexus requirement still persisted specifically in relation to the crime of persecution with reference to Art 7(1)(h) and (2)(g) of the ICC Statute: *Prosecutor v Kupreškić et al* (Trial Chamber Judgment) IT-95-16-T (14 January 2000) paras 577–8. The Trial Chamber explained that the nexus requirement to other crimes in the context of Nuremberg, ie war crimes and aggression, implied an armed conflict requirement, whereas this is not the case with the connection requirement of Art 7(1)(h) of the Statute given that genocide and other crimes against humanity can also be committed in peacetime.

[25] ibid.

[26] *Draft Code of Crimes Against the Peace and Security of Mankind* ('ILC Draft Code'), Report of the International Law Commission on the Work of its Forty-eighth session, 6 May–26 July 1996, GAOR 51st Sess Supp No 10, 30, UN Doc A/51/10.

[27] 'Report of the Secretary-General pursuant to paragraph 2 of Security Council resolution 808 (1993)', UN Doc S/25704 (3 May 1993) para 47.

[28] *Prosecutor v Mrksić et al* (Trial Chamber Judgment) IT-95-13/1T (27 September 2007) para 431.

[29] *United States of America v Alstötter et al* (the *Justice* case) (1951) 3 TWC 954, 963 (United States Military Tribunal).

To deny this independence would make the change devoid of meaning'.[30] The only evidence provided in the *Ohlendorf* case for the finding that there was not a nexus requirement was a reference to the opening statement of the prosecution in the *Flick* case.[31] However, in the *Flick* case, the United States Military Tribunal IV had disagreed with the prosecutor and found that there was no clear support for the argument that the omission had been deliberate. Instead, the Tribunal argued that the joint purpose of the London Agreement, the Nuremberg Charter, and Control Council Law No 10 was to try *war* criminals. This vision entailed an inherent requirement that the crimes prosecuted were linked to the war.[32] As some authors have indicated, the *Weizsäcker* case (the *Ministries* case), which was not mentioned by the ICTY, also endorsed the requirement of a linkage.[33] So, the jurisprudence emanating from Control Council Law No 10 was not unequivocal on the linkage requirement. Subsequent developments show a rather similar diverse picture, and it may have been for that reason that the drafters included the linkage requirement in the ICTY's Statute.[34] Yet, the ICTY judges in *Tadić* decided that the linkage requirement was jurisdictional and particular to the ICTY statute, rather than substantive and an inherent part of the definition.

The *Tadić* determination that the link to an armed conflict was not a legal ingredient of crimes against humanity has subsequently been codified in the Rome Statute. However, in the course of the negotiations, the proposal to omit the armed conflict requirement met with some resistance and a number of states argued in favour of this element.[35] Schabas has submitted that the opposition of states to the elimination of the armed conflict requirement might conceivably be taken as evidence that the armed conflict requirement does still exist under customary international law.[36] This argument implies that the *Tadić* Appeals Chamber was wrong in its identification of customary international law.[37] Alternatively, it can be argued that the eventual disappearance of the armed conflict requirement from the definition of crimes against humanity is the final outcome of a process, and that no specific moment in time can be identified at which point the nexus requirement was dispensed with.[38] The ICTR statutory definition, in conjunction with the *Tadić* appeal decision, have certainly given this process a vital shove. The Rome Statute and in particular the implementing legislation of state parties to the ICC may well definitely settle this process and consolidate the existence of a customary international rule discarding the armed conflict requirement from the definition of crimes against humanity.

[30] *United States v Otto Ohlendorf et al* (the *Einsatzgruppen* case) 4 TWC 49. [31] ibid.

[32] *United States v Friedrich Flick et al* (the *Industrialist* case) 6 TWC 1213.

[33] Cassese (n 3 above) 108, fn 27; R Cryer *et al*, *International Criminal Law and Procedure* (Cambridge: CUP, 2007) 191. [34] S Ford (n 10 above) 125–200.

[35] WA Schabas, *An Introduction to the International Criminal Court* (Cambridge: CUP, 3rd edn, 2007) 100–1. [36] ibid.

[37] Similarly, Shraga and Zacklin have put forward an argument that to consider the ICTR definition of crimes against humanity as extending the application of crimes against humanity to peacetime would imply an advancement of the law rather than a declaration of a settled rule of customary international law. A Shraga and R Zacklin, 'The International Criminal Tribunal for Rwanda' (1996) 7 EJIL 501, 509. [38] Ford (n 10 above) 197.

IV. The Policy Requirement

When the ICTY effectively minimized the importance of the statutory requirement of an armed conflict on the basis of its understanding of customary international law, it also added a new element to the definition of crimes against humanity. In interpreting the word 'population', the ICTY presented a requirement that the acts be committed as part of a widespread or systematic attack, viewing this as an unmentioned but inherent element of crimes against humanity.[39] The ICTR statutory definition did explicitly include this element. After some discussion, mainly at the ICTR,[40] it was settled that the two adjectives 'widespread' and 'systematic' were disjunctive rather than conjunctive. The attack had to be either widespread or systematic. Widespread has generally been interpreted as referring to the large-scale nature of the attack and the number of victims, whereas systematic refers to the organized nature of the attack and the improbability that individual acts occurred randomly.[41] It has been pointed out that in practice the two criteria will often overlap.[42] This was particularly the case at the ICTR, where crimes against humanity were often charged in relation to a rather uniform set of acts. Generally crimes against humanity charges concerned genocidal acts committed pursuant to governmental policy and they were often placed in the indictment alongside genocide charges. The field of operation of the ICTY provided a much more diverse crime scene, where, for instance, the crimes committed in Bosnia differed in nature and scale from crimes committed in the former Yugoslav Republic of Macedonia. Moreover, in contrast to the ICTR, the ICTY's prosecutorial policy targeted a much more varied number of actors related to different parties to the conflict, including members of rebel groups such as the Kosovo Liberation Army. Therefore, questions regarding state involvement and the policy requirement were more pertinent to the ICTY than they were to the ICTR.

Chambers of the ICTY have pointed out that 'due to structural factors and organizational and military capabilities' an attack comprising crimes against

[39] *Prosecutor v Tadić* (Trial Chamber Judgment) IT 94-1-T (7 May 1997) paras 644–9. In the *Mrkšić* 1996 Review Decision, this element was said to be one of the distinctions between war crimes and crimes against humanity: *Prosecutor v Mrkšić et al* (Trial Chamber Review Decision) IT-95-13-R61 (3 April 1996) para 30.

[40] The ICTY Trial Chamber in *Tadić* found that the elements were disjunctive. However, given that the French version of the ICTR Statute required that the attack be 'généralisé *et* systématique', ICTR Chambers had to explain in more detail why a disjunctive interpretation as followed from the English text prevailed over the conjunctive interpretation as required by the French text: *Prosecutor v Semanza* (Trial Chamber Judgment) ICTR-97-20-T (15 May 2003) para 328. See more elaborately, LJ van den Herik, *The contribution of the Rwanda Tribunal to the development of international law* (Leiden: Martinus Nijhoff, 2005) 163–4.

[41] *Blaškić* (Appeals Chamber Judgment) (n 17 above) para 101.

[42] Schabas (n 19 above) 192; S Chesterman, 'An altogether different order: defining the elements of crimes against humanity' (2000) 10 Duke JCIL 307, 312–13.

humanity will be most often committed at the behest of a state.[43] In the words of the Trial Chamber in the *Limaj* case:

> Being the *locus* of organized authority within a given territory, able to mobilize and direct military and civilian power, a sovereign State by its very nature possesses the attributes that permit it to organize and deliver an attack against a civilian population; it is States which can most easily and efficiently marshal the resources to launch an attack against a civilian population on a 'widespread' scale, or upon a 'systematic' basis.[44]

But earlier Trial Chambers had agreed that state involvement was not a legal requirement for crimes against humanity.[45] This led to the subsequent question regarding the circumstances under which non-state actors could launch an attack independently of a state and meet the requirements of the definition of crimes against humanity. Although the Trial Chamber in *Tadić* alluded to the possibility that terrorist organizations could carry out such an attack,[46] it also indicated that in fact only state-like entities with *de facto* power over a given territory can launch an attack that meets the requirements.[47]

A matter closely related to the identity of the non-state actor is the question of a policy requirement. Is the existence of a policy an inherent legal ingredient of crimes against humanity? In the *Tadić* judgment, the Trial Chamber referred to the Dutch *Menten* case and the French *Barbie* case as domestic examples where the policy requirement was understood to be a legal ingredient of crimes against humanity. The Chamber noted that there was some discussion as to whether these domestic examples requiring the existence of policy actually represented the state of the law,[48] although in the end it concurred that a policy had to exist.[49] After some internal controversy between ICTY Chambers, the Appeals Chamber took a clear position in the *Kunarac* case in 2002, in which it concluded that despite the ICTY debates there was in fact 'overwhelming' evidence that supported its conclusion that policy was not a legal element of the crime under customary international law.[50] This finding has been followed in subsequent ICTY case law. In the *Limaj* case, the Trial Chamber repeated that:

> [t]he existence of a policy or plan (or that the crimes were supported by a policy or plan to carry them out) may evidentially be relevant, but is not a legal requirement, to establish

[43] *Prosecutor v Limaj et al* (Trial Chamber Judgment) IT-03-66-T (30 November 2005) para 191; also see *Tadić* (Trial Chamber Judgment) (n 39 above) para 654.

[44] ibid para 191.

[45] *Tadić* (Trial Chamber Judgment) (n 39 above) para 654; *Kupreškić* (Trial Chamber Judgment) (n 24 above) paras 552–5; *Prosecutor v Blaškić* (Trial Chamber Judgment) IT-95-14-T (3 March 2000) para 205.

[46] *Tadić* (Trial Chamber Judgment) (n 39 above) para 654.

[47] ibid para 654; *Kupreškić* (Trial Chamber Judgment) (n 24 above) para 552; *Limaj* (Trial Chamber Judgment) (n 43 above) para 213.

[48] *Tadić* (Trial Chamber Judgment) (n 39 above) para 653.

[49] ibid para 655.

[50] *Prosecutor v Kunarac* (Appeals Chamber Judgment) IT-96-23 and IT-96-23/1-A (12 June 2002) para 98 and fn 114.

the widespread or systematic nature of the attack and that it was directed against a civilian population.[51]

However, in applying these abstract findings to the specificities of the case concerning crimes committed at the behest of the Kosovo Liberation Army, the Trial Chamber conceded that:

> . . . although not a legal element . . . evidence of a policy or plan is an important indication that the acts in question are not merely the workings of individuals acting pursuant to haphazard or individual design, but instead have a level of organizational coherence and support of a magnitude sufficient to elevate them into the realm of crimes against humanity.[52]

Still, the formal line of reasoning at the ICTY is that customary international law does not require a policy element, as concluded in the *Kunarac* appeal judgment.[53]

The Appeals Chamber supported its conclusion in the *Kunarac* case that no policy requirement existed under customary international law with a number of sources, none of which seems to be entirely unequivocal. First of all, it referred to Article 6(c) of the Nuremberg Charter, the Nuremberg judgment, and in particular, those parts of the judgment that related to Streicher and von Schirach, as well as Article II(1)(c) of Control Council Law No 10.[54] The fact that the two cited provisions do not mention the policy requirement could be taken to show that the policy requirement did not exist. However, most relevant domestic judgments have perceived policy as an inherent ingredient, even if it was not expressly required by the letter of the Statute.[55] Moreover, the two provisions emanated from an era in which state involvement was still a legal ingredient of crimes against humanity and might be understood as subsuming the policy requirement.

In relation to the reference to the Nuremberg judgment, it is not immediately clear how the exact pages mentioned sustain the finding that no policy is required.[56] In fact, on one such page the crimes against humanity committed by the Nazis are described as a policy of terror.[57] Mettraux has made the argument

[51] *Limaj* (Trial Chamber Judgment) (n 43 above) para 184. [52] ibid para 212.

[53] The ICTR also adopted the *Kunarac* jurisprudence, eg *Prosecutor v Kajelijeli* (Trial Chamber Judgment) ICTR-98-44A-T (1 December 2003) para 873.

[54] *Kunarac* (Appeals Chamber Judgment) (n 50 above) para 98, fn 114.

[55] eg Hoge Raad der Nederlanden (Supreme Court of the Netherlands) 13 January 1981, LJ Number: 72244 (Dutch) para 8.1, as quoted in *Tadić* (Trial Chamber Judgment) (n 39 above) para 653: 'The concept of "crimes against humanity" also requires—although this is not expressed in so many words in the above definition [Art 6(c) of the Nürnberg Charter]—that the crimes in question form a part of a system based on terror or constitute a link in a consciously pursued policy directed against particular groups of people.'

[56] The Appeals Chamber in the *Kunarac* judgment refers to *Trial of the Major War Criminals before the International Military Tribunal* (Judgment) 14 November 1945–1 October 1946, 84, 254, 304, and 318–19.

[57] ibid 254. Cf WA Schabas, 'State policy as an element of international crimes' (2008), 98 *Journal of Criminal Law & Criminology* 953, 961–2: 'The conviction of these Nazi figures at Nuremberg [Streicher and von Schirach] may support the position that a perpetrator of crimes

that policy serves a descriptive function and is not expressly required as a legal ingredient by the Nuremberg Tribunal.[58]

Upon closer scrutiny of the domestic cases put forward by the ICTY Appeals Chamber in support of its finding regarding the policy ingredient, it seems that these cases might not unequivocally support the conclusion that was reached. First of all, the reference to the Dutch *Ahlbrecht* case of 1949 was not explained, and in that judgment the Dutch Supreme Court held that crimes against humanity are characterized 'either by their gravity and barbarity, or by their dimension, or by the fact that they form a part of a system based on terror or constitute a link in a consciously pursued policy directed against particular groups of people'.[59] The judgment does not clearly dispense with the policy requirement, but rather presents it as one of a few distinct characterizing factors of crimes against humanity. In the later Dutch *Menten* case, to which the *Tadić* judgment also referred as evidence of a policy requirement, the Supreme Court there held that it was an inherent element of crimes against humanity that they 'form a part of a system based on terror or constitute a link in a consciously pursued policy directed against particular groups of people'.[60] The *Menten* judgment was set aside by the ICTY Appeals Chamber in *Kunarac* based on the reasoning that the Dutch court had gone beyond the statute to be applied. In its judgment, the Dutch Supreme Court did indeed indicate that policy was not required by the letter of the text, but nevertheless considered it as a necessary inherent ingredient.[61]

The Appeals Chamber also referred to the Australian case *Polyukhovich* as support for the conclusion that a policy requirement did not exist under customary international law. This decision addressed the question as to whether Australia had the right to try Polyukhovich for war crimes and crimes against humanity committed during the Second World War in occupied Ukraine. The High Court of Australia answered this question in the affirmative, with only one dissenting opinion. The judgment is generally understood to support the view that the existence of policy is a requirement.[62] In contrast, the ICTY seemingly invoked the judgment to rebut the *Alstötter* precedent, which is also often invoked in support of the policy requirement. Hence, *Polyukhovich* was invoked to make the claim that *Alstötter* is not an authoritative statement of customary international law rather than as direct evidence of the removal of the policy requirement.[63] In addition to the indirectness of the evidence, it is also worth noting that the observation

against humanity need not be an "insider" in the plan. However, it cannot buttress the argument that crimes against humanity do not require the existence of a plan, something of which there was no shortage in Nazi Germany.'

[58] G Mettraux, 'Crimes against humanity in the Jurisprudence of the International Criminal Tribunals for the Former Yugoslavia and for Rwanda' (2002) 43 Harv ILJ 237, 271–4.

[59] Bijzondere Raad van Cassatie (Special Court of Cassation) NJ 1949, No 425 (11 April 1949).

[60] Hoge Raad der Nederlanden (n 55 above) para 8.1.

[61] ibid. Also see the argument related to (n 55 above).

[62] See eg Cryer *et al* (n 33 above) 196, fn 49.

[63] This is how Mettraux invokes the judgment: Mettraux (n 58 above) 275–6.

on the *Alstötter* case comes from Judge Brennan, the dissenting judge, who argued that Australia did not have any right to exercise jurisdiction over crimes against humanity, as this crime did not exist as a separate crime before 1945.[64]

As is the case in relation to most of the relevant references given in the *Kunarac* judgment,[65] the particular paragraph numbers of the *Eichmann* case, which the ICTY relied upon, are not explicitly indicated in the judgment. It should be noted in this respect that, as with the Nuremberg references, the *Eichmann* case concerned a case of a crime against humanity with clear state involvement that might have subsumed the policy requirement. At a given occasion in the *Eichmann* judgment, the district court even cites the *Alstötter* case in which it was stated that 'governmental participation is a material element of the crime against humanity'.[66] It further observes that the persecution of the Jews had become official policy.[67] The question of whether or not policy was a formal requirement was thus not pertinent in that case. Interestingly, some cases which did require policy were set aside for this reason, namely that they in fact merely highlighted the factual circumstances of the case at hand, rather than that they imposed an independent constitutive element.[68]

The case of *Trajković*, also referred to, did not squarely address the issue as to whether policy was an inherent requirement for crimes against humanity. Notably, Trajković was convicted for crimes against humanity because his acts were committed 'within a concerted plan aiming systematic atrocities' [*sic*].[69] This would seem to provide evidence of the requirement for the existence of a policy rather than being an instance of a national tribunal denying that policy is a legal ingredient. Even more disturbingly, it has to be noted that the *Trajković* judgment was overturned on appeal and returned to the same court for retrial.[70] This was all done before the *Kunarac* appeal judgment was rendered.

Finally, three Canadian cases were invoked to corroborate the Appeals Chamber's conclusion regarding the policy requirement.[71] It is interesting to note that these are administrative cases concerning the refusal of refugee status based on Article 1F of the 1951 Refugee Convention. Whereas the *Moreno* case concerns crimes committed by the army of El Salvador and is thus less

64 Brennan J, *Polyukhovich v the Commonwealth of Australia and anor* (1991) 172 CLR 501 (High Court of Australia).

65 *Kunarac* (Appeals Chamber Judgment) (n 50 above) para 98 and fn 114.

66 *A-G Israel v Eichmann* (1968) 36 ILR 5 (Criminal Case No 40/61, District Court, Jerusalem) para 28, cited: *Alstötter et al* (n 29 above) 984.

67 ibid para 56.

68 This happened to the following case: Supreme Court for the British Zone, OGH br Z, Vol I, 19.

69 *Momcilo Trajković* (District Court of Gjilan) P Nr 68/2000 (6 March 2001).

70 *Momcilo Trajković* (Supreme Court of Kosovo in Pristina) AP nr 145/2001 (30 November 2001).

71 *Mugesera et al v Minister of Citizenship and Immigration* (Federal Court of Canada, Trial Division) IMM-5946-98 (10 May 2001); *Moreno v Canada (Minister of Employment and Immigration)* (Federal Court of Canada, Court of Appeal) 1 FC 298 (14 September 1993); *Sivakumar v Canada (Minister of Employment and Immigration)* (Federal Court of Canada, Court of Appeal) 1994 1 FC 433 (4 November 1993).

directly relevant, and the *Mugesera* case mainly focuses on the question of incitement, the case against *Sivakumar* directly addresses the policy question. This case concerns a former leader of the Tamil Tigers and in the case the court noted the ongoing discussion between academics and judges on the question of whether state involvement or policy is an element of crimes against humanity. The court referred to the *Alstötter* case and the writings of Bassiouni as evidence in favour of the state policy ingredient. On the other hand the court observed that there was evidence of a practice and legal opinion that individuals unrelated to a state could commit crimes against humanity. Referring to the *Flick* case, the *Advisory Opinion on Reservations to the Genocide Convention* of the International Court of Justice, and the work of the ILC, the court held: 'Based on these latter authorities, therefore, it can no longer be said that individuals without any connection to the state, especially those involved in paramilitary or armed revolutionary movements, can be immune from the reach of international criminal law.'[72]

The court thus seemed to side with the argument that governmental policy is not required as an element of crime, and the case could thus serve as an instance of practice supporting the *Kunarac* appeal conclusion. However, in its subsequent reasoning, the court did not clearly distinguish between the question of whether an organizational policy is required as an element of crime and the question as to whether persons unaffiliated with the state can commit crimes against humanity. Even if the latter question is answered in the affirmative, one might conceivably still require state involvement in the overarching attack. Here again, the *Sivakumar* case does not present an unequivocal instance of state practice on the policy requirement.

In the context of citing Canadian cases in relation to the definition of crimes against humanity, it is further noteworthy that the leading Canadian case on crimes against humanity, *Finta*, was not referred to at all. In this case, the Canadian court characterized policy as a 'central concern'.[73] Other domestic cases that are generally seen as authoritative on the law on crimes against humanity, such as the cases against *Touvier* and *Barbie*, were not mentioned either.[74]

In addition to the instances of national case law, the Appeals Chamber also made reference to the Report of the Secretary-General in relation to the establishment of the ICTY, as well as to the work of the ILC. Finally, it is observed that it had reached the same conclusion that policy was not an element of crime in relation to the crime of genocide.[75] Interestingly, the Appeals Chamber did not make any mention of the Rome Statute, which does seemingly require a state or

[72] *Sivakumar* (n 71 above). [73] *R v Imre Finta* [1994] 1 SCR 701 (24 March 1994).

[74] The case of *Barbie* was cited in Trial Chamber in the *Tadić* case as an instance in which policy was required, whereas the case of *Touvier* was cited in the context of discussing policy in *Kupreškić* (Trial Chamber Judgment) (n 24 above) para 552.

[75] *Prosecutor v Jelisić* (Appeals Chamber Judgment) ICTY-95-10-A (5 July 2001) para 48.

organizational policy.[76] Given the analysis above, it does not come as a surprise that the *Kunarac* judgment on the policy requirement has been subject to serious criticism in terms of its legal foundation and for opening the door to a concept of crimes against humanity that would include widespread but random crimes.[77]

Article 7(2)(a) of the ICC Statute closed this door in that it requires policy for all crimes against humanity and does not allow for a concept of crimes against humanity that covers widespread but unorganized crimes. From a broader perspective, the ICC provision can thus be seen as an amendment to the disjunctive approach of the tribunals in relation to the adjectives 'widespread' and 'systematic' that qualify the attack requirement. While the ICC definition accepts that crimes against humanity can be committed as part of an attack that is systematic but not widespread, the policy requirement of Article 7(2)(a) excludes the possibility that crimes against humanity are committed as part of an attack that is widespread but not systematic. In contrast to the *Kunarac* legacy, the ICC requires that all crimes against humanity are committed as part of an attack 'that follows a regular pattern'.[78] However, perhaps inspired by *Kunarac*, the ICC did proceed beyond the ICTY legacy on a closely related aspect, namely the identity of the non-state actor capable of launching an attack. In the *Katanga* and *Bemba* confirmation of charges decisions, the ICC Pre-Trial Chambers held that an organizational policy could be made not only by groups which govern a specific territory—the *Tadić* dictum—but also by 'any organization with the capability to commit a widespread or systematic attack against a civilian population'.[79] In its Article 15 decision in relation to the situation in Kenya, the Pre-Trial Chamber even went one step further and held that any 'group that has the capability to perform acts which infringe on basic human values' can be the author of a crime against humanity.[80] In his dissenting opinion, Judge Kaul proposed a more rigid interpretation confining the organizations capable of committing crimes against

[76] This ICC requirement was mentioned in *Blaškić* (Trial Chamber Judgment) (n 45 above) para 205. In other instances where the ICTY deviated from the ICC Statute, it has more clearly referred to Art 10 of the ICC Statute and expressly articulated its finding that a given provision of the ICC Statute, namely Art 7(1)(h) on persecution, was not consonant with customary international law: *Kupreškić* (Trial Chamber Judgment) (n 24 above) para 580. Cf Schabas (n 57 above) 962–3.

[77] Schabas (n 57 above); Cryer (n 33 above) 197–8.

[78] *Prosecutor v Bemba* (Pre-Trial Chamber Decision on the Confirmation of Charges) ICC-01/05–01/08 (15 June 2009) para 81. cf also *Prosecutor v Katanga and Ngudjolo Chui* (Pre-Trial Chamber Decision on the Confirmation of Charges) ICC-01/04–01/07 (30 September 2008) para 396: 'Accordingly, in the context of a widespread attack, the requirement of an organizational policy pursuant to Article 7(2)(a) of the Statute ensures that the attack, even if carried out over a large geographical area or directed against a large number of victims, must still be thoroughly organized and follow a regular pattern.'

[79] *Katanga and Ngudjolo Chui* (Confirmation of Charges Decision) (n 78 above) para 396 and *Bemba* (Confirmation of Charges Decision) (n 78 above) para 81.

[80] *Situation in the Republic of Kenya* (Pre-Trial Chamber Decision pursuant to Article 15 of the Rome Statute on the authorization of an investigation into the situation in the Republic of Kenya) ICC-01/09 (31 March 2010) para 90. Further considerations on whether a given group qualified as an organization under the Rome Statute were given in para 93.

humanity to state-like entities, which would have a certain degree of hierarchical structure and some policy level, with the capacity to impose the policy on their members and to sanction them.[81] But Kaul's attempt to not let 'Article 7(2)(a) of the Statute [be broadened] infinitely beyond its conceptual confines' seems to have been in vain. While closing the *Kunarac* door on policy, the ICC has opened up another one on the identity of the non-state actor capable of launching a crime against humanity. Quite possibly, the ICC judges were stirred by the same motivations as had prompted the *Kunarac* Appeals Chamber.

Yet, as is often the case, the proof of the pudding is in the eating and it may well be that, when applying this new criterion to a factual situation, it will be difficult to prove that there is an organization, ie a clearly defined entity rather than a loosely connected group of people, which has the capability to launch an attack without having *de facto* territorial control. In summary, an attack must be planned, directed, or organized to come within the purview of the ICC definition of crimes against humanity and thus the *Kunarac* legacy has not been directly followed. At most, the attempt of *Kunarac* to broaden the crime and not to include policy as a legal requirement may have inspired the ICC vision on the identity of non-state actors.

V. The *Civilian* Population

In addition to introducing a new element, the ICTY also re-emphasized the statutory requirement that a crime against humanity had to be 'directed against a civilian population'. This requirement is often characterized as the core element of crimes against humanity.[82] It has been argued that this element, along with the nexus requirement, denotes the international humanitarian law origins of crimes against humanity.[83] This is underscored by the fact that the Martens clause is often invoked as the legal basis for the concept of crimes against humanity[84] and also because the concept of civilian status is essential in international humanitarian law and the principle of distinction between civilians and combatants is central to that branch of law.[85] However, as noted, the concept of crimes against humanity has developed beyond the laws of war in that it has lost the nexus requirement. Therefore, the meaning of 'civilian' as a residue in the reconceptualized crimes against humanity was open to interpretation.

[81] *Situation in the Republic of Kenya* (Decision pursuant to Article 15 of the Rome Statute on the authorization of an investigation into the situation in the Republic of Kenya, Dissenting opinion of Judge Kaul) ICC-01/09 (31 March 2010) para 51. Following the ICC jurisprudence (as quoted in n 78 above), Judge Kaul did not consider territorial control a condition *sine qua non*: see eg fn 56 of the Opinion.

[82] Dinstein (n 2 above) 383.

[83] Ambos and Wirth (n 12 above) 4.

[84] M Lippman, 'Crimes against humanity' (1997) 17 BC TWLJ 171, 173–4.

[85] F Kalshoven and L Zegveld, *Constraints on the waging of war* (Geneva: International Committee of the Red Cross, 2001) 96–100.

In the *Kayishema and Ruzindana* case, the ICTR embarked upon an interpretation of 'civilian' outside the context of armed conflict. It held:

> Traditionally, legal definitions of 'civilian' or 'civilian population' have been discussed within the context of armed conflict. However, under the Statute, crimes against humanity may be committed inside or outside the context of an armed conflict. Therefore, the term civilian must be understood within the context of war as well as relative peace. The Trial Chamber considers that a wide definition of civilian is applicable and, in the context of the situation of Kibuye Prefecture where there was no armed conflict, includes all persons except those who have the duty to maintain public order and have the legitimate means to exercise force. Non-civilians would include, for example, members of the FAR, the RPF, the police and the Gendarmerie Nationale.[86]

The Trial Chamber did not provide any legal basis for its finding. The approach has been qualified as erroneous by scholars.[87] They point out that policemen in armed conflict who do not participate in the conflict are considered civilian under international humanitarian law, but those same policemen executing the same acts would not be qualified as civilian under the proposed *Kayishema* definition. These scholars argue that, instead of the *Kayishema* approach, the starting point for a correct interpretation should be international humanitarian law and on that basis a wider interpretation for peacetime situations can be developed.[88]

This suggestion was in line with the *Akayesu* approach.[89] In this case, the ICTR did seek guidance from international humanitarian law, despite the emancipation of crimes against humanity from the laws of war-context and despite the absence of a direct link to an armed conflict in the case at hand. Building on *Akayesu*, the authoritative interpretation of the word 'civilian' as used in the *chapeau* of Article 5 of the ICTY Statute was given by the ICTY Appeals Chamber in the *Blaškić* case. It held that Article 50 of Additional Protocol I reflected customary international law and was therefore relevant for the interpretation of crimes against humanity.[90] Article 50 provides a negative definition, stipulating that anyone who does not belong to the armed forces, a militia, or a resistance group, is a civilian. Pursuant to this interpretation, persons *hors de combat*, such as prisoners of war or wounded soldiers, do not qualify as civilian. The presence of some persons *hors de combat* or even soldiers in an otherwise predominantly civilian population would not deprive the population of its civilian character.

Subsequently, the question arose as to whether the actual victims had to be civilian as well. In the *Mrkšić* case, the Trial Chamber held that '[t]here is insufficient evidence in support of the proposition that the notion of crimes against humanity has expanded, under customary international law, so as to include

[86] *Prosecutor v Kayishema and Ruzindana* (Trial Chamber Judgment) ICTR-95-1-T (21 May 1999) para 127.

[87] Ambos and Wirth (n 12 above) 22–3.

[88] ibid.

[89] *Prosecutor v Akayesu* (Trial Chamber Judgment) ICTR-96-4-T (2 September 1998) para 582.

[90] *Blaškić* (Appeals Chamber Judgment) (n 17 above) para 110.

crimes against combatants.'[91] In contrast, in the *Martić* judgment, the ICTY Appeals Chamber drew a distinction between the *chapeau* element and the actual victims.[92] It endorsed the *Blaškić* jurisprudence on the *chapeau* element, but held that the actual victims of the act that was qualified as a crime against humanity did not have to be civilians, and could also be persons *hors de combat*. In its reasoning in support of this conclusion, the Appeals Chamber referred to reports of the Secretary-General and the Commission of Experts that had referred to common Article 3 in the context of a discussion on crimes against humanity.[93] In addition, it referred to its own case law, and finally held that its approach reflected customary international law. In relation to the last finding, it first of all referred to subsequent practice in the context of the drafting of the Genocide Convention.[94] Secondly, a number of Second World War cases were cited,[95] and although the cited parts of the judgments did not address the precise legal question of the correct interpretation of the words 'civilian' or the character of the individual victims, the jurisprudence did show that those courts also characterized as crimes against humanity acts where partisans, enemy belligerents, and prisoners of war were the actual victims. The Appeals Chamber also referred to the two French cases, *Barbie* and *Touvier*, in which acts against resistance fighters had been characterized as crimes against humanity.[96]

In their totality, the cited cases could also support a finding that enemy combatants and resistance fighters actively participating in an armed conflict can be actual victims of crimes against humanity, and possibly even the finding that the word 'civilian' has become superfluous under customary international law and that attacks against soldiers can also qualify as crimes against humanity.

[91] *Prosecutor v Mrkšić et al* (Trial Chamber Judgment) IT-95-13/1T (27 September 2007) para 460. Footnote 1716 corroborates this point as follows: Cassese quotes a number of precedents in support of his proposition that applying Art 5 to enemy combatants is recognized by customary international law (Cassese (n 3 above) 64): there are some cases of the British Occupation Tribunals under Allied Control Council Law No 10 that entered convictions for crimes against humanity in cases where the victims were servicemen (ibid, 86–8), but there are also examples of decisions that exclude from the definition of victims of crimes against humanity persons who belonged or who had belonged to the military (see eg the *Neddermeier* case, quoted at 88). In his commentary to the article on crimes against humanity in the Rome Statute (Art 7), Cassese admits that, in the current state of the law, crimes against humanity (at least the 'murder variety'), can only apply where the victims are civilians: A Cassese, *The Rome Statute of the International Criminal Court: a commentary*, Vol I (Oxford: OUP, 2002) 375.

[92] For an insightful note, see J Dungel, 'Defining victims of crimes against humanity: *Martić* and the International Criminal Court' (2009) 22 LJIL 727–52.

[93] *Prosecutor v Martić* (Appeals Chamber Judgment) IT-95-11-A (8 October 2008) para 306.

[94] ibid paras 309–11, fn 828.

[95] Such as the case of *United States v von Leeb et al* (the *High Command* case) X–XI TWC; *United States v von Weizsaecker et al* (the *Ministries* case) XII–XIV TWC; *British Occupied Zone* case (n 68 above).

[96] For this and more generally on these cases, see L Sadat, 'The interpretation of the Nuremberg Principles by the French Court of Cassation: from *Touvier* to *Barbie* and back again' (1994–1995) 32 Col JTL 289; C Fournet, 'Reflection of the separation of powers: The law of genocide and the symptomatic French paradox' in R Henham and P Kim (eds), *The Criminal Law of Genocide: international, comparative and contextual aspects* (Aldershot: Ashgate, 2007) 211–22.

The alleged rule of customary international law would thus actually seem to stretch beyond the Appeals Chamber's proposed interpretation, which raises the question of whether the interpretation is in fact well grounded in customary international law. So far, the ICC has not explicitly pronounced on this question. It has generally stated that 'the term civilian population refers to persons who are civilians, as opposed to members of armed forces and other legitimate combatants'.[97] When the issue comes before the ICC, the judges may be well advised by Kaul's belief that, even if the ICC is part of the broader normative environment of international criminal law and may thus be inspired by the case law of other international criminal courts and tribunals, it is still not released from 'ascertaining for itself in a given instance whether eg, the constitutive elements of custom, namely state practice and *opinio iuris sive necessitatis*, are met'.[98]

VI. Assessing the ICTY's Means and Methods

In its findings regarding three of the cardinal elements of the definition of crimes against humanity, the ICTY consistently referred to customary international law in support of its proposed interpretations. The ICTY thus seemingly followed the guidance of the UN Secretary-General, who had cautioned the tribunal in his report on its establishment to rely on customary international law in order that the principle of *nullum crimen sine lege* would not be violated.[99] Given the lack of an underlying treaty on crimes against humanity, it seemed natural for the *ad hoc* Tribunals to turn to customary international law as a primary source of law, in light of its position in Article 38 of the ICJ Statute, in cases of ambiguities or gaps in its Statute. However, the reliance on this source of international law has generated much criticism, given that a perceived vagueness regarding its content sits uneasily with the criminal law requirements of certainty and specificity of offences. There has also been more 'public international law-oriented' criticism of the 'arbitrary and haphazard' selection of national case law presented as evidence of a customary international rule.[100] Against this setting, it is worth appraising the ICTY's identification and use of customary international law in its case law on crimes against humanity.

97 *Situation in the Republic of Kenya* (Pre-Trial Chamber Decision) (n 80 above) para 82.

98 *Situation in the Republic of Kenya* (Dissenting opinion of Judge Kaul) (n 81 above) para 30.

99 Report of the Secretary-General (n 27 above) para 34.

100 A Nollkaemper, 'Decisions of National Courts as Sources of International Law: An Analysis of the Practice of the ICTY' in G Boas and WA Schabas (eds), *International Criminal Law Developments in the Case Law of the ICTY* (Leiden: Martinus Nijhoff, 2003) 285.

A. Identifying custom: inter-state international law versus international law of the community

The traditional textbook approach to identifying customary international law emphasizes actual state practice and *opinio juris* as the basis for a rule of customary international law.[101] The existence of state practice, coupled with a belief that they were acting out of a legal obligation, was taken as a basis from which customary international rules could be identified. The requirements for determining state practice were spelled out by the International Court of Justice in the 1969 *North Sea Continental Shelf* case:

> State practice, including that of States whose interests are specially affected, should have been both extensive and virtually uniform in the sense of the provision invoked; and should moreover have occurred in such a way as to show a general recognition that a rule of law or legal obligation is involved.[102]

These requirements were later softened in the *Nicaragua* judgment to requiring general consistency rather than virtual uniformity of state practice.[103] Moreover, this judgment marked the beginning of a trend towards a more modern and deductive approach to customary international law. Pursuant to this modern approach, *opinio juris* is first identified and subsequently corroborating state practice sought.[104] Moreover, the modern approach also accepts official statements of states as instances of practice,[105] and would even allow non-state actors to have a certain role in the formation of custom.[106]

The combination of increased emphasis on *opinio juris* and the acceptance of evidence of state practice that is other than a state's actual behaviour has led Bruno Simma and Philip Alston to speak of an 'identity crisis' for customary international law. They contend that the *opinio juris* evidence, which is the articulation of a rule, is in fact counted twice.[107] In relation to the field of human rights law specifically, these scholars point out that customary international law may not be the most adequate basis to explain the universally binding nature of human rights. First of all, in light of contrary material state practice which

[101] H Thirlway, 'The sources of international law' in MD Evans (ed), *International law* (Oxford: OUP, 2nd edn, 2006) 121–7.

[102] *North Sea Continental Shelf (Federal Republic of Germany/Denmark; Federal Republic of Germany/Netherlands)* (Judgment, 20 January 1969) [1969] ICJ Rep 3, para 74.

[103] *Military and Paramilitary Activities in and against Nicaragua (Nicaragua v United States of America)* (Merits Judgment) [1986] ICJ Rep 14, para 186.

[104] AE Roberts, 'Traditional and modern approaches to customary international law: a reconciliation' (2001) 95 AJIL 757–91.

[105] A more relaxed approach to the requirements of state practice was taken by the ICJ in the *Nicaragua* case in relation to findings on the customary nature of common Arts 1 and 3 of the 1949 Geneva Conventions, as set out by T Meron, 'Revival of Customary Humanitarian Law' (2005) 99 AJIL 817, 819.

[106] B Simma and P Alston, 'The sources of human rights law: custom, *jus cogens*, and general principles' (1988–1989) 12 Aus YBIL 84.

[107] ibid 96.

violates rather than promotes a given human right such as the prohibition of torture, the element of state practice is downplayed to breaking point.[108] Simma and Alston speak of the manipulation of the established concept of customary international law. Secondly, they indicate that the field of human rights lacks the 'constant interaction' between states which is intrinsic to state practice, leading to customary international law.[109] Human rights do not entail contractual obligations between states and therefore violation of certain human rights obligations by State A towards its own citizens may not result in a reaction by State B at all, or in any event not one that is similar to State B's reaction in a situation where State A violates obligations owed directly to State B. The lack of interaction between states is also inherent to international criminal law and leads to the question of whether customary international law is in fact an adequate source of law for international criminal law.

What is important to note here is that the quest for customary international law was not undertaken by the ICTY to determine the existence of a rather general rule prohibiting and penalizing crimes against humanity, but rather, the ICTY turned to customary international law to identify rules on particular elements of the definition of the crime. It was thus a more detail-oriented exercise. The question is whether customary international law is an apt source of law to assist in such an exercise and, if so, what kind of evidence should be relevant to identify such a customary rule of international criminal law.

In light of these questions, it is first of all important to take account of the particular nature of international criminal law in addition to the lack of state interaction. In this respect, Hélène Ruiz Fabri has emphasized that international criminal tribunals exist precisely because domestic courts often fail properly to execute their task in the area of punishing international crimes. Given this state of affairs, it is only logical that there are few national decisions to be taken into account when evaluating state practice.[110] As a consequence of this observation and based on a particular interpretation of the Martens clause, Cassese has set forth that the requirement of state practice should be loosened, whereas the requirement of *opinio juris* should be elevated to a rank higher than normally admitted.[111] Furthermore, Cassese has submitted that, in the context of

[108] ibid. [109] ibid.

[110] H Ruiz Fabri, 'Commentaire sur le rapport de Lorenzo Gradoni' in M Delmas-Marty *et al* (eds), *Les sources du droit international pénal: l'expérience des tribunaux pénaux internationaux et le statut de la Cour Pénale Internationale* (Paris: Société de legislation comparée, 2005) 385.

[111] A Cassese, *International Law* (Oxford: OUP, 2nd edn, 2005) 160–1. This is in line with the sliding scale theory of Kirgis: see FL Kirgis, 'Custom on a Sliding Scale' (1987) 81 AJIL 146–51. Cf also the *Kupreškić* judgment over which Cassese presided: 'This is however an area where *opinio iuris sive necessitatis* may play a much greater role than *usus*, as a result of the aforementioned Martens Clause. In the light of the way States and courts have implemented it, this Clause clearly shows that principles of international humanitarian law may emerge through a customary process under the pressure of the demands of humanity or the dictates of public conscience, even where State practice is scant or inconsistent. The other element, in the form of *opinio necessitatis*, crystallising as a result of the imperatives of humanity or public conscience, may turn out to be the decisive

international humanitarian law, *opinio juris* can equally be formed by legal views from entities other than states, such as international organizations. In her dissenting opinion in the *Arrest Warrant* case, Judge Van den Wyngaert put forward the view that 'the opinion of civil society... cannot be completely discounted in the formation of customary international law today'.[112] These observations are in line with the trend towards a more modern formation of customary international law. Nevertheless, despite these valuable observations, questions remain as to what minimum level of evidence is needed to demonstrate the existence of a norm of customary international law, and to what extent the requirements of state practice and *opinio juris* can be stretched to take account of the particularities of international criminal law as a separate branch of international law. The next section analyses how the tribunals grappled with these questions in their jurisprudence on crimes against humanity.

B. Evaluating the identification of custom in relation to findings on crimes against humanity

In relation to the process undertaken by the tribunals to identify customary rules on crimes against humanity, a number of observations may be made. First of all, it is notable that the chambers generally did not specify which customary law elements were fulfilled by the evidence adduced. They did not make a clear distinction between state practice and *opinio juris*.[113] It is also remarkable that, on occasion, customary international law appeared to play a secondary role in being used to validate a given interpretation.[114] The ICTY would establish a given rule first, for instance what the correct interpretation and scope of the *chapeau*-word 'civilian' was, and would only subsequently determine that this interpretation accorded with customary international law.

The evidence adduced by the ICTY to support a finding of the existence of particular rules of customary law falls broadly in two categories: (1) national legislation and case law; and (2) international documents, such as treaties, the Secretary-General's report, and ILC documents. In addition, it is notable that the

element heralding the emergence of a general rule or principle of humanitarian law.' *Kupreškić* (Trial Chamber Judgment) (n 24 above) para 527.

112 *Arrest Warrant of 11 April 2000 (Democratic Republic of the Congo v Belgium)* (Judgment) [2002] ICJ Rep 3, Dissenting Opinion Judge Van den Wyngaert, para 27. Relevant scholarly and advocacy organizations would include the Institut de Droit International, the International Law Association, Amnesty International, and the International Commission of Jurists.

113 It has been pointed out on several occasions that it is difficult if not impossible to disentangle the two elements: see JM Henckaerts, 'Study on customary international humanitarian law' (2005) 87 IRRC 175, 182.

114 This is a function generally ascribed to general principles of law. On this source of law in the context of international criminal law, see FO Raimondo, *General principles of law in the decisions of international criminal courts and tribunals* (Leiden: Martinus Nijhoff, 2008) and his contribution to this collection (Ch 2 above).

chambers consistently referred to earlier ICTY case law, apparently also as evidence of custom. Of these sources, national case law generally provided the best and most detailed guidance for the specific questions at hand. As such, national laws and case law are well accepted as evidence of state practice or *opinio juris*,[115] but it may be problematic if they have to fulfil both requirements at the same time. Specifically in relation to international criminal law, one may note in addition to Ruiz-Fabri's observation, that crimes against humanity were not codified in a treaty and consequently there has been sparse domestic legislation and case law. The dearth of relevant case law may have had its effects on the requirements of generality and consistency and the ICTY may have been justified in adopting a more lenient approach. Given the low number of pertinent cases, one expects a systematic inquiry into all pertinent cases on crimes against humanity for each element. However, the ICTY appeared to engage in a more random approach in its case selection. Leading cases on crimes against humanity, such as *Barbie*, *Touvier*, and *Finta* were sometimes cited as evidence of a given customary rule regarding a particular element,[116] whereas these same cases were ignored in relation to other elements.[117]

A substantive enquiry into the cases cited also demonstrates that these cases did not always fully corroborate with the presented outcome and, moreover, cases were occasionally considered outside their context. The three elements of crimes against humanity are interrelated and if the element of armed conflict, for example, is part of the definition in a given legal context, this may result in de-emphasizing or subsuming the policy element in the jurisprudence emanating from that legal context. This does not necessarily mean that the courts in that particular legal context also agreed that the policy element would not be a relevant legal ingredient if the element of armed conflict was absent. That was a matter that did not have to be addressed in the legal construction in which that specific court was operating. Similarly, the views of courts addressing crimes against humanity that were clearly committed with state involvement may be less pertinent for determining the rules of customary international law on the policy requirement than the findings of courts that specifically dealt with crimes against humanity committed by rebel groups.[118] However, the precise problem for the ICTY was that there were few if any examples of these latter types of finding.

In addition to its use of national case law, a brief remark can be made on the ICTY's use of treaties as evidence of custom. These were used rather arbitrarily at times, with the Rome Statute, for instance, sometimes having been quoted as

[115] M Akehurst, 'Custom as a source of international law' (1974–1975) 47 BYBIL 1, 8–10; Nollkaemper (n 100 above) 281–6.

[116] Such as the cases of *Barbie* and *Touvier* in relation to determining who can be actual victims of crimes against humanity: *Martić* (Appeals Chamber Judgment) (n 93 above) para 308, fn 831.

[117] The cases of *Barbie* and *Touvier* were not mentioned in the context of the finding in the *Kunarac* Appeals Chamber Judgment (n 50 above) that policy was not a legal ingredient of the definition of crimes against humanity.

[118] cf *Situation in the Republic of Kenya*, Dissenting opinion of Judge Kaul (n 81 above) para 30.

evidence of the existence of customary international law,[119] whereas in relation to the policy element of crimes against humanity, customary international law was identified by the ICTY without regard to the Rome Statute. Of the three treaties most referred to in the context of crimes against humanity, only one is concerned with crimes against humanity *per se* rather than a specific type of crime against humanity, namely genocide or apartheid.[120] Hence, it might at best be argued that taken together the treaties evinced a certain trend. The specific value of treaties as evidence of customary international law depends on a number of factors, such as most importantly similar practice of non-state parties, and also the number of state parties and the existence of reservations to the rule in question. These factors have different standing depending on whether a treaty is declaratory of customary international law or whether it is constitutive of customary international law.[121] Whether a given treaty is declaratory or constitutive of customary international law can be ascertained in a number of ways. For instance, the language of *travaux préparatoires* may reveal whether the negotiating and/or signatory states considered the treaty or specific treaty rules as declaratory of existing customary international law. If it is not declaratory of customary international law, a treaty may become constitutive of customary international law. Whether this is the case is generally determined by international tribunals.[122] For this determination, it is important to consider the practice of states that are not parties to the treaty, or other practice showing that state parties are not just complying with the rules because of the principle that *pacta sunt servanda*. Richard Baxter has observed that often decisions of tribunals that treaty norms are constitutive of customary norms are not accompanied by an explanation as to how this conclusion was reached.[123] The ICTY's approach fits well in this pattern, as it generally did not provide any further explanation of why certain treaties would be indicative of the status of customary international law.

In relation to the evidentiary standards required for the determination of the existence of custom, the ICTY Appeals Chamber made some notable observations

[119] See above (n 17 above).

[120] Convention on the Prevention and Punishment of the Crime of Genocide (adopted in New York, 9 December 1948, entered into force 12 January 1951) 78 UNTS 277, number of state parties in 1990: 101, in 2009: 141; International Convention on the Suppression and Punishment of the Crime of Apartheid (adopted in New York, 30 November 1973, entered into force, 18 July 1976) 1015 UNTS 243, number of state parties in 1990: 88, in 2009: 107; Convention on the non-applicability of statutory limitations to war crimes and crimes against humanity (adopted in New York, 26 November 1968, entered into force 11 November 1970) 754 UNTS 73, number of state parties in 1990: 28, in 2009: 53.

[121] A treaty provision that is declaratory of customary international law codifies an existing rule of customary nature whereas a treaty provision that is constitutive of a rule of customary international law lies at the origins of a new rule of customary international law that did not exist previously.

[122] RR Baxter, 'Treaties and Customs', *Recueil des Cours*, Collected courses of The Hague Academy of International Law (1970) Vol 129, 27–105.

[123] ibid.

in the *Tadić* judgment concerning the issue as to whether discriminatory intent was a general element of crimes against humanity:

> The letter of these provisions [ie the Nuremberg and Tokyo Charter as well as Control Council Law No 10] is clear and indisputable. Consequently, had customary international law developed to restrict the scope of those treaty provisions which are at the very origin of the customary process, uncontroverted evidence would be needed. In other words, both judicial practice and possibly evidence of consistent State practice, including national legislation, would be necessary to show that customary law has deviated from treaty law by adopting a narrower notion of crimes against humanity.[124]

This approach confirms the idea that the evidentiary standard differs per situation. In general it has been argued that, in the absence of conflicting state practice, a small amount of practice may suffice to create a rule of customary international law.[125] In contrast, a large number of judicial decisions and other acts may be needed to overturn an existing customary rule.[126] The finding quoted above on the discriminatory intent element accords with this approach. It does appear, though, that in relation to the armed conflict requirement, which was also mentioned in the Nuremberg Charter and which gave rise to diverse jurisprudence under Control Council Law No 10, a more relaxed approach was taken by the ICTY. This may be explained by the fact that there were two judgments based on Control Council Law No 10 that sustained the elimination of the armed conflict requirement. However, it may also have been that the finding was the result of the assumption apparently implicit in natural law that the evidentiary standard is lower for customary international law, adopting a broader notion of crimes against humanity rather than introducing more restrictive elements.

VII. Conclusion

Despite the pitfalls of customary international law as a source of international criminal law, it also presents significant advantages in terms of development of the law. Had crimes against humanity been codified immediately after Nuremberg, as was done with genocide, it is most likely that the requirement of an armed conflict would still be present today.[127] The lack of a general treaty provided the tribunals with an enormous possibility to develop the law, an opportunity that they fully exploited. In relation to discarding the armed conflict requirement, the ICTY's *Tadić* Appeals Chamber decision crucially fomented an ongoing process

[124] *Tadić* (Appeals Chamber Judgment) (n 17 above) para 290.

[125] Akehurst (n 115 above) 18–19.

[126] ibid 19.

[127] As Timothy McCormack has observed: 'the lack of an existing treaty definition...proved liberating in that delegates were not beholden to some past compromise text paraded as sacrosanct and somehow beyond re-negotiation': TLH McCormack 'Crimes against humanity' in D MacGoldrick *et al* (eds), *The Permanent International Criminal Court: legal and policy issues* (Oxford: Hart, 2004) 180–1.

towards the application of crimes against humanity in peacetime. The jurisprudence on the policy requirement has to be read in conjunction with jurisprudence on the identity of non-state actors as the key organizers of crimes against humanity. Even if the *Kunarac* finding on policy was not codified in the ICC Statute, the ICC Pre-Trial Chambers may have been inspired by the flexible approach that opened the door, perhaps too widely, to accepting that non-state actors can organize attacks that lead to crimes against humanity. Possibly in relation to the interpretation of the word 'civilian', the tribunals were most hesitant to fully discard the Statute or to embark on a novel interpretation. They generally stuck to the old humanitarian law roots of crimes against humanity and only at a later stage gradually moved away. It remains to be seen whether the ICTY jurisprudence on this point of law will serve as a source of inspiration to the ICC or whether the ICC will replace this jurisprudence with its own interpretation and understanding of customary international law.[128]

Intertwined with the reconceptualization of crimes against humanity, the ICTY may also have contributed to a renewed conception of customary international law as a source of international criminal law that fits in the modern conception of customary international law. Yet questions as to the adequacy of this source of law for international criminal law remain. These doubts may have been reinforced by criticisms related to the means and methods by which the ICTY identified customary norms. Specifically, in relation to crimes against humanity, the identification process on crucial aspects was at times rather haphazard: decisions cited did not provide any direct evidence for the proposed rule, key decisions were invoked or ignored in a sometimes arbitrary fashion, and treaties were invoked without indicating how these were relevant in the process of identifying a customary norm. Despite all these valid criticisms, it is also true that the Tribunals have made a remarkable contribution to the reconceptualization of crimes against humanity, in particular in removing the armed conflict linkage requirement. In so doing the Tribunals have paved the way for a contemporary application of this crime and have rendered it apt to address present-day realities.

[128] On jurisprudential references more generally, see Judge Kaul (n 81 above) paras 28–32, in particular para 30.

5

The Reinvention of War Crimes by the International Criminal Tribunals

Shane Darcy[*]

I. Introduction

At one of the very first international conferences dedicated to the legal regulation of warfare, it was suggested that justice and the repression of wartime excesses necessitated the creation of 'a general penal code for crimes, offences or contraventions committed in violation of international law'.[1] This earnest proposal was viewed as somewhat premature by the majority of the delegates at the 1874 Brussels Conference on the Rules of Military Warfare,[2] and like other attempts at developing the laws of war, the proposal fell by the wayside until subsequent conflicts and peace conferences involving the 'Great Powers' brought the questions of law and war back to the table. In the period of the Hague Peace Conferences of 1899 and 1907 and the First World War, the concept of war crimes gained currency in international politics and legal scholarship.[3] Writing in 1916, Cyril M Picciotto considered that, in light of the degree of uncertainty surrounding aspects of war crimes, belligerent reprisals, and the responsibility of States for breaches of the laws of war '[t]he judgment of a Hague Tribunal would be of the greatest assistance.'[4] Some ninety years later and Picciotto would no doubt be impressed with the wealth of jurisprudence on war crimes and related matters that has emerged from the Hague-based International Criminal Tribunal for the former Yugoslavia (ICTY) and its

* The author would like to thank Adam Grieser for the assistance provided.

1 'Correspondence Respecting the Proposed Conference at Brussels on the Rules of Military Warfare', *United Kingdom Parliamentary Papers*, Miscellaneous No 1 (1875) (c-1128) 313.

2 ibid 313–14.

3 AP Higgins, *The Hague Peace Conferences and Other International Conferences Concerning the Laws and Usages of War: Texts of Conventions with Commentaries* (Cambridge: CUP, 1909); CA Hereshoff Bartlett, 'Liability for Official War Crimes' (1919) 35 LQR 177; HH Bellott, 'War Crimes and War Criminals' (1916) 36 *Canadian Law Times* 754.

4 CM Picciotto, 'War Crimes' (1916) 1 *International Law Notes* 69, 70.

sister tribunal in Arusha, the International Criminal Tribunal for Rwanda (ICTR).

The law of war crimes is arguably where the *ad hoc* Tribunals have made their most significant and far-reaching contribution to the development of international criminal law. While the Security Council-created statutory instruments provided a platform for the Tribunals' judges to address violations of the laws of armed conflict, it was the judiciary itself which expanded the scope of the concept of war crimes and expounded on the meaning and content of numerous individual crimes of war. This chapter considers the judicial development of war crimes at the ICTR and ICTY and the lasting influence of this frequently ground-breaking jurisprudence. In addition to progressing the law of war crimes, the *ad hoc* Tribunals demonstrated considerable creativity in related areas of the laws of armed conflict, such as the rules applicable in non-international armed conflicts,[5] command responsibility,[6] and the meaning of concepts such as armed conflict[7] and belligerent occupation.[8]

This chapter begins by considering the war crimes provisions in the statutes of the *ad hoc* Tribunals and the inclusion of the concept of war crimes in non-international armed conflicts in the ICTR Statute. The war crimes cases at the *ad hoc* Tribunals represent the first application of the criminal provisions of humanitarian law by international criminal courts. Section III explores judicial treatment with regard to the two categories of war crimes before the Tribunals, grave breaches of the 1949 Geneva Conventions and 'violations of the laws and customs of war'. Judicial creativity has been more significant for the latter category of war crimes, and has led to the expansion of the scope of the law of war crimes and the identification of new offences not previously established in positive international law. Such creativity in a criminal context prompts consideration of whether the expansive treatment of the law of war crimes is in keeping with the principle of *nullum crimen sine lege* and the traditional international lawmaking process. Section IV concludes with a consideration of the legacy of the *ad hoc* Tribunals' creativity towards war crimes.

II. War Crimes in the Statutes of the *Ad Hoc* Tribunals

According to the United Nations War Crimes Commission '[t]he trials of war criminals by victorious opponents can be traced back to the dawn of modern

[5] *Prosecutor v Tadić* (Appeals Chamber Decision on the Defence Motion for Interlocutory Appeal on Jurisdiction) IT-9-1-AR72 (2 October 1995) paras 119–26.

[6] See the contribution of Robert Cryer (Ch 7 below).

[7] *Tadić* (Appeals Chamber Jurisdiction Decision) (n 5 above) para 70.

[8] *Prosecutor v Naletilić et al* (Trial Chamber Judgment) IT-98-34-T (31 March 2003) para 217.

international law.'[9] Several important nineteenth-century documents on the laws of war indeed recognized the enforcement role of penal prosecutions,[10] although it was only in the twentieth century that international agreements and treaties addressed the concept of war crimes. Until the creation of the *ad hoc* Tribunals for Rwanda and the former Yugoslavia in the early 1990s, international agreement on war crimes could be found in the Report of the 1919 Commission on the Responsibility of the Authors of the War and on Enforcement of Penalties,[11] the December 1946 affirmation by the United Nations of the principles of international law in the Nuremberg Charter and judgment,[12] and, in a truly multilateral treaty sense, in the provisions of the 1949 Geneva Conventions and the 1977 Additional Protocol I addressing 'grave breaches'.[13] The ICTY Statute, adopted by the United Nations Security Council in 1993, draws on the content and language of these earlier developments and establishes jurisdiction over grave breaches of the Geneva Conventions and 'violations of the laws or customs of war'.[14]

Article 2 of the ICTY Statute empowers the Tribunal to prosecute persons committing or ordering the commission of grave breaches of the 1949 Geneva Conventions. Grave breaches consist of certain acts directed against persons or property protected by the Conventions, namely:

(a) wilful killing;
(b) torture or inhuman treatment, including biological experiments;
(c) wilfully causing great suffering or serious injury to body or health;
(d) extensive destruction and appropriation of property, not justified by military necessity and carried out unlawfully and wantonly;

[9] The United Nations War Crimes Commission, *History of the United Nations War Crimes Commission and the Development of the Laws of War* (London: HM Stationery Office, 1948) 30.

[10] See eg 'Instructions for the Government of Armies of the United States in the Field', Prepared by Francis Lieber, promulgated as General Orders No 100 by President Lincoln, 24 April 1863, art 71; 1880 Oxford Manual on the Laws of War on Land, Article 84, reprinted in D Schindler and J Toman (eds), *The Laws of Armed Conflict: A Collection of Conventions, Resolutions and Other Documents* (Dordrecht: Martinus Nijhoff, 1988) 3, 35.

[11] 'Commission on the Responsibility of the Authors of the War and on the Enforcement of Penalties, Report Presented to the Preliminary Peace Conference, March 19, 1919' (1920) 14 AJIL 95, 112–15.

[12] 'Affirmation of the Principles of International Law recognised by the Charter of the Nürnberg Tribunal', UNGA Res 95(I), Fifty-fifth plenary meeting, 11 December 1946.

[13] Geneva Convention I for the Amelioration of the Condition of Wounded and Sick in Armed Forces in the Field (1949) 75 UNTS 31, Art 50; Geneva Convention II for the Amelioration of the Condition of Wounded, Sick and Shipwrecked Members of Armed Forces at Sea (1949) 75 UNTS 85, Art 51; Geneva Convention III Relative to the Treatment of Prisoners of War (1949) 75 UNTS 135, Art 130; Geneva Convention IV Relative to the Protection of Civilian Persons in Time of War (1949) 75 UNTS 287, Art 147; Protocol Additional to the Geneva Conventions of 12 August 1949, and Relating to the Protection of Victims of International Armed Conflicts (1977) 1125 UNTS 3, Arts 11 and 85.

[14] Statute of the International Tribunal for the Prosecution of Persons Responsible for Serious Violations of International Humanitarian Law Committed in the Territory of the Former Yugoslavia since 1991, UN Doc S/25704 at 36, Annex (1993) and S/25704/Add.1, (1993) UN Doc S/RES/827.

(e) compelling a prisoner of war or a civilian to serve in the forces of a hostile power;
(f) wilfully depriving a prisoner of war or a civilian of the rights of fair and regular trial;
(g) unlawful deportation or transfer or unlawful confinement of a civilian;
(h) taking civilians as hostages.

Article 3 of the Statute gives the Tribunal jurisdiction over persons 'violating the laws or customs of war', and provides examples of such violations:

(a) employment of poisonous weapons or other weapons calculated to cause unnecessary suffering;
(b) wanton destruction of cities, towns or villages, or devastation not justified by military necessity;
(c) attack, or bombardment, by whatever means, of undefended towns, villages, dwellings, or buildings;
(d) seizure of, destruction or wilful damage done to institutions dedicated to religion, charity and education, the arts and sciences, historic monuments and works of art and science;
(e) plunder of public or private property.

The *chapeau* of Article 3 states that such offences will 'not be limited' to this list, whereas the list in Article 2 is clearly exhaustive, through use of the word 'namely'. In its practice, discussed below, the ICTY has included, within the category of Article 3 offences, unenumerated crimes such as murder, torture, cruel treatment, outrages upon personal dignity, rape, unlawful attacks on civilian persons and objects, terror, and unlawful labour.

The ICTR Statute does not contain a provision on grave breaches, but gives the Tribunal jurisdiction over serious violations of Common Article 3 of the 1949 Geneva Conventions and 1977 Additional Protocol II.[15] Article 4 of the Statute contains an illustrative list of such violations:

(a) violence to life, health and physical or mental well-being of persons, in particular murder as well as cruel treatment such as torture, mutilation or any form of corporal punishment;
(b) collective punishments;
(c) taking of hostages;
(d) acts of terrorism;
(e) outrages upon personal dignity, in particular humiliating and degrading treatment, rape, enforced prostitution and any form of indecent assault;
(f) pillage;
(g) the passing of sentences and the carrying out of executions without previous judgement pronounced by a regularly constituted court, affording all the judicial guarantees which are recognised as indispensable by civilised peoples;
(h) threats to commit any of the foregoing acts.

[15] Statute of the International Criminal Tribunal for the Prosecution of Persons Responsible for Genocide and Other Serious Violations of International Humanitarian Law Committed in the Territory of Rwanda 1994, UN Doc S/Res/955.

The ICTR has not to date charged any individual with a war crime not explicitly included in Article 4 of the Statute,[16] although the innovation of the provision is not in the list itself, but rather in the creation of international criminal responsibility for breaches of the laws applying to internal armed conflicts.

Prior to the adoption of the Statutes, the view of the International Committee of the Red Cross and the Commission of Experts established by the United Nations Security Council to investigate crimes in the former Yugoslavia was that war crimes applied only to situations of international armed conflict.[17] The concept of war crimes in internal conflict had not been provided for in either the Geneva Conventions or the Additional Protocols, and the Secretary-General recognized that the ICTR Statute 'for the first time criminalizes common Article 3'.[18] The Secretary-General explained that:

> ...the Security Council has decided to take a more expansive approach to the choice of the applicable law than the one underlying the statute of the Yugoslav Tribunal, and included within the subject-matter jurisdiction of the Rwanda Tribunal international instruments regardless of whether they were considered part of customary international law or whether they have customarily entailed the individual criminal responsibility of the perpetrator of the crime.[19]

It was conceded by the Secretary-General that it was 'still debatable' as to whether Common Article 3 entailed criminal responsibility for an individual breaching its rules and that Additional Protocol II as a whole had not been universally considered as being customary international law,[20] and accordingly the creativity of the Security Council here has not gone without criticism.[21]

In assessing the collective input of the ICTY and the ICTR to the development of the law of war crimes, the pioneering article of the ICTR Statute is matched, if not surpassed, by the jurisprudential contribution of the ICTY itself, where war crimes charges have featured in a majority of its completed cases, which now number almost 90.[22] In the practice of the ICTR, war crimes charges have been laid against around 40 accused persons, although successful convictions have been obtained against just 8 to date,[23] the first of which was

[16] Although there was a notable lack of specificity in the early indictments as regards the war crimes charges. See eg *Prosecutor v Kayishema and Ruzindana* (First Amended Indictment) ICTR-95-1-I.

[17] As noted by WA Schabas, *The UN International Criminal Tribunals* (Cambridge: CUP, 2006) 232.

[18] Report of the Secretary-General Pursuant to Paragraph 5 of Security Council Resolution 955 (1994), UN Doc S/1995/134 (13 February 1995) para 12.

[19] ibid.

[20] ibid para 12, fn 8.

[21] See eg A Marsten Danner, 'When Courts Make Law: How the International Criminal Tribunals Recast the Laws of War' (2006) 59 *Vanderbilt Law Review* 1, 23.

[22] As of July 2009, the ICTY had 86 completed cases: see *Sixteenth Annual Report of the International Criminal Tribunal for the Former Yugoslavia*, A/64/205–S/2009/394 (31 July 2009) 3.

[23] *Prosecutor v Rutaganda* (Appeals Chamber Judgment) ICTR-96-3-A (26 May 2003) paras 580–85; *Prosecutor v Semanza* (Appeals Chamber Judgment) ICTR-97-20-A (20 May 2005) paras 370–71; *Prosecutor v Imanishimwe* (Appeals Chamber Judgment) ICTR-99-46-A (7 July 2006) para 129; *Prosecutor v Bagosora et al* (Trial Chamber Judgment) ICTR-98-41-T (18 December

only secured in May 2003, and was an overruling by the Hague-based Appeals Chamber of the previous acquittal by the Trial Chamber.[24] Guénaël Mettraux has noted that the nature of the conflict in Rwanda has meant that 'the relevancy of war crimes as a criminal idiom capable of labelling the sort of crimes committed in Rwanda appears much less potent than it may be in the Yugoslav context'.[25] It is the ICTY that has made the greater and perhaps most lasting impact on the law of war crimes, by way of judicial creativity towards both its Statute and customary international law.

While positive international law regarding war crimes was reasonably well-developed when the *ad hoc* Tribunals commenced their work, judicial treatment of the matter was largely limited to the trials conducted by the Allies in the aftermath of the Second World War. The Nuremberg Charter had described war crimes as 'violations of the laws and customs of war', and according to Charles Garraway, this approach 'gave considerable discretion to the judges themselves in deciding what fell within their jurisdiction and what did not'.[26] A similar interpretative licence can be said to have been granted and adopted by judges at the *ad hoc* Tribunals, one which has led to a broad revision of the meaning and content of the law of war crimes.

III. Judicial Creativity and the Law of War Crimes

The parameters of international humanitarian law extend far beyond the law of war crimes and it has been a recurring question since the inception of war crimes as to which breaches of humanitarian law are to be considered as international crimes.[27] Not every breach of a rule of humanitarian law amounts to a war crime, and over the years various authorities and scholars have sought to define the latter concept. Cyril Picciotto felt in 1916 that a war crime was 'the technical expression for such an act of enemy soldiers and enemy civilians as may be visited by punishment or capture of the offenders'.[28] More recently, the International Committee of the Red Cross considered that 'serious violations of international humanitarian law constitute war crimes'.[29] Answering this question in the contemporary

2008) paras 2242–5, 2250–54; *Prosecutor v Renzaho* (Trial Chamber Judgment) ICTR-97-31-T (14 July 2009) paras 795–811; *Prosecutor v Setako* (Trial Chamber Judgment) ICTR-04-81-T (25 February 2010) paras 483–92.

[24] *Rutaganda* (Appeals Chamber Judgment) ibid paras 580–85.

[25] G Mettraux, *International Crimes and the* ad hoc *Tribunals* (Oxford/New York: OUP, 2005) 28.

[26] C Garraway, 'War Crimes', in E Wilmshurst and S Breau (eds), *Perspective on the ICRC Study on Customary International Humanitarian Law* (Cambridge: CUP, 2007) 377.

[27] See generally P Gaeta, 'International Criminalization of Prohibited Conduct' in A Cassese (ed), *The Oxford Companion to International Criminal Justice* (Oxford: OUP, 2009) 63.

[28] Picciotto (n 4 above) 69.

[29] J-M Henckaerts and L Doswald-Beck, *Customary International Humanitarian Law, Volume I: Rules* (Cambridge: CUP, 2005) 568, Rule 156.

context is made easier by the existence of several international treaty provisions providing for war crimes, although recourse must also be made to the more malleable source of customary international law. Michael Bothe has pertinently observed that:

> [r]ules concerning the punishment of 'war crimes' are secondary rules in relation to the primary rules concerning behaviour which is prohibited in case of armed conflict. Thus, the concept of war crimes is a dynamic concept, as it is bound to change with the development of the primary or substantive rules relating to that behaviour. But for that very reason, it is in the interest of the certainty of the law, which in criminal matters is enshrined in the principle *nulla poena sine lege*, that acts which may be punished as war crimes are clearly defined. This is necessary because of the vague and general character of some of the primary rules, but also because not every breach of those rules may necessarily be characterized as a war crime.[30]

The approach adopted by the *ad hoc* Tribunals, particularly the ICTY, can be said to involve something of a departure from this traditional formula for war crimes. The determination of the existence of new crimes has been made by looking at issues such as the existence of a prohibition under the laws of armed conflict, its customary international law status, the seriousness of the acts in question, and whether such can be said to give rise to individual criminal responsibility in positive or customary law.

A. Grave breaches

Grave breaches as a distinct category of war crimes were first included in the 1949 Geneva Conventions and their content was derived primarily from the war crimes trials of the post-Second World War period.[31] The idea of prosecuting and punishing those responsible for grave breaches, even under universal jurisdiction, is not controversial, as evidenced by the near universal ratification of the Conventions themselves and the replication of the grave breaches provisions in both the ICTY Statute and the Rome Statute of the International Criminal Court (ICC).[32] Nevertheless, the application of the grave breaches regime to the conflicts in the former Yugoslavia presented particular challenges, to which the ICTY responded with some creative judicial interpretation.

Article 2 of the ICTY Statute specifies that grave breaches consist of certain prohibited acts directed against persons or property protected by the Geneva Conventions, and common Article 2 of those treaties states that the Conventions apply to wars or armed conflicts 'which may arise between two or more of the

[30] M Bothe, 'War Crimes' in A Cassese, P Gaeta, and JRWD Jones (eds), *The Rome Statute of the International Criminal Court: A Commentary, Vol. I* (Oxford/New York: OUP, 2002) 379, 381.

[31] Henckaerts and Doswald-Beck (n 29 above) 574.

[32] Rome Statute, Art 8(2)(a), 1998, UN Doc A/CONF.183/9, 2187 UNTS 3.

High Contracting Parties'. Grave breaches accordingly can arise only in situations of international armed conflict, a position that is further evidenced, for example, by the inclusion of crimes against prisoners of war, a category of protected persons that does not exist in internal armed conflicts.[33] In 1995, the *Tadić* Appeals Chamber corrected an earlier Trial Chamber decision on jurisdiction which sought to extend the grave breaches regime to non-international conflicts.[34] The Appeals Chamber explained that:

> [t]he international armed conflict element generally attributed to the grave breaches provisions of the Geneva Conventions is merely a function of the system of universal mandatory jurisdiction that those provisions create. The international armed conflict requirement was a necessary limitation on the grave breaches system in light of the intrusion on State sovereignty that such mandatory universal jurisdiction represents.[35]

The Chamber concluded that, as the law stood at that time, Article 2 of the ICTY Statute was applicable only to offences committed in the context of an international armed conflict.[36] This 'relatively conservative approach'[37] was tempered by the broadening of the grave breaches regime's reach through progressive interpretation of the concept of 'protected persons' and of the element of control required in instances of extra-territorial state-sponsored military activities in order to classify a conflict as international in nature.

The *Tadić* Appeals Chamber's very first decision sought to address the meaning of the concept of 'armed conflict' and its findings have had a lasting effect on international humanitarian law. It took the view that 'an armed conflict exists whenever there is a resort to armed force between States or protracted armed violence between governmental authorities and organized armed groups or between such groups within a State'.[38] The threshold for an internal armed conflict proposed was more flexible than that in Additional Protocol II and was replicated in the Rome Statute of the ICC and upheld in one of the first decisions of the

[33] Chambers of the ICTY, however, applied the protections of the Third Geneva Convention without clarifying whether the conflict was international or internal in nature. See *Prosecutor v Mrkšić et al* (Trial Chamber Judgment) IT-95-13/1-T (27 November 2007); *Prosecutor v Mrkšić et al* (Appeals Chamber Judgment) IT-95-13/1-A (5 May 2009).

[34] See *Prosecutor v Tadić* (Trial Chamber Decision on the Defence Motion on Jurisdiction) IT-94-1-T (10 August 1995) paras 46–56. See C Greenwood, 'The Development of International Humanitarian Law by the International Criminal Tribunal for the Former Yugoslavia' (1998) 2 MP YB UNL 97, 112.

[35] *Tadić* (Appeals Chamber Jurisdiction Decision) (n 5 above) para 80.

[36] ibid para 84. See, however, the Separate Opinion of Judge Abi-Saab where he favours 'a teleological interpretation of the Conventions in light of their object and purpose of the effect of including internal conflicts within the regime of "grave breaches"'.

[37] W Fenrick, 'The Development of the Law of Armed Conflict Through the Jurisprudence of the International Criminal Tribunal for the Former Yugoslavia' (1998) 3 JACL 197, 200. See also T Meron, 'The Hague Tribunal: Working to Clarify International Humanitarian Law' (1998) 13 AU ILR 1511, 1516.

[38] *Tadić* (Appeals Chamber Jurisdiction Decision) (n 5 above) para 70.

ICC.[39] In the *Tadić* case the question subsequently arose as to what level of support would be necessary if an 'organized armed group' was controlled by another state, to convert the armed conflict from non-international to international and thus trigger the application of the grave breaches regime. Tadić had been acquitted of grave breaches charges by the Trial Chamber on the basis that the conflict in Bosnia and Herzegovina to which the acts were related was not international in nature, and the victims could not be considered as 'protected persons', ie individuals who find themselves in situations of international armed conflict or occupation 'in the hands of a Party to the conflict or Occupying Power of which they are not nationals'.[40] It found that at the relevant time and place, the *Republika Srpska* forces could not be considered as either *de facto* organs or agents of the Federal Republic of Yugoslavia and therefore:

> ...each of the victims of the acts ascribed to the accused...enjoy the protection of the prohibitions contained in Common Article 3, applicable as it is to all armed conflicts, rather than the protection of the more specific grave breaches regime applicable to civilians in the hands of a party to an armed conflict of which they are not nationals, which falls under Article 2 of the Statute.[41]

Similar issues confronted the *Čelebići* Trial Chamber, and it decided not to pronounce on the question of whether grave breaches could apply in internal armed conflicts, but rather held that the issue was whether or not the victims in question were 'protected persons'.[42]

The majority of the *Tadić* Appeals Chamber overturned the Trial Chamber in relation to grave breaches, by adopting a broader understanding of the type of control needed to be exercised by a state over armed forces outside its territory and by loosening the requirement of nationality of victims in order for them to be considered 'protected persons'. It confirmed that Article 2 of the Statute on grave breaches can only apply to international armed conflicts, a view that was uncontested by the parties in the case.[43] As regards the issue of control, the Chamber departed from the test of 'effective control' adopted by the International Court of Justice in *Nicaragua v United States*, holding that for attribution to arise, it needed to be proven that a state 'wields overall control over the group, not only by equipping and financing the group, but also by coordinating or helping in the general planning of its military activity'.[44] The acts of the group or its members can then be considered as those of *de facto* State organs, 'regardless of any specific instruction by the controlling State concerning the commission of each of those

[39] Rome Statute, Art 8(2)(f); *Prosecutor v Thomas Lubanga Dyilo* (Pre-Trial Chamber Decision on the Confirmation of Charges) ICC-01/04–01/06 (29 January 2007) para 233.

[40] Fourth Geneva Convention, Art 4(1); *Prosecutor v Tadić* (Trial Chamber Judgment) IT-94-1-T (7 May 1997) para 608.

[41] *Tadić* (Trial Chamber Judgment) ibid para 607.

[42] *Prosecutor v Delalić et al* (Trial Chamber Judgment) IT-96-21-T (16 November 1998) para 235.

[43] *Prosecutor v Tadić* (Appeals Chamber Judgment) IT-94-1-A (15 July 1999) para 83.

[44] ibid paras 115, 130.

acts'.[45] The application of this 'overall control test' allowed for the relevant conflict in *Tadić* to be treated as international in nature.[46] This test has been cited approvingly in the early jurisprudence of the ICC.[47]

As regards the definition of 'protected persons', the Appeals Chamber expanded on the definition in the Fourth Geneva Convention as it considered that 'substantial relations' were of more importance than 'formal bonds' in modern international armed conflicts involving the break-up of states. It held that 'ethnicity rather than nationality may become the grounds for allegiance' and that:

> [u]nder these conditions, the requirement of nationality is even less adequate to define protected persons. In such conflicts, not only the text and the drafting history of the Convention but also, and more importantly, the Convention's object and purpose suggest that allegiance to a Party to the conflict and, correspondingly, control by this Party over persons in a given territory, may be regarded as the crucial test.[48]

The Appeals Chamber overturned the Trial Chamber's acquittal of the accused for the grave breaches charges.[49]

The ICTY did not completely overhaul the law regarding grave breaches, resisting attempts to extend its scope to internal conflicts which did not contain any international element. Nonetheless, it expanded the understanding of the 'protected persons' category, although 'in such a way that it can only exist in an international armed conflict'.[50] Theodor Meron, subsequently President of the ICTY, had considered that it would have been 'the height of legalism' to enforce a strict nationality requirement in the Balkans' conflicts.[51] Defence counsel have sought to argue that this expanded interpretation amounts to a judicial 're-creation' of the law on grave breaches and a violation of the principle of legality, arguments that were found to be 'unpersuasive' by successive Appeals Chambers.[52]

The ICTY's creative approach to grave breaches, specifically the definition of 'protected persons', has been adopted in a novel way by Pre-Trial Chamber I of the ICC. In considering the charge in *Lubanga* of conscripting or enlisting children under the age of 15 years into the national armed forces, the Chamber observed that the ICTY Appeals Chamber had construed 'national' in the Fourth Geneva Convention 'as referring not solely to nationality as such, but also to the fact of belonging to the opposing party in an armed conflict'.[53] It concluded that 'national armed forces' was not limited to the governmental armed forces of a

[45] ibid para 137. [46] ibid para 162.

[47] *Lubanga* (Pre-Trial Chamber Confirmation of Charges) paras 210–11. See, however, International Court of Justice, *Case Concerning the Application of the Convention on the Prevention and Punishment of the Crime of Genocide* (*Bosnia and Herzegovina v Serbia and Montenegro*) (Judgment) 26 February 2007, General List No 91, paras 402–6.

[48] *Tadić* (Appeals Chamber Judgment) (n 43 above) para 166. [49] ibid paras 170–71.

[50] Greenwood (n 34 above) 112. [51] Meron (n 37 above) 1516–17.

[52] See eg *Prosecutor v Delalic et al* (Appeals Chamber Judgment) IT-96-21-A (20 February 2001) para 73; *Prosecutor v Blaškić* (Appeals Chamber Judgment) IT-95-14-A (29 July 2004) para 180.

[53] *Lubanga* (Pre-Trial Chamber Confirmation of Charges) paras 277–80.

state and to limit the meaning in such a way undermined the object and purpose of the Statute of ensuring crimes do not go unpunished.[54] It seems that the creative approach to interpretation espoused by the ICTY is contagious. But compared to the jurisprudence on grave breaches, the approach of the *ad hoc* Tribunals to the other category of war crimes, violations of the laws and customs of war, has been significantly more creative and profoundly influential.

B. Violations of the laws and customs of war

The second category of war crimes over which the *ad hoc* Tribunals have jurisdiction has proved to be a fertile ground for judicial creativity. The ICTY in particular has extended the scope of Article 3 to internal armed conflicts, as well as identifying individual war crimes not previously enunciated in positive international law, and clarifying the scope and content of more established offences against the laws and customs of war. It was again in the landmark *Tadić* case that the ICTY began its expansive treatment of the law of war crimes by unveiling a formula which allowed for the exercise of jurisdiction over violations of the laws applicable to non-international armed conflicts.

(1) Internal armed conflicts

Responding to a jurisdictional challenge that Article 3 of the Statute applied only to international armed conflicts, the *Tadić* Trial Chamber took the view that jurisdiction 'extends to serious violations of international humanitarian law that are a part of customary law'.[55] The rules in Common Article 3 prohibit acts that are 'criminal in nature' and as these rules are to be considered customary law, criminal responsibility could be imposed on individuals for their violation without contravening the *nullum crimen sine lege* principle.[56] As discussed further below, the Trial Chamber considered that individual criminal responsibility for a person breaching rules of humanitarian law 'need not be explicitly stated in a convention for its provisions to entail individual criminal liability'.[57] The Appeals Chamber agreed with the result of the Trial Chamber, but distinguished its approach by developing a set of criteria to be applied to the 'residual clause' of Article 3 of the Statute, which had been 'designed to ensure that no serious violation of international humanitarian law is taken away from the jurisdiction of the International Tribunal'.[58] For the Tribunal to try offences under Article 3: (1) there must have been a violation of a rule of international humanitarian law; (2) the rule comprised customary law, or if found in treaty law, the rule was applicable under the treaty's conditions; (3) the violation was 'serious', breaching a rule 'protecting important values', and involving 'grave consequences for the victim';

54 ibid para 281.
55 *Tadić* (Trial Chamber Jurisdiction Decision) (n 34 above) para 60.
56 ibid paras 65, 68.
57 ibid para 70.
58 *Tadić* (Appeals Chamber Jurisdiction Decision) (n 5 above) para 91.

and (4) the violation of the rule gave rise to individual criminal responsibility under either treaty or customary law.[59] Although an armed conflict needed to have taken place, with a nexus between the offence and the conflict,[60] the nature of the armed conflict was immaterial, if each criterion was satisfied.[61]

Customary international law played a significant role in both Chambers' treatment of the issue, ostensibly in keeping with the Secretary-General's stipulation that the Tribunal was to apply rules which are 'beyond any doubt part of customary law'.[62] The Appeals Chamber relied on custom to overcome the lack of an 'explicit reference' to criminal liability in Common Article 3, drawing inspiration from the practice at Nuremberg where the International Military Tribunal pointed to statements by government officials and international organizations and the trials by national courts and military tribunals for breaches of the laws of war as evidence of state practice indicating an intention to criminalize such violations.[63] As evidence of the same intention regarding Common Article 3, the Appeals Chamber gave a few examples of state practice indicating (or implying) that breaches of Common Article 3 or Additional Protocol II were crimes and two Security Council Resolutions regarding Somalia.[64] It held:

> All of these factors confirm that customary international law imposes criminal liability for serious violations of common Article 3, as supplemented by other general principles and rules on the protection of victims of internal armed conflict, and for breaching certain fundamental principles and rules regarding means and methods of combat in civil strife.[65]

The Appeals Chamber concluded that 'substantive justice and equity' fully warranted taking the position that serious violations of humanitarian law applicable to non-international armed conflicts should give rise to individual criminal responsibility in the context of the former Yugoslavia.[66] An issue that was deemed 'still debatable' by the Secretary-General the previous year was resolved to the satisfaction of the majority of the Appeals Chamber, and has not been departed from since.

Although the Statute of the ICTR expressly provides for criminal jurisdiction over violations of the international laws governing internal armed conflict, the Trial Chamber in *Akayesu* also decided to explore the question of individual criminal responsibility under customary international law. It decided that:

> . . . it must also be shown that an individual committing serious violations of these customary norms incurs, as a matter of custom, individual criminal responsibility thereby.

[59] ibid para 94.

[60] The Appeals Chamber considered in *Tadić* that it was 'sufficient that the alleged crimes were closely related to the hostilities occurring in other parts of the territories controlled by the parties to the conflict' (ibid para 70). See also *Prosecutor v Kunarac, Kovaić and Vuković* (Trial Chamber Judgment) IT-96-23-T and IT-96-23/1-T (22 February 2001) para 568.

[61] *Prosecutor v Furundžija*, (Trial Chamber Judgment) IT-95-17/1-T (10 December 1998) para 132.

[62] 'Report of the Secretary-General Pursuant to Paragraph 2 of Security Council Resolution 808 (1993)', UN Doc S/25704 (3 May 1993) para 34.

[63] *Tadić* (Appeals Chamber Jurisdiction Decision) (n 5 above) para 128.

[64] ibid paras 130–33. [65] ibid para 134. [66] ibid para 135.

Otherwise, it might be argued that these instruments only state norms applicable to States and Parties to a conflict, and that they do not create crimes for which individuals may be tried.[67]

In the Trial Chamber's view, the findings in the *Tadić* case were 'convincing and dispositive of the issue, both with respect to serious violations of Common Article 3 and of Additional Protocol II'.[68] The Chamber noted that, in addition to an argument based on custom, Rwanda had also signed the Geneva Conventions and the Additional Protocols, which were in force at the time of the alleged offences, and at that time, the offences set out in Article 4 of the Statute had been included as crimes under Rwandan domestic law. It held that 'Rwandan nationals were therefore aware, or should have been aware, in 1994 that they were amenable to the jurisdiction of Rwandan courts in case of commission of those offences falling under Article 4 of the Statute.'[69]

The *Tadić* Appeals Chamber's decision that the law of war crimes extended to internal armed conflicts was endorsed not only by subsequent benches of both *ad hoc* Tribunals, but also by the drafters of the Rome Statute of the ICC, who were similarly guided by its pioneering jurisprudence on crimes against humanity.[70] According to Theodor Meron, the influential United States position at the Rome Conference regarding war crimes in non-international conflicts would not have been possible without the ICTY jurisprudence in *Tadić*.[71] Article 8 of the widely ratified Rome Statute establishes that the Court's war crimes jurisdiction covers grave breaches, serious violations of Common Article 3, and violations of the laws and customs of war applicable in both international and non-international armed conflicts. The ICTY decision beat a new path with regard to war crimes in internal conflicts, after the ICTR statute had broken the ice, and states subsequently followed suit. Accordingly, it is not an overstatement to view the decision in *Tadić* as one of the most important war crimes cases since Nuremberg itself.[72] Nonetheless, the means by which the *ad hoc* Tribunals reached the conclusion that the concept of war crimes applies to internal conflicts has been challenged, in large part on the basis of a somewhat cavalier attitude to the existence of customary international law.[73] Judge Li considered that the Appeals Chamber's decision was 'an unwarranted assumption of legislative power which has never been given to this Tribunal by any

[67] *Prosecutor v Akayesu* (Trial Chamber Judgment) ICTR-96-4-T (2 September 1998) para 610.

[68] ibid para 614.

[69] ibid para 616.

[70] See the contribution of Larissa van den Herik (Ch 4 above).

[71] T Meron, 'Panel Commentary: War Crimes Tribunals: The Record and Prospects: The Contribution of the *Ad Hoc* Tribunals to International Humanitarian Law' (1998) 13 AU ILR 1509, 1538. See also Bothe (n 30 above) 420.

[72] DF Orentlicher, 'Internationalizing Civil War' in B Cooper (ed), *War Crimes: The Legacy of Nuremberg* (New York: TV Books, 1999) 154, 154.

[73] See *Prosecutor v Tadić* (Separate Opinion of Judge Li on the Defence Motion for Interlocutory Appeal on Jurisdiction) IT-9-1-AR72 (2 October 1995) paras 10–13.

authority'.[74] As criminal Tribunals, this gives rise also to concerns regarding the principle of legality, an issue which also arose in other decisions concerning the existence and content of individual war crimes.

(2) Unenumerated war crimes

Article 3 of the ICTY Statute was described by the *Tadić* Appeals Chamber as a 'residual clause' designed to ensure that the jurisdiction of the Tribunal over all serious violations of humanitarian law as war crimes is 'watertight and inescapable'.[75] In subsequent cases, the application of the formula adopted to effectuate this article gave rise to expansive development of the law of war crimes and the trying of several crimes not enumerated in Article 3's illustrative list. Examples include hostage-taking,[76] unlawful labour,[77] outrages upon personal dignity,[78] rape,[79] humiliating and degrading treatment,[80] unlawful attacks on civilian persons and objects,[81] and murder, torture, and cruel treatment of prisoners of war.[82] Judicial errors have been made at times, such as when the Trial Chamber in *Blaškić* held that 'targeting civilians is an offence when not justified by military necessity'.[83] This finding was corrected by the Appeals Chamber which affirmed the absolute prohibition of targeting civilians under customary international law.[84] More generally though, the practice of the ICTY under Article 3 has often been said to leave the Tribunal open to a charge of 'creating new law',[85] and criticism of judicial legislation and its perils has even been voiced from the bench. This was particularly apparent in the *Galić* case concerning the prosecution of the war crime of terror in the context of the 'siege of Sarajevo'.[86]

[74] ibid para 13. [75] *Tadić* (Appeals Chamber Jurisdiction Decision) (n 5 above) para 91.

[76] *Prosecutor v Blaškić* (Trial Chamber Judgment) IT-95-14-T (3 March 2000) para 187.

[77] *Prosecutor v Naletilić and Martinović* (Trial Chamber Judgment) IT-98-34-T (31 March 2003) paras 250–61.

[78] *Prosecutor v Aleksovski* (Trial Chamber Judgment) IT-95-14/1-T (25 June 1999) paras 48–57; *Prosecutor v Aleksovski* (Appeals Chamber Judgment) IT-95-14/1-A (24 March 2000) paras 17–28; *Furundžija* (Trial Chamber Judgment) (n 61 above) paras 270–75.

[79] *Kunarac, Ković and Vuković* (Trial Chamber Judgment) (n 60 above) paras 436–64. See further the contribution of Niamh Hayes (Ch 6 below).

[80] *Prosecutor v Češić* (Trial Chamber Sentencing Judgment) IT-95-10/1-S (11 March 2004).

[81] *Prosecutor v Jokic* (Trial Chamber Judgment) IT-01-42/1-T (18 March 2004).

[82] *Prosecutor v Mrkšić et al* (Trial Chamber Judgment) (n 33 above); *Prosecutor v Mrkšić et al* (Appeals Chamber Judgment) (n 33 above).

[83] *Blaškić* (Trial Chamber Judgment) (n 76 above) para 180. See also *Prosecutor v Kordić and Čerkez* (Trial Chamber Judgment) IT-95-14/2-T (26 February 2001) paras 326–8.

[84] *Blaškić* (Appeals Chamber Judgment) (n 52 above) para 109. See also *Prosecutor v Kordić and Čerkez* (Appeals Chamber Judgment) IT-95-14/2-A (17 December 2004) para 54; *Prosecutor v Kordić and Čerkez* (Appeals Chamber Corrigendum to Judgment) IT-95-14/2-A (17 December 2004) 26 January 2005.

[85] See eg G Pinzauti, 'Protecting Prisoners of War; The *Mrkšić et al* Appeal Judgment' (2010) 8 JICJ 1 199, 200. The conviction was based on aiding and abetting by omission, a form of liability discussed by Gideon Boas in Ch 9 of this collection.

[86] *Prosecutor v Galić* (Trial Chamber Judgment) IT-98-29-T (5 December 2003) para 2.

Major-General Galić had been charged with 'unlawfully inflicting terror upon civilians', and in having to address this charge, the Trial Chamber was faced with a dearth of international precedent, noting itself that this was the first time the matter had been dealt with by an international tribunal.[87] Although the Geneva Conventions and Additional Protocols outlaw 'measures of intimidation and terrorism' directed at a civilian population in occupied territories and 'Acts or threats of violence the primary purpose of which is to spread terror among the civilian population', a war crime of terror had not been defined in conventional law at the time of the offences.[88] The Trial Chamber deemed that the actual infliction of terror was not an element of the offence, which it defined as: 'Acts of violence directed against the civilian population or individual civilians not taking part in hostilities causing death or serious injury to body or health within the civilian population . . . committed with the primary purpose of spreading terror among the civilian population'.[89] The Trial Chamber decided also that the question of whether this crime of terror had a foundation in customary international law was not one 'which the Majority is required to answer'.[90]

In his separate and partially dissenting opinion, Judge Nieto-Navia took the view that a war crime of terror was not within the Tribunal's jurisdiction and to conclude otherwise was contrary to the principle set out by the Secretary-General that the ICTY 'cannot create new criminal offences, but may only consider crimes already well established in international humanitarian law'.[91] He supported the view that:

> . . . under no circumstances may a court create new criminal offences after the act charged against an accused either by giving a definition to a crime which had none so far, thereby rendering it prosecutable or punishable, or by criminalizing an act which had not until the present time been regarded as criminal.[92]

Judge Nieto-Navia rebuked the majority for failing to pronounce on the customary nature of the war crime of terror and criticized its reliance on conventional law and an agreement between the parties, rightly pointing out that it did not satisfy the requirement that the violation in question attracted individual criminal responsibility.[93] He concluded that 'the Majority is furthering a conception of international humanitarian law which I do not support'.[94]

87 ibid para 66.

88 See Geneva Convention IV, Art 33; Additional Protocol I, Art 51(2); Additional Protocol II, Art 13.

89 *Galić* (Trial Chamber Judgment) (n 86 above) paras 133–4.

90 ibid paras 94–5, 138.

91 *Prosecutor v Galić* (Trial Chamber Separate and Partially Dissenting Opinion of Judge Nieto-Navia) IT-98-29-T (5 December 2003) paras 108–9.

92 ibid para 109, citing *Prosecutor v Vasiljević* (Trial Chamber Judgment) para 196.

93 *Galić* (Trial Chamber Nieto-Navia Opinion) (n 91 above) paras 112–13.

94 ibid para 113. See, however, D Kravetz, 'The Protection of Civilians in War: The ICTY's *Galić* Case' (2004) 17(3) LJIL 521.

Disagreement regarding the crime of terror continued at the appeals stage, and the issues surrounding its customary status prompted several of the judges to pass comment in their separate individual opinions. The majority judgment explained why it was necessary to demonstrate the existence of the offence in customary law:

> ...in most cases, treaty provisions will only provide for the prohibition of a certain conduct, not for its criminalisation, or the treaty provision itself will not sufficiently define the elements of the prohibition they criminalise and customary international law must be looked at for the definition of those elements.[95]

Having made a convincing argument as to the customary status of the terror prohibition in the Additional Protocols,[96] the Appeals Chamber then drew on the 1919 Commission, national legislation, and military manuals to assert that individual criminal responsibility had arisen for violation of the prohibition at least since the 'siege of Sarajevo'.[97] Judge Shahabuddeen agreed that 'terror as charged is a crime known to customary international law', although more as a core concept, rather than a comprehensive definition.[98] As regards individual criminal responsibility, he was satisfied that a serious violation of the laws or customs of war under Article 3 'namely, by resorting to the core of terror, gives rise to such responsibility'.[99] In Judge Meron's opinion, the majority finding could also be based on the well-established rule that forbids declaring that no quarter will be given: 'And if threats that no quarter will be given are crimes, then surely threats that a party will not respect other foundational principles of international law—such as the prohibition against targeting civilians—are also crimes. The terrorization at issue here is exactly such a threat.'[100] He drew on the Nuremberg judgment to argue that '[i]t is a crime to violate principles of customary international law identified in the Fourth Hague Convention'.[101]

Judge Schomburg took issue in his forceful opinion with both the majority and Judge Meron's view regarding the crime of terror. He felt that 'there is no basis to find that this prohibited conduct as such was penalized beyond any doubt under customary international criminal law at the time relevant to the Indictment'.[102] He agreed that the first three elements of the *Tadić* test were satisfied, but not the fourth, a position which he persuasively supports by reference to the limited instances of state practice provided by the majority.[103] Judge Schomburg felt that the analogy with the denial of quarter was incorrect, 'since it could be made in any context in relation to any and every violation of international humanitarian

[95] *Prosecutor v Galić* (Appeals Chamber Judgment) IT-98-29-A (30 November 2006) para 83.
[96] ibid paras 87–90. [97] ibid paras 91–8.
[98] *Prosecutor v Galić* (Appeals Chamber Separate Opinion of Judge Shahabuddeen) IT-98-29-A (30 November 2006) para 3. [99] ibid para 5.
[100] *Prosecutor v Galić* (Appeals Chamber Separate and Partially Dissenting Opinion of Judge Meron) IT-98-29-A (30 November 2006) para 2. [101] ibid.
[102] *Prosecutor v Galić* (Appeals Chamber Separate and Partially Dissenting Opinion of Judge Schomburg) IT-98-29-A (30 November 2006) para 2. [103] ibid paras 8–11.

law'.[104] While the prohibitions may have shared similar aims, that was insufficient because 'as an international criminal court, we are under the obligation to define what is a crime under our Statute *with precision* in order to avoid any violation of the fundamental principle of *nullum crimen sine lege certa*'.[105] The Rome Statute did not include a crime of terror in 1998, although Judge Schomburg favoured the idea that the prohibited conduct would be criminalized:

> However, this Tribunal is not acting as a legislator... The International Tribunal is required to adhere strictly to the principle of *nullum crimen sine lege praevia* and must ascertain that a crime was 'beyond any doubt part of customary law'. It would be detrimental not only to the Tribunal but also to the future development of international criminal law and international criminal jurisdiction if our jurisprudence gave the appearance of inventing crimes—thus highly politicizing its function—where the conduct in question was not without any doubt penalized at the time when it took place.[106]

Judge Schomburg felt that the majority could have avoided these controversies by overturning the crime of terror conviction and treating the terrorization element as an aggravating factor in sentencing a conviction of the well-established war crime of attacks against civilians.[107]

Judge Liu favoured this approach as advocated by Judge Schomburg in the subsequent case against Dragomir Milošević, although the majority of the Appeals Chamber, which included three judges who sat in *Galić*, unsurprisingly upheld its previous findings.[108] Judge Liu was critical of the holding in *Galić*, taking the view that the elements of the crime of terror did not adequately define a criminal charge: 'this problem stems from the simple conversion of the prohibition, as proscribed by the Additional Protocols, into an international crime'.[109] He went further than Judge Schomburg and actually proposed a set of elements for a war crime of terror, so that it might be 'properly defined and prospectively confirmed as part of the canon of war crimes either by convention or clear custom'.[110]

The treatment of the crime of terror at the ICTY demonstrates the difficulty of satisfying the fourth *Tadić* criterion when the war crime in question has not previously been codified in treaty law. Robert Cryer was not persuaded as to the existence of the terror offence and considered that the fourth *Tadić* requirement has led to 'some of the most questionable argumentation in international tribunals'.[111] The jurisprudence regarding this offence also points to the risks of judicial creativity in the context of international criminal law. The potential drawbacks include compromising the rights of accused persons and harming the reputation

[104] ibid para 17. [105] ibid (original emphasis). [106] ibid paras 20–21.

[107] ibid paras 2, 22. See the similar suggestion in R Cryer, '*Prosecutor v Galić* and the War Crime of Terror Bombing' (2005–6) 2 *Israeli Defense Forces Law Review* 73.

[108] *Prosecutor v Milošević* (Appeals Chamber Judgment) IT-98-29/1-A (12 November 2009) para 30; *Prosecutor v Milošević* (Partly Dissenting Opinion of Judge Liu Daqun) IT-98-29/1-A (12 November 2009) para 1.

[109] *Milošević* (Partly Dissenting Opinion of Judge Liu Daqun) ibid para 14.

[110] ibid para 24. [111] Cryer (n 107 above) 90.

and legitimacy of these significant mechanisms of international justice in the eyes of victims, wider society, and even states. Cryer considered that if a war crime of terror was to be created 'it ought to be done by those who have the authority to make international law, States, rather than by courts stretching existing international law'.[112]

It is in the overstating of existing law that problems with judicial creativity may arise. This approach is perhaps facilitated by the fluid nature of customary international law and, as Judge Wald points out in her foreword to this collection, by the at times skeletal nature of the Statues of the *ad hoc* Tribunals themselves. The Appeals Chamber has noted that:

> [t]he Statute of the ICTY is not and does not purport to be, unlike for instance the Rome Statute of the International Criminal Court, a meticulously detailed code providing explicitly for every possible scenario and every solution thereto. It sets out in somewhat general terms the jurisdictional framework within which the Tribunal has been mandated to operate.[113]

That being said, the shifting parameters of the customary law of war crimes should not prevent the *ad hoc* Tribunals from presenting sufficient evidence of state practice and *opinio juris* to support the criminalization of a particular humanitarian law prohibition, if such do exist. In seeking to provide evidence of the existence of war crimes, the *ad hoc* Tribunals have often over-emphasized the illegality of a particular practice in order to demonstrate its criminality. It is worth recalling the distinction highlighted by Michael Bothe between primary and secondary rules of international humanitarian law in this regard, which the *Galić* Appeals Chamber seemingly did when it noted that usually 'treaty provisions will only provide for the prohibition of a certain conduct, not for its criminalisation'.[114] From the outset, the *ad hoc* Tribunals have drawn on the Nuremberg judgment to hold that the criminal nature of violations does not have to be explicitly stated in a treaty to give rise to criminal liability, with Judge Meron in *Galić* asserting that all violations of the principles of customary international law in the Hague Fourth Convention are war crimes. The question arises as to whether the approach of the Nuremberg Tribunal to the existence of war crimes, one involving the 'conflation of illegality and criminality',[115] is permissible in contemporary international criminal law in light of the comparatively significant fair trial protections now accruing to persons accused of international crimes.[116]

[112] Cryer (n 107 above) 101. On the existence of the crime, see also Mettraux (n 25 above) 129.

[113] *Prosecutor v Milutinović et al* (Appeals Chamber Decision on Dragoljub Ojdanić's Motion Challenging Jurisdiction—*Joint Criminal Enterprise*) IT-99-37-AR72 (21 May 2003) para 18.

[114] *Galić* (Appeals Chamber Judgment) (n 95 above) para 83.

[115] Beth van Schaack, '*Crimen Sine Lege*: Judicial Lawmaking at the Intersection of Law and Morals', (2008) 97 *Georgetown Law Journal* 119, 127.

[116] This charge has also been levelled against the *ad hoc* Tribunals: see Mettraux (n 25 above) 129.

Shortly after it affirmed the Nuremberg Charter and judgment, the United Nations adopted the Universal Declaration of Human Rights in an attempt to herald a new era of respect for the rights of individuals, including those persons facing criminal charges.[117] Article 11 states that: '[n]o one shall be held guilty of any penal offence on account of any act or omission which did not constitute a penal offence, under national or international law, at the time when it was committed.' The International Covenant on Civil and Political Rights replicates this articulation of the principle of legality, adding, however, that it would not 'prejudice the trial and punishment of any person for any act or omission which, at the time when it was committed, was criminal according to the general principles of law recognized by the community of nations'.[118] The principle of legality is framed here primarily as a rule against retroactive legislation, prohibiting the creation of crimes and penalties *ex post facto*, although it is clear that the principle also incorporates the requirement that the offences were defined with sufficient clarity at the time they were committed.[119] Adjudging respect for the principle of legality is less taxing in a national context, where offences are normally specified in legislation or penal codes, whereas international law derives from a variety of sources, including unwritten custom and general principles.[120]

The *ad hoc* Tribunals have certainly been cognizant of the importance of the principle of legality, but have stressed that the limits it imposes on judicial activity do not prevent a court from 'interpreting and clarifying the elements of a particular crime'.[121] Challenges on the basis of *nullum crimen sine lege* have been 'practically ubiquitous' at the *ad hoc* Tribunals, 'as criminal defendants attempt to stem this jurisprudential tide'.[122] Lawyers, judges, and commentators, however, have been at odds as to the content of the principle of legality. The Appeals Chamber of the ICTY has stated that the principle does not 'preclude the progressive development of the law by the court':

> But it does prevent a court from creating new law or from interpreting existing law beyond the reasonable limits of acceptable clarification. This Tribunal must therefore be satisfied that the crime or the form of liability with which an accused is charged was sufficiently foreseeable and that the law providing for such liability must be sufficiently accessible at the relevant time, taking into account the specificity of international law when making that assessment.[123]

[117] Universal Declaration of Human Rights (1948), UNGA Res 217A (III), UN Doc A/810, para 71.

[118] International Covenant on Civil and Political Rights (1966), 999 UNTS 171, Art 15(2).

[119] UN Human Rights Committee, 'General Comment No. 29—Article 4: Derogations during a state of emergency', UN Doc CCPR/C/21/Rev.1/Add.11, (2001), para 7.

[120] Statute of the International Court of Justice, Art 38(1).

[121] *Milutinović* (Appeals Chamber Jurisdiction Decision) (n 113 above) para 38 (footnotes omitted).

[122] van Schaack (n 115 above) 125.

[123] *Milutinović* (Appeals Chamber Jurisdiction Decision) (n 113 above) para 38 (footnotes omitted).

In *Tadić*, the Trial Chamber held squarely that imposing criminal responsibility for violations of Common Article 3 'does not violate the principle of *nullum crimen sine lege*'.[124] The Chamber cited the scholarly view that 'the principle *nullum crimen* is designed to protect a person only from being punished for an act that he or she reasonably believed to be lawful when committed'.[125] In addition to the precedent of Nuremberg relying on the 1907 Hague Regulations and the 1929 Geneva Prisoners of War Convention as a basis for prosecutions, the Trial Chamber cited the customary nature of Common Article 3 as proof of the unlawfulness of the acts it prohibits.[126] Christopher Greenwood agreed that the ICTY did not breach the principle of legality in this context as there was clearly wrongfulness and any doubt as to criminality was only with regard to the question of under which particular system of law.[127]

The *ad hoc* Tribunals have not interpreted the principle of legality as requiring 'a prior written criminal statute specifically accompanying the act charged', as Kenneth Gallant suggests it does.[128] Rather, the view seems to be that the existence of the offence must first be established in customary law, drawing on positive law where available, and secondly that the crime must have been 'sufficiently foreseeable' and the law providing for its liability, irrespective of its source, sufficiently accessible at the time of commission. The Trial Chamber in *Galić* took the view expressed similarly by the *Tadić* Trial Chamber that *nullum crimen* 'is meant to prevent the prosecution and punishment of a person for acts which were reasonably, and with knowledge of the laws in force, believed by that person not to be criminal at the time of their commission'.[129] This subjective approach seems to contrast with the view of Judge Nieto-Navia:

> Once it is satisfied that a certain act or set of acts is indeed criminal under customary international law, a Trial Chamber must finally confirm that this offence was defined with sufficient clarity under international customary law for its general nature, its criminal character and its approximate gravity to have been sufficiently foreseeable and accessible.[130]

Judge Schomburg, in relation to the first requirement, drew on the Secretary-General's Report to assert that there must be 'penalization beyond any doubt'.[131]

Consideration of the principle of legality is thus tied up with the issue of jurisdiction at the *ad hoc* Tribunals, and customary international law has played a central and at times controversial role. The unsatisfactory treatment of customary international law at the *ad hoc* Tribunals has been noted by other contributors to

[124] *Tadić* (Trial Chamber Jurisdiction Decision) (n 34 above) para 65.

[125] ibid paras 68–9, referring to T Meron, 'International Criminalization of Internal Atrocities' (1995) 89 AJIL 554, 566.

[126] ibid paras 70–72.

[127] Greenwood (n 34 above) 132–3.

[128] KS Gallant, *The Principle of Legality in International and Comparative Law* (Cambridge: CUP, 2009) 321.

[129] *Galić* (Trial Chamber Judgment) (n 86 above) para 93.

[130] *Galić* (Trial Chamber Nieto-Navia Opinion) (n 91 above) para 111.

[131] *Galić* (Appeals Chamber Schomburg Opinion) (n 102 above) para 2.

this collection.[132] It is certainly problematic to assert the existence of particular war crimes where the supporting evidence of state practice and *opinio juris* is weak or contradictory. Even so, a legal system which relies on customary law is not seen to be best placed for ensuring respect for the principle of *nullum crimen*, particularly the elements of foreseeability and accessibility.[133] If reasonable disagreement exists among international judges and scholars as to the existence of particular crimes in customary international law, then surely this casts doubt on whether an accused would have been sufficiently appraised as to the existence and nature of criminal liability attaching to their actions at the time of their commission? This is particularly so with regard to war crimes, which derive from a branch of international law involving complex sets of rules, categories, and principles. The prohibition of certain practices, such as murder or torture, is absolute and relatively straightforward,[134] while the legality or criminality of other wartime practices is subject to caveats such as military necessity and proportionality. Acts such as the transfer or confinement of civilians are war crimes only if committed 'unlawfully', while the destruction of civilian property is not a war crime if carried out as an absolute military necessity. Kenneth Gallant concludes his study on the legality principle by observing that international criminal courts 'have not applied the strictest definition of legality', with the ICTY merely asking 'whether the act of the accused was a crime as generally understood at the time of the offense charged'.[135]

IV. Conclusion

When the jurisdiction of the International Military Tribunal at Nuremberg was challenged on the basis of the principle of legality, it famously held that:

> ... the maxim *nullum crimen sine lege* is not a limitation of sovereignty, but is in general a principle of justice. To assert that it is unjust to punish those who in defiance of treaties and assurances have attacked neighbouring states without warning is obviously untrue, for in such circumstances the attacker must know that he is doing wrong, and so far from it being unjust to punish him, it would be unjust if his wrong were allowed to go unpunished.[136]

[132] See also Danner (n 21 above); A Zahar and G Sluiter, *International Criminal Law* (Oxford/New York: OUP, 2008) 110–12, 115, fn 33; Schabas (n 17 above) 228–9, 235. See, however, A Cassese, 'The International Criminal Tribunal for the Former Yugoslavia and the implementation of international humanitarian law' in L Condorelli, A-M La Rosa, and S Scherrer (eds), *The United Nations and International Humanitarian Law* (Paris: Editions Pedone, 1996) 229, 237–8.

[133] van Schaack (n 115 above) 138.

[134] See *Kononov v Latvia* (App No 36376/04) ECHR Grand Chamber 17 May 2010. On the question of *nullum crimen*, note the dissenting opinion of Judges Costa, Kalaydjieva, and Poalelungi.

[135] Gallant (n 123 above) 321.

[136] *Judgment of the Nuremberg International Military Tribunal 1946* (1947) 41 AJIL 1 172, 217.

This approach chimes somewhat with that taken by the *ad hoc* Tribunals towards war crimes. There has not always been an insistence that war crimes were clearly defined in customary international law, nor sufficient evidence of the existence of some of those war crimes in the first place. Judge Shahabuddeen has commented that 'provided that the acts alleged bore the fundamental criminality of the crime charged, it does not appear to be necessary to show that at the time at which they were done, they exhibited every detail of that crime'.[137] This approach has certainly provided for a rich jurisprudence on war crimes and allowed the *ad hoc* Tribunals to exercise a broad jurisdiction in fulfilling their mandates.

The era of judicial creativity for the law of war crimes which began at Nuremberg and continues through the life of the *ad hoc* Tribunals may, however, be coming to an end. The importance of the principle of legality in international criminal law was reiterated at the opening plenary of the diplomatic conference leading to the creation of the ICC; President Scalfaro of Italy commended the 'positive advances' of the *ad hoc* Tribunals, but urged that '[c]riminal law should always precede crimes; it should be known that the crimes were punishable by law and what the penalties would be'.[138] The ICC may become the sole international justice mechanism for trying war crimes and the detailed, exhaustive approach of Article 8 of the Rome Statute and the 'Elements of Crimes' may preclude its judges from straying too far from the letter of the written law. Additionally, the Rome Statute enshrines various rights of accused persons, including the principle that '[t]he definition of a crime shall be strictly construed and shall not be extended by analogy. In case of ambiguity, the definition shall be interpreted in favour of the person being investigated, prosecuted or convicted.'[139]

There is little doubt that the judicial creativity demonstrated at the international criminal tribunals in the area of war crimes has amounted to judicial law-making, albeit law which does not formally extend beyond the jurisdiction of the tribunals. This is law that has been created by the tribunals for their own purposes, although states or other international courts may follow the precedent, and at times have done so. Sovereign states, of course, solely possess the general power to create international law, and have usually refrained from explicitly granting such a power to judicial bodies.[140] Judicial decisions are 'a subsidiary

[137] M Shahabuddeen, 'Does the Principle of Legality Stand in the Way of Progressive Development of the Law?' (2004) 2 JICJ 1007, 1010.

[138] *United Nations Diplomatic Conference of Plenipotentiaries on the Establishment of an International Criminal Court*, Rome (June 1998) *Official Records, Vol II, Summary records of the plenary meetings*, 1st Plenary Meeting, 15 June 1998, para 16, p 62.

[139] Rome Statute of the International Criminal Court, Art 22, para 2.

[140] See eg the Security Council debate leading to the ICTY's creation, S/P V3217, 25 May 1993, reprinted in V Morris and MP Scharf, *An Insider's Guide to the International Criminal Tribunal for the Former Yugoslavia, Vol 2* (New York: Transnational Publishers, 1995) 182. Note, however, the power of the *ad hoc* Tribunals to adopt their own rules of procedure and evidence, as discussed elsewhere in this collection.

means for the determination of rules of law',[141] and the judiciary in war crimes trials has noted that judges themselves do not create new law, but only 'apply it as we find it'.[142] It is an obvious truism that it is a fine line which separates development of the law from its creation. The Nuremberg tribunal noted the variety of sources in which the law of war is to be found and observed that '[t]his law is not static, but by continual adaptation follows the need of a changing world'.[143] This is undeniably the case, but the jurisprudence of the *ad hoc* Tribunals challenged the traditional understanding that such law is to be developed by states as the traditional creators of international legal rules, rather than by tribunals whose duty ostensibly is to apply those rules. As Charles Garraway notes:

> Codified international law is the subject of agreement amongst States after lengthy negotiations. It is inevitably subject to compromise and practical reality, which may water down the desirable to the feasible. If States find that customary law is being used to 'raise the bar' so that requirements are being imposed which States would not be prepared to accept at the conference table on grounds of practicality, then the whole structure of customary law, as providing a foundation for treaty law and underpinning the legal system, may be cast in doubt.[144]

In general, states are bound by the jurisprudence of the *ad hoc* Tribunals only to the extent that they agree to be or where findings reflect an accurate picture of customary international law. For the international law of war crimes, the *ad hoc* Tribunals have taken a creative, progressive and at times lawmaking approach, generating a considerable body of jurisprudence across the spectrum of war crimes. They may have departed from the prior will of states at times, but like the law itself, the will of states is not static, and significant war crimes rulings by the *ad hoc* Tribunals have been adopted and transformed into positive international law.

[141] Statute of the ICJ (n 120 above) Art 38(1)(d).

[142] *United States of America v Wilhelm List et al* (Judgment) 19 February 1948, Case No 7, XI *Trials of War Criminals before the Nuernberg Military Tribunals under Control Council Law No. 10* 757, 1249.

[143] *Nuremberg* (n 136 above) 219.

[144] Garraway (n 26 above) 397.

6

Creating a Definition of Rape in International Law: The Contribution of the International Criminal Tribunals

Niamh Hayes

I. Introduction

In any analysis of the contribution of the Yugoslavia and Rwanda Tribunals to the prosecution of rape and sexual violence as international crimes, it would be remiss to overlook the obvious yet disheartening fact that one of their most significant achievements was in prosecuting such crimes at all. Although the prohibition of rape in time of war has existed as a legal rule for centuries[1] and its origins in modern humanitarian law can be traced as far back as the Lieber Code of 1863,[2] there was extraordinarily little appetite historically to prosecute the crime, in part due to the continuing perception that sexual violence was simply one of the 'spoils of war'.[3] Rape was not included in the Charter of the International Military Tribunal at Nuremberg, nor was it prosecuted as an international crime in those proceedings.[4] While the relegation of sexual violence in the Second World War to a handful of mentions in the transcript of

[1] Theodor Meron acknowledged that '[r]ape by soldiers has of course been prohibited by the law of war for centuries', citing the national military codes of Richard II (1385) and Henry V (1419) as examples. T Meron, 'Rape as a Crime Under International Humanitarian Law' (1993) 87(3) AJIL 424.

[2] F Lieber, 'Instructions for the Government of the United States in the Field by Order of the Secretary of War', United States War Department, Adjutant General's Office, General Orders No 100, 24 April 1863. Art 44 of the Lieber Code stated that the crime of rape was prohibited under penalty of death.

[3] See further KD Askin, *War Crimes Against Women: Prosecution in International War Crimes Tribunals* (The Hague: Kluwer Law International, 1997) Chs I–V.

[4] See R Goldstone, 'Prosecuting Rape as a War Crime' (2002) 34 CWR JIL 277, 279 and Agreement for the Prosecution and Punishment of the Major War Criminals of the European Axis and Establishing the Charter of the International Military Tribunal (8 August 1945) 82 UNTS 279.

the Nuremberg proceedings is a glaring omission,[5] even the most resounding judicial pronouncements on sexual violence would have rung a little hollow coming, for example, from the Soviet representatives to the Tribunal.[6] Rape was successfully prosecuted as a war crime by the International Military Tribunal for the Far East, however, and was included as a crime against humanity—though not prosecuted—under Control Council Law No 10.[7]

Despite the continuing codification of the prohibition of rape in post-Second World War humanitarian law instruments,[8] at the time of the establishment of the International Criminal Tribunal for the former Yugoslavia (ICTY) there was still a noticeable degree of hesitancy in recognizing that rape and sexual violence could constitute grave breaches of the Geneva Conventions. The International Committee of the Red Cross and the US Department of State came out in support of a progressive interpretation of the Geneva Conventions, arguing that rape could be prosecuted as a grave breach under the rubric of 'wilfully causing great suffering or serious injury to body or health'.[9] Rape was explicitly included in the Statute of the ICTY as a crime against humanity,[10] and was repeatedly emphasized in the Report of the Secretary-General annexed to Security Council Resolution 808.[11] International outrage at the systematic nature of rape and sexual violence committed in the former Yugoslavia had been a major contributing factor to the establishment of the Tribunal,[12] but it remained to be seen how

[5] Askin (n 3 above) 137–8.

[6] Several commentators have argued that the lack of will to prosecute sexual violence at Nuremberg, which was possible under the Charter (under the rubric of other inhumane acts or enslavement) was due to the awareness that Allied forces had also committed rape on a mass scale. See Askin (n 3 above) 163; Anne-Marie de Brouwer, *Supranational Criminal Prosecution of Sexual Violence: The ICC and the Practice of the ICTY and ICTR* (Antwerp, Oxford: Intersentia, 2005) 7–8; R Copelon, 'Gender Crimes as War Crimes: Integrating Crimes Against Women into International Criminal Law' (2000–2001) 46 *McGill Law Journal* 217, 222.

[7] De Brouwer (n 6 above) 6–9. See also Allied Control Council Law No 10, Punishment of Persons Guilty of War Crimes, Crimes Against Peace and Against Humanity (20 December 1945), published in *Official Gazette of the Control Council for Germany* No 3 (1946) 50, Art II.

[8] Geneva Convention (IV) Relative to the Protection of Civilian Persons in Time of War (12 August 1949) 75 UNTS 287, Art 27; Protocol Additional I to the Geneva Conventions of 12 August 1949, and Relating to the Protection of Victims of International Armed Conflicts (12 December 1977) 1125 UNTS 3, Arts 76(1) and 85; Protocol II Additional to the Geneva Conventions of 12 August 1949, and Relating to the Protection of Victims of Non-International Armed Conflicts (8 June 1977) 1125 UNTS 609, Art 4(2)(e).

[9] Meron (n 1 above) 426–7. Meron argued that, in certain circumstances, rape could also constitute the grave breach of 'torture or inhuman treatment'.

[10] Statute of the International Criminal Tribunal for the former Yugoslavia, UN Doc S/RES/827, UN Security Council, 1994, Annex, Art 5(g).

[11] UNSC, 'Report of the Secretary-General Pursuant to Paragraph 2 of Security Council Resolution 808' (1993) UN Doc S/25704.

[12] See eg UNSC Res 827 (1993) UN Doc S/RES/827, which deplored the 'continuing reports of widespread and flagrant violations of international humanitarian law occurring within the territory of the former Yugoslavia . . . including reports of . . . massive, organised and systematic detention and rape of women' and reiterated the Security Council's intention to put an end to such crimes and take effective measures to prosecute those responsible; Karen Engle argued that '[a]ttention to the rapes in Bosnia and Herzegovina coincided with increasing support in general for an international

effective the Tribunal would be in finally providing a legal framework for and judicial response to a crime which, up to that point, had been significant only in its absence from international prosecutions.

The range and breadth of sexual violence case law which has since been articulated by the judges of both the Yugoslavia and Rwanda Tribunals is a tremendous achievement in and of itself. The international crime of rape is no longer couched in euphemism or relegated to the catch-all bin of 'other inhumane acts'; it is firmly established in international criminal law and capable of being prosecuted as an act of genocide, as a crime against humanity in its own right or as an act of torture, enslavement, or persecution, as a grave breach or as a war crime. If the only contribution of the *ad hoc* Tribunals to the case law on rape had been convictions for such crimes, they would still have had tremendous import. However, this chapter seeks to further identify the substantive law in this area as interpreted, applied, and in some cases created by the judges of the ICTY and the International Criminal Tribunal for Rwanda (ICTR), and to critically appraise their repeated attempts to identify an international definition for the crime of rape, with particular emphasis on the vexed question of the significance of consent.

II. Identifying the Definition

The first judgment by the *ad hoc* Tribunals to address rape—and that which continues to be most frequently extolled as a landmark in international law—arose from the prosecution of Jean Paul Akayesu.[13] The judgment of Trial Chamber I of the Rwanda Tribunal marked the first conviction of an individual for genocide by an international tribunal since the adoption of the Genocide Convention 50 years earlier.[14] Its significance was compounded by being the first conviction to emanate from the Rwanda Tribunal,[15] the first conviction for rape as a crime against humanity, and, most notably, the first judicial recognition that rape can constitute an act of genocide. The *Akayesu* judgment has been rightly hailed as groundbreaking, particularly for the ramifications of its findings on

criminal law that could be enforced through tribunals and courts': K Engle, 'Feminism and its (Dis)contents: Criminalising Wartime Rape in Bosnia and Herzegovina' (2005) 99(4) AJIL 778, 778; and Christine Chinkin noted in 1994 that '[t]he substantive law on rape in armed conflict has now become entangled with the question of arenas for its application': C Chinkin, 'Rape and Sexual Abuse of Women in International Law' (1994) 5 EJIL 326, 334.

[13] *Prosecutor v Akayesu* (Trial Chamber Judgment) ICTR-96-4-T (2 September 1998).

[14] See generally W Schabas, 'The Genocide Convention at Fifty', United States Institute of Peace Special Report (7 January 1999).

[15] Although Jean Kambanda pleaded guilty at his initial appearance before the ICTR in May 1998, his conviction and sentence were not handed down until 4 September 1998, just two days after the *Akayesu* judgment: *Prosecutor v Kambanda* (Judgment and Sentence) ICTR-97-23-S (4 September 1998). The first conviction from either Tribunal was that of Duško Tadić at the ICTY in May 1997.

sexual violence. However, it is somewhat unsettling to note that the case most immediately associated with positive international jurisprudence on rape did not initially contain any charges of sexual violence. The impetus for redressing this oversight, as well as the legal innovation shown in the judgment, came from Judge Navanethem Pillay.

The original indictment against Akayesu contained 12 counts of genocide, crimes against humanity, and violations of Common Article 3 relating to his role as *bourgemestre* of Taba commune during the genocide.[16] In the course of the trial, a witness spontaneously testified about acts of rape which had taken place, including the gang rape of her 6-year-old daughter.[17] Another witness testified that she had been raped and had witnessed multiple rapes at or near the *bureau communal*.[18] Judge Pillay, along with Judge Kama and Judge Aspegren, immediately began questioning the witnesses regarding sexual violence,[19] and following the judges' intervention, the trial was adjourned while the prosecutor initiated further investigations of sexual violence in Taba.[20] The indictment was amended in June 1997 to include charges of rape and sexual violence as genocide, crimes against humanity (rape and other inhumane acts), and violations of Common Article 3 (outrages on personal dignity).[21] Following the amendment of the indictment, several additional witnesses testified at length about rape and sexual violence in Taba commune. The defence closing statement suggested that the indictment had been amended in response to public pressure from NGOs to include rape charges.[22] However, the trial judgment made clear that the spontaneous testimony of the two crime base witnesses had given rise to the renewed prosecution investigation of sexual violence, although it noted that international interest in the issue was 'indicative of public concern over the historical exclusion of rape and other forms of sexual violence from the investigation and prosecution

[16] Original Indictment (confirmed on 16 February 1996); *Akayesu* (Trial Chamber Judgment) (n 13 above) para 6.

[17] *Akayesu* (Trial Chamber Judgment) (n 13 above) para 416.

[18] ibid.

[19] For a description of the initial witness testimony of rape and the questioning of the judges, see E Neuffer, *The Key to My Neighbour's House: Seeking Justice in Bosnia and Rwanda* (London: Bloomsbury, 2003) 279–83; and B van Schaack, 'Engendering Genocide: The *Akayesu* Case Before the International Criminal Tribunal for Rwanda', Santa Clara University School of Law, Legal Studies Research Paper Series, Working Paper No 08-55, July 2008, available at <http://ssrn.com/abstract=1154259> 6–7.

[20] *Akayesu* (Trial Chamber Judgment) (n 13 above) para 417.

[21] Amended Indictment, 17 June 1997, Counts 1, 13, 14, and 15; *Akayesu* (Trial Chamber Judgment) (n 13 above) para 6. See also K Askin, 'Sexual Violence in Decisions and Indictments of the Yugoslav and Rwandan Tribunals: Current Status' (1999) AJIL 97, 105–6.

[22] See eg Human Rights Watch/Federation Internationale des Ligues des Droits de l'Homme, 'Shattered Lives: Sexual Violence During the Rwandan Genocide and its Aftermath' (24 September 1996), available at <http://www.hrw.org/sites/default/files/reports/1996_Rwanda_ShatteredLives.pdf>, which extensively documented incidents of rape committed during the genocide and called on the ICTR to amend existing indictments to include rape charges. For a discussion of the *amicus curiae* brief submitted to the Chamber urging the investigation and inclusion of rape charges against Akayesu, see Askin (n 21 above) 106, fn 45; Copelon (n 6 above) 225–6; and Neuffer (n 19 above) 283.

of war crimes'.[23] However, Judge Pillay herself undoubtedly played a significant role in encouraging the prosecution to further investigate and amend the indictment in light of the witness evidence.[24]

The *Akayesu* judgment constitutes an archetypal example of judicial creativity, which may be at least partially explained by the relative paucity of international criminal precedents at that point in the Tribunals' development. However, the *Akayesu* Trial Chamber went far further than merely filling in the gaps, instead demonstrating a palpable determination to provide an innovative progressive interpretation of international law, most significantly in its definition of the crime of rape.[25] Judge Pillay has stated that the testimony of one victim of sexual violence in the case 'motivated me to re-examine traditional definitions of rape'.[26]

In the *Akayesu* judgment, the Trial Chamber noted that there was 'no commonly accepted definition of [rape] in international law',[27] but described it as inherently a form of aggression, and argued that 'the central elements of the crime of rape cannot be captured in a mechanical description of objects and body parts'.[28] Instead, the judgment set out a broad conceptual definition of rape as 'a physical invasion of a sexual nature, committed on a person under circumstances which are coercive',[29] not limited to penetration and capable of including 'the insertion of objects and/or the use of bodily orifices not considered to be intrinsically sexual'.[30] Sexual violence was likewise defined as 'any act of a sexual nature which is committed on a person under circumstances which are coercive',[31] a definition which was considerably broader than that used in the indictment.[32] Evidence of physical force was not required to prove coercion; it could be created by threats, intimidation, extortion, duress, fear, or desperation and could likewise be inherent in certain situations (such as armed conflict or the military presence of *Interahamwe*).[33] Crucially, the judgment also recognized that rape and sexual violence, if committed with the requisite specific intent, could constitute genocide by means of the infliction of serious bodily or mental harm; the Chamber

[23] *Akayesu* (Trial Chamber Judgment) (n 13 above) para 417.

[24] D Amann, '*Prosecutor v Akayesu*—Case note' (1999) 93 AJIL 195, 196. See also Copelon (n 6 above) 225–6.

[25] It is worth noting that the *Akayesu* judgment also suggested that, in line with its perception of the drafters' intention, the Genocide Convention could be expansively interpreted to protect not only national, ethnic, racial, or religious groups, but any 'stable and permanent group'. *Akayesu* (Trial Chamber Judgment) (n 13 above) paras 516, 701. For further discussion of this issue, see the contribution of William Schabas (Ch 3 above).

[26] N Pillay, 'Equal Justice for Women' (2008) 50 *Arizona Law Review* 657, 666.

[27] *Akayesu* (Trial Chamber Judgment) (n 13 above) para 596.

[28] ibid paras 597, 687.

[29] ibid paras 598, 688.

[30] ibid para 596.

[31] ibid para 598. Sexual violence did not need to include penetration 'or even physical contact' (ibid para 688).

[32] The Amended Indictment defined sexual violence as including 'forcible sexual penetration of the vagina, anus or oral cavity by a penis and/or of the vagina or anus by some other object', as distinct from acts of 'sexual abuse' such as forced nudity. Amended Indictment, 17 June 1997, para 10A.

[33] *Akayesu* (Trial Chamber Judgment) (n 13 above) para 688.

went further and stated that rape was one of the worst ways to inflict such harm as the victim suffered 'both bodily and mental harm'.[34]

As Judge Pillay has publicly explained, the definition of rape in *Akayesu* intentionally excluded descriptive elements of penetration or issues of consent, but rather was intended to reconstitute 'the law's perception of women's experience of sexual violence'.[35] The judgment made a very telling comparison to the Convention Against Torture, which did not attempt to provide an exhaustive list of acts which could constitute torture, instead focusing on the 'conceptual framework of state-sponsored violence'.[36] The advantages of the *Akayesu* definition in this respect are clear, particularly in light of the understandable reluctance of witnesses to publicly divulge explicit anatomical details of the assaults perpetrated against them.[37] The displacement of the issue of consent in favour of the concept of coercion, which would prove to be highly contentious in subsequent jurisprudence, nevertheless appears entirely sensible when one considers rape as an international crime. As Wolfgang Schomburg and Ines Peterson have noted, consent is central to crimes of sexual violence in domestic jurisdictions, acting as the distinguishing factor between legal sexual contact and punishable sexual violence.[38] However, when committed in circumstances which amount to an international crime, it seems reasonable to define the act of rape with reference to the overwhelming circumstances which are knowingly exploited by the perpetrator, rather than to restrict the context and criminality of the act to the internal acquiescence of the victim. When considered in light of one incident held to be rape in *Akayesu*—the forcing of a piece of wood into the vagina of a dying Tutsi woman[39]—any discussion of consent appears utterly misguided.

The conceptual nature of the definition also enabled the Chamber to address rape as committed in the context of an ongoing genocide and widespread, systematic attack against a civilian population, rather than as isolated criminal occurrences. The exceptional nature of the sexual violence which took place in Rwanda was acknowledged by the Chamber as a systematic 'integral part of the process of destruction',[40] in which Tutsi women were specifically targeted for rape on the basis of their ethnicity. The judgment damningly concluded that '[s]exual violence was a step in the process of destruction of the Tutsi group—destruction of the spirit, of the will to live, and of life itself.'[41]

[34] ibid para 731. [35] Pillay (n 26 above) 666–7.

[36] *Akayesu* (Trial Chamber Judgment) (n 13 above) paras 597, 687. Significantly, the Chamber noted that rape could constitute an act of torture when committed by, at the instigation of, or with the consent of a person acting in an official capacity. [37] ibid para 687.

[38] W Schomburg and I Peterson, 'Genuine Consent to Sexual Violence under International Criminal Law' (2007) 101(1) AJIL 121, 124.

[39] *Akayesu* (Trial Chamber Judgment) (n 13 above) paras 429, 686. [40] ibid para 731.

[41] ibid para 732.

The *Akayesu* judgment has been widely praised for its creativity and progressiveness.[42] Louise Arbour, then Prosecutor of the ICTY and ICTR, commended the 'remarkable' vision and sensitivity of the judgment.[43] Kelly Dawn Askin has repeatedly emphasized the 'monumental legal significance' of *Akayesu*,[44] openly crediting the 'crucial' contribution of Judge Pillay,[45] without whose participation the judgment was 'highly unlikely... [to have exemplified such] a heightened awareness of crimes committed against women'.[46] Catharine MacKinnon has described the definition of rape in *Akayesu* as 'the single biggest substantive accomplishment' of the Rwanda Tribunal.[47] Diane Amann praised the Chamber's 'choice of a definition focusing on the concept of rape rather than on methodological detail', thereby 'properly reflect[ing] the aim of international humanitarian law' to protect the most vulnerable victims of conflict.[48] However, the judgment was not without its flaws. The inclusion and definition of the crime of sexual violence was categorized under the rubric of other inhumane acts, outrages upon personal dignity, and serious bodily or mental harm,[49] but it has been criticized as being insufficiently clear and potentially in violation of the principle of specificity.[50] Kelly Askin, although unfailingly supportive of the jurisprudential significance of the judgment, has also criticized it as 'abundant on facts but short on law and reasoning'.[51]

It is certainly true that, for many of its most significant legal findings, the *Akayesu* judgment is frustratingly silent on the interpretational basis for its conclusions. Alison Cole has rightly criticized the Chamber for its 'failure to follow two international norms in identifying the content of international law—namely,

[42] See eg van Schaack (n 19 above), highlighting judicial precedents of the judgment other than recognition of genocidal rape, including 'incitement, complicity, cumulative charging, individual criminal responsibility in non-international armed conflicts and the constitutive elements of the crime of genocide'; FT Pilch, 'The Crime of Rape in International Humanitarian Law' (1998–1999) 9 *USAF Academic Journal of Legal Studies* 99, describing the judgment as 'a milestone in the conceptualization of rape as a crime under international law'; Kofi Annan described it as 'a landmark decision in the history of international criminal law... [that]... brings to life, for the first time, the ideals of the Genocide Convention' (quoted in J Kirk, 'Forecasting the Legacy of the International Criminal Tribunal for Rwanda' (2007) 15 ISLR 26, 30).

[43] Statement by Justice Louise Arbour, Prosecutor of the International Criminal Tribunal for Rwanda, Press Release CC/PIU/342-E (4 September 1998), available at <http://www.icty.org/sid/7642>.

[44] K Askin, 'Prosecuting Wartime Rape and Other Gender-Related Crimes Under International Law: Extraordinary Advances, Enduring Obstacles' (2003) 21 Berk JIL 288, 318; see also K Askin, 'A Decade of the Development of Gender Crimes in International Courts and Tribunals: 1993 to 2003' (2004) 11(3) *Human Rights Brief* 16, describing the judgment as '[p]erhaps the most groundbreaking decision advancing gender jurisprudence worldwide'; and Askin (n 21 above) 107, praising the judgment for providing a 'broad, progressive international definition of both rape and sexual violence'.

[45] Askin, 'Extraordinary Advances, Enduring Obstacles' (n 44 above) 318.

[46] Askin (n 21 above) 98, fn 8.

[47] C MacKinnon, 'The ICTR's Legacy on Sexual Violence' (2008) 14(2) *New England Journal of International and Comparative Law* 101, 102.

[48] Amann (n 24 above) 199.

[49] *Akayesu* (Trial Chamber Judgment) (n 13 above) para 688.

[50] Amann (n 24 above) 199.

[51] Askin (n 21 above) 110, fn 63.

the application of the *nullum crimen sine lege* principle, and the identification of the proper sources of international law'.[52] In relation to the judgment's most innovative holding on the definition of rape, beyond the bare declaration that 'there is no commonly accepted definition ... in international law' and a comparison to the conceptual definition in the Convention Against Torture,[53] no legal instruments or case law are cited in support of the proposed definition, nor is there any discussion of the position of rape in customary international law at the time of the commission of the indicted crimes. One could argue that the ICTR Statute does not require as crucial an emphasis on customary international law as would be the case at the ICTY,[54] or indeed that, as only the second trial judgment to emanate from either of the *ad hoc* Tribunals, such tropes of judicial composition were not yet firmly established. However, given that the *Akayesu* judgment provides scrupulous references to sources of international law elsewhere in its legal holdings and pursues an originalist interpretation of the Genocide Convention,[55] it seems far more likely that the Chamber quite consciously intended to create a *sui generis* definition. Had the judgment provided a more detailed legal pedigree for the definition, it is likely that the precedent set by *Akayesu* would have been followed in far more subsequent jurisprudence.[56]

Initially, the ICTY appeared content to follow the definition laid down in the *Akayesu* case. The Trial Chamber in the *Čelibići* case was the first to attempt to define the crime of rape at the ICTY.[57] The judgment provided a detailed examination of the historical prohibition of rape in international humanitarian law,[58]

[52] A Cole, '*Prosecutor v Gacumbitsi*: The New Definition for Prosecuting Rape Under International Law' (2008) 8 ICLR 55, 77.

[53] *Akayesu* (Trial Chamber Judgment) (n 13 above) paras 596–7 and 686–7.

[54] 'Report of the Secretary-General Pursuant to Paragraph 5 of Security Council Resolution 955 (1994)', UN Doc S/1995/134, para 12, which notes 'the Security Council has elected to take a more expansive approach to the choice of applicable law than the one underlying the statute of the Yugoslav Tribunal', including international instruments within the subject-matter jurisdiction of the ICTR 'regardless of whether they were considered part of customary international law or whether they have customarily entailed the individual criminal responsibility of the perpetrator'. Schabas has described this Report as providing 'helpful guidance for purposes of interpretation'; W Schabas, *The UN International Criminal Tribunals: The former Yugoslavia, Rwanda and Sierra Leone* (Cambridge: CUP, 2006) 30.

[55] Referring to the 'particularly important' need 'above all, to respect the intent of the drafters of the Genocide Convention'. *Akayesu* (Trial Chamber Judgment) (n 13 above) paras 516, 701.

[56] The definition of rape identified in *Akayesu* was clearly considered appropriately specific to incorporate into domestic civil law in Illinois and California (where gender violence is defined as 'a physical invasion of a sexual nature under coercive conditions') as well as the criminal law of South Africa. See California Civil Code, §52.4(c)(2); Illinois Gender Violence Act, 740 ICLS 82/5(2); Pillay (n 26 above) 667.

[57] Rape charges had initially been included in the case against Duško Tadić, but were dropped after the withdrawal of one prosecution witness and the discrediting of another. Tadić was, however, convicted of persecution, other inhumane acts, and cruel treatment in relation to his role in the rape and sexual violence committed against both male and female detainees in the Omarska, Keraterm, and Trnopolje camps. See Askin (n 21 above) 101–5.

[58] Albeit incorrectly stating that rape was enumerated as a crime against humanity under the Nuremberg Charter, Art 6(c): *Prosecutor v Delalić* (Trial Chamber Judgment) IT-96-21-T (16 November 1998) para 476.

but concluded that 'there is no convention or other international instrument containing a definition of the term itself'.[59] After quoting the *Akayesu* definition and agreeing with its reasoning, the Chamber stated that it '[saw] no reason to depart from the conclusion of the ICTR...on this issue'.[60] Interestingly, the *Čelibići* judgment also contains an extensive and extremely well-reasoned finding that rape can constitute torture.[61] Having defined the criminal elements of torture (including as prohibited purposes obtaining information, punishment, intimidation, coercion, and discrimination), the judgment concluded that it was 'difficult to envisage circumstances in which rape by, or at the instigation of a public official, or with the consent or acquiescence of an official, could be considered as occurring for a purpose that does not, in some way, involve punishment, coercion, discrimination or intimidation'.[62] Significantly, the Chamber went on to state that 'this is inherent in situations of armed conflict'.[63] Despite the obvious importance of such a finding in relation to the crime of torture, the rationale of the judges appeared to be the omission of rape from the grave breaches provisions of the Geneva Conventions and Common Article 3, leading them to categorize rape as torture or cruel treatment.[64] The *Čelebići* judgment is an early but extremely pertinent example of a trend which has been continually evidenced in judgments from both of the *ad hoc* Tribunals, emphasizing the extraordinary harm caused by sexual violence in wartime and interpreting facts of widespread rape and sexual violence as capable of exemplifying the constituent elements of a range of different international crimes not immediately or explicitly related to such acts.[65]

Less than a month later, however, the *Furundžija* trial judgment all but abandoned the conceptual definition set out in the *Akayesu* case in favour of exactly the kind of mechanistic focus on penetration that the ICTR Trial Chamber had explicitly rejected. Just as in *Čelibići* before it, the *Furundžija* Trial Chamber examined the prohibition of rape throughout the evolution of international humanitarian and international criminal law, before concluding that no definition was to be found in international law. Unlike *Akayesu* or *Čelibići*, however, the *Furundžija* judgment made overt reference to the requirements of the principle of specificity and concluded that 'to arrive at an accurate definition

[59] *Delalić* (Trial Chamber Judgment) ibid para 478.

[60] ibid.

[61] ibid paras 475–97, citing jurisprudence from the Inter-American Commission on Human Rights, the European Court of Human Rights, the United Nations Special Rapporteur on Torture, and the comparisons drawn between torture and rape in the *Akayesu* judgment.

[62] *Delalić* (Trial Chamber Judgment) ibid para 495. The judgment found that one victim had been raped simply because she was a woman, and that this was equally capable of amounting to discrimination constituting a prohibited purpose under the definition of torture (ibid para 941). Significantly, the Chamber also held that forcing two male detainees to perform fellatio on each other (which was charged as the offences of inhuman treatment and cruel treatment) could have constituted rape if it had been charged as such (ibid paras 1056–66).

[63] ibid para 495.

[64] ibid para 475.

[65] Including genocide (serious bodily or mental harm and measures intended to prevent births within the group), torture, enslavement, extermination, persecution, other inhumane acts, grave breaches, cruel treatment, and outrages on personal dignity.

of rape ... it is necessary to look for principles of criminal law common to the major legal systems of the world ... [which] may be derived, with all due caution, from national laws'.[66] The Chamber duly examined the legislative provisions of a very broad range of (both common and civil law) national jurisdictions before determining that 'most legal systems ... consider rape to be the forcible sexual penetration of the human body by the penis or the forcible insertion of any other object into either the vagina or the anus'.[67] The Chamber could not determine a consensus in domestic criminal legislation on the issue of whether forcible oral penetration should be categorized as rape or sexual assault; having regard to general principles of international law and the importance of respect for human dignity therein, the Chamber held that 'such a serious sexual outrage' should be classified as rape.[68]

The resulting definition identified the objective elements of the crime of rape as (1) the sexual penetration, however slight: (a) of the vagina or anus of the victim by the penis of the perpetrator or any other object used by the perpetrator; or (b) of the mouth of the victim by the penis of the perpetrator; (2) by coercion or force or threat of force against the victim or a third person.[69] The judgment noted that both rape and sexual assault were criminal under international law, and therefore held that the distinction between the two categories was relevant principally for the purposes of sentencing.[70] The judgment is also significant as precedent for the fact that even a single rape against one individual can constitute a serious violation of international humanitarian law entailing individual criminal responsibility.[71]

It is clear that the Trial Chamber in the *Furundžija* case—which consisted of Judge Mumba, Judge Cassese, and Judge May—was at pains to strictly observe the general rules of interpretation for international law. In its definition of rape, and indeed its discussion of torture and aiding and abetting, the judgment obediently and consistently makes reference to recognized sources of international law and subsidiary aids to interpretation; the judgment draws on international instruments, international criminal and international human rights jurisprudence, general principles of international law, and, where necessary, general principles of law as extrapolated from a survey of domestic legislation. However, it is somewhat puzzling that, having concluded that international law contained no definition of rape, the judgment went on to quote at length the definition set forth in *Akayesu* and confirmed in *Čelibići*.[72] The Chamber offered

[66] *Prosecutor v Furundžija* (Trial Chamber Judgment) IT-95-17/1-T (10 December 1998) para 177.

[67] ibid para 181.

[68] ibid para 183.

[69] ibid para 185.

[70] ibid para 186. On the issue of individual criminal responsibility, Furundžija was convicted of both torture and rape as a war crime. Furundžija had been present for the rape and sexual assault of a female detainee under interrogation (which was held to be torture), but had not raped the victim himself. He was convicted as a co-perpetrator of torture, but merely an aider and abettor of rape (ibid paras 264–75).

[71] Askin, 'Extraordinary Advances, Enduring Obstacles' (n 44 above) 327.

[72] *Furundžija* (Trial Chamber Judgment) (n 66 above) para 176.

no explanation of why it did not or should not consider the *Akayesu* definition as having filled the gap it identified in international law, beyond its somewhat pointed reference to the principle of specificity. Catharine MacKinnon scathingly rejected this emphasis and criticized the *Furundžija* Trial Chamber for suggesting, in her view, that 'without such specification, the defendants—guards of concentration camps charged with sexual assault on prisoners in their custody—might not have known with sufficient precision that what they were accused of doing was a crime'.[73] It is difficult to tell whether the judges responsible for drafting the *Furundžija* trial judgment were more uncomfortable with the absence of traditional references to international law provisions in *Akayesu* or its obvious preference for a necessarily vague conceptual definition over an exhaustive one. However, if the latter was the deciding factor, Alison Cole has pointed out that *Furundžija* attaches its own conceptual underpinning to the definition of rape by its repeated reference to the importance of the concept of human dignity and its use of that concept to justify 'broadening the definition of rape' to include oral penetration.[74]

The *Furundžija* definition is also noteworthy for its explicit incorporation of force or threat of force, along with coercion, as an element of the crime of rape. The basis for this can be seen in the Chamber's conclusion that 'all jurisdictions surveyed... require an element of force, coercion, threat, or acting without the consent of the victim'.[75] The Chamber also noted the unchallenged definition in the prosecution's pre-trial brief that rape is a forcible act, accomplished by force or express or implied threats of force against the victim or a third person which places them in reasonable fear that they will be subjected to violence, detention, duress, or psychological oppression.[76] This effectively introduced a mental element into the crime of rape and marked the first (albeit *obiter*) articulation of the requirement of non-consent. Indeed, the judgment made clear that, in the view of the Trial Chamber, 'any form of captivity vitiates consent'.[77] In light of that analysis, it is worth noting that Schomburg and Peterson have argued that it would have been more appropriate, if relying on domestic criminal provisions to extrapolate an international definition, to have made reference to national laws criminalizing sexual acts between individuals in unequal positions of power (such as prison guards and inmates) instead of general criminal provisions regulating consensual sex between individuals in presumptively peaceful circumstances.[78]

[73] C MacKinnon, 'Defining Rape Internationally: A Comment on *Akayesu*' (2006) 44 Col JTL 940, 946.

[74] *Furundžija* (Trial Chamber Judgment) (n 66 above) paras 183–4; Cole argued that '[i]t therefore appears that the Trial Chamber in *Furundžija* disapproved of the conceptual basis for defining rape in *Akayesu*, and yet founded its own definition upon a similarly conceptual basis.' Cole (n 52 above) 59.

[75] *Furundžija* (Trial Chamber Judgment) (n 66 above) para 180.

[76] ibid para 174.

[77] ibid para 271.

[78] Schomburg and Peterson (n 38 above) 138–9.

The definition of the crime of rape articulated in the *Furundžija* trial judgment was upheld on appeal. The Appeals Chamber acknowledged that the *Akayesu* definition had been followed in the *Čelibići* case, but ruled that, as the definition had not been at issue between the parties, the Trial Chamber 'was entitled to interpret the law as it stood'.[79] The next case at the ICTR to address the definition of rape attempted to provide a harmonious interpretation of the apparently divergent approaches in the *Akayesu* and *Furundžija* cases. The *Musema* trial judgment (unsurprisingly, given that the Trial Chamber contained the same three judges as in *Akayesu*) praised the *Akayesu* definition for providing a clear framework for judicial determination of whether individual acts of sexual violence constitute rape. It determined that this 'clearly encompasse[d] all the conduct described in the definition of rape set forth in *Furundžija*'.[80] The *Musema* Trial Chamber noted the reliance in *Furundžija* on the principle of human dignity to justify its inclusion of oral penetration within the definition of rape, as well as its acknowledgement of the trend in national legislation in favour of broadening the definition.[81] The Chamber therefore concluded that 'a conceptual definition is preferable to a mechanical definition of rape', as the conceptual definition would 'better accommodate evolving norms of criminal justice'.[82] For that reason, the *Musema* judgment adopted the definition of rape set out in *Akayesu*.[83]

III. The Question of Consent

Thus far, the efforts by the *ad hoc* Tribunals to identify a workable definition of rape as an international crime had diverged primarily on the issue of the *actus reus* of the crime. The *Akayesu* definition, as approved and applied in the *Čelibići* and *Musema* cases, hinged on the relatively broad descriptor of 'a physical invasion of a sexual nature', while the *Furundžija* definition required an act of penetration falling within one of the expressly specified combinations of objects and body parts. Both definitions were in agreement about the centrality of coercion within the offence, although *Furundžija* also introduced the element of force or threat of force. However, two crucial judgments of the Appeals Chamber, in *Kunarac* and *Gacumbitsi*, were to fundamentally shift the contention to the issue of *mens rea*, specifically the role of non-consent as an element of the international crime of rape.

[79] *Prosecutor v Furundžija* (Appeals Chamber Judgment) IT-95-17/1-A (21 July 2000) paras 211–12.

[80] *Prosecutor v Musema* (Trial Chamber Judgment) ICTR-96-13-T (27 January 2000) para 227.

[81] *Musema* (Trial Chamber Judgment) ibid para 228; *Furundžija* (Trial Chamber Judgment) (n 66 above) para 179.

[82] *Musema* (Trial Chamber Judgment) ibid.

[83] ibid para 229.

The *Kunarac* trial before the ICTY was extremely significant even before the rendering of the judgment in the case, as it was the first indictment from either of the *ad hoc* Tribunals to focus exclusively on crimes of sexual violence.[84] The mass rape of women in the municipality of Foča in Bosnia-Herzegovina during the war—in which Muslim women and girls were repeatedly raped in the local gymnasium and sports hall, and in some cases detained for months in nearby apartments to be systematically raped by Serb forces—was charged as both a crime against humanity and a war crime, and classified as rape, torture, and enslavement.[85] The resulting judgment contained the ICTY's first conviction for rape as a crime against humanity, as well as the first conviction for enslavement as a crime against humanity.[86] It also marked the first express introduction of non-consent into the definition of rape.

The *Kunarac* Trial Chamber agreed that the elements of penetration set out in *Furundžija*, if proven, 'constitute the *actus reus* of the crime of rape in international law'.[87] However, the Chamber took issue with the *Furundžija* definition for its excessively narrow focus on coercion and force, which failed to 'refer to other factors which would render an act of sexual penetration *non-consensual or non-voluntary* on the part of the victim'.[88] The Chamber considered that the true common denominator which could be drawn from the national jurisdictions surveyed in *Furundžija* was not force *per se*, but violations of sexual autonomy.[89] The *Kunarac* judgment classified the common factors from domestic legislation on the crime of rape into three categories:

(1) the sexual activity is accompanied by force or threat of force to the victim or a third party;
(2) the sexual activity is accompanied by force *or* a variety of other specified circumstances which made the victim particularly vulnerable or negated her ability to make an informed refusal; or
(3) the sexual activity occurs without the consent of the victim.[90]

The Chamber found that the absence of consent could be evidenced by the presence of factors such as force or threats of force, but that the fundamental principle underlying the crime of rape was that '[s]exual autonomy is violated wherever the person subjected to the act has not freely agreed to it or is otherwise not a voluntary participant.'[91] Accordingly, the *Kunarac* trial judgment concluded that the

[84] Askin, 'Extraordinary Advances, Enduring Obstacles' (n 44 above) 333; D Buss, 'Prosecuting Mass Rape: *Prosecutor v Dragoljub Kunarac, Radomir Kovac and Zoran Vukovic*' (2002) 10 *Feminist Legal Studies* 91.

[85] Copelon (n 6 above) 230; see also M Fiori, 'The Foča "Rape Camps": A Dark Page Read Through the ICTY's Jurisprudence' (2007) 2 *Hague Justice* J 9.

[86] Kelly Askin has noted that it is regrettable the judgment does not use the phrase 'sexual slavery', as enslavement for the primary purpose of facilitating continuous sexual abuse would most appropriately be characterized as such. Askin, 'Extraordinary Advances, Enduring Obstacles' (n 44 above) 340.

[87] *Prosecutor v Kunarac et al* (Trial Chamber Judgment) IT-96-23-T & IT-96-23/1-T (22 February 2001) para 438.

[88] ibid (emphasis in original).

[89] ibid para 439–41.

[90] ibid para 442.

[91] ibid paras 457–8.

correct definition of the crime of rape consisted of both a physical and a mental element. The *actus reus* of rape, as defined by the Trial Chamber, amounts to any of the various forms of penetration enumerated in *Furundžija*, 'where such sexual penetration occurs without the consent of the victim'.[92] The *mens rea* of the crime is 'the intention to effect this sexual penetration, and the knowledge that it occurs without the consent of the victim'.[93]

The *Kunarac* trial judgment thereby placed the issue of consent at the very heart of both the physical and mental elements of its definition of rape (penetration without consent and knowledge of non-consent, respectively). Like *Furundžija*, the *Kunarac* case 'mentioned the *Akayesu* definition only to ignore it'.[94] However, the judgment approvingly quoted the reference to the principle of specificity in the *Furundžija* case and the need to turn to national criminal jurisdictions to identify general principles of law 'in the absence of customary or conventional international law on the subject'.[95] It seems likely, therefore, that once again *Akayesu*'s failure to provide a solid interpretational basis for its definition proved unpalatable to the ICTY Trial Chamber, and once again they felt obliged to go back to the drawing board to extrapolate a clear and appropriately specific definition. Unlike *Furundžija*, however, the examination of domestic jurisdictions in *Kunarac* identified the violation of sexual autonomy, rather than force or coercion, as the basic principle common to most national definitions of rape. The logic of the *Kunarac* Trial Chamber was that the concepts of coercion and force were to be given a broad interpretation, and that 'coercion in particular would encompass *most* conduct which negates consent'.[96] The Chamber held that 'consent for this purpose must be consent given voluntarily, as a result of the victim's free will, assessed in the context of the surrounding circumstances'.[97]

Somewhat offensively, the issue of consent was explicitly raised by one of the defendants in the case, Kunarac, who claimed that, since a particular victim witness had initiated sex, he was unaware that she had not consented.[98] Given that the victim in question was in captivity and had only done so after being threatened by one of Kunarac's associates that she would be killed unless his boss was satisfied,[99] the Chamber unsurprisingly found that she had not freely consented. Moreover, since Kunarac was aware of the context of war and of the 'specifically delicate' situation of Muslim women detained by Serb forces at that time, as well

[92] ibid para 460. The full definition of the *actus reus* provided by the judgment is as follows: 'the sexual penetration, however slight: (a) of the vagina or anus of the victim by the penis of the perpetrator or any other object used by the perpetrator; or (b) of the mouth of the victim by the penis of the perpetrator; where such sexual penetration occurs without the consent of the victim.'

[93] ibid para 460.

[94] MacKinnon (n 73 above) 945 (in reference to the *Furundžija* judgment).

[95] *Kunarac* (Trial Chamber Judgment) (n 87 above) paras 437, 439.

[96] ibid para 459.

[97] ibid para 460.

[98] ibid paras 643–7.

[99] Alison Cole has described the argument advanced by Kunarac 'that he was effectively raped by the victim' as ridiculous. Cole (n 52 above) 79. See also Askin, 'Extraordinary Advances, Enduring Obstacles' (n 44 above) 336.

as the fact that the witness had previously been raped by several other soldiers, the Chamber held that he had engaged in sexual intercourse with the witness 'in the full knowledge that she did not freely consent', regardless of whether he had heard the specific threat against her life.[100]

On the issue of consent as an element of the crime of rape, the reasoning of the judgment is frustratingly circular. Coercion and force were held to be too narrow to be the central elements of the crime of rape, as the crucial principle common to national jurisdictions was the issue of sexual autonomy and consent. The presence of force could be taken as evidence of non-consent, coercion was held to encompass most conduct which would negate consent, and consent itself was to be defined in the context of the surrounding circumstances (presumably to assess whether they included coercion or force).[101] It is questionable, therefore, what benefit was adduced by the addition of consent to the definition that was not already implicit in the concepts of coercion and force. Cole has suggested that the shift of emphasis away from force in favour of non-consent in *Kunarac* came about in order to adequately reflect the factual subject matter of the case, involving enslavement and effective detention.[102]

The definition of rape outlined in the *Kunarac* trial judgment was addressed on appeal. The Appeals Chamber emphatically rejected the submission by the appellant defendants proposing an additional element of the crime of rape, which would require a display of 'continuous and genuine resistance' on the part of the victim throughout the duration of sexual contact, without which it could be concluded that the victim had consented.[103] The Chamber noted that the appellants had offered no basis for this contention in customary international law, and rejected the proposed element on the grounds that the 'bald assertion that nothing short of continuous resistance provides adequate notice to the perpetrator that his attentions are unwanted is wrong on the law and absurd on the facts'.[104] The Appeals Chamber largely upheld the *Kunarac* Trial Chamber's definition of rape, albeit with some important modifications. The Trial Chamber's emphasis on consent rather than force was interpreted as intending to avoid circumstances in which too narrow a focus on force 'could permit perpetrators to evade liability for sexual activity to which the other party had not consented by taking advantage of coercive circumstances without relying on physical force'.[105] However, the Appeals Chamber noted that 'the circumstances... that prevail in most cases charged as either war crimes or crimes against humanity will be almost universally coercive', concluding that in such circumstances 'true consent will not be possible'.[106] The appeal judgment noted several examples of strict liability provisions in national jurisdictions criminalizing sexual relations in situations

[100] *Kunarac* (Trial Chamber Judgment) (n 87 above) para 647.

[101] Cole has argued that the *Kunarac* definition essentially retained the *Akayesu* definition's emphasis on coercive circumstances, albeit not explicitly: Cole (n 52 above) 61.

[102] ibid 61.

[103] *Prosecutor v Kunarac et al* (Appeals Chamber Judgment) IT-96-23 and IT-96-23/1-A (12 June 2002) para 125.

[104] ibid para 128.

[105] ibid para 129.

[106] ibid para 130.

involving 'unequal positions of power and... inherent coerciveness', such as relations between prisoners and correctional officers, in which consent is not an element of the crime.[107] The existence of such criminal provisions, designed 'to protect prisoners who enjoy substantive legal protections... highlight[ed] the need to presume non-consent' in the instant case.[108]

Based on the facts of the case, including *de facto* detention, systematic and repeated rape of the victims, and increased brutality in response to resistance, the Appeals Chamber concluded that 'such detentions amount to circumstances that were so coercive as to negate any possibility of consent' and that 'the coercive circumstances present in this case made consent... impossible'.[109] The Appeals Chamber's emphasis on the innately coercive nature of the background factual circumstances of international criminal prosecutions, while entirely accurate and commendable, ultimately makes the additional element of the definition of rape expressed in *Kunarac* redundant, as it 'both requires and presumes lack of consent'.[110] The Appeals Chamber upheld the Trial Chamber's definition, which specifically requires non-consent (rather than evidence of force or coercion) as an element of the crime of rape, while simultaneously holding that consent will be impossible in the coercive circumstances common to most international criminal prosecutions. One could argue that it would have been far more logical and effective for the Appeals Chamber to have taken a similar approach to the ICTR Trial Chamber in *Musema* and attempted to harmonize the varying definitions. The Appeals Chamber's repeated emphasis on coercive circumstances was clearly reminiscent of *Akayesu*, although the *Akayesu* judgment was not even mentioned in the Chamber's discussion of the definition.[111] The *Akayesu* formulation that rape is 'committed under circumstances which are coercive' appears particularly relevant given the Appeals Chamber's finding in *Kunarac* that coercive circumstances vitiate consent.

Given that *Kunarac* represented the first case before the Appeals Chamber to directly address the definition of rape, several subsequent judgments of the Rwanda Tribunal applied the *Kunarac* definition, considering it to be persuasive authority.[112] The trial judgments in the *Kajelijeli* and *Kamuhanda* cases both found the definition of rape as the commission of an enumerated act of

[107] ibid para 131.

[108] ibid. Cole notes that the Appeals Chamber's reference to strict liability offences, such as those criminalizing sexual contact between inmates and prison guards, is further evidence 'that the national crime of rape may not be the best analogy for international crimes': Cole (n 52 above) 62.

[109] *Kunarac* (Appeals Chamber Judgment) (n 103 above) paras 132–3.

[110] Engle (n 12 above) 804.

[111] The Appeals Chamber noted that the *Kunarac* Trial Chamber had departed from previous definitions of rape, but only cited the *Furundžija* trial judgment as an example: *Kunarac* (Appeals Chamber Judgment) (n 103 above) para 129.

[112] *Prosecutor v Semanza* (Trial Chamber Judgment) ICTR-97-20-T (15 May 2003) paras 344–6; *Prosecutor v Kajelijeli* (Trial Chamber Judgment) ICTR-98-44A-T (1 December 2003) paras 910–15; *Prosecutor v Kamuhanda* (Trial Chamber Judgment) ICTR-95-54A-T (22 January 2004) paras 705–9.

penetration without the consent of the victim and in the knowledge that consent was absent to be persuasive authority on the basis that it had been endorsed by the Appeals Chamber in *Kunarac*.[113] Interestingly, the *Semanza* trial judgment acknowledged that the mechanical style of defining rape had initially been rejected by the Rwanda Tribunal, but found the 'comparative analysis' on which the *Kunarac* definition was based to be persuasive.[114] Some other ICTR cases continued to apply the more conceptual definition of rape contained in the *Akayesu* trial judgment, regardless of the Appeals Chamber's backing for the mechanistic *Kunarac* definition. In the *Niyitegeka* trial judgment, the *Akayesu* definition of rape was applied without discussion.[115]

In *Muhimana*, just as in the *Musema* case, the ICTR Trial Chamber valiantly attempted to reconcile the competing definitions of the crime of rape.[116] Both the defence and prosecution in that case had endorsed the conceptual definition of rape as a 'physical invasion of a sexual nature' identified in *Akayesu*.[117] The Chamber somewhat disingenuously considered that the *Kunarac* trial judgment, by not commenting adversely on the *Akayesu* definition, had thereby 'tacitly accepted' it.[118] The Chamber held that the judgments in *Furundžija* and *Kunarac* were actually 'substantially aligned' to the *Akayesu* definition and that the elements of each were 'not incompatible or substantially different in their application', despite the findings in *Semanza* and other ICTR cases that the 'penetration without consent' *Kunarac* definition had effectively supplanted that of *Akayesu*.[119] The *Kunarac* definition was held to merely 'provide additional details on the constituent elements of acts considered to be rape'. In order to combine the two definitions, the Chamber endorsed the conceptual definition of rape set out in *Akayesu* but interpreted the mechanical elements of *Kunarac* as 'articulat[ing] the parameters of what would constitute a physical invasion of a sexual nature'.[120]

The *Muhimana* Trial Chamber deserves to be praised for attempting to reconcile the disparate jurisprudence on the definition of rape. As can be seen from the discussion above, elements of the *Akayesu* definition, particularly its emphasis on coercion, are implicit in and complementary to both the *Furundžija* and *Kunarac* formulations. An interpretation which combines the conceptual and mechanistic approaches to construe *Kunarac* as providing a (presumably non-exhaustive) enumeration of acts of penetration which may constitute a 'physical invasion of a sexual nature' is appealingly inclusive, not least in light of the con-

[113] See *Kajelijeli* (Trial Chamber Judgment) ibid para 915 and *Kamuhanda* (Trial Chamber Judgment) ibid para 709. The *Kamuhanda* judgment does not refer to *Kajelijeli* in its findings on the definition, yet uses identical wording throughout its discussion of the evolving jurisprudence on rape.

[114] *Semanza* (Trial Chamber Judgment) (n 112 above) para 345.

[115] *Prosecutor v Niyitegeka* (Trial Chamber Judgment) ICTR-96-14-T (16 May 2003) para 456.

[116] *Prosecutor v Muhimana* (Trial Chamber Judgment) ICTR-95-1B-T (28 April 2005).

[117] ibid para 535.

[118] ibid para 541.

[119] ibid paras 549–50.

[120] 'On the basis of the foregoing analysis, the Chamber endorses the conceptual definition of rape established in *Akayesu*, which encompasses the elements set out in *Kunarac*' (ibid paras 550–51).

tinuing viability of the *Akayesu* definition up to that point. The Chamber also noted approvingly that both *Furundžija* and *Kunarac* had acknowledged that the element of coercion was capable of obviating the relevance of the element of consent.[121] However, the *Muhimana* judgment does not provide sufficient detail as to whether non-consent or coercion should be the decisive element of the crime of rape, particularly in relation to the *mens rea* of the offence. Ultimately, it is difficult to assess whether the net effect of the *Muhimana* trial judgment is to reduce *Kunarac* to an interpretational handbook for the broad but laconic *Akayesu* definition, or to provide an almost sentimental endorsement of the conceptual definition set out in *Akayesu* while acknowledging the necessary specificity provided by *Kunarac*.

The efforts of so many trial and appeal judgments to provide a comprehensive definition of the crime of rape, or even to provide a coherent interpretation of the apparently divergent jurisprudence on the issue, had not yet provided much-needed clarity. It was clear that Trial Chambers in the Rwanda Tribunal still felt the influence of the conceptual definition set out in *Akayesu*, while those in the Yugoslavia Tribunal were more comfortable with a mechanistic interpretation drawn from a survey of national jurisdictions, yet did not go so far as to expressly reject the interpretation of the Trial Chamber in *Akayesu* as incorrect. Despite the persuasive authority of the Appeals Chamber judgment in *Kunarac*, the elements of the crime of rape still appeared to be up for discussion. Because of the general significance of the issue to the Tribunal's jurisprudence, rather than any allegation that it had constituted an error which invalidated the trial judgment, the Appeals Chamber in *Gacumbitsi* agreed to address the question of whether consent was an element of the crime of rape.[122]

The *Gacumbitsi* Trial Chamber, similarly to that in *Musema* and *Muhimana*, had applied a definition which sought to combine the conceptual and mechanical approaches, by stating that 'any penetration of the victim's vagina by the rapist with his genitals or with any object constitutes rape, although the definition of rape… is not limited to such acts alone', and citing (without further comment) both *Akayesu* and *Kunarac*.[123] The Trial Chamber did not explicitly comment on whether coercion or non-consent was included as an element of the definition, but, in commenting on the factual evidence, it concluded that the statements made by the accused (that if rape victims resisted they should be killed 'in an atrocious manner') and the fact that victims were attacked by those they were fleeing from constituted adequate evidence of the victims' lack of consent to the rapes.[124] The prosecution appealed the question of whether non-consent constituted an element of the crime of rape or whether consent could merely amount to

[121] ibid paras 544–6.

[122] *Prosecutor v Gacumbitsi* (Appeals Chamber Judgment) ICTR-2001-64-A (7 July 2006) para 150.

[123] *Prosecutor v Gacumbitsi* (Trial Chamber Judgment) ICTR-2001-64-T (17 June 2004) para 321.

[124] ibid para 325.

an affirmative defence to a charge of rape.[125] It pointed out two arguments which would undermine the assumption that non-consent could constitute an element of the crime: namely, (1) that in order for a crime to come within the Tribunal's jurisdiction, it must occur in the context of genocide, armed conflict, or a widespread and systematic attack on a civilian population, circumstances in which (as the *Kunarac* Appeals Chamber had acknowledged) genuine consent would not be possible;[126] and (2) that rape should be viewed in the same light as torture, enslavement, and other crimes against humanity, for which proof of the absence of consent is not required.[127] Indeed, it should be noted that rape has repeatedly been held to constitute an act of torture, and in its findings on enslavement (brought about for the purposes of facilitating repeated and systematic rape and sexual assault), the *Kunarac* Appeals Chamber had specifically stated that lack of consent was not an element of the crime of enslavement.[128]

The Appeals Chamber was not called upon to address the issue of the correct definition of rape in the abstract; rather, it sought to provide clarity on the issue of whether lack of consent was an element of the crime of rape or an affirmative defence to it. Nonetheless, (although unsurprisingly given that four of the five judges had presided over both decisions)[129] the Chamber chose to adopt the definition of rape set out by the ICTY Appeals Chamber in *Kunarac*.[130] In response to the specific issue raised by the prosecution, the Chamber took the position that lack of consent and knowledge thereof *are* elements of the crime of rape, which must be proven beyond a reasonable doubt by the prosecution.[131] Rule 96 of the Rules of Procedure and Evidence refers to the 'defence of consent' and sets limitations on the circumstances in which it will be impermissible.[132] However, the Appeals Chamber interpreted Rule 96 as merely defining the circumstances in which evidence of the element of consent will be admissible rather than creating or establishing a defence to the crime of rape.[133] Having conclusively held

[125] *Gacumbitsi* (Appeals Chamber Judgment) (n 122 above) para 147.

[126] ibid para 148 and *Kunarac* (Appeals Chamber Judgment) (n 103 above) para 130.

[127] *Gacumbitsi* (Appeals Chamber Judgment) (n 122 above) para 149.

[128] *Kunarac* (Appeals Chamber Judgment) (n 103 above) para 120.

[129] The Appeals Chamber bench sitting in the *Kunarac* appeal was made up of Judge Jorda, Judge Shahabuddeen, Judge Schomburg, Judge Güney, and Judge Meron, while the Appeals Chamber in *Gacumbitsi* was composed of Judge Shahabuddeen, Judge Schomburg, Judge Güney, Judge Meron, and Judge Daqun.

[130] 'The *actus reus* of the crime of rape in international law is constituted by: the sexual penetration, however slight: (a) of the vagina or anus of the victim by the penis of the perpetrator or any other object used by the perpetrator; or (b) the mouth of the victim by the penis of the perpetrator; where such sexual penetration occurs without the consent of the victim. Consent for this purpose must be consent given voluntarily, as a result of the victim's free will, assessed in the context of the surrounding circumstances. The *mens rea* is the intention to effect this sexual penetration, and the knowledge that it occurs without the consent of the victim': *Kunarac* (Appeals Chamber Judgment) (n 103 above) para 127.

[131] *Gacumbitsi* (Appeals Chamber Judgment) (n 122 above) para 153.

[132] See *Kunarac* (Trial Chamber Judgment) (n 87 above) paras 461–4 and *Gacumbitsi* (Trial Chamber Judgment) (n 123 above) para 156.

[133] *Gacumbitsi* (Appeals Chamber Judgment) (n 122 above) para 154.

that lack of consent is an element of the crime of rape, the Appeals Chamber examined the means by which it may be proven, and in so doing, attempted to address the practical difficulties raised by the prosecution. In order to prove the absence of consent, it is not necessary for the prosecution to introduce evidence of force, the words or conduct of the victim, or their relationship to the perpetrator. Non-consent can be proven beyond a reasonable doubt 'by proving the existence of coercive circumstances under which meaningful consent is not possible'. The Trial Chamber may also infer a lack of consent from the background circumstances of the case 'such as an ongoing genocide campaign or the detention of the victim'.[134] Similarly, the *mens rea* requirement of knowledge of the absence of consent can be proven by establishing that the accused 'was aware, or had reason to be aware, of the coercive circumstances that undermined the possibility of genuine consent'.[135]

Once again, the inclusion of consent as an element of the definition of rape was upheld by the Appeals Chamber, and once again 'coercive circumstances' were held to vitiate the possibility of genuine consent. Yet, unlike *Kunarac*, the Appeals Chamber in *Gacumbitsi* did not refer to national jurisdictions in support of its conclusion that non-consent was a central element of the offence under international law, nor did it provide a logical or interpretational basis for including non-consent in the definition of rape yet centralizing coercion as the means of proving it. In the absence of the resort to national criminal legislation as a subsidiary source of law, it is not immediately obvious what advantage is gleaned by insisting on non-consent as an element of rape in preference to coercion. Perhaps the most glaring omission in the Appeals Chamber judgment is the question, raised by the prosecution but left unanswered, as to why lack of consent should constitute a criminal element of sexual violence if charged as rape, but not if the same conduct is charged as torture, enslavement, outrages on personal dignity, persecution, or genocide. This question is particularly galling in light of the prevalence of cumulative charging.[136]

The position of non-consent as an element of the crime of rape appears to have become settled since the judgment of the Appeals Chamber in *Gacumbitsi*,[137] and yet the *Akayesu* judgment continues to be approvingly cited, in the Rwanda Tribunal at least.[138] The following section will attempt to analyse the reasoning of the Trial and Appeal Chambers in their insistence on emphasizing consent rather than coercion, and will highlight some of the legal, practical, and logical pitfalls which the established definition unwittingly entails.

134 ibid para 155.

135 ibid para 157.

136 See eg G Werle, *Principles of International Criminal Law* (The Hague: TMC Asser Press, 2nd edn, 2009) 243.

137 See *Prosecutor v Muvunyi* (Trial Chamber Judgment) ICTR-00-55A-T (12 September 2006) paras 517–22 and *Prosecutor v Bagosora* (Trial Chamber Judgment) ICTR-98-41-T (18 December 2008) paras 2199–2200.

138 *Muvunyi* (Trial Chamber Judgment) ibid paras 517–22.

IV. The Judicial Interpretation of Rape

The judges of the *ad hoc* Tribunals have had an inescapable impact on the evolution of rape as an international crime and on the concurrent efforts to arrive at a cogent, workable definition of the crime under international law.[139] It is clear from the above discussion of the jurisprudence that the challenge of defining rape was one to which consecutive Trial and Appeals Chambers continued to return, and yet one over which the initial effort of the Trial Chamber in *Akayesu* continued to loom large. It is worth examining the definition as it has apparently settled to analyse the legal and practical ramifications of the result of so much judicial exertion.

It is at last clear that the working definition of rape before the Yugoslavia and Rwanda Tribunals involves one of several enumerated acts of penetration, carried out without the free consent of the victim and in the knowledge that such consent is absent. Crucially, from an evidentiary perspective, the element of non-consent can be proven by establishing coercive circumstances.[140] It is clear—particularly in relation to the Appeals Chamber jurisprudence—that there was a conscious decision to emphasize non-consent as the decisive element of the crime of rape in preference to coercion.[141] The genesis of this line of interpretation can be found in the *Furundžija* Trial Chamber's resort to general principles of law derived from national jurisdictions as a subsidiary source of international law, which was modified by the *Kunarac* Trial Chamber to highlight violations of sexual autonomy as the fundamental unifying principle underlying national legislation on rape. As Wolfgang Schomburg and Ines Peterson (and, implicitly, the *Kunarac* Appeals Chamber) have pointed out,[142] it is questionable whether the domestic crime of

[139] Mark Ellis has noted that '[t]he work of the ICTY and ICTR in creating a more precise definition of rape meant that the ICC could more easily establish an agreed upon definition within its Statute.' M Ellis, 'Breaking the Silence: Rape as an International Crime' (2006–2007) 38 CWR JIL 225, 231.

[140] It is interesting to note that the use of a finding of coercive circumstances to create a rebuttable presumption of non-consent had been suggested in academic writings as early as 1994. See J Green, R Copelon, P Cotter, and B Stephens, 'Affecting the Rules for the Prosecution of Rape and Other Gender-Based Violence before the International Criminal Tribunal for the Former Yugoslavia: A Feminist Proposal and Critique' (1994) 5 *Hastings Women's Law Journal* 171, 202.

[141] Significantly, the ICC has not taken a similar approach. The Elements of Crimes require only that the crime is committed 'by force, or by threat of force or coercion, such as that caused by fear of violence, duress, detention, psychological oppression, or abuse of power, against such person or another person, or by taking advantage of a coercive environment or . . . was committed against a person incapable of giving genuine consent'. Incapability of genuine consent can be affected by 'natural, induced or age-related incapacity'. See International Criminal Court Elements of Crimes, ICC-ASP/1/3(part II-B), Art 7(1)(g)-1, Art 8(2)(b)(xxii)-1, and Art 8(2)(e)(vii)-1. Given the state of the ICTY and ICTR jurisprudence at the time of the drafting of the ICC's Elements of Crimes, it appears that the *Furundžija* trial judgment had a particularly persuasive impact on the drafting process.

[142] Schomburg and Peterson (n 38 above) 138–9; *Kunarac* (Appeals Chamber Judgment) (n 103 above) para 131.

rape is even the correct paradigm from which to interpret a definition for the international crime of rape. Alison Cole has likewise argued that 'the national crime of rape may not be the best analogy for international crimes'.[143] When viewed in comparison to domestic offences which criminalize sexual contact with individuals who are incapable of freely exercising agency over their own sexual autonomy (such as prison inmates or those with a mental disability), Cole notes that 'even domestic law is not alien to the notion that the determining factor is the surrounding context of coercive circumstances rather than consent'.[144] It is also interesting, given both the presumption that true consent will not be possible in the coercive circumstances giving rise to international criminal prosecutions and the frequency of sexual violence against children in armed conflict, to question whether the offence of statutory rape would have been a better point of comparison within national jurisdictions.

The most problematic aspect of the definition of rape as it has been developed in the *ad hoc* Tribunals is not the inclusion of the issue of consent in the abstract, but the circular logic required to address the inappropriateness of discussions of consent given the practical realities of international crimes. In order for a prosecution which includes acts of rape to come within the subject-matter jurisdiction of an international criminal tribunal, it must be established that the crimes in question qualify as war crimes, crimes against humanity, or acts of genocide. Before any analysis of the criminality of the rapes charged, the *chapeau* requirements for the relevant category of offence must be proven; namely, that the crimes in question took place in the context of an international or non-international armed conflict, a widespread or systematic attack on a civilian population, or a campaign targeting individuals on the basis of their membership of a national, ethnic, racial, or religious group. In addition, it must be shown that a sufficient nexus existed between the crimes and the existence of the armed conflict, that they were carried out as part of the widespread or systematic attack on a civilian population, or that they were committed with the specific intent to destroy, in whole or in part, the national, ethnic, racial, or religious group as such. Against such background circumstances, it is difficult to envisage any scenario where a Trial Chamber would be willing to find that consent had *not* been vitiated, particularly when one considers that the *Furundžija*, *Kunarac*, and *Gacumbitsi* cases all acknowledged that true consent would not be possible under such circumstances. Why, therefore, introduce an element which will be presumed to have been proven once jurisdiction has been established?[145]

Judge Pillay has stated that she framed the judgment in *Akayesu* to focus on coercion 'because it was evident that, in the circumstances that were being described, there was no place whatsoever for the consideration of consent'.[146]

143 Cole (n 52 above) 62. 144 ibid 76.

145 ibid 75; Schomburg and Peterson (n 38 above) 138.

146 'Sexual Violence: Standing by the Victim', Address by Ms Navanethem Pillay, United Nations High Commissioner for Human Rights, to the Hague Colloquium on Sexual Violence as

Indeed, when one considers the factual context for many of the decisions discussed in this chapter alone—including systematic mass rape of women on the basis of their ethnicity, multiple acts of rape committed in public, forcible detention of girls as young as 12 for the purposes of repeated sexual assault, sexual slavery, and the impaling of women on sticks forced into their sexual organs—it seems crass and counterintuitive even to discuss questions of consent in such circumstances, to say nothing of entering into a legal analysis of whether lack of consent has been proven beyond a reasonable doubt.

The choice of consent rather than coercion as the central element of the crime of rape under international criminal law is problematic on a theoretical as well as a practical level. In order to avoid the need for insensitive and potentially re-traumatizing questioning of witnesses as to whether they did or did not consent to their rapes,[147] the Appeals Chamber in *Gacumbitsi* held that non-consent could be inferred from background circumstances.[148] However, repeated judicial findings that true consent is not possible in circumstances of armed conflict or an ongoing attack against a civilian population, although introduced in order to solve the evidentiary problem caused by their own insistence that non-consent should be an element of the crime, has the inadvertent effect of giving rise to a presumption that no consensual sexual relations are possible in such circumstances. Schomburg and Peterson have pointed out that, even in protracted armed conflicts, 'individuals may decide to engage in sexual relationships for a variety of reasons that did not result from coercive circumstances negating any possibility of genuine consent'.[149] If the definition of rape was predicated solely on the issue of coercion, such findings would give rise to nothing more than the uncontroversial recognition that situations of widespread use of force or attacks on a civilian population are inherently coercive. Likewise, the element of non-consent presupposes the existence of a degree of sexual autonomy which, given the unequal position of women in many societies, would struggle to manifest itself even without the aggravating factors of genocide or armed conflict.

A focus on coercion, on the other hand, addresses the crime of rape through the lens of aggression, vulnerability, and inequality, which in the context of international crimes appears far more sensible. Moreover, the emphasis on consent makes the acts and thoughts of the victim the central concern,[150] whether a particular sexual act was welcome or whether they found themselves in a situation

an International Crime—Cross-Disciplinary Approaches to Evidence, The Hague, 16 June 2009 (original text on file with author).

[147] De Brouwer (n 6 above) 122–3. For an excellent discussion of the psychological impact and potential for re-traumatization for victims of sexual violence arising from testimony before international criminal tribunals, see N Henry, 'Witness to Rape: The Limits and Potential of International War Crimes Trials for Victims of Wartime Sexual Violence' (2009) 3(1) *International Journal of Transitional Justice* 114.

[148] *Gacumbitsi* (Appeals Chamber Judgment) (n 122 above) para 157.

[149] Schomburg and Peterson (n 38 above) 130–1, 125.

[150] ibid 139.

which allowed for meaningful consent, rather than those of the perpetrator in consciously exploiting a situation of duress, captivity, or widespread violence. It is interesting to consider how the Tribunals' definition would address a situation such as that which developed during the fall of Berlin at the end of the Second World War, where some German women would actively seek sexual relationships with higher-ranking Soviet officers in order to protect themselves from rape by non-commissioned troops.[151] The *Gacumbitsi* appeals judgment conceded that even evidence of consent which is admissible under Rule 96 can be disregarded if the Trial Chamber concludes that 'under the circumstances, the consent given was not genuinely voluntary'.[152] One can only hope that the nominal consent of victims whose sexual autonomy extends only to choosing between rapists would, in practice, be dismissed under the Appeals Chamber's holding.

The very concept of coercion implies a lack of consent, and the context of coercive circumstances was very consciously included in the original definition of rape outlined by the Trial Chamber in *Akayesu*. It is regrettable that subsequent Trial and Appeals Chambers elected to marginalize it to the status of proof of non-consent rather than the crux of the offence of rape. It would perhaps have been more logical and more practical had the Appeals Chamber in *Gacumbitsi* followed the urging of the prosecution and allowed consent only as a positive defence to the crime of rape.[153] Rule 96 of the Rules of Procedure and Evidence initially provided that consent should not be allowed as a defence; this was later amended to permit evidence of consent only in the absence of the presence or threat of 'violence, detention, duress or psychological oppression'.[154] Interpreting consent as a defence rather than an element of the crime would have allowed for the introduction of evidence of positive consent only in exceptional circumstances (not including those that were pleaded in *Kunarac*), rather than placing the burden of proof on the prosecution to prove its absence in every case of rape by reference to coercive background circumstances. It appears utterly illogical to require proof of non-consent in relation to an act of rape only where it is charged as rape, and not if the same act is concurrently charged as genocide, torture, enslavement, persecution, outrages upon personal dignity, or other inhumane

[151] See eg *A Woman in Berlin* (London: Virago Press, 2006) or G Köpp, *Warum War Ich Bloß ein Mädchen? Das Trauma einer Flucht 1945* (Munich: Herbig Verlag, 2010), which is significant for being the first book written under the author's own name to describe first-hand accounts of rape by advancing Soviet troops in 1945. See also Cole (n 52 above) 79, giving other examples of 'factually challenging' circumstances.

[152] *Gacumbitsi* (Appeals Chamber Judgment) (n 122 above) para 156.

[153] Schomburg and Peterson (n 33 above) 139.

[154] Rule 96(ii) provides that 'consent shall not be allowed as a defence if the victim (a) has been subjected to or threatened with or has had reason to fear violence, duress, detention, or psychological oppression, or (b) reasonably believed that if the victim did not submit, another might be so subjected, threatened or put in fear.' MacKinnon has noted that Rule 96(ii) initially ruled out consent as a defence to charges of rape entirely before being amended to its current form, a change which badly damaged the ICTY's credibility with survivors of sexual violence: MacKinnon (n 73 above) 947.

acts.[155] Alison Cole has noted that most national jurisdictions acknowledge that it is not legally possible to consent to grievous bodily harm or a violent attack.[156] Given the repeated emphasis in the jurisprudence of both Tribunals on the severity of bodily and mental harm caused by rape, it is arguable that an interpretation which surveyed national jurisdictions on the basis of 'analogous acts, instead of the analogous "name" of the crime'[157] would have found the concept of consent to be legally incompatible with the international crime of rape rather than central to it.

The focus thus far has been on the contextual or mental element of the crime of rape, rather than the physical element. The *actus reus* of the crime as defined in the *Furundžija*, *Kunarac*, and *Gacumbitsi* cases undoubtedly provides a greater degree of specificity than the *Akayesu* formulation of a 'physical invasion of a sexual nature'. It may be argued that a mechanistic emphasis on penetration leads only to humiliating questioning of the victim.[158] Conversely, the extremely broad *Akayesu* definition gave rise to some acts being clearly miscategorized in subsequent indictments as rape.[159] On an evidentiary level, although Rule 96 clearly states that no corroboration is required in cases of sexual violence,[160] judgments such as *Kunarac* contain lengthy factual descriptions of systematic rape yet ultimately provide for acquittal on individual charges of rape on the grounds of insufficient evidence.[161] There is also a discernible tendency to conclude that evidence of superior responsibility has been sufficiently established in relation to acts of murder but not acts of rape.[162] Although the *Furundžija* trial judgment specifically rejected the suggestion that a witness suffering from post-traumatic stress disorder should be considered unreliable,[163] Kelly Askin has criticized the

[155] Schomburg and Peterson (n 38 above) 126. Patricia Sellers has noted regretfully that, although rape has been held to be capable of constituting an act of genocide, torture, and enslavement (all prohibited as peremptory norms), it is only through a form of 'legal piggybacking' that it can be held to have 'reach[ed] the glory of *jus cogens*'. See P Sellers, 'Sexual Violence and Peremptory Norms: The Legal Value of Rape' (2002) 34 CWR JIL 287, 296.

[156] Cole (n 52 above) 76.

[157] ibid 78.

[158] Pillay (n 26 above) 666–7, describing an example from *Akayesu* where the victim of multiple rapes was repeatedly questioned by the prosecution: 'I am sorry to keep on asking you each time—did your attacker penetrate you with his penis?'

[159] eg in the *Muhimana* case, the Chamber rejected the classification as rape of the disembowelling of a pregnant woman, who was cut open with a machete from her breasts to her vagina and had her unborn baby removed. This act was instead dealt with in the Chamber's legal findings on murder. *Muhimana* (Trial Chamber Judgment) (n 116 above) para 557.

[160] Rules of Procedure and Evidence of the ICTY, Rule 96(i). The Rules of Procedure and Evidence of the ICTR, Rule 96(i) likewise states that no corroboration is required in cases of sexual assault, notwithstanding the provisions of Rule 90(C), which states that a judgment cannot be based on the testimony of a child who has testified without taking the solemn declaration.

[161] Buss (n 84 above) 98.

[162] See MacKinnon (n 47 above) 104–5, citing the *Muvunyi* and *Niyitegeka* cases and the extremely strong dissent of Judge Ramaroson in *Kajelijeli*. See *Kajelijeli* (Trial Chamber Judgment—Dissenting Opinion of Judge Ramaroson) (n 112 above).

[163] '[T]he Trial Chamber finds that Witness A's memory regarding material aspects of the events was not affected by any disorder which she may have had... The Trial Chamber bears in mind that even when a person is suffering from PTSD, this does not mean that he or she is necessarily

Chamber for its previous decision ordering the disclosure of a witness's medical, psychological, and psychiatric records, which raised 'moral, legal medical and public policy issues that could have had devastating and far-reaching consequences not only for victims of sexual violence, but for all survivors of traumatic events'.[164]

The judges of both tribunals should be praised for their continuing willingness to address evidence of sexual violence in judgments even where rape or related offences have not been included in the indictment.[165] This provides vital recognition of the pervasive and destructive role of rape and sexual violence in conflict, and enables the judgments to reflect accurately the reality of the circumstances addressed in the case. Such acknowledgement is all the more significant when Trial Chambers have refused leave to amend indictments to include charges of sexual violence or entered an acquittal on individual charges on the grounds of procedural fairness.[166] In particular, the jurisprudence of the ICTY has made a unique contribution to the recognition of rape and sexual abuse in conflict of male victims, which has been marginalized and overlooked historically to an even greater extent than sexual violence against women, and which occurred on a significant scale in the former Yugoslavia, particularly against male detainees in prison camps.[167]

One of the most significant elements of the judicial interpretation of the crime of rape by the *ad hoc* Tribunals has undoubtedly been the role played by female judges. As discussed at length above, Judge Pillay continues to be hailed as the driving force behind the extraordinary, creative, and progressive judgment of the ICTR in *Akayesu*. However, it is revealing to note that each of the trial judgments discussed above for their substantial contribution to the development of the law on rape and sexual violence emanated from a Chamber containing a female judge—Judge Navanethem Pillay in *Akayesu* and *Musema*, Judge Elizabeth Odio-Benito in *Delalić*, Judge Florence Mumba in *Furundžija* and *Kunarac*, Judge Andresia

inaccurate in the evidence given. There is no reason why a person with PTSD cannot be a perfectly reliable witness': *Furundžija* (Trial Chamber Judgment) (n 66 above) paras 108–9.

[164] Askin (n 21 above) 111. See also K Askin, 'The International War Crimes Trial of Anto Furundžija: Major Progress Toward Ending the Cycle of Impunity for Rape Crimes' (1999) 12 LJIL 935.

[165] See eg K Askin, 'Gender Crimes Jurisprudence in the ICTR—Positive Developments' (2005) 3 JICJ 1007, 1013, 1017, discussing the inclusion of evidence of sexual violence in the *Kayishema* and *Barayagwiza* cases.

[166] eg leave to amend the indictments to include sexual violence charges was refused in the *Lukić* case at the ICTY, while in the *Muvunyi* trial the ICTR Trial Chamber refused a prosecution request to withdraw the original rape charges only a few weeks prior to trial. For a discussion of the *Lukić* case, see F de Londras, 'Prosecuting Sexual Violence in the *ad hoc* International Criminal Tribunals for Rwanda and the former Yugoslavia', UCD Working Papers in Law, Criminology and Socio-Legal Studies, Research Paper No 06/2009, available at <http://papers.ssrn.com/sol3/papers.cfm?abstract_id=1393298>, 12–13.

[167] See eg Goldstone (n 4 above) 277; P Sellers, 'Sexual Torture as a Crime Under International Criminal and Humanitarian Law' (2007–2008) 11 *NY City Law Review* 339; ES Carlson, 'The Hidden Prevalence of Male Sexual Assault During War: Observations on Blunt Trauma to the Male Genitals' (2006) 46 *British Journal of Criminology* 16.

Vaz in *Gacumbitsi*, and Judge Khalida Khan in *Muhimana*. The role of female judges in proceedings has not gone unnoticed by the defence. Judge Pillay has noted that, although all three judges in *Akayesu* introduced questions regarding sexual violence, only her alleged impartiality was raised as an issue on appeal.[168] Similarly, Judge Mumba was accused not only of bias but of advancing a 'legal and political agenda' in the *Furundžija* judgment on the basis of her membership of the United Nations Commission on the Status of Women.[169] It would be reductive and unfair even to suggest that rape and sexual violence would have been ignored by the *ad hoc* Tribunals in the absence of female judges. However, that does not mean that the empathy, inquisitiveness, and undeniable legal expertise provided by the above-mentioned judges as individuals should not be highlighted and celebrated.[170] This trend is equally evident outside the ICTY and ICTR, with the contribution of Judge Teresa Doherty of the Special Court for Sierra Leone to the recognition of forced marriage as a crime against humanity, and the willingness of Judge Odio-Benito, now at the International Criminal Court, to reclassify the charges against Thomas Lubanga to include sexual slavery.[171]

V. Conclusion

The extensive attempts of the judges of the Yugoslavia and Rwanda Tribunals to identify and develop the definition of rape as an international crime provide a classic illustration of judicial interpretation in action. The *Akayesu* judgment is a perfect archetype of judicial creativity (if not judicial activism) to address a glaring *lacuna* in the law and to provide a progressive, purposive, and conceptual definition of a crime which, up until that point, had mouldered unused in the recesses of international law.[172] The *Furundžija* and *Kunarac* judgments exemplify

[168] Pillay (n 26 above) 666.

[169] *Furundžija* (Appeals Chamber Judgment) (n 79 above) para 169.

[170] See eg E Rackley, 'Judicial Diversity, the Woman Judge and Fairytale Endings' (2007) 27 *Legal Studies* 74, 90 (discussing the contribution of Judge Pillay). Great credit is also due to Patricia Viseur Sellers, who worked as the Gender Advisor in the Office of the Prosecutor and was intimately involved in progressively charging sexual and gender-based violence in both the Yugoslavia and Rwanda Tribunals.

[171] See Judge Doherty's dissenting judgment in the AFRC case before the Special Court for Sierra Leone, *Prosecutor v Brima et al* (Trial Chamber Judgment) SCSL-2004-16-A (22 February 2008), discussed in J Gong-Gershowitz, 'Forced Marriage: A "New" Crime Against Humanity?' (2009) 8 Nw JIHR 53. See also *Situation in the Democratic Republic of the Congo: Prosecutor v Lubanga* (Decision Giving Notice to the Parties and Participants that the Legal Characterisation of the Facts May be Subject to Change in Accordance with Regulation 55(2) of the Regulations of the Court) ICC-01/04-01/06 (14 July 2009). This decision was overturned by the Appeals Chamber in December 2009 on procedural grounds.

[172] As one commentator has put it, 'this brilliant postulation of international humanitarian law must stand for what it is: a revolution in legal thinking': K Chiedu Moghalu, 'International Humanitarian Law from Nuremberg to Rome: The Weighty Precedents of the International Criminal Tribunal for Rwanda' (2002) 14 *Pace International Law Review* 273, 285.

a more cautious approach, deferential to the traditional sources of international law and at pains to emphasize the doctrinal importance of the principle of specificity. The Appeals Chamber decisions in *Kunarac* and *Gacumbitsi* could be viewed both as developmentalist and contextualist: they support and include incremental additions to previous definitions of rape, while at the same time interpreting the content of the offence in light of the factual circumstances of its commission and the *chapeau* requirements of international crimes. Other decisions, such as those in *Musema* and *Muhimana*, attempt to devise a harmonious interpretation of the existing jurisprudence. It is clear that the efforts of the judges of the ICTY and ICTR have had a tremendous impact, not only in defining rape but also in acknowledging the role of rape and sexual violence in the commission of a huge range of international crimes such as genocide, extermination, enslavement, torture, persecution, other inhumane acts, grave breaches, outrages on personal dignity, and cruel treatment. As Judge Wald has written in her foreword to this collection '[i]f that be creativity, blessed be its name'.

PART III

FORMS OF CRIMINAL LIABILITY

7

The *Ad Hoc* Tribunals and the Law of Command Responsibility: A Quiet Earthquake

*Robert Cryer**

I. Introduction

There is no doubt that the judiciary have a role in developing international law.[1] This is at least as true in international criminal law as it is anywhere else, and possibly more.[2] That this is the case was given a backhanded recognition by the fact that the drafters of the Rome Statute were so uncomfortable about granting the International Criminal Court (ICC) a broad mandate to interpret customary international law.[3] Command responsibility has a lengthy history, probably about as long as that of the law of war crimes,[4] but it is not too much to say that many, if not the majority of the developments (positive or otherwise) in the

* Many thanks to all at the Irish Centre for Human Rights.

[1] Sir Hersch Lauterpacht, *The Development of International Law by the International Court* (London: Stevens, 1958); RY Jennings, 'The Judiciary, National and International, and the Development of International Law' (1996) 45 ICLQ 1; G Schwarzenberger, *International Law as Applied By International Courts and Tribunals Vol 1* (London: Stevens, 3rd edn, 1957).

[2] T Meron, 'War Crimes in Yugoslavia and the Development of International Law' (1994) 88 AJIL 78; C Greenwood, 'The Development of International Humanitarian Law by the International Criminal Tribunal for the Former Yugoslavia' (1998) 2 MP YB UNL 97; W Fenrick, 'The Development of the Law of Armed Conflict Through the Jurisprudence of the International Criminal Tribunal for the Former Yugoslavia' (1998) 3 JACL 197; LJ van den Herik, *The International Criminal Tribunal for Rwanda and the Development of International Law* (The Hague: Brill, 2005); IP Blischenko, 'Judicial Decisions as a Source of International Humanitarian Law' in A Cassese (ed), *The New Humanitarian Law of Armed Conflict* (Naples: Editoriale Scientifica, 1979) 41, 51; G Mettraux, *International Crimes and the Ad Hoc Tribunals* (Oxford: OUP, 2005).

[3] See eg M McAuliffe de Guzman, 'Article 21' in Otto Triffterer (ed), *Commentary on The Rome Statute of the International Criminal Court* (Oxford: Hart, 2nd edn, 2008) 701, 702.

[4] See eg W Hays Parks, 'Command Responsibility for War Crimes' (1973) 62 *Military Law Review* 1, 120

concept since the beginning of the twentieth century have occurred as a result of judicial activity.

It is true that in 1919 states, in the inter-Allied Commission, were willing to accept that liability accrued to a commander when he knew of offences occurring, but failed to intervene to prevent them;[5] a result, it is worth noting, which was dissented from by both the American and Japanese members of the Commission.[6] However, the *locus classicus* of the law of command responsibility, at least until the 1990s, was the much discussed *Yamashita* case:[7] a case, it bears remembering, in which two dissenting judges of the US Supreme Court failed to identify a violation of the laws of war.[8] The principle was not directly contained in either the Nuremberg or Tokyo International Military Tribunal (IMT) Charters, but this did not prevent the Tokyo IMT from expanding the applicability of this form of liability (considered by two of the judges to be novel)[9] to civilian superiors.[10] The main treaty-based development of the concept came in Articles 86 and 87 of Additional Protocol I, which provided some codification of the concept.[11] Still, it must be said that, at the start of the 1990s, the details of the ambit of command responsibility remained uncertain. The post-Second World War jurisprudence was helpful, but not voluminous.[12] This chapter will look at how the International Criminal Tribunal for the former Yugoslavia (ICTY) and International Criminal Tribunal for Rwanda (ICTR) have approached the question of their role in developing the law, and how this has played out in relation to the nature of command responsibility.[13]

[5] 'Report of the Commission on the Responsibility of the Authors of the War' (1920) 14 AJIL 95, 121.

[6] ibid 143, 152.

[7] *Re Yamashita* (1945) 4 Law Reports of Trials of War Criminals 1, 2 (Military Commission) 37 (Supreme Court).

[8] ibid 51–4 (Murphy), 57 (Rutledge).

[9] These were Judges Röling and Pal (the latter of whom would not countenance liability beyond where a person was, in essence, directly complicit in war crimes). See N Boister and R Cryer, *The Tokyo International Military Tribunal: A Reappraisal* (Oxford: OUP, 2008) 232–3.

[10] See Majority Judgment, in N Boister and R Cryer (eds), *Documents on the Tokyo International Military Tribunal: Charter, Indictment, and Judgments* (Oxford: OUP, 2008) 82–4. Given the proof of the relevant orders in the Nuremberg IMT, that Tribunal did not deal in any major way with command responsibility: see LC Green, 'Command Responsibility in International Law' (1995) 5 *Transnational Law and Contemporary Problems* 319, 333.

[11] Protocol I Additional to the Geneva Conventions of 8 August 1949 and Relating to the Protection of Victims in International Armed Conflict, 1125 UNTS 3. See Y Sandoz (ed), *Commentary on the Additional Protocols of 8 June 1977 to the Geneva Conventions of 12 August 1949* (Dordrecht: Nijhoff, 1986) 1005–23 and M Bothe, K Partsch, and W Solf, *New Rules for Victims of Armed Conflicts* (The Hague: Nijhoff, 1982) 523–9.

[12] Sandoz, *Commentary* (n 11 above) 1014 does use such jurisprudence.

[13] Or at least, aspects thereof; detailed discussion of the area is now genuinely beyond the scope of a single chapter: for a book-length treatment, see G Mettraux, *The Law of Command Responsibility* (Oxford: OUP, 2009).

II. The Provisions of the ICTY and ICTR Statutes

It was against the background of the post-Second World War cases and Additional Protocol I that the ICTY Statute was drafted, and the rather undeveloped state of the details of the law are reflected in Article 7(3) of the ICTY Statute (to which Article 6(3) of the ICTR Statute is, in all material regards, identical),[14] which reads:

> The fact that [crimes were] committed by a subordinate does not relieve his superior of criminal responsibility if he knew or had reason to know that the subordinate was about to commit such acts or had done so and the superior failed to take the necessary and reasonable measures to prevent such acts or to punish the perpetrators thereof.

When the ICTY came to determine the ambit of command responsibility, this was almost all the guidance that it was given. As a result, it is unsurprising that, against the background of the UN Secretary-General's strident views on the *nullum crimen sine lege* principle,[15] the ICTY has consistently determined that Article 7(3) was a *renvoi* to the customary law on command responsibility.[16] This has, of course, enabled the judges there to engage in significant discussion of the relevant principles of command responsibility in customary law, and by doing so, develop it.[17] It is the purpose of this chapter to evaluate the extent to which it has simply crystallized, or developed the law, and the extent to which it has, in fact, judicially created the law. This is, of course, a matter of degree rather than always one of kind, something that the European Court of Human Rights has traditionally been fairly relaxed upon from the point of view of the *nullum crimen* principle, especially, although not solely, when discussion has centred on international crimes.[18]

[14] On this see WJ Fenrick, 'Some International Law Problems Related to Prosecutions before the International Criminal Tribunal for the Former Yugoslavia' (1995) 6 Duke JICL 103, 111–12.

[15] Report of the Secretary-General Pursuant to Paragraph 2 of Security Council Resolution 808, UN Doc S/25704, 34.

[16] See eg *Prosecutor v Hadžihasanović, Alagić and Kubura* (Appeals Chamber Decision on Interlocutory Appeal Challenging Jurisdiction in Relation to Command Responsibility) IT-01-47-AR72 (16 July 2003) paras 24–31, 44 (hereinafter *Hadžihasanović*); Partially Dissenting Opinion of Judge Shahabuddeen, para 31; *Prosecutor v Bagilishema* (Appeals Chamber Judgment) IT-95-1A-A, (3 July 2002) (hereinafter *Bagilishema*) paras 26–37 (albeit implicitly).

[17] There are clear overlaps in this regard with the seminal decision in *Prosecutor v Tadić* (Appeals Chamber Decision on the Defence Interlocutory Appeal on Jurisdiction) IT-94-1-AR72 (2 October 1995), on which see T Meron, 'The Continuing Role of Custom in the Formation of International Humanitarian Law' in T Meron (ed), *War Crimes Law Comes of Age* (Oxford: OUP, 1998) 262, 263–8; GR Watson, 'The Humanitarian Law of the Yugoslavia War Crimes Tribunal: Jurisdiction in *Prosecutor v Tadic*' (1996) 36 Va JIL 687, 709–28.

[18] See eg M Shahabuddeen, 'Does the Principle of Legality Stand in the Way of Progressive Development of the Law?' (2004) 1 JICJ 1007. In *Jorgić v Germany* (App No 74613/01) ECHR 12 July 2007, the European Court was willing to accept convictions in Germany for genocide on a broader interpretation of the concept than has been accepted in the international criminal tribunals. On the ECHR generally on point see P van Dijk, Fr van Hoof, A van Rijn and L Zwaak (eds),

Nonetheless, it is possible to draw a tolerably clear line between the situations in which a tribunal develops and clarifies the law simply by the reflexive process of application of the law to facts,[19] and an attempt to reshape the entire law on point. The ICTY, as any criminal court perhaps ought to (and any court working against the background of a relatively unexplored area almost certainly has to), has clarified the law in the former manner.[20] In many ways, it might be noted that, at times, the ICTY's approach to command responsibility has been to assert that customary law is essentially the same as the rules in Additional Protocol I.[21] They might have a fair argument that in doing so they have done nothing more than reflect what states have already accepted (some might say that with respect to the *mens rea*, though, it has taken a narrower view than states).[22] This, however, is not the focus of this chapter.

This is because it can feasibly be argued that the ICTY has recently sought to go beyond this, and, in addition to taking a broad approach to what custom requires (which is not necessarily wrong), it has effectively reformulated the principle of command responsibility in a manner which, whilst laudable in some ways, may well alter the fundamental basis upon which command responsibility has traditionally been seen by states. This is not to say that states cannot be wrong. As most international lawyers could be relied upon to say, there is no oxymoron in saying that a state, on occasion, 'misunderstands' international law. Still, it remains a fact of life in the international community that states create international law. However, the relationship between the way the ICTY has sought to rationalize this with important principles of criminal law, in particular the principle of individual liability, has proved, shall we say, complex. So, let us join the fray.

Theory and Practice of the European Convention on Human Rights (Antwerp: Intersentia, 4th edn, 2006) Ch 11.

[19] Which is perhaps a common-lawyer's conceit, but it is not necessarily an unacceptable one: see G Abi-Saab, 'Harvard and International Law: A Foreign View' (1959–1960) 2 *Harvard International Law Club Bulletin* 57, 57–8.

[20] For a detailed analysis of the *ad hoc* Tribunal's practice in this regard, see G Boas, J Bischoff, and N Reid, *International Criminal Law Practitioner Library Volume I, Forms of Responsibility in International Criminal Law* (Cambridge: CUP, 2007) Ch 3; W Schabas, *The UN International Criminal Tribunals: The Former Yugoslavia, Rwanda and Sierra Leone* (Cambridge: CUP, 2006) 314–24.

[21] See eg *Prosecutor v Delalić, Mucić, Delić and Landžo* (Appeals Chamber Judgment) IT-96-21-A (20 February 2001) (hereinafter *Čelebići* Appeal) para 393.

[22] See eg R Kolb, 'The Jurisprudence of the Yugoslav and Rwanda Criminal Tribunals on their Jurisdiction and on International Crimes' (2000) 71 BYBIL 259, 309–12. The matter is, though largely settled given that the prosecutor decided not to challenge the *Čelebići* appeal when the matter came up in the *Blaškić* appeal: *Prosecutor v Blaškić* (Appeals Chamber Judgment) IT-94-14-A (29 July 2004) paras 58–64. The ICC has seemingly taken a broader view about what states thought of the *mens rea* for command responsibility in the Rome Statute: see *Prosecutor v Bemba* (Decision on Confirmation of Charges) ICC-01/05–01/08 (15 June 2009) paras 432–5.

III. The General Approach to Custom and Development

A. The *Hadžihasanović* decision

It is in the context of command responsibility that some of the most open statements have been made about the role of the Yugoslavia Tribunal with respect to developing international criminal law. This occurred in a case to which we will return on a number of occasions, *Prosecutor v Hadžihasanović*. This case involved some bitter exchanges between the judges, and remains controversial. There were two issues which arose in the case, the first of which was whether or not the principle of command responsibility applied to non-international armed conflict, the second was if a commander could be responsible on the basis of failure to punish offences that occurred prior to his or her taking up command. Neither issue was simple on the approach that the ICTY—at least in that case—took, namely that it is not a current principle of international criminal law that, unless excluded, the same general principles of liability apply to all international crimes equally.[23]

On the first issue, however, the court was unanimous, with respect to the result, if not the reasoning that underlay it. The majority averred on point that:

> the Appeals Chamber is aware that it is incorrect to assume that, under customary international law, all the rules applicable to an international armed conflict automatically apply to an internal armed conflict. More particularly, it appreciates that to hold that a principle was part of customary international law, it has to be satisfied that State practice recognized the principle on the basis of supporting *opinio juris*. However, it also considers that, where a principle can be shown to have been so established, it is not an objection to the application of the principle to a particular situation to say that the situation is new if it reasonably falls within the application of the principle.[24]

This is, understandably, self-denying. The judges of the ICTY know very well that their ability to affect the law is related to the extent to which they can convince states that their interpretation of the law is acceptable. This is more certainly the case when customary law is at issue, as it is meant to be an interpretation of state practice and (states') *opinio juris*. The difficulty, of course, is whether or not a principle reasonably falls within it, requiring us to understand, beforehand, what the principle is.

When it came to the question of the applicability of command responsibility to war crimes in non-international armed conflicts, the entire Appeals Chamber was

[23] More generally, it must be said that the ICTY and ICTR have largely assumed that the same general principles of liability apply to all international crimes and have used cases relating to one international crime to prove that a principle of liability exists for another international crime. As it happens, I think that this is acceptable; however, a defence of that position must await another time.

[24] *Hadžihasanović* (Appeals Chamber Jurisdiction Decision) (n 16 above) para 12.

happy enough to accept that the principle did apply.[25] Since in non-international armed conflict there was some requirement of responsible command (for war crimes), this implied that command responsibility applied to non-international armed conflicts. There is, undoubtedly, on their reasoning, a rather broad level of deductivism here. This is not to say that they were wrong, but their reasoning left something to be desired.[26]

However, the Chamber determined by a three to two majority that command responsibility did not extend to a failure to punish offences committed prior to a commander exercising effective control.[27] Both sides in this imbroglio looked at the previous applications of the principle of command responsibility, and agreed that there was no specific case where a person had been convicted on such a basis, and the Rome Statute appeared to exclude it. The majority therefore opined that, although they accepted that opinions differed, 'this Tribunal can impose criminal responsibility only if the crime charged was clearly established under customary law at the time the events in issue occurred. In case of doubt, criminal responsibility cannot be found to exist, thereby preserving full respect for the principle of legality'.[28] In other words, even though custom is not static, nor inelastic, the customary rule on point did not apply here, as it did not extend to accepting superior responsibility liability for offences committed prior to a person taking up their post.

This did not pass without significant comment from the two dissenters, Judges Shahabuddeen and Hunt. Judge Shahabuddeen gave an opinion that, even given the judicious idiom to which it conformed,[29] expressly disavowed any intention to assert a right to change customary international law. Instead, he acknowledged the judicial right to interpret and apply an existing customary principle in light of new factual circumstances before a court:

> If State practice and *opinio juris* have thrown up a relevant principle of customary international law, the solution turns on the principle. But that does not bar all forward movement: a principle may need to be interpreted before it is applied...In the process of clarification, the Tribunal has the competence, which any court of law inevitably has, to interpret an established principle of law and to consider whether, as so interpreted, the principle applies to the particular situation before it...The competence is inseparable from the judicial function; it does not invite to open horizons, but, within disciplined limits, it has to be exercised...The particular question whether that responsibility extends to acts of a subordinate committed before the commander assumed duty has

[25] ibid para 31.

[26] For a defence of it (from one of the judges) see T Meron, 'The Revival of Customary Humanitarian Law' (2005) 99 AJIL 817, 823–4.

[27] *Hadžihasanović* (Appeals Chamber Jurisdiction Decision) (n 16 above) paras 54–6.

[28] ibid para 51.

[29] Judge Shahabuddeen all but openly criticized the majority's strong framing of their critiques of the views of the dissentients. He had a point, as we will see, since the majority were decidedly undiplomatic in their tone: see *Hadžihasanović* (Appeals Chamber Jurisdiction Decision Shahabuddeen Partial Dissent) (n 16 above) para 41.

> not fallen to be so far dealt with—at any rate, in any reported instance. That, however, does not mean that such a situation is not capable of being governed by the established principle. If it is capable of being governed by the established principle, that principle must be held to prevail. In acting accordingly, the Appeals Chamber will not be changing customary international law but will be carrying out its true intent by interpreting and applying one of its existing principles.[30]

The implication of the majority in this case was that the minority were attempting to act *ultra vires*, by changing the law, rather than merely interpreting it. In paragraphs not designed, it would appear, to encourage judicial collegiality they argued that:

> [u]nable to muster any significant evidence of State practice or *opinio juris* supporting their view, the dissenting Judges rely on a broad interpretation of treaty texts which do not address in terms the question of responsibility for crimes committed before the assumption of command. Their method is flawed. First, it represents a departure from our consistent jurisprudence requiring that criminal liability be grounded not only on statutory language but on firm foundations of customary law. Second, to interpret texts speaking of command responsibility as imposing a duty to punish, after the assumption of command, crimes committed before the assumption of command, is counterintuitive and contrary to the plain meaning of 'command' responsibility. Although the duty to prevent and the duty to punish are separable, each is coterminous with the commander's tenure. Third, an expansive reading of criminal texts violates the principle of legality, widely recognized as a peremptory norm of international law, and thus of the human rights of the accused.[31]

The point of this suggestion is indicative of one of the core issues surrounding this mode of criminal liability, namely, what is the fundamental principle of command responsibility? Judges Shahabuddeen and Hunt asserted both that customary law is malleable and also that, once a customary rule is established, that which comes within its ambit is *a priori* included.[32] In many ways this is a difficulty which is not unique to customary international law: the interpretation of treaty-based rules has similar problems—and both often involve judgement calls.[33] The majority, however, whilst agreeing with the dissenters on the general points of international law, disagreed on the specifics. Starting off in a manner in which

[30] ibid paras 9–10. See similarly *Prosecutor v Hadžihasanović, Alagić and Kubura* (Appeals Chamber Decision on Interlocutory Appeal Challenging Jurisdiction in Relation to Command Responsibility—Partially Dissenting Opinion of Judge Hunt) IT-01-47-AR72 (16 July 2003) paras 4, 7, 8, 13.

[31] *Hadžihasanović* (Appeals Chamber Jurisdiction Decision Hunt Partial Dissent) (n 30 above) para 55.

[32] As Judge Shahabuddeen explained, in his separate opinion in *Orić*, the basic point is that the majority were unwilling to accept that the general principle covered the case, whilst the minority did: *Prosecutor v Orić* (Appeals Chamber Judgment) IT-03-68-A (3 July 2008) paras 16–17.

[33] On custom, see A Roberts, 'Traditional and Modern Approaches to Customary International Law: A Reconciliation' (2001) 95 AJIL 757. On treaty interpretation, see A Aust, *The Modern Law of Treaties* (Cambridge: CUP, 2nd edn, 2007) Ch 13.

anyone who has heard a sentence beginning with the phrase 'with the greatest of respect' will know that something disrespectful is about to be uttered, the majority stated that they agreed that custom changes, and that it can be applied to new situations, but:

> [i]t is quite a different matter, however, to stretch an existing customary principle to establish criminal responsibility for conduct falling beyond the established principle. Whether the principle of command responsibility extends to crimes committed prior to the assumption of command is a difficult legal question, and reasonable minds may certainly debate the point. To assert, as the dissenting Judges do, that such a dereliction *clearly* carries individual criminal liability under existing principle seems indefensible. It is trite to observe that in international criminal law, imposition of criminal liability must rest on a positive and solid foundation of a customary law principle. It falls to the distinguished dissenting Judges to show that such a foundation exists; it does not fall to the Appeals Chamber to demonstrate that it does not.[34]

It must be said that the majority did not here deal in any useful way with the interplay of treaty and custom, which is notable given the way in which treaties on point have tended to be drafted to reflect, at least in broad terms, custom rather than to demolish it.[35] Judge Hunt, in response, also made a telling point about the implications of the majority's reasoning:

> It is (in the view of the majority) necessary, before a principle accepted in customary international law can be applied to any particular circumscribed factual situation, to demonstrate that custom already exists supporting its application to that situation. Surely it is the purpose of the relevant principle of customary international law which dictates the scope of its application, not the facts of the situation to which the principle is sought to be applied. And, if that scope or purpose is not sufficiently rigorous or precise, it may be defined by reference to the 'principles of humanity' and 'dictates of public conscience' as provided for in the Martens Clause. If the view of the majority is correct, no principle of customary international law could ever be applied to a new situation, simply because it *is* a new situation.[36]

Other than the rather broad use of the Martens Clause, which is not really applicable in this sort of situation,[37] there is some truth to his view, since custom develops by application to new situations. The ICTY has certainly applied custom to new situations. However, the problem with it is that custom is at times nebulous, so

[34] *Hadžihasanović* (Appeals Chamber Jurisdiction Decision) (n 16 above) para 52.

[35] In relation to the Rome Statue, see eg C Garraway, 'Command Responsibility: Victor's Justice or Just Desert?' in R Burchill, ND White, and J Morris (eds) *International Conflict and Security Law: Essays in Memory of Hilaire McCoubrey* (Cambridge: CUP, 2005) 68. This is not to say that the Rome Statute is, in all its aspects customary, for it is not. The point here is simply that, for the most part, the drafters were guided by their views of custom.

[36] *Hadžihasanović* (Appeals Chamber Jurisdiction Decision Hunt Partial Dissent) (n 30 above) para 40.

[37] See eg T Meron, *The Humanization of International Law* (Leiden: Nijhoff, 2006) 16–29.

the line between applying an existing rule to a new situation and inventing a new rule is a difficult one to draw.[38]

That said, the quotation from the majority set out above nonetheless also raises another important matter, the burden of proof, which was a major part of the issue between the majority and the minority. The majority took a firm view on the point, asserting that:

> [a]ware of these difficulties, the distinguished dissenting Judges seem to suggest that the criminal responsibility of a commander to punish crimes committed before his assumption of command is *ab initio* part and parcel of the customary law principle of command responsibility, and, that the rest is simple application of the law to the facts. But surely this claim of prior existence of such a broader principle of command responsibility is nothing more than a *petitio principii*. Relying on such a proposition, without any support in customary law, does not compensate for the failure of the dissents to carry the burden of demonstrating that such a principle exists in positive international law.[39]

This in itself might be seen as begging the point, as what it requires is delineation between the elaboration of a customary principle, application of that principle, and an expansion of it. This is a matter of appreciation, and perhaps both sides were guilty of using the malleability of those concepts to move towards their predetermined positions on whether it is appropriate to hold a person responsible for crimes committed before they took up command. As we will see, this is closely linked to their respective views of what the nature of command responsibility was. There is perhaps a hint of an accusation of this (on the part of the majority) in Judge Hunt's comparison of the approach they took to the two issues in the case (ie whether command responsibility in non-international armed conflicts fell within the principle of responsible command, and whether that principle covered failure to punish liability for offences prior to the taking up of command). As he said, the majority's approach seemed inconsistent: 'Somehow, and without explanation, the majority has moved... from a requirement that the particular factual situation falls "reasonably" within the principle to one that it "clearly" falls within that principle.... There is a very real distinction between the two requirements.'[40] Could it really be said that the majority's view about the development of custom on command responsibility in relation to international crimes in non-international armed conflicts was that different to the minority's view about the scope of command responsibility? According to Judge Hunt, customary law appears, for the majority, at one moment to stretch like bubblegum, but at another to be as rigid as concrete.

[38] See eg W Schabas, 'Customary Law or "Judge-Made" Law: Judicial Creativity at the UN Criminal Tribunals' in J Doria *et al* (eds), *The Legal Regime of the International Criminal Court: Essays in Honour of Igor Blischenko* (The Hague: Nijhoff, 2009) 77, 100. Schabas likens the approach to custom in the ICTY to common-law development of the law.

[39] *Hadžihasanović* (Appeals Chamber Jurisdiction Decision) (n 16 above) para 56.

[40] *Hadžihasanović* (Appeals Chamber Jurisdiction Decision Hunt Partial Dissent) (n 30 above) para 38.

Whilst it is true that the principle of legality has something to do with this, it ought to apply equally to both issues, and as such Judge Hunt has a point: the majority here is trying to have its cake and eat it, adopting one standard when it comes to the general applicability of command responsibility, and another when it comes to the question of liability for failure to punish. There is no articulated reason for their change of approach.

As such, and given the fact that opinion was split on the question of whether or not it would be appropriate to impose liability in the latter situation, it is no surprise that the matter arose again before the Appeals Chamber. The judgment on point was, in addition to the views expressed on the relevant law, interesting owing to the approach taken to the judicial function in relation to developing international criminal law.

B. *Orić* and overruling

This next judgment arose in one of the more politically contentious cases (even against the backdrop of most of the cases being seen by many as controversial) the ICTY has dealt with. This was the case of Naser Orić, the Bosniak commander of the forces defending Sarajevo. Given this, Orić was seen by many as a Bosniak war hero, and any criticism of him was seen as a calumny. At trial, Orić was nonetheless found guilty on the basis of command responsibility for certain offences, and sentenced to two years' imprisonment.

At trial level, the Chamber expressly followed *Hadžihasanović*, holding that there was no duty to punish offences devolving on a commander for crimes committed prior to his or her taking up command.[41] They reached this decision only on the basis of the ICTY's rules of precedent though, as set out in the *Aleksovski* Appeal, which require Trial Chambers of the ICTY to follow Appeals Chambers' decisions, even if they are of the view they are wrong.[42] The Trial Chamber in *Orić* (which included the renowned international criminal lawyer Albin Eser) made no effort to hide its discomfort with *Hadžihasanović*, and after a lengthy disquisition on the logic behind the principles underlying command responsibility, found that 'for a superior's duty to punish, it should be immaterial whether he or she had assumed control over the relevant subordinates prior to their committing the crime',[43] but accepted that they were obliged to hold differently.

Whatever their view on the appropriateness of the majority opinion in *Hadžihasanović*, the Trial Chamber's view on the rules of precedent in the ICTY

[41] *Prosecutor v Orić* (Trial Chamber Judgment) IT-03-68-T (30 June 2006) para 335.

[42] *Prosecutor v Aleksovski* (Appeals Chamber Judgment) IT-95-14/1-A (24 March 2000) para 113. See also R Cryer, 'Neither Here nor There? The Status of International Criminal Jurisprudence in the International and UK Legal Orders' in M Bohlander and K Kaikobad (eds), *International Law and Power: Perspectives on Legal Order and Justice: Essays in Honour of Colin Warbrick* (The Hague: Brill, 2009) 183.

[43] *Orić* (Trial Chamber Judgment) (n 41 above) para 335.

was impeccable, as the Appeals Chamber itself admitted.[44] On appeal, however, the prosecution decided to open up an assault on the *Hadžihasanović* precedent, and sought to persuade the Appeals Chamber to revisit the decision and overturn it. The defence countered that it cannot be an error of law for a trial chamber to follow a binding precedent (which must be right), and that there were no cogent reasons for changing the *Hadžihasanović* decision. A bare majority of the Appeals Chamber decided that they would not address the prosecution challenge.[45] They did so on the basis that, on the facts as they determined them on appeal, the question of whether Orić may have had a duty to punish offences prior to his taking up post, was irrelevant to the outcome of the appeal. There were two highly dissatisfied dissents on point from Judges Liu and Schomburg. Interestingly, the bare majority in *Orić* was made up of Judges Vaz, Meron, and Shahabuddeen. Vaz was not on the Appeals Panel in *Hadžihasanović*, Meron was one of the majority, whilst Shahabuddeen was one of the dissenters. The latter two are thus, on this issue, strange bedfellows indeed.

For present purposes, the most interesting aspect of this is Judge Shahabuddeen's concurring (in the result) opinion. It might have been expected that he would have joined the two dissentients, Judges Schomburg and Liu, who shared the view he expressed in *Hadžihasanović* that there was a duty to punish crimes committed prior to a commander taking office included in the ambit of customary command responsibility. He decided not to, even though the early parts of the opinion gave reason to believe that he might. He noted, for example, that the Trial Chamber felt bound by *Hadžihasanović*, but supported its expression of its view that the (majority of the) Appeals Chamber were wrong, albeit binding. As he noted though, given the fact that Judges Liu and Schomburg dissented on point, 'there is a new majority of appellate thought. The question is whether that new majority of appellate thought should be translated into a formal decision of the present bench of the Appeals Chamber acting through a bare majority.'[46]

Shahabuddeen was unconcerned that the issue had not been fully argued before them, as the defence had the opportunity to do so, but had chosen not to.[47] He also spoke clearly, and forcefully, of his view that there was a role for the Appeals Chamber in setting out the law, in language that came close to accepting a semi-legislative role, noting that '[i]n an oft-cited remark, it was said that doubtful issues have to be resolved and the law knows no better way of resolving them than by the considered majority opinion of the ultimate tribunal'.[48] He did accept that there are reasons for judicial caution, but said that 'they are not

[44] *Orić* (Appeals Chamber Judgment) (n 32 above) para 165.

[45] ibid paras 166–7. The earlier decision is *Hadžihasanović* (Appeals Chamber Jurisdiction Decision) (n 16 above). On which see C Greenwood, 'Command Responsibility and the *Hadžihasanović* Decision' (2004) 2 JICJ 598.

[46] *Orić* (Appeals Chamber Judgment) (n 32 above) para 3 (Shahabuddeen).

[47] ibid para 4. Given that certain aspects (such as the nature of command responsibility) had been fully argued, this is a surprising statement.

[48] ibid para 10.

enough to neutralise the duty of the Appeals Chamber to state fundamental law correctly: There is no legislature to which the task can be left'.[49] This latter point is a strong assertion of the right (and perhaps even the duty) of a court to take on, if necessary, a quasi-legislative role.

Ultimately, however, he decided not to join the two other dissenters to form a three to two majority to overturn *Hadžihasanović*, as:

> [a] decision to reverse turns upon more than theoretical correctness; it turns upon larger principles concerning the maintenance of the jurisprudence, judicial security and predictability. Included in those principles is, I believe, a practice for a judge to observe restraint in upholding his own dissent. I do not assert that a dissenting judge can never form part of a subsequent majority upholding his earlier dissent, but I think that the preferred lesson of the cases is that he is expected to do so with economy. Since I was one of the two dissenting judges in the earlier case . . . I consider that, in the circumstances of the present case, a reversal should await such time when a more solid majority shares the views of those two judges [ie Schomburg and Liu]. Meanwhile, the decision in *Hadžihasanović* continues to stand as part of the law of the Tribunal.[50]

This is, although indubitably honest, more than a little perplexing, in that as Shahabuddeen accepted, it would mean that Trial Chambers would be bound to follow a decision which a majority of the Appeals Chamber thinks is wrong. In addition, given that Shahabuddeen appeared, simply, on the basis of his own opinion, to be biding his time, Trial Chambers are going to have to follow a decision that can be expected to be reversed.

This is not simply a matter of interest to pedants or those who feel that to describe something is to understand it and all its implications. As Judge Shahabuddeen noted, it is a fundamental matter.[51] The question of whether or not there is a duty to punish pre-command offences is one which is intrinsically linked to the question of the nature of command responsibility (ie whether it is a form of responsibility for the crime itself or a *sui generis* form of responsibility). It appears that the Appeals Chamber is at least on course to take the latter view,[52] which, as we will see, would genuinely be a form of legislation, one which fundamentally puts the ICTY's conception of the mode of liability at odds with the way that command responsibility has traditionally been seen, and is seen (uncontroversially during its drafting) by those that drafted the Rome Statute.[53]

49 ibid para 12. 50 ibid paras 14–15. 51 ibid para 11.

52 *Prosecutor v Hadžihasanović* (Appeals Chamber Judgment), IT-01-47-A (22 April 2008) para 39: 'Takes into consideration' *Prosecutor v Halilović* (Trial Chamber Judgment) IT-01-48-T (16 November 2005) para 78, which takes this view.

53 Which is not to say that the Rome Statute is, on all points, reflective of customary law, but simply that against a backdrop of many controversies, both legal and political in relation to it, the nature of command responsibility was not among the contentious matters. See P Saland, 'International Criminal Law Principles' in RS Lee (ed), *The International Criminal Court* (The Hague: Kluwer, 1999) 189, 202–4: there is no mention of the matter as being controversial, unlike a number of other issues.

To understand this matter fully, it is necessary to go back in time, to the early post war era, and the trials that were undertaken then.

IV. The Nature of Command Responsibility

A. The nature of command responsibility at the end of the Second World War

The disagreement here surrounded whether command responsibility was a principle of liability, making someone responsible for the crimes committed by those who were being commanded, or whether it was some form of serious dereliction of duty charge. There was some confusion that goes right back to the *Yamashita* case.[54] The charge Yamashita faced was that '[he] unlawfully disregarded and failed to discharge his duty as commander to control the operations of the members of his command, permitting them to commit brutal atrocities ... [and] ... thereby violated the law of war'.[55] The US Supreme Court also appeared, at times, to conceive of it as such, opining at one point that 'the gist of the charge is an unlawful breach of duty by the petitioner as an army commander to control the operations of the members of his command'.[56] This interpretation of *Yamashita* can be supported by the review of the Yamashita case by the Staff Judge-Advocate, in which the charge was considered to be 'criminal dereliction of duty'.[57]

This is not the end of the matter, though, as the quotes above do not explain what responsibility arises as a result of the breach of duty. In particular, they do not make clear whether the responsibility arising from the breach is simply for the breach of duty, or whether that breach leads to responsibility for the offences that followed. The case is not expressly on point, and contains much, in fact, that contradicts the idea that it was setting out a form of simple dereliction of duty. For example, the Commission convicting *Yamashita* averred that, even though it 'would be absurd to consider a commander a murderer or rapist because one of his soldiers commits a murder or a rape', where crimes are widespread and the commander does nothing, 'such a commander may be held responsible, even criminally liable, for the lawless acts of his troops'.[58]

As Meloni points out, the almost overwhelming majority of the post-Second World War jurisprudence considered command responsibility to be a form of liability for the underlying offences, rather than a separate dereliction offence. Some cases, such as the *High Command Case*, with its reference to 'acquiescence', cannot really be rationalized any other way and on the basis that command

[54] See *Yamashita* (n 7 above) 5–8. [55] *US v Yamashita*, Transcript, 23.
[56] *Yamashita* (n 7 above) 66. [57] Parks (n 4 above) 32.
[58] IV Law Reports of Trials of War Criminals 1, 35.

responsibility was a form of responsibility for the underlying crimes. This strong trend appeared, albeit not completely unambiguously, to be the view taken up until the adoption of the ICTY Statute.[59] The language of Additional Protocol I, which was intended as a codification of the post-Second World War jurisprudence, speaks of 'penal or disciplinary responsibility' without referring to whether this is for the failure to exercise control or for the underlying offences. Still this was intended to draw upon the *Yamashita* case,[60] which on balance looked more like responsibility for the underlying crimes. Even Judge Shahabuddeen, who, as we will see, has taken the lead in adopting a significantly different view of the nature of command responsibility, accepted that 'the language of several of the cases does suggest that the commander himself committed the crime of the subordinate'.[61]

B. The nature of command responsibility before the ICTY: early cases

In the early practice of the ICTY, the Court appeared to take the view that the principle was liability for the offences of the subordinate. For example, in the *Čelebići* case the Trial Chamber, in its first major discussion of customary law on point, said:

> That military commanders and other persons occupying positions of superior authority may be held criminally responsible for the unlawful conduct of their subordinates is a well-established norm of customary and conventional international law. This criminal liability may arise either out of the positive acts of the superior (sometimes referred to as 'direct' command responsibility) or from his culpable omissions ('indirect' command responsibility or command responsibility *strictu sensu).* Thus, a superior may be held criminally responsible not only for ordering, instigating or planning criminal acts carried out by his subordinates, but also for failing to take measures to prevent or repress the unlawful conduct of his subordinates.[62]

This was picked up on in the *Aleksovski* case, and the Trial Chamber stated that '[a] superior is held responsible for the acts of his subordinates if he did not prevent the perpetration of the crimes of his subordinates or punish them for the crimes'.[63] Slightly later, in the *Blaškić* Trial Chamber judgment (which included Judge Shahabuddeen), the Chamber opined that 'a commander may

[59] C Meloni, 'Command Responsibility: Mode of Liability for Subordinates or Separate Offence of the Superior?' (2007) 5 JICJ 619, 621–3. See also eg *The Manual of Military Law* (London: HMSO, 1958) 178.

[60] Bothe, Partsch, and Solf (n 11 above) 525.

[61] *Orić* (Appeals Chamber Judgment) (n 32 above) para 25 (Shahabuddeen). This perhaps does not quite reflect what the cases said, in that they did not say that the commander committed the crimes, but that he was being held responsible for them; the two are not quite the same.

[62] *Prosecutor v Delalić, Mucić, Delić and Landžo* (Trial Chamber Judgment) IT-96-21-T (16 November 1998) (hereinafter *Čelebići* Trial) para 333. At para 334 they reiterate the 'imputed' nature of the liability.

[63] *Prosecutor v Aleksovski* (Trial Chamber Judgment) IT-95-14/1-T (25 June 1999) para 67.

incur criminal responsibility for crimes committed by persons who are not formally his (direct) subordinates, insofar as he exercises effective control over them'.[64]

The *locus classicus*, though, at least in the early jurisprudence of the ICTY, is the *Čelebići* appeal (upon which Judge Hunt sat). The Appeals Chamber looked at the analysis by the Trial Chamber of the Second World War jurisprudence and agreed with it, that command responsibility was a form of liability for the underlying acts.

> Based on an analysis of Second World War jurisprudence, the Trial Chamber also concluded that the principle of superior responsibility reflected in Article 7(3) of the Statute encompasses political leaders and other civilian superiors in positions of authority. The Appeals Chamber found no reason to disagree with the Trial Chamber's analysis of this jurisprudence. The principle that military and other superiors may be held criminally responsible for the acts of their subordinates is well established in conventional and customary law.[65]

It is notable that all these cases came after the Rome Statute, and in that treaty command responsibility is treated as a form of liability for the underlying offence. Although some elements of Article 28 of the Rome Statute could be read as creating a dereliction of duty-type offence,[66] it quite clearly imputes the crimes of the subordinates to the superior,[67] rather than giving rise to a different type of liability. It is of course true that the Rome Statute is questionable in some of its details on command responsibility, for example with respect to the *mens rea* of civilian superiors. However, the nature of the principle was not a bone of contention at Rome. Professor (now Judge) Christopher Greenwood was therefore right to say that:

> [i]n a command responsibility case, the commander is punished for his failure to control those under his command—not for participation in the crimes which they commit. Yet the commander is punished not for a separate offence of failure to control, but for the actual offences committed by his subordinates.[68]

A perusal of the disposition of many cases where command responsibility is at issue shows that a person is found responsible for the actual crime. It is true that sentencing, with the notable exception of the *RTLM* case,[69] for command

[64] *Prosecutor v Blaškić* (Trial Chamber Judgment) IT-95-14-T (3 March 2000) para 301. In para 303 they are perhaps even clearer, saying that 'the Trial Chamber holds that the test of effective control exercised by the commander implies that more than one person may be held responsible for the same crime committed by a subordinate'. Both paragraphs cite the earlier *Aleksovski* Trial Chamber Judgment.

[65] *Čelebići* Appeal (n 21 above) para 195.

[66] K Ambos, 'Superior Responsibility' in A Cassese, JRWD Jones, and P Gaeta (eds), The *Rome Statute of the International Criminal Court: A Commentary* (Oxford: OUP, 2002) 823, 850–5.

[67] Art 28 provides that the commander 'shall be criminally responsible for crimes within the jurisdiction of the Court committed by forces under his or her effective command and control'.

[68] Greenwood (n 45 above) 599. See also S Darcy, 'Imputed Criminal Liability and the Goals of International Justice' (2007) 20 LJIL 377, 387–9.

[69] *Prosecutor v Nahimana, Barayagwiza and Ngeze* (Appeals Chamber Judgment) ICTR-99-52-A (28 November 2007).

responsibility convictions alone tends to be fairly low,[70] but the point remains that the responsibility is for the crime. The ICTY appears to be on the road to changing this.

C. *Hadžihasanović*: redux

This journey began in earnest in *Hadžihasanović*. In this case, the majority, basing itself on the Rome Statute, and, it must be said, the traditional way in which the principle has been seen, treated command responsibility as a form of complicity or liability for the underlying offences.[71] They, at least implicitly, took the view that it is a step too far to hold a person responsible for the crimes committed by another person when they took control after the offences were committed. The minority took a different view. Judge Shahabuddeen challenged the idea that command responsibility is a form of complicity, opining that '[c]ommand responsibility imposes responsibility on a commander for failure to take corrective action in respect of a crime committed by another; it does not make the commander party to the crime committed by that other.'[72] As he accepted, the ambit of superior responsibility is intrinsically linked to its conceptualization.[73] Judge Hunt essentially agreed.[74]

So, how did they go about this? Judge Shahabuddeen is at one point very candid, basically accepting that this was simply a preference:

> I prefer to interpret the provision as making the commander guilty for failing in his supervisory capacity to take the necessary corrective action after he knows or has reason to know that his subordinate was about to commit the act or had done so. Reading the provision reasonably, it could not have been designed to make the commander a party to the particular crime committed by his subordinate.[75]

[70] See eg *Prosecutor v Strugar* (Appeals Chamber Judgment) IT-01-42-A (17 July 2008). I am grateful to William Schabas for this point.

[71] It is at least implicit in *Hadžihasanović* (Appeals Chamber Jurisdiction Decision) (n 16 above) paras 42–3, 46 and 51. Judge Shahabuddeen certainly sees them as having taken that view (*Hadžihasanović* (Appeals Chamber Jurisdiction Decision Shahabuddeen Partial Dissent) (n 16 above) para 32), although he refers to a non-existent paragraph. See also International Criminal Court Act 2001, s 65.

[72] *Hadžihasanović* (Appeals Chamber Jurisdiction Decision Shahabuddeen Partial Dissent) (n 16 above) para 33. See also *Orić* (Appeals Chamber Judgment) (n 32 above) para 294.

[73] *Hadžihasanović* (Appeals Chamber Jurisdiction Decision Shahabuddeen Partial Dissent) (n 16 above) para 33.

[74] *Hadžihasanović* (Appeals Chamber Jurisdiction Decision Hunt Partial Dissent) (n 30 above) para 9.

[75] *Hadžihasanović* (Appeals Chamber Jurisdiction Decision Shahabuddeen Partial Dissent) (n 16 above) para 32. This jars a little with his disavowal of 'policy-oriented law' in the Tribunals: see M Shahabbuddeen, 'Policy Oriented Law in the International Criminal Tribunal for the Former Yugoslavia' in LC Vohrah *et al* (eds), *Man's Inhumanity to Man: Essays in Honour of Antonio Cassese* (Dordrecht: Kluwer, 2003) 889.

He does, in support, however, refer to the Secretary-General's report preceding the adoption of the ICTY statute, noting that it read:

> A person in a position of superior authority should, therefore, be held individually responsible for giving the unlawful order to commit a crime under the present statute. But he should also be held responsible for failure to prevent a crime or to deter the unlawful behaviour of his subordinates. This imputed responsibility or criminal negligence is engaged if the person in superior authority knew or had reason to know that his subordinates were about to commit or had committed crimes and yet failed to take the necessary and reasonable steps to prevent or repress the commission of such crimes or to punish those who had committed them.[76]

He went on to say that this showed that the Secretary-General carefully distinguished being a party to an offence (ie through ordering it) from command responsibility, which 'does not make the commander a party to the crime committed by that other'.[77] This does not seem to be the natural reading of the provision: the Secretary-General was distinguishing liability under Article 7(1) and 7(3) of the Statute, and at no point does the report use the term parties. The only ambiguity is where it refers to responsibility for failing to prevent, but this is made clearer when it clearly refers to 'imputed responsibility' in the next sentence. The reference to 'criminal negligence' does muddy the waters slightly, but this could be read as referring to the *mens rea*. At the most, it adds a note of possible doubt. It does not bear the strong weight that Judge Shahabbudeen seeks to place upon it.

Judge Hunt, on the other hand, relies on three main cases, *Yamashita*, *Čelebići*, and the *Bagilishema* appeal, alongside commentary from Professor Ambos on Article 28 of the Rome Statute.[78] Unfortunately for him, none of the cases supports the position taken. *Yamashita*, as discussed above, is in fact at the very best slightly ambiguous about the nature of liability, but the fairly clear upshot is that it imposed responsibility for the underlying crimes rather than a breach of duty alone; in the very quote he uses, the Court refers to the fact that he 'permitted' the offences. In addition, neither the Trial nor Appeals Chamber decisions support him. Although the Trial Chamber decided that causation was not a necessary aspect of command responsibility, this does not mean that responsibility is not imposed for the underlying offences; many forms of complicity do not require causation. In any event, the Trial Chamber was, as was shown above, clear that command responsibility is a form of responsibility for the underlying crimes. His use of the Appeals Chamber decision is also misplaced, when he states that the

[76] Report of the Secretary-General (n 15 above) para 56.

[77] *Hadžihasanović* (Appeals Chamber Jurisdiction Decision Shahabuddeen Partial Dissent) (n 16 above) para 33.

[78] *Hadžihasanović* (Appeals Chamber Jurisdiction Decision Hunt Partial Dissent) (n 30 above) fn 23.

Appeals Chamber decided that it was not a form of vicarious liability. What the Appeals Chamber actually said was that:

> ... as correctly held by the Trial Chamber, as the element of knowledge has to be proved in this type of cases, command responsibility is not a form of strict liability. A superior may only be held liable for the acts of his subordinates if it is shown that he 'knew or had reason to know' about them. The Appeals Chamber would not describe superior responsibility as a vicarious liability doctrine, insofar as vicarious liability may suggest a form of *strict* imputed liability.[79]

As is clear, they are speaking, first, of the *mens rea* and not the nature of command responsibility, which they had already opined was a form of responsibility for the underlying offences. Here, the 'insofar' is doing a lot of work, which is ignored by Judge Hunt. So, let us turn to the last case Judge Hunt uses, the decision of the ICTR Appeals Chamber (ie the joint Appeals Chamber) in *Bagilishema*, which included Judges Shahabuddeen and Hunt and in which they said:

> References to 'negligence' in the context of superior responsibility are likely to lead to confusion of thought, as the Judgement of the Trial Chamber in the present case illustrates. The law imposes upon a superior a duty to prevent crimes which he knows or has reason to know were about to be committed, and to punish crimes which he knows or has reason to know had been committed, by subordinates over whom he has effective control. A military commander, or a civilian superior, may therefore be held responsible if he fails to discharge his duties as a superior either by deliberately failing to perform them or by culpably or wilfully disregarding them.[80]

This statement is not a strong authority for the point as it does not identify responsibility for what. As a result, it is worth looking into the reference the Appeals Chamber used. They referred for authority to the Australian post war case of *Baba Masao*.[81] This, admittedly rather obscure, case is perhaps the best authority they cite. It does refer to the breach of duty being a war crime, and so does not require twisting too far to support the idea that that is the nature of command responsibility, but they in turn referred for authority to *Yamashita*, which is subject to what was said about it above. In addition, the context in which the Appeals Chamber made their comments needs to be understood. The Trial Chamber had:

> ... identified criminal negligence as a 'third basis of liability'. This form was qualified as a liability by omission, which takes the form of 'criminal dereliction of a public duty'. The Appeals Chamber wishes to recall and to concur with the *Čelebići* jurisprudence, whereby a superior's responsibility will be an issue only if the superior, whilst some general information was available to him which would put him on notice of possible unlawful acts by his subordinates, did not take the necessary and reasonable measures to prevent the acts or to punish the perpetrators thereof. The Statute does not provide for criminal liability

[79] *Čelebići* Appeal (n 21 above) para 239 (footnote omitted).
[80] *Bagilishema* (Appeals Chamber Judgment) (n 16 above) para 35.
[81] XI Law Reports of Trials of War Criminals 56–60.

other than for those forms of participation stated therein, expressly or implicitly. In particular, it would be both unnecessary and unfair to hold an accused responsible under a head of responsibility which has not clearly been defined in international criminal law.[82]

As such, the Appeals Chamber noted that:

> ... there is a difference, breaches of duties imposed by the laws of war may entail a disciplinary rather than a criminal liability of a superior who is subject to military discipline. The line between those forms of responsibility which may engage the criminal responsibility of the superior under international law and those which may not can be drawn in the abstract only with difficulty, and the Appeals Chamber does not need to attempt to do so in the present Judgement.[83]

Given their comments, it is difficult to read this as a ringing endorsement of the idea that command responsibility is equivalent responsibility simply for the breach of duties, rather than responsibility for the underlying crimes. It appears to be distinguishing general duties to control troops (equivalent to those in the *chapeau* of Article 28 of the Rome Statute) from command responsibility properly so called in international criminal law.

To finish, Hunt supports his opinion by reference to Kai Ambos' commentary to the Rome Statute, which does indeed take the view that command responsibility is a separate omission-type offence, and not a form of complicity. However, in spite of the logical and structural case made by Professor Ambos that this ought to be the way in which command responsibility is seen, it does not make a strong case that it is so seen in state practice and *opinio juris*, and in Article 28. Indeed he accepts that his idea 'is not sufficiently reflected in the case law which ... normally does not clearly distinguish between accomplice liability and liability for failure to supervise'.[84] Ambos' view also does not reflect the clear terminology of the Rome Statute, which imposes liability 'for crimes within the jurisdiction of the Court committed by forces'. As Roberta Arnold has said:

> ... even though in some jurisdictions command responsibility may be considered an offence *per se*, indicating a superior's liability for the mere fact of failing to properly supervise his/her subordinates, the ICC Statute considers it as a form of participation to the crimes enlisted in Article 5 [ie genocide, crimes against humanity, and war crimes].[85]

As such it cannot be said that the dissenters have managed to make the case here.

D. The next steps

However, the *Hadžihasanović* decision was barely cold from the printer when the Appeals Chamber, in an extraordinary comment, given its earlier comments on point, appeared to completely reject its earlier views, stating that '[i]t cannot

[82] *Bagilishema* (Appeals Chamber Judgment) (n 16 above) paras 32–4. [83] ibid.

[84] Ambos (n 66 above) 852.

[85] O Triffterer and R Arnold, 'Article 28' in Triffterer (n 3 above) 795, 827.

be overemphasised that, where superior responsibility is concerned, an accused is not charged with the crimes of his subordinates but with his failure to carry out his duty as a superior to exercise control'.[86] This comment is, astonishingly, entirely unreasoned. It is true that the ICTY has in the past decided upon controversial matters rather quickly,[87] but here, a matter which had been the subject of considerable earlier comment was covered by an unreferenced *ipse dixit*. It must be said, the breezy manner in which it makes this comment has been the subject of some disagreement: in the next appeal we will deal with, the prosecutor described it as a 'passing reference', whereas Judge Shahabuddeen considered it a 'studied, deliberate and unanimous one'.[88] Given its remarkable lack of reference to any cases, documents, or commentary, it is difficult to see it as the latter.

This was followed by a number of Trial Chamber opinions which sought to separate command responsibility from the underlying crimes. The first of these was the Trial Chamber in *Halilović* which, partly relying on Shahabuddeen's dissent, attempted to square the circle, by asserting that:

> ... command responsibility is responsibility for an omission. The commander is responsible for the failure to perform an act required by international law. This omission is culpable because international law imposes an affirmative duty on superiors to prevent and punish crimes committed by their subordinates. Thus 'for the acts of his subordinates' as generally referred to in the jurisprudence of the Tribunal does not mean that the commander shares the same responsibility as the subordinates who committed the crimes, but rather that because of the crimes committed by his subordinates, the commander should bear responsibility for his failure to act. The imposition of responsibility upon a commander for breach of his duty is to be weighed against the crimes of his subordinates; a commander is responsible not as though he had committed the crime himself, but his responsibility is considered in proportion to the gravity of the offences committed.[89]

This is elegant, but the support they give is a brief review of the post war jurisprudence and the documents that followed it, which showed really, rather than a major split, that the trend of the case law was against it being the idea of command responsibility being a form of dereliction of duty.[90] Next, it noted that the ICTY had been practically uniform in its imposition of command responsibility on the basis that it is a form of liability for the underlying offences.[91] However,

[86] *Prosecutor v Krnojelac* (Appeals Chamber Judgment) IT-97-25-A (13 September 2003) para 171.

[87] One example is the disavowal of a policy requirement in crimes against humanity, in a single paragraph, with one footnote: see eg R Cryer, H Friman, D Robinson, and E Wilmshurst, *An Introduction to International Criminal Law and Procedure* (Cambridge: CUP, 2007) 197.

[88] *Orić* (Appeals Chamber Judgment) (n 32 above) para 20 (Shahabuddeen).

[89] *Halilović* (Trial Chamber Judgment) (n 52 above) para 54.

[90] ibid paras 42–52. See, on point, *Prosecutor v Orić* (Prosecutor's Appeal Brief) IT-03-68-A (16 October 2006) (hereinafter *Orić* Appeal Brief) paras 200–203 which, on point, is accurate.

[91] *Halilović* (Trial Chamber Judgment) (n 52 above) para 53.

it asserted that the Trial Chamber in *Aleksovski* noted that Article 7(1) and 7(3) formed different bases of liability, on the basis of its comment that:

> [t]he doctrine of superior responsibility makes a superior responsible not for his acts sanctioned by Article 7(1) of the Statute but for his failure to act. A superior is held responsible for the acts of his subordinates if he did not prevent the perpetration of the crimes of his subordinates or punish them for the crimes.[92]

This is true, but does not necessarily support the view that the liability is for complicity in the offences in the manner required in Article 7(1), rather than being liability for those offences. Thus, they are rather left with Shahabuddeen's dissent as authority, as, inexplicably, they did not refer to *Krnojelac*. Still, this did not stop the Trial Chamber in *Hadžihasanović*, in a manner which rather ignored the interlocutory appeal in that very case, from subscribing instead to the findings in *Halilović*,[93] and rationalizing *Čelebići* on the basis that it was not dealing directly with the nature of command responsibility, but its existence in custom.[94] This may be true, but does not undermine the fact that, on the basis of a considerable review of practice, they came to that conclusion on the form of responsibility it represents. In any event, as the prosecutor later noted, in both cases the Trial Chambers convicted the defendants of the relevant offence, not of a breach of duty *per se*.[95]

E. *Orić*: the deferred dénouement

The same cannot be said of the last major case that falls for discussion, *Orić*. Here, the Trial Chamber purported to rely on *Halilović* and *Hadžihasanović*, but considered the Article 7(3) charges not to be for the offences themselves, but for '[f]ailure to discharge his duty as a superior to take necessary and reasonable steps' to prevent the offences.[96] The prosecutor was unimpressed, and appealed this characterization of the charges.[97] Given that the Appeals Chamber acquitted Orić on the relevant counts, the majority decided that it was not necessary to pronounce on this directly. However, it will probably come as no surprise to find that the dissentients (and Judge Shahabuddeen) had something to say on the matter. To begin with the dissents, Judge Liu essentially asserted that he agreed with Judges Shahabuddeen and Hunt in *Hadžihasanović*, that custom supported liability for failure to punish pre-command offences,[98] only commenting that

[92] *Aleksovski* (Appeals Chamber Judgment) (n 42 above) para 67.

[93] *Prosecutor v Hadžihasanović* (Trial Chamber Judgment) IT-01-47-T (15 March 2006) paras 74–5.

[94] ibid para 70.

[95] *Orić* Appeal Brief (n 90 above) paras 200–202. As such, the fact that their comments on the nature of command responsibility were not mentioned on appeal does not mean that the finding was necessarily agreed with.

[96] *Orić* (Trial Chamber Judgment) (n 41 above) para 782.

[97] *Orić* Appeal Brief (n 90 above) paras 159 *et seq.*

[98] *Prosecutor v Hadžihasanović, Alagić and Kubura* (Appeals Chamber Decision on Interlocutory Appeal Challenging Jurisdiction in Relation to Command Responsibility—Separate and Partially Dissenting Opinion of Judge Liu) IT-01-47-AR72 (16 July 2003) para 27.

owing to the nature of command responsibility, causation is not a necessary aspect of liability,[99] which, as discussed above, does not mean that liability is not for the underlying crime (and, to be fair, Judge Liu did not claim it did). Judge Schomburg, in a typically forthright and thoughtful opinion, expressly supported Judge Shahabuddeen's opinion on the nature of command responsibility in the case.[100] Therefore, it is most instructive to look to the opinion of this exceptional judge.[101] Judge Shahabuddeen, in spite of his decision not to revisit the *Hadžihasanović* opinion, gave further comments on the nature of command responsibility that deserve some considerable discussion, not least as they illustrate an important point in relation to international criminal law and interpretation.

Judge Shahabuddeen began by claiming that, even though perhaps the majority of commentators took the view that it was a form of participation in the underlying offence, the matter had already been dealt with deliberately and 'studiously' by the Appeals Chamber in *Krnojelac*, and thus was not really an issue.[102] This is not really satisfying; the Appeals Chamber had, in the past, prior to *Krnojelac*, repeatedly expressed the view that this was not the case. As discussed above, *Krnojelac*, if it were to be authoritative, needed to deal with all the other Appeals Chamber jurisprudence, and reject it. Judge Shahabuddeen, nonetheless, added to what he had said before about the nature of command responsibility, even though he thought that the issue was now moot.[103] He referred to *Yamashita*, alongside the Trial Chambers in *Halilović* and *Hadžihasanović*, all of which have been dealt with above,[104] but then sought to deal with the various pieces of earlier jurisprudence, by saying that:

> [t]he language of several cases does suggest that the commander himself committed the crime of the subordinate. However, in my view those cases are to be construed as resting on the basis that punishment for the actual crime actually committed by the subordinate

[99] ibid para 32.

[100] *Prosecutor v Hadžihasanović, Alagić and Kubura* (Appeals Chamber Decision on Interlocutory Appeal Challenging Jurisdiction in Relation to Command Responsibility—Separate and Partially Dissenting Opinion of Judge Schomburg) IT-01-47-AR72 (16 July 2003) para 12.

[101] This chapter might be read as a screed against Judge Shahabuddeen. Nothing could be further from the truth. Judge Shahabuddeen is an exceptional scholar and judge; although on point, this piece disagrees with his view, it is intended as a positive contribution to the debate, rather than an attack.

[102] *Hadžihasanović* (Appeals Chamber Jurisdiction Decision Shahabuddeen Partial Dissent) (n 16 above) paras 18–19. It ought to be said that this is not quite the issue: it is about whether the liability is for the underlying crime, rather than for participation in it. In such issues, uses of terms such as 'participation' are unhelpful insofar as they seek to analogize command responsibility and participation.

[103] A pedant might note that the Appeals Chamber had pronounced on the matters a number of times before *Krnojelac*, which did not deal with the previous decisions.

[104] *Orić* (Appeals Chamber Judgment) (n 32 above) paras 22–3. He does note that the holding in *Hadžihasanović* was not dealt with on appeal, but that does not prove that it was agreed with. *Orić* was the first time that the question was expressly dealt with on appeal after the *Hadžihasanović* Appeals Chamber Jurisdiction Decision.

> is only the measure of the punishment of the commander for his failure to control the subordinate. Considered in this way, those cases are correct. If they are not to be so construed and have as a result led to punishment of the commander for participating in the actual crimes committed by his subordinates, they have misrepresented the true nature of command responsibility in international criminal law. Practitioners are familiar with the procedure of construing a case to reconcile it, if possible, with common sense. One should speak only of a contradiction where such a procedure fails to achieve harmony. I do not consider that there is a contradiction in this case, and so do not propose to express a view on the assumption that there is.[105]

This is an exceptionally interesting statement, in that it seems to take the view that there is a 'true' nature of command responsibility that exists somewhere in the ether, and simply requires an interpreter to find it. This is not inconsistent with other aspects of Judge Shahabuddeen's thought as expressed, for example, in the *Nuclear Weapons* advisory opinion, when he dealt with the Martens clause.[106] Nonetheless, his statements both here and in the *Hadžihasanović* case imply that it is appropriate to recast cases if it is possible to do so, to see them as supporting a particular point of view, and that a judge's personal view on point is an acceptable grounding for such a re-reading. As such, given the clear overlaps in their thought on point, it is worth seeing if there is a basis for such a view.

Whether the influence or similarity was conscious or not, there are very clear overlaps between Judge Shahabuddeen's views and those of Ronald Dworkin. For example, Dworkin has been a strong supporter of the idea that the personal views of a judge are an appropriate part of the interpretative mandate of an international judge.[107] Similarly, the idea of finding, against a background of a certain level of indeterminacy, a constructive re-reading of cases that narrates an answer that fits best with the moral views of the judge is acceptable, so long as it does not undermine the integrity of the legal system.[108] Hence, as Dworkin says, 'propositions of law are true if they figure or follow from the principles of justice or fairness or procedural due process'.[109] In addition, there are those in international law, particularly with reference to customary law, that have taken the view that a Dworkinian (re-)reading of previous practice is the appropriate way of approaching what has gone before in a fashion that supports the best view of the relevant law.[110] As such, Dworkin's view of the judicial function is something that cannot simply be dismissed when we discuss the appropriate interpretative role of judges in international tribunals.

[105] *Orić* (Appeals Chamber Judgment) (n 32 above) para 25 (Shahabuddeen).

[106] See *Legality of the Threat or Use of Nuclear Weapons* (Advisory Opinion) [1994] ICJ Rep 4, 405 *et seq* (Dissenting Opinion of Judge Shahabuddeen).

[107] R Dworkin, 'The Judge's New Role: Should Personal Convictions Count?' (2003) 1 JICJ 4.

[108] The most detailed version of this can be found in R Dworkin, *Law's Empire* (Oxford: Hart, 1998). He describes his view (briefly) as follows: 'constructive interpretation is a matter of imposing purpose on an object or practice in order to make of it the best possible example of the form or genre to which it is taken to belong' (ibid 52).

[109] ibid 255.

[110] See eg Roberts (n 33 above).

Dworkin's approach, is, as is well known, not universally accepted.[111] For good reason, not all areas of law are necessarily subject to the same interpretative canons—as Oscar Schachter said many years ago, the UN Charter is not to be interpreted like an insurance contract.[112] Criminal law, with its penal consequences, is (and ought to be) subject to more stringent standards of interpretation than other areas of international law. The *nullum crimen sine lege* principle is a hugely important principle in criminal law.[113] Therefore, the integrity of international criminal law would be compromised by a re-reading of cases that is designed to increase the substantive coverage of that law retrospectively. To be fair to Dworkin, it is likely that he would not dissent from this. Even so, this provides a reason to question the way in which Judge Shahabuddeen sought to approach the earlier cases.

This does not alter the fact, though, that the Appeals Chamber seems to be shifting towards the view that command responsibility is not a form of responsibility for the underlying crimes. Most recently, in the *Hadžihasanović* appeal judgment, the Appeals Chamber took into account the Trial Chamber's view on causation, which was linked to their view of the nature of command responsibility.[114] It thus appears that the Appeals Chamber is close to on taking, or perhaps has already made, a truly legislative move, fundamentally altering the basis of command responsibility.[115] This would be a mistake, for at least two reasons in addition to those mentioned above. The first is that it would further fragment international criminal law, creating more disjunction between the Rome Statute and the ICC's views on international criminal law, which is to be resisted, as far as possible.[116] The second reason is that, as Judge Shahabuddeen has said, the ambit of command responsibility is linked to its conceptualization. Most of the early cases, which have been extensively used by the ICTY to delimit the elements of command responsibility, conceived of command responsibility as a form of liability for the underlying offences, and structured their approaches to what is required for a superior/subordinate relationship, and perhaps most importantly, the *mens rea* against that background. To reframe command responsibility as a different type of liability would create a Frankenstein's monster, with elements developed in one context being used for a different type of responsibility to which they may not be suited.

[111] See eg (the sympathetic, albeit not uncritical) S Hershowitz (ed), *Exploring Law's Empire: The Jurisprudence of Ronald Dworkin* (Oxford: OUP, 2006) and J Burley (ed), *Dworkin and His Critics* (Oxford: Blackwell, 2004).

[112] O Schachter, 'Review of Kelsen, *The Law of the United Nations*' (1951) 60 Yale LJ 189, 193.

[113] See eg the International Covenant on Civil and Political Rights, 999 UNTS 171 Art 15, European Convention on Human Rights, 223 UNTS 221, Art 7.

[114] *Prosecutor v Hadžihasanović* (Appeals Chamber Judgment) IT-01-47-A (22 April 2008) para 39.

[115] Some take the view that the ICTY, as a whole (ie including the Trial Chambers) has already succeeded in 'clarifying' the matter such that we now know the nature of the liability is not that for the underlying crimes: see eg Mettraux (n 13 above) Ch 4 and Boas *et al* (n 20 above) 177–8.

[116] See R Cryer, 'Royalism and The King: Article 21 of the Rome Statute and the Politics of Sources' (2009) 12 *New Criminal Law Review* 390.

V. Conclusion

Command responsibility was a doctrine that was almost born, as Guénaël Mettraux has said, 'in sin', of judicial creativity.[117] And judges have been developing it ever since. At times their approach has probably been within the application/interpretation level. This probably even extends to the minority's view in the *Hadžihasanović* case, and that of the majority of the judges in *Orić*, that custom may extend to crimes committed prior to a commander taking up post. It is at least arguably within the margin of appreciation that lies in the difficult grey zone between interpretation/application and legislation. On the question of the nature of command responsibility, though, there is a considerable likelihood that the ICTY has embarked on a course of seismic legislative activity, which is neither clearly referable to customary law nor within a legitimate theory of the judicial function.

The approach seems to be a genuine attempt to make command responsibility a form of responsibility which is more closely tied to individual culpability. However, what we ought to bear in mind is that states, in the end, are those that make international law, and the ICTY is treading on thin ice here. As it happens, both views of command responsibility are problematic, as they assume a unitary model of culpability in command responsibility, which does not tie up with the various different situations the principle covers.[118] It covers too many and too different situations to be appropriately considered under one rubric. However, we have what we have—and this is not an essay in criminal law theory, but authority to create international law—in that states get the international law they decide upon, not that which they deserve, or we necessarily want. It is entirely appropriate to appraise the existing law with regard to the moral/political principles which we apply to domestic criminal law. This ought to be the case: in both situations we are dealing with the justification for depriving someone of their liberty, and labelling them with a pejorative adjective. However, neither sense nor sensibility are sources of international criminal law and, as such, it is difficult to support what the ICTY may be about to do.

[117] Mettraux (n 13 above) 5.

[118] See R Cryer, 'General Principle of Liability in International Criminal Law' in D McGoldrick, P Rowe, and E Donnelly (eds), *The Permanent International Criminal Court: Legal and Policy Issues* (Oxford: Hart, 2004) 233, 258–60; Meloni (n 59 above); V Nerlich, 'Superior Responsibility Under Article 28 of the Rome Statute: For Exactly What is the Superior Held Responsible?' (2007) 5 JICJ 665.

8

Judicial Creativity and Joint Criminal Enterprise

Mohamed Shahabuddeen

The topic 'Judicial Creativity in International Criminal Law' is on the table; it is interesting, but wide. Accepting an invitation to contribute, the writer limits himself to 'Judicial Creativity and Joint Criminal Enterprise'. He notes that it is said that joint criminal enterprise is not a theory known to international criminal law. Taking the opposite view, he begins by asking the preliminary question as to what is judicial creativity; he considers it to be valid but to be exercised with caution. Then follows a discussion of joint criminal enterprise; he recognizes that co-perpetratorship is a meritorious theory, but prefers joint criminal enterprise. The concluding view is then expressed that judicial creativity enabled the International Criminal Tribunal for the former Yugoslavia (ICTY) to opt for joint criminal enterprise. The discussion of these branches overlaps.

I. Judicial Creativity

International law has developed out of West European law.[1] Two schools of thought were dominant there: the common law and the civil law. In the common law, the name of Blackstone is associated with the notion that the judges declare the law, but do not make it. In the view of other common law jurists, in addition to declaring the law, the judges make it but only interstitially and by a process of binding precedent: a decision of a higher court binds the lower courts, subject to qualifications which are not now being examined. The civil law highlighted the position of the legislature. In relation to the courts, it adopted an

[1] In a system which prides itself on scientific inquiry wherever it will lead, it is remarkable that, by a mysterious process of self-combustion, the genesis of international law is ordinarily placed in Portugal, Spain, and Italy, countries which faced others in the south with a notable intellectual past; no further inquiry is usually undertaken. See AG Koroma, 'International Law and Multi-Culturalism', an address delivered at Stanford University in April 2008.

attitude somewhat similar to that of the common law, except that, instead of the law of binding precedent, there was the doctrine known as *jurisprudence constante*. The law as pronounced by a court—however exalted—did not bind lower courts; the law was as it was declared to be by a series of concurring decisions of the courts.

The central idea which emerged from both systems was that a change of the law was for the lawgiver and that the role of the judge was to carry out the will of the former, subject to this: as indicated above, there was room for judge-made law. In fact, judge-made law has long been regarded as 'one of the existing realities of life'.[2] Judges will not needlessly call attention to it, but historically they (including international judges)[3] have had recourse to it. When they do so, they are faced with a barrage of criticisms: they do not have the facility enjoyed by the legislature of the matter being first studied by other agencies, and legions of remarks to similar effect. Criticized judges are likely to be old, male, rich, upper class—people who mechanically reflect the outlook of their kind without concerning themselves with the interests of the wider society.

A solution was needed. In searching for it, the term 'judicial activism' was introduced into the discussions by Arthur Schlesinger Jr in 1947. But this was accompanied by disputes, some of which preceded that year. The term 'judicial creativity' was thought of. But what is the precise boundary between it and 'judicial activism'? The divisional line is not clear. This contribution will proceed on the footing that judicial activism fashions new law on the basis of personal predilections of the judges not anchored in existing law. Judicial creativity also fashions new law but, by contrast with judicial activism, does so on the basis of the policy of the law as it can be extracted from the roots of the law.

The position in England was put thus by Lord Steyn in a 2004 lecture:

> In construing statutes the courts have no law-making role. On the other hand, in the exposition of the common law, the courts have a creative role. If this statement causes surprise in some quarters, one need only to point to the fact the whole common law is judge made law. On the other hand, it is necessary for courts, when developing the common law, to proceed with caution lest they undermine confidence in their judgments. The courts may not make law contrary to the will of Parliament. The courts are therefore constrained when Parliament has spoken. But in general courts are not so constrained when Parliament has not spoken since Parliament's silence and inaction is usually ambiguous. The courts do not have the last word. Parliament may reverse any decision unacceptable to it.[4]

[2] B Cardozo, *The Nature of the Judicial Process* (New Haven: Yale University Press, 1921) 10, cited in G Mettraux, *The Law of Command Responsibility* (Oxford: OUP, 2009) 8.

[3] Mettraux (n 2 above) 9.

[4] Lord Steyn, 'Deference: A Tangled Story', 2004 Judicial Studies Board Lecture, Belfast (25 November 2004) 4. Lord Steyn's speech was referred to by Mr Justice Howie of the South African Law Reform Commission, 'Judges and Law Reform: Judicial Creativity or judicial activism?', ALRAESA Law Reform Conference (2005).

Every court possesses judicial creativity subject to those limitations; the power is inherent in the activities of a court; it is not necessary for it to be the subject of a specific grant.

Judicial creativity is more satisfactory than the pretence that the many propositions produced by an international criminal tribunal for its work flow directly from customary international law. That seldom convinces anyone. All that is found is a chance statement by the Nuremberg Tribunal or by an author. If it is asked what is behind the statement, one is answered with generalities. Save where conventional law or customary law was clearly at work, it is more satisfactory to cite judicial creativity. As to the field covered by judicial creativity in international criminal law, it should be recalled that international criminal law has not quite gone through the early phase of general international law, when the latter borrowed with relative freedom from West European domestic law. Perhaps that is not very material for present purposes, but it should be kept in mind. As to making out a case that a field of human activity within the general mandate of a judicial forum requires the application of judicial creativity, all that has to be shown is that, if judicial creativity did not apply, there would be an intolerable gap in the law and in the capacity of the tribunal to deliver that justice which it was established to give. The showing of this, one way or another, would be self-evident; time would not be spent on the subject. What demands closer study is the subsidiary, if thornier, question as to which of any number of rival propositions in a given field is enjoined as law by judicial creativity.

There is a limitation to be noticed. It could well have been the intention of the lawgiver to leave some matters not subject to law. *South West Africa* has been justly criticized. However, the criticisms do not affect the validity of the pronouncement of the International Court of Justice (ICJ) that in 'the international field, the existence of obligations that cannot in the last resort be enforced by any legal process, has always been the rule rather than the exception'.[5] It is possible that the same self-denying posture underlay a 1996 advisory opinion in *Legality of the Threat or Use of Nuclear Weapons*.[6] There the ICJ took the position that there could be a *lacuna* in the law which even that court was powerless to fill,[7] notwithstanding that what was at risk there was the survival of humanity at large. As Immanuel Kant saw it two hundred years before, 'the greatest problem for the human species is that of attaining a civil society which can administer universal justice.'[8] The difficulty was that it was not practicable to devise a scheme under

[5] [1966] ICJ Rep 6, 46, para 86.

[6] [1996] ICJ Rep 226, para 105(2)(E).

[7] cf the statement in RY Jennings and A Watts (eds), *Oppenheim's International Law: Volume I: Peace* (London/New York: Longmans, 9th edn, 1996) 13, that it is 'not permissible for an international tribunal to pronounce a *non liquet*...'.

[8] Cited in JL Gaddis, *The Cold War, A New History* (New York: Penguin, 2005) 158, from 'Idea for a Universal History with a Cosmopolitan Purpose' in H Reiss (ed), *Kant: Political writings* (HB Nisbet (trans), Cambridge: CUP, 2nd edn, 1991) 45. The passage in the latter reads: 'The greatest problem for the human species, the solution of which nature compels him to seek, is that of attaining a civil society which can administer justice universally.'

which justice could be universal. That is true of the administration of international justice to states; it is equally true of the administration of international justice to individuals. And, though improvements have been made, it remains true to this day.

So, judicial creativity cannot be used to fill any conceivable gap in the law. A reasonable limitation must be found. There is a reasonable limitation in the idea that the gap in the law must be one which prevents a court from dispensing justice as it is required to do under its constituent instrument. Judicial creativity is not licence for unregulated action. A view is that it was really fear of unregulated action which underlay some of the more spectacular episodes of judicial reticence in the past. In conclusion, it appears that there is a basis for holding that states, having established an international criminal court, are to be regarded as also vesting it with a power of judicial creativity. The power is intrinsic and fundamental to the judicial process. It does not have to be justified under any more specific grant of jurisdiction. References to a specific grant of jurisdiction will be made but only for purposes of determining the nature of a particular competence, and not for the purpose of determining whether it is available to the court.

II. The Legal Milieu

The state of international criminal law was meagre at the time of the establishment of the ICTY. The subject has developed enormously through the workings of the Tribunal. It is understandable that, in a relatively new field of law, some part of the growth is regarded as due to judicial creativity where no lines of formal legal development can be traced. And that is true. For example, customary law admitted the competence of conquering states to create criminal courts for the trial of persons accused of war crimes. In the *Yerodia* case the ICJ recognized the like competence of an international criminal tribunal founded by all states,[9] and not only by conquering states. That is important to the ICTY, as it was not instituted by conquering states. But the holding of the ICJ was not clearly grounded in positive law and the courts could only have upheld it through the idea of judicial creativity.

Likewise, in the *Krstić* case the Appeals Chamber of the ICTY approved of a person being ordered by the Tribunal to attend an out-of-court meeting with defence counsel for the latter to decide whether the defence would call him as a witness.[10] The action of the Tribunal was unusual as it was not based on any law in the normal sense. What the Tribunal did was to use judicial creativity in order to have a fair hearing where a hearing was required. One may take it that the duty

[9] *Case Concerning the Arrest Warrant of 11 April 2000 (Democratic Republic of DRC v Belgium)* [2002] ICJ Rep 3.

[10] *Prosecutor v Krstić* (Decision on Application for Subpoenas) IT-98-33-A (1 July 2003).

to hold a fair hearing where a hearing is required is by now part of customary international law,[11] but competence to summon a person to attend such an out-of-court meeting is less clearly so.

Krstić may be compared with *Stakić*. In the latter case, the Appeals Chamber of the ICTY, speaking more conservatively, held that 'it is not the role of the Appeals Chamber to either provide "authorization" to contact a witness, nor to provide the means to facilitate that contact'.[12] But on reflection, the decision in *Krstić* dealing with a specific situation can seek justification from judicial creativity. So too with the *Milošević* case, in which an *amicus curiae* was allowed, as such, to appeal.[13] The Appeals Chamber of the ICTY was obviously concerned to adopt a procedure which ensured that the justice of the case ensued from a hearing on all material points. There being no law which permitted it to do what it thought was right, the Appeals Chamber nevertheless acted to defend its concern.

Other instances of judicial creativity in the ICTY can be cited. It was at first proposed to mention them *seriatim*, but, on reconsideration, it seemed preferable to deal with one only. This is the theory of joint criminal enterprise, with its rival, the theory of co-perpetratorship—two important but controversial theories. The question is which of the two (considered with the question of intent) is more in keeping with the law. The theories will be discussed with a view to showing that the ICTY was not in error in selecting joint criminal enterprise in preference to co-perpetratorship. However, before treating of them, it will be convenient to notice certain initial matters.

It is usual to speak of the 'theory' of joint criminal enterprise and of the 'theory' of co-perpetratorship. That is a convenient course, and it will be followed in this contribution. However, it should not be lost sight of that what is involved is the law represented by those theories. Joint criminal enterprise has roots in the common law and co-perpetratorship has roots in the civil law. Neither, considered with the problem of intent, can claim the status of customary international law. It is recognized that universality of support is not needed for the development of customary international law;[14] generality approaching universality will do, depending on the particular situation. But in this case such generality of support is lacking: each of the two theories is supported by a considerable part of the world. That is not consistent with either theory being regarded as customary international law.

[11] See, to the contrary, *Prosecutor v Gbao* (Decision on Prosecution Motion for Immediate Protective Measures for Witnesses and Victims and for Non-Public Disclosure) SCSL-2003-09-PT (10 October 2003) para 41.

[12] *Prosecutor v Stakić* (Appeals Chamber Judgment) IT-97-24-A (22 March 2006) fn 968.

[13] *Prosecutor v Milošević* (Decision on the Interlocutory Appeal by the *Amici Curiae* Against the Trial Chamber Order Concerning the Presentation and Preparation of the Defence Case) IT-02-54-AR73.6 (20 January 2004). The decision on the point was not unanimous.

[14] *Military and Paramilitary Activities in and against Nicaragua (Nicaragua v United States of America)* (Merits, Judgment) [1986] ICJ Rep, para 186.

The reader will be acquainted with the three categories of criminal liability which are involved in joint criminal enterprise, including in particular category III. In respect of that category, references to the primary offender are references to the actual perpetrator of an additional crime; references to the secondary offender are references to the member of the joint criminal enterprise who had foresight of the risk of an additional crime being committed by the primary offender and who was willing to take that risk.

English cases are for the most part referred to, not of course by way of authority,[15] but only for the value of their reasoning. It is strange that there could be misunderstanding on the propriety of that course, even admitting that it happens to be easier for the writer. And it is appropriate to discuss national law because it is that law which determines the international behaviour of a state. One has of course to bear in mind the distinction between domestic law and international law, but there is no reason to be overwhelmed by the distinction. As to the kind of court visualized, this is any judicial body administering international criminal justice. The ICTY is used in this contribution as the institutional model.

Part of the criticism of joint criminal enterprise relates to terminology. Common law courts have not been consistent in the language used to refer to the idea. In *Brdanin and Talić*, the Trial Chamber sharply observed:[16]

> The Appeals Chamber labelled this concept [common criminal purpose] variously, and apparently interchangeably, as a common criminal plan,[17] a common criminal purpose,[18] a common design or purpose,[19] a common criminal design,[20] a common purpose,[21] a common design,[22] and a common concerted design.[23] The common purpose is also described, more generally, as being part of a criminal enterprise,[24] a common enterprise,[25] and a joint criminal enterprise.[26] For reasons which will become clear, the Trial Chamber prefers the last of these labels, a 'joint criminal enterprise', to describe a common purpose case. It proposes to adhere to that label wherever possible.

When painstakingly collected in one place, the various terms piled one on another do look curious. However, there is no doubt that they portray a basic idea of the common law, which will be intelligible to the average reader. The writer had occasion to note elsewhere that:[27]

> ...there seems to be some flexibility even within the greater coherence of a single national system. In the Court of Criminal Appeal of England and Wales, reference was

[15] Largely, it seems, as a matter of internal discipline, it has been decided by the Appeals Chamber of the ICTY that Trial Chambers must follow the decisions of the Appeals Chamber. It is hard to see any exemption from the general principle that there is no doctrine of binding precedent in international law. Nevertheless, there are elements of the Tribunal's jurisprudence which mimic that doctrine.

[16] *Prosecutor v Brdanin and Talić* (Decision on Form of Further Amended Indictment and Prosecution Application to Amend) IT-99-36-PT (26 June 2001) para 24.

[17] *Prosecutor v Tadić* (Appeals Chamber Judgment) IT-94-1-A (15 July 1999) para 185.

[18] ibid para 187. [19] ibid para 188. [20] ibid paras 191, 193.

[21] ibid paras 193, 195, 204, 225. [22] ibid paras 196, 202, 203, 204.

[23] ibid para 203. [24] ibid para 199. [25] ibid para 204. [26] ibid para 220.

[27] *Prosecutor v Milutinović* (Separate Opinion) IT-99-37-AR72 (21 May 2003) paras 4 and 5.

made in the same case, at the same page, to 'joint enterprise' and to 'common enterprise'.[28] In a Privy Council case, inclusive of a number of authorities which it cited, references were made to 'joint enterprise', 'common unlawful enterprise', 'common enterprise', 'planned enterprise', 'common plan', and 'common purpose'.[29] A common law work of authority uses a subheading, 'Joint enterprise/common design'.[30] Leading common law authors speak of 'common purpose'.[31] That expression seems to be also acceptable in Canada[32] and South Africa.[33] In Australia, it appears that one may speak of 'the doctrine of common purpose—or as it is called, joint venture, common venture, common enterprise, etc'.[34]

The law looks to the substance. The substance in this case is of venerable origin. Lord Mustill referred to 'joint enterprise' and Lord Steyn referred to 'joint criminal enterprise'. It is true that these references were made in a case determined by the House of Lords at the end of the last century,[35] but that was only the shadow of a long past.

III. Category III and the Problem of Intent

Developing a response to the contention that joint criminal enterprise is not a theory known to international criminal law is not without difficulty. As has been submitted, neither co-perpetratorship nor joint criminal enterprise (including liability to conviction without intent) is customary international law. Conventional law is not in point; indeed, save for judicial creativity, there is no basis on which those theories could be recognized as law. Judicial creativity shows that the Tribunal was nevertheless competent to take the required action. Competence to act includes power to select the theory which in the judgement of the Tribunal is most in keeping with judicial creativity. The ICTY has chosen joint criminal enterprise, although there is merit also in co-perpetratorship. The question is which of these two theories was indicated by judicial creativity: was the choice made by the ICTY correct? It is submitted that the decision of the ICTY in favour of joint criminal enterprise should stand.

The subject of joint criminal enterprise was ably discussed by learned counsel before the Appeals Chamber of the ICTY in several cases, including *Krajišnik*,[36]

[28] *R v Anderson* [1966] 2 QB 110, 118; the catchwords of the report also spoke of 'common design'. [29] *Chan Wing-Siu v R* (1985) 80 Cr App R 117.

[30] *Archbold Criminal Pleading, Evidence and Practice 2000* (Sweet & Maxwell, London 2003) ch 18, para 15.

[31] Sir John Smith and B Hogan, *Criminal Law* (London: Butterworths, 8th edn, 1996) 148–9.

[32] D Stuart, *Canadian Criminal Law, A Treatise* (Toronto: Carswell, 3rd edn, 1995) 561–2.

[33] CR Snyman, *Criminal Law* (Durban: Butterworths, 3rd edn, 1995) 249 *et seq*.

[34] P Gillies, *Criminal Law* (New South Wales: Law Book Co, 4th edn, 1997) 174. See also the references to 'common purpose' in *Johns v R* [1980] 28 ALR 155, 173.

[35] *R v Powell* [1999] 1 AC 10–11, 23.

[36] *Prosecutor v Krajišnik* (Appeals Chamber Judgment) IT-00-39-A (17 March 2009).

the last case in which the matter was raised before that Tribunal. In that case, a challenge to the legitimacy of the concept was rejected, an appeal being partially allowed on a point not germane to the present discussion.[37] It is recognized that readers may find it convenient to have the whole matter before them,[38] but, for reasons of achieving priority in a limited contribution, the present argument will be confined to category III of joint criminal enterprise, the essential ground of criticism of categories I and II being more manageably met. The ground of criticism of category III is worrying; it is dealt with below.

A prefatory remark concerns the appellant's statement in the *Krajišnik* case, made in the course of a criticism of joint criminal enterprise, to the effect that category III 'has much in common with American notions of *Pinkerton* liability (vicarious liability for foreseeable crimes committed in furtherance of the conspiracy)'.[39] In a footnote to *Tadić*, the Appeals Chamber of the ICTY referred to *Pinkerton*.[40] The Appeals Chamber was engaged in a more general discussion which showed, as it said, that 'the notion of common purpose upheld in international criminal law has an underpinning in many national systems'.[41] The observation was correct.

The worrying criticism (alluded to above) is that category III allows for conviction of a crime of specific intent without need for proof of intent. As a general matter, intent is, of course, a requirement of the criminal law.[42] Distinguishing it from a concept with which it is apt to be confused, it has been pointed out that '[f]oresight and intention are not synonymous terms'.[43] An accused may have foresight of an event but no intention to cause it to happen. Thus, it is said that the secondary offender may have foresight of an additional crime perpetrated by the primary offender, but that foresight, not being intent, does not justify the conviction of the secondary offender for the additional crime. Chiefly on this ground, joint criminal enterprise is challenged. Two solutions are suggested: (a) the normal requirement to prove intent is removed by analogy with the law relating to accessories; and (b) if that is wrong so that there is a requirement for proof of intent, the requirement is satisfied by regarding the secondary offender as sharing the intent of the primary offender to commit the additional crime.

[37] ibid paras 729–30.

[38] A larger discussion is attempted in the separate opinion filed by the writer in *Krajišnik's* case.

[39] Para 53 of the Dershowitz Brief (so referred to in the *Krajišnik* case), referring to *Pinkerton v United States*, 328 US 640 (1946). See in this connection, J Meierhenrich, 'Conspiracy in International Law' (2006) 2 *Annual Review of Law and Social Science* 341–57.

[40] *Tadić* (Appeals Chamber Judgment) (n 17 above) fn 289.

[41] ibid para 225.

[42] It may be a necessary implication of a statute that intent is not required for a crime, as in cases of 'strict liability' offences. See *Warner v Metropolitan Police Commissioner* [1969] 2 AC 256.

[43] *Powell* (n 35 above) 13. The distinction supplied a reason why the appeal of Mr Sary was allowed by the Pre-Trial Chamber of the Extraordinary Chambers in the Courts of Cambodia (ECCC) on 20 May 2010. See section V of this chapter.

A. Intent was removed

As to the first solution, it can be argued that the normal requirement for proof of intent was removed by close analogy with the law relating to accessories. In the words of Lord Steyn, 'it does not follow that "intent" has precisely the same meaning in every context in the criminal law';[44] the meaning may change. In this case, there has not been a mere change: the normal requirement for proof of intent has been altogether removed, leaving only a requirement to prove foresight. And the existence of foresight is, of course, evident.

(1) The law relating to accessories

In the *Powell* case, it was noted that the liability of a secondary offender in joint criminal enterprise cases is founded on the accessory principle, which is one of general application in criminal law.[45] It was held that '[u]nder the accessory principle criminal liability is dependent on proof of subjective foresight on the part of a participant in the criminal enterprise that the primary offender might commit a greater offence.'[46] In contrast to the general requirement of the criminal law relating to intent, 'foresight is a necessary and sufficient ground of the liability of accessories'.[47]

There would be the anomaly noted by Lord Steyn in his observation that:

[a]t first glance... it is anomalous that a lesser form of culpability is required in the case of a secondary party, *viz.* foresight of the possible commission of the greater offence, whereas in the case of the primary offender the law insists on proof of the specific intention which is an ingredient of the offence.[48]

Giving his answer to this anomaly, that learned judge said:

The answer to this supposed anomaly, and other similar cases across the spectrum of criminal law, is to be found in practical and policy considerations. If the law required proof of the specific intention on the part of a secondary party, the utility of the accessory principle would be gravely undermined. It is just that a secondary party who foresees that the primary offender might kill with the intent sufficient for murder, and assists and encourages the primary offender in the criminal enterprise on this basis, should be guilty of murder. He ought to be criminally liable for harm which he foresaw and which in fact resulted from the crime he assisted and encouraged. But it would in practice almost invariably be impossible for a jury to say that the secondary party wanted death to be caused or that he regarded it as virtually certain. In the real world proof of an intention sufficient for murder would be well nigh impossible in the vast majority of joint enterprise cases.[49]

[44] Lord Steyn in *R v Woollin* [1999] 1 AC 82, 90. [45] *Powell* (n 35 above) 12.
[46] ibid 12. [47] ibid 13 (Lord Steyn). [48] ibid 14. [49] ibid 23.

Further, the appearance of anomaly vanishes when it is borne in mind that cases which stressed the need for proof of intent concerned the primary offender[50]—it was he who perpetrated the additional crime, and, in a charge against him for doing so, he must be proved to have intended to do so. A secondary offender does not perpetrate the additional crime himself; the applicable principle is that deriving from accessory liability, under which foresight is enough. In his case, the requirement for proof of intent has been removed.

(2) This conclusion is in keeping with the objects of the criminal law

The exclusion of the normal requirement for proof of intent by analogy with the law relating to accessories is in keeping with the objects of the criminal law. Dealing with the anomaly referred to above, Lord Steyn said:

> Moreover, ... [t]he criminal justice system exists to control crime. A prime function of that system must be to deal justly but effectively with those who join with others in criminal enterprises. Experience has shown that joint criminal enterprises only too readily escalate into the commission of greater offences. In order to deal with this important social problem the accessory principle is needed and cannot be abolished or relaxed.[51]

Lord Steyn's statement that the 'criminal justice system exists to control crime' refers to a reality which the law must take into account; it is the criminal justice system, as it is, which the law enforces, and not an intellectual construct or a logical remake of what the system should be. Lord Steyn's explanation was that the 'liability is imposed because the secondary party [through the joint criminal enterprise] is assisting in and encouraging a criminal enterprise which he is aware might result in the commission of a greater offence'.[52] As he added, it 'is just that a secondary party who foresees that the primary offender might kill with the intent sufficient for murder, and assists and encourages the primary offender in the criminal enterprise on this basis, should be guilty of murder',[53] ie although the secondary offender lacked the specific intent to murder. The normal requirement to prove intent on the part of the secondary offender is dispensed with.

In *Powell*, Lord Hutton likewise observed:

> I recognise that as a matter of logic there is force in the argument advanced on behalf of the Appellants, and that on one view it is anomalous that if foreseeability of death or really serious harm is not sufficient to constitute *mens rea* for murder in the party who actually carries out the killing, it is sufficient to constitute *mens rea* in a secondary party. But the rules of the common law are not based solely on logic but relate to practical concerns and, in relation to crimes committed in the course of joint enterprises, to the need to give effective protection to the public against criminals operating in gangs. As Lord Salmon stated in *R v. Majewski* [1977] AC 443, 482E, in rejecting criticism based

[50] ibid 13. [51] ibid 23. [52] ibid 14. [53] ibid 23.

on strict logic of a rule of the common law, 'this is the view that has been adopted by the common law of England, which is founded on common sense and experience rather than strict logic'.[54]

In short, Lord Hutton considered that 'there are practical considerations of weight and importance related to considerations of public policy... which prevail over considerations of strict logic'.[55] The remark recalls that of Oliver Wendell Holmes: 'The life of the law is not logic, but experience.'[56] That well-known aphorism does not mean that logic has no place in the law; as the cases will easily attest, it has. Logic has to be applied to the fruits of experience; when so applied, logic supports the conclusion reached by Lord Steyn and Lord Hutton to the effect that the objects of the criminal law require only proof of foreseeability in these cases, proof of specific intent not being required.

B. The secondary offender shares the intent of the primary offender to commit the additional crime

As to the second solution, if, contrary to the foregoing, proof of intent is required, such proof is available. Some of the difficulty has been caused by a neglect to appreciate that the ICTY jurisprudence on joint criminal enterprise is not speaking only of foresight, but is speaking of foresight in the context of willingness of the secondary offender to accept responsibility for a further crime committed by the primary offender, as shown by the active support and encouragement of the secondary offender for the primary offender. Lord Steyn described the secondary offender as one who 'assists and encourages the primary offender in the criminal enterprise'.[57] What then is the result in law?

According to the Appeals Chamber in the *Tadić* case,[58] 'the event must have been predictable';[59] murder may occur where there is a 'forcible removal of civilians at gunpoint'.[60] In the *Borkum Island* case, the murder convictions were presumably 'on the basis that the accused, whether by virtue of their status, role or conduct, were in a position to have predicted that the assault would lead to the killing of the victims by some of those participating in the assault'.[61] In *Manelli*, the Italian Court of Cassation said 'he who requests somebody else to wound or kill cannot answer for a robbery perpetrated by the other person,

[54] ibid 25. [55] ibid.

[56] O Wendell Holmes, *The Common Law* (Boston: Macmillan, 1881) 1, a remark which has spawned much commentary. See also the comments of Lords Steyn and Hutton in *Powell* (n 35 above) 14 and 25. For the view that the judicial function is an art, see Sir Robert Y Jennings, 'The Judicial Function and the Rule of Law in International Relations' in *International Law at the Time of its Codification, Essays in Honour of Roberto Ago*, Vol III (Milan: Giuffrè, 1987) 148.

[57] *Powell* (n 35 above) 14. The idea was referred to in the recent Cambodian case concerning Mr Ieng Sary but given scant juridical emphasis. See the decision of the Pre-Trial Chamber of the ECCC dated 20 May 2010, para 39. [58] *Tadić* (Appeals Chamber Judgment) (n 17 above).

[59] ibid para 218. [60] ibid para 204. [61] ibid para 213.

for this crime does not constitute the logical development of the intended offence'.[62]

The emphasis has been on the need for proof of circumstances from which the additional crime perpetrated by the primary offender could have been 'predicted' by the secondary offender, or regarded by him as a 'logical development' of the original crime. The situation must be such as to associate the secondary offender with the intent of the primary offender to commit the additional crime. How far is the secondary offender from sharing the intent of the primary offender? As was correctly said in *Tadić*, 'more than negligence is required';[63] it must be a case in which 'the accused *willingly took [the] risk*' that an additional crime would be committed.[64] What does '*willingly*' taking the risk mean? A reasonable interpretation is that the secondary offender '*willingly*' takes the risk of an additional crime being committed by the primary offender if the secondary offender identifies himself with the additional crime. So, in putting forward the idea of the third category, the *Tadić* Appeals Chamber did not have in mind foresight and intent as wholly separate notions; it assumed a vital link between them.

Tadić was a case in which a commander (the secondary offender) ordered his soldiers to remove civilian villagers at gunpoint. As the Appeals Chamber of the ICTY said, it was 'foreseeable' that compliance with the order 'might well result in the deaths of one or more of those civilians'.[65] The secondary offender, being engaged in a joint criminal enterprise for the forcible removal of the civilians at *gunpoint* and being therefore aware of the risk of death resulting from the execution of the criminal enterprise by that dangerous method, is identified with the intent of the primary offender (the particular soldier) who causes a death in the course of such a removal. The requirement that there should be this kind of connection between foreseeability on the part of the secondary offender and intent on the part of the primary offender removes the gravamen of the criticism that the secondary offender is being convicted of a crime in respect of which he lacks the necessary intent.

The position is apt to be obscured by the concept of recklessness. But nothing in the discussion of recklessness impairs this vital link between foreseeability and intent. To adopt the explanation given by Sir John Smith, a leading English jurist, in the case of murder (which requires proof of specific intent),[66] the secondary offender 'must be proved to have been reckless, not merely whether death might be caused, but whether murder might be committed; he must have been aware, not merely that death or grievous bodily harm might be caused, but that it

[62] *Giustizia penale*, 1950, Part II, cols 696–7 cited in *Tadić* (Appeals Chamber Judgment) (n 17 above) para 218.

[63] *Tadić* (Appeals Chamber Judgment) (n 17 above) para 220.

[64] ibid para 228 (emphasis in original).

[65] ibid para 204.

[66] Murder is a crime of specific intent. See *Archbold* (n 30 above) paras 17-35(a) and 17-37, and *Blackstone's Criminal Practice 2007* (Oxford: OUP, 2007) para B1.11(a).

might be caused intentionally'.[67] Thus, in cases of recklessness the foresight of the secondary offender has to be of the *intent* of the primary offender.

Indeed, there is a view that the secondary offender may be taken to agree to the commission by the primary offender of the additional crime if particular circumstances were to arise. Recalling the attitude to this of British courts, Lord Mustill said in *Powell*:[68]

> Throughout the modern history of the law on secondary criminal liability ... the responsibility of the secondary defendant has been founded on his participation in a *joint enterprise* of which the commission of the crime by the principal offender formed part. Any doubts on this score were set at rest by *R v. Anderson*; *R v. Morris* [1966] 2 QB 110 by reference to which countless juries have been directed over the years. As it seemed to me the House should not depart from this long-established principle without the strongest reasons. The problem is to accommodate in the principle the foresight of the secondary party about what the main offender might do. Two aspects of this problem are simple. If S did not foresee what was actually done by P he is not liable for it [S being the secondary offender, P being the primary offender], since it could not have been part of any *joint enterprise*. This is what the court decided in *R v. Anderson*; *R v. Morris*. Conversely, if S did foresee P's act this would always, as a matter of *common sense*, be relevant to the jury's decision on whether it formed part of a course of action to which both S and P *agreed*, albeit often on the basis that the action would be taken if particular circumstances should arise.[69]

A secondary offender, although guilty of the first crime, is not guilty of an additional crime committed by the primary offender if he does not foresee it or if the additional crime is wholly outside the ambit of the joint criminal enterprise. It is otherwise if the secondary offender foresees a crime within that ambit being committed by the primary offender in addition to the crime originally agreed. Why? Because, as Lord Mustill said, the additional crime would have 'formed part of a course of action to which both [the secondary offender and the primary offender] *agreed*, albeit often on the basis that the action would be taken if particular circumstances should arise'.[70] The secondary offender being *agreed* with the primary offender on the commission of the additional crime by the primary offender in certain circumstances, the secondary offender shares the primary offender's intent to commit that crime if those circumstances arise. What is left to the secondary offender is the decision whether those circumstances have arisen, not the formation of the intent. That intent was and remains an intent

[67] Sir John Smith, 'Criminal Liability of Accessories: Law and Law Reform' (1997) 113 LQR 453, 464, cited by Lord Steyn in *Powell* (n 35 above) 13–14.

[68] *Powell* (n 35 above) 10–11. The case is still good law. See *R v Mendez* (2010) EWCA Crim 516, (2010) 107 (14) LSG 19 CA (Crim Div). *Powell* is referred to in A Cassese, 'The Proper Limits of Individual Responsibility under the Doctrine of Joint Criminal Enterprise' (2007) 5(1) JICJ 109. See also in the same volume articles by JD Ohlin, H van der Wilt, K Gustafson, K Ambos, and E van Sliedregt.

[69] *Powell* (n 35 above) 14 (emphasis added).

[70] Emphasis added.

which was fully formed by the secondary offender: it continues at the time of the crime.

The ICTY has been thoughtfully reminded of the consequences of 'a failure to understand the philosophical significance of knowledge and intentionality in criminal law theory'.[71] However, it is not knowledge alone which is concerned here; it is knowledge coupled with willingness (as evidenced by active support) to take the risk of an additional crime being committed by the primary offender. That willingness forms a sufficiently substantial link between knowledge and intent to justify the secondary offender being regarded as sharing the intent of the primary offender and so liable to be convicted for the additional crime perpetrated by the latter. The secondary offender intended it, though conditionally. In short, in cases of this kind, knowledge amounts to intent. In international law, even more than in national law, it is the substance which matters.[72]

C. Summary of the position in joint criminal enterprise

It is argued in section A above, that the requirement for proof of intent in a prosecution against the secondary offender was removed by analogy with the law relating to accessories. If that is correct, the only requirement thereafter remaining was a requirement to prove foresight. But it is not disputed that that foresight existed. Alternatively, it is argued in section B above, that the secondary offender shared the intent of the primary offender to commit the additional crime. If that is correct, it is not disputed that, if proof of intent is required in these cases, the secondary offender has it. The road leading to these two conclusions is a common law one; but the conclusions are based on a course of reasoning which commends itself for adoption by the ICTY in international criminal law, provided that a mechanism of adoption can be found. There being no positive law supporting the adoption of these two conclusions as part of international criminal law, and such adoption being necessary for the fulfilment of the mission of the ICTY to administer international criminal justice, it is permissible for the Tribunal to draw on judicial creativity. Judicial creativity supplies the needed mechanism of adoption. For these reasons, it is respectfully submitted that joint criminal enterprise is a theory known to international criminal law.

[71] JD Ohlin, 'Three Conceptual Problems with the Doctrine of Joint Criminal Enterprise' (2007) 5 JICJ 69, 79.

[72] *Barcelona Traction, Light and Power Company Ltd* (Preliminary Objections) [1964] ICJ Rep 62–3, Judge Koo; *Barcelona Traction, Light and Power Company Ltd* (Second Phase) [1970] ICJ Rep 127, Judge Tanaka.

IV. Co-perpetratorship

A. A criticism of joint criminal enterprise

Joint criminal enterprise has come in for much criticism. Judge Lindholm has offered one which, in its substance, may be taken as representative of the views of adherents of co-perpetratorship. In his interesting remarks, Judge Lindholm said that the 'so-called basic form of joint criminal enterprise does not, in my opinion, have any substance of its own. It is nothing more than a new label affixed to a long since well-known concept or doctrine in most jurisdictions as well as in international criminal law, namely co-perpetration.'[73] The judge added, severely, that 'the concept or "doctrine" [of joint criminal enterprise] has caused confusion and a waste of time and is in my opinion of no benefit to the work of the Tribunal or the development of international law'.[74]

The theory[75] of co-perpetratorship (including indirect perpetratorship)[76] is subscribed to by several countries. It is understandable that there is a preference by some jurists for it, but it is prudent to be wary of a 'doctrinal disposition to come out differently'.[77] Preference for a certain doctrine is not the same as asserting that another doctrine has no merit. When another doctrine is suggested, it has to be looked at carefully. It is appropriate for the ICTY to take respectful notice of it if its judges, who are from various national jurisdictions, are to produce a jurisprudence which belongs to all.

B. Control

In the *Tadić* case the ICTY Appeals Chamber affirmed that 'the foundation of criminal responsibility is the principle of personal culpability'.[78] Similar statements are to be found elsewhere. To respect that important principle, the supporters of co-perpetratorship take the view that it is necessary in every case to establish that the accused himself perpetrated the additional crime, as distinguished from his simply being imputed with its commission. Co-perpetratorship seeks to do the former by laying down a juridical link which would make the secondary offender liable for the additional crime on the basis that he had personally perpetrated it. That link depends upon control being exercised by the secondary offender over the primary offender.

[73] *Prosecutor v Simić* (Judge Lindholm Separate and Partly Dissenting Opinion) IT-95-9-T (17 October 2003) para 2. [74] *Simić* (Judge Lindholm) (n 73 above) para 5.

[75] It is said that one should not speak of 'the theory of control'. The 'forbidden' term is used in chapter VII of *Videla and ors* National Appeals Court (Criminal Division) for the Federal District of Buenos Aires, Docket No 13 (9 December 1985).

[76] See the *Politbüro* case (BGHSt) 40, 236 *et seq* (26 July 1974); and *Videla* (n 75 above).

[77] See *Lewis v A-G Jamaica and anor* [2001] 2 AC 50, 90, Lord Hoffmann dissenting.

[78] *Tadić* (Appeals Chamber Judgment) (n 17 above) para 186.

The concept of control was illustrated in this example given by Claus Roxin, a leading exponent of co-perpetratorship. Speaking of 'the bank robber with the gun or the perpetrator of the murder holding the victim', he said:

> The co-perpetrator can achieve nothing on his own: the intimidation of the bank employees and the seizing of the victim do not ensure success. The plan only 'works' if the accomplice works with the other person. That other person is just as helpless however; if the bank employees are not fully controlled, he will be arrested; and if no one seizes the victim, he will defend himself or flee. Both are therefore in the same position: they can only realize their plan in so far as they act together, but each individually can ruin the whole plan if he does not carry out his part. To this extent he is in control of the act.[79]

Thus, to make the secondary offender personally liable for the additional crime of the primary offender as if it had been perpetrated by the secondary offender himself, it has to be proved that the secondary offender exercised control over the primary offender. Control is not an element of joint criminal enterprise, as it links the secondary offender's liability to his willingness to accept responsibility for the primary offender's additional crime and to his active support for it.

C. Joint criminal enterprise and co-perpetratorship compared

How did the ICTY react to the issues raised? On 15 July 1999 the ICTY Appeals Chamber in the *Tadić* case referred to 'the notion of co-perpetratorship' but did not adopt it.[80] The notion was not chosen in *Stakić*, decided by the ICTY Appeals Chamber on 22 March 2006.[81] The ICTY Appeals Chamber in that case unanimously affirmed its preference for joint criminal enterprise over co-perpetratorship, finding that the former was 'firmly established in customary international law',[82] as had been found in *Tadić* in 1999 after an examination of post-Second World War cases. Many decisions have followed the *Tadić* holding. After a hesitant start at the ICTR, joint criminal enterprise is now enthroned in that Tribunal's jurisprudence.[83] Did the ICTY err in giving support to joint criminal enterprise?

On reflection, the writer would respectfully doubt the *Tadić* finding (to which he was a party) that joint criminal enterprise is customary international law insofar as it permits a conviction without proof of intent: the known fact is that a

[79] C Roxin, *Täterschaft und Tatherrschaft* (Berlin/New York: de Gruyter, 6th edn, 1994) 278.

[80] *Tadić* (Appeals Chamber Judgment) (n 17 above) para 201.

[81] *Stakić* (Appeals Chamber Judgment) (n 12 above) para 62.

[82] ibid, repeating the holding of *Tadić* (Appeals Chamber Judgment) (n 17 above) para 220.

[83] See *Prosecutor v Kayishema and Ruzindana* (Appeals Chamber) ICTR-95-1-A (1 June 2001) paras 191–3; *Prosecutor v Rwamakuba* (Appeals Chamber Decision on Interlocutory Appeal Regarding Application of Joint Criminal Enterprise to the Crime of Genocide) ICTR-98-44-AR72.4 (22 October 2004) para 31; *Prosecutor v Ntakirutimana* (Appeals Chamber Judgment) ICTR-96-17-A (13 December 2004) para 468; and *Karemera* (Appeals Chamber Decision on Jurisdictional Appeals: Joint Criminal Enterprise) ICTR-98-44-AR72.5 and ICTR-98-44-AR72.6 (12 April 2006) paras 13, 16, 17.

considerable part of the world prefers co-perpetratorship. But that concerns a question of classification of the theories and does not necessarily affect the question as to what are the legal incidents to which the theories give rise. On this point, it is difficult to find superior merit in co-perpetratorship. Proponents of co-perpetratorship stress that under it the delinquent 'behind the scenes' would be liable.[84] But in this respect there is no difference from joint criminal enterprise if there is evidence of appropriate incriminating activity 'behind the scenes'—a requirement which, on ordinary principles of the criminal law, applies to both theories.

Insofar as the ICTY Appeals Chamber affirmed in *Tadić* that 'the foundation of criminal responsibility is the principle of personal culpability',[85] any difficulties in reconciling this with the position of the secondary offender in the common law are resolved by the circumstance that (though he himself did not perpetrate the additional crime) he willingly accepted liability for it and actively supported and encouraged its commission by the primary offender. Admittedly, that is based on inferential reasoning. But inferential reasoning is not confined to one theory. The example given by Claus Roxin shows that it is by a series of inferences, based on the concept of control, that the conclusion is reached that the secondary offender himself perpetrated the additional crime.

With regard to Judge Lindholm's cited views, it is, with respect, not a matter of a 'new label'; if it were, argument on the substance would be foreclosed. In fact, there are material differences: as seen, co-perpetratorship restricts criminal liability to cases in which there was control. Joint criminal enterprise does not know of that limitation and accordingly provides room for growth. What is interesting is that it follows from the above that a secondary offender can have criminal liability under joint criminal enterprise when he could not under co-perpetratorship. Views may differ as to whether he should have such liability; it is respectfully submitted that he should. His culpability for the additional crime is not diminished by the fact that he was not in 'control' if he willingly accepted responsibility for it and actively gave aid and encouragement to its perpetration.

Co-perpetratorship requires that the contribution of the secondary offender to the criminal enterprise has to be substantial. This may be compared with the position in joint criminal enterprise. In 'general, there is no specific legal requirement [in joint criminal enterprise] that the accused make a substantial contribution to [a] joint criminal enterprise.'[86] Exceptionally such a requirement may exist, but only 'to determine whether [the accused] participated in the joint criminal enterprise'.[87] It is therefore apparent that, in a joint criminal enterprise, 'the

[84] See the *Politbüro* case (n 76 above), which concerned the criminal responsibility of East German high political officials for the killings of escaping citizens; and *Videla* (n 75 above), which concerned the criminal responsibility of Argentine leaders for 'disappearances'. Both cases involved accused who were 'behind the scenes'.

[85] *Tadić* (Appeals Chamber Judgment) (n 17 above) para 186.

[86] *Prosecutor v Kvočka* (Appeals Chamber Judgment) IT-98-30/1-A (28 February 2005) para 97 (footnotes omitted).

[87] ibid. See also *Krajišnik* (Appeals Chamber Judgment) (n 36 above) paras 675, 680, 729, 730.

Prosecutor need not demonstrate that the accused's participation is a *sine qua non*, without which the crimes could or would not have been committed'.[88] This applies also to the additional crime. The position on both counts is otherwise in co-perpetratorship; but there is no overriding merit in requiring proof of a substantial contribution by the secondary offender if there is proof of willingness of the secondary offender to accept responsibility for the additional crime together with proof that the secondary offender actively supported and encouraged the primary offender to perpetrate it.

If it is understood correctly, the example of control given by Roxin relates to a case in which the secondary offender is *particeps* in the perpetration of the additional crime. That is not required in joint criminal enterprise. The idea of co-perpetratorship suggests that there are participants in the forbidden activity who are not within the control of a member of the plan and who cannot therefore be prosecuted under that theory. Under joint criminal enterprise, they can, control not being an ingredient of a prosecution under this theory. The exemption of some participants from prosecution is a matter for prosecutorial discretion or the authority setting up the tribunal. A tendency to glide over the point will not do. It is safer for the ICTY to proceed in a way which does not present the problem of control, namely, on the footing of the willingness of the secondary offender to accept responsibility for the additional crime of the primary offender and his active support for it, ie on the basis of joint criminal enterprise.

It is hoped that the foregoing has outlined the main differences between the two theories, considered as wholes. It cannot be said that all the differences favour one theory. But the balance inclines in favour of joint criminal enterprise. Co-perpetratorship lacks needed flexibility. Admitting that it has merit, it does not appear that this is sufficient to warrant the substitution of co-perpetratorship for joint criminal enterprise in the existing decision of the Tribunal. The writer had the honour of presiding over the bench of the Appeals Chamber of the ICTY which adopted joint criminal enterprise. And he agrees with its judgment on that point. But, to remove any impression to the contrary, he desires to state that he does not claim authorship; that distinction belongs to another member of the bench.[89]

V. Postscript

On 20 May 2010, a decision was rendered by the Cambodia Pre-Trial Chamber under the title 'Decision on the Appeals against the Co-Investigative Judge for the Crime of Joint Criminal Enterprise (JCE)'. The suggestion was that the

[88] *Kvočka* (Appeals Chamber Judgment) (n 86 above) para 98 (footnotes omitted).

[89] The text of the judgment was authored by Judge Antonio Cassese; information to that effect was set out in para 11 of Radovan Karadžić's motion filed on 27 March 2009 in *Prosecutor v Radovan Karadžić* IT-95-5/18-PT.

case had much to say on joint criminal enterprise, but this does not appear to be borne out. In paragraph 88 of the decision, the Pre-Trial Chamber said: it 'upholds the appeal insofar as the applicability of JCE III before the ECCC is concerned'. Paragraphs 77 and 83 were also broad. But in paragraph 87, the Pre-Trial Chamber explained:

> The Pre-Trial Chamber is of the view that it does not need to decide whether a number of national systems, which can be regarded as representative of the world's major legal systems, recognise that a standard of *mens rea* lower than direct intent may apply in relation to crimes committed outside the common criminal purpose and amount to commission. Indeed, even if this were the case and the Chamber found that the third form of JCE was punishable in relation to international crimes, the Pre-Trial Chamber is not satisfied that such liability was foreseeable to the charged persons in 1975–1979, that is that crimes falling outside the common criminal purpose but [which] were natural consequences of the realization of that purpose and foreseeable to them could trigger their responsibility as co-perpetrators.

Thus, the Pre-Trial Chamber (comprising five judges) did not pronounce on the question whether, in the absence of proof of direct intent, a person could be convicted under category III of joint criminal enterprise; it held that, even if that were so, the necessary proof of foreseeableness was wanting. The decision was not in conflict with the holding in *Tadić* that, in the absence of proof of intent, a person could be convicted under joint criminal enterprise category III. If there was no customary international law authorizing a prosecution where there was no intent, a solution has to be sought by exploring the concept of judicial creativity. The latter is part of international law. The ICTY was entitled to take the view that international creativity authorized a prosecution on the basis that there was no intent. That there is no explicit averment that judicial creativity was so used is not a barrier to recourse to that concept.

VI. Conclusion

A comment, though seemingly striking, can miss the opposing point of view. On the other hand, an author has to know when it is time to give up. On the basis that the law is as stated by the court, a judge may join colleagues in implementing the disposition of the court, much as he may have previously disagreed with the underlying reasoning. As to inconsistencies in the jurisprudence, every law student knows that they exist. This is not a matter for pride. But, subject to clarity, it helps to recall that judicial discourse inclines before courtesy.

The writer has referred to an error of the Tribunal, to which he was a party; it concerns the question whether joint criminal enterprise was customary international law insofar as it permits of a conviction without proof of intent. In this respect, two rival theories—joint criminal enterprise and co-perpetratorship—hold sway in major parts of the world, but not generally; neither is therefore entitled to be regarded as customary international law. Excepting judicial creativity, there is no basis on which they could apply in this case. By contrast, there can be need for one or the other theory to apply if the Tribunal is to fulfil its mission of administering international criminal justice. Is there some body of law lurking around which authorizes the application of either theory? There is: that body of law is represented by judicial creativity. Pursuant to judicial creativity, a tribunal can validly say that it will apply one theory or the other. The ICTY has made its decision: it has opted for joint criminal enterprise. The admitted merit of co-perpetratorship is not sufficient to warrant its substitution for joint criminal enterprise.

Thus, judicial creativity enables the ICTY to say that joint criminal enterprise forms part of international criminal law, arguably on the basis that states which establish an international criminal court are presumed to vest it with that power. It is submitted, however, that recourse to judicial creativity should only be had where it is necessary to fill a gap in the law which would disable the court from administering justice in accordance with its mission. The new law should be consistent with the old; it should not represent a break. Recourse to judicial creativity should not be allowed to degenerate into mere judicial activism, in the sense of a personal predilection of a judge which is sought to be given the force of law by his *ipse dixit*.

9

Omission Liability at the International Criminal Tribunals—A Case for Reform

Gideon Boas

I. Introduction

It is clearly tempting, when examining forms of individual responsibility in the context of substantive international criminal law,[1] to look to their respective elements and application in domestic criminal law systems. Indeed, the international criminal tribunals regularly examine common law and civil law systems with the aim of extracting general principles of international law,[2] or even for evidence of state practice and *opinio juris* that might lead to the articulation of a rule of customary international law.[3] On occasion, this analysis has led to productive and supportable conclusions that an international legal rule exists;[4] at other times, superficial reference to a handful of cases, scattered practice, or (less often) *opinio juris* has been used to assert the existence of general principles or custom, where in fact little evidence of a rule of international law can be shown to exist.[5] The effect of this developing practice in international criminal law

[1] See G Boas, J Bischoff, and N Reid, *Forms of Responsibility in International Criminal Law* (Cambridge: CUP, 2007) 2–4 (for a preliminary discussion of the forms of responsibility and how they are structured) and generally (for a discussion of all the forms of international criminal responsibility). The articulations of the forms of responsibility are derived from the Statutes of the international criminal tribunals, including the ICC Statute, Art 25; the ICTY Statute, Art 7; the ICTR Statute, Art 6. It is worth noting briefly that complicity is sometimes referred to as a form of responsibility as it relates to the crime of genocide; it is, however, more properly identified as a substantive crime in its own right (complicity to commit genocide) (chapter 4, s 4.2).

[2] See Statute of the International Court of Justice (adopted 26 June 1945, entered into force 24 October 1945) (1945) 39 AJIL Supplement 215, Art 38(1)(c).

[3] ICJ Statute (n 2 above) Art (1)(b).

[4] See eg *Prosecutor v Furundžija* (Trial Chamber Judgment) IT-95-17/1-T (10 December 1998) paras 165–86, setting out the basis in custom for the international crime of rape and the elements of the offence in general principles of international law.

[5] See eg *Prosecutor v Simić* (Trial Chamber Decision on the Prosecution Motion Under Rule 73 for a Ruling Concerning the Testimony of a Witness) IT-95-9-PT (27 July 1999) paras 73–4, concluding that the Geneva Conventions and the general practice of states under those treaties with regard to the International Committee of the Red Cross (ICRC) established a customary

may at times be to weaken the fundamental legal rights of accused persons[6] and substantially dilute custom as a source of international (or at least international criminal) law.[7]

One such way in which the *ad hoc* Tribunals (the International Criminal Tribunal for the former Yugoslavia (ICTY) and the International Criminal Tribunal for Rwanda (ICTR)) have stretched the available evidence of a form of responsibility in international criminal law is in the area of omission liability relating to aiding and abetting. Through a string of rulings dating back to the *Aleksovski* trial judgment in 1999,[8] the *ad hoc* Tribunals—at the trial and appellate levels—have held that fulfilment of the requirement that an aider and abettor lend assistance or support to the perpetration of a relevant crime may occur not only by means of positive action, but also through omission.[9] This legal

international legal right against disclosure of such information; but see, in the same decision, the Separate Opinion of Judge David Hunt, dissenting from the majority's conclusion that customary international law requires recognition of an absolute privilege, and noting that 'it is an enormous step to assume' that states had ever contemplated an absolute immunity of the ICRC from giving evidence in international courts, particularly in light of the role of such courts in enforcing the Geneva Conventions. See also T Meron, 'Editorial Comment: Revival of Customary Humanitarian law' (2005) 99 AJIL 817, in particular arguing (at 818 and 821 *et seq*) that international criminal tribunals have taken an essentially conservative and traditional approach to the identification and application of customary international law principles—an assertion that is often contradicted by the tribunals' actual practice. These issues are at times referred to in some of the literature: see eg A Zahar and G Sluiter, *International Criminal Law: A Critical Introduction* (Oxford/New York: OUP, 2008) 79–105; S Ratner, J Abrams, and J Bischoff, *Accountability for Human Rights Atrocities in International Law: Beyond the Nuremberg Legacy* (Oxford/New York: OUP, 3rd edn, 2009) 22; R Cryer *et al*, *An Introduction to International Criminal Law and Procedure* (Cambridge: CUP, 2007) 111; G Mettraux, *International Crimes and the Ad Hoc Tribunals* (Oxford/New York: OUP, 2005) 13–18.

6 A point well made by Mettraux (n 5 above) 15–16.

7 The *ad hoc* Tribunals are not alone in their watering-down of the elements of custom. The International Court of Justice (ICJ) itself has recently relaxed or largely ignored its own articulation of the required standards to be met for evidence of custom to be established. Indeed, despite there being no formal system of precedent in international law (ICJ Statute, Art 59), the ICJ has increasingly begun to rely upon its own past decisions respecting statements of the customary international legal status of a proposition, or to simply state that it has reviewed state practice without articulating clearly the sources of such a review: see eg *Case Concerning the Arrest Warrant of 11 April 2000 (Democratic Republic of Congo v Belgium)* [2002] ICJ Rep 3, para 58. An example of the relaxation of its previously rigorous requirement that state practice and *opinio juris* be identified before custom can be said to exist is the heavy reliance on UN Resolutions: see eg *Legal Consequences of the Construction of a Wall in the Occupied Palestinian Territories* (Advisory Opinion) [2004] ICJ Rep 136, paras 18–23.

8 *Prosecutor v Aleksovski* (Trial Chamber Judgment) IT-95-14/1-T (25 June 1999) para 88.

9 See eg *Prosecutor v Mrkšić* (Appeals Chamber Judgment) IT-95-13-T (5 May 2009) para 135; *Prosecutor v Orić* (Appeals Chamber Judgment) IT-03-68-A (3 July 2008) para 523; *Nahimana v Prosecutor* (Appeals Chamber Judgment) ICTR-99-52-A (28 November 2007) para 482; *Prosecutor v Simić* (Appeals Chamber Judgment) IT-95-9-A (28 November 2006) paras 85–6; *Prosecutor v Seromba* (Appeals Chamber Judgment) ICTR-2001-66-A (12 March 2008) para 56; *Prosecutor v Blagojević and Jokić* (Appeals Chamber Judgment) IT-02-60-A (9 May 2007) para 127; *Prosecutor v Blaškić* (Appeals Chamber Judgment) IT-95-14-A (29 July 2004) para 47; *Prosecutor v Aleksovski* (Appeals Chamber Judgment) IT-95-14/1-A (24 March 2000) para 162; *Prosecutor v Milutinović et al* (Trial Chamber Judgment) IT-05-87-T (26 February 2009)

proposition reached its zenith in the *Mrkšić* appeal judgment in 2009, in which the Appeals Chamber confirmed the Trial Chamber's statement that aiding and abetting by omission is a recognized mode of liability under the International Tribunal's jurisdiction.[10] Nonetheless, aiding and abetting by omission is often asserted in passing and, when it is applied to facts in a given case, the Chamber has never articulated what the legal foundation for this form of responsibility is in international law.

In preliminary motions filed by the accused in the *Karadžić* case in 2009, the ICTY was given an opportunity to consider whether there is indeed such a form of responsibility. One such motion challenged the often cited proposition that aiding and abetting by omission exists. The Tribunal approach has been to simply state the existence of this form of omission liability without explaining either its content or its legal foundation in international law.[11] Both the Trial and Appeals Chambers in the *Karadžić* case determined that the question of aiding and abetting by omission was not one of jurisdiction and declined to consider the substantive issue prior to the commencement of the trial.[12]

While there are a variety of forms of individual criminal responsibility available to the international criminal courts and tribunals, many such forms share domestic analogues and are readily identifiable as reflecting approaches to the attribution of guilt in most national criminal justice systems. Some forms of responsibility, on the other hand, are quintessentially representative of international criminal law and reflect the preoccupation with attributing guilt to senior level accused. Such forms are command (or superior) responsibility and joint criminal enterprise, particularly as developed in the case law of the ICTY.[13] Both these forms of responsibility are the subject of separate chapters in this book.[14]

For the most part, the other forms of responsibility—reflecting accomplice or accessory liability—have not given rise to a great deal of controversy or complexity. Accordingly, they are not dealt with in any depth either in this chapter or

para 90 (Vol 1); *Prosecutor v Muvunyi* (Trial Chamber Judgment and Sentence) ICTR-00-55A-T (12 September 2006) para 470; *Prosecutor v Orić* (Trial Chamber Judgment) IT-03-68-T (30 June 2006) para 283; *Prosecutor v Strugar* (Trial Chamber Judgment) IT-01-42-T (31 January 2005) para 349; *Prosecutor v Brđanin* (Trial Chamber Judgment) IT-99-36-T (1 September 2004) para 271; *Prosecutor v Galić* (Trial Chamber Judgment and Opinion) IT-98-29-T (5 December 2003) para 168; *Aleksovski* (Trial Chamber Judgment) (n 8 above) para 88.

[10] *Mrkšić* (Appeals Chamber Judgment) (n 9 above) paras 133–5.

[11] See *Prosecutor v Karadžić* (Preliminary Motion on Lack of Jurisdiction Concerning Omission Liability) IT-95-5/18-AR72.1 (25 March 2009), and the substantive ruling of the Trial Chamber: *Prosecutor v Karadžić* (Decision on Six Preliminary Motions Challenging Jurisdiction) IT-95-5/18-AR72.1 (28 April 2009). The author of this chapter drafted the motions on behalf of Dr Karadžić in respect of this issue.

[12] ibid.

[13] See Boas *et al* (n 1 above) 3.

[14] See the contributions of Robert Cryer and Mohamed Shahabuddeen (Chs 7 and 8 above).

this book. One exception to this proposition, however, is the development by the *ad hoc* Tribunals of aiding and abetting by omission.

This chapter will consider the determination at the *ad hoc* Tribunals that aiding and abetting by omission is a form of responsibility in international criminal law. The elements and history of this form of responsibility will first be examined. The chapter will also consider the challenge made in the *Karadžić* case to the proper foundation in international law for the existence of this form of omission liability. The failure by the *ad hoc* Tribunals to articulate adequate evidence of the existence of this form of omission liability serves as an example of declaratory lawmaking, by which the *ad hoc* Tribunals have at times shown a tendency to assert the existence of a rule of customary international law without satisfying the elemental requirements of this important process of international lawmaking. In this way, the judicial creativity shown by the *ad hoc* Tribunals can at times extend beyond the proper limits of a court in applying existing law. The early position at the International Criminal Court (ICC) will also be briefly considered, as will the importance of the Rome Statute's position on omission liability.

It will be argued that, unlike command responsibility, aiding and abetting by omission has not been shown to have a foundation in customary international law and it does not have a clear or coherent place in the realm of international criminal law. Command responsibility is, it will be posited, the only true form of omission liability in international criminal law, and the development of aiding and abetting by omission is legally flawed.

II. Aiding and Abetting by Omission—An Incoherent Development

A. The elements of aiding and abetting

As with all forms of responsibility in international criminal law, the physical and mental elements of aiding and abetting must be established before a person can be held responsible for such participation in an international crime.[15] While the early case law of the *ad hoc* Tribunals explains that the phrase 'aiding and abetting' refers to two discrete activities (aiding meaning 'giving assistance to someone' and abetting 'facilitating the commission of an act by being sympathetic

[15] Much of the *ad hoc* Tribunal case law, as well as literature discussing forms of (international) criminal responsibility, erroneously refers to the physical and mental elements of the forms of responsibility as *actus reus* and *mens rea*. Reference in this chapter will be made to these forms of responsibility as having physical and mental elements. This is because 'they are not in themselves criminal, but only serve to attribute criminality to the accused when combined with the criminal conduct and mental state of the physical perpetrator' (Boas *et al* (n 1 above) 4).

thereto'),[16] prosecutors have consistently charged—and chambers have consistently applied—these forms of liability as a single legal concept.[17]

B. The mental elements of aiding and abetting

The mental elements of aiding and abetting are: (1) that an accused must have knowledge or awareness that their acts assist the physical perpetrator in the commission of the crime;[18] and (2) they must be aware of the essential elements of the crime ultimately committed by the perpetrator.[19] Some early jurisprudence suggested that the aider and abettor must have intended to assist or facilitate the commission of the crime through their act;[20] the *Blaškić* appeal judgment, however, rejected this proposition and instead adopted a less stringent approach: 'knowledge on the part of the aider and abettor that his acts assist in the commission of the principal perpetrator's crime suffices for the *mens rea* requirement of this mode of participation'.[21] This less stringent approach with respect to the aider and abettor's required intent was articulated coherently in the *Kunarac* case, where the Trial Chamber held that the accused must take 'the conscious decision to act in the knowledge that he thereby supports the commission of the crime'.[22]

[16] *Milutinović* (Trial Chamber Judgment) (n 9 above) Vol I, fn 107; *Prosecutor v Akayesu* (Trial Chamber Judgment) ICTR-96-4-T (2 September 1998); *Prosecutor v Kvočka et al* (Trial Chamber Judgment) IT-98-30/1-T (2 November 2001) para 254; *Prosecutor v Blaškić* (Trial Chamber Judgment) IT-95-14-T (3 March 2000) 92, fn 510.

[17] See eg *Prosecutor v Ndindabahizi* (Trial Chamber Judgment and Sentence) ICTR-2001-71-I (15 July 2004) para 457; *Prosecutor v Kajelijeli* (Trial Chamber Judgment and Sentence) ICTR-98-44A-T (1 December 2003) para 765; *Prosecutor v Semanza* (Trial Chamber Judgment and Sentence) ICTR-97-20-T (15 May 2003) para 384. However, there are a few examples of chambers apparently convicting only of abetting in respect of a given count in the indictment: eg *Prosecutor v Muhimana* (Trial Chamber Judgment and Sentence) ICTR-95-1B-T (28 April 2005) para 553; *Prosecutor v Musema* (Trial Chamber Judgment and Sentence) ICTR-96-13-T (27 January 2000) para 908; *Akayesu* (Trial Chamber Judgment) (n 16 above) para 707.

[18] See *Mrkšić* (Appeals Chamber Judgment) (n 9 above) para 49; *Blaškić* (Appeals Chamber Judgment) (n 9 above) para 49. Accord *Simić* (Appeals Chamber Judgment) (n 9 above) para 86; *Prosecutor v Vasiljević* (Appeals Chamber Judgment) IT-98-32-A (25 February 2004) para 102; *Prosecutor v Kayishema and Ruzindana* (Appeals Chamber Judgment (Reasons)) ICTR-95-1-A (1 June 2001) para 186; *Aleksovski* (Appeals Chamber Judgment) (n 9 above) para 162; *Prosecutor v Tadić* (Appeals Chamber Judgment) IT-94-1-A (15 July 1999) para 229.

[19] See eg *Mrkšić* (Appeals Chamber Judgment) (n 9 above) para 49; *Simić* (Appeals Chamber Judgment) (n 9 above) para 86; *Aleksovski* (Appeals Chamber Judgment) (n 9 above) para 162; *Prosecutor v Mpambara* (Appeals Chamber Judgment) ICTR-01-65-T (11 September 2006) para 17.

[20] See eg *Prosecutor v Kamuhanda* (Trial Chamber Judgment and Sentence) ICTR-99-54A-T (22 January 2003) para 597; *Kajelijeli* (Trial Chamber Judgment) (n 17 above) para 766; *Kvočka* (Trial Chamber Judgment) (n 16 above) para 255; *Blaškić* (Trial Chamber Judgment) (n 16 above) para 286.

[21] *Blaškić* (Appeals Judgment) (n 9 above) para 42 (following the *Vasiljević* Appeals Chamber Judgment (n 18 above) para 102).

[22] *Prosecutor v Kunarac et al* (Trial Chamber Judgment) IT-96-23-T and IT-96-23/1-T (22 February 2001) para 392. See also *Aleksovski* (Trial Chamber Judgment) (n 8 above) para 61; *Prosecutor v Tadić* (Trial Chamber Opinion and Judgment) IT-94-1-T (7 May 1997) para 674.

A significant aspect of the mental requirements of this form of responsibility is the understanding that the intention of the aider and abettor to facilitate the crime by acting is separate to the intention of the perpetrator committing the crime. This point was explained by Judge Shahabuddeen when discussing the application of aiding and abetting to the specific intent crime of genocide in the *Krstić* appeal:

> Intent must always be proved, but the intent of the perpetrator of genocide is not the same as the intent of the aider and abettor. The perpetrator's intent is to commit genocide. The intent of the aider and abettor is not to commit genocide; his intent is to provide the means by which the perpetrator, if he wishes, can realise his own intent to commit genocide.[23]

In addition to being aware that their acts or omissions lend assistance or encouragement to the actions of the physical perpetrator, the accused aider and abettor must be aware of the essential elements of the crime that is in fact committed by the perpetrator.[24]

There is an apparent conflict in the jurisprudence of the ICTY concerning whether fulfilment of this element requires that the accused know the precise crime of the physical perpetrator committed with the aider and abettor's assistance or encouragement,[25] or rather whether they need only have knowledge that 'one of a number of crimes will probably be committed, one of those crimes is in fact committed, and the aider and abettor intended to facilitate the commission of that crime'.[26] Surprisingly, despite the *Simić* trial judgment raising this contradiction, subsequent trial and appeal judgments have either endorsed one or the other approach, or endorsed both approaches as being available to a chamber in the determination of an accused's responsibility for aiding and abetting a crime. This contradictory authority is difficult to resolve; however, the following formulation provides some guidance:

> In the absence of a clear statement by the Appeals Chamber, the most appropriate and safest approach to this issue is that which places a greater burden on the prosecution to

[23] *Prosecutor v Krstić* (Appeals Chamber Judgment) IT-98-33-A (19 April 2004) Partially Dissenting Opinion of Judge Shahabuddeen, para 66.

[24] See eg *Simić* (Appeals Chamber Judgment) (n 9 above) para 86; *Aleksovski* (Appeals Judgment) (n 9 above) para 162; *Mpambara* (Trial Chamber Judgment) (n 18 above) para 17.

[25] This line of jurisprudence commenced with the *Tadić* Appeals Judgment (n 17 above) para 229, and was followed in a number of trial judgments and the following appeal judgments: *Aleksovski* (Appeals Chamber Judgment) (n 9 above); *Vasiljević* (Appeals Chamber Judgment) (n 18 above); *Prosecutor v Kvočka et al* (Appeals Chamber Judgment) IT-98-30/1-A (28 February 2005); and *Simić* (Appeals Chamber Judgment) (n 9 above).

[26] *Furundžija* (Trial Chamber Judgment) (n 4 above) para 246 and followed in a line of trial judgments, including: *Strugar* (Trial Chamber Judgment) (n 9 above) para 350; *Brđanin* (Trial Chamber Judgment) (n 9 above) para 272; *Prosecutor v Naletilić and Martinović* (Trial Chamber Judgment) IT-98-34-T (31 March 2003) para 63; *Blaškić* (Trial Chamber Judgment) (n 16 above) para 287. The contradictory approach in the jurisprudence to this element was first articulated in *Prosecutor v Simić et al* (Trial Chamber Judgment) IT-95-9-T (17 October 2003) para 163.

establish this element. In other words, the accused must have had the specific crime with which he is charged in mind when he rendered the assistance or encouragement, whether or not he simultaneously had other crimes in mind as well. This requirement constitutes a key distinction between aiding and abetting and participation in a joint criminal enterprise.[27]

C. The physical elements of aiding and abetting

The physical elements for aiding and abetting in international criminal law are: (1) that the accused must lend practical assistance, encouragement, or moral support to the physical perpetrator or perpetrators in committing a crime; and (2) this practical assistance, encouragement, or moral support must have a substantial effect on the commission of a crime by the physical perpetrator or perpetrators.[28]

For the purposes of this chapter, it is the articulation of the conduct of an accused that may fulfil the physical elements that is most significant. The *ad hoc* Tribunal Statutes clearly state that aiding and abetting may occur in the 'planning, preparation or execution of a crime',[29] which has led to the consistent articulation by these tribunals that the act of assistance may occur before, during, or after the crime of the physical perpetrator.[30] Such assistance may include providing the means to commit the crime or promising to perform certain acts once the crime has been committed;[31] meanwhile, acts of assistance occurring too long after the crime may lack the 'substantial effect' required of aiding and abetting. In the *Strugar* case, the prosecution argued that, because Strugar failed to subsequently punish his troops for shelling the Old Town of Dubrovnik, this omission amounted to aiding and abetting the unlawful shelling. The Trial Chamber held that 'conduct of this nature, *well after the offences were committed*, could [not] have a direct and substantial effect on the commission of the offences',[32] and the Chamber acquitted Strugar as an aider and abettor of these offences. Significantly, the Chamber held that the most appropriate description of the conduct of the accused in that case was that he failed to prevent or to punish his subordinates for their acts constituting violations of international humanitarian law. As will be discussed later in this chapter, where aiding and abetting by omission

[27] Boas *et al* (n 1 above) 323–4 (and 321–4 for a full discussion of this issue).

[28] See *Mrkšić* (Appeals Chamber Judgment) (n 9 above) para 49; *Orić* (Appeals Chamber Judgment) (n 9 above) para 43; *Nahimana* (Appeals Chamber Judgment) (n 9 above) para 482; *Simić* (Appeals Chamber Judgment) (n 9 above) para 85; *Blaškić* (Appeals Chamber Judgment) (n 9 above) para 45; *Vasiljević* (Appeals Chamber Judgment) (n 18 above) para 102.

[29] ICTY Statute, Art 7(1); ICTR Statute, Art 6(1).

[30] See eg *Mrkšić* (Appeals Chamber Judgment) (n 9 above) para 81; *Simić* (Appeals Chamber Judgment) (n 9 above) para 85; *Blaškić* (Appeals Chamber Judgment) (n 9 above) para 48.

[31] *Mpambara* (Trial Chamber Judgment) (n 19 above) para 23; *Orić* (Trial Chamber Judgment) (n 9 above) para 285; *Aleksovski* (Trial Chamber Judgment) (n 8 above) para 62.

[32] *Strugar* (Trial Chamber Judgment) (n 9 above) para 355 (emphasis in original).

is pleaded and applied by the *ad hoc* Tribunals, invariably the conduct in question is more appropriately characterized either as a positive act coupled with the other requisite elements of aiding and abetting or—more often—as failure to act as a superior. This deduction is also consistent with the argument, set out below, that superior responsibility is the only established form of omission liability in customary international law.

In another case before the ICTY, Blagojević was held not to be responsible for aiding and abetting the mass executions of Srebrenica victims by permitting the use of personnel and resources for the reburial of victims. The Trial Chamber held that there was insufficient evidence that the reburial operation was agreed upon or even foreseen at the time of the planning, preparation, or execution of the killings.[33]

The *ad hoc* Tribunal jurisprudence requires the aider and abettor's acts of practical assistance, encouragement, or support to have a 'substantial effect' on the perpetration of the crime.[34] From the first trial judgment of the ICTY, the *Tadić* Trial Chamber stated that a substantial contribution 'calls for a contribution that in fact has an effect on the commission of the crime'.[35] While the accused's lending of assistance must have some real effect on the crime's commission, it has been consistently held that the prosecution need not prove that the crime would not have been committed but for the accused's participation.[36] However, it clearly remains the case that the anticipated crime must actually have been committed for the aider and abettor to incur liability.[37]

D. Aiding and abetting by omission

Chambers of the *ad hoc* Tribunals have held on a number of occasions that the requirement that a person accused of aiding and abetting 'lend assistance or support' may occur not only by means of positive action, but also through an omission.[38]

[33] *Blagojević and Jokić* (Trial Chamber Judgment) (n 9 above) paras 731, 745. But see *Naletilić and Martinović* (Trial Chamber Judgment) (n 26 above) para 507.

[34] See *Simić* (Appeals Chamber Judgment) (n 9 above) para 85; *Kvočka* (Appeals Chamber Judgment) (n 25 above) 90; *Blaškić* (Appeals Chamber Judgment) (n 9 above) para 46; *Vasiljević* (Appeals Chamber Judgment) (n 18 above) para 102; *Prosecutor v Delalić et al* (Appeals Chamber Judgment) IT-96-21-A (20 February 2001) para 352; *Tadić* (Appeals Chamber Judgment) (n 18 above) para 229; *Muvunyi* (Trial Chamber Judgment) (n 9 above) para 469; *Mpambara* (Trial Chamber Judgment) (n 19 above) para 17.

[35] *Tadić* (Trial Chamber Judgment) (n 22 above) para 688.

[36] See *Simić* (Appeals Chamber Judgment) (n 9 above) para 85; *Blaškić* (Appeals Chamber Judgment) (n 9 above) para 48; *Kajelijeli* (Trial Chamber Judgment) (n 17 above) para 766.

[37] See eg *Krstić* (Appeals Chamber Judgment) (n 23 above) para 140; *Vasiljević* (Appeals Chamber Judgment) (n 18 above) para 142; *Brđanin* (Trial Chamber Judgment) (n 9 above) para 273; *Prosecutor v Stakić* (Trial Chamber Judgment) IT-97-24-T (29 October 2003) para 534.

[38] See sources cited in n 9 above. See also *Prosecutor v Mrkšić* (Trial Chamber Judgment) IT-95-13/1-T (27 September 2007) para 553.

The Trial Chamber in the *Milutinović* judgment considered the *ad hoc* Tribunal precedent and concluded that:

> ... along with the 'approving spectator' doctrine, [aiding and abetting] also encompasses culpable omissions, where (a) there is a legal duty to act, (b) the accused has the ability to act, (c) he fails to act either intending the criminal consequences or with awareness and consent that the consequences will ensue, and (d) the failure to act results in the commission of the crime.[39]

The Chamber considered the content of the requirement that the accused be under a legal duty to act. It noted that the Trial Chamber in the ICTR case of *Ntagerura* had stated that a culpable omission required the accused to 'have had a duty to act mandated by a rule of criminal law'.[40] On appeal, the Appeals Chamber, without resolving the question, queried the requirement that the duty incumbent upon an accused must be a rule of *criminal law*. The *Milutinović* Trial Chamber referred to subsequent ICTY Appeals Chamber judgments raising the same query as that raised by the *Ntagerura* Appeals Chamber.[41] Without a clear appellate ruling on the issue, the Trial Chamber determined that the test required a legal duty only, and not a legal duty mandated by criminal law.[42] In this way, the evolution of this test of aiding and abetting by omission follows the same path as other developments of this form of responsibility: statements *obiter* followed by reference in other judgments and, eventually, consolidation as established law—all without there ever being a clear articulation of a basis in international law for such a holding.[43]

A review of the jurisprudence reveals that only two concrete examples of aiding and abetting by omission have been proffered by the Tribunal judges, and these have mostly been postulated as hypothetical examples of this species of criminal responsibility.

E. Presence at the scene as aiding and abetting by omission

The first example is of a person present at the scene who stands idly by while his or her associates commit a crime—the 'approving spectator'. It was held by the Trial Chamber in the *Furundžija* case that, while an accused's mere presence at the scene is not conclusive evidence of aiding and abetting, where such presence demonstrates what has been described in one case as a 'significant legitimising or encouraging effect on the principals', the accused may be held to have aided and

39 *Milutinović* (Trial Chamber Judgment) (n 9 above) para 90 (Vol 1).

40 *Prosecutor v Ntagerura et al* (Trial Chamber Judgment and Sentence) ICTR-99-46-T (15 May 2008) para 659.

41 *Prosecutor v Galić* (Appeals Chamber Judgment) IT-98-29-A (30 November 2006) para 175; *Orić* (Appeals Chamber Judgment) (n 9 above) para 43.

42 *Milutinović* (Trial Chamber Judgment) (n 9 above) para 91 (Vol 1).

43 The *Mrkšić* appeals judgment also endorsed this approach without any further discussion: *Mrkšić* (Appeals Chamber Judgment) (n 9 above) para 134.

abetted the crime of a principal offender.[44] As discussed in respect of the physical elements of this form of responsibility, most chambers of the *ad hoc* Tribunals refer to the requirement that the accused's acts have a 'substantial effect' on a principal offender.[45] It is unclear whether the *Furundžija* Trial Chamber, whose language was subsequently endorsed in other ICTY and ICTR judgments,[46] meant to impose a different standard to the 'substantial effect' standard most chambers apply to all examples of aiding and abetting. It is probable that, as has been articulated, 'through these words *Furundžija* was simply emphasising that the aider and abettor must be something more than just another spectator'.[47]

The presence of an accused at the scene as a basis for criminal responsibility represents an example of 'intangible' aiding and abetting: in other words, aiding and abetting through encouragement and/or moral support.[48] In *Furundžija*, the Trial Chamber convicted the accused of rape as a violation of the laws or customs of war for continuing his interrogation while the person being interrogated was subjected to sexual violence.[49] In *Aleksovski*, the accused was a detention camp warden whose presence, without objection, was enough to render him guilty as an aider and abettor of physical abuse of inmates of the camp:

> In his capacity as prison warden [Aleksovski] was clearly in charge of organizing ... body-searches of detainees and of supervising them. By being present during the mistreatment, and yet not objecting to it notwithstanding its systematic nature and the authority he had over its perpetrators, the accused was necessarily aware that such tacit approval would be construed as a sign of his support and encouragement. He thus contributed substantially to the mistreatment. Accordingly, the accused must be held responsible for aiding and abetting under Article 7(1) in the physical and mental abuse which detainees were subjected to ...[50]

In the *Tadić* case, the Trial Chamber convicted the accused of aiding and abetting through mere presence in circumstances where the accused had previously played an active role in similar acts of beating:

> Moreover, when an accused is present and participates in the beating of one person and remains with the group when it moves on to beat another person, his presence would

[44] *Furundžija* (Trial Chamber Judgment) (n 4 above) para 232. This standard was endorsed by the Trial Chamber in *Kunarac et al* (Trial Chamber Judgment) (n 22 above) para 393.

[45] See sources cited in n 34 above.

[46] *Kunarac et al* (Trial Chamber Judgment) (n 22 above) para 393; *Prosecutor v Vasiljević* (Trial Chamber Judgment) IT-98-32-T (29 November 2002) para 70; *Prosecutor v Kvočka et al* (Trial Chamber Judgment) IT-98-30/1-T (2 November 2001) para 257; *Prosecutor v Krnojelac* (Trial Chamber Judgment) IT-97-25-T (15 March 2002) para 88; *Simić et al* (Trial Chamber Judgment) (n 26 above) para 165; *Ndindabahizi* (Trial Chamber Judgment) (n 17 above) para 457.

[47] Boas *et al* (n 1 above) 308.

[48] See *Kayishema and Ruzindana* (Appeals Chamber Judgment) (n 18 above) para 201; *Prosecutor v Kayishema and Ruzindana* (Trial Chamber Judgment) ICTR 95-1-T (21 May 1999) para 200; *Furundžija* (Trial Chamber Judgment) (n 4 above) para 232.

[49] *Furundžija* (Trial Chamber Judgment) (n 4 above) para 274.

[50] *Aleksovski* (Trial Chamber Judgment) (n 8 above) para 87.

have an encouraging effect, even if he does not physically take part in this second beating, and he should be viewed as participating in this second beating as well. This is assuming that the accused has not actively withdrawn from the group or spoken out against the conduct of the group.[51]

The *Blaškić* Trial Chamber regarded the position of superior authority of the person who is present at a crime scene as a 'probative indication for determining whether that person encouraged or supported the perpetrators of the crime'.[52] ICTR judgments have also held that the accused's position of authority alone might engage his responsibility for complicity,[53] but these judgments are in the minority.[54] The majority of judgments have followed the approach of the *Aleksovski* Trial Chamber, which was restated by the *Brđanin* Trial Chamber in the following way: 'An individual's position of superior authority does not suffice to conclude from his mere presence at the scene of the crime that he encouraged or supported the crime. However, the presence of a superior can be perceived as an important *indicium* of encouragement or support.'[55]

Even though an accused's position of authority provides strong evidence of aiding and abetting, 'responsibility is not automatic and merits consideration against the background of the factual circumstances'.[56] In the *Akayesu* case, the Trial Chamber referred to Akayesu's leadership status in the Taba commune as evidence that his silence in the face of nearby rapes was a 'clear signal of official tolerance for sexual violence, without which these acts would not have taken place'.[57] This signal of official tolerance was an element leading to the Trial Chamber holding Akayesu guilty as an aider and abettor of rape and other inhumane acts as crimes against humanity.[58]

F. Failure to act as aiding and abetting by omission

The second scenario to which trial chambers have referred is where the aider and abettor has a legal duty to act and fails to do so, irrespective of his presence at or absence from the scene of the crime.[59]

[51] *Tadić* (Trial Chamber Judgment) (n 22 above) para 690.

[52] *Blaškić* (Trial Chamber Judgment) (n 16 above) para 284, affirmed in *Blaškić* (Appeals Chamber Judgment) (n 9 above) para 47.

[53] *Furundžija* (Trial Chamber Judgment) (n 4 above) para 207.

[54] See *Kayishema and Ruzindana* (Appeals Chamber Judgment) (n 18 above) para 201; *Ndindabahizi* (Trial Chamber Judgment) (n 17 above) para 457; *Prosecutor v Bagilishema* (Trial Chamber Judgment) ICTR-95-1A-T (7 June 2001) para 34.

[55] *Brđanin* (Trial Chamber Judgment) (n 9 above) para 271 (emphasis in original). Accord *Muvunyi* (Trial Chamber Judgment) (n 9 above) para 472; *Mpambara* (Trial Chamber Judgment) (n 34 above) para 22; *Orić* (Trial Chamber Judgment) (n 9 above) para 283; *Strugar* (Trial Chamber Judgment) (n 9 above) para 349; *Kamuhanda* (Trial Chamber Judgment) (n 20 above) para 600; *Kajelijeli* (Trial Chamber Judgment) (n 20 above) para 769.

[56] *Aleksovski* (Trial Chamber Judgment) (n 8 above) para 65. Accord *Mpambara* (Trial Chamber Judgment) (n 34 above) para 22.

[57] *Akayesu* (Trial Chamber Judgment) (n 16 above) para 693.

[58] ibid.

[59] See discussion and sources in nn 40–43 above, and accompanying text.

Aleksovski was a prison warden of the Kaonik prison and was therefore responsible for the conditions in which inmates were detained.[60] The Trial Chamber considered the position of the accused in the context in which crimes were committed and held that his position of authority, coupled with his presence at the scene and failure to stop the crimes, while not amounting to ordering the crimes, constituted aiding and abetting. In respect of beating meted out during body searches at which the accused was present the Trial Chamber held:

> [Aleksovski] aided and abetted in the commission of these acts. In his capacity as prison warden he was clearly in charge of organising the body-searches of detainees and of supervising them. By being present during the mistreatment, and yet not objecting to it notwithstanding its systematic nature and the authority he had over its perpetrators, the accused was necessarily aware that such tacit approval would be construed as a sign of his support and encouragement. He thus contributed substantially to the mistreatment. Accordingly, the accused must be held responsible for aiding and abetting under Article 7(1) in the physical and mental abuse which detainees were subjected to . . .[61]

The Chamber also held Aleksovski responsible as an aider and abettor for a broader range of mistreatments in the prison:

> It is also similarly satisfied that the recurring brutality the two detainees were subsequently subjected to in the absence of the accused was aided and abetted by him. Abuse of this kind was frequent and was committed day and night near the accused's office so that the accused could hardly not have not been aware of it. Yet he did not oppose or repress it, as his position required. On the contrary, his silence could only be taken as a sign of his approval, given that he participated actively in the initial abuse of these two detainees; the accused could hardly have been unaware that his silence would amount to encouragement to the perpetrators. This silence evinces a culpable intent of aiding and abetting such acts as contemplated in Article 7(1).[62]

An example of the treatment of this issue before the ICTR is the ruling of the Trial Chamber in the *Rutaganira* case. The accused, the *conseiller* of the Mubuga *secteur*, was convicted of aiding and abetting in exterminations because he remained inactive while the civilian population under his watch joined armed attackers in massacring the Tutsis taking refuge in the Mubuga church.[63] The Trial Chamber referred to the failure of the accused under the Rwandan Penal Code to stop persons over whom he had responsibility from committing acts of violence and to report them to the appropriate authorities as the crucial factor which transformed his idleness into culpable aiding and abetting.[64] As will be discussed further below, this articulation of the accused's responsibility for aiding and abetting is more appropriately discussed in the context either of superior responsibility or positive acts giving rise to criminal responsibility.

[60] *Aleksovski* (Trial Chamber Judgment) (n 8 above) para 86. [61] ibid para 87.
[62] ibid para 88.
[63] *Prosecutor v Rutaganira* (Trial Chamber Judgment and Sentence) ICTR-95-1C-T (14 March 2005) paras 74, 100. [64] ibid paras 81, 84, 91, 99–100.

This issue is crystallized somewhat by consideration of the *Strugar* trial judgment, where the Trial Chamber considered whether an accused may be found guilty as an aider and abettor for failing to discharge a duty. The prosecution alleged that, even though Strugar was not physically present to witness the unlawful shelling of the Old Town of Dubrovnik by his troops, he should still be responsible as an aider and abettor for failing to stop them from doing so. Strugar had issued a ceasefire order, but only did so three hours after he discovered that his troops might be engaging in unlawful shelling, and he took no steps subsequently to launch an adequate investigation into the events.[65] While the Trial Chamber referred to the statement in the *Blaškić* appeal judgment that referred *obiter* to the possibility 'that in the circumstances of a given case an omission may constitute the *actus reus* of aiding and abetting',[66] the *Strugar* Chamber held that a finding that Strugar aided and abetted the crimes in these circumstances was an inappropriate one:[67]

> In view of the fact that the Accused made an effort, albeit ineffective, to stop the firing, and in the absence of more settled jurisprudence as to whether, and if so in what circumstances, an omission may constitute the *actus reus* of aiding and abetting, in circumstances such as the present, it is the view of the Chamber that the Accused's failure to take more effective measures to stop the unlawful shelling of the Old Town is more properly regarded in the context of the Accused's responsibility as a superior under Article 7(3) of the Statute.[68]

In doing so, the Trial Chamber held that a superior should not be held liable as an aider or abettor (at least in the absence of 'more settled jurisprudence') for crimes committed in these circumstances. What the *Strugar* Trial Judgment did was to articulate how inappropriate it is to impose liability for aiding and abetting on a superior who fails to stop the criminal conduct by his subordinates or to carry out a proper investigation, as well as, by logical analogy, for failing to punish those responsible for committing crimes. What it does not do—and this is true of each decision of the *ad hoc* Tribunals relating to aiding and abetting by omission—is explain whether there is even a basis for the proposition that aiding and abetting by omission exists in international criminal law. As the remainder of this chapter will assert, no such foundation exists.

III. Aiding and Abetting by Omission—a Legal Fallacy?

A proper review of the *ad hoc* Tribunal jurisprudence suggests that attempts by trial and appeals chambers to articulate a form of responsibility known as aiding

[65] *Strugar* (Trial Chamber Judgment) (n 9 above) paras 352–5.
[66] ibid para 349.
[67] ibid para 356.
[68] ibid para 355.

and abetting by omission is simply not supportable.[69] Two arguments will be made in an effort to respond to the evolution and now consolidation of the view that aiding and abetting by omission is a form of responsibility in international criminal law. First, building on the discussion above and despite what is said in the jurisprudence, the conduct offered as examples of aiding and abetting by omission is more properly to be interpreted either as acts, not omissions, or as an instance of superior responsibility. Secondly, and more significantly, not a single chamber, nor the *ad hoc* Tribunal prosecutors, have ever satisfactorily articulated the foundation for this form of responsibility in international law. As a consideration of the jurisdictional motions in the *Karadžić* case reveals, little beyond the mere assertion that aiding and abetting by omission is part of international criminal law has been offered, and certainly no evidence of state practice and *opinio juris*—required to identify a rule of customary international law[70]—has been articulated.

A. Examples of omissions are in fact positive acts

As the discussion in the previous section of this chapter suggests, a proper examination of the *ad hoc* Tribunal jurisprudence shows that examples of inactive presence at the scene of a crime are not properly characterized as aiding and abetting 'by omission'. In most cases in which a chamber would find the requisite 'significant encouraging effect',[71] the aider and abettor intentionally made himself available at the scene, or intentionally stayed on the scene if already there, for the express purpose of showing solidarity with the physical perpetrators or approval of their actions.[72] By intentionally being present, the accused is in fact *actively* aiding and abetting the crime, even though he or she may take no overt action or say anything once at the scene.

The only other circumstance in which aiding and abetting by omission might be said to arise is where a superior with a duty to act fails to take action—the scenario envisaged or mentioned by the Trial Chambers in *Galić*, *Simić*, and *Rutaganira*. A careful consideration of the articulation of the form of responsibility leads to the

[69] For a detailed analysis of this issue, see Boas *et al* (n 1 above) Ch 4, section 4.3.1.1.3.

[70] See ICJ Statute, Art 38(1)(b); *Continental Shelf (Libya v Malta)* [1985] ICJ Rep 29; *Case Concerning Military and Paramilitary Activities in and against Nicaragua (Nicaragua v United States)* (Merits) [1986] ICJ Rep 14, 97; P Malanczuk, *Akehurst's Modern Introduction to International Law* (London/New York: Routledge, 7th revsd edn, 1997). For a discussion of the lax methodology for identifying customary rules at the *ad hoc* Tribunals, see nn 5–7 above, and accompanying text.

[71] See *Ndindabahizi* (Trial Chamber Judgment) (n 17 above) para 457; *Strugar* (Trial Chamber Judgment) (n 9 above) para 349; *Simić* (Trial Chamber Judgment) (n 26 above) para 165; *Vasiljević* (Trial Chamber Judgment) (n 46 above) para 70; *Krnojelac* (Trial Chamber Judgment) (n 46 above) para 88; *Kvočka et al* (Trial Chamber Judgment) (n 46 above) para 257; *Kunarac et al* (Trial Chamber Judgment) (n 22 above) para 393.

[72] See eg *Aleksovski* (Trial Chamber Judgment) (n 8 above).

conclusion that the failure to act scenario is the one uncontroversially recognized form of omission liability—superior responsibility.[73] One scholarly view states:

> Superior responsibility, which covers exactly the circumstances discussed in these cases, is a well-developed and clear form of indirect liability under customary international law which arises out of the superior–subordinate relationship, and which is explicitly included within the jurisdiction of all contemporary international criminal tribunals. Unlike aiding and abetting by omission, the foundation, purpose, elements, and meaning of superior responsibility have all been expounded and are comprehensible.[74]

The creation and application of aiding and abetting by omission as a form of international criminal responsibility, bending the physical elements to fit into a scenario that is already clearly articulated as superior responsibility, is counterintuitive and exposes the tribunals applying international criminal law to the criticism that they are making up rules to suit the facts.

Despite the strong statement about the existence of this form of omission liability in the *Mrkšić* appeals judgment, in the cases in which aiding and abetting has been discussed in close association with the facts of the case, a clear picture emerges. In the *Muvunyi* case before the ICTR, the Trial Chamber again repeated the statement that liability for aiding and abetting may be incurred by way of omission; notably, however, the Chamber could not provide an example of where such responsibility might arise beyond the approving-spectator scenario dealt with above.[75]

In the *Mpambara* case, while the Trial Chamber again stated that the physical elements of aiding and abetting might be fulfilled by omission, the Chamber itself was clearly not convinced by the proposition. While stating that evidence 'which is characterised as an omission can be used to show that an accused aided and abetted a crime',[76] it then referred to the presence of a person in a position of authority at the scene of a crime as a possible example of aiding and abetting by omission, and stated that '[o]ther examples of aiding and abetting through failure to act are not to be easily found in the annals of the *ad hoc* Tribunals'.[77] The Chamber went on to actually hold that an accused, by choosing to be present, is in fact taking a *positive step* which may contribute to the crime,[78] while subsequently asserting that aiding and abetting liability in such circumstances is established 'from the omission combined with the choice to be present'.[79] On this reasoning, it appears as though the choice to be present is action while mere presence is omission. The following has been stated in respect of this case:

> The struggle in which the Trial Chamber engages to try to establish the proposition that at least part of the culpable conduct of an accused in such circumstances constitutes

[73] See also section IV of the contribution of Robert Cryer (Ch 7 above).

[74] Boas *et al* (n 1 above) 313. For a comprehensive discussion of the evolution and elements of this form of omission liability, see G Mettraux, *The Law of Command Responsibility* (Oxford/New York: OUP, 2009).

[75] See *Muvunyi* (Trial Chamber Judgment) (n 9 above) para 472.

[76] *Mpambara* (Trial Chamber Judgment) (n 19 above) para 22.

[77] ibid para 23.

[78] ibid para 22.

[79] ibid.

omission further demonstrates the farcicality of seeking to establish 'aiding and abetting by omission' as a form of responsibility recognised in international criminal law and applicable in the *ad hoc* Tribunals.[80]

B. No support for aiding and abetting by omission in customary international law

In his jurisdictional motion challenging aiding and abetting as a form of responsibility available at the ICTY, Radovan Karadžić raised four central arguments against the existence of aiding and abetting by omission as constituting a form of responsibility in international criminal law:

(1) The ICTY may not consider any form of responsibility of an accused or crime (as substantive international criminal law) without first establishing its existence and availability in customary international law. A thorough review of the post-Second World War jurisprudence, the jurisprudence of the *ad hoc* Tribunals, and the drafting history of Article 28 of the Rome Statute of the International Criminal Court (ICC), reveals a lack of *evidence* establishing that liability for omissions has become recognized in customary international law, beyond superior responsibility, as a means of attributing criminal responsibility to an individual in international criminal law.

(2) None of the forms of responsibility applied in the jurisprudence of the ICTY has in fact identified the existence of responsibility for omissions outside responsibility as a superior under Article 7(3) of the ICTY Statute. In particular, despite reference in the ICTY jurisprudence to the concept of omission in relation to aiding and abetting... all such examples of omission liability contemplated are, properly interpreted, references to positive acts (not omissions).

(3) Superior responsibility, as set out in Article 7(3) of the ICTY Statute, is *lex specialis* for omission liability in international criminal law. Therefore, punishing someone for failing to carry out their duty to act must be limited to this recognized form of criminal responsibility, or the *nullum crimen sine lege* principle will have been violated.

(4) It is for the prosecution to establish the existence of the forms of liability upon which it intends to rely; it is not for Dr Karadžić to prove the absence of the existence of such rules.[81]

The first and last points relate to the fundamental proposition that customary international law does not support the existence of aiding and abetting by omission as a form of international criminal responsibility.

[80] Boas *et al* (n 1 above) 314.

[81] *Karadžić* (Motion on Omission Liability) (n 11 above) para 2.

In answer to the *Karadžić* motion, arguing that there is insufficient evidence of the existence in international law of support for the existence of aiding and abetting as a form of omission liability, the prosecution argued that there was indeed evidence that aiding and abetting by omission existed as a form of responsibility prior to 1991.[82] The prosecution referred to the post-First World War Report of the Commission on the Responsibility of the Authors of the War and on Enforcement of Penalties of 1919[83] (post-First World War Commission on Responsibility) and five post-Second World War cases[84] as evidence for the existence of omission liability for aiding and abetting.

In fact, the content of the post-First World War Commission on Responsibility report, contrary to the meaning attributed to it by the prosecution, reveals that the Commission was referring exclusively to superior responsibility and none of the language in that report can be reasonably construed as 'broad enough to cover omission liability beyond superior responsibility'.[85] Furthermore, the post-Second World War cases referred to by the prosecution did not articulate a cogent basis for determining the existence of omission liability as asserted, for reasons articulated by Karadžić in his reply:

(1) contrary to the prosecution's assertions, the cases cited do not reflect clear cases of omission liability; instead, they variously reflect conduct more properly described as positive acts, something like a form of vicarious liability, or they are insufficiently clear as to the conduct giving rise to conviction (or acquittal);

(2) the comments in these cases that might provide for such a possibility are vague or inferential and at no point articulate a clear list of elements supporting evidence of a rule of international law;

(3) post-Second World War cases are just that—they are not primary sources of international law; they are, as stated in Article 38(1) of the International Court of Justice (ICJ) Statute, subsidiary sources. Furthermore, no system of precedent exists in international law and, although the *ad hoc* Tribunals have claimed for themselves a doctrine of *stare decisis*, decisions of chambers cannot create rules of international law but can only serve to interpret existing rules. Therefore, while a judgment of an international tribunal might contain an explanation of a rule that has attained the status of customary international law by articulating the *evidence* upon which this assertion is made, none of the cases cited by the prosecution, to the

[82] See *Prosecutor v Karadžić* (Prosecution Response to 'Preliminary Motion on Lack of Jurisdiction Concerning Omission Liability') IT-95-5/18-AR72.1 (7 April 2009).

[83] Reprinted in (1920) 14 AJIL 95, 121.

[84] The *Synagogue Fire*, *Essen Lynching*, *High Command*, *Fire Brigade* and *Velpke Children's Home* cases, *Karadžić* (Prosecution Response) (n 82 above) para 10.

[85] *Karadžić* (Prosecution Response) (n 82 above) para 9. See also section I of the contribution of Robert Cryer (Ch 7 above).

> extent that they genuinely address the question of omission liability, do this. These cases are, therefore, of no assistance in determining the *actual existence* of a rule of customary international law that an individual may be held criminally responsible for an omission beyond the doctrine of superior responsibility in international criminal law.[86]

The prosecution, in its response, also argued that the provisions of certain treaties having customary international law status (the Geneva Conventions[87] and their two Additional Protocols)[88] refer to omissions as a basis of liability. However, these treaties stand as evidence of the existence in customary international law of omission liability based on superior responsibility and say nothing about responsibility for omissions beyond this established form of responsibility. Significantly, these provisions are contained in multilateral treaties giving rise to state obligations to behave in certain ways. They do not articulate rules relating to individual responsibility and, at any rate, their articulation of the concept of omission is vague and does not indicate with the required specificity what such a rule might entail.[89]

An assessment of the available evidence suggests that aiding and abetting by omission is a form of responsibility that has not been coherently and convincingly established in customary international law. It has been favourably referred to in the jurisprudence and has now been applied to actual cases. However, while a system of binding precedent operates at the *ad hoc* Tribunals, the fact that an appellate court has said this form of responsibility exists—and has articulated

[86] *Prosecutor v Karadžić* (Reply to Prosecution Response to 'Preliminary Motion on Lack of Jurisdiction Concerning Omission Liability') IT-95-5/18-AR72.1 (14 April 2009).

[87] The four Geneva Conventions of 12 August 1949, which entered into force on 21 October 1950 are: (1) Geneva Convention for the Amelioration of the Condition of the Wounded and Sick in Armed Forces in the Field (opened for signature 12 August 1949, entered into force 21 October 1950) 75 UNTS 31; (2) Geneva Convention for the Amelioration of the Condition of Wounded, Sick and Shipwrecked Members of Armed Forces at Sea (opened for signature 12 August 1949, entered into force 21 October 1950) 75 UNTS 85; (3) Geneva Convention relative to the Treatment of Prisoners of War (opened for signature 12 August 1949, entered into force 21 October 1950) 75 UNTS 135 (Third Geneva Convention); (4) Geneva Convention relative to the Protection of Civilian Persons in Time of War (opened for signature 12 August 1949, entered into force 21 October 1950) 75 UNTS 287.

[88] The two Additional Protocols of 1977 to the 1949 Geneva Conventions, which entered into force on 7 December 1978, are: (1) Protocol Additional to the Geneva Convention of 12 August 1949, and Relating to the Protection of Victims of International Armed Conflict, 1125 UNTS 3 (opened for signature 8 June 1977, entered into force 7 December 1978) (Additional Protocol I); and (2) Protocol Additional to the Geneva Conventions of 12 August 1949, and Relating to the Protection of Victims of Non-International Armed Conflicts, 1125 UNTS 609 (Additional Protocol II).

[89] The *Karadžić* (Reply) (n 86 above) further responded that 'the provisions cited by the Prosecution in support of its argument relate largely to the responsibility of a detaining power to provide for the protection of prisoners of war—provisions which clearly relate to the chain of command and are, at any rate, too vague in content to articulate a rule giving rise to criminal responsibility beyond superior responsibility' (ibid para 7).

elements for its application—does not mean that it is derived from an accepted source of international law.

The second argument made in the *Karadžić* motion relates to the proposition that none of the forms of conduct characterized in the jurisprudence in fact amount to omissions, but are rather positive acts. These issues have been comprehensively discussed in the preceding section of this chapter.

C. The only true form of omission liability established as custom in international criminal law is superior responsibility

The final argument made in the *Karadžić* motion, that the only form of omission responsibility that can properly be said to exist in customary international law is that of superior responsibility, related to that form as the *lex specialis* of omission liability in international criminal law.[90] The *Halilović* trial judgment offers a good description of superior responsibility as a species of omission liability: 'The commander is responsible for the failure to perform an act required by international law. This omission is culpable because international law imposes an affirmative duty on superiors to prevent and punish crimes committed by their subordinates.'[91]

The doctrine of superior responsibility is well established as a form of responsibility recognized in international criminal law, with early articulation of the principle appearing in the post-Second World War jurisprudence.[92] An accused convicted pursuant to the doctrine of superior responsibility is not held liable for the substantive crime of a subordinate, but rather for an accused's own wrongdoing in having failed to honour a legal obligation, placed upon that accused by customary or conventional international law, to take action to promote and ensure law-abiding behaviour among subordinates.[93]

At the heart of this point is the proposition that the finding of criminal responsibility for failing to act requires the establishment of a legal duty to act and an attendant failure to do so. Where the *ad hoc* Tribunal jurisprudence has sought to identify circumstances beyond superior responsibility in which omission liability exists in international criminal law, not only has it rather identified positive acts

[90] See section IV of Robert Cryer's contribution (Ch 7 above).

[91] *Prosecutor v Halilović* (Trial Chamber Judgment) IT-01-48-T (16 November 2005) para 54. See also *Prosecutor v Krnojelac* (Appeals Chamber Judgment) IT-97-25-A (17 September 2003) para 75.

[92] See Boas *et al* (n 1 above) Ch 3. See also section I of Robert Cryer's contribution (Ch 7 above).

[93] *Prosecutor v Krnojelac* (Appeals Chamber Judgment) IT-97-25-A (17 September 2003) para 171: 'It cannot be overemphasised that, where superior responsibility is concerned, an accused is not charged with the crimes of his subordinates but with his failure to carry out his duty as a superior to exercise control.' See also *Prosecutor v Bagilishema* (Appeals Chamber Judgment) ICTR-95-1A-A (3 July 2002) para 35; *Prosecutor v Delalić et al* (Appeals Chamber Judgment) IT-96-21-A (20 February 2001) para 239.

that form part of the objective elements of the form of responsibility, in addition none of the jurisprudence or other sources considered has provided evidence to support the existence of omission liability as a form of responsibility in international criminal law apart from the superior responsibility doctrine.

In its response to the *Karadžić* motion on this matter, the prosecution first sought to rely upon the position expressed in the jurisprudence. It referred to the following passage in the *Orić* appeal judgment:

> The Appeals Chamber recalls that omission proper may lead to individual criminal responsibility under Article 7(1) of the Statute where there is a legal duty to act. The Appeals Chamber has never set out the requirements for a conviction for omission in detail. However, at a minimum, the offender's conduct would have to meet the basic elements of aiding and abetting. Thus, his omission must be directed to assist, encourage or lend moral support to the perpetration of a crime and have a substantial effect upon the perpetration of the crime (*actus reus*). The aider and abettor must know that his omission assists in the commission of the crime of the principal perpetrator and must be aware of the essential elements of the crime which was ultimately committed by the principal (*mens rea*).[94]

This extract itself acknowledges that the 'Appeals Chamber has never set out the requirements for a conviction for omission in detail'. Neither the *Orić* nor *Blaškić* comments, and certainly not the *Galić* ruling,[95] do anything more than reinforce the fact that, beyond vague comments in *obiter*, liability for omissions beyond superior responsibility has no articulated basis in international criminal law. This position is only reinforced in the most recent pronouncement in the *Mrkšić* appeals judgment.

D. No omission liability under the Rome Statute for the International Criminal Court

The Rome Statute of the ICC is often cited as a foundation for asserting the development of a rule of customary international criminal law.[96] This is not always appropriate given that the process of compromise that gave rise to certain provisions might not accurately reflect the views of states. An early draft of Article 28 of the Rome Statute by the Preparatory Committee, which dealt with individual criminal responsibility, expressly contemplated liability for omission.[97] However,

[94] *Orić* (Appeals Chamber Judgment) (n 9 above) para 43.

[95] These are the judgments extracted for specific discussion by the prosecution: see *Karadžić* (Prosecution Response) (n 82 above) paras 4–6.

[96] Rome Statute of the International Criminal Court (opened for signature 17 July 1998, entered into force 1 July 2002) 2187 UNTS 90 (Rome Statute), Art 25(3)(c): 'aids, abets or otherwise assists in its commission or its attempted commission'.

[97] See draft reproduced in M Cherif Bassiouni, *The Legislative History of the International Criminal Court: An Article-by-Article Evolution of the Statute* (Ardsley, New York: Transnational, 2005) Vol 2, 195.

states parties in negotiating this provision could not reach any agreement on a rule expressing the existence of omission liability for any form of responsibility excepting superior responsibility. The article contemplating omission liability was deleted, 'because it was not possible to reach consensus on the definition of an omission'.[98]

The prosecution, in its response to the *Karadžić* motion, played down the significance of a large number of states negotiating the Rome Statute of the ICC failing to agree on the existence of individual criminal responsibility for omissions beyond superior responsibility.[99] The point is extremely important. The fact is that, as recently as 1998, numerous states found it 'almost impossible to negotiate a solution'[100] to this issue. Indeed, they did find it impossible. The *Karadžić* reply addresses this point:

> The Prosecution confuses the rule-making process in international law and inverts the meaning of this issue. To create custom, a significant number of States must behave in a certain way in relation to a rule of international law (state practice) and must believe they are bound by such rule, clearly identifiable (*opinio juris*). The point Dr Karadžić made in the Motion was that where a significant number of States could not agree on the existence of omission liability beyond superior responsibility as a rule of international law, this was a powerful statement that such a rule does not exist. The ICC Statute is indeed an instrument of compromise and caution must be exercised in asserting that because a rule appears in the Statute it is necessarily reflective of customary international law. However, where these States could not reach agreement, even compromising as they were, this can be taken as strongly suggesting that no such rule exists.[101]

IV. Conclusion

Like the elements of substantive crimes, all elements of the forms of individual responsibility in international criminal law must be sourced in international law and each time a court enters a conviction for a crime it must articulate the basis for criminality and the fulfilment of each of the required elements beyond a reasonable doubt; if this is not done, the principle of legality may be infringed. Identification of the elements of forms of responsibility is a requirement that cannot be fulfilled by simply referring to previous rulings of the same tribunal, even at the appellate level. The *ad hoc* Tribunals are required to apply customary international law at the inception of their jurisdiction. This means that to convict a person for aiding and abetting a crime by omission, the chamber must identify the basis in customary international law for fulfilment of the physical elements

[98] O Triffterer and K Ambos, *Commentary on the Rome Statute of the International Criminal Court: Observers' Notes, Article by Article* (Portland: Hart, 2nd edn, 2008) 770.

[99] *Karadžić* (Prosecution Response) (n 82 above) para 13.

[100] Prosecution citing a Working Group Chair, Per Saland, in its response, ibid para 14.

[101] *Karadžić* (Reply) (n 86 above) para 9.

of the crime by omission. None of the tribunals that have raised such a prospect of aiding and abetting by omission, or applied it to the facts of a case, have done this. Custom requires evidence of state practice and *opinio juris*—this is not fulfilled by simply stating a line of authority, unless somewhere along that line of authority is an articulation of such evidence.

Another way in which prosecutors and chambers have avoided dealing with this fundamental requirement, particularly at the preliminary motion stage of proceedings, is to sidestep it by referring to a form of responsibility as having 'contours'. The prosecution in the *Karadžić* case argued that, 'even if international law sources do not specifically reflect omission liability for all of the separate modes of liability of Article 7(1) of the Statute, the Tribunal will define their contours'.[102] Such vague references to 'contours'[103] or 'interpretation' cannot excuse the prosecution from its responsibility to establish the existence of such a rule, nor the chamber's obligation under international criminal law. If the sources of international law do not *specifically* establish a rule, then no rule of international law can be said to exist—this is particularly apposite in a criminal jurisdiction where the deprivation of a person's liberty is at stake.

Neither the Trial Chamber nor the Appeals Chamber in the *Karadžić* jurisdiction challenge chose to engage directly in consideration of these arguments concerning the customary international law basis for the existence of omission liability for aiding and abetting. The Trial Chamber, for its part, simply repeated that a long line of jurisprudence existed, that the matter was not properly one of jurisdiction and that the accused would have an opportunity to address the issue at trial.[104] It ostensibly ignored the arguments relating to the lack of foundation in customary international law, reinforcing the longstanding reluctance of the *ad hoc* Tribunals to address, once a line of (particularly appellate) authority exists, the legal foundation for a form of responsibility in international criminal law.

On 25 June 2009, the Appeals Chamber finally dismissed this and other applications by Karadžić challenging the jurisdiction of the Tribunal.[105] In doing so, the Chamber strategically avoided dealing with some crucial aspects of the Tribunal's jurisdiction, including its compliance with customary international law. This outcome was unfortunate. Given the important questions posed, the anticipated reluctance from the appellate jurisdiction of the *ad hoc* Tribunals to

[102] *Karadžić* (Prosecution Response) (n 82 above) para 16.

[103] This reference to 'contours' has been made in respect of interpreting aspects of the joint criminal enterprise doctrine (see *Prosecutor v Milutinović et al* (Decision on Ojdanić's Motion Challenging Jurisdiction: Indirect Co-Perpetration) IT-05-87-PT (22 March 2006) paras 23–4). It has some relevance to the identification of the nuance of a particular form of responsibility but not to such a major question as whether the Tribunal has jurisdiction over omission liability beyond the doctrine of superior responsibility.

[104] See *Karadžić* (Jurisdiction Decision) (n 11 above) paras 67–78.

[105] *Prosecutor v Karadžić* (Appeals Chamber Decision on Radovan Karadžić's Motions Challenging Jurisdiction) (Omission Liability, JCE-III—Special Intent Crimes, Superior Responsibility) IT-95-5/18-AR72.1–3 (25 June 2009).

answer questions of jurisdiction makes the likelihood of any further serious development in the articulation of this area of international criminal law before those Tribunals most unlikely. Where fundamental questions of an accused's criminal responsibility come before the Appeals Chamber on a question of jurisdiction, sidestepping it on the casual reference to the convenient 'contours' argument indicates a lack of intent to grapple with some of the remaining tough issues.

Aiding and abetting by omission may exist as a form of individual responsibility in international criminal law; if so, its legal foundation and content should be explained—that is the minimum requirement of a jurisdiction applying such forms of responsibility to actual accused persons. While the Appeals Chamber explains that the Trial Chamber hearing the *Karadžić* case can deal with the substantive arguments in its final judgment, there is nothing to suggest that the Trial Chamber, and following it the Appeals Chamber on a merits appeal, will do any more than once again refer to the line of ICTY and ICTR authority stating that such a form of responsibility exists. This conclusory reasoning will not answer the important questions posed as to whether the existence of aiding and abetting by omission is properly founded in customary international law.

While the *ad hoc* Tribunals have produced outstanding examples of judicial creativity that balance the crucial guarantees of a right to a fair trial and the principle of legality with the jurisdictional imperative to develop and explain international criminal law, aiding and abetting by omission is an example of a lack of creativity. Instead of examining the foundation for such a form of responsibility in international law, these tribunals have hidden behind a self-constructed system of precedent that, when interpreted in this context, reflects the proposition: it is law because we have said it is. Far from creative, this is a retrograde approach to an important question of law. The more the opportunity has arisen to engage the issue directly, the greater the endeavours of the tribunals have been to avoid it. It may well be that, given the concern of the *ad hoc* Tribunals (mindful of their completion strategies) to expedite the disposal of cases, consideration of these and other important substantive issues will fall to the growing body of work being undertaken by the International Criminal Court.

PART IV

DEFENCES AND FAIR TRIAL RIGHTS

10

Judicial Development of the Law of Defences by the International Criminal Tribunals

Caroline Fournet

I. Introduction

Defences are an essential component of international criminal justice, but the law of defences has not been fully clarified within international criminal law. It is unsurprising, therefore, that the development of the law of defences has relied heavily on judicial input. This jurisprudential contribution has proved invaluable in elaborating a coherent set of norms on admissible defences in international criminal law. Neither the Statute of the International Criminal Tribunal for Rwanda (ICTR) nor that of the International Criminal Tribunal for the former Yugoslavia (ICTY) enunciate a clear set of rules on admissible defences, although this silence should not be interpreted as meaning that valid defences cannot be raised.[1] The relative silence of the law is not to be equated with a lack of practice and, on the contrary, a notable degree of judicial creativity was generated in this context.

Such a judicial reaction had been anticipated by the Secretary-General of the United Nations in his report to the Security Council on the draft ICTY Statute. In the report he noted that '[t]he International Tribunal itself will have to decide on various personal defences which may relieve a person of individual criminal responsibility, such as minimum age or mental incapacity, drawing upon general principles of law recognised by all nations'.[2] This was a role which the *ad hoc* Tribunals accepted, with the ICTY Trial Chamber in *Kordić* stating that defences 'form part of the general principles of criminal law which the International Tribunal must take into account in deciding the cases before it'.[3] Over the life of

[1] WA Schabas, *The UN International Criminal Tribunals—The former Yugoslavia, Rwanda and Sierra Leone* (Cambridge: CUP, 2006) 325.

[2] 'Report of the Secretary-General Pursuant to Paragraph 2 of Security Council Resolution 808 (1993)', UN Doc S/25704 (1993), para 58. Cited in Schabas (n 1 above) 325.

[3] *Prosecutor v Kordić and Čerkez* (Trial Chamber Judgment) IT-95-14/2-T (26 February 2001) para 449.

the international criminal tribunals, they have 'developed a considerable body of case law concerning defences to charges of genocide, crimes against humanity and war crimes'.[4]

With respect to admissible defences, the Statutes of the *ad hoc* Tribunals fall somewhere between the approach of the Charter of the International Military Tribunal (IMT) at Nuremberg and that of the Rome Statute of the International Criminal Court (ICC). Similar to the Nuremberg Charter, both Statutes are almost silent on the law of defences. It might be worth recalling here that the brevity of the Nuremberg Charter generated active judicial lawmaking, perhaps unsurprisingly and even necessarily.[5] The rules of procedure of the Nuremberg Tribunal, including those relating to admissible defences, showed an equal lack of loquacity and thus did not escape the interpretative artistry of the judges.[6] Article 7 of the Charter merely enunciated that '[t]he official position of defendants, whether as Heads of State or responsible officials in Government Departments, shall not be considered as freeing them from responsibility or mitigating punishment'.[7] Article 8 stated briefly that '[t]he fact that the Defendant acted pursuant to order of his Government or of a superior shall not free him from responsibility, but may be considered in mitigation of punishment if the Tribunal determines that justice so requires'.[8] The door was clearly opened to judicial interpretation and possible judicial lawmaking by Article 19 of the Charter, which empowered the Tribunal to adopt its own procedural rules.[9] In contrast, the Rome Statute of the ICC sets out a detailed list of admissible 'grounds for excluding criminal responsibility' which may be raised by an accused, although judges also have scope to consider potential defences not included in the Statute.[10] The instrument appears to deviate significantly from the judicial precedents elaborated since Nuremberg with respect to certain defences, thus leaving some uncertainty hanging over the law of defences.

[4] Schabas (n 1 above) 325–6.

[5] The same remark may be made with respect to the Tokyo Charter of the International Military Tribunal for the Far East (IMTFE), 19 January 1946, *United States Treaties and Other International Acts Series* 1589.

[6] See *Uniform Rules of Procedure, Military Tribunals, Nuremberg*, adopted 29 October 1945 and revised 8 January 1948, in *Trial of the Major War Criminals Before the International Military Tribunal, Nuremberg, 14 November 1945–1 October 1946*, Vol 1 (International Military Tribunal, Nuremberg 1947–1949).

[7] Agreement for the Prosecution and Punishment of the Major War Criminals of the European Axis, and Charter of the International Military Tribunal, London, 8 August 1945, in *Trial of the Major War Criminals Before the International Military Tribunal, Nuremberg, 14 November 1945–1 October 1946*, Vol 1 (International Military Tribunal, Nuremberg 1947–1949), Art 7.

[8] ibid Art 8.

[9] ibid Art 19.

[10] Rome Statute of the International Criminal Court, UN Doc A/CONF.183/9, (1998) 2187 UNTS 90, Arts 31–3. See generally S Darcy, 'Defences to international crimes' in WA Schabas and N Bernaz (eds), *Routledge Handbook of International Criminal Law* (Oxford: forthcoming: Routledge, 2010).

To appreciate the contribution of the *ad hoc* Tribunals to the law of defences, the following analysis focuses on the case law related to the principle of legality, to factors mitigating punishment, and to grounds for excluding responsibility, including defence pleas specifically raised in the context of armed conflicts. Reference will be made where relevant to the Nuremberg precedent and to the Rome Statute of the ICC in order to assess adequately the contribution of the international criminal tribunals to defences. The dichotomy between the case law of the Tribunals and the Rome Statute on the qualification of pleas as either mitigating factors or grounds excluding responsibility, as well as on the admissibility of certain defence pleas, will arguably allow for further judicial creativity at the ICC itself.

II. The Principle of Legality: A Defence of Sorts

Nullum crimen, nulla poena sine lege praevia, the principle of legality, implies that there can be no crime without pre-existing law. Although a well-known principle of law in both domestic and international systems, neither statute of the *ad hoc* Tribunals makes direct reference to it, despite the fact that the Report of the Secretary-General places significant emphasis on its centrality to the legitimacy of the ICTY.[11] The absence of an express provision is surprising given the fact that international criminal law has had to face harsh criticism as to its legitimacy since its inception after the Second World War. Since Nuremberg, defendants before international criminal courts have regularly challenged jurisdiction on the basis of an alleged failure to respect the legality principle.[12]

One of the sternest criticisms of the Nuremberg Charter and trial, which has led to fierce and fervent debates, is the alleged contravention of the legality principle through the creation of new crimes and the simultaneous recognition of individual criminal responsibility attached to their perpetration. While the principle can be seen as a safeguard against injustice, it is also arguable that it is 'an ethical principle rather than a rule of law, [and] it may be set aside if considerations of justice demand it'.[13] As Julius Stone has observed: 'Where it has been adopted

[11] 'Report of the Secretary-General' (n 2 above) para 34.

[12] For instance, with respect to the ICTY, Slobodan Milošević argued that he did not 'recognise this court' and had 'no intention of appointing counsel for a non-existent court': *Prosecutor v Milošević* (Trial Transcript) IT-02-54 (25 July 2002) p 8632, lines 24–5. In the same vein, Radovan Karadžić has also threatened to boycott his trial, thus failing to appear before the Trial Chamber. See *Prosecutor v Karadžić* (Trial Transcript) IT-95-5/18-I (26 October 2009, 27 October 2009, 2 November 2009). Karadžić nonetheless maintained that he did not 'want to boycott... these proceedings' but could not 'take part in something that has been bad from the start and where [his] fundamental rights have been violated': *Prosecutor v Karadžić* (Trial Transcript) IT-95-5/18-I (3 November 2009) p 676, lines 12–14.

[13] RK Woetzel, *The Nuremberg Trials in International Law. With a Postlude on the Eichmann Case* (London: Stevens and Sons, 1962) 112.

into a legal system, it is usually with exceptions and qualifications; and in many countries, including most British countries, it is not a *rule of law* at all.'[14] Hans Kelsen also maintained that an act may be punished as a crime if it was clearly *illegal in character* at the time of its commission.[15] Although admittedly prompted by the circumstances and driven by the facts, it seems obvious that the law of the Nuremberg Charter ultimately criminalized acts which were illegal *per se*.

The defendants at Nuremberg were swift in invoking the *nullum crimen, nulla poena sine lege praevia* principle when attempting to refute the jurisdiction of the IMT.[16] Equally swift were the judges in their dismissal of this challenge and in their confirmation of jurisdiction. As they boldly asserted, 'it is to be observed that the maxim *nullum crimen sine lege* is not a limitation of sovereignty, but is *in general* a principle of justice'.[17] In other words, the judges admitted the legality principle but, considering the circumstances and the amplitude of the crimes, voluntarily chose to reject it. As they controversially held:

> [t]he Charter is not an arbitrary exercise of power on the part of the victorious Nations, but in the view of the Tribunal, as will be shown, it is the *expression of international law existing at the time of its creation*; and to that extent is itself a contribution to international law.[18]

And while it may be, in the words of Yoram Dinstein, 'virtually irrefutable that present-day international law reflects the Judgment',[19] it remains that the Nuremberg judges acknowledged the legal novelty of the Charter and knowingly established new law. Had they refrained from adopting a proactive and constructive attitude with respect to the challenge based on the legality principle, international criminal law would have remained dormant.

This approach raises the question of respect for the principle of legality. While contemporary human rights law treats the principle of non-retroactive criminal law as a fundamental right, it nonetheless recognizes certain limits to its application[20] and essentially views the principle as a safeguard against abusive and unfair judicial proceedings and as a guarantee of credibility for proceedings.

[14] J Stone, *Legal Controls of International Conflict—A Treatise on the Dynamics of Disputes—And War—Law* (London: Stevens and Sons, 2nd revsd impression, 1959) 368.

[15] H Kelsen, 'Will the Judgment in the Nuremberg Trial Constitute a Precedent in International Law?' (1947) 1 ILQ 153, 165. It may also be noted here that in the *Llandovery Castle* case, the German Supreme Court at Leipzig ruled that an individual may be punished for violations of international law which may not have been defined as crimes, but which were clearly illegal in character. See Woetzel (n 13 above) 114.

[16] For an extensive analysis of the 'arguments bearing on the issues of legality' raised by the defence at Nuremberg, see KS Gallant, *The Principle of Legality in International and Comparative Criminal Law* (Cambridge: CUP, 2009) 99–110.

[17] *Judgment of the Nuremberg International Military Tribunal 1946* (1947) 41(1) AJIL 172, 217 (emphasis added).

[18] ibid 189 (emphasis added).

[19] Y Dinstein, 'The Distinctions between War Crimes and Crimes Against Peace' in Y Dinstein and M Tabory (eds), *War Crimes in International Law* (The Hague: Martinus Nijhoff, 1996) 2.

[20] See the International Covenant on Civil and Political Rights, Art 15(2); and the European Convention for the Protection of Human Rights and Fundamental Freedoms, Art 7(2).

In the contemporary context, the silence of the Statutes of the international criminal tribunals as regards the principle may also be problematic. William Schabas has observed that '[a]lthough formally professing rigid adherence to the *nullum crimen* principle, in practice judges at the *ad hoc* tribunals have taken a relatively relaxed approach, much in the spirit of their predecessors at Nuremberg...'.[21]

This 'relatively relaxed approach' may be illustrated by the rather wide interpretation given to the legality principle by the ICTY Appeals Chamber in the *Aleksovski* case:

> That principle does not prevent a court, either at the national or international level, from *determining an issue through a process of interpretation and clarification* as to the element of a particular crime; nor does it prevent a court from relying on previous decisions which reflect an interpretation as to the meaning to be ascribed to particular ingredients of a crime.[22]

The drafters of the Rome Statute of the ICC departed from the approach of previous statutes and chose to give due consideration to the *nullum crimen sine lege* principle in Article 22:

> 1. A person shall not be criminally responsible under this Statute unless the conduct in question constitutes, at the time it takes place, a crime within the jurisdiction of the Court.
> 2. The definition of a crime shall be strictly construed and shall not be extended by analogy. In case of ambiguity, the definition shall be interpreted in favour of the person being investigated, prosecuted or convicted.
> 3. This article shall not affect the characterization of any conduct as criminal under international law independently of this Statute.[23]

The inclusion of the principle of legality in the Rome Statute is to be welcomed, and while it should not prevent the ICC judges from equally adopting a 'relatively relaxed approach', it should however pre-empt criticism as to the legality of the proceedings in The Hague.

The principle of legality is used by defence counsel as a basis for challenging the legal qualification of an act as a crime and thus the jurisdiction of a court or tribunal, rather than questioning the criminal responsibility of an individual, and accordingly is not a defence *per se*. The next section considers defences proper before the *ad hoc* Tribunals and occasions where defences are treated as mitigating factors in sentencing.

[21] Schabas (n 1 above) 63.

[22] *Prosecutor v Aleksovski* (Appeals Chamber Judgment) IT-95-14/1A (24 March 2000) para 127 (emphasis added).

[23] ICC Statute, Arts 22–4. See Rome Statute of the International Criminal Court, adopted by the United Nations Diplomatic Conference of Plenipotentiaries on the Establishment of an International Criminal Court on 17 July 1998, UN Doc A/Conf.183/9.

III. Factors Mitigating Punishment or Admissible Defences?

A. Obedience to superior orders

Both Statutes of the *ad hoc* Tribunals address the issue of obedience to superior orders and expressly exclude it as a valid defence, stressing that it may only be considered as a mitigating circumstance: 'The fact that an accused person acted pursuant to an order of a Government or of a superior shall not relieve him of criminal responsibility, but may be considered in mitigation of punishment if the International Tribunal determines that justice so requires.'[24]

This approach arguably contrasts with military law, which is based on a hierarchical system where discipline and obedience to superior orders, supposedly legitimate and lawfully executed, are values to be preserved.[25] Nonetheless, the provision merely mirrors the Nuremberg Charter, which had indicated that this argument would not free defendants from responsibility and would only mitigate punishment 'if the Tribunal determines that justice so requires'.[26] The Nuremberg Tribunal accordingly ruled that the true test was 'not the existence of the order, but whether a moral choice was in fact possible', explaining that:

> [s]uperior orders, even to a soldier, cannot be considered in mitigation when crimes as shocking and extensive have been committed consciously, ruthlessly and without military excuse or justification... It was... submitted on behalf of most of these defendants that in doing what they did they were acting under the orders of Hitler, and therefore cannot be held responsible for the acts committed by them in carrying out these orders... The

[24] ICTY Statute, Art 7(4); and ICTR Statute, Art 6(4).

[25] As explained by Yoram Dinstein, '*respondeat superior* is based on the demands of military discipline, on the one hand, and on the elements of mistake of law and compulsion, on the other. It removes the responsibility from the shoulders of one person, the recipient of the order, and places it on the shoulders of another, the superior who issued the order'. Y Dinstein, *The Defence of 'Obedience to Superior Orders' in International Law* (The Hague: AW Sijthoff, 1965) 59–60.

[26] IMT Charter, Art 8. For a valid precedent, see the Report of Commission on the Responsibility of the Authors of the War and on Enforcement of Penalties: 'civil and military authorities cannot be relieved from responsibility by the mere fact that a higher authority might have been convicted of the same offence. It will be for the court to decide whether a plea of superior orders is sufficient to acquit the person charged with responsibility': 'Commission on the Responsibility of the Authors of the War and on Enforcement of Penalties—Report Presented to the Preliminary Peace Conference, March 29, 1919' (1920) 14 AJIL 117. It is interesting to note here that, although Art 227 of the 1919 Versailles Treaty failed to mention such a defence and only included criminal provisions to punish war crimes committed by nationals of the Central Powers, the defence of obedience to superior orders was judicially addressed and admitted but only in a restrictive fashion. In the *Llandovery Castle* case, the Court recognized that it was a relevant factor for mitigation of punishment but held that German military law did not excuse subordinates who exceeded orders or who carried out orders that they knew were illegal. See *Judgment in Case of Lieutenants Dithmar and Boldt, Hospital Ship 'Llandovery Castle'*, Leipzig Supreme Court (German War Trials), 16 July 1921, reprinted in (1922) 16 AJIL 708–24. For an excellent analysis of the historical development of the defence of superior orders, see M Lippman, 'Conundrums Of Armed Conflict: Criminal Defenses To Violations Of The Humanitarian law of War' (1996) 15 *Dickinson Journal of International Law* 1.

> provisions of... Article [8] are in conformity with the law of all nations. That a soldier was ordered to kill or torture in violation of the international law of war has never been recognized as a defense to such acts of brutality, though, as the Charter here provides, the order may be urged in mitigation of the punishment.[27]

These findings highlight the distinction between defences and mitigating factors in sentencing, but more importantly illustrate the approach of the Nuremberg judges who refrained from using the brevity of the text of Article 8 as an excuse to depart from its ordinary meaning. Finch is correct in his view that, if superior orders had been accepted as a defence at Nuremberg, 'the rule *respondeat superior* would have served merely as *reductio ad absurdum* for the purpose of frustrating the law. Upon such a theory it would have been impossible to punish anyone for the crimes of this war.'[28] Although a popular argument raised by most of the defendants at Nuremberg and in the subsequent proceedings related to the crimes perpetrated by the Nazis, courts and tribunals have generally rejected this plea as a ground for excluding criminal responsibility.[29] It has been noted by Schabas that '[t]his is in stark contrast with the... United Nations *ad hoc* tribunals, where the defence of superior orders has been raised only rarely'.[30] Alexander Zahar and Göran Sluiter have observed that:

> [d]espite significant academic discussion on the defence of superior orders, it is almost by definition not a live defence at the tribunals. Persons accused before the tribunals are senior military or civilian leaders, or, if low-ranking, they are accused of very serious crimes. In neither case can they have been unaware of the illegal nature of the orders resulting

[27] *Nuremberg Judgment* (n 17 above) 223–4.

[28] GA Finch, 'The Nuremberg Trial and International Law' (1947) 41 AJIL 20, 21.

[29] See *United States v Ohlendorf et al* (Case No 9, Military Tribunal II) 4 Nuremberg Subsequent Proceedings 470–1 and 666; *United States v Flick et al* (Case No 5, Military Tribunal IV) 6 Nuremberg Subsequent Proceedings 1213; *United States v Krauch et al* (Case No 6, Military Tribunal VI) 7–8 Nuremberg Subsequent Proceedings; *United States v Milch et al* (Case No 2, Military Tribunal II) 2 Nuremberg Subsequent Proceedings 42 and 791; *United States v Greifelt et al* (Case No 8, Military Tribunal I) 5 Nuremberg Subsequent Proceedings 153–4; *United States v von Leeb et al* (Case No 12, Military Tribunal V) 10–11 Nuremberg Subsequent Proceedings 507–9; *United States v von List et al* (Case No 7, Military Tribunal) 11 Nuremberg Subsequent Proceedings 1236–8. At the domestic level, see *A-G Israel v Eichmann* [1968] 36 ILR 5 (District Court, Jerusalem), where the District Court held that an order should not be obeyed blindly but rather questioned by conscience, finding that '[s]ince the order was manifestly unlawful, it cannot be used as an excuse' and that 'the accused acted in accordance with general directives from his superiors, but there still remained to him wide powers of discretion which extended also to the planning of operations on his own initiative'. See also *Fédération Nationale des Déportés et Internés Résistants et Patriotes et Autres v Klaus Barbie*, cass crim, 6 October 1983; reprinted in (1984) RGDIP 88, 509, where the French Cour de cassation unequivocally recalled the scope of application of the Nuremberg Charter, Art 8, reiterating that this disposition was never meant to be an excuse nor a mandatory mitigating circumstance. Contra, see (1947–49) 3 LRTWC 23, cited by Dinstein as 'one unique case, and it seems to be an anomalous phenomenon and an historical anachronism, which does not fall into line with all the other post-Second World War cases': Dinstein (n 25 above) 194–6. See also *Regina v Finta* [1994] 1 SCR 701 (24 March 1994) where the Supreme Court of Canada ruled that the superior order defence was available to defendants charged with war crimes and crimes against humanity.

[30] Schabas (n 1 above) 331.

in the alleged crimes. If they did perform the acts they are accused of pursuant to orders, then they (or any reasonable person in their position) would have realized that the orders were illegal.[31]

Superior orders were, however, a central issue in relation to sentencing in the *Erdemović* case at the ICTY. Trial Chamber I, after considering the fact that the Nuremberg Tribunal had rejected the plea of superior orders as a mitigating factor in the case of the major war criminals, decided that it could nonetheless be accepted for 'low ranking accused'. In other words, the importance of superior orders as a mitigating factor would vary according to the rank of the accused:

> ...the Trial Chamber considers that the rejection by the Nuremberg Tribunal of the defence of superior orders, raised in order to obtain a reduction of the penalty imposed on the accused, is explained by their position of superior authority and that, consequently, the precedent setting value of the judgment in this respect is diminished for low ranking accused.[32]

The Trial Chamber further specified that, to be validly claimed as a mitigating factor, the superior orders invoked must have influenced the defendant in his criminal behaviour: 'If the order had no influence on the unlawful behaviour because the accused was already prepared to carry it out, no such mitigating circumstances can be said to exist.'[33]

The Rome Statute of the ICC is in contrast to the approach at Nuremberg and the *ad hoc* Tribunals and, in Article 33, deviates unjustifiably from both public international law precedents[34] and customary international law[35] by

[31] A Zahar and G Sluiter, *International Criminal Law: A Critical Introduction* (Oxford: OUP, 2007) 425.

[32] *Prosecutor v Erdemović* (Trial Chamber Sentencing Judgment) IT-96-22-T (29 November 1996) para 51.

[33] ibid para 53.

[34] See eg the 1946 UN Resolution on the Affirmation of the Principles of International Law recognized by the Charter of the Nuremberg Tribunal, which expressly recalled the validity of Art 8 of the Charter, while the 1950 International Law Commission's Report on the Nuremberg Principles declared that 'the fact that a person acted pursuant to order of his government or of a superior does not relieve him from responsibility under International Law provided a moral choice was in fact possible to him' ([1950] II *ILC Yearbook*, Principle IV). In its 1996 Draft Code of Crimes, the Commission reaffirmed that 'the existing rule of international law under which the mere fact that an individual committed a crime while acting pursuant to the order of his Government or his superior will not shield him from criminal responsibility for his conduct but may constitute a mitigating factor in certain situations when justice so requires' (Art 5, [1996] II (2) *ILC Yearbook* 23). See the Convention against Torture and Other Cruel, Inhuman or Degrading Treatment or Punishment (adopted 10 December 1984, entered into force 26 June 1987) Art 2(3).

[35] See A Cassese, 'The Statute of the International Criminal Court: Some Preliminary Reflections' (1999) 10 EJIL 144, 157. See also P Gaeta, 'The Defence of Superior Orders: The Statute of the International Criminal Court versus Customary International Law' (1999) 10 EJIL 172–91. For an opposite view, see H McCoubrey, 'From Nuremberg to Rome: Restoring the defence of superior orders' (2001) 50 ICLQ 386–94, in which the author convincingly argues that the Rome Statute, far from representing a 'softening of the international legal approach to war crimes', has in fact 'merely recognised the essential doctrine of superior orders as it existed prior to 1945 and which, properly understood, should not have been thought essentially to have been changed even in 1945' (ibid 386).

adopting a conditional liability approach.[36] Unlike other legal instruments, the Rome Statute does not exclude the defence of superior orders and provides that an accused may be relieved of criminal responsibility if such a person had been 'under a legal obligation to obey orders of the Government or the superior in question', had no knowledge 'that the order was unlawful', and '[t]he order was not manifestly unlawful'.[37] This is a departure from the precedent at the *ad hoc* Tribunals.

The Rome Statute also draws a questionable distinction between crimes against peace and war crimes, on the one hand, and crimes against humanity and genocide, on the other. By expressly stating that 'orders to commit genocide or crimes against humanity are manifestly unlawful',[38] and thereby excluding the 'obedience to superior orders' defence in such cases, Article 33 automatically implies that orders to commit crimes against peace and war crimes are not always manifestly unlawful and can therefore be validly invoked as a defence. Considering the seriousness of all international crimes, the suggestion that orders to perpetrate either crimes against peace or war crimes could not be manifestly unlawful is difficult to comprehend. It seems improbable that any order to commit one of the acts listed in Article 8 of the Rome Statute as a war crime could not be manifestly unlawful. As Antonio Cassese rightly recalled, according to customary international law, any order to commit an international crime—regardless of its classification—is illegal and thus may not be urged in defence.[39] He further considered that:

> given the specificity of Article 8, one fails to see under what circumstances the order to commit one of the crimes listed therein may be regarded as not manifestly unlawful, ie if nothing else, it would be 'manifest' in the text of the Rome Statute itself... On this score... Article 33 must be faulted as marking a retrogression with respect to existing customary law.[40]

It remains to be seen how the ICC judges will interpret Article 33 and whether they will opt for a literal interpretation of the text of the Statute or choose to depart from it and return to the precedent of Nuremberg and the *ad hoc* Tribunals, thus staying within the ambit of pre-existing law.

The ICC judges might also have to clarify the link between the defence of obedience to superior orders and that of duress, a matter which has yet to be definitely settled. As identified by Schabas, 'difficulties with superior orders sometimes arise because of confusion with the defence of duress',[41] insofar as the link

[36] According to Paola Gaeta, this new approach is due to the concern of the United States to protect their servicemen on the battlefield from international criminal responsibility if they obey orders in order to carry out military operations. See P Gaeta (n 35 above) 189.

[37] ICC Statute, Art 33(1).

[38] ibid.

[39] Cassese (n 35 above) 157.

[40] ibid. See also Gaeta (n 35 above).

[41] WA Schabas, *Genocide in International Law—The Crime of Crimes* (Cambridge: CUP, 2nd edn, 2009) 385.

between superior orders and duress is two fold. Indeed, duress, which forces a person to act in a criminal way and to harm another in order to avoid a greater or equal personal harm, could be present alongside superior orders. As the United States Military Tribunal held in the *Einsatzgruppen* case:

> But were any of the defendants coerced into killing Jews under the threat of being killed themselves if they failed in their homicidal mission? The test to be applied is whether the subordinate acted under coercion or whether he himself approved of the principle involved in the order. If the second proposition be true, the plea of superior orders fails. The doer may not plead innocence to a criminal act ordered by his superior if he is in accord with the principle and intent of the superior. When the will of the doer merges with the will of the superior in the execution of the illegal act, the doer may not plead duress under superior orders.[42]

In this context, the opinion expressed by Dinstein is worth recalling:

> The correct legal position is that the fact that a defendant acted in obedience to superior orders cannot constitute a defence *per se*, but is a factual element which may be taken into account—in conjunction with other circumstances—within the compass of an admissible defence based on lack of *mens rea* (specifically, duress or mistake).[43]

The admissibility of such 'other circumstances', and particularly duress, in defence has led to judicial controversies and debates and has put the constructive role of the international criminal judge into a greater and more obvious limelight.

B. Duress

The defence of duress, which will be raised by an accused claiming to have been coerced into engaging in criminal behaviour so as to avoid a greater or equal personal harm, is highly controversial in international criminal law and is absent from both Statutes of the *ad hoc* Tribunals. Post-Second World War international criminal jurisprudence established that the defence of duress had to be based on firm evidence that the accused was genuinely unwilling to commit the crime in question and that he would have avoided perpetrating the crime but for the duress.[44] The case law also revealed the unease of judges towards this defence, given their recognition of the possibility that one might not have had a choice when perpetrating an international crime. In the *Einsatzgruppen* case, the United States Military Tribunal found that this defence was unavailable where the crime was perpetrated after the duress had ended and where the actual harm caused by

[42] *Ohlendorf* (n 29 above) 480.

[43] Y Dinstein, *War, Aggression and Self-Defence* (Cambridge: CUP, 3rd edn, 2001) 131. See also Dinstein (n 19 above) 12–14; Dinstein (n 25 above) 252.

[44] See *United States v Krupp et al* (Case No 10, Military Tribunal III) 9 Nuremberg Subsequent Proceedings 1439; *Ohlendorf* (n 29 above) 470–1 and 666; *Flick* (n 29 above) 1213; *Krauch* (n 29 above).

the crime was disproportionately greater than the potential harm to the accused, or to those individuals close to him:

If one claims duress in the execution of an illegal order it must be shown that the harm caused by obeying the illegal order is not disproportionately greater than the harm which would result from not obeying the illegal order. It would not be an adequate excuse, for example, if a subordinate under orders killed a person known to be innocent, because by not obeying it he himself would risk a few days of confinement. Nor if one acts under duress, may he, without culpability, commit the illegal act once the duress ceases.[45]

The Tribunal in this instance also made the questionable finding that, in the context of mass killings of Jews by Nazi extermination squads, 'there is no law which requires that an innocent man must forfeit his life or suffer serious harm in order to avoid committing a crime which he condemns'.[46] This position was sharply criticized on the grounds that 'no degree of duress can justify murder, let alone genocide. It can scarcely be contested today that atrocities, and even plain murder, cannot be exonerated on the ground of duress under international criminal law.'[47]

The issue of duress also arose before the ICTY and prompted much judicial debate among members of the Appeals Chamber. Judge Cassese, in his Separate and Dissenting Opinion in the *Erdemović* case, upheld the finding in the *Einsatzgruppen* case.[48] The case also brought to the fore the overlap between the defence of superior orders and duress; as explained by the Trial Chamber:

The order of a superior must, however, also be examined in the light of the related issue of duress. The Secretary-General, conscious of a link between the two, suggested in his report that acting upon an order of a Government or a superior may be considered 'in connection with other defences such as coercion or lack of moral choice'. (Report of the Secretary-General, S/25704, para. 57). The Trial Chamber notes that when duress was not accepted as grounds for exculpating the accused—the analysis it made when reviewing the guilty plea in this case—the tribunals have nevertheless acknowledged that it might be a mitigating circumstance entailing a more lenient sentence.[49]

Judge Cassese, in his Separate and Dissenting Opinion, explained further:

It is also important to mention that, in the case-law, duress is commonly raised in conjunction with superior orders. However there is no necessary connection between the two. Superior orders may be issued without being accompanied by any threats to life or limb. In these circumstances, if the superior order is manifestly illegal under international

[45] *Ohlendorf* (n 29 above) 470–1. [46] ibid 480. [47] Dinstein (n 19 above) 9–11.

[48] See *Prosecutor v Erdemović* (Separate and Dissenting Opinion of Judge Cassese) IT-96-22-A (7 October 1997) para 27.

[49] *Erdemović* (Trial Chamber Sentencing Judgment) (n 32 above) para 54. See also *Prosecutor v Blaškić* (Trial Chamber Judgment) IT-95-14 (3 March 2000) para 769: 'Duress, where established, does mitigate the criminal responsibility of the accused when he had no choice or moral freedom in committing the crime. This must consequently entail the passing of a lighter sentence if he cannot be completely exonerated of responsibility.'

law, the subordinate is under a duty to refuse to obey the order. If, following such a refusal, the order is reiterated under a threat to life or limb, then the defence of duress may be raised, and superior orders lose any legal relevance. Equally, duress may be raised entirely independently of superior orders, for example where the threat issues from a fellow serviceman. Thus, where duress is raised in conjunction with manifestly unlawful superior orders, the accused may only have a defence if he first refused to obey the unlawful order and then only carried it out after a threat to life or limb.[50]

The ICTY judges had to overcome the silence of the Statute as regards duress and although, in this particular case, the Trial Chamber found insufficient evidence to accept the duress plea, it nonetheless accepted as relevant the fact that the accused had followed orders and had held a subordinate position in the military hierarchy.[51] The majority of the Appeals Chamber found 'that duress does not afford a complete defence to a soldier charged with a crime against humanity and/or a war crime involving the killing of innocent human beings'.[52] Duress could, however, be considered as a mitigating circumstance. The majority's finding was disputed and as noted by Schabas: 'The finding of the Appeals Chamber left great uncertainty about the question, because it settled the issue by only the barest of majorities.'[53] Judges Cassese and Stephen dissenting insofar as they both favoured the admissibility of the defence of duress. As explained by Judge Cassese:

> I do not see any point in contending that, since duress can be urged in mitigation, a court of law could take account of the situations just discussed by sentencing the person who acted under duress to a minimum or token penalty. Any such contention would neglect a critical, inescapable point, namely that the purpose of criminal law, including international criminal law, is to punish behaviour which is criminal, ie, morally reprehensible or injurious to society, not to condemn behaviour which is 'the product of coercion that is truly irresistible' or the choice of the lesser of two evils. No matter how much mitigation a court allows an accused, the fundamental fact remains that if it convicts him, it regards his behaviour as criminal, and considers that he should have behaved differently. I have tried to demonstrate that this may be unjust and unreasonable where the accused can do nothing to save the victims by laying down his own life.[54]

The judicial approach advocated by the dissenting members of the Appeals Chamber was favoured during the drafting of the Rome Statute of the ICC. The instrument endorses the position taken by Judges Cassese and Stephen by including duress and necessity as valid grounds for excluding individual criminal

[50] *Erdemović* (Separate and Dissenting Opinion of Judge Cassese) (n 48 above) para 15.

[51] ibid paras 91–5.

[52] *Prosecutor v Erdemović* (Appeal of Sentencing Judgment) IT-96-22 (7 October 1997) para 19 and Joint Separate Opinion of Judges McDonald and Vohrah appended to the *Erdemović* Sentencing Appeal, para 66. See also *Prosecutor v Krstić* (Trial Chamber Judgment) IT-98-33 (2 August 2001) para 714.

[53] Schabas (n 41 above) 391.

[54] *Erdemović* (Separate and Dissenting Opinion of Judge Cassese) (n 48 above) para 48 (footnote omitted).

responsibility for all crimes.[55] Article 31(1)(d) states that a person shall not be criminally responsible for conduct if at the time of commission:

(d) The conduct which is alleged to constitute a crime within the jurisdiction of the Court has been caused by duress resulting from a threat of imminent death or of continuing or imminent serious bodily harm against that person or another person, and the person acts necessarily and reasonably to avoid this threat, provided that the person does not intend to cause a greater harm than the one sought to be avoided. Such a threat may either be:

(i) Made by other persons; or
(ii) Constituted by other *circumstances beyond that person's control* [emphasis added].

The inclusion of duress as a defence in the Rome Statute triggered a reaction from Ilias Bantekas and Susan Nash, for whom '[t]he poor drafting of Article 31(1)(d) has its roots not in the ignorance of its drafters, but rather on the divergent and inflexible views of the negotiating parties'.[56] ICC judges may have an opportunity to settle the law on the matter of duress, although they will be bound to respect the unambiguous terms of the Rome Statute. Accordingly, they are likely to depart from the failed attempt at judicial lawmaking by the majority of the *Erdemović* Appeals Chamber, which had excluded such a defence for crimes against innocent persons.

C. Mental incapacity and intoxication

Statutory silence did not prevent the ICTY Appeals Chamber in the *Delalić* case from admitting mental incapacity or insanity as a defence. Based on a review of domestic law, the Chamber held that:

...if the defendant raises the issue of *lack* of mental capacity, he is challenging the presumption of sanity by a plea of insanity. That is a defence in the true sense, in that the defendant bears the onus of establishing it—that, more probably than not, at the time of the offence he was labouring under such a defect of reason, from disease of the mind, as not to know the nature and quality of his act or, if he did know it, that he did not know that what he was doing was wrong. Such a plea, if successful, is a complete defence to a charge and it leads to an acquittal.[57]

To justify its decision and probably to pre-empt and dismiss any accusation of excessive judicial activism, the Appeals Chamber felt the need to specify the

[55] William Schabas explains that '[t]he defence of necessity is closely related to duress, in that the accused argues that the material act was committed under circumstances where there was an absence of moral choice. In the case of duress, the exterior pressure comes from an individual; in the case of necessity, it results from natural causes' (footnote omitted). Schabas (n 41 above) 392–3.

[56] I Bantekas and S Nash, *International Criminal Law* (London: Routledge-Cavendish, 3rd edn, 2003) 61.

[57] *Prosecutor v Delalić et al* (Appeals Chamber Judgment) IT-96-21-A (20 February 2001) para 582 (footnotes omitted).

'rule-making powers of the judges', stressing that 'there is . . . no power to adopt rules which constitute new defences'. It stated that:

> . . . there is no reference to any defence of diminished mental responsibility in the Tribunal's Statute. The description of diminished mental responsibility as a 'special defence' in Rule 67(A)(ii) is insufficient to constitute it as such. The rule-making powers of the judges are defined by Article 15 of the Tribunal's Statute, which gives power to the judges to adopt only—
>
> > . . . *rules of procedure and evidence* for the conduct of the pre-trial phase of the proceedings, trials and appeals, the admission of evidence, the protection of victims and witnesses and other appropriate matters.
>
> The Appeals Chamber has held that this power does not permit rules to be adopted which constitute new *offences*, but only *rules of procedure and evidence* for the conduct of matters falling within the jurisdiction of the Tribunal. It follows that there is, therefore, no power to adopt rules which constitute new *defences*. If there is a 'special defence of diminished responsibility known to international law, it must be found in the usual sources of international law—in this case, in the absence of reference to such a defence in established customary or conventional law, in the general principles of law recognised by all nations.[58]

Drawing a distinction between mental incapacity and 'diminished mental responsibility', the ICTY Appeals Chamber specified that the latter could only be invoked as a factor mitigating punishment:

> The Appeals Chamber accepts that the relevant general principle of law upon which, in effect, both the common law and the civil law systems have acted is that the defendant's diminished mental responsibility is relevant to the sentence to be imposed and is not a defence leading to an acquittal in the true sense. This is the appropriate general legal principle representing the international law to be applied in the Tribunal. Rule 67(A)(ii)(b) must therefore be interpreted as referring to diminished mental responsibility where it is to be raised by the defendant as a matter in mitigation of sentence.[59]

This position of the Appeals Chamber was endorsed by the *Vasiljević* Trial Chamber, which held that 'the issue of diminished mental responsibility is relevant only to the sentence to be imposed. It is not a defence that if established would lead to the acquittal of the Accused.'[60]

The Rome Statute is explicit on this defence and accepts mental defect as a ground for excluding criminal responsibility. According to Article 31(1)(a) of the Statute, a person may escape criminal liability if '[t]he person suffers from a mental disease or defect that destroys that person's capacity to appreciate the unlawfulness or nature of his or her conduct, or capacity to control his or her conduct to conform to the requirements of law'. In other words, a valid plea of mental

[58] ibid para 583 (emphasis in original, footnotes omitted).

[59] ibid para 590.

[60] *Prosecutor v Vasiljević* (Trial Chamber Judgment) IT-98-32-T (29 November 2002) para 282.

incapacitation may be entered when it deprived the defendant of the mental ability to appreciate the wrongfulness of an act.

The Rome Statute, unlike the statutes of the *ad hoc* Tribunals, also addresses the defence of intoxication, and states in its Article 31(1)(b) that a person shall not be criminally responsible if, at the time of his or her conduct:

> The person is in a state of intoxication that destroys that person's capacity to appreciate the unlawfulness or nature of his or her conduct, or capacity to control his or her conduct to conform to the requirements of law, unless the person has become voluntarily intoxicated under such circumstances that the person knew, or disregarded the risk, that, as a result of the intoxication, he or she was likely to engage in conduct constituting a crime within the jurisdiction of the Court.

As explained by Cassese:

> Being in an intoxicated state as a result of taking alcohol, drugs, or other intoxicants may amount to an excuse only under very strict conditions: (1) the intoxication is so serious as to negate *mens rea* (that is, it alters the agent's mental state to such a point that he is not in a position to be aware of his actions and to appraise the unlawfulness of his conduct); (2) in the case of voluntary intoxication, the person has not become voluntarily intoxicated knowing the risk that, as a result of his state, he was likely to engage in criminal action.[61]

Although this has arisen only rarely before the *ad hoc* Tribunals, reference may still be made to the *Kvočka* case, where an ICTY Trial Chamber rejected the defendant's claim that intoxication should be a mitigating factor and instead found it to be an aggravating circumstance, considering the 'extreme gravity of the crimes committed'.[62]

IV. Admissible Defences and the Law of Armed Conflict

A. Self-defence

Jens David Ohlin explains that: 'Self-defence is recognized either implicitly or explicitly in every legal system as a ground for excluding criminal responsibility. It is best regarded as a justification, ie a defence that negates not the culpability of the defendant but rather the very existence of wrongdoing itself.'[63] While the right to self-defence is widely admitted at the domestic level, the issue becomes more controversial when it is claimed as a ground for excluding individual criminal

[61] A Cassese, *International Criminal Law* (Oxford: OUP, 2nd edn, 2008) 266.

[62] *Prosecutor v Kvočka et al* (Trial Chamber Judgment) IT-98-30/1-T (2 November 2001) para 748.

[63] J Ohlin, 'Self-Defence' in A Cassese (ed), *The Oxford Companion to International Criminal Justice* (Oxford: OUP, 2009) 506.

responsibility for international crimes. Self-defence has been raised before the *ad hoc* Tribunals, albeit in a confused manner, as it:

> ... has been presented in a collective sense, justifying the use of force rather than specific atrocities. In this way, it is closer to the concept of self-defence as used in article 51 of the Charter of the United Nations, although with respect to the tribunals the argument has been put with respect to internal armed conflicts instead of as a justification for the use of force in international relations.[64]

Karadžić provided a recent example in his opening defence statement where he expressed his intention of defending his nation and its 'just and holy' cause[65] and qualified the Bosnian war as one of self-defence by the Bosnian Serbs against Muslims, referring to 'everything Serbs did as part of their own legitimate defence'.[66] This argument had previously been raised by Plavšić, who argued that she had convinced herself that the war against Croats and Muslims was 'a matter of survival and self-defence'.[67] In a similarly incorrect manner, self-defence was also invoked under the labels of 'civil defence' or 'auto defence' before the ICTR in relation to the extermination of Tutsis.[68]

This confusion was adequately addressed by the ICTY Appeals Chamber, which clearly specified that military operations in self-defence were not admissible defences excluding individual criminal responsibility:

> Of particular relevance to this case is the last sentence of the above provision to the effect that the involvement of a person in a 'defensive operation' does not 'in itself' constitute a ground for excluding criminal responsibility. It is therefore clear that any argument raising self-defence must be assessed on its own facts and in the specific circumstances relating to each charge. The Trial Chamber will have regard to this condition when deciding whether the defence of self-defence applies to any of the charges. The Trial Chamber, however, would emphasize that military operations in self-defence do not provide a justification for serious violations of international humanitarian law.[69]

Schabas has noted that:

> because of the very individual dimension of self-defence as an admissible defence, and the requirement that it be in response to 'an imminent and unlawful use of force', to borrow the words of the Rome Statute, it is unlikely to arise in prosecutions of the type undertaken by the *ad hoc* tribunals.[70]

64 Schabas (n 1 above) 336.

65 *Prosecutor v Karadžić* (Trial Transcript) IT-95-5/18-I (1 March 2010) p 808, line 12.

66 ibid p 815, lines 14–15.

67 *Prosecutor v Plavšić* (Trial Chamber Sentencing Judgment) IT-00-39 and 40/1-S (27 February 2003) para 72.

68 *Prosecutor v Kayishema and Ruzindana* (Appeals Chamber Judgment Reasons) ICTR-95-1-A (1 June 2001) para 145; *Prosecutor v Bagilishema* (Trial Chamber Judgment) ICTR-95-1A-T (7 June 2001) para 883.

69 *Prosecutor v Kordić and Čerkez* (Trial Chamber Judgment) IT-95-14/2-T (26 February 2001) para 452.

70 Schabas (n 1 above) 336–7.

In the *Kordić and Čerkez* case, the ICTY rejected the plea of self-defence but held that self-defence was admissible under customary international law, as reflected by Article 31(1)(c) of the Rome Statute of the ICC:

> The principle of self-defence enshrined in this provision reflects provisions found in most national criminal codes and may be regarded as constituting a rule of customary international law. Article 31(1)(c) of the ICC Statute sets forth two conditions which must be met in order for self-defence to be accepted as a ground for excluding criminal liability: (a) the act must be in response to 'an imminent and unlawful use of force' against an attack on a 'protected' person or property; (b) the act of defence must be 'proportionate to the degree of danger'. In relation to the specific circumstances of war crimes, the provision takes into account the principle of military necessity.[71]

What is noticeable from this judicial finding is the implied assertion that Article 31(1)(c) constitutes a faithful reflection of customary international law. The Trial Chamber may have erred in law here; several commentators have questioned this disposition, characterizing it as 'extraneous to customary international law'.[72] Article 31(1)(c) stipulates that, with respect to war crimes, self-defence may exonerate responsibility when exercised in order to defend property. One commentator has described this provision as 'a Pandora's box that is rigorously incompatible with the law of armed conflict'.[73] The Rome Statute seems to contribute here to the establishment of a hierarchy of international crimes—to the detriment of war crimes—and it remains to be seen whether the ICC judges will confirm this hierarchy and whether they will feel encouraged by the *Kordić and Čerkez* finding to consider Article 31 of the Rome Statute as a whole as encapsulating customary international law.

While not a defence proper, military necessity is often raised by an accused to justify behaviour during an armed conflict, similarly to self-defence. The absence of military necessity is an element of various war crimes, such as 'extensive destruction and appropriation of property' and 'wanton destruction of cities, towns or villages, or devastation' in the ICTY Statute.[74] Trial Chambers at the ICTY initially failed to grasp the meaning of the concept; in *Blaškić* it was held that '[t]argeting civilians or civilian property is an offence when not justified by military necessity'.[75] Subsequent chambers responded promptly and in *Galić*, Trial Chamber I asserted that:

> the Trial Chamber does not however subscribe to the view that the prohibited conduct set out in the first part of Article 51(2) of Additional Protocol I is adequately described as 'targeting civilians when not justified by military necessity'. This provision states in clear

[71] *Kordić and Čerkez* (Trial Chamber Judgment) (n 69 above) para 451.

[72] A Cassese (n 61 above) 261.

[73] E David, *Principes de droit des conflits armés* (Brussels: Bruylant, 2nd edn, 1999) cited in WA Schabas, *An Introduction to the International Criminal Court* (Cambridge: CUP, 3rd edn, 2007) 229.

[74] ICTY Statute, Arts 2(d) and 3(b).

[75] *Prosecutor v Blaškić* (Trial Chamber Judgment) (n 49 above) para 180. See also *Kordić and Čerkez* (Trial Chamber Judgment) (n 69 above) para 328.

language that civilians and the civilian population as such should not be the object of attack. It does not mention any exceptions. In particular, it does not contemplate derogating from this rule by invoking military necessity.[76]

More authoritatively, the ICTY Appeals Chamber in both the *Blaškić* and *Kordić* cases corrected the Trial Chambers on military necessity, acting 'essentially on its own initiative and without this being part of the grounds of appeal'.[77] The Appeals Chamber recalled in unequivocal terms that 'there is an absolute prohibition on the targeting of civilians in customary international law'[78] and clarified that:

> ... the prohibition against attacking civilians and civilian objects may not be derogated from because of military necessity. The prohibition against attacking civilians stems from a fundamental principle of international humanitarian law, the principle of distinction, which obliges warring parties to distinguish *at all times* between the civilian population and combatants, between civilian objects and military objectives and accordingly to direct military operations only against military objectives.[79]

It remains to be judicially settled whether military necessity could be validly invoked as a defence against a charge of crimes against humanity. The *Blagojević* Trial Chamber found that, although the destruction of personal property could amount to persecution, and forcible transfer of population to a crime against humanity, such actions might be justified by military necessity.[80]

B. Reprisals and *tu quoque*

Belligerent reprisals are defined as the retributive practices of a state acting in violation of the laws of armed conflict against another state or its nationals in order to force the latter to return respect for the international rules governing conduct during armed conflicts.[81] Insofar as they might indiscriminately punish persons on a collective basis, it would seem reasonable to leave reprisals out of possible grounds for excluding criminal responsibility. Yet, the silence in the statutes of the ICTR and ICTY left the door open for judicial determination of reprisals as a possible defence.

In the *Martić* case, Trial Chamber I of the ICTY firmly ruled that:

> the rule which states that reprisals against the civilian population as such, or individual civilians, are prohibited in all circumstances, even when confronted by wrongful

[76] *Prosecutor v Galić* (Trial Chamber Judgment) IT-98-29-T (5 December 2003) para 44 (footnotes omitted).

[77] Schabas (n 1 above) 346.

[78] *Prosecutor v Blaškić* (Appeals Chamber Judgment) IT-95-14-A (29 July 2004) para 109.

[79] *Prosecutor v Kordić and Čerkez* (Appeals Chamber Judgment) IT-95-14/2-A (17 December 2004) para 54 as amended by *Prosecutor v Kordić and Čerkez* (Corrigendum to Appeals Chamber Judgment of 17 December 2004) IT-95-14/2-A (26 January 2005).

[80] *Prosecutor v Blagojević* (Trial Chamber Judgment) IT-02-60-T (17 January 2005) paras 593 and 598.

[81] See F Kalshoven, *Belligerent Reprisals* (Leyden: AW Sijthoff, 1971).

behaviour of the other party, is an integral part of customary international law and must be respected in all armed conflicts.[82]

In *Kupreskić*, Trial Chamber II of the ICTY further reiterated the prohibition of reprisals against civilians as 'inherently a barbarous means of seeking compliance with international law',[83] explaining that:

> [a]s for reprisals against civilians, under customary international law they are prohibited as long as civilians find themselves in the hands of the adversary. With regard to civilians in combat zones, reprisals against them are prohibited by Article 51(6) of the First Additional Protocol of 1977, whereas reprisals against civilian objects are outlawed by Article 52(1) of the same instrument.[84]
>
> [. . .]
>
> The most blatant reason for the universal revulsion that usually accompanies reprisals is that they may not only be arbitrary but are also not directed specifically at the individual authors of the initial violation. Reprisals typically are taken in situations where the individuals personally responsible for the breach are either unknown or out of reach. These retaliatory measures are aimed instead at other more vulnerable individuals or groups. They are individuals or groups who may not even have any degree of solidarity with the presumed authors of the initial violation; they may share with them only the links of nationality and allegiance to the same rulers.[85]

The *Kupreskić* Trial Chamber also noted a 'trend towards the humanisation of armed conflict', which would entail a customary law prohibition of reprisals:

> the reprisal killing of innocent persons, more or less chosen at random, without any requirement of guilt or any form of trial, can safely be characterized as a blatant infringement of the most fundamental principles of human rights. It is difficult to deny that a slow but profound transformation of humanitarian law under the pervasive influence of human rights has occurred. As a result belligerent reprisals against civilians and fundamental rights of human beings are absolutely inconsistent legal concepts.[86]

The lawmaking attitude of the ICTY judges in these cases was sharply criticized insofar as state practice seems to contradict the assertion that there exists a customary law prohibition of reprisals in the contexts described.[87] It is to be hoped that, in the silence of the Rome Statute regarding this defence, the ICC judges will follow the *Kupreskić* precedent and recognize that:

> . . . while reprisals could have had a modicum of justification in the past, when they constituted practically the only effective means of compelling the enemy to abandon unlawful acts of warfare and to comply in future with international law, at present they can no longer be justified in this manner. A means of inducing compliance with international

[82] *Prosecutor v Martić* (Trial Chamber Decision) IT-65-11-R61 (8 March 1996) para 17.

[83] *Prosecutor v Kupreskić et al* (Trial Chamber Judgment) IT-95-16-T (14 January 2000) para 528.

[84] ibid para 527.

[85] ibid para 528.

[86] ibid para 529.

[87] See S Darcy, *Collective Responsibility and Accountability under International Law* (Ardsley, New York: Transnational, 2007) 156–66.

law is at present more widely available and, more importantly, is beginning to prove fairly efficacious: the prosecution and punishment of war crimes and crimes against humanity by national or international courts. This means serves the purpose of bringing to justice those who are responsible for any such crime, as well as, albeit to a limited extent, the purpose of deterring at least the most blatant violations of international humanitarian law.[88]

The statutes of the tribunals and of the ICC are equally silent on the related defence of *tu quoque*. Also involving a violation of international law, the defence of *tu quoque* could be seen as the modern interpretation of the Old Testament's 'an eye for an eye, and a tooth for a tooth' and aims at justifying the unlawful conduct of a state on the grounds that the state upon which the harm was caused has engaged in a similar conduct. Yet, unlike in the case of reprisals, the complete exclusion of this argument as a defence is unequivocal. At Nuremberg, the International Military Tribunal remained categorical in its rejection of all the defendants' allegations of violations of the law of armed conflict perpetrated by the Allies. Some commentators have nonetheless argued that the *tu quoque* argument could constitute a valid defence, even if not absolute:

> Only if there is sufficient evidence to conclude that the act is practised with impunity by a large number of other persons, would it be justified to assume that it was not a crime, since international custom and general practice condoned it. On these grounds, the International Military Tribunal at Nuremberg decided not to assess in the sentence of Doenitz certain charges of unrestricted submarine warfare in violation of international treaties.[89]

Such a position appears to be incorrect, and relying on the existence of impunity to prove legality is unconvincing. In any event, contemporary international criminal case law confirmed the Nuremberg precedent, with the ICTY Trial Chamber in *Kupreskić* specifying unequivocally that:

> ... evidence that Bosnian Muslims may have committed atrocities against Bosnian Croat civilians in villages in the vicinity of Ahmici or elsewhere in the Lasva River valley is, as such, *irrelevant* because it does not tend to prove or disprove any of the allegations made in the indictment against the accused, and that, likewise, evidence which is adduced to show that one Party to the Croat–Muslim conflict was responsible for starting the conflict is equally irrelevant and hence inadmissible in these proceedings.[90]

The Trial Chamber took the view that the notion of *tu quoque* is not applicable to international humanitarian law. This branch of international law does not set:

> ... synallagmatic obligations, ie obligations based on reciprocity, but obligations *erga omnes* (or, in the case of treaty obligations, obligations *erga omnes contractantes*) which are

[88] *Kupreskić* (Trial Chamber Judgment) (n 83 above) para 530.
[89] Woetzel (n 3 above) 120–1.
[90] *Prosecutor v Kupreskić et al* (Trial Chamber Decision on Evidence of the Good Character of the Accused and the Defence of *Tu Quoque*) IT-95-16-T (17 February 1999) 3–4.

designed to safeguard fundamental human values and therefore must be complied with regardless of the conduct of the other party or parties.[91]

In its judgment, the Trial Chamber further held that 'there is in fact no support either in State practice or in the opinions of publicists for the validity of such a defence'[92] and that:

> ... the *tu quoque* argument is flawed in principle. It envisages humanitarian law as based upon a narrow bilateral exchange of rights and obligations. Instead, the bulk of this body of law lays down absolute obligations, namely obligations that are unconditional or in other words not based on reciprocity.[93]

Adopting a similar view, the ICTY Appeals Chamber equally held that:

> ... when establishing whether there was an attack upon a particular civilian population, it is not relevant that the other side also committed atrocities against its opponent's civilian population. The existence of an attack from one side against the other side's civilian population would neither justify the attack by that other side against the civilian population of its opponent nor displace the conclusion that the other side's forces were in fact targeting a civilian population as such. Each attack against the other's civilian population would be equally illegitimate and crimes committed as part of this attack could, all other conditions being met, amount to crimes against humanity.[94]

Trial Chamber III of the ICTR has also dismissed the defence of *tu quoque*, recalling that 'such a line of *tu quoque* defence against the serious crimes that this Tribunal is prosecuting is inadmissible'.[95] Judges at the *ad hoc* Tribunals have clarified the inadmissibility of the *tu quoque* defence at the international level, although the success of the attempts at judicial activism with regard to reprisals is as yet unproven.

V. Conclusion

> There was a time when it was a thought almost indecent to suggest that judges make law... Those with a taste for fairytales seem to have thought that in some Aladdin's cave there is hidden the Common Law in all its splendour and that on a judge's appointment there descends on him knowledge of the magic words Open Sesame. Bad decisions are given when the judge has muddled the password and the wrong door opens. But we do not believe in fairytales any more.[96]

[91] ibid. [92] *Kupreskić* (Trial Chamber Judgment) (n 83 above) para 516.

[93] ibid para 517.

[94] *Prosecutor v Kunarac* (Appeals Chamber Judgment) IT-96-23-A (12 June 2002) para 87 (footnotes omitted).

[95] *Prosecutor v Gacumbitsi* (Trial Chamber Judgment) ICTR-2001-64-T (17 June 2004) para 165.

[96] Lord Reid, 'The Judge as Lawmaker' (1972) 12 *Journal of Society of Public Teachers of Law* 23, cited in M Kirby, *Judicial Activism—Authority, Principle and Policy in the Judicial Method* (London: Sweet & Maxwell, 2004) 43–4.

The expression 'judicial lawmaking' may be viewed by some as blasphemous and there is little doubt that the judiciary, including the international criminal judiciary, is closely scrutinized and sharply criticized when it adopts a normative and legislative attitude. Indeed, judicial creativity, and especially lawmaking, carries with it an element of risk. Notwithstanding these risks, the Nuremberg and *ad hoc* Tribunals have voluntarily and knowingly engaged with lawmaking at times and may have had no other option if international criminal law was to emerge in positive international law. The ICTY Appeals Chamber itself recognized and assumed this role when it held that 'the progressive development of the criminal law through judicial law-making is a well entrenched and necessary part of legal tradition'.[97] As illustrated by this analysis of the law of defences in the context of international criminal justice, international judges have occasionally broken new ground and clarified or established legal principles. As observed by Guénaël Mettraux:

> . . . because international criminal law is still a body of law in need of legal precision, international criminal tribunals from Nuremberg to The Hague and Arusha, have had to give it substance and precision and have eased many meta-legal standards into proper legal prohibitions. Without judicial input, such legal standards, in and of themselves, would rarely have attained the degree of precision and certainty required from a legal norm to warrant more than a vain hope of compliance. In the history of international criminal law, international tribunals have done more than merely give jural *imprimatur* to norms in waiting . . . so that international criminal law may owe more to judges than any other part of international law.[98]

The importance of judicial input in the development of international law is well illustrated by the *ad hoc* Tribunals' appreciation of available defences related to the law of armed conflict. While recalling the limited admissibility of self-defence and military necessity, the Tribunals have also confirmed the prohibition of certain practices, such as reprisals and *tu quoque*, sometimes going as far as to read in the law and practice an improbable customary law prohibition. As has been highlighted, such findings were controversial—if not incorrect in law—and, as pointed out by Mettraux:

> First, the credibility and acceptability of international norms and standards depend to a large extent upon the readiness of states (and individuals) to comply with them and states will not easily do so in relation to norms or standards that ignore their position on a given issue and their practice in that regard. Secondly, international tribunals risk losing the trust that states have placed in them if they are seen to assume too much discretion when determining what the law is, regardless of what states consider it to be. Thirdly, from the point of view of customary international law, judicial intrusion into the process of custom-making is conceptually somewhat awkward.[99]

[97] *Prosecutor v Multinović* (Appeals Chamber Decision on Dragoljub Ojdanić's Motion Challenging Jurisdiction—Joint Criminal Enterprise) IT-99-37-AR72 (21 May 2003) para 15.

[98] G Mettraux, *International Crimes and the* ad hoc *Tribunals* (Oxford: OUP, 2005) 14.

[99] ibid 16–17 (footnotes omitted).

It must nonetheless be recognized that if the *ad hoc* Tribunals' extensive understanding of international customary law fails to convince and thus to fully contribute to the 'trend towards the humanisation of armed conflict',[100] it is to be hoped that, in time, their findings will participate in the development and humanization of humanitarian law itself. In any event, the judicial creativity of the *ad hoc* Tribunals should not be over stated insofar as they have generally remained within the confines of their mandate, usually walking in their predecessors' footsteps and following the Nuremberg precedent. In codifying the law of admissible defences while at times departing from these precedents, it is undeniable that the Rome Statute has generated a certain legal ambivalence, particularly with its recognition as grounds for excluding individual criminal responsibility pleas which had, until then, been judicially characterized as mitigating factors only. Albin Eser has written that the Rome Statute is 'not yet in the very best shape, both from substance and format' when it comes to grounds for excluding criminal responsibility.[101] As further noted by Matjaž Ambrož, defences 'are listed in the ICC Statute relatively haphazardly, without suggesting any legal categorisation of the defences or drawing any other distinction between them'.[102]

It remains to be seen how the judges at the ICC will consider admissible defences insofar as they now have the arduous task of striking a coherent equilibrium between the text of the ICC Statute and the case law of the *ad hoc* Tribunals. Furthermore, the Rome Statute expressly allows those judges to consider grounds for excluding criminal responsibility not expressly included in the instrument,[103] a power which, if not handled with care, might ultimately lead to an abusive self-empowerment. That said, it might also lead to the establishment of a harmonized and coherent international criminal law of defences. It is apt to conclude with the oft-quoted statement of the Nuremberg Tribunal, that 'this law is not static, but by *continual adaptation* follows the needs of a changing world'.[104]

[100] *Kupreskić* (Trial Chamber Judgment) (n 83 above) para 529.

[101] A Eser, 'Article 31: Grounds for excluding criminal responsibility' in O Triffterer (ed), *Commentary on the Rome Statute of the International Criminal Court: Observers' Notes, Article by Article* (Oxford: Hart Publishing, 2nd revsd edn, 2008) 863, 878.

[102] M Ambrož, 'A Need for Differentiation between Justification and Excuse in International Criminal Law' in T Kruessmann (ed), *ICTY: Towards a Fair Trial?* (Vienna: Neuer Wissenschaftlicher Verlag, 2008) 65, 76.

[103] See ICC Statute, Art 31(3).

[104] *Trials of the Major War Criminals before the International Military Tribunal, Nuremberg, 14 November 1945–1 October 1946*, Vol 1 (International Military Tribunal, Nuremberg 1947–1949) 221 (emphasis added).

11

The Development of the Right to Self-Representation before the International Criminal Tribunals

Gillian Higgins[*]

I. Introduction

The right of self-representation before the International Criminal Tribunal for the former Yugoslavia (ICTY) is protected by Article 21(4)(d) of the Statute, which provides that the accused shall be entitled to the minimum guarantee in full equality, 'to be tried in his presence, and to defend himself in person or through legal assistance of his own choosing'. An identical provision is set out in Article 20(4)(d) of the Statute of the International Criminal Tribunal for Rwanda (ICTR). With the exception of the Supreme Iraqi Criminal Tribunal, the statutes of all international and internationalized courts and tribunals protect a defendant's right to self-representation.[1] On 4 November 2008, the ICTY adopted Rule 45*ter* which provides that a Chamber may decide that it is in the interests of justice to instruct the Registrar to assign counsel to represent the interests of the accused. An identical provision was adopted by the ICTR on 6 July 2002.

The precise nature and remit of the right in proceedings before the ICTY, and to a lesser extent the ICTR, has been the subject of significant controversy and creative judicial development. Over the past decade, the *ad hoc* Tribunals have tried and tested various models of assistance and representation of those accused who have sought to represent themselves. The tension between the principles of fairness and efficiency has led to sporadic restrictions of the right as the judiciary attempt to walk the discretionary tightrope requiring the balancing of fundamental rights and the need to ensure the expeditious conclusion of highly complex criminal trials. More recently, the Appeals Chamber of the ICTY has

* The author would like to thank Cindy Nesbit.

[1] See the ECCC Statute, Art 35(d); ICC Rome Statute, Art 67(1)(d); SCSL Statute, Art 17(4); STL Statute, Art 16(4)(d).

recognized the practical limitations of the imposition of counsel upon an accused who seeks to represent himself.

This chapter will examine the ways in which the right to self-representation has been developed by the *ad hoc* Tribunals, and the mechanisms which have been employed to assist or represent those who seek to represent themselves. It is only through means of creative judicial interpretation that the *ad hoc* Tribunals have been able to marry the rights of the accused with the attendant demands of expeditious international criminal justice. As will be demonstrated, the jurisprudence on this subject is extensive and continues to develop. This chapter charts this development and highlights the role played by the bench in its progression.

II. Early ICTR Jurisprudence: The Enabling Provision of Article 20(4)(d) ICTR to Appoint Standby Counsel and Initial Restrictions of the Right to Self-Representation

The ICTR was the first of the *ad hoc* Tribunals to grapple with the meaning of Article 20(4)(d). In the *Barayagwiza* case, the Trial Chamber was not concerned with the assertion of the right to self-representation by the defendant but rather with an application by his lawyers to withdraw from the case. The defendant had instructed his lawyers 'not to represent him in any respect during the trial'.[2] Barayagwiza's conduct was interpreted by the Chamber as a boycotting of the proceedings. In a separate opinion, Judge Gunawardana seized the opportunity to interpret Article 20(4)(d) as an 'enabling provision for the appointment of a "standby counsel"' in circumstances where an accused boycotts his trial and instructs his lawyers not to represent him.[3] This expansive interpretation of Article 20(4)(d) was to pave the way for future Trial Chambers to justify the appointment of counsel to unwilling accused.

The Chamber further held that 'where an accused has been duly informed of his ongoing trial, neither the Statute nor human rights law prevent the case against him from proceeding in his absence'.[4] Assigned counsel 'represents the interest of the Tribunal to ensure that the Accused receives a fair trial'.[5] The impact of Judge Gunawardana's interpretation of Article 20(4)(d) was cited extensively at

[2] *Prosecutor v Barayagwiza* (Trial Chamber Decision on Defence Counsel Motion to Withdraw) ICTR-97-19-T (2 November 2000) para 2.

[3] *Barayagwiza* (Trial Chamber Decision) ibid, Concurring and Separate Opinion of Judge Gunawardana. Defence counsel for Mr Barayagwiza were allowed to withdraw pursuant to the Trial Chamber's oral decision on 6 February 2001. The Trial Chamber then ordered the appointment of two lawyers to represent him at trial. Mr Barayagwiza did not attend his trial.

[4] *Barayagwiza* (Trial Chamber Decision) (n 2 above) para 6.

[5] *Prosecutor v Barayagwiza* (Trial Chamber Judgment) ICTR-97-19-T (3 December 2003) para 21. In the circumstances, Barayagwiza chose not to communicate with counsel assigned by the court, provide instructions, or attend his trial.

the ICTY in the trials of Milošević and Šešelj, both of whom were assigned counsel against their will.

The following year, the ICTR dealt directly with the right of self-representation in the context of a request by an accused to represent himself during the replacement of his counsel. Ntahobali requested the withdrawal of his defence counsel on the grounds of lack of professionalism. He expressed his willingness to conduct his own defence, pending assignment of new counsel of his choice from the Registry's list.[6] The Chamber accepted his request for the withdrawal of counsel but denied his application to represent himself in the interim period. In this case, the Chamber considered the seriousness of the charges pending against him and the prosecution's objections to the defendant directly cross-examining witnesses given that he was charged with rape. The Chamber determined *proprio motu* that it was in the interests of justice that a duty counsel be immediately appointed.[7] The bench did not, however, use this as an opportunity to develop the test to be applied or expand upon the concept of the 'interests of justice' which would become the touchstone for the future assignment of counsel to unwilling defendants.

III. Self-Representation and the Role of *Amici Curiae*

The trial of Slobodan Milošević was the first international criminal trial at the *ad hoc* Tribunals in which the mechanism of *amici curiae* was employed by the court in order to ensure fair trial protection while respecting the right of an accused to represent himself.

During his first appearance, Milošević informed the Chamber that he did not want to be represented by a lawyer.[8] The Trial Chamber duly noted that the accused was entitled to represent himself and determined that, in order to ensure the trial was fair and the rights of the accused fully respected, the Registrar was invited to appoint *amici curiae* to assist it in the proper determination of the case. The Chamber made it clear that the appointment of the *amici curiae* did not equate to any form of representation of the accused. Their task was to provide assistance to the Chamber to ensure the fairness of the trial. The Chamber ordered the *amici* to assist the court by:

> (i) making any submissions properly open to the accused…and cross-examining witnesses as appropriate; (ii) drawing to the attention of the Trial Chamber any exculpatory

[6] *Prosecutor v Ntahobali* (Trial Chamber Decision on Ntahobali's Motion for Withdrawal of Counsel) ICTR-97-21-T (22 June, 2001) para 2. [7] ibid para 20.

[8] *Prosecutor v Milošević* (Written Note by the Accused, 3 July 2001 and Initial Appearance, 3 July 2001) IT-99-37-I, Trial Transcript, 1–2.

or mitigating evidence; and (iii) acting in any other way considered appropriate in order to secure a fair trial.[9]

It was not the role of the *amici curiae* to put forward a positive defence case.[10] The appointment of *amici curiae* with a precise mandate to assist the Trial Chamber with a self-representing accused was a unique instance of judicial creativity in the field of international criminal procedural law.

Milošević's assertion of his right to represent himself was challenged immediately by the prosecution in the first Status Conference during which it argued that, in addition to the *amici curiae*, the Chamber should also assign defence counsel. At this stage in the proceedings, the Chamber dismissed the argument and observed that 'the accused has a right to counsel, but he also has a right not to have counsel'.[11] The role of the *amici curiae*, which had been carefully crafted by the bench, did not impinge upon or restrict Miloševic's right to represent himself. Instead, it ensured a continuity of legal expertise throughout the prosecution's case which in practice assisted both the judges and the accused.

IV. A Trend towards the Assignment of Counsel

The *Milošević* case is undoubtedly the most significant instance of the ICTY's grappling with the issue of self-representation. At various points during the proceedings, three different mechanisms of assistance or representation were employed by the Tribunal. Following the initial engagement of the *amici curiae* during Milošević's period of self-representation, the Trial Chamber imposed assigned counsel with a mandate to represent the accused against his will, followed by the Appeals Chamber's restoration of the accused's right to self-representation, while retaining counsel in the event that his health prevented him from presenting his own defence. The reasoning behind these fundamental decisions reveals the difficulties faced by both the judiciary and the accused when the latter seeks to exercise his right to self-representation. These difficulties are also evident from the Trial Chamber's handling of the *Krajišnik* case in which the accused sought to represent himself mid-trial. Both cases reflect a trend towards the assignment of counsel and will be explored in detail in this section.

In the initial phase of the *Milošević* trial, the prosecution requested the Trial Chamber to appoint defence counsel to represent the accused, notwithstanding the appointment of the *amici curiae*.[12] At the outset the Chamber rejected the

[9] *Prosecutor v Milošević* (Status Conference) IT-99-37-PT (30 August 2001) Trial Transcript, 7. See Further Order Inviting Designation of *Amicus Curiae* (30 August 2001); and Order Concerning *Amici Curiae* (11 January 2002).

[10] *Milošević* (Status Conference) (n 9 above) Trial Transcript, 18.

[11] ibid.

[12] See eg *Prosecutor v Milošević* (Submission from the Office of the Prosecutor on the Future Conduct of the Case in the Light of the State of the Accused's Health and the Length and Complexity of the Case) IT-02-54-T (8 November 2002) para 14.

prosecution's submission,[13] and noted that 'the imposition of a defence counsel upon an accused who does not want one is a feature of inquisitorial systems, but not of adversarial systems'.[14] The United States Supreme Court case of *Faretta v California* was expressly considered, wherein the Court found that:

> [t]he language and spirit of the Sixth Amendment contemplate that counsel, like the other defence tools guaranteed by the Amendment, shall be an aid to a willing defendant—not an organ of the state interposed between an unwilling defendant and his right to defend himself personally. To thrust counsel upon the accused, against his considered wish, thus violates the logic of the Amendment.[15]

The Chamber noted that the obligation of counsel to put a case pursuant to Rule 90(H) cannot 'be fulfilled by counsel who is not instructed by an accused as to the defence to put forward'.[16] The bench distinguished the case of *Croissant v Germany* (cited by the prosecution in support of a qualified right to self-representation)[17] and held that it was not 'concerned with an accused seeking to represent himself' but rather with the objection by an accused to the appointment of additional counsel by the court. The Chamber also noted the findings of the Human Rights Committee in the case of *Michael and Brian Hill v Spain* that an accused has a right to defend himself pursuant to Article 14(3)(d) of the ICCPR.[18] Significantly, however, the Trial Chamber stated that 'the right to defend oneself in person is not absolute'[19] and considered that 'there may be circumstances, as envisaged by Judge Gunawardana, where it is in the interests of justice to appoint counsel', but concluded that such circumstances had not yet arisen in the trial although it would 'keep the position under review'.[20]

Soon after the close of the prosecution case on 25 February 2004, Presiding Judge May retired on grounds of ill-health.[21] On 10 June 2004, the ICTY President assigned Judge Bonomy to the Trial Chamber.[22] Judge Bonomy's involvement in the trial marked a new stage of development in the setting of limitations upon the right of an accused to represent himself. In July 2004, the

[13] *Prosecutor v Milošević* (Trial Chamber Reasons for Decision on the Prosecution Motion Concerning Assignment of Counsel) IT-02-54-T (4 April 2003) para 18.

[14] ibid para 21.

[15] ibid para 22.

[16] ibid para 25.

[17] ibid para 31 referring to *Croissant v Germany* (Case No 62/1001/314/385) ECHR, 25 September 1992.

[18] ibid para 33 referring to *Michael and Brian Hill v Spain*, Human Rights Committee, Communication No 526/1993, UN Doc CCPR/C/59/D/526/1993 (2 April 1997).

[19] ibid para 40.

[20] ibid.

[21] On 12 March 2004, President Meron held a hearing in which he sought Milošević's consent to the continuation of the trial with a replacement judge, pursuant to Rule 15*bis*(C). Predictably, Milošević refused to declare his views, a position interpreted by Judge Meron as a 'refusal to consent'. The issue then reverted back to the Trial Chamber where, pursuant to Rule 15*bis*(D), the remaining trial judges ordered that it was nonetheless in the interests of justice for the trial to proceed with a substitute judge: see *Prosecutor v Milošević* (Order Pursuant to Rule 15*bis*(D)) IT-02-54-T (29 March 2004).

[22] *Prosecutor v Milošević* (Order Replacing a Judge in a Case before a Trial Chamber) IT-02-54-T (10 June 2004).

Chamber noted that the trial had been marked by a number of interruptions due to the accused's ill-health, amounting to the loss of 66 trial days by 25 February 2004, and a period of illness during the 3-month period allocated to him for the preparation of his defence. The medical report indicated that Milošević's health problems were expected to recur. The newly-composed Chamber determined that it would review the issue of the assignment or imposition of defence counsel and noted the decision in *Šešelj* in which standby counsel had been assigned against the wishes of the accused.[23] It was time to conduct a 'radical review' of the future conduct of the trial.[24]

After several adjournments due to the ill-health of the accused, the defence case started on 31 August 2004 with an opening statement presented by Milošević. On 1 September 2004, the parties were invited by the Chamber to make oral submissions on the recent medical reports concerning his health and the issue of the assignment of counsel. The medical reports confirmed that Milošević was suffering from 'severe essential hypertension and that his condition was such that a hypertensive emergency, a potentially life-threatening condition could develop'.[25] The following day, the Trial Chamber gave an oral ruling assigning counsel to Milošević on the basis of his ill-health.[26] It was determined that it would be irresponsible to allow the accused to continue to represent himself and that it was necessary to relieve the accused of the burden of conducting his own case in order to stabilize his health. It was important for the trial to proceed with the 'minimum of interruption' in order to permit the orderly presentation of his case and to ensure the completion of trial in a reasonable time.

On 3 September 2004, the Registrar assigned Steven Kay QC and Gillian Higgins as defence counsel to Mr Milošević. Subsequent to the assignment, the Trial Chamber issued an order on modalities to be followed by the assigned counsel. The modalities of the assignment were crucial to determining the manner in which the trial would thereafter unfold. The order instructed the assigned counsel to determine how to present the case for the accused and, in particular, to represent the accused by preparing and examining those witnesses that they deemed appropriate to call.[27] The order also instructed counsel to make 'all submissions on fact and law that they deem it appropriate to make', to 'seek from the Trial Chamber such orders as they consider necessary to enable them to present the Accused's case properly, including the issuance of subpoenas', 'to discuss with the Accused the conduct of the case', and to 'act throughout in the best interests of the Accused'.[28] The Trial Chamber made it clear that the participation of

[23] See *Prosecutor v Šešelj* (Decision on Prosecution's Motion for Order Appointing Counsel to Assist Vojislav Šešelj with his Defence) IT-03-67-PT (9 May 2003).

[24] *Prosecutor v Milošević* (Order on Future Conduct of the Trial) IT-02-54-T (6 July 2004).

[25] *Prosecutor v Milošević* (Reasons for Decision on Assignment of Defence Counsel) IT-02-54-T (22 September 2004) para 1.

[26] ibid.

[27] *Prosecutor v Milošević* (Order on the Modalities to be Followed by Court-Assigned Counsel) IT-02-54-T (3 September 2004).

[28] ibid.

Milošević would be secondary to that of assigned counsel and strictly contingent on the discretionary permission of the Chamber. The minimum guarantees set out in Article 21(4) of the Statute were described as 'elements of the overarching requirement of a fair trial' and it was stated that it was in this context that the accused's right to defend himself must be interpreted.

The Chamber determined that '[i]f at any stage of a trial there is a real prospect that it will be disrupted and the integrity of the trial undermined with the risk that it will not be conducted fairly, then the Trial Chamber has a duty to put in place a regime which will avoid that'. The sporadic ill-health of the accused had shifted the focus of concern away from the practical difficulties of assignment towards the goal of completing the trial efficiently, a shift which brought with it radical change. Erroneously, the Chamber appeared to equate the ill-health of the accused with deliberate misconduct, stating that there was no 'difference in principle between deliberate misconduct which disrupts the proceedings and any other circumstance which so disrupts the proceedings as to threaten the integrity of the trial'.[29] The Chamber did, however, recognize that extensive research had not led to the identification of any case in any jurisdiction where counsel had been assigned to an accused person because he was unfit to conduct his case as the result of impaired physical health.[30] Equally, it had not identified any international or domestic authority which was inconsistent with its interpretation of Articles 20 and 21 of the ICTY Statute and thus believed that the matter might be one of first impression because of the exceptional circumstances of the present trial.[31]

Reliance was placed upon jurisprudence from the ICTR and the Special Court for Sierra Leone (SCSL) in which both institutions have recognized that there may be circumstances where it is competent and appropriate for a Chamber to insist that the defence is presented by counsel and not by the accused in person. The Chamber referred specifically[32] to the cases of *Norman*[33] and *Barayagwiza*,[34] and to the ICTY approach in *Šešelj*.[35] Reliance was also placed on the civil law tradition, which often provides for mandatory defence counsel in domestic criminal procedures,[36] and the assignment of counsel to accused persons in relation to certain sexual offence crimes in common law jurisdictions.[37] While the Trial Chamber expressed concern as to drugs found in Milošević's blood and in his

[29] *Milošević* (Reasons for Decision on Assignment of Defence Counsel) (n 25 above) para 33.

[30] ibid para 37. [31] ibid. [32] ibid paras 39–41.

[33] See *Prosecutor v Norman et al* (Decision on the Application of Samuel Hinga Norman for Self Representation Under Article 17(4)(d) of the Statute of the Special Court) SCSL-04-14-T (8 June 2004) para 8.

[34] See *Prosecutor v Barayagwiza* (Decision on Defence Counsel Motion to Withdraw) ICTR-97-19-T (2 November 2000) para 21.

[35] See *Prosecutor v Šešelj* (Decision on Prosecution's Motion for Order Appointing Counsel to Assist Vojislav Šešelj with his Defence) IT-03-67-PT (9 May 2003) para 20.

[36] *Milošević* (Reasons for Decision on Assignment of Defence Counsel) (n 25 above) para 49.

[37] ibid paras 46–8.

possession, significantly it did not base its decision on the prosecution submission that Milošević had wilfully manipulated the trial timetable through these and other means.[38]

On appeal,[39] the assigned counsel submitted on behalf of Milošević that insufficient weight had been given to the practical considerations of assigning counsel to an accused against his will. Such considerations include the fact that the defence put forward by counsel cannot accurately represent an accused's actual defence in the absence of his or her cooperation and instructions. Furthermore, there was a sufficient likelihood that a significant number of defence witnesses would not cooperate with assigned counsel, and the accused might decide not to testify as a witness in his own case. The defective way in which the defence may be conducted by an assigned counsel could constitute grounds of appeal, and the imposition of unwanted counsel upon an unwilling defendant who refuses to cooperate may in fact be the source of increased stress to the accused.[40] Unlike the cases of *Norman* before the SCSL, and *Šešelj* at the ICTY, where standby counsel had been assigned to *assist* the accused, the Trial Chamber in *Milošević* had created an unworkable situation in circumstances where instructions had not been provided to counsel and there was no cooperation between counsel and the accused. The Chamber's decision to allow the accused merely to ask additional questions at its discretion infringed the accused's right to examine his own witnesses in circumstances where the examination conducted by assigned counsel without instructions could never accurately reflect his case. Unlike Šešelj, Milošević's behaviour had not been deemed to be obstructionist and he had at no point in time waived his right to represent himself by his own conduct. It was noted that the circumstances in which counsel had previously been assigned to an unwilling defendant before the ICTY and the ICTR were limited to circumscribed situations, largely concerning obstructionist behaviour by defendants.[41]

[38] ibid para 67.

[39] *Prosecutor v Milošević* (Appeal Against the Trial Chamber's Decision on Assignment of Defence Counsel) IT-02-54-AR73.7 (29 September 2004) para 93. Given that Milošević had not filed any written submissions during the trial, on 8 September 2004 the assigned counsel, acting in his best interests, mounted the appeal against their own assignment. The appeal was heard by the Appeals Chamber on 21 October 2004.

[40] ibid.

[41] ibid para 57. In *Šešelj*, the main reason for the imposition of standby counsel was because the accused was 'increasingly demonstrating a tendency to act in an obstructionist fashion, while at the same time revealing a need for legal assistance' (ibid para 59). In *Norman*, before the SCSL, the accused informed the court that he wished to dispense with his counsel and represent himself on the date which had been set for the start of his trial. The Court specifically distinguished the situation from that facing *Milošević* on the basis that (i) Norman was being jointly tried with two others, (ii) the Special Court had a limited time-span which created 'a serious case for concern' in relation to 'further disruption to the Court's timetable' which might have been caused if the accused were to be allowed to dispense with counsel at the outset of the trial proceedings, and (iii) the accused attempted to exercise the right to self-representation only at the outset of the trial, after more than a year in pre-trial detention, with a defence team having prepared his case for trial. The Special Court qualified Norman's right to self-representation and chose to assign standby counsel to 'assist' him during the course of the trial (ibid para 61).

The assigned counsel experienced first-hand the dilemmas and practical reality of the task. After the initial assignment, counsel had requested an adjournment of the proceedings pending appeal, which was rejected by the Trial Chamber. In the circumstances, the assigned counsel called three witnesses from Milošević's defence witness list and requested that Milošević be allowed to examine the witnesses first. This application was, however, rejected. The overwhelming majority of defence witnesses contacted by the assigned counsel refused to testify in circumstances where Miloševic was no longer conducting his own defence. On 26 October 2004, the assigned counsel requested the Registrar to permit their withdrawal from the proceedings on the basis that the absence of instructions from Milošević prevented them from knowing and abiding by his objective of representation, from fulfilling their duty to communicate with him, and from knowing and protecting his best interests pursuant to the ICTY Code of Conduct.[42] The Appeals Chamber's decision affirmed the assignment of defence counsel, but reversed the Trial Chamber's order on modalities and took the opportunity to develop a proportionate approach to the manner in which assigned counsel can function, which signified a radical departure from the role ascribed originally by the Trial Chamber.

The interpretation adopted purported to recognize the fact that the:

> ... drafters of the Statute clearly viewed the right to self-representation as an indispensable cornerstone of justice, placing it on a structural par with defendant's rights to remain silent, to confront witnesses against them, to a speedy trial, and even to demand a court-appointed attorney if they cannot afford one themselves.

The right may, however, be curtailed, the Appeals Chamber held, on the grounds that a defendant's self-representation is substantially and persistently obstructing the proper and expeditious conduct of his trial. As to the preliminary issue of the bare decision to assign counsel, the Appeals Chamber concluded that the Trial Chamber had not abused its discretion in doing so.[43] The Chamber remarked that 'the doctors who examined Milošević in July each concluded that, given his condition at the time, Milošević was not fit to continue defending himself'.[44]

[42] *Prosecutor v Milošević* (Letter from Assigned Counsel to Registrar, 'Re: The Prosecutor *v* Slobodan Milošević, IT-02-54-T—Withdrawal of Assigned Counsel') (26 October 2004) 8. For a review of the litigation concerning the unsuccessful request by the assigned counsel to withdraw, see the following: *Prosecutor v Milošević* (Appeals Chamber Decision on Interlocutory Appeal of the Trial Chamber's Decision on the Assignment of Defense Counsel) IT-02-54-AR73.7 (1 November 2004); *Prosecutor v Milošević* (Assigned Counsel's Motion for Withdrawal with Annex A) IT-02-54-T (8 November 2004); *Prosecutor v Milošević* (Decision on Assigned Counsel's Motion for Withdrawal) IT-02-54-T (7 December 2004); *Prosecutor v Milošević* (Decision Affirming the Registrar's Denial of Assigned Counsel's Application to Withdraw) IT-02-54-T (7 February 2005).

[43] *Milošević* (Appeals Chamber Decision on Interlocutory Appeal) (n 42 above) para 15.

[44] ibid.

Given that finding, 'it was within the Trial Chamber's discretion to assign counsel to Milošević notwithstanding his opposition'.[45]

The Appeals Chamber did not, however, agree with the Trial Chamber's order on modalities. This development is significant as the Appeals Chamber recalibrated the mechanism by which such assigned counsel may be expected to function in the future. The excessive demands placed upon counsel by the Trial Chamber were tempered by the principle of proportionality. The Trial Chamber's original order had sharply restricted Milošević's ability to participate in the conduct of his case in any way, making it contingent on the discretionary decision of the Trial Chamber. The order relegated 'Milošević to a visibly second tier role in the trial', sharp restrictions which were grounded on a fundamental error of law. The Appeals Chamber emphasized that the Trial Chamber should have recognized that 'any restrictions on Milošević's right to represent himself must be limited to the minimum extent necessary to protect the Tribunal's interest in assuring a reasonably expeditious trial'.

In the circumstances, the restrictions were excessive given that the medical reports relied upon explicitly rejected the notion that Milošević's condition was permanent, there was no evidence that he had suffered from any health problems since late July 2004, and he had made a vigorous two-day opening statement without interruption or apparent difficulty.

The Appeals Chamber decided that, when physically able to do so, Milošević would take the lead in presenting his case. If his health problems resurfaced with sufficient gravity, the presence of assigned counsel would enable the trial to continue even if he was temporarily unable to participate. The precise point at which a reshuffling of trial roles should occur would be a matter for the Trial Chamber.[46] The retention of the assigned counsel and restructuring of the role to be played by Milošević was a significant and radical departure from the framework established by the Trial Chamber. After having lost the battle to withdraw, the assigned counsel no longer determined or controlled the public presentation of the defence case or the calling of the witnesses, but rather they assisted by performing a complementary yet essential role as protectors of Milošević's fair trial rights. Such assistance took the form of filing motions, and making oral submissions on matters of law and evidence on Milošević's behalf. It is noteworthy that the Trial Chamber did not fashion a new set of modalities, neither did it seek further to define the role of the assigned counsel. It may be argued with hindsight that this was an opportunity missed by the ICTY judges to develop the role and function of assigned counsel. However, in many respects, the broad mandate set by the Appeals Chamber afforded both Milošević and the assigned counsel an opportunity to develop a working relationship in a brave new legal world. For the rest of the journey, assigned counsel rode behind Milošević as

[45] ibid. [46] ibid para 20.

vigilant passengers in a trial which required their procedural skills and knowledge to ensure the continued protection of the defendant. A reshuffling of roles between him and the assigned counsel, as envisaged by the Appeals Chamber, never in fact took place.

Commentators have observed that the assigned counsel in *Milošević* essentially functioned as 'hybrid' counsel, sharing the role of defence counsel with the accused.[47] This post-appeal model has been described as the most appropriate in the circumstances, as '[f]amiliarity with the vast and countless facts, figures, locations and witnesses made the Accused more suited to conducting certain aspects of his defence'.[48] Hybrid representation 'allowed Milošević to publicly conduct cross-examination and examination-in-chief while relinquishing to counsel those procedural and substantive tasks which required the legal skills at which they excel'.[49] In the *Krajišnik* case, the Trial Chamber was confronted with a request from the accused to represent himself mid-trial, having been previously represented by defence counsel. On this occasion, the Chamber had to grapple not only with the question of whether Krajišnik's request was unequivocal but also with the issue of potential disruption to the trial proceedings should the accused be allowed to start to represent himself part-way through the case. Krajišnik's request was based on his claim that, his defence team was unable to assist him in establishing the truth. In a provisional decision on 26 May 2005,[50] the Trial Chamber determined that, pending resolution of the request, Krajišnik, who was represented by defence counsel, was allowed to supplement counsel's cross-examination by asking questions himself.

Thereafter, the Trial Chamber denied his request and determined that Krajišnik had not unequivocally decided to proceed with the trial unrepresented. The Chamber interpreted his request to represent himself as a 'drive' for 'financial and structural improvements to be made to the defence team'[51] and that what Krajišnik actually wanted was a more effective defence and not to unequivocally represent himself. The Chamber went on to deal with the right of self-representation and observed that a relevant factor is the disruption to proceedings that self-representation may cause and that when a request is made during trial, the judge has a broader discretion to reject it. The concern about potential disruption to the trial proceedings due to the ill-health of the accused, the stage of the trial, or the conduct of the accused have been recurrent elements in the progressive development of this issue by the Tribunals.

[47] J Williams, 'Slobodan Milošević and the Guarantee of Self-Representation' (2007) 32(2) *Brooklyn Journal of International Law*, section 4.2. [48] ibid.

[49] ibid. [50] *Prosecutor v Krajišnik* (Trial Transcript) IT-00-39-T (26 May 2005) 13439.

[51] *Prosecutor v Krajišnik* (Reasons for Oral Decision Denying Mr Krajišnik's Request to Proceed Unrepresented by Counsel) IT-00-39-T (18 August 2005) para 10.

V. Obstructionism and Standby Counsel: Assistance or Representation?

A distinct category of jurisprudence has developed before the *ad hoc* Tribunals concerning the waiver of the right to self-representation by those whose conduct is deemed to be obstructionist. One mechanism which has been employed to tackle this situation is the engagement of standby counsel. The concept of standby counsel was introduced in the *Barayagwiza* case before the ICTR. The distinct character of the concept was not, however, fleshed out until the surrender of Vojislav Šešelj to the ICTY.[52] Šešelj wanted to defend himself but his conduct was deemed to be obstructionist by the Trial Chamber. The ensuing litigation on the right to self-representation in this case pushed the boundaries of the debate to new extremes. The Appeals Chamber addressed significant procedural law issues, including the possibility of restricting an accused's right to represent himself at the pre-trial stage and the issue of whether or not a warning was required before standby counsel could be assigned to an accused against his will. The issue of obstructionism also arose in the *Stanković* case before the ICTY.

A. Development of the role of standby counsel in the *Šešelj* case

Šešelj declared his intention to represent himself at his initial appearance on 26 February 2003.[53] Two days later, the prosecution requested the Trial Chamber to direct that counsel be appointed to *assist* him with his defence. The prosecution argued that he had 'expressed publicly his intent to cause harm to the Tribunal and to use these proceedings as a forum for Serb national interests' rather than as a means to defend himself.[54] At this early stage, the prosecution left open the possibility that 'there might nevertheless remain some limited scope for the accused to participate directly in the proceedings with the leave of the Chamber', provided that he did not interfere with the normal conduct of the proceedings.[55] This initial request that counsel be assigned to Šešelj to 'assist' as opposed to 'represent' him marked a radical shift from the model which had previously been proposed in the *Milošević* case.[56] On 9 May 2003, the Trial Chamber issued a decision on the prosecution's request.[57] It noted the practice within many civil law countries

[52] Vojislav Šešelj is currently President of the Serbian National Party and is charged with crimes of persecution on political, racial, or religious grounds, inhumane acts, murder, torture, cruel treatment, and property destruction in Croatia and Bosnia between August 1991 and September 1993.

[53] *Prosecutor v Šešelj* (Trial Transcript) IT-03-67-1 (26 February 2003) 5–6.

[54] *Prosecutor v Šešelj* (Prosecution's Motion for Order Appointing Counsel to Assist Vojislav Šešelj with his Defence) IT-03-67-PT (28 February 2003) para 9.

[55] ibid para 14.

[56] For Šešelj's response, see *Prosecutor v Šešelj* (Reply to the Prosecutor's Motion to Impose Defence Counsel on me Against my Will) IT-03-67-PT (20 March 2003).

[57] *Prosecutor v Šešelj* (Decision on Prosecution's Motion for Order Appointing Counsel to Assist Vojislav Šešelj with his Defence) IT-03-67-PT (9 May 2003).

of the mandatory assignment of counsel in serious cases, a subject which had been explored in the *Milošević* litigation,[58] and cited the same jurisprudence,[59] concluding that Article 21 of the Statute left open the possibility of assigning counsel to an accused on a case-by-case basis in the interests of justice.[60]

The Chamber determined that the complex legal, evidential, and procedural issues which arise in cases of such magnitude may fall outside the competence even of a legally qualified accused, especially where that accused is in detention without access to all the facilities he may need. The recurrent theme of trial efficiency was also considered alongside the legitimate interest of the Trial Chamber to ensure that the trial proceeds in a timely manner without interruptions, adjournments, or disruptions.[61] The Chamber held that the accused's intention to harm or destroy the Tribunal had been shown 'following his declared intention to attempt to use the Tribunal as a vehicle for the furtherance of his political beliefs and aspirations'.[62] Šešelj was displaying a need for legal assistance as his motions were not only excessively long but also largely irrelevant. His attitudes and actions as set out in the decision were deemed to be indicative of his obstructionism. Accordingly, the Chamber determined that the best way to preserve his rights while at the same time satisfying the interests of justice was to assign standby counsel.[63] Interestingly, the Chamber emphasized that Šešelj's right to defend himself was 'left absolutely untouched' and that standby counsel was not an *amicus curiae* but an assistant operating in the sphere of the accused only, who would serve to safeguard a fair and expeditious trial.[64] Although the terms of reference of the mandate of the standby counsel were couched largely in terms of assistance, not representation, the Chamber included a provision which clearly provided that, in exceptional circumstances, counsel were to ensure that they would be in a position to take over the representation of the accused if, after a warning, the accused was removed from the courtroom for disruptive conduct under Rule 80(B).[65]

Following the initial assignment of a Bosnian/Croatian/Serbian speaker,[66] who was subsequently withdrawn on the basis of a conflict of interest, the Registry subsequently assigned Tjarda Eduard van der Spoel, a Dutch non-Bosnian/Croatian/Serbian-speaking lawyer.[67] Thereafter, once again, Šešelj reasserted his intention to defend himself in person and to use an expert team to assist him.[68] As a professor of Law at Belgrade University, he argued that there was no material hindrance to him conducting his own defence and that he fulfilled the

58 ibid paras 16–17.
59 ibid paras 18–19.
60 ibid para 20.
61 ibid para 21.
62 ibid para 22.
63 ibid para 27.
64 ibid para 28.
65 ibid para 30.
66 *Prosecutor v Šešelj* (Registry Decision) IT-03-67-PT (5 September 2003).
67 Instead of appealing the decision to assign standby counsel, on 26 May 2003 Šešelj submitted a lengthy letter directly to the Appeals Chamber. He was informed that he must file an appeal in accordance with the Rules, advice he did not subsequently act upon.
68 *Prosecutor v Šešelj* (Motion by the Accused for Normalization of Conditions for Preparing a Defence) IT-03-67-PT (9 November 2004).

requirements of Rule 44 for counsel to practice before the ICTY. He maintained that the appointment of defence counsel without his agreement represented 'the most egregious violation of fundamental human rights'.[69] Šešelj requested the Trial Chamber to re-examine its decision[70] and argued that standby counsel, van der Spoel, did not even fulfil the criteria set out by the Trial Chamber due to his lack of knowledge of the Bosnian/Croatian/Serbian language.

The Chamber issued a decision on 1 March 2005[71] and held that Šešelj's arguments that the establishment of the office of standby counsel was not consistent with international human rights law were without merit.[72] Further, there had been no change in circumstances to warrant revoking the Trial Chamber's decision. In a dissenting opinion, Judge Antonetti interestingly determined that, given the accused's repeated desire to represent himself, it would be more desirable and in the interests of the good administration of justice for an *amicus curiae* to have been designated, not to represent him, but to provide assistance.[73] The use of the *amici curiae* model in the *Milošević* proceedings as a fair trial mechanism had clearly been influential as an appropriate method for providing a form of assistance which did not trample on the rights of the accused.

In January 2006, Šešelj filed a further request before the Chamber for the revocation of the decision to assign standby counsel.[74] Four months later, the prosecution sought an order from the Trial Chamber to appoint defence counsel to assist the accused with the exclusive right to file submissions, to put a stop to Šešelj's 'frivolous, repetitive or irrelevant filings'.[75] It was argued that the experience during the pre-trial phase showed that the figure of standby counsel was ineffective and did not prevent the defendant from obstructing the proceedings. Equally, the concept of *amici curiae* would not work with an obstructionist like Šešelj. Interestingly, the prosecution motion did not address the role of either Šešelj or defence counsel in the courtroom, a potentially glaring omission given its obvious future significance in the trial proceedings. It was argued that Šešelj thrived on the creation of scandal, conspiracies, and publicity,[76] and had repeatedly claimed that the robes worn by the ICTY personnel in the courtroom are 'just like an SS or Gestapo uniform'.[77] It was also alleged that the defendant

[69] ibid 1, 6.

[70] *Prosecutor v Šešelj* (Request by the Accused to the Trial Chamber to Re-examine the Decision to Assign Standby Counsel to the Accused filed by the Accused Vojislav Šešelj) IT-03-67-PT (9 November 2004) para 5. For the prosecution's position, see *Prosecutor v Šešelj* (Prosecution's Response to the Accused's Motion to Re-examine the Decision to Assign Standby Counsel) IT-03-67-PT (23 November 2004) paras 5–6.

[71] *Prosecutor v Šešelj* (Decision on the Accused's Motion to Re-examine the Decision to Assign Standby Counsel) IT-03-67-PT (1 March 2005).

[72] ibid 4.

[73] ibid, dissenting opinion, 12.

[74] *Prosecutor v Šešelj* (Request of Dr Vojislav Šešelj for the Revocation of the Decision to Assign Standby Counsel (Submission No 125)) IT-03-67-PT (3 January 2006).

[75] *Prosecutor v Šešelj* (Prosecution's Second Motion for Order Appointing Counsel to Assist Vojislav Šešelj with his Defence) IT-03-67-PT (5 May 2006) para 25.

[76] ibid para 9.

[77] ibid para 12.

had repeatedly targeted the Trial Chamber, the Registrar, the prosecution, and standby counsel with false allegations, used abusive and insulting language,[78] and repeatedly threatened and intimidated witnesses.[79]

On 21 August 2006, the Trial Chamber issued a decision on the assignment of counsel.[80] It was called upon to make a determination as to whether to restrict Šešelj's right to represent himself during the remainder of the proceedings on the basis of his conduct during the pre-trial phase.[81] The decision cited the post-*Faretta* case of *United States v Brock*, in which the 7th Circuit Court of Appeals indicated that disruptive behaviour at the pre-trial stage, including the 'steadfast refusal to answer the court's questions', justified the revocation of a defendant's *pro se* status at trial. It was sufficient to allow the district judge to conclude that there was a strong indication that Brock would continue to be disruptive at trial.[82] In *McKaskle v Wiggins* the US Supreme Court upheld a lower court decision appointing standby counsel to assist a *pro se* defendant. The *pro se* defendant was nevertheless to be allowed to control the organization of his own defence, submit motions, argue points of law, question witnesses, and address the court at appropriate points in the trial. The *pro se* defendant was also to be 'able and willing to abide by the rules of procedure and courtroom protocol'.[83]

The Chamber noted that, in the *Krajišnik* case, where the accused was represented by counsel, the Trial Chamber granted him the possibility of asking follow-up questions to witnesses and under certain circumstances requesting the Chamber to call witnesses that his counsel did not decide to call.[84] The Chamber reminded itself of the proportionality requirement when assigning counsel against the wishes of an accused, as set out by the Appeals Chamber in *Milošević*,[85] and determined that Article 21(4)(d) of the Statute enshrines not only the right of an accused to represent himself, but also his right to be tried in his presence. However, just as the former right is not absolute, the latter may also be restricted in cases of substantial trial disruption. The Chamber agreed with the US Supreme Court, which held in *Illinois v Allen* that:

> ... a defendant can lose his right to be present at trial if, after he had been warned by the judge that he will be removed if he continues his disruptive behaviour, he nevertheless insists on conducting himself in a manner so disorderly, disruptive and disrespectful of the court that his trial cannot be carried on with him in the courtroom.[86]

When considering whether or not Šešelj had engaged in obstructionist conduct, the Chamber held that it would not consider the substance of his published books, but only their 'clearly offensive' titles, which included the *Genocidal Israeli Diplomat Theodor Meron*, *In the jaws of the whore Del Ponte*, and *the Lying Hague homosexual Geoffrey Nice*. In the pre-trial phase, the Chamber

[78] ibid para 10. [79] ibid para 16.
[80] *Prosecutor v Šešelj* (Decision on Assignment of Counsel) IT-03-67-PT (21 August 2006).
[81] ibid para 73. [82] ibid paras 18 and 73. [83] ibid para 19. [84] ibid para 22.
[85] ibid para 23. [86] ibid.

determined that the 191 written submissions constituted the bulk of Šešelj's interaction with the Tribunal[87] and that Šešelj had raised irrelevant or specious matters amounting to obstructionist behaviour. The Chamber cited the example of the defendant considering the attire of the judges in court to be inappropriate, since in his view, it was 'reminiscent of the Catholic inquisition or of German SS or Gestapo uniforms'.[88] It found that the defendant had often hinted at information in his possession allegedly demonstrating plots and machinations against him or against other individuals. Such 'unsubstantiated statements of this kind' were held to constitute a waste of the Tribunal's time and resources.[89] In a reworded and watered-down version of the *Brock* test, the Trial Chamber concluded that it must be satisfied that the accused's behaviour 'considered as a whole provides a strong indication that self-representation *may* substantially and persistently obstruct the proper and expeditious conduct of the proceedings'. The Chamber held that Šešelj had been put 'on notice through a number of warnings, some specific and some general' about his behaviour and the possible consequences but that he had 'nonetheless persisted in his tactic of trying to turn the Tribunal into a stage for his private non-forensic purposes'.[90] Šešelj's conduct as a whole led the Chamber to conclude that there was a strong indication that his self-representation *might* substantially and persistently obstruct the proper and expeditious conduct of a fair trial. Accordingly, the Chamber found that there was a proper basis for the exercise of its discretion to impose restrictions on his right to represent himself during the remainder of the proceedings.[91]

In terms of the restrictions to be imposed during the trial phase, the Chamber determined that it saw no alternative that would sufficiently protect the fairness and integrity of the proceedings than to order that Šešelj participate in the proceedings through counsel only. The Chamber would consider whether and to what extent the interests of justice would allow for any personal participation of the accused.[92] The Registry was instructed to assign counsel and ordered standby counsel to represent the accused until the Registry had made the necessary arrangements. On 30 August 2006, the Registry assigned a British barrister, David Hooper, as counsel for the defendant. The transition from standby counsel (whose function it was to assist the accused), to assigned counsel (who was to represent Šešelj against his will) was a marked development in the handling of obstructionist accused.[93] On appeal, the Appeals Chamber[94] relied heavily upon the decision in *Milošević* where the right to self-representation may only be

[87] ibid para 30. [88] ibid para 34. [89] ibid para 37. [90] ibid para 78.
[91] ibid para 79. [92] ibid para 80.

[93] For Šešelj's appeal, see *Prosecutor v Šešelj* (Appeal Against the Trial Chamber's Decision on Assignment of Counsel) IT-03-67-AR73.3 (4 September 2006). For the prosecution's response, see *Prosecutor v Šešelj* (Prosecution Response to Appeal against the Trial Chamber's Decision on Assignment of Counsel) IT-03-67-AR73.3 (13 September 2006).

[94] *Prosecutor v Vojislav Šešelj* (Appeals Chamber Decision on Appeal Against the Trial Chamber's Decision on Assignment of Counsel) IT-03-67-AR73.3 (20 October 2006).

curtailed 'on the grounds that a defendant's self-representation is substantially and persistently obstructing the proper and expeditious conduct of his trial'.[95]

The issue of whether a warning was required before assigning counsel to an accused was 'a matter of first impression'.[96] The Chamber found guidance in Rule 80(B) which allows for a Trial Chamber to order the removal of an accused from the courtroom and continue proceedings in his absence if he has persisted in disruptive conduct following a warning that such conduct may warrant his removal from the courtroom. The Appeals Chamber considered that the right to self-representation should not be treated differently. Due to the fundamental nature of both rights, an accused should be duly warned before any restriction. Although such a requirement was a feature of domestic law, the need for a specific previous warning that an accused's right to represent himself would be taken away in the event of continued obstructionist behaviour marked a significant development in the procedural law of the Tribunal. The Appeals Chamber in *Šešelj* noted that none of the warnings mentioned by the Trial Chamber sufficed given that they did not specifically state that he would lose his right to self-representation as a sanction if his obstructionist behaviour persisted.[97] It determined that the Trial Chamber should satisfy itself that the defendant's pre-trial behaviour when considered as a whole provides a strong indication that continued self-representation *would* (not 'may' as the Trial Chamber had determined) substantially and persistently obstruct the proper and expeditious conduct of the trial proceedings.[98] The Appeals Chamber noted the test in *United States v Brock* and in *Prosecutor v Janković and Stanković*.[99]

Although the Appeals Chamber made significant findings concerning Šešelj's pre-trial behaviour,[100] it reversed the impugned decision in light of the absence of a specific warning to Šešelj before assigning him counsel. Thereafter, the Appeals Chamber explicitly stated that, should Šešelj's self-representation subsequent to this decision substantially obstruct the proper and expeditious proceedings in his case, the Trial Chamber would be justified in promptly assigning him counsel after allowing him the right to be heard.[101] Remarkably, only five days after the Appeals Chamber's decision, the Trial Chamber ordered the Registrar to re-appoint standby counsel to Šešelj with a mandate to assist, advise, and crucially, to be prepared to temporarily or permanently take over the conduct of the defence from the accused should the Trial Chamber find, following a warning, that he was engaging in disruptive conduct.[102] On 30 October 2006, the Registrar withdrew David Hooper and his co-counsel, Andreas O'Shea, as assigned defence counsel, and reassigned them as standby counsel in accordance

[95] ibid para 20. [96] ibid para 22. [97] ibid para 26. [98] ibid para 28.
[99] ibid. [100] ibid para 29. [101] ibid para 52.
[102] *Prosecutor v Šešelj* (Order Concerning Appointment of Standby Counsel and Delayed Commencement of Trial) IT-03-67-PT (25 October 2006) para 6.

with the Trial Chamber's decision.[103] No warning was issued to Šešelj before the Trial Chamber made its decision.

In response to the Trial Chamber's order, Šešelj began a hunger strike on 10 November 2006. The Chamber noted on 22 November 2006 that he did not attend the Status Conference and explicitly refused to appear in court. The Chamber ordered that Šešelj must be warned that his conduct was found to be substantially obstructive and warranted the imposition of defence counsel. The Chamber invited the accused to make representations in writing or orally and expressly stated that, should the accused choose not to make any submissions on this matter, the Trial Chamber would interpret this as a waiver of his right to be heard and would proceed to a final decision.[104] Shortly thereafter, the Trial Chamber issued reasons for its decision to instruct standby counsel to permanently take over the conduct of Šešelj's defence.[105] The Chamber held that he had repeatedly disrupted court hearings by deliberately and unreasonably interrupting the proceedings and by refusing to appear in court to represent himself. He had been put on notice and specifically warned by the Trial Chamber that, should his disruptive and obstructionist conduct continue, the Chamber would consider imposing counsel.[106] Two days later, an appeal was filed by Šešelj before the Appeals Chamber.[107] In its second decision on the assignment of counsel,[108] the Appeals Chamber noted the extraordinary circumstances of the situation in that Šešelj had persisted in his refusal to take food or medicine since 11 November 2006 and was seriously damaging his health, which could in turn have grave consequences.[109] The Appeals Chamber took the view that Šešelj had not been given a 'clean slate' by the Trial Chamber[110] and that the Chamber had abused its discretion by immediately ordering the imposition of standby counsel, without first establishing additional obstructionist behaviour on the part of Šešelj.[111]

The impugned decision assigning standby counsel to Šešelj was reversed and the Appeals Chamber directed the Trial Chamber not to impose standby counsel unless he exhibited obstructionist behaviour fully satisfying the Trial Chamber that, in order to ensure a fair and expeditious trial, he required the assistance of standby counsel.[112] Alternatively, the Appeals Chamber stated that 'should the full restoration of Šešelj's right to self-representation fail to curb his obstructionist behaviour, the Trial Chamber would be permitted to proceed to assign counsel. Again such a decision may only be taken once Šešelj has been given a real chance

[103] *Prosecutor v Šešelj* (Decision of Registrar) IT-03-67-PT (30 October 2006).

[104] *Prosecutor v Šešelj* (Invitation to Accused to Make Submissions) IT-03-67-PT (22 November 2006).

[105] *Prosecutor v Šešelj* (Reasons for Decision (No 2) on Assignment of Counsel) IT-03-67-T (27 November 2006).

[106] ibid para 13.

[107] *Prosecutor v Šešelj* (Submission for Motion 226) IT-03-67-AR73.4 (7 December 2006).

[108] *Prosecutor v Šešelj* (Appeals Chamber Decision on Appeal Against the Trial Chamber's Decision (No 2) on Assignment of Counsel) IT-03-67-AR73.4 (8 December 2006).

[109] ibid para 14.

[110] ibid paras 24 and 26.

[111] ibid para 27.

[112] ibid para 28.

to effectively exercise the right to self-representation' and if the Trial Chamber felt justified in making such a decision.[113] The Appeals Chamber nullified the opening of the proceedings and ordered that the trial must restart.[114] The prosecution attempted again to terminate Šešelj's self-representation and have counsel assigned to him,[115] alleging that the accused was substantially and persistently obstructing the proceedings both in and out of court.[116] It was alleged that Šešelj and his associates had conducted a campaign of witness harassment and intimidation in order to obstruct the proceedings.[117] On 27 November 2008, the Trial Chamber stayed a decision on this matter as the allegations requiring consideration were no longer within the Chamber's jurisdiction.[118]

On 21 January 2009, the Trial Chamber issued a decision and order in which it initiated contempt proceedings against Šešelj 'for knowingly and wilfully disclosing information in knowing violation of an order of a Chamber'.[119] He was accused of having disclosed the names and other personal details of three witnesses whose identity had been ordered by a Trial Chamber to be withheld from the public. Šešelj was alleged to have authored a book in which the information was published, along with other material such as excerpts of the written statement of one of these witnesses, the disclosure of which was prohibited. In a confidential decision on 24 July 2009, he was found guilty by the Trial Chamber and sentenced to 15 months' imprisonment.[120]

In a decision on 24 November 2009, the Trial Chamber examined whether conditions had been met to assign counsel for the remainder of his trial.[121] First, the Court found that Šešelj's conviction for contempt did not automatically mean that counsel should be appointed.[122] Furthermore, while Mr Šešelj was found guilty of a:

> ... serious and grave [act, it was] ... nevertheless an isolated act that cannot legitimately be considered as continually disruptive ... such that it would substantially and persistently obstruct the proper and expeditious conduct of the trial ... [The] conduct that led to his conviction ... does not in itself justify the assignment of counsel.[123]

[113] ibid. [114] ibid para 29.

[115] *Prosecutor v Šešelj* (Prosecution's Motion to Terminate the Accused's Self-Representation) IT-03-67-T (28 July 2008 (confidential and *ex parte*); public version filed 8 August 2008 (redacted)). [116] ibid para 2.

[117] ibid para 13.

[118] *Prosecutor v Šešelj* (Trial Chamber Redacted Version of the 'Redacted Version of the "Decision on Prosecution Motion to Terminate the Accused's Self-Representation" filed Confidentially and *Ex Parte* on 25 November 2008') IT-03-67-T (27 November 2008) paras 26–7.

[119] *Prosecutor v Šešelj* (Trial Chamber Decision on Allegations of Contempt) IT-03-67-R77.2 (21 January 2009) para 14.

[120] See eg <http://www.haguejusticeportal.net/eCache/DEF/11/431.TGFuZz1FTg.html>.

[121] *Prosecutor v Šešelj* (Trial Chamber Public Version of the 'Consolidated Decision on Assignment of Counsel, Adjournment and Prosecution Motion for Additional Time with Separate Opinion of Presiding Judge Antonetti in Annex') IT-03-67-T (24 November 2009) paras 66–87.

[122] ibid para 67. [123] ibid para 73.

Moreover, while he was warned that certain obstructive behaviour could lead to restrictions on his right of self-representation, those warnings were not issued to him in relation to the conduct that led to his conviction in the contempt case.[124] When examining the issue of proportionality, the Chamber noted that the prosecution's case was almost concluded and that should counsel be appointed at this point in the trial, it 'would be felt by the Accused primarily at the Defence stage of the case'.[125] Additionally, assigning counsel would cause significant delay,[126] which did not 'seem proportional to the conduct for which the Accused [was] charged in the Judgement of 24 July 2009'.[127] The Chamber did not believe that assigning counsel would prevent such conduct from occurring in the future.[128] Therefore, it refrained from assigning counsel.[129]

Further contempt charges were filed against Šešelj in a decision in December 2009 by the Appeals Chamber[130] for knowingly disclosing confidential information and thereby creating 'a hostile environment that demonstrates an intention to interfere with witnesses'.[131] On 4 February 2010, the Appeals Chamber initiated the contempt proceedings by way of order in lieu of an indictment.[132] In a hearing on 6 May 2010, Šešelj refused to enter a plea, thereby forcing the presiding judge to register a not guilty plea on his behalf.[133] At the time of writing, he continues to represent himself with contempt proceedings pending.

B. Obstructionism and the self-representing accused: guidance from the *Stanković* case

The *Stanković* case provided the ICTY with another opportunity to deal with obstructionism and its impact upon the right of self-representation. Stanković was transferred from the ICTY to the State Court of Bosnia and Herzegovina on 29 September 2005 and thereafter sentenced to 20 years' imprisonment for crimes against humanity.[134] During the period of his detention before the ICTY, Milenko Radović had been originally assigned to represent him. However, due to allegations of professional misconduct, he was suspended from his position as

[124] ibid para 75. [125] ibid para 78. [126] ibid para 79. [127] ibid para 80.
[128] ibid para 81. [129] ibid para 87.

[130] *Prosecutor v Šešelj* (Appeals Chamber Decision on Prosecution's Appeal against the Trial Chamber's Decision of 21 August 2009) IT-03-67-R77.3 (17 December 2009) para 28. See also 'Order Assigning Judges to a Case Before a Trial Chamber and Replacing a Judge' issued confidentially and *ex parte* by the President of the Tribunal on 18 December 2009, p 3, ordering that the bench in this matter shall be composed of Judges O-Gon Kwon, Kevin Parker, and Burton Hall.

[131] *Prosecutor v Šešelj* (Prosecution's Motion under Rule 77 Concerning Further Breaches of Protective Measures) IT-03-67-R77.3 (26 January 2009) para 31.

[132] *Prosecutor v Šešelj* (Appeals Chamber Public Redacted Version of Second Decision on Prosecution's Motion under Rule 77 Concerning Further Breaches of Protective Measures (Three Books) Issued on 3 February 2010) IT-03-67-R77.3 (4 February 2010) para 20(a)–(b).

[133] ICTY Weekly Press Briefing, 12 May 2010, available at <http://www.icty.org/sid/10400>.

[134] On 25 May 2007, Stanković escaped from prison in Foca, Bosnia Herzegovina. To date, he has not been traced.

counsel.[135] Stanković was given time to choose a new lawyer from the Tribunal's list and informed that, if he did not select someone, counsel would be chosen for him. After Stanković refused to assign counsel, the Registry took the decision to assign Victor Koppe. Thereafter, Stanković informed the Court that he wished to represent himself.

In a decision on 19 August 2005, the Trial Chamber relied upon earlier jurisprudence and recognized that while an accused 'has a presumptive right to self-representation', this right is qualified.[136] The defendant must be literate and competent. Moreover, this right 'must be exercised voluntarily, unequivocally and intelligently'.[137] The Chamber determined that Stanković was literate, and appeared able to defend himself. He was aware of the consequences of waiving his right to counsel, and that he had to act in accordance with the Rules of Procedure and Evidence.[138] In his written statements, Stanković said that he would represent himself *if* he could not have Radović to represent him. In this regard, the Chamber determined that Stanković's request for self-representation was 'an alternative position, advanced as a fall-back to a primary request for different counsel', and that as such, it was not equivocal.[139] Stanković made the choice to represent himself of his own free will.[140] However, the Chamber reiterated that there may be circumstances in which it is appropriate to *insist* that a case is presented by counsel and not a self-represented accused in order to ensure that the fairness of the trial is not obstructed.[141] Such decisions must be made on a case-by-case basis. Factors to be considered include the accused's ability to conduct his defence, his attitude, and his actions.[142]

[135] *Prosecutor v Gojko Stanković and Radovan Stanković* (Decision Following Registrar's Notification of Radovan Stanković's Request for Self-representation) IT-96-23/2-PT (19 August 2005) para 3.

[136] ibid paras 8–9, citing *Prosecutor v Milošević* (Decision on Interlocutory Appeal of the Trial Chamber's Decision on the Assignment of Defence Counsel) (1 November 2004) para 11.

[137] ibid para 9 of the *Stanković* decision, referring to *Faretta v California* 422 US 806 (1975): 'In the Joint Opinion of Judge McDonald and Judge Vohrah attached to the Appeals Chamber's Judgment in *Prosecutor v Drazen Erdemovic* IT-96-22-A, 7 October 1997, and in the context of the validity of a guilty plea, the judges construed the word "voluntary" as a statement if made by an accused whose mental state allows him to understand the consequences of his choice and who is not making a choice forcefully. In relation to "not equivocal", the judges considered a statement not equivocal if not accompanied by contrary words' (para 8). In *United States v Denno* 348 F 2d 12 (1965), 16, the court found equivocation where an accused had failed to 'unmistakably commit himself' to the alternative of conducting his own defence. In *Faretta v California* the court said that 'a statement is intelligently made if made in full awareness of the possible consequences of waiving the opportunity for skilled legal representation'.

[138] ibid para 15.

[139] ibid para 16.

[140] ibid paras 17–18.

[141] ibid para 10, referencing *Prosecutor v Šešelj* (Decision on Prosecution's Motion for Order Appointing Counsel to Assist Vojislav Šešelj with his Defence) IT-03-67-PT (9 May 2003) para 20.

[142] ibid referencing *Prosecutor v Milošević* (Reasons for Decision on the prosecution Motion Concerning Assignment of Counsel) IT-02-54-T (4 April 2003) para 40.

The Chamber determined that Stanković was charged 'with serious crimes [the defence of which would] require particular legal skills'.[143] Stanković was also charged with sexual crimes, in respect of which the Chamber held that it was not appropriate for him to examine 'witnesses who are also alleged victims of those crimes'.[144] It was found that, throughout the proceedings, Stanković had been deliberately disrespectful and inappropriate and that his behaviour showed his intention to disrupt the proceedings. It was determined that Stanković's disruptions, including abusive language in court and in written documents, sufficed to demonstrate that his obstructive behaviour 'would disrupt the conduct of the proceedings and seriously impair the effective and fair defence of the Accused if he were to defend himself in person'.[145] In the circumstances, it was not 'in the interests of justice, in particular that of a fair trial, to allow the Accused to waive his right of legal assistance'. Stanković's 'deliberate and serious' misbehaviour required the Chamber to insist upon the imposition of legal assistance in this case.[146]

VI. The Right to Self-Representation Upheld

In recent years, the right to self-representation before the ICTY has been upheld on three separate occasions, although it is perhaps too early to interpret this development as a permanent change in approach. Recent developments in this area include recognition of an accused's right to represent himself on appeal and the notion of *partial* self-representation at the appellate stage.

In the *Krajišnik* case the majority of the Appeals Chamber upheld the defendant's right to represent himself on appeal, determining that the Statute is silent on the opportunity to restrict the right at that juncture of the proceedings.[147] Five months later, the Appeals Chamber held that an accused who elects to represent himself may be permitted to engage legal counsel with regard to certain issues.[148] The Chamber concluded that '[t]here is no fundamental reason why a defendant may not make different choices—self-representing or engaging legal counsel—with regard to different issues.'[149] In this case, the Chamber permitted defence counsel to represent Krajišnik with respect to the discrete legal issue of the concept of joint criminal enterprise on condition that his involvement did

[143] ibid para 20. [144] ibid para 21. [145] ibid para 23. [146] ibid para 25.

[147] *Prosecutor v Krajišnik* (Appeals Chamber Decision on Momcilo Krajišnik's Request to Self-Represent) IT-00-39-A (11 May 2007).

[148] *Prosecutor v Krajišnik* (Appeals Chamber Decision on Momcilo Krajišnik's Motion to Reschedule Status Conference and Permit Alan Dershowitz to Appear) IT-00-39-A (28 February 2008). [149] ibid para 8.

not cause substantial or persistent obstruction or delay.[150] This development of partial self-representation on appeal may help to ensure in future cases that where accused represent themselves, complicated legal concepts such as joint criminal enterprise can still be addressed competently by a legal professional, to the benefit of both the accused and the Tribunal.

In the *Tolimir* case, the accused expressed his desire to represent himself only after his request to be represented by a particular lawyer as lead counsel was denied.[151] The lawyer in question, Nebojsa Mrkić, was Tolimir's family lawyer, and served as assistant counsel to Ljubiša Beara, a defendant in *Popović et al.* Tolimir explained that he wanted to be represented by Mrkić as he had previously appeared before the Tribunal and was thus familiar with its rules.[152] He also expressed the importance of his confidence in Mrkić, particularly when dealing with crimes of such gravity. The prosecution argued that various conflicts of interest would arise if Mrkić were to be appointed as Tolimir's lead counsel.[153] The Registry determined that Mrkić did not meet the requirements of Rule 45 (qualifications for the assignment of counsel) and that a conflict of interest might arise due to Mrkić's involvement in Beara's case. Thereafter, the Deputy Registrar acknowledged Tolimir's election to conduct his own defence, terminated representation by duty counsel, and ordered his former duty counsel to surrender all papers and case-related materials to Tolimir.[154]

On 29 April 2008, the prosecution requested the assignment of permanent counsel to Tolimir on the basis that: (1) Tolimir had failed to accept or review documents provided to him;[155] (2) he had refused to allow his legal advisers to receive documents from the Court on his behalf;[156] and (3) he had refused to meet with the prosecution.[157] The prosecution characterized Tolimir's conduct as obstructive[158] and reiterated that the right to self-representation may be curtailed at the pre-trial stage.[159] The pre-trial test in *Šešelj* was cited in addition to the proportionality requirement that the restrictions on an accused's right of self-representation must be the minimum necessary to ensure a fair and expeditious

150 ibid para 9.

151 *Prosecutor v Tolimir* (Submission by the Accused to the Registrar for Leave to Conduct his own Defence or to Appoint Counsel of His Own Choosing Pursuant to Article 21(4)(d), and Rule 45(F) and Amended Rule 62(C) of the Rules) IT-05-88/2-I (6 August 2007) para 7.

152 ibid para 2.

153 *Prosecutor v Tolimir* (Prosecutor's Response to Submission by the Accused for Assistance of the Trial Chamber on Appointment of Permanent Counsel) IT-05-88/2-PT (18 July 2007) para 3.

154 *Prosecutor v Tolimir* (Notification by the Deputy Registrar [of accused's election to conduct his own defence and termination of representation by duty counsel]) IT-05-88/2-PT (27 August 2007).

155 *Prosecutor v Tolimir* (Prosecution's Motion Requesting Appointment of Permanent Counsel for Accused Tolimir) IT-05-88/2-PT (29 April 2008) paras 2, 5, and 7.

156 ibid paras 10–11, 13.

157 ibid para 14.

158 ibid para 16, citing *Prosecutor v Šešelj* (Appeals Chamber Decision on Appeal Against the Trial Chamber's Decision on Assignment of Counsel) IT-03-67-AR73.3 (20 October 2006).

159 ibid para 17, citing *Šešelj* (Appeals Chamber Decision) (n 158 above) para 28.

trial.[160] Tolimir argued that the prosecution must disclose case materials to him directly and not through his legal advisers, who were not his defence counsel.[161] The function of his advisers at the pre-trial stage was to assist him in the preparation of his defence. In respect of his decision not to meet with the prosecution, Tolimir argued that he would 'not like any meetings with anyone from the Prosecution to be interpreted in any way whatsoever' and that he wanted to have a clear and unambiguous record of communication in writing.[162] Tolimir's request to receive material in the Serbian language in Cyrillic script had previously been dismissed by the Pre-Trial Judge, Kimberly Prost, in an oral decision on 11 December 2007, on the basis that she was satisfied that Tolimir was able to read and understand the documents that had been served on him. His appeal of the decision and a request for reconsideration were dismissed by the Appeals Chamber on 28 March and 18 June 2008, respectively.

The prosecution's request for the assignment of counsel was only dealt with 22 months later on 25 February 2010, the day before the commencement of trial. The Chamber pronounced in an oral decision that 'the reasons stated in the motion for imposing counsel do not appear to the Chamber to be pertinent at this time'.[163] The Chamber warned Tolimir, as it had before, that the trial phase would be demanding and that he could engage counsel at any time if he felt unable to continue representing himself.[164] The Chamber further recalled the possibility provided by ICTY Rule 45*ter* of imposing counsel on him in the interests of justice. The Chamber stressed that it would 'closely monitor [his] conduct in this trial and any impact it may have on the progress of this trial'.[165] Tolimir is assisted by a team of legal advisers. However, the precise role and responsibilities of his advisers as a self-representing accused has yet to be determined. While Tolimir's request to have his assistant Aleksandar Gajic in the courtroom has been granted by the Trial Chamber,[166] the issue of whether or not he will be allowed to present legal arguments, raise objections, and conduct the examination of witnesses has still to be addressed by the

[160] ibid paras 19–20, citing *Prosecutor v Milošević* (Appeals Chamber Decision on Interlocutory Appeal of the Trial Chamber's Decision on the Assignment of Defence Counsel) IT-02-54-AR73.7 (1 November 2004) para 17, and *Prosecutor v Norman* (Decision on the Application of Samuel Hinga Norman for Self-Representation Under Article 17(4)(d) of the Statute of the Special Court) SCSL-04-14-T (8 June 2004) para 26.

[161] *Prosecutor v Tolimir* (Response to the Prosecution's Motion Requesting the Appointment of Permanent Counsel for the Accused Tolimir) IT-05-88/2-PT (2 June 2008) para 8.

[162] ibid para 29.

[163] *Prosecutor v Tolimir* (Pre-Trial Conference Transcript) IT-05-88-2/PT (25 February 2010) 317.

[164] ibid 317–18.

[165] ibid 318.

[166] *Prosecutor v Tolimir* (Decision on Motion Requesting the Chamber to Allow the Accused's Legal Advisor to be Present in the Courtroom) IT-05-88/2-PT (22 February 2010) 2. The prosecution did not oppose Tolimir's request. See *Prosecutor v Tolimir* (Response to Accused's Request for the Chamber to Allow his Legal Advisor, Aleksandar Gajić, to be present in the Courtroom) IT-05-88/2-PT (18 February 2010).

Chamber.[167] The prosecution has interpreted Tolimir's request as one whereby his assistant can 'appear before the Trial Chamber in a representational capacity substantively coextensive with that of appointed Counsel'.[168] However, a decision on this matter remains pending.

Radovan Karadžić asserted his right to represent himself at his initial appearance on 31 July 2008.[169] He is the first individual to do so since the introduction of Rule 45*ter* which provides that '[t]he Trial Chamber may, if it decides that it is in the interests of justice, instruct the Registrar to assign a counsel to represent the interests of the accused'. This Rule was adopted on 4 November 2008.

During the initial appearance, Judge Orie took the opportunity to read certain 'key words' to the defendant concerning self-representation:

> . . . the right to self representation is a qualified right but not an absolute right. That right may be restricted under certain circumstances. If an accused would elect to represent himself, then he also should accept responsibility for disadvantages which result from self representation in the absence of qualified counsel. An accused who represents himself is not given special treatment. Further, there is no provision for legal aid to be given to a self-represented accused. Some funding may be allowed for assistance by legal associates who fulfil the necessary requirements under the Rules of Procedure and Evidence, but the right to privileged access to such legal associates cannot be guaranteed. These and other related matters such as communication and translation facilities for self representation should be further discussed by the Registrar.[170]

Karadžić responded that he would defend himself before the institution as he would defend himself before any 'natural catastrophe'.[171] At a further initial appearance on 29 August 2008 he was advised by Judge Bonomy of the 'highly complex matters' which might arise should the prosecution seek to amend the indictment, an area in which the defendant 'would significantly benefit from having a trained legal representative' to assist him in responding effectively to the arguments raised.[172] Judge Bonomy informed Karadžić that he had requested the Registry to make a member of staff available to act as a liaison with a view to assisting in the preparation and delivery of documents,[173] a tool which had been employed effectively during the trial of Slobodan Milošević.

[167] See *Prosecutor v Tolimir* (Request to the Trial Chamber) IT-05-88/2-T (1 March 2010) paras 1, 3. See also *Prosecutor v Tolimir* (Prosecution Response to Tolimir's Request to the Trial Chamber) IT-05-88/2-T (5 March 2010) para 3.

[168] *Tolimir* (Prosecution Response) (n 167 above) para 4.

[169] *Prosecutor v Karadžić* (Hearing on 31 July 2008) IT-95-5/18 Trial Transcript, p 2, lines 11–12.

[170] ibid p 19, lines 1–25 to p 20, line 1.

[171] ibid p 20, lines 12–23. On 5 August 2008, Karadžić filed notice of his intention to represent himself to the Registrar pursuant to Rule 45(F).

[172] *Prosecutor v Karadžić* (Trial Transcript) IT-95-5/18-I (29 August 2008) p 30, lines 8–19.

[173] ibid p 36, lines 18–24.

On 14 October 2009, the Trial Chamber issued a scheduling order setting a trial date of 26 October 2009,[174] which was followed by Karadžić's Submission on Commencement of Trial, in which he stated that he would not appear, as the defence was not yet ready for trial.[175] True to his word, Karadžić did not appear on 26 October, or the following day. Judge Kwon, presiding, stated that since the accused had ignored the Chamber's oral and written request and warnings:

> he...must accept that consequences will inevitably flow from the choice... Should the accused persist in his refusal to attend the trial and fail to appear...at the next hearing...the Chamber may decide to continue trial in his absence. In addition, counsel may, in the interests of justice, be assigned to represent the interests of the accused for the remainder of the proceedings.[176]

The accused was again absent on the next trial date of 2 November 2009. While he attended proceedings on 3 November, he informed the Court that he was not prepared and would not attend any future proceedings until he deemed himself ready to do so.[177] On 5 November 2009, the Trial Chamber determined that since 'the accused substantially and persistently obstructed the proper and expeditious conduct of his trial by refusing to attend the proceedings',[178] the overall interests of justice would best be served by appointing counsel, and ordered the Registrar to do so.[179] In making this decision, the Court acknowledged the 'fundamental nature of the right to self-representation, which cannot be diminished lightly' and therefore stated that counsel was being appointed for the specific task of assisting at trial.[180] The accused would still be responsible for representing himself by 'dealing with the day-to-day matters that arise, such as the filing of motions and responses to motions filed by the Prosecution, and further preparing himself for the trial'.[181] Moreover, the Trial Chamber warned that, should Karadžić continue to be absent from the trial, he would forfeit his right of self-representation, no longer be entitled to assistance from his assigned defence team, and would have his appointed counsel take over his case as assigned counsel.[182]

When the accused failed to indicate a preference in respect of the five counsel approved by the Registrar, the latter appointed Mr Richard Harvey.[183] Shortly thereafter, Karadžić filed a motion to vacate that appointment on 4 December 2009.[184] In his motion, Karadžić stated that the Registrar erred by providing

[174] *Prosecutor v Karadžić* (Scheduling Order for the Commencement of Trial) IT-95-5/18 (14 October 2009).

[175] *Prosecutor v Karadžić* (Submission on Commencement of Trial) IT-95-5/18 (21 October 2009).

[176] *Prosecutor v Karadžić* (Trial Transcript) IT-95-5/18 (27 October 2009) 510–11.

[177] *Prosecutor v Karadžić* (Trial Transcript) IT-95-5/18 (3 November 2009) 676–8.

[178] *Prosecutor v Karadžić* (Trial Chamber Decision on Appointment of Counsel and Order on Further Trial Proceedings) IT-95-5/18 (5 November 2009) para 21.

[179] ibid para 28.

[180] ibid para 25.

[181] ibid.

[182] ibid para 27.

[183] *Prosecutor v Karadžić* (Decision [of the Registrar]) IT-95-5/18 (19 November 2009) 2–3.

[184] *Prosecutor v Karadžić* (Motion to Vacate Appointment of Richard Harvey) IT-95-5/18 (4 December 2009).

him with a list of only five names from which to choose instead of the complete approved counsel list[185] and that he would never consent to Mr Harvey's appointment, given submissions he had made as counsel for Lahi Brahimaj. Karadžić explained that Mr Harvey could not be expected to 'attack Serbs in one trial and turn around and defend them in another'.[186] In dealing with this matter, the Court first had to determine its competence to review the Registrar's decision. It found that the rules relied upon by the accused in the Directive on the Assignment of Counsel did not apply to this case.[187] The Directive does not specifically deal with a situation such as the present case, in which counsel had been appointed to prevent obstruction.[188] However, the Trial Chamber determined that, as the Registrar's decision to appoint Mr Harvey went to the fairness of the trial, it had the power to review the Registrar's decision.[189]

In examining the decision, the Trial Chamber stated that, while Article 21 sets out the rights of an accused wishing to self-represent or be represented by counsel, under Article 21(4)(d) only an accused being represented by counsel is entitled to counsel of his choice.[190] Since Karadžić always maintained his intention to represent himself, and is in fact still representing himself, this rule did not apply to him.[191] The Court stated that 'accepting the Accused's argument would mean that the Accused is simultaneously entitled to exercise both the right to self-representation and the right to have counsel of his choosing'.[192] Moreover, even in cases where an accused is represented by counsel, his right to counsel of his choosing is not absolute[193] and may be limited due to conflicts of interest or unavailability.[194] Furthermore, Mr Harvey was not assigned counsel but rather counsel assisting for a specific task.[195] Whether that relationship would exist in the future was entirely dependent upon the accused's behaviour and willingness to attend the trial proceedings.[196] The Court, therefore, found that Karadžić's rights had not been violated by the Registrar's decision and that his continued right to represent himself was not affected.[197]

Karadžić relied on the *Šešelj* decision, in which the Court provided Šešelj with a complete list of standby counsel.[198] However, in that case, Šešelj had had a well-documented and troubled history with the assigned standby counsel.[199] Whereas, apart from Karadžić's complaints in respect of Mr Harvey's submissions in the Lahi Brahimaj final brief and his observation that Mr Harvey had never represented a Serb, Karadžić appeared 'to have been impressed by Richard Harvey and his "ethical standards" '.[200] The Court went on to state that:

> [t]he logic of a pre-condition to any appointment of counsel to a self-represented accused intent on preserving his right to self-represent that he must be able to choose his counsel

[185] ibid paras 2–4. [186] ibid paras 11–16.

[187] *Prosecutor v Karadžić* (Trial Chamber Decision on the Accused's Motion to Vacate Appointment of Richard Harvey) IT-95-5/18 (23 December 2009) 22. [188] ibid.

[189] ibid para 23. [190] ibid para 26. [191] ibid. [192] ibid.

[193] ibid para 27. [194] ibid para 40. [195] ibid paras 27–8.

[196] ibid para 28. [197] ibid. [198] ibid para 35. [199] ibid paras 36–7.

[200] ibid para 37.

(or stand-by counsel) from Rule 45(B) list or ('Rule 44 list') is somewhat wanting. That logic is even less compelling when the counsel in question has been appointed simply to prepare himself to represent the interests of an accused sometime in the future, if that should be required.[201]

Furthermore, that the Registrar should be expected to provide names of counsel who could not represent the accused because of a conflict or those unwilling to represent the accused would have been counterproductive.[202] The Court was not persuaded by Karadžić's argument that Mr Harvey was unsuitable because he 'has represented Kosovo Albanians, has never represented Serbs, and has made statements that the Accused regards as critical of Serbs'.[203] Instead, it found that 'on the basis of his past considerable experience, the Chamber has no doubt that [he] . . . would be able to provide effective and professional legal assistance without any divided loyalties'.[204] The Chamber, therefore, denied the motion.[205]

On appeal, the Appeals Chamber confirmed that Article 21(4)(d) does not give an accused both the right to self-represent and the right to counsel of his choice but rather provides the right to one or the other.[206] Since Karadžić chose to remain self-represented, he 'does not enjoy any rights that are derived from choosing to be represented by counsel'.[207] Likewise, the Court was not persuaded by his argument that since the Trial Chamber attempted to override his right to self-represent, he should be afforded the rights of those choosing to be represented.[208] It found it was within the Trial Chamber's powers to appoint counsel in this case because of Karadžić's obstructionist behaviour.[209] Moreover, should such an appointment occur, it would not occur because of Karadžić's:

> . . . voluntary decision to cease self-representation. Instead, it will be because the Trial Chamber found that Karadžić's persistent obstructive behaviour has made it necessary, in the interests of justice, to limit his right of self-representation by assigning counsel to represent his interests.[210]

In relation to the *Šešelj* argument, the Appeals Chamber stated that the '*Šešelj* decision was rendered in a unique factual and procedural context very different from Karadžić's' and a 'Chamber's context-limited decision to provide for processes beyond those guaranteed by the Statute and the Rules does not create an automatic right to these processes'.[211] In the *Šešelj* case, the Appeals Chamber found that the Trial Chamber had violated Šešelj's right of self-representation by failing to warn him that should his obstructionist behaviour continue, counsel

[201] ibid para 38. [202] ibid para 40. [203] ibid para 43. [204] ibid.
[205] ibid para 48.
[206] *Prosecutor v Karadžić* (Appeals Chamber Decision on Radovan Karadžić's Appeal from Decision on Motion to Vacate Appointment of Richard Harvey) IT-95-5/18-AR73.6 (12 February 2010) para 26. [207] ibid.
[208] ibid para 27. [209] ibid. [210] ibid. [211] ibid para 31.

could be appointed.[212] Karadžić, on the other hand, had been warned on numerous occasions that this could happen.[213] Moreover, given the flexibility shown to him by the Registrar, the Appeals Chamber found 'no basis for requiring that he be provided... greater opportunities to select personally between individuals available to serve as standby counsel'.[214] The Appeals Chamber, therefore, dismissed the appeal.[215] At the time of writing, Karadžić continues to represent himself in the courtroom, and is aided by a team of lawyers and assistants who help to prepare his case for trial. Mr Richard Harvey continues to act in his role as standby counsel.[216]

VII. Legal Aid and the Right to Self-Representation

The thorny issue of whether or not a self-representing accused is entitled to receive legal aid, and if so, to what extent, has been considered most recently in the case of Karadžić before the ICTY. On 29 September 2008, Karadžić declared himself indigent and applied for the appointment and remuneration of three legal advisers at the level of counsel and five members of support staff. The Registry responded by relying on an Appeals Chamber decision in *Krajišnik*[217] and argued that a self-represented accused is 'not entitled to receive legal aid funds' but that, in order to give effect to Article 21(4)(b), the Registry considered it 'appropriate to provide some funding, outside the Tribunal's legal aid system'. The Registry determined that legal associates of a self-representing accused would be paid at the same rate as those who would normally assist counsel. The Registry refused a request by Karadžić to reconsider its decision.

Thereafter, Karadžić filed a motion arguing that, notwithstanding his desire to represent himself, he still required assistance from legal professionals and that the 'Registrar's refusal to provide... [him] with anything more than support staff' frustrates his right to defend himself and 'makes a fair trial at this Tribunal impossible'.[218] Specifically, Karadžić requested the Tribunal to pay his legal team what they would 'pay other legal teams because lawyers who are as skilled as required for his case will not work for 15 or 25 Euros per hour'.[219] Karadžić argued that, while the Appeals Chamber in Krajišnik held that a self-representing accused is not entitled to legal assistance *per se*, he is entitled to adequate facilities under Article 21(4)(b).[220] These facilities include 'adequately

[212] ibid para 32. [213] ibid. [214] ibid. [215] ibid para 36.

[216] *Prosecutor v Karadžić* (Trial Chamber Decision on Designation of Standby Counsel) IT-95-5/18-T (15 April 2010).

[217] *Prosecutor v Karadžić* (Appeals Chamber Decision on Krajišnik Request and on Prosecution Motion) IT-00-39-A (11 September 2007).

[218] *Prosecutor v Karadžić* (Motion for Adequate Facilities and Equality of Arms: Legal Services) IT-95-05/18-PT (24 November 2008) paras 1–3. [219] ibid paras 4 and 6.

[220] ibid para 10, citing *Krajišnik* (Appeals Chamber Decision) (n 217 above) paras 41–2.

reimburs[ing] the legal associates for their coordinating work and for related legal consultation'.[221]

Karadžić relied upon the liberal approach taken in *Šešelj*, in which the Trial Chamber had held that 'the duty to ensure the proper administration of justice can be fulfilled only if a team of associates assists the accused in preparing and presenting his defence at every stage of the proceedings'.[222] In *Šešelj*, Judge Antonetti held that an accused without means who 'wishes, for reasons of his own, to represent himself' must be positively assisted to do so, and this at the very least requires that he or she ought not to be denied the right to legal aid.[223] Judge Antonetti observed that the Tribunal's regulations do not include a procedure for self-representing defendants to obtain legal aid and that this was a gap in the law.

On 28 January 2009, the Trial Chamber dismissed Karadžić's motion and in reviewing the Registrar's decision held that it was unable to identify an error in the Registry's reasoning to merit overturning the decision.[224] On appeal, in rejecting Karadžić's arguments, the Appeals Chamber held that the effect of the *Krajišnik* appeal decision is that:

> ... where an accused lacks the requisite knowledge of the law or legal procedures to the extent that it will substantially and persistently obstruct the proper and expeditious conduct of the trial, the solution is not the funding of highly experienced legal associates, but rather the curtailment of his right of self-representation.[225]

The *Krajišnik* appeal decision recognized that: '[t]o the extent that the Registry requires or encourages indigent self-representing accused to co-ordinate their defences through designated legal associates', it 'should adequately reimburse the legal associates for their coordinating work and for related legal consultation'.[226] However, it concluded that such funding should not be comparable to that paid to counsel for represented accused.[227] The Appeals Chamber clearly adopts the view that to grant such level of facilities would be to enable the self-representing accused to have 'his cake and eat it too'.[228] However, a different approach has been taken in *Karadžić* by the President of the Tribunal, who made it clear that it is incumbent upon the Registrar to take relevant factors into account, when he stated that 'no reasonable person having taken the circumstances of this case into account could have arrived at the decision that an allocation of only

[221] ibid para 11.

[222] ibid para 25, citing *Prosecutor v Šešelj* (Decision on the Financing of the Defence of the Accused) IT-03-67-PT (30 July 2007) para 53.

[223] See A Zahar, 'Legal Aid, Self-Representation, and the Crisis at the Hague Tribunal' (2008) 19 *Criminal Law Forum* 241, 248.

[224] *Prosecutor v Karadžić* (Decision on Accused Motion for Adequate Facilities and Equality of Arms: Legal Associates) IT-95-5/18-PT (28 January 2009) para 37.

[225] *Prosecutor v Karadžić* (Appeals Chamber Decision on Interlocutory Appeal of the Trial Chamber's Decision on Adequate Facilities) IT-95-5/18-AR73.2 (7 May 2009) para 14.

[226] ibid para 16, citing *Krajišnik* (Appeals Chamber Decision) (n 217 above) para 42.

[227] ibid.

[228] ibid para 13, citing *Krajišnik* (Appeals Chamber Decision) (n 217 above) para 41.

500 additional pre-trial hours above and beyond the Remuneration Scheme was sufficient in the given circumstances'.[229]

In the *Karadžić* 'Decision on Request for Review of OLAD Decision on the Trial Phase Remuneration', the President stressed the need for reasonableness in relation to remuneration, and stated that he did 'not consider that Karadžić can reasonably be expected to deal with [the review of 300,000 documents disclosed by the prosecution after the commencement of trial] during the adjournment phase with the assistance of only two staff members'. Judge Robinson considered the 'high volume of... disclosure, coupled with the timing of the disclosure, the complexity of Karadžić's case, and the other outstanding tasks Karadžić cites in support of his Request for additional resources'.[230] Judge Robinson also pointed out that the *Krajišnik* appeal decision confirmed that Article 31(4)(b) did not call merely for 'some legal consultation and coordination', as claimed by the Registrar, but that it requires the provision of ' "certain technical and logistical support" and "conceivabl[y]" the assignment of a Tribunal-paid "investigator and/or (an) expert(s), depending on the stage of the proceedings", as well as "translation assistance" '.[231] Judge Robinson added that, given the complexity of the case, the allotment of only one support staff member to Karadžić was unreasonable.[232] The President determined that, during the trial period, Karadžić should be allotted 750 hours,[233] equating to five support members.[234] The President stressed that his decision cannot, however, be read as allowing '*all* self-represented accused... [to] be allocated the same number of support staff as allocated to represented accused with cases of similar complexity'.[235] Decisions can only be made on a case-by-case basis taking into careful

[229] *Prosecutor v Karadzić* (Decision on Appeal of OLAD Decision in Relation to Additional Pre-Trial Funds) IT-95-5/18-T (17 December 2009) para 29: 'It is therefore apparent that the 7,500 remunerable hours applied for in the Request for Review is not comparable to the funding received by Counsel of represented accused under the Pre-Trial Legal Aid policy.' See also *Prosecutor v Karadžić* (President Decision on Request for Review of OLAD Decision on Trial Phase Remuneration) IT-95-5/18-T (19 February 2010) para 34: 'In light of the significant amount of work involved in reviewing 300,000 disclosure documents [provided by the Prosecution after the commencement of trial], I find that it was unreasonable for the Registrar to conclude that most of the outstanding work cited by Karadžić in support of his Request was covered in the pre-trial allotment.'

[230] *Prosecutor v Karadžić* (President Decision on Request for Review of OLAD Decision on Trial Phase Remuneration) IT-95-5/18-T (19 February 2010) para 36.

[231] ibid para 37.

[232] ibid para 43.

[233] Because of exceptional circumstances, the number of support staff had been increased from four to eight during pre-trial. Due to the high volume of disclosure after the beginning of the trial and the number of witnesses and prospective witnesses, the President concluded that those exceptional circumstances still existed and 1,200 hours should be granted until the resumption of trial. Once the trial resumed the situation might be different (ibid paras 45, 46).

[234] The President observed that, under the Trial Legal Aid Policy for represented accused, five support members are allocated for a level three case; each for 150 hours/month (ibid para 46).

[235] ibid para 46 (emphasis added).

consideration the specific circumstances of each self-represented accused.[236] In respect of the remuneration of one of Karadžić's legal associates (Mr Peter Robinson), given that he has been granted rights of audience, the President considered that such work 'more closely reflects work normally undertaken by co-counsel' and 'goes beyond the tasks, functions and levels of responsibility of legal associates as envisaged by the Appeals Chamber'.[237] In the circumstances, the President determined that the associate should be paid the same rate as co-counsel even though, technically, Karadžić will not 'receive funds to remunerate a lead counsel or co-counsel'.[238]

VIII. Conclusion

In proceedings before the ICTY, the introduction of Rule 45*ter* in November 2008 represents a codification of the Chamber's discretion to assign counsel in the interests of justice against the will of an accused. The Rule has been in force at the ICTR since 2002. In 2005, the Appeals Chamber in *Milošević* affirmed that counsel may be assigned to a defendant against his will and that the right to self-representation is not unqualified. The interests of justice have been used as the touchstone for assignment in various guises in all cases before the ICTY. Factors taken into account in qualifying the right have included: the accused's ill-health; the risk that the accused will engage in obstructionist misconduct; and the assertion of the right at a late stage in the proceedings, coupled with general considerations such as the seriousness, complexity, and magnitude of the case; the public interest in the expeditious completion of the trial; and the effect on the rights of co-accused.[239] Ultimately, if the right to self-representation is to be 'subjected to revocation or qualification, it is necessary to determine the threshold for interference with it'.[240] The capacious concept of the interests of justice must be scrutinized with great care in order to avoid the procedural and substantive pitfalls of premature or disproportionate assignment of counsel, a feature of the early jurisprudence before the ICTY.

In the *Milošević* case the Trial Chamber recognized that the 'assignment of counsel against the wishes of the accused is a developing area of the law both in national and international jurisdictions'.[241] However, as the work of the *ad hoc* Tribunals slowly comes to an end, it is noteworthy that the most proportionate

[236] ibid para 47.

[237] ibid para 51. The President further considered the instructions of the Appeals Chamber that 'legal associates must be adequately compensated for their work, and that rate of pay is determined not only by experience but also the functions and tasks undertaken by legal associates, as well as the level of responsibility assumed by them' (ibid).

[238] ibid para 55.

[239] NHB Jorgensen, 'The Problem of Self-Representation at International Criminal Tribunals' (2006) 4 JICJ 64, 70.

[240] ibid.

[241] *Prosecutor v Milošević* (Decision on Assigned Counsel's Motion for Withdrawal) IT-02-54-T (7 December 2004) para 22.

form of assignment of counsel has yet to be perfected. Many commentators have observed that the imposition of counsel against the will of an accused is no more than a 'legal fiction' and that the 'cure may be worse than the disease'.[242] Imposed or assigned defence counsel cannot 'effectively advocate on behalf of someone who does not want assistance'.[243] Even in respect of standby counsel, often defined as assistants 'operating in the sphere of the accused only',[244] the ICTY has regularly made provision for such counsel to take over conduct of the defence from the accused should the need arise. Once again, in the absence of cooperation and instructions, such an assignment may amount to little more than a fiction.

As the Tribunals continue to grapple with the circumstances in which the right to self-representation may be qualified, the practical difficulties confronted by assigned, imposed, or standby counsel cannot be underestimated. Not only is it impossible for counsel to ensure the presentation of a robust defence in the absence of any cooperation with an accused, but the situation also presents significant issues in terms of a lawyer's ethical obligations to retain independence and ensure the protection of their 'client's' best interests. Ultimately, there is a grave risk that the imposition of counsel against the will of an accused may 'harm the integrity of the legal profession and, more broadly, the fairness of the proceedings'.[245] But is there a viable alternative in a situation where an accused declares an intention not to cooperate with counsel assigned against his will?

In retrospect, one of the most effective mechanisms for harmonizing an accused's right to self-representation with the need for fair and expeditious proceedings was devised in *Milošević*, where the Chamber decided to appoint *amici curiae* to assist it in the proper determination of the case. The Chamber made it clear that the appointment of the *amici curiae* did not equate to any form of representation of the defendant. Their task was to provide assistance to the Chamber to ensure the fairness of the trial. The *amici* filed written motions, objected to evidence, questioned witnesses, and drew possible defences to the attention of the judges. Several commentators have observed the benefits of the assignment of a neutral assistant to the court who is able to protect the rights of the accused while not burdened by a duty of representation in the absence of cooperation and instructions from the accused.[246] As an *amicus*, counsel can act independently and is not dependent on either instructions or communication with an accused. The absence of a counsel–client relationship also means that an *amicus* may act

[242] See G Sluiter, 'Karadžić on Trial: Two Procedural Problems' (2008) 6 JICJ 617, 619; JT Tuinstra, 'Assisting an Accused to Represent Himself: Appointment of *Amici Curiae* as the Most Appropriate Option' (2006) 4 JICJ 47, 57.

[243] M Ellis, 'The Saddam Trial: Challenges to Meeting International Standards of Fairness with Regard to the Defence' (2006–2007) 39 CWR JIL 171, 183.

[244] *Prosecutor v Šešelj* (Decision on Prosecution's Motion for Order Appointing Counsel to Assist Vojislav Šešelj with his Defence) IT-03-67-PT (9 May 2003) para 28.

[245] Tuinstra (n 242 above) 48.

[246] Jorgensen (n 239 above) 72; Tuinstra (n 242 above) fn 42.

without fear of breaching his ethical obligations. There is nonetheless a need for clarity as to the extent to which an *amicus curiae* is bound by the Code of Professional Conduct for Defence Counsel. Whether or not the appointment of an *amicus* can assist in cases of extreme obstructionism remains to be seen. In such cases, the accused is deemed to have waived his right to self-representation. The practical solution of how to ensure his representation thereafter by counsel in an international setting has yet to be mastered. Other developments in the field of self-representation before the *ad hoc* Tribunals include the necessity of a warning prior to assigning counsel in the case of obstructionist defendants, the possibility of curtailing the right at the pre-trial stage of proceedings, and the advent of self-representation on appeal, including partial self-representation.

Future international courts and tribunals must endeavour to provide clarity as to the methods and modalities to be employed when assigning counsel, standby counsel, or *amici curiae* to defendants against their will. These institutions will undoubtedly seek to draw upon the experiences and lessons to be learnt from the *ad hoc* Tribunals. The ICC's Rome Statute sets out clearly in Article 67(1)(d) the right of the accused to 'conduct the defence in person or through legal assistance of the accused's choosing', although to date, none of the current accused have sought to exercise the right to represent themselves. It is the pragmatic and ethical issues embodied in the issue of assignment which require rigorous analysis in order to avoid the adoption of improvised approaches and ensure the future fairness of international criminal proceedings and the protection of fundamental fair trial rights in a manner which is rational, methodical, and defensible.

12

The Right to be Informed of the Nature and Cause of the Charges: A Potentially Formidable Jurisprudential Legacy

Wayne Jordash and John Coughlan

I. Introduction

The statutes of the International Criminal Tribunals for the former Yugoslavia (ICTY) and Rwanda (ICTR) mirror the major human rights instruments in guaranteeing an accused prompt notification of the nature and cause of the charges against them, in recognition of the fundamental nature of the right to the maintenance of an effective defence and fair trial.[1] The strength of this guarantee can only be judged by an assessment of the *ad hoc* Tribunals' jurisprudence and particularly that which relates to the requirement of specificity of indictments. The jurisprudential history of the Tribunals, and the paucity of information contained in the early indictments, suggests that this guarantee was inadequately enforced at the beginning of the lives of these institutions. In the latter years, the *ad hoc* Tribunals have made significant strides forward in understanding the importance of this right, not only by providing an accused with the tools necessary for mounting an effective defence but also as a means of ensuring more focused trials with corresponding efficiency benefits.

This chapter will discuss how the judges of the *ad hoc* Tribunals, with little statutory guidance and a dearth of international judicial precedent, have come to approach this minimum guarantee with an increasing degree of creativity, establishing the role of the indictment as the primary accusatory instrument and developing jurisprudence that has led to an enhancement of an accused's right to an effective defence and a fairer trial in international criminal law.

[1] See the Statute of the ICTY, Art 21(4)(a); and the Statute of the ICTR, Art 20(4)(a) ('the accused shall be entitled to the following minimum guarantees, in full equality: (a) to be informed promptly and in detail in a language which he understands of the nature and cause of the charge against him').

That being said, it is apparent that the Tribunals continue to make too many unhelpful concessions to perceived prosecutorial difficulties in providing specificity to indictments and the jurisprudential developments remain unhelpfully tethered to these concerns. Nonetheless, as the *ad hoc* Tribunals near the completion of their respective mandates, they hand to their successor in international criminal law, the International Criminal Court (ICC), a potentially formidable jurisprudential legacy that can provide for the significant enhancement of the right of an accused to be informed promptly and in detail of the nature and cause of the charges against them.

II. The Human Rights Standards and the *Ad Hoc* Tribunals' Approach

The right of accused persons to be informed promptly and in detail of the nature and cause of the charges against them has been recognized as a fundamental right in the major human rights instruments. The International Covenant on Civil and Political Rights, for example, provides in Article 14(3)(a) that '[i]n the determination of any criminal charges against him, everyone shall be entitled to the following minimum guarantees, in full equality... to be informed promptly and in detail in a language which he understands of the nature and cause of the charges against him'.[2] An accused must be made aware of the cause (the material facts alleged) and the nature (the legal qualification of those acts) of the charges being made.[3] According to the European Court of Human Rights, the 'provision of full, *detailed* information to the defendant concerning the charges against him—and consequently the legal characterisation that the court might adopt in the matter—is an essential prerequisite for ensuring that the proceedings are fair'.[4]

[2] See also the European Convention on Human Rights (ECHR), Art 6(3)(a); and the American Convention on Human Rights (ACHR), Art 8(2)(b). The African Charter on Human and People's Rights does not contain a provision to this effect but in the case of *Media Rights Agenda* (on behalf of Niran Malaolu) *v Nigeria*, Communication No 224/98, decision adopted during the 28th session, 23 October–6 November 2000 the African Commission on Human and Peoples' Rights held, para 43, that the right to a fair trial includes the requirement that persons arrested 'shall be informed at the time of arrest, in a language which they understand of the reason for their arrest and shall be informed promptly of any charges against them'.

[3] *IH and ors v Austria* (App No 42780/98) ECHR 20 April 2006, para 30; *Mattoccia v Italy* (App No 23969/94) ECHR 25 July 2000, para 59; and *Kamasinski v Austria* (App No 9783/82) ECHR 19 December 1989, para 79.

[4] *Soering v UK* (App No 14038/88) ECHR 7 July 1989, para 113 (emphasis added). See also: *Einhorn v France* (App No 71555/01) ECHR 16 October 2001; *Brozicek v Italy* (App 10964/84), ECHR 19 December 1989; *Pélissier and Sassi v France* (App No 25444/94) ECHR 25 March 1999; and *Mattoccia v Italy* (n 3 above).

The right to be promptly and properly informed at the time of arrest of the nature and cause of the charges is, therefore, one of the most fundamental procedural rights of a person facing criminal prosecution. The guarantee stems from the right of an accused not to be deprived of liberty arbitrarily,[5] but must also be seen in light of the right to have adequate time and materials to prepare an effective defence.[6] As Stefan Trechsel has noted, the 'right to defend oneself can only be exercised effectively, ie with a minimum of chances of success, if the accused knows what he or she is accused of. Otherwise a Kafkaesque situation arises.'[7]

The right encompasses the factual information and any changes in the accusation necessitating new or additional facilities so that the accused might react and organize an effective defence.[8] Therefore the right to be informed can be seen to have two different aspects:

> [the] first and primary one concerns the right of the defence to receive the information immediately—or at least early enough in the course of the proceedings—of the allegations which they must meet... [t]he second aspect is a logical consequence of the first—once the information has been communicated, the charge cannot be modified unless there is a new communication and a sufficient period of time to allow the defence to adapt to the new situation. This principle is known as the 'principle of immutability'.[9]

It is the view of the European Court of Human Rights, that the question of 'whether the content and the promptness of the information conveyed were sufficient is to be assessed in each case according to its special features'.[10]

The prosecution must inform accused persons of the accusations against them and provide them with enough detail for the preparation of an adequate defence and to secure a fair trial.[11] The duty to inform is an active, rather than passive one and remains with the prosecution.[12] Information must be given promptly and must set out the accusation 'in a precise and reliable way'.[13] Such information forms an essential part of the charge and, as Trechsel has pointed out, this requirement necessarily implies that the communication must be given at the end of the investigation, rather than at any stage before its completion. The instrument containing the information required must therefore be the indictment.[14]

Although purporting to rely upon human rights law in their approach to this guarantee, the *ad hoc* Tribunals have been unwavering in their insistence that the 'uniqueness' of their proceedings should determine the degree of particularization

[5] See eg ECHR, Art 5(2); and ACHR, Art 7(2). See further D Harris, M O'Boyle, and C Warwick, *Law of the European Convention of Human Rights* (London: Butterworths, 1995) 250.

[6] See eg ICCPR, Art 14(3)(b); ECHR, Art 6(3)(b); and ACHR, Art 8(2)(c).

[7] S Trechsel, *Human Rights in Criminal Proceedings* (Oxford: OUP, 2005) 193.

[8] *Mattoccia v Italy* (n 3 above) para 61.

[9] Trechsel (n 7 above) 195.

[10] *Campbell and Hartley* (Apps No 12244/86, 12245/86, and 12383/86) ECHR 30 August 1990, para 40.

[11] *Kamasinski v Austria* (n 3 above), paras 80–81.

[12] See also *D Monguya Mbenge et al v Zaire* Communication No 16/1977 (Views adopted on 25 March 1983), in UN Doc GAOR A/38/40 and *Mattoccia v Italy* (n 3 above) para 65.

[13] Trechsel (n 7 above) 199–200.

[14] ibid.

required from an indictment.[15] This approach has indubitably been premised on the assumption that:

> ... the degree of particularity required in indictments before the International Tribunal is different from, and perhaps not as high as, the particularity required in domestic criminal law jurisdictions ... The massive scale of the crimes with which the International Tribunal has to deal makes it impracticable to require a high degree of specificity in such matters as the identity of the victims and the dates for the commission of the crimes—at any rate, the degree of specificity may not be as high as that called for in domestic jurisdictions.[16]

That is not to argue that this approach *per se* departs from the requirements of human rights law. Throughout their existence the ICTY and ICTR have consistently stated that the touchstone criterion is 'whether or not the accused can prepare his defence',[17] a functionalist approach that is consistent with the approach taken by the European Court of Human Rights.[18] Nonetheless, the 'slippery slope' of the *ad hoc* Tribunals' approach is obvious: a preconceived assumption of the scale of the crimes, and the associated assumption that the prosecution has a nigh-on impossible task to perform, was always likely to encourage loose drafting, less particularization, and less rigorous scrutiny of indictments, both at the time of confirmation and during the trial. This approach is evident in the jurisprudence of the Tribunals discussed below, which has seen, until recently, the prosecution provided with excessive latitude both in the drafting of indictments and in ensuring confirmation.

For many years the prosecutorial refrain that 'it can provide no better particulars',[19] had not provoked any proper judicial scrutiny, such as an enquiry into the efficiency of the underlying investigative practices. The assumption that it is always impracticable to obtain the level of detail envisaged in domestic cases was not put to the test. Despite the occasional cautionary note in earlier cases that 'there is a floor below which the level of information must not fall if the indictment is to be valid as to form',[20] and that this 'may itself demonstrate sufficient

[15] This proposition is constantly rehearsed both in the jurisprudence and by legal commentators: see eg G Boas and WA Schabas (eds), *International Criminal Law Developments in the Case Law of the ICTY* (Boston/Leiden: Martinus Nijhoff, 2003) 202, arguing that the situation in international criminal law is more complex than municipal law and so the ICTY has developed more elaborate procedures to ensure fulfilment of the obligation to inform the accused.

[16] *Prosecutor v Kvočka* (Trial Chamber Decision on Defence Preliminary Motions on Form of the Indictment) IT-98-30/1 (12 April 1999) para 17.

[17] *Prosecutor v Blaškić* (Trial Chamber Decision on the Defence Motion to Dismiss the Indictment Based upon Defects in the Form Thereof (Vagueness/Lack of Adequate Notice of Charges)) IT-95-14 (4 April 1997) para 32.

[18] See Trechsel (n 7 above) 194, referring, *inter alia*, to: *Sipavičius v Lithuania* (App No 49093/99) ECHR 21 February 2002, para 29; and *Mattoccia v Italy* (n 3 above) para 71: 'the defence was confronted with exceptional difficulties'.

[19] *Prosecutor v Krnojelac* (Trial Chamber Decision of Preliminary Motion on Form of Indictment) IT-97-25-PT (11 February 2000) para 37.

[20] *Prosecutor v Kolundjiža* (Decision of Preliminary Motions) IT-97-25-PT (10 February 2000) para 8; and *Kvočka* (Trial Chamber Decision) (n 16 above) para 14.

prejudice to an accused person as to make a trial upon the relevant charge necessarily unfair',[21] the emphasis has been predominantly upon the perceived need to prosecute a particular individual, the seriousness of the charges, and the *inherent* difficulties faced by the prosecution. This emphasis has been used to justify restrictions on the right of an accused to specificity in the indictment, rather than providing the basis for a challenge to the jurisdiction of the tribunal to conduct the anticipated trials.[22]

This overbearing emphasis has led to a body of unhelpful jurisprudence. Whilst there was acknowledgement in the early jurisprudence that the right was important, this did not translate into a practical guarantee. Therefore, whilst the absence of a process of review of the grounds of arrest should have meant that the importance of the indictment clearly stating the nature and cause of the case against an accused could not be overemphasized—indeed, the very jurisdiction of the Tribunal over the accused depended upon it,[23] nonetheless, the Appeals Chamber in *Kovačević* established—purportedly in accordance with human rights jurisprudence—that an accused's right to be promptly informed of charges will be violated only where there was a failure to charge him with any crime at the time of the arrest.[24]

The dangers inherent in this type of minimal approach to an accused's fair trial rights are obvious. At its extreme, when indictments remain insufficiently examined or unchallenged by judicial disquiet or curiosity, the end results are shockingly unfair, reducing indictments to the barest of legal and factual generalizations devoid of meaningful or useful content—justified by contextual considerations traded against an accused's fundamental and minimum rights.[25] Fortunately, the emphasis at the ICTY and the ICTR in recent years has altered considerably and yielded tangible results. In the late 1990s there developed an appreciation that the particularization of an indictment was not just a function of the complexity or scale of the alleged crimes. With the growth of judicial experience, the looming closure of the Tribunals, and the increased threat to resources, judges at the *ad hoc* Tribunals began to understand that prosecutorial claims of being unable to provide further and better particulars in indictments were not necessarily accurate and may have been in fact somewhat self-serving. The judiciary has since shown a greater willingness to enquire into such claims

[21] *Prosecutor v Krnojelac* (Trial Chamber Decision of Preliminary Motion on Form of Indictment) IT-97-25-PT (24 February 1999) para 40.

[22] G McIntyre, 'Defining Human Rights in the Arena of International Humanitarian Law: Human Rights in the Jurisprudence of the ICTY' in Boas and Schabas (n 15 above) 217.

[23] ibid 214–15.

[24] ibid 215, citing *Prosecutor v Kovačević* (Appeals Chamber Decision Stating Reasons for Appeals Chamber's Order of 29 May 1998) IT-97-24-AR73 (2 July 1998) paras 34–6.

[25] eg *Prosecutor v Issa Hassan Sesay* (Trial Chamber Decision and Order on Defence Preliminary Motion for Defects in the Form of the Indictment) SCSL-2003-05-PT (13 October 2003) para 9. See also: *Prosecutor v Sesay, Kallon and Gbao* (Corrected Amended Consolidated Indictment) SCSL-04-15-PT (2 August 2006); and *Prosecutor v Sesay, Kallon and Gbao* (Trial Judgment) SCSL-04-15-T (2 March 2009) para 330.

and to impose more stringent and more human rights-compliant pleading standards.[26]

III. The Development of the Jurisprudence

A. Jurisprudential vacuum and deference to the disclosure of evidence

It is perhaps understandable that the pleading practices in the early years of the *ad hoc* Tribunals left much to be desired as the Trial Chambers, eschewing valuable assistance from experience at the national level, had little else to draw upon. The International Military Tribunals established after the Second World War could not offer much by way of practical guidance. Article IV of IMT Ordinance No 7 merely provided that, in order to ensure a fair trial, defendants had to be furnished at a reasonable time before trial with a copy of the indictment and all the documents lodged with it, translated into a language which they could understand. The indictments before the International Military Tribunals had to 'state the charges, plainly concisely and with sufficient particulars to inform defendant of the offenses charged'.[27] Consequently, the *ad hoc* Tribunals had little but bald legal enunciations to provide a steer and had to rely upon the fruits of their own judicial creativity. As is plain from an examination of the *Tadić* experience—the first trial at the ICTY—this process was to commence slowly. The rules initially crafted were rudimentary, making huge concessions to perceived prosecution difficulties and paying little regard to the rights of the accused to be informed through the indictment of the nature and cause of the charges.

In the *Tadić* case a challenge to the lack of specificity for most of the 33 counts was largely dismissed by the Trial Chamber with the following rebuff:

> The Rules of the International Tribunal require, in Rule 47(B), that the indictment set forth the name and particulars of the suspect and, echoing the words of Article 18 of the Statute, 'a concise statement of the facts of the case and of the crime with which the suspect is charged'. These eight paragraphs provide those particulars; they identify the accused, state paragraph by paragraph the facts of each incident and in separate counts specify particular provisions of international humanitarian law that have been violated by him. Rule 47(B) has accordingly been complied with and it follows that, in relation to

[26] See eg *Prosecutor v Ntakirutimana* (Appeals Chamber Judgment) ICTR-96-10-A and 96-17-A (13 December 2004) para 33; *Prosecutor v Blagojević* (Trial Chamber Decision on Motions Challenging the Form of the Amended Joinder Indictment) IT-02-60-PT (1 August 2002) para 13; *Prosecutor v Kupreškić et al* (Appeals Chamber Judgment) IT-95-16-A (23 October 2001) para 91.

[27] International Military Tribunal (IMT) Ordinance No 7, Art IV(a); see *Trials of War Criminals Before the Nuremberg Military Tribunals under Council Control Law No. 10*, Vol XV, Procedure, Practice and Administration, Nuernberg, October 1946–April 1949, 218.

paragraphs 5 to 12 and the counts under these paragraphs, the Motion founded on lack of specificity of the Indictment is denied.[28]

The Trial Chamber's approach here was replicated in much of the ICTY and ICTR jurisprudence throughout the 1990s. The provision in Article 21(4)(a) of the ICTY Statute and Article 20(4)(a) of the ICTR Statute guaranteeing the right of an accused to be informed in detail of the nature and cause of the charges was given little emphasis and was treated as subsumed by the interrelated right in Article 21(4)(b) of the ICTY Statute and Article 20(4)(a) of the ICTR Statute to have adequate time and facilities for the preparation of a defence. The predominant approach was to regard the accused's rights as being assured by the disclosure of evidence. Thus, the accused in *Tadić* was to have regard to the 'supporting material which accompanied the indictment when confirmation was sought and the names of the witnesses to be called in proof of guilt of the accused'.[29] If the defence, nevertheless, regarded 'the material currently before it . . . not adequate to permit of the preparation of the defence to [the counts the subject of the motion] it is open to it, by motion under Rule 54, to seek further particulars'.[30] Accordingly, as regards the right of the accused to be informed through the indictment, the Chamber took the view that the specificity required in the indictment was satisfied by a strict adherence to the letter—and not the spirit—of Article 18 of the ICTY Statute and Rule 47(B).[31]

Despite the adoption of the prosecutor's minimal approach to particularization, the Chamber in *Tadić* did take issue with paragraph 4 of the indictment, deciding that it needed to be amended so as to provide the necessary specificity. This paragraph stated:

Between about 23 May 1992 and about 31 December 1992, Duško TADIĆ participated with Serb forces in the attack, destruction and plunder of Bosnian Muslim and Croat residential areas, the seizure and imprisonment of thousands of Muslims and Croats under brutal conditions in camps located in Omarska, Keraterm and Trnopolje, and the deportation and/or expulsion of the majority of Muslim and Croat residents of Opstina Prijedor by force or threat of force. During this time, Serb forces, including Duško TADIĆ, subjected Muslims and Croats inside and outside the camps to a campaign of terror which included killings, rapes, assaults and other physical and psychological abuse. By his participation in these acts, Duško TADIĆ committed:

COUNT 1:
a CRIME AGAINST HUMANITY recognised by Articles 5(h) (persecution on political, racial and/or religious grounds) and 7(1) of the Statute of the Tribunal; and,

COUNT 2:
a CRIME AGAINST HUMANITY recognised by Articles 5(d) (deportation) and 7(1) of the Statute of the Tribunal; and,

[28] *Prosecutor v Tadić* (Trial Chamber Decision on the Defence Motion on the Form of the Indictment) IT-97-25-PT (14 November 1995) para 7.
[29] ibid para 8.
[30] ibid.
[31] ibid para 7.

COUNT 3:
a GRAVE BREACH recognised by Article 2(g) (unlawful deportation or transfer or unlawful confinement of a civilian) and 7(1) of the Statute of the Tribunal.[32]

The Chamber found that:

> ... paragraph 4 clearly enough does not, in its very generalised form, provide the accused with any specific, albeit concise, statement of the facts of the case and of the crimes with which he is charged. It says nothing about the accused's conduct, about what was the nature and extent of his participation in the several courses of conduct which are alleged over the months in question ... there should ... be some clear identification of particular acts of participation by the accused in such an attack.[33]

The focus on the acts of the accused as a litmus test of the adequacy of pleadings was to become a central theme in the Tribunals' pleading jurisprudence, as was, unfortunately, the acceptance therein of the failure of the prosecution to provide specificity as to the specific head of responsibility under Article 7(1) of the ICTY Statute and the corresponding provision in Article 6(1) of the ICTR Statute.

It is worthwhile to note the rigidly minimal approach taken by the prosecution in the *Tadić* case as regards specificity. Unfortunately it was to become the hallmark of many international prosecutors and the benchmark of much of the subsequent jurisprudence. It must have been obvious even at that stage in the life of the institution that the paucity of information in paragraph 4 could not secure a fair trial for the accused nor could such a pleading be properly justified by any claim to the impossibility or impracticality of providing better particulars due to the 'massive scale of the crimes'.[34] Nevertheless, the prosecution in this and most of the subsequent cases have routinely resisted greater specificity. As the jurisprudence shows, the development of pleading requirements—and the corresponding enhancement of the rights of the accused—has been largely resisted by international prosecutors, slowing the development of meaningful and fair trial-compliant pleading principles. This recurrent prosecutorial approach laid the foundation for the specificity of indictments to be subordinated to prosecutorial difficulties and *perceived* difficulties in collating evidence of international crimes.[35]

The early decisions of the ICTY Trial Chamber were a model of applying the letter of Rule 47(B) and little else. By June 1996, the time that the *Delalić*

[32] *Prosecutor v Tadić* (First Amended Indictment) IT-94-1-I (1 September 1995).

[33] *Prosecutor v Tadić* (Trial Chamber Decision) (n 28 above) para 12.

[34] *Kvočka* (Trial Chamber Decision) (n 16 above) para 17.

[35] See eg the respective approaches adopted by the prosecution in: *Prosecutor v Brđanin and Talić* (Trial Chamber Decision on Objections by Radoslav Brđanin to the Form of the Amended Indictment) IT-99-36-PT (23 February 2001); *Prosecutor v Krajišnik* (Trial Chamber Decision Concerning Preliminary Motion on the Form of the Indictment) IT-00-369-PT (1 August 2000); and *Krnojelac* (Trial Chamber Decision) (n 19 above).

'Decision on the Accused's Mucić's Motion for Particulars' was delivered,[36] the approach to the specificity of an indictment remained unhelpfully restricted to this literalist approach. As observed by the *Delalić* Trial Chamber: 'When tested by the standard set out in previous cases [*Tadić* and *Djukić*][37] the indictment is not vague.'[38] As was recognized many years later, however, this standard was inadequate. The 11-page indictment against Mucić (and others), alleging Article 7(3) responsibility for 49 counts of war crimes, including wilful killings, torture, rape, unlawful detentions, and plunder, provided only 2 descriptions of *his* alleged participation: (1) that he, along with 2 other accused, had 'responsibility for the operation of Čelebići camp and were in positions of superior authority to all the camp guards and to those other persons who entered the camp and mistreated detainees'[39] and; (2) that:

> ...he knew or had reason to know that persons in positions of subordinate authority to them were about to commit those acts resulting in the inhumane conditions, or had already committed those acts, and failed either to take the necessary and reasonable steps to prevent those acts or to punish the perpetrators after the acts had been committed.[40]

The Chamber's overall approach to notice was clear from its dismissal of the defence request for greater specificity of the identity of the detainees allegedly abused by the use of an electrical device, which was stated as having occurred between 'around 20 May 1992 and continuing until the latter part of September 1992...on many detainees, including Milenko Kuljanin and Novica Dordic'.[41] The Trial Chamber declined to order further specification on the basis that the indictment specified two of the detainees and this, if proved, would suffice to convict the accused of the offence as alleged.[42] The Trial Chamber concluded that this was adequate to give Zdravko Mucić 'warning of the nature of the crimes with which he is charged and sets out the factual basis of the charges'.[43] It appears that this *warning* was considered sufficient to meet the standard of clearly informing the accused of the nature and cause of the charges against him so as to enable him to prepare his defence effectively and efficiently.

Once again, as in *Tadić*, the Trial Chamber in the *Mucić* case endorsed the use of particulars as a means of providing, pursuant to Article 21(2) of the Statute, a fair and public hearing and in accordance with Article 21(4)(b), compliance with the right to adequate time and facilities for the preparation of the defence.[44] This approach appears to have been based on the view that the preparation of an

[36] *Prosecutor v Delalić* (Trial Chamber Decision on the Accused Mucić's Motion for Particulars) IT-96-21-T (26 June 1996).

[37] *Tadić* (Trial Chamber Decision) (n 28 above) 14 November 1995; *Prosecutor v Djukić* (Trial Chamber Decision on Preliminary Motions of the Accused) IT-96-20-T (26 April 1996).

[38] *Delalić* (Trial Chamber Decision) (n 36 above) para 6.

[39] *Prosecutor v Delalić* (Indictment) IT-96-21 (21 March 1996) para 7.

[40] ibid, eg para 35.

[41] ibid para 33.

[42] *Delalić* (Trial Chamber Decision) (n 36 above) para 16.

[43] ibid para 6.

[44] ibid para 7 (internal quotations omitted).

accused's defence 'assumes a more detailed level of information which may not be available at the time the indictment is framed'.[45] The 'nature and cause' text of Article 21(4)(a) was interpreted as 'a concept which includes not only the acts but also the evidence in support of the indictment'.[46] This appears to have misled the *ad hoc* Tribunals into concluding that the accused's rights could be protected through the subsequent service of evidence, rather than through an indictment providing specificity as to the legal classification and the facts underlying the charges.

As observed in the *Blaškić* case the Trial Chamber had:

> ...intended already to emphasise the distinction...between the *minimum demands* required for the presentation of the indictment to the accused and all the guarantees which the accused must enjoy after the indictment in respect of the subsequent production of the additional or supplementary evidence permitting him to prepare his defence in due time.[47]

In other words, the right of an accused to prompt and detailed information was viewed through the disclosure of the evidence 'as soon as practicable after the initial appearance of the accused'[48] and the *overall* 'guarantee that the accused will be in a position to prepare his defence in due time with complete knowledge of the matter',[49] rather than through the information contained in the indictment. In the words of an ICTR Trial Chamber, 'the accused will have ample opportunity and adequate means to prepare his defence once he has received supporting documentation in accordance with Rule 66(A)(i) and disclosure of witness statements in terms of Rule 66(A)(ii) of the Rules'.[50]

Ultimately, it was through this myopic prism that the ICTY considered whether the requirement was met that indictments contained information which permitted the accused to prepare his defence in order to avoid prejudicial surprise.[51]

[45] *Blaškić* (Trial Chamber Decision) (n 17 above) para 11. [46] ibid.

[47] ibid para 19, referring to *Djukić* (Trial Chamber Decision) (n 37 above) (emphasis added).

[48] Quoting Rule 66(A) of the Rules of Procedure and Evidence of the ICTY. This language was removed at the 12th review of the Rules of Procedure and Evidence on 12 November 1997 (IT-32-Rev. 12) and replaced as follows:

> '(A) Subject to the provisions of Rules 53 and 69, the Prosecutor shall make available to the defence:
> (i) within thirty days of the initial appearance of the accused, copies of the supporting material which accompanied the indictment when confirmation was sought as well as all prior statements obtained by the Prosecutor from the accused, and
> (ii) no later than sixty days before the date set for trial, copies of the statements of all witnesses whom the Prosecutor intends to call to testify at trial; copies of the statements of additional prosecution witnesses shall be made available to the defence when a decision is made to call those witnesses.'

[49] *Blaškić* (Trial Chamber Decision) (n 17 above) para 11.

[50] *Prosecutor v Ntakirutimana* (Trial Chamber Decision on a Preliminary Motion Filed by Defence Counsel for an Order to Quash Counts 1, 2, 3, 6 and 7 of the Indictment) ICTR-96-17-T (23 March 1998) para 9; cited in *Prosecutor v Ntakirutimana* (Trial Chamber Decision on a Preliminary Motion Filed by Defence Counsel for an Order to Quash Counts 1, 2, 3 and 6 of the Indictment) ICTR-96-10-T (30 June 1998) para 10. [51] ibid para 20.

Accordingly, any prejudice was assumed to be remedied by the disclosure of evidence, as required by Rules 66 and 67. Consequently all that was required was that an indictment met the criteria set out in Rule 47(B)[52] and that it was inevitable that it would be nothing more than 'succinct and summary' in nature.[53] The jurisprudence that developed through these early years defining the appropriate specification of an indictment was constrained and premised upon these restrictive expectations.

B. Dominance of the prosecution's approach and limited defence success

Initially there was a marked reluctance on the part of ICTY and ICTR Trial Chambers to develop and impose more stringent requirements for the preparation of indictments. The (perceived) elasticity of the requirement that the information in the indictment had to allow an accused to prepare his defence, combined with the paucity of jurisprudential guidance available (or regarded as applicable), provided individual Trial Chambers with considerable discretion. This led to an unhelpful variance in the approaches taken to the issue. At one end of the spectrum, certain Trial Chambers emphasized expansiveness, as the following statements from *Kunarac* demonstrate:

> ...the capacity in which the accused allegedly committed the charged offence must be clearly defined. The indictment must also leave no doubt as to what the accused is alleged to have done at a particular venue on a particular date during a particular time period, with whom, to whom, or to what purpose. It must describe the full conduct complained of which amounts to the crime(s) charged. It must identify with reasonable clarity other persons involved, or affected, where necessary.
>
> It further follows that neither the supporting material nor the witness statements made available to an accused under Rule 66 of the Rules of Procedure and Evidence ('Rules') can be used to fill in any gaps in the indictment. An accused could be prejudiced were the Prosecutor to be allowed, for example, to introduce material facts through the calling of additional witnesses at trial instead of applying for leave to amend the indictment.[54]

At the other end of the scale, emphasis was placed on the 'very real differences between a domestic criminal jurisdiction and the system administered by the International Tribunal':

> The massive scale of the crimes with which the International Tribunal has to deal makes it impracticable to require a high degree of specificity in such matters as the identity of the

[52] *Prosecutor v Delalić* (Trial Chamber Decision on Application for Leave to Appeal (Form of the Indictment)) IT-96-21-AR72.3 (15 October 1996) para 7.

[53] *Blaškić* (Trial Chamber Decision) (n 17 above) para 23. See also *Prosecutor v Delalić* (Trial Chamber Decision on the Accused Zejnil Delalić Based on Defect in the Indictment) IT-96-21-T (2 October 1996) paras 22–3.

[54] *Prosecutor v Kunarac* (Trial Chamber Decision on the Form of the Indictment) IT-96-23 (4 November 1999) paras 6–7.

victims and the dates for the commission of the crimes—at any rate, the degree of specificity may not be as high as that called for in domestic jurisdictions. *However, there may be cases in which more specific information can be provided as to the time, the place, the identity of victims and the means by which the crime was perpetrated; in those cases, the Prosecution should be required to provide such information.* The Trial Chamber understands and accepts the findings in the *Krnojelac* Decision as to Form as to the degree of particularity required in an indictment subject to the above-mentioned qualification.[55]

It is worth scrutinizing the foregoing statement of legal principle from the *Kvočka* case as it is illustrative of an approach that placed greater emphasis on the perceived difficulties in prosecuting, than on the rights of an accused to a minimal level of clarity in the indictment. This approach qualified even the *Blaškić* minimal right to an indictment that specified the means used to perpetrate the crime.[56] The provision of this information was explicitly stated as possible only in 'some cases' and logically this was to be determined with regard to prosecutorial claims to 'impracticability'.[57] Given that prosecutors, or at least some of them, were convinced that their interests were best served by specifying as little as possible in the indictment in order to make the 'allegations as broad and as comprehensive as possible without giving any real idea of what the case actually is',[58] this emphasis did not bode well for the rights of the accused or act as an encouragement to jurisprudential developments.

It ought to have been apparent to the *ad hoc* Tribunals that placing such excessive emphasis on the needs and rights of the prosecution was unlikely to produce clearer or more precise indictments. This emphasis was resisted by some judges and consequently there were some fierce battles between individual chambers seeking to bring clarity to indictments and prosecutors determinedly resistant to any attempt to move away from the reliance on the strict application of Rule 47(B) and towards a more purposive approach entailing greater specificity.

For example, Trial Chamber II of the ICTY in *Krnojelac* ordered the prosecution to amend paragraph 5.2 of the indictment which comprised the 'sole foundation' for a charge of the crime against humanity of persecutions on political, racial, and/or religious grounds.[59] The paragraph stated:

MILORAD KRNOJELAC persecuted the Muslim and other non-Serb males by subjecting them to prolonged and routine imprisonment and confinement, repeated torture and beatings, countless killings, prolonged and frequent forced labour, and inhumane conditions within the KP Dom detention facility. As part of the persecution, MILORAD

[55] *Kvočka* (Trial Chamber Decision) (n 16 above) paras 16 and 17 (emphasis added), referring to *Krnojelac* (Trial Chamber Decision) (n 21 above).

[56] ibid para 20.

[57] Retorting to the Trial Chamber in *Kvočka*, Trial Chamber II in *Krnojelac* stated that it agreed with the caveat expressed by the former Chamber inasmuch as specificity required in a case alleging superior responsibility was less important in respect of acts by subordinates because the 'relevant facts will usually be stated with less precision, and that is because the detail of those acts (by whom and against whom they are done) are often unknown—and because the acts themselves often cannot be greatly in issue': see *Krnojelac* (Trial Chamber Decision) (n 19 above) para 18.

[58] *Krnojelac* (Trial Chamber Decision) (n 19 above) para 23.

[59] ibid para 12.

KRNOJELAC assisted in the deportation or expulsion of the majority of Muslim and non-Serb males from the Foča municipality.[60]

The prosecution stated that this 'sufficiently identified the accused's course of conduct that gave rise to his individual responsibility for persecutions'.[61] The Chamber emphasized, however, the importance of pleading material facts as these were integral to the nature of the case that the prosecution sought to make and held that the greater the proximity of the accused to the events the more precision was required. The relevant paragraph of the indictment was used by the prosecution to charge the accused with personally committing the offence of persecution and had to, so far as it was possible, identify the victim or victims, the place and the approximate date of the alleged offence, and the means by which it was committed.[62] The prosecutor's approach of erroneously conflating the right to be informed of the factual allegations through the indictment with the distinct right to disclosure of evidence was firmly and properly rejected.

The ICTY's Trial Chamber II, with Judge Hunt presiding, was to continue to engage with this issue in a series of interlocutory decisions in 2001 in the *Brđanin* case. The prosecution had again insisted that the detail omitted from the indictment should be the subject of a request for further and better particulars. In a forthright decision that brought some finality to the debate, the Chamber emphasized the distinction between an accused's right to be informed of the nature and cause through the vehicle of a specified indictment and that which arose separately and later through disclosure of the evidence. The Chamber stated that:

> [t]he right of an accused to seek further and better particulars of an allegation in the indictment does *not* overcome a deficiency in the form of the indictment. The indictment *must* state all of the *material* facts upon which the prosecution relies to establish the charges laid. If the evidentiary material provided by the prosecution during the pre-trial discovery process does not sufficiently identify the *evidence* upon which the prosecution relies to establish those material facts, then—and only then—is it appropriate for an application to be made to the Trial Chamber for an order that the prosecution supply particulars (and even then only if a request to the prosecution for such particulars has not been satisfactorily answered).[63]

In a decision three days later, in equally robust terms, Trial Chamber II dealt with the prosecution's suggestion that it was entitled to wait until service of the pre-trial brief before particularizing 'the precise role the accused is said to

60 *Prosecutor v Krnojelac* (First Amended Indictment) IT-97-25 (21 July 1999) para 5.2.

61 *Krnojelac* (Trial Chamber Decision) (n 19 above) para 17.

62 ibid paras 12–21.

63 *Prosecutor v Brđanin and Talić* (Trial Chamber Decision on Objections by Momir Talić to the Form of the Amended Indictment) IT-99-36-PT (20 February 2001) para 27 (emphasis in original).

have played' pursuant to Article 7 of the Statute and the nature of the alleged individual criminal responsibility.[64] The Chamber stated:

> An indictment must fairly apprise the accused of the nature of the case against him, and place him in possession of its broad outlines and the facts which constitute his responsibility. These are the 'material facts' which must be pleaded. How broadly the outlines may be given depends, as this Trial Chamber has said, upon the proximity of the accused to the particular events pleaded. But it is *essential* for the accused to know from the indictment just what that alleged proximity is. The Trial Chamber cannot determine whether the form of the *indictment* is sufficient in answer to a preliminary motion if the issue of proximity is not to be revealed until the Pre-Trial Brief is filed, after the preliminary motion is disposed of.[65]

As stated, the firm stance taken by Trial Chamber II was not typical of that era at the ICTY. Conversely, the decidedly confident stance taken by the prosecution in cases such as *Krnojelac* and *Brđanin* was due to the fact that the prosecution recognized that the specification being ordered was unusual and not supported by jurisprudence. In *Brđanin*, for example, as outlined above, the prosecution relied upon the approach taken in *Krajišnik* in August 2000.[66] The defence in *Krajišnik* complained that the scope of the accused's individual criminal responsibility was not clearly defined and, *inter alia*, that there was no specification concerning the accused's mode of responsibility under Article 7(1) or Article 7(3) of the Statute.[67] The prosecution argued that it had provided sufficient precision because of the widespread and massive nature of the allegations and the accused's high level of responsibility. It opined further that it was under no obligation to choose between liability under Article 7(1) and Article 7(3) and that it was 'a matter for the fact finder to determine the legal characterisation of the accused's conduct from the evidence presented'.[68] The fact that the prosecution took this stance was surprising enough. That this submission was partially accepted by both the Trial Chamber and the Appeal Chamber was even more so.[69] The latter

[64] *Brđanin and Talić* (Trial Chamber Decision) (n 35 above) para 8, citing *Prosecutor v Brđanin and Talić* (Prosecution's Response to 'Motion Objecting to the Form of the Amended Indictment' Filed by the Accused Brđanin on 5 February 2001) IT-99-36-PT (6 February 2001).

[65] ibid para 13 (emphasis in original).

[66] *Krajišnik* (Trial Chamber Decision) (n 35 above), see also *Prosecutor v Martić* (Trial Chamber Decision on Preliminary Motion Against the Amended Indictment) IT-95-11-PT (2 June 2003), which arguably takes the same approach.

[67] ibid para 2.

[68] ibid para 5.

[69] The *Krajišnik* defence sought leave to appeal the 1 August 2000 Trial Chamber Decision on the grounds that, *inter alia*, the Trial Chamber had abused its discretion by finding that the prosecution satisfied the requirements for specificity as regards the criminal responsibility alleged against the accused. The Appeals Chamber deemed this finding of the Trial Chamber to have been a discretionary one and held that the defence had failed to show any error on the part of the Trial Chamber in reaching this conclusion. In the absence of any perceived good cause, the Appeals Chamber rejected the Defence Application for Leave to Appeal. See *Prosecutor v Krajišnik* (Appeals Chamber Decision on Application for Leave to Appeal the Trial Chamber's Decision Concerning Preliminary Motion on the Form of the Indictment) IT-39-A (13 September 2000).

even concluded that these details *were* necessary, but their revelation could wait until service of the pre-trial brief[70]

The *Krajišnik* approach was illustrative of the judicial mindset that ran through the jurisprudence at this time that asking for too much specification, too early, or at all, would hinder the prosecution of those considered guilty or, somehow, create too onerous a task for the prosecutors. As a result, the jurisprudence, whilst appearing to be developing enhanced rights for the accused by clarifying the distinction between the right of the accused to be informed through the indictment and that which arises through disclosure of the evidence, for example, continued to provide prosecutors with too much latitude. They were not required to identify the precise basis of criminal responsibility alleged under Article 7(1) and/or Article 7(3) of the Statute, to plead factual allegations in detail, to identify the requisite *mens rea*, nor to specify the legal elements of the offences alleged. Moreover, they were permitted to plead cumulatively and also to plead ostensibly inconsistent factual allegations between indictments.[71]

C. The beginnings of a new approach

The approach as outlined was unhelpful from many different perspectives, including effective trial management and the maintenance of fair trial standards. It is an approach that has changed significantly in more recent years. As was observed by one legal commentator with regard to the ICTY:

> . . . as the Tribunal has become more comfortable with its jurisdiction, and as the international community has begun to put pressure upon the Tribunal to complete its mandate, it has begun to accept that part of the problem of the vagueness of indictments is due to the fact that the Prosecution does not know what its case is with sufficient clarity.[72]

The increased acceptance of this view marked the emergence of a willingness to develop new and more precise standards and acted, hence, as a significant catalyst for jurisprudential development in this field. The indictment has been acknowledged in *Kupreškić* to be the 'primary accusatory instrument' and it is required to plead with 'sufficient detail the essential aspect of the Prosecution case'.[73] The prosecution is expected to know its case before it goes to trial. It is not acceptable for the prosecution 'to omit the material aspects of its main allegations in the indictment with the aim of moulding the case against the accused in the course of the trial depending upon how the evidence unfolds'.[74] The increased

[70] ibid para 13.
[71] McIntyre (n 22 above) 217–18 (internal citations omitted).
[72] ibid 220.
[73] *Kupreškić* (Appeals Chamber Judgment) (n 26 above) para 114. See also *Prosecutor v Blaškić* (Appeals Chamber Judgment) IT-95-14-A (29 July 2004) para 220.
[74] ibid para 92, citing *Krnojelac* (Trial Chamber Decision) (n 19 above) para 23. See also WA Schabas, *The UN International Criminal Tribunals, The former Yugoslavia, Rwanda and Sierra Leone* (Cambridge: CUP, 2006) 361–2.

acceptance of these fundamentals was to spearhead the advancements in the jurisprudence, and consequently the rights of the accused, that have occurred over the last decade.

The effect of the October 2001 ICTY Appeal Chamber judgment in *Kupreškić* was to confirm and consolidate the approach taken by Judge Hunt when he presided over Trial Chamber II in *Krnojelac* and *Brđanin*. Whilst many of the underlying principles had been outlined in previous decisions, the emphasis in *Kupreškić* was new and sought to address both the difficulties that *might* be encountered in prosecuting international crimes *and* the rights of the accused to receive a minimum of information in the indictment so as to be informed of the nature and cause of the case against them. The Appeal Chamber emphasized that the specificity of an indictment was inextricably linked to the requirements of Article 21(4)(a) *and* (b) of the ICTY Statute, thus marking a significant departure from much of the previous jurisprudence.[75] The Appeal Chamber emphasized that the prosecution was required to state in the indictment 'the material facts underpinning the charges', even though the degree of specificity required would depend upon the nature of the alleged criminal conduct.[76] In other words the indictment must plead 'what the accused is alleged to have done, or failed to have done, at a particular venue on a particular date, during a particular period and in what capacity'.[77] In a case where the prosecution alleged that an accused personally committed the criminal acts, the identity of the victim, the time and place of the events, and the means by which the acts were committed had to be pleaded in detail.[78]

Crucially, the 'sheer scale' exception to specificity that had pervaded previous decisions was recalibrated. Instead of an assumption that it *was* impracticable to require a high degree of specificity in such matters as the identity of the victims and the dates for the commission of the crimes,[79] the Appeal Chamber re-emphasized this as a narrow exception.[80] The Chamber indicated that this exception might apply in the event that there was an allegation that the accused participated in the 'killing of hundreds of men' or had been 'charged with having participated as a member of a military force in an extensive number of attacks on civilians that took place over a prolonged period of time and resulted in large numbers of killings and forced removals'.[81] In such circumstances:

> [t]he Prosecution need not specify every single victim that has been killed or expelled in order to meet its obligation of specifying the material facts of the case in the indictment.

[75] *Kupreškić* (Appeals Chamber Judgment) (n 26 above) para 88. [76] ibid.

[77] A Obote-Odora, 'Drafting of Indictments for the International Criminal Tribunal for Rwanda' (2001) 12 *Criminal Law Forum* 335, 349.

[78] *Kupreškić* (Appeals Chamber Judgment) (n 26 above) para 89, referring to *Krnojelac* (Trial Chamber Decision) (n 19 above) para 18; and *Brđanin and Talić* (Trial Chamber Decision) (n 63 above) para 22.

[79] *Kvočka* (Trial Chamber Decision) (n 16 above) paras 16 and 17 (emphasis added).

[80] *Kupreškić* (Appeals Chamber Judgment) (n 26 above) para 89. [81] ibid para 90.

Nevertheless, since the identity of the victim is information that is valuable in the preparation of the defence case, if the Prosecution is in a position to name the victims, it should do so.[82]

The guidance was clear: the rule could not be invoked in instances where the victims or the attacks were few. Clearly, as the Chamber noted, the arguments advanced in an attempt to rely upon this rule in the *Kupreškić* case, a case limited to allegations of personal participation in attacks on two houses resulting, *inter alia*, in the killing of six people, were less than persuasive.[83]

The prosecution had a duty to particularize the material facts of the alleged conduct that described the accused's role, even for a crime such as persecution where a course of conduct was alleged.[84] Accordingly, this lack of detail would constitute a defective indictment and this might itself amount to a basis for the reversal of a conviction.[85] The Appeals Chamber conceded, however, that it could not exclude the possibility that, in some instances, a defective indictment could be cured if the prosecution provided the accused with timely, clear, and consistent information detailing the factual basis underpinning the charges against them. However, in light of the factual and legal complexities associated with the crimes within the jurisdiction of the Tribunal, there would only be a limited number of cases that fall within this category.[86]

Further, whilst recognizing that the prosecution could not plead material facts that were not in its possession, as previous jurisprudence had repeatedly emphasized, the Appeals Chamber endorsed the cautionary note in *Krnojelac* that 'in such a situation, doubt must arise as to whether it is fair to the accused for the trial to proceed'.[87] The overall approach of the Appeal Chamber was to root firmly the requirement that the indictment pleads material facts with the accused's ability to have a fair trial, thus heralding a new era in the jurisprudence.

D. Current pleading requirements

The import of these developments was that individual trial chambers had, for perhaps the first time, a set of general guiding appellate court principles that could be gainfully employed. Subsequent interlocutory challenges to the specificity of the indictment were addressed with reference to these minimum prerequisites. The jurisprudence was increasingly to recognize that specified indictments benefit not only the accused but also the prosecution and make for more efficient and fairer trials. This changed approach was manifested in a more interventionist approach by the judiciary and consequently real developments in the

[82] ibid para 90, referring to *Kvočka* (Trial Chamber Decision) (n 16 above) para 23.

[83] ibid para 91. [84] ibid para 98. [85] ibid para 114.

[86] As noted by the ICTR Appeals Chamber in *Ntakirutimana* (Appeals Chamber Decision) (n 26 above) para 125. See also Schabas (n 74 above) 362.

[87] ibid para 92, citing *Krnojelac* (Trial Chamber Decision) (n 21 above) para 40.

jurisprudence, crafted on a case-by-case basis to meet the challenges of a particular prosecution. Chambers began to demand 'objective reasons' to support prosecutors' claims not to be able to provide more particulars in providing, for example, a classification of the group that a victim belonged to or a time frame during which the acts were committed.[88] There was a greater expectation that the indictment should be at the forefront of a fair trial process, even to the extent that the prosecution should commit themselves to a guarantee of sorts in some situations to affirming in the indictment that the detail provided was the best information available.[89]

The overall approach of the Appeal Chamber in *Kupreškić* was to fuse the requirement that the indictment plead material facts with the accused's ability to have a fair trial, thus recognizing that the rights of the accused could be secured and the admittedly unique demands of prosecuting international crimes met. It became a stated norm that the expectation that '[w]here the evidence at trial turns out differently than expected the indictment may be required to be amended, an adjournment granted or certain evidence excluded as not within the scope of the indictment'.[90] This led to a helpful clarification of some of the nebulous definitions that had bedevilled the jurisprudence and made it difficult to enforce particularized indictments. Trial Chambers began to recognize and identify the introduction of material facts constituting fresh allegations amounting either to separate charges or to a new allegation in respect of an existing charge and to demand that they be the subject of an amendment to an indictment. This critical focus on the assessment of new material facts not pleaded in the indictment, combined with the recognition that new charges should be defined as a basis for conviction 'that is factually and/or legally distinct from any already alleged in the indictment',[91] represented a significant improvement in the jurisprudence and

[88] *Blagojević* (Trial Chamber Decision) (n 26 above) para 13. See also *Ntakirutimana* (Appeals Chamber Decision) (n 26 above) para 33.

[89] *Prosecutor v Ntagerura* (Trial Chamber Judgment and Sentence) ICTR-99-46-T (25 February 2004) para 32.

[90] *Prosecutor v Deronjić* (Trial Chamber Decision on Form of Indictment) IT-02-61-PT (25 October 2002) para 10, referring to *Kupreškić* (Appeals Chamber Judgment) (n 26 above) para 114. It is noteworthy that the Trial Chamber in *Deronjić*, when referring to the *Kupreškić* appeal, went further, noting that '[i]t can be left open whether the view expressed by the Appeals Chamber (at para 88) is an *obiter dictum* only, and whether there may not be exceptional cases in which the Prosecution may be required to plead the evidence in an indictment' (see para 34 and fn 29 of *Deronjić*).

[91] *Prosecutor v Halilović* (Trial Chamber Decision on Prosecutor's Motion Seeking Leave to Amend the Indictment) IT-01-48-PT (17 December 2004) para 30. See also *Prosecutor v Prlić* (Trial Chamber Decision on Prosecution Application for Leave to Amend the Indictment and on Defence Complaints on Form of Proposed Amended Indictment) IT-04-74-PT (18 October 2005) para 13: 'If a new allegation does not expose an Accused to an additional risk of conviction, then it cannot be considered a new charge'; and *Prosecutor v Krnojelac* (Trial Chamber Decision on Prosecutor's Response to Decision of 24 February 1999) IT-27-95-PT (20 May 1999) para 19, in which it was observed that the presence or absence of new counts in the indictment did not determine whether the prosecution had sought to add new charges: 'the Trial Chamber has obtained the impression that the prosecution may have taken the opportunity to add new charges for which

the rights of the accused. It was explicitly accepted that a Chamber had a duty to approach the task of assessing the significance of material facts and differences between the wording of the indictment and the evidence adduced in a rigorous manner; before making findings that such additions or changes were minor and insignificant, the issue was to determine whether an accused could reasonably identify the crime and conduct specified in each paragraph of the indictment.[92]

It is clear that the trial process benefits if the prosecution knows its case before it goes to trial. The fact that its case must be stated provides the essence of an (ostensibly) adversarial process: that which is stated must be proven. It was demonstrably unfair to the accused that the previous jurisprudence permitted the prosecution to omit material aspects of its case from the indictment in order to be able to mould the case during the trial depending on how the evidence unfolded.[93] It is obvious that the right of an accused to be informed promptly and in detail of the charges against them through the indictment benefits the accused in innumerable ways. Crucially, the defence investigation can begin from that point, rather than being handicapped until the service of the evidence or the disclosure of the prosecution's pre-trial brief.[94] Doubt must arise concerning the fairness of continuing a trial in circumstances where the prosecution's lack of specification causes impairment to the accused's ability to prepare an effective defence.[95]

In summary, the attempts by the judges at the *ad hoc* Tribunals to create and develop jurisprudence to define and refine the role of an indictment have been undoubtedly successful. As the Tribunals began their work, precedent at an international level was almost wholly absent and the rights of the accused ill defined and untested. Whilst it might be correct to observe that the developments were driven by pragmatic considerations relating to case management and efficiency

leave is required pursuant to Rule 50(A). It is true, as the prosecution says, that no new counts have been added to the indictment. But that is only because of the pleading style adopted by the prosecution in this case: each count has been pleaded only in the terms of the Statute, and thus in terms of absolute generality, leaving it to the material facts pleaded in respect of that count to reveal specific details which are required.'

92 *Prosecutor v Hadžihasonović* (Trial Chamber Decision on Motion of the Accused Hadžihasonović Regarding the Prosecution's Examination of Witnesses on Alleged Violations Not Covered by the Indictment) IT-01-47-T (16 March 2004) p 4.

93 See eg *Ntakirutimana* (Appeals Chamber Decision) (n 26 above) paras 124, 125; *Prosecutor v Rutaganda* (Appeals Chamber Judgment) ICTR-96-3-A (26 May 2003) paras 301–3; and *Prosecutor v Niyitegeka* (Appeals Chamber Judgment) ICTR-96-14-A (9 July 2004) para 194.

94 *Brđanin and Talić* (Trial Chamber Decision) (n 35 above) para 8. See also *Prosecutor v Zigiranyirazo* (Trial Chamber Decision on Defence Urgent Motion to Exclude some parts of the Prosecution Pre-Trial Brief) ICTR-2001-73-PT (30 September 2005), reiterating the now firmly established role of the pre-trial brief to assist the Chamber and the defence in understanding the prosecution strategy and how it intends to establish through evidence its case. It is relevant to the case only insofar as it *develops* the theory that has been promptly and in detail particularized in the indictment.

95 See eg *Ntakirutimana* (Appeals Chamber Decision) (n 26 above) para 26; *Rutaganda* (Appeals Chamber Judgment) (n 93 above) paras 301–3; and *Niyitegeka* (Appeals Chamber Judgment) (n 93 above) para 194.

considerations, it is nonetheless the case that through the creative endeavours of the *ad hoc* Tribunals the rights of the accused in this fundamental area of procedure have been substantially enhanced. As the following summary of the modern pleading standards illustrates, these principles stand as a considerable jurisprudential legacy.

IV. Pleading of Essential Factual Ingredients and Modes of Criminal Responsibility

The fundamental question in determining whether an indictment is pleaded with sufficient particularity is whether accused persons have enough detail to prepare their defence.[96] The fundamental role of the indictment is to identify each of the essential factual ingredients of the offences charged.[97] These essential factual ingredients must be pleaded expressly, although in some circumstances it is sufficient that they are expressed by necessary implication.[98] According to the ICTY Trial Chamber in *Brđanin*, this rule is no 'mere technicality', but rather compliance is necessary to enable an accused to know the nature of the case against them.[99] In this regard, the legal prerequisites underlying a crime constitute material facts.[100] This fundamental rule of pleading is not complied with if the pleading merely assumes the existence of the prerequisites.[101]

This approach has been approved by the Trial and Appeal Chambers of the ICTR such that the question of whether certain facts are material to an indictment will depend on the nature of the case at hand,[102] ie the form of participation alleged in the indictment and the proximity of the accused to the underlying crime.[103] The judgment of the ICTY Appeals Chamber in *Blaškić* provides a helpful overview of the specificity requirements for the different forms of criminal responsibility contained in Article 7 of the ICTY Statute.[104] The Appeals

[96] *Prosecutor v Semanza* (Trial Chamber Judgment) ICTR-97-20-T (15 May 2003) para 44, citing *Kupreškić* (Appeals Chamber Judgment) (n 26 above) para 88.

[97] *Krnojelac* (Trial Chamber Decision) (n 21 above) para 12, fn 19.

[98] *Prosecutor v Krnojelac* (Trial Chamber Decision on Form of Second Amended Indictment) IT-97-25-PT (11 May 2000) para 22.

[99] *Brđanin and Talić* (Trial Chamber Decision) (n 63 above) para 48.

[100] *Prosecutor v Hadžihasonović* (Trial Chamber Decision on Form of Indictment) IT-01-47 (7 December 2001) para 10.

[101] *Prosecutor v Brđanin and Talić* (Trial Chamber Decision on Form of Third Amended Indictment) IT-99-36 (21 September 2001) para 48.

[102] *Rutaganda* (Appeals Chamber Judgment) (n 93 above) para 301; *Ntagerura* (Trial Chamber Judgment) (n 89 above) para 31.

[103] *Kupreškić* (Appeals Chamber Judgment) (n 26 above) para 89; *Prosecutor v Karemera* (Trial Chamber Decision on Defects in the Form of the Indictment) ICTR-98-44-R72 (5 August 2005) para 17.

[104] *Blaškić* (Appeals Chamber Judgment) (n 73 above) paras 207–21: the Appeals Chamber disagreed with the Trial Chamber's suggestion that Article 21(4)(a) ('nature and cause of the charge') only 'establishes the context for the accused's entitlement to disclosure as set forth in Rule 66'. The

Chamber observed that a distinction can be drawn between the following three categories:

(1) individual responsibility under Article 7(1), where the accused is alleged to have carried out the act(s) in question: this form of liability has been described as 'personal' or 'direct' liability;[105]

(2) individual responsibility under Article 7(1), where the accused is not alleged to have carried out the acts underlying the crimes charged but may have planned, instigated, ordered, or otherwise aided and abetted in the planning, preparation, or execution of a crime; and

(3) superior responsibility under Article 7(3).[106]

In the *Krnojelac* case the ICTY Appeals Chamber held that 'the practice by the Prosecution of merely quoting the provisions of Article 7(1) in the indictment is likely to cause ambiguity, and it is preferable that the Prosecution indicate in relation to each individual count precisely and expressly the particular nature of the responsibility alleged'.[107] Accordingly, the jurisprudence of the ICTR and ICTY require that in instances in which the accused is alleged to have personally carried out the acts underlying the crime in question, the prosecution is under an obligation to set out the identity of the victim, the place and approximate date of the alleged criminal acts, and the means by which they were committed 'with the greatest precision'.[108]

The Appeals Chamber of the ICTY has approved of a lower standard of specificity where an accused is alleged to have planned, instigated, ordered, or aided and abetted in the planning, preparation, or execution of the alleged crimes under Article 7(1) of the Statute.[109] In such instances, the prosecution has an obligation

Appeals Chamber noted that Articles 18(4) and 21(4) of the Statute and Rule 47(B) 'accord the accused an entitlement that translates into an obligation on the part of the Prosecution to state the material facts underpinning the charges in an indictment, but not the evidence by which such material facts are to be proven' (ibid para 209).

105 The Trial Chamber in *Krnojelac* referred to this form of liability as 'personal' responsibility: see *Krnojelac* (Trial Chamber Decision) (n 19 above) para 18. The Appeals Chamber, in its judgment in the case of *Krnojelac*, referred to this form of liability as 'direct' responsibility: see *Prosecutor v Krnojelac* (Appeals Chamber Judgment) IT-97-25-A (17 September 2003) para 138, as cited in *Blaškić* (Appeals Chamber Judgment) (n 73 above) fn 435.

106 *Blaškić* (Appeals Chamber Judgment) (n 73 above) para 211. See also *Rutaganda* (Appeals Chamber Judgment) (n 93 above) para 301; *Ntagerura* (Trial Chamber Judgment) (n 89 above) para 31; *Kupreškić* (Appeals Chamber Judgment) (n 26 above) para 89; and *Karemera* (Trial Chamber Decision) (n 103 above) para 17.

107 *Krnojelac* (Trial Chamber Decision) (n 19 above) paras 59–60.

108 *Blaškić* (Appeals Chamber Judgment) (n 73 above) para 213, citing *Tadić* (Trial Chamber Decision) (n 28 above) paras 11–13; *Krnojelac* (Trial Chamber Decision) (n 19 above) para 18; *Kupreškić* (Appeals Chamber Judgment) (n 26 above) para 89; and *Deronjić* (Trial Chamber Decision) (n 90 above) para 37. See also *Ntakirutimana* (Appeals Chamber Decision) (n 26 above) para 32; *Karemera* (Trial Chamber Decision) (n 103 above) para 12; and *Ntagerura* (Trial Chamber Judgment) (n 89 above) para 32.

109 *Blaškić* (Appeals Chamber Judgment) (n 73 above) para 213.

to identify the 'particular acts' or 'the particular course of conduct' of the accused which has given rise to charges in the indictment.[110] This language was cited with approval by ICTR Trial Chamber III in *Karemera*.[111] In order to ensure that an accused is left in no doubt as to the form of liability charged under Article 6(1) and 7(1) of the ICTR and ICTY Statutes respectively, the indictment must, in the interests of a fair and expeditious trial, plead only the type of responsibility that the prosecution intends to rely upon at trial on the basis of specific factual allegations.[112]

The ICTY Appeals Chamber in *Krnojelac* held that, in the same way that the prosecution must distinguish between 'direct' commission under Article 7(1) and other forms of individual criminal responsibility articulated in that article, when the prosecution charges the 'commission' of one of the crimes under the Statute within the meaning of Article 7(1), it must specify whether the term is to be understood as physical commission by the accused, or participation in a joint criminal enterprise, or both.[113] In William Schabas's words, the indictment must specify between 'explicit' participation, the planning, instigation, ordering, commission or aiding and abetting of the crime, and 'implicit' participation, participation as a member of a joint criminal enterprise.[114] Moreover, an indictment alleging responsibility on the part of an accused as a participant in a joint criminal enterprise should also refer to whether the form envisaged is basic or extended.[115] The ICTR Trial Chamber in *Zigiranyirazo* determined, based on the relevant jurisprudence from the ICTY, that where an accused is charged with participation in a joint criminal enterprise, the indictment should:

> ...indicate the nature and the purpose of the joint criminal enterprise in which the Accused allegedly participated, its period of existence, its other participants, the implication of the Accused in it and any facts and circumstances from which the Prosecution infers the existence of and the Accused's participation in the alleged joint criminal enterprise.[116]

The *ad hoc* Tribunals have concluded that the facts underlying a charge of superior responsibility will necessarily be stated with less precision than those alleging 'personal' or 'direct' responsibility. Nonetheless, where an accused is alleged to be criminally responsible for the acts of subordinates, the accused is entitled to know the prosecution allegations as to (a) his conduct as a superior and (b) the

[110] ibid citing: *Krnojelac* (Trial Chamber Decision) (n 21 above) para 13; *Krnojelac* (Trial Chamber Decision) (n 19 above) para 18; *Brđanin and Talić* (Trial Chamber Decision) (n 63 above) para 20. [111] *Karemera* (Trial Chamber Decision) (n 103 above) para 12.

[112] ibid. [113] *Krnojelac* (Appeals Chamber Judgment) (n 105 above) para 138.

[114] Schabas (n 74 above) 362.

[115] ibid. See also *Ntagerura* (Trial Chamber Judgment) (n 89 above) para 34.

[116] *Prosecutor v Zigiranyirazo* (Trial Chamber Decision on the Defence Preliminary Motion Objecting to the Form of the Amended Indictment) ICTR-2001-73-I (15 July 2004) para 39.

conduct of those for whom he is alleged to be responsible.[117] In the *Zigiranyirazo* case the ICTR Trial Chamber cited with approval the ICTY pleading criteria, insofar as charges of superior responsibility are concerned,[118] such that where superior responsibility is alleged at the ICTR, the indictment should outline the relationship of the accused to his subordinates, his knowledge of the crimes, and the necessary and reasonable measures that he failed to take to prevent the crimes or to punish his subordinates.[119]

In the *Brđanin* case the Trial Chamber outlined the pleading requirements insofar as the *mens rea* requirement of crimes alleged are concerned, noting that 'where the state of mind with which the accused carried out his alleged acts is relevant, state of mind is just as much a fact to be proved by the prosecution as are the accused's acts themselves'.[120] In other words, where the state of mind is relevant to the crime charged, that state of mind is a material fact that must be pleaded in the indictment. In order to satisfy this requirement, the prosecutor may plead the evidentiary facts from which the state of mind is necessarily inferred or the relevant state of mind itself as the material fact. Where the latter approach is followed, the grounds on which the material facts are to be established will be evidentiary matters and will not be pleaded in the indictment.[121]

V. Conclusion

The pleading standards employed by the *ad hoc* Tribunals have advanced beyond recognition since the first indictments were drafted. The developments in the pleading standards were resisted by international prosecutors and are the result of concerted struggles. Once gained, they began to provide a measure of the guarantees of fairness and equality of arms that accord with those accepted on the national level and are commensurate with the modern human rights regime. It is right, though, to strike a cautionary note. As the history of the jurisprudence demonstrates, the standards that have been developed guarantee rights only inasmuch as the ICTY, the ICTR, and future tribunals remain confident in the ability of prosecutors to bring viable prosecutions. There are still too many examples of standards being sacrificed in the interests of the exigencies of prosecutions or as a result of the judiciary not grasping the central importance of the right to be

[117] *Krnojelac* (Trial Chamber Decision) (n 21 above) para 38; and *Krnojelac* (Trial Chamber Decision) (n 19 above) para 18.

[118] *Zigiranyirazo* (Trial Chamber Decision) (n 116 above) para 32.

[119] *Ntagerura* (Trial Chamber Judgment) (n 89 above) para 32, citing *Prosecutor v Mejakić* (Trial Chamber Decision on Željko Mejakić Preliminary Motion on the Form of the Indictment) IT-02-65-PT (14 November 2003) p 3; *Deronjić* (Trial Chamber Decision) (n 90 above) para 7; and *Zigiranyirazo* (Trial Chamber Decision) (n 116 above) para 32.

[120] *Prosecutor v Brđanin and Talić* (Trial Chamber Decision on Form of Further Amended Indictment and Prosecution Application to Amend) IT-99-36 (26 June 2001) para 31.

[121] ibid para 33.

informed of the nature and cause of the charges and conducting correspondingly elastic assessments of the minimum detail required for the effective preparation of a defence.

The pleading standards require further development and more stringent enforcement. Given the investigative resources provided to the prosecution there is little to justify an approach that deprives an accused of the optimum conditions to contest serious charges of violations of international law. The continual reliance on the catch-all claim of the 'uniqueness' of international proceedings must be put to the test in each individual case. The requirement that the indictment should particularize the count or charge and the material facts that underpin each count or charge should be interpreted strictly.[122] Accordingly, there is little to justify jurisprudence that consistently recognizes that pleading all of the forms of liability pursuant to Article 7(1) or Article 6(1) is likely to cause ambiguity and yet repeatedly warns that it is only *preferable* that an indictment indicates with precision the specific form.[123] The prosecution has an expansive cache of liabilities, both direct and indirect, to choose from.[124] Each is sufficiently encompassing to capture an extremely wide range of conduct and there is simply no justification for charging all heads of liability. The less the particularization the more the accused is hampered in his or her preparation and the more restricted the opportunity to rebut the charges. There is little to distinguish the prejudice that arises from indictments where details are omitted from those where the 'real case' is buried in an overloaded indictment containing multiple, cumulative, and alternative charges, most of which have no realistic prospect of leading to conviction. Unless a compelling justification is demonstrated, the prosecution should be compelled to do that which has been identified as best practice.

Best practice should mean that it is mandatory that the prosecution use the expression 'joint criminal enterprise' if that is being charged.[125] This fertile but now futile debate about terminology has run its course and no sensible reason exists to justify anything less than the use of this term. Similarly, it is difficult to justify the jurisprudential admonishment that it is only '*preferable* for an indictment alleging the accused's responsibility as a participant in a JCE to refer also to the particular form (basic or extended) of JCE envisaged'.[126] There is no basis

[122] *Prosecutor v Kupreškić* (Appeals Chamber Judgment) IT-95-16-A (23 October 2001) para 88. See also *Krnojelac* (Appeals Chamber Judgment) (n 105 above) para 131.

[123] See eg *Prosecutor v Karemera* (Trial Chamber Decision on Severance of Rwamakuba and for Leave to File Amended Indictment) ICTR-98-44-PT (14 February 2005) para 45; *Semanza* (Trial Chamber Judgment) (n 96 above) para 59; and *Prosecutor v Delalić* (Appeals Chamber Judgment) IT-96-21-A (20 February 2001) para 351.

[124] See eg *Prosecutor v Mrkšić* (Trial Chamber Decision on Form of the Indictment) IT-95-13/1-PT (19 June 2003) para 62.

[125] See eg *Prosecutor v Simić* (Appeals Chamber Judgment) IT-95-9-A (28 November 2006) para 22; and *Prosecutor v Gacumbitsi* (Appeals Chamber Judgment) ICTR-01-64-A (7 July 2006) para 167.

[126] *Krnojelac* (Appeals Chamber Judgment) (n 105 above) para 138 (emphasis added).

for requiring anything less than the identification of all 'known' participants by name in such a joint criminal enterprise. The alternative of omitting individuals of lesser importance may be consistent with the 'jurisdictional criterion of proximity' of the accused to the alleged criminal events,[127] but such an approach hampers the defence with little reason other than prosecutorial convenience.

Finally, as this chapter has outlined, international prosecutors have, largely, been resistant to the developments in the jurisprudence and continue to appear to regard the requirements as an unwelcome and unhelpful straitjacket.[128] The judiciary have innovated and crafted pleading standards without the assistance that might have been derived from a realistic or measured prosecutorial response. Nonetheless, whilst this creativity has produced significant advances in the jurisprudence, too many concessions to this unhelpful prosecutorial perspective continue to create worrying caveats. Newer institutions, such as the Special Court for Sierra Leone (SCSL), are particularly vulnerable to these prosecutorial interests and are too willing to sacrifice the rights of the accused, rather than raise questions concerning the viability of fair trials.[129] Notwithstanding that the Trial Chambers at the SCSL were able to draw on almost all of the significant case law, the indictments fail in almost all instances to abide by these modern pleading requirements.[130] Trial Chamber I in the *RUF* case, with which the Appeals Chamber agreed, whilst purporting to abide by the modern pleading standards, reinterpreted and abandoned them, explaining that the prosecution were excused from providing information on the indictment due to the fact that the trials at the SCSL were 'intended [presumably, by the United Nations] to proceed as expeditiously as possible in an immediate post-conflict environment'.[131] The indictments at the SCSL and this prosecution-centred approach are a salutary reminder that the *ad hoc* Tribunal's jurisprudential legacy is far from secure and too easily sacrificed to prosecutorial expediency and the misconception that any trial is better than none.

It is still too early to ascertain the approach that the ICC will take to the *ad hoc* Tribunals' legacy. The Rome Statute was drafted prior to the development of this area of international criminal law by the *ad hoc* Tribunals. However the ICC Statute, and the elaborate confirmation of the charges regime provided

[127] *Prosecutor v Gotovina* (Trial Chamber Decision on Ante Gotovina's Preliminary Motions Alleging Defects in the Form of the Joinder Indictment) IT-06-90-PT (19 March 2007) paras 14–15.

[128] See eg the inadequate pleading practices of the prosecution in *Gotovina* ibid; and *Karemera* (Trial Chamber Decision) (n 103 above).

[129] For an analysis of how the pleading practices of the prosecution at the Special Court for Sierra Leone—particularly with respect to joint criminal enterprise and sex-based crimes—have undermined the rights of the accused, see C Rose, 'Troubled Indictments at the Special Court for Sierra Leone: The Pleading of Joint Criminal Enterprise and Sex-Based Crimes' (2009) 7 JICJ 353–72.

[130] Available at <http://www.sc-sl.org/>.

[131] *Prosecutor v Sesay, Kallon and Gbao* (Trial Chamber Judgment) SCSL-04-15-T (2 March 2009) para 330; and *Prosecutor v Sesay, Kallon and Gbao* (Appeals Chamber Judgment) SCSL-04-15-A (26 October 2009) para 60.

for therein, creates a number of procedural safeguards which could, alongside this jurisprudence, provide even greater protection for the rights of the accused during the trial process.[132] Nonetheless, despite signs that the ICC is prepared to adopt and afford the accused with many of the protections envisaged in this jurisprudence,[133] there are other indications emerging from the *Lubanga* trial that the judiciary has not fully grasped the importance of the accused's right to be informed in detail of the charges against them. The recent decision in the Trial Chamber by the majority in the *Lubanga* case, with Judge Fulford dissenting, concluded that the addition of (effectively) new charges at the close of the prosecution case was permissible pursuant to Regulation 55 of the Regulations of the Court, thus discarding the ICTY and ICTR jurisprudence in almost all respects.[134] The majority claim that Sub-Regulation 55(2) permitted the legal re-characterization of facts 'at any time during the trial',[135] and that this was not limited to the facts and circumstances described in the initial charges, was clearly an interpretation that violated the accused's right to be informed of the nature and cause of the charges.

Whilst the Appeal Chamber rejected the Trial Chamber's interpretation of Regulation 55 and ruled that its scope was limited to 'the facts and circumstances,

[132] The ICC Statute, Art 61(1) provides that the Pre-Trial Chamber of the Court shall hold a hearing to confirm the charges on which the prosecutor intends to seek trial. The hearing shall be held in the presence of the prosecutor and the person charged, as well as his or her counsel. Art 61(3) provides that '[w]ithin a reasonable time before the hearing, the [charged] person shall (a) Be provided with a copy of the document containing the charges on which the Prosecutor intends to bring the person to trial; and (b) Be informed of the evidence on which the Prosecutor intends to rely at the hearing'. Rule 121(3) of the Rules of Procedure and Evidence provides that 'the Prosecutor shall provide to the Pre-Trial Chamber and the [charged] person, no later than 30 days before the date of the confirmation hearing, a detailed description of the charges together with a list of the evidence which he or she intends to present at the hearing'. Art 61(6) establishes that '[a]t the hearing, the [charged] person may: (a) Object to the charges; (b) Challenge the evidence presented by the Prosecutor; and (c) Present evidence.'

[133] In its decision on the confirmation of charges in the case of *Bemba Gombo*, for example, the Pre-Trial Chamber of the ICC in considering the 'basic principles on framing a document containing the charges' relies on the case law of the *ad hoc* Tribunals to the effect that the document containing the charges 'must state the material facts underpinning the charges and that the material facts underpinning the charges shall be specific enough to clearly inform the suspect of the charges against him or her, so that he or she is in a position to prepare properly his or her defence'. See *Situation in the Central African Republic in the case of the Prosecutor v Jean-Pierre Bemba Gombo* (Pre-Trial Chamber Decision Pursuant to Article 61(7)(a) and (b) of the Rome Statute on the Charges of the Prosecutor Against Jean-Pierre Bemba Gombo) ICC-01/05–01/08 (15 June 2009) para 208, citing *Kupreškić* (Appeals Chamber Judgment) (n 122 above) paras 88, 92, and 98; and *Prosecutor v Ntakirutimana* (Trial Chamber Judgment and Sentence) ICTR-96-10 and ICTR-96-17-T (2 February 2003).

[134] *Situation in the Democratic Republic of the Congo in the Case of the Prosecutor v Thomas Lubanga Dyilo* (Trial Chamber Decision giving notice to the parties and participants that the legal characterization of the facts may be subject to change in accordance with Reg 55(2) of the Regulations of the Court) ICC-01/04–01/06 (12 July 2009); and *Situation in the Democratic Republic of the Congo in the Case of the Prosecutor v Thomas Lubanga Dyilo* (Trial Chamber Decision giving notice to the parties and participants that the legal characterization of facts may be subject to change in accordance with Reg 55(2) of the Regulations of the Court) ICC-01/04–01/06 (17 July 2009).

[135] ibid para 28.

described in the charges and any amendment thereto', it nonetheless ruled that it was permissible for a Trial Chamber to modify the legal characterization of the facts on its own motion once the trial had commenced.[136] The Appeal Chamber, remitting the issue back to the Trial Chamber to make a decision on the specific facts of the case, noted that the modification must not render the trial unfair, but declined to interpret Regulation 55 to prohibit the modification of a legal characterization to a more serious offence, observing that 'the particular circumstances of the case will have to be taken into account'.[137] The Chamber appeared to have been heavily influenced in this conclusion by its interpretation that 'a principal purpose of Regulation 55 is to close accountability gaps' in order to achieve the statutory aim of putting 'an end to impunity'.[138] This, unfortunately, appears to foreshadow a return at the ICC to a narrow focus on prosecutorial interests that, in the cases at the SCSL, and those in the early days of the ICTY and ICTR, militated against the development and application of a human rights-compliant jurisprudence.

There is no basis in the *ad hoc* Tribunals' jurisprudence for any future ICC decision allowing an accused to be convicted for a more serious offence than those disclosed in the original or amended charges. The provision of full, detailed information concerning the charges and the applicable legal characterization is an essential prerequisite to ensuring a fair trial. Accordingly, it is hoped that Trial Chambers at the ICC, which will be called upon to address this issue, will accept the need to adopt and build upon the *ad hoc* Tribunals' jurisprudence, further strengthening the accused's right to be informed promptly and in detail of the nature and cause of the charges, rather than taking a permissive approach to the modification of a legal characterization to a more serious offence. This would be a fitting testimonial to the work of the ICTY and the ICTR and would ensure that this potentially formidable jurisprudential legacy is fully maintained for the benefit of future international criminal adjudication.

[136] ibid para 93. [137] ibid para 100. [138] ibid para 77.

PART V
PROCEDURE

13

Procedural Lawmaking at the International Criminal Tribunals

*Göran Sluiter**

I. Introduction

The judges at the *ad hoc* Tribunals fulfil an intriguing double function. They not only adjudicate the most serious international crimes, but they also act as legislator with respect to the determination of institutional criminal procedure. And what zealous legislators they are! From the moment of their creation in 1994, the Rules of Procedure and Evidence (RPE)—the International Criminal Tribunal for the former Yugoslavia's (ICTY) procedural code—have been revised no less than 44 times, as of early 2010.[1] This means that there has been an average of almost three amendments a year.

The role of the judges of the *ad hoc* Tribunals as procedural lawmakers tends to be accepted as an inevitable aspect of *ad hoc* institutions that were created under great pressure and time constraints, and for which no detailed procedural framework could be created by the drafters of their constituent Statutes. Yet the position of judges as procedural lawmakers is highly unusual and raises a number of pertinent questions. The central question in this chapter is whether the position of judges as lawmakers, and their perception of their role as active lawmakers, has been a defendable experiment given the circumstances in which international criminal justice systems have been forced to operate, or whether the experiences of the *ad hoc* Tribunals are not worth repeating. Given that the ICTY Rules of Procedure and Evidence were the first to be crafted and that they, as a result, served as a model for both the International Criminal Tribunal for

* Professor in the Law of International Criminal Procedure, University of Amsterdam. The author wishes to acknowledge funding received from the Netherlands Organisation for Scientific Research (NWO) which facilitated research for this chapter, as part of the research project 'International Criminal Procedure—In Search of General Rules and Principles'.

[1] The judges of the International Criminal Tribunal for Rwanda were less active; in early 2010 they had amended their Rules of Procedure and Evidence 17 times. The Special Court for Sierra Leone judges amended their RPE 11 times.

Rwanda (ICTR) and the Special Court for Sierra Leone (SCSL), this chapter will concentrate on procedural lawmaking by the ICTY judges exclusively.

Addressing this research question requires a short introduction to the origin and development of the ICTY's procedural law, and the role of the judges therein (section II). An even-handed approach to the chapter's central research question requires particular attention to be paid to the need for a dynamic procedural system. Working on the basis of a comparison with the International Criminal Court (ICC), it will be argued that, while one may be critical of the number of amendments made to the ICTY's procedural law, almost full legislative inaction may be an even greater problem for the effective functioning of international criminal law (section III). This having been said, the next section sets out the risks inherent in the pronounced legislative role of ICTY judges, while also addressing credible alternatives to the status quo (section IV). In order to avoid this becoming a theoretical exercise only, it is imperative to examine whether the exercise of legislative functions by judges has given birth to 'bad law'. Section V will explore one unfortunate procedural creation as an example, without this implying, however, that this makes ICTY judges bad lawmakers. It is, however, a necessary element in the critical analysis of the function of the judges, which ultimately allows us to draw some conclusions as to the lessons that can be learned from the ICTY experiment (section VI).

II. A Short History of the ICTY's Procedural Law

There is some similarity among the main international criminal tribunals when it comes to the crafting of procedural rules. While their creators, ie states, are keen on maintaining control over matters such as jurisdiction and substantive international criminal law, they tend to delegate the creation of the vast majority of procedural norms to the respective bench.

This approach started with the post-Second World War Nuremberg and Tokyo International Military Tribunals. Article 13 of the Charter of the International Military Tribunal (IMT) at Nuremberg stipulated that the Tribunal should be responsible for the drafting of its own procedural rules. Eleven rules were adopted on 29 October 1945 and together with relevant provisions in the Charter—Articles 14 and 29—they made up the procedural law of the IMT at Nuremberg. Article 7 of the Charter of the International Military Tribunal for the Far East (IMTFE) authorized the Tribunal to draft and amend rules of procedure consistent with the fundamental provisions of the Charter. These Rules were drafted by the IMTFE judges, with input from a US Judge Advocate General.[2] Not unsurprisingly, the rules adopted closely corresponded to those in place before the US military commissions established pursuant to Control Council Law No 10.[3]

[2] N Boister and R Cryer, *The Tokyo International Military Tribunal—A Reappraisal* (Oxford: OUP, 2008) 86–7. [3] ibid 87.

It cannot be said of the post-Second World War tribunals that the bench was the primary designator of procedure. The drafters of the respective Charters laid down the essentials and gave general direction to the procedural approach to be followed. Compared with the ICTY and the ICTR, the judges of the IMT and IMTFE had far less of an impact on the creation of procedural rules. Several factors may explain this. First, the allied powers had more time to prepare for the creation of the procedural edifice than was the case with the ICTY, which had to become operational at very short notice, as a result of being established under Chapter VII with a view to restoring international peace and security. Secondly, without a firmly established international human rights *corpus juris* to guide judges, it may very well have been quite difficult for them to reach agreement on key procedural issues. In evaluating the procedural law of the IMT and the IMTFE, one apprehends diverging views as to their fairness; indeed, it was often the case that individual judges either expressed dissatisfaction about, or defended the fairness of, the applicable procedural rules.[4] A common ground—which states currently find in internationally recognized human rights norms—was lacking immediately after the Second World War and made the role of judges as lawmakers a difficult task.[5] It is therefore difficult to assess their endeavours and one should be cautious in using them as a point of reference in respect of the ICTY.[6] What can be said, however, is that the procedural lawmaking undertaken by the judges at the IMT and the IMTFE did not constitute an excessive exercise of judicial activism. It seems that there was not enough time, too much influence from outside, too much divergence, and also it seems, too much restriction in the specific texts of the respective Charters to allow them to be supplemented by significant procedural legislation. The observations of President Webb of the IMTFE in relation to the admissibility of evidence are quite illustrative in this respect, revealing powerlessness rather than a sense of legislative opportunities:

> We cannot lay down technical rules. We might spend months in trying to agree upon them and then fail to reach an agreement. The Charter does not allow us to adopt them in any event. It is contrary to the spirit of the Charter. The decision of the Court will vary with its constitution from day to day. There is no way of overcoming it.[7]

[4] ibid 86–8; EJ Wallach, 'The Procedural and Evidentiary Rules of the Post-World War II War Crimes Trials: Did They Provide an Outline for International Legal Procedure?' (1999) 37 Col JTL 868–83.

[5] Wallach (n 4 above) 882, mentions the lack of standardized rules as a major problem in respect of international criminal trials; he concludes that the lack of predictability in procedure was seen as a most troubling problem in the post-Second World War tribunals.

[6] Criticism has been voiced that the procedural precedents of Nuremberg and Tokyo have nevertheless been used as a basis for procedural solutions at the ICTY, without, however, a thorough inquiry into their quality; see A Zahar and G Sluiter, *International Criminal Law—A Critical Introduction* (Oxford: OUP, 2008) 38.

[7] Cited in the dissenting opinion of Judge Pal (India), printed in BVA Röling and CF Rüter (eds), *The Tokyo Judgement—Volume II* (Amsterdam: Amsterdam University Press, 1977) 655.

Things were different with the creation of the ICTY. It is true that Article 15 of the ICTY Statute[8]—attributing to the judges a procedural lawmaking power, along with an obligation to exercise this power—is reminiscent of Article 13 of the IMT Charter. However, the ICTY Statute contains fewer provisions on procedure than the IMT and IMFTE Charters, irrespective of contemporary demands for the detailed regulation of criminal procedure as follows from various human rights treaties. This simply meant that the judges had to fill far more gaps than their predecessors had to at the IMT and IMFTE; furthermore, the unanticipated longevity of the ICTY's activities also allowed, even obliged, the bench to continue to exercise their legislative functions based on experience in practice.

The drafting process of the ICTY Statute suggested a strong focus on jurisdiction and substantive criminal law.[9] With respect to procedure, the Statute lays down the basic contours. The prosecutor has the power to start investigations, collect evidence, and no judge is involved in this stage (Articles 16 and 18); the pre-trial involvement of the judges is confined to the confirmation of the indictment, following which the judge may issue the necessary orders and warrants for the preparation of the trial (Article 19).[10] The preference for the adversarial model of criminal procedure set out in the Statute not only follows from the absence of a judicial role in the pre-trial stage, but also from the accused having to enter a plea of guilty or not guilty and from the prohibition of trials in the accused's absence. The latter is a deviation from the procedural law of the IMT and the IMTFE and seemed to have been one of the biggest procedural issues for the UN Secretary-General's team drafting the Statute.[11] It was, somewhat erroneously, considered by the Secretary-General that trials *in absentia* would violate Article 14 of the International Covenant on Civil and Political Rights (ICCPR).[12] Another novelty in the Statute was the particular concern for victims, triggered by the ongoing conflict in the former Yugoslavia, and this resulted in the adoption of

[8] Statute of the International Tribunal for the Prosecution of Persons Responsible for Serious Violations of International Humanitarian Law Committed in the Territory of the Former Yugoslavia since 1991, UN Doc S/25704, p 36, Annex (1993) and S/25704/Add.1, (1993) UN Doc S/RES/827.

[9] See the account thereof in V Morris and MP Scharf, *An Insider's Guide to the International Criminal Tribunal for the Former Yugoslavia* (Irvington-on-Hudson: Transnational, 1995) 17–84.

[10] Interestingly, the latter provision only allows for the prosecutor to trigger such orders and warrants, which is not only at odds with the principle of equality of arms, but also makes the judge highly passive in that process. It has been rectified by the adoption of Rule 54.

[11] See R Zacklin, 'Some Major Problems in the Drafting of the ICTY Statute' (2004) 2 JICJ 364–5. See the contribution of Håkan Friman (Ch 14 below). For an analysis of the return of the possibility of trials *in absentia* very recently in international criminal justice at the Special Tribunal for Lebanon, see W Schabas, 'In Absentia Proceedings before International Criminal Courts' in G Sluiter and S Vasiliev (eds), *International Criminal Procedure—Towards a Coherent Body of Law* (London: CMP Publishing, 2009) 327–72.

[12] See Report of the Secretary-General pursuant to Paragraph 2 of Security Council Resolution 808 (1993) (presented 3 May 1993), UN Doc S/25704 (1993) para 101.

Article 22, ordering the judges to provide for adequate protection in the Rules of Procedure and Evidence.

Compared to its post-Second World War predecessors, much more (legislative) responsibility was vested in the judiciary. For example, the admissibility of evidence—which was flexible at the IMT and IMTFE as a result of provisions in the respective Charters stipulating that the Tribunals shall not be bound by technical rules of evidence[13]—was left fully at the discretion of the judges. Commentators have explained this approach mainly on the basis of practical considerations, such as time constraints.[14] But it was also expressed by a participant in the drafting process: 'It was felt that it would be quite inappropriate for a political body to be involved in the drafting or even approval of such Rules; the integrity and impartiality of the proceedings require that only the judicial branch of the Tribunal be responsible.'[15] This is remarkable; the contrary could be argued just as easily, maybe even better, because procedural law is within the domain of the legislator, a political organ, in many criminal justice systems, as discussed in section IV below. An active procedural rulemaking role for the judiciary is encountered in common law systems and international tribunals, but it is not generally shared among criminal justice systems and unlikely to go as far as was the case with the ICTY.

The drafting of the initial set of Rules was not only a judicial responsibility; one may even wonder how many of the Rules have been directly drafted by the judges. Rather, they were drafted and adopted by judges working together on the basis of proposals submitted by states and organizations.[16] The procedure for discussing these proposals and amending the first set of Rules, on 11 February 1994, was not public. But it is common knowledge that the set of rules proposed by the United States was most influential and strengthened the common law nature of ICTY procedure.[17] It has been submitted by a judge who was involved in the drafting and adoption of the Rules that the adversarial system could be considered to perhaps better safeguard the rights of the accused.[18] Irrespective of the merits of this proposition, it raises the question of the degree to which it has been influential in the creation of the ICTY's procedural law.

In order to provide some 'counterweight' to a 'predominant' adversarial procedure, the ICTY judges also underlined the unique and mixed nature of its procedural edifice and pointed out three important civil law elements in its procedure: the absence of plea bargaining, an active judiciary, and the absence of technical rules of evidence.[19] Interestingly, this mixed nature and subsequent development was never really seriously assessed in light of the Statute, to which the Rules are

[13] IMT Charter, Art 19; and IMTFE Charter, Art 13(a).
[14] Morris and Scharf (n 9 above) 176.
[15] L Johnson, 'Ten Years Later: Reflections on the Drafting' (2004) 2 JICJ 374–5.
[16] Morris and Scharf (n 9 above) 176. [17] ibid 177.
[18] A Cassese, *International Criminal Law* (Oxford: OUP, 2008) 369.
[19] For more detail, see Zahar and Sluiter (n 6 above) 37–45.

subordinate. One could say that the Statute contains too many gaps to be directive or even guiding, but the fact is that the Statute contains no basis for a mixed procedure, as in procedural terms it is purely adversarial. For example, an active fact-finding role for the judiciary and the creation of a pre-trial judge are outspoken legislative procedural choices that seem not to be in keeping with the Statute.

There is the widely shared perception that the ICTY procedure was initially predominantly adversarial in nature but has come to incorporate more and more civil law elements.[20] While it is true that, under the pressure of the Security Council's completion strategy, judges have increasingly sought to tighten their grip on procedure, it would be wrong to assess this in terms of a more inquisitorial or more adversarial approach. In their urge to finalize trials and to expedite proceedings, the judges appear to have embarked upon a managerial model, which may be difficult to evaluate along the lines of the traditional adversarial–inquisitorial distinction.[21] The following example illustrates very well that there is no real and significant move towards the inquisitorial procedural system. Recent years at the ICTY reveal a significant increase in the number of cases in which a guilty plea has materialized. These cases are not fully tried and are disposed of quite quickly.[22] We thus witness a preference for elements of every system and legal tradition which assist the judges in disposing quickly of their case load. Given the prominent role of the uniquely adversarial phenomenon of plea bargaining, an unequivocal trend towards the inquisitorial system at the ICTY is still difficult to sustain, in the present author's view.

III. The Need for a Dynamic Procedural System

While one may at times be critical in respect of the frequency with which changes in the procedural law of the ICTY have occurred, this serves the interests of a dynamic procedural system. Even in national jurisdictions, which are generally the stable result of decades, even centuries, of practice and development, there are still regular changes in and constant monitoring of procedural law. There, the competing demands of efficiency and fairness also trigger regular amendments. In the Netherlands, for example, important changes over the past decades were predicated on these competing demands; at the risk of a degree of generalization,

[20] See D Mundis, 'From "Common Law" towards "Civil Law": The Evolution of the ICTY Rules of Procedure and Evidence' (2001) 14 LJIL 367–82; K Ambos, 'International Criminal Procedure: "Adversarial", "Inquisitorial" or Mixed?' (2003) 3 ICLR 1–37.

[21] In this sense, see M Langer, 'The Rise of Managerial Judging in International Criminal Law' (2005) 53 AJCL 835–909.

[22] For a detailed analysis of guilty pleas in international criminal law, see N Combs, *Guilty Pleas in International Criminal Law: Constructing a Restorative Justice Approach* (Stanford: Stanford University Press, 2006).

it can be said that fairness changes were often stimulated by outside pressure, such as decisions of the European Court of Human Rights; efficiency, on the other hand, is a continuing demand of the general public.

The starting point of the ICTY differs radically from that in national criminal jurisdictions. The first vital distinction is that the ICTY was only expected to respond to some of the international crimes committed. There were no pre-existing expectations as to output, contrary to national systems, where each serious crime is expected to be investigated and prosecuted. This, in terms of its operational effectiveness, is an enormous luxury for the ICTY, which, however, also harbours risks: it may take away or reduce the incentive to be as efficient and organized as possible. The second key difference is the aspect of 'instant procedure'. The ICTY had no meaningful precedent and no proper societal context to fall back on. As a result, it is self-evident that its procedural edifice would be in need of regular 'revision'. In the unique circumstances surrounding the ICTY, nobody could expect there to be a procedural framework which would be perfect from the beginning and would require no future amendment. A dynamic procedural system would seem to be inevitable.

Some experiences of the ICC illustrate the problems which may arise in cases where the procedural law is not sufficiently dynamic. The drafters of the Rome Statute deliberately reserved the mandate of (procedural) lawmaking to the state parties; the Statute of the ICC, which contains many important procedural provisions, and the Rules of Procedure and Evidence cannot be amended by the judges.[23] Their legislative activities are confined to the 'Regulations of the Court', which are, pursuant to Article 52, to be adopted as necessary for the 'routine functioning' of the Court. Subordinate to the Statute and the RPE, the Regulations cannot meaningfully alter the procedural law of the ICC.

The absence of meaningful procedural lawmaking powers for the ICC judges need not be by definition problematic. It may even be preferred in light of the problems to be addressed, if the states parties, in their legislative role, live up to the needs and expectations of a new procedural system. They can only do that if they actively monitor the ICC's law in operation and have in place regular and effective amendment mechanisms relating to procedural defects. At present, in this author's view, such mechanisms are not in place and this absence may have negative consequences. A good example is the problem regarding disclosure of information handed to the prosecutor under the condition of confidentiality. The prosecutor's ability to receive and possess information on a confidential basis under the Statute (Article 54(3)(d)) appears in direct contrast with the defendant's absolute right to receive from the prosecutor potentially exonerating evidence (Article 67(2)). The absence in the Statute of a mechanism resolving the

[23] However, the ICC Statute, Art 51(3) allows the drawing-up of provisional rules by ICC judges in urgent cases. But the Statute, which contains most important procedural rules, cannot be (provisionally) amended. Judges have never made use of the power to draw up provisional rules.

conflicting wording of these provisions almost resulted in the dismissal of the case in the *Lubanga* proceedings.[24] It seems that this inconsistency should have been resolved in the Statute urgently and that the legislator, the state parties, carries an important responsibility here.[25] Undeniably, the need for a dynamic procedural system finds better protection in the ICTY context.

The ICTY judges have clearly sought to operate in the best interests of a dynamic procedural system. They have made very frequent amendments to the ICTY's procedural law. However, these amendment proceedings are not transparent at all. The decisions on new or amended rules are taken in closed sessions of the plenary of judges. There are no public minutes of these sessions and the only explanations one encounters are some very brief remarks provided in the annual reports.[26] In addition, one may find some explanation as to the new or amended rule's intended object and purpose in relevant case law, although these accounts may differ among judges.[27] What is more, the case law never refers to debates within the plenary as a tool in proper interpretation.

In the absence of any sort of 'explanatory memorandum', it is practically impossible to learn what are the precise considerations and rationale underlying changes in the rules. For example, it would be highly relevant for all participants to learn the factors indicating resort to legislation instead of relying on judicial discretion and precedent. One indeed wonders why certain matters have made it to rules and

[24] Because of the inability to provide a fair trial—the prosecutor refusing to disclose confidential information to the defence—the *Lubanga* Trial Chamber ordered a stay on proceedings and in fact decided that the accused should be released: *Situation in the Democratic Republic of the Congo in the case of the Prosecutor v Thomas Lubanga Dyilo* (hereinafter *Lubanga*) (Trial Chamber Decision on the consequences of non-disclosure of exculpatory materials covered by Article 54(3)(e) agreements and the application to stay the prosecution of the accused, together with certain other issues raised at the Status Conference on 10 June 2008) ICC 01/04–01/06 (13 June 2008); *Lubanga* (Trial Chamber Decision on the release of Thomas Lubanga Dyilo) ICC-01/04–01/06 (2 July 2008). Similar problems arose in the second case, *Katanga and Ngudjolo Chui*, but that case was too far removed from the trial phase to require a stay of proceedings: *Situation in the Democratic Republic of Congo in the case of the Prosecutor v Germain Katanga and Mathieu Ngudjolo Chui* (Pre-Trial Chamber Decision on Article 54(3)(e) Documents Identified as Potentially Exculpatory or Otherwise Material to the Defence's Preparation for the Confirmation Hearing) ICC 01/04–01/07 (20 June 2008). The matter was remedied, but just barely, with the Appeals Chamber suspending the Trial Chamber's release decision and with the lifting of confidentiality for most documents, allowing either their disclosure to the defence or their inspection by the judges.

[25] One way of resolving the incongruence would be a reference to Art 67(2) in Art 54(3)(d). In the author's view, the latter would, in its application, have to be made subject to the individual's rights set out in Art 67(2).

[26] Recent reports, however, offer no explanation at all. In the Annual Reports for 2006, 2007, and 2008 there is only mention of the Rules which have been amended. In other reports there is very little information, although they may mention the object and purpose of amendments (eg in the Annual Report for 2005, para 32: 'The amendments are based on a combination of judicial economy and expedition in a way that strengthens the rights of the accused.')

[27] A striking example of very different interpretation is the criticism of Judge Hunt directed towards his colleagues at the Appeals Chamber regarding the interpretation of Rule 92*bis*: *Prosecutor v Milošević* (Appeals Chamber Decision on Interlocutory Appeal on the Admissibility of Evidence-in-Chief in the Form of Written Statements—Dissenting Opinion of Judge Hunt) IT-02-54-AR73.4 (30 September 2003).

other matters have never been the object of procedural legislation. An example of the former is Rule 45*ter*, adopted on 4 November 2008: 'The Trial Chamber may, if it decides that it is in the interests of justice, instruct the Registrar to assign a counsel to represent the interests of the accused.' This was already a matter within the discretion of the judges and the Rule adds nothing to the case law on self-representation, such as, for example, the manner in which the discretion must be exercised.[28] An example where rule-making would be welcome is in the practice of early release. In the interests of justice and legal certainty there is much to be said for codifying the currently prevailing practice of early release after two-thirds of the sentence has been served. It is a fundamental issue for both the convicted person and participants in trials. Furthermore, victims and the international community should be in a position to assess what it effectively means if an individual is sentenced to, for example, 20 years' imprisonment.

This example and the absence of transparency in the legislative process are important factors to consider when addressing the question of whether the rule-making at a closed plenary of judges is a defensible means of making procedural law. The matter will be further explored in the next section.

IV. Judges as Lawmakers: Unacceptable Risk or the Only Feasible Alternative?

It follows from the above that an active legislator is indispensable in the dynamic field of international criminal procedure. The key question, however, is whether judges should do this or whether this creates an unacceptable risk. The central issue here is the right of the accused to be tried by an independent tribunal and the importance generally attached to separating the legislative from the adjudicative functions.

The independence of international criminal tribunals is generally a sensitive point. It tends to be dealt with mostly in terms of 'victor's justice', and thus concerns the perceived dependence of judges/prosecutors on the victorious side in an armed conflict.[29] Furthermore, the relationship to political organs, especially

[28] For an overview and analysis of the ever-growing case law on self-representation, see the contribution of Gillian Higgins (Ch 11 above). See also NHB Jorgensen, 'The Problem of Self-Representation at International Criminal Tribunals: Striking a Balance between Fairness and Effectiveness' (2006) 4 JICJ 64–77; MP Scharf, 'Self-Representation versus Assignment of Defence Counsel at International Criminal Tribunals' (2006) 4 JICJ 31–46; J Temminck Tuinstra, 'Assisting an Accused to Represent Himself: Appointment of *Amicus Curiae* as the Most Appropriate Option' (2006) 4 JICJ 47–63; M Damaska, 'Assignment of Counsel and Perceptions of Fairness' (2005) 3 JICJ 3–8; and G Sluiter, 'Fairness and the Interests of Justice: Illusive Concepts in the *Milošević* Case' (2005) 3 JICJ 9–19.

[29] The criticism of international criminal tribunals as representing victor's justice or as reflecting power dominance in international relations is of all ages and concerns all tribunals.

the UN Security Council, is also a recurring matter in relation to judicial independence.[30]

With the focus on the executive–judiciary relationship, little attention has been given to the problematic aspects of the accumulation of judicial and legislative functions in the same body. This is surprising, because legislation has to be the result of a political process, and transparent in its creation. Judges may have a different perspective on this, emphasizing their managerial function, and may pay little attention to fundamental issues underlying criminal procedure, such as the goals and objectives it should pursue in international society and what procedural model would best correspond to that. Clearly, one can wonder whether any international body is yet in a position to take on this role, but it is clear that judges are not meant to be legislators.

The position of legislator makes judges particularly vulnerable. They are, as a result, not only accountable for applying and interpreting the law—which is difficult enough—but also for making the law. The interpretation of the Rules of Procedure and Evidence, as if they were some external source of law, is a sensitive exercise. When judges try to establish the proper interpretation of a particular rule, one is tempted to submit that they, having made a certain rule, should at least know what this rule is about. Thus, the judges pore over all the necessary information to interpret a rule in light of its object and purpose, but they are in no position to share this information publicly.

Both on a macro- and micro-level one might question the ability of judges to legislate. The macro-level concerns the fact that the ICTY Rules of Procedure and Evidence have been revised no fewer than 44 times. While the importance of an active legislator has been emphasized above, the number of amendments may be said to exceed what has been reasonably necessary. One cannot help but have the impression that the ICTY judges actually *like* lawmaking, instead of adopting a highly reserved attitude towards it, as they should do, in the present author's view. On a micro-level, there is a question regarding the quality of certain rules. One such 'less fortunate' rule is discussed below. At this stage, it suffices to mention that the existence of bad or defective rules puts the judges in an awkward position. They may be called upon to assess the validity and quality of a rule—either in relation to the Statute or in relation to other sources of

30 At the ICTY and ICTR judges have sought to emphasize their independence in relation to the Security Council: *Prosecutor v Kanyabashi* (Trial Chamber Decision on the Defence Motion on Jurisdiction) ICTR-96-15-T (18 June 1997) paras 40–42. However, the completion strategy is said to unduly interfere with judicial independence: see *Milošević* (Dissenting Opinion Judge Hunt) (n 27 above) para 32: 'This Tribunal will not be judged by the number of convictions which it enters, or by the speed with which it concludes the Completion Strategy which the Security Council has endorsed, but by the fairness of its trials.' In the context of the ICC, similar concerns have been expressed regarding the position of the Security Council and its possible undermining of judicial independence: cf S Zappalà, 'The Reaction of the US to the Entry into Force of the ICC Statute: Comments on UN SC Resolution 1422 (2002) and Article 98 Agreements' (2003) 1 JICJ 114–34.

international law—by one of the parties. Can they reasonably be expected to set aside or explore critically the result of their own legislative activity? Interestingly, parties to the proceedings, especially defence counsel, have never challenged the (adverse) interpretation and application of the rules as the inevitable result of a lack of independence. More specifically also, when challenging a certain rule, to this author's knowledge, parties have never inquired as to whether the judges on the panel have voted in favour of that rule, which could display an appearance of bias in relation to the dispute before them.

Generally speaking, the accumulation of functions in a single of body is problematic, but it is especially problematic when there is no proper mechanism of supervision. On the occasion of the departure of Carla Del Ponte from the role of Chief Prosecutor, this critical comment appeared in the media:

> At the same time, the ICTY has fallen short of its original purposes and the hopes of its founders. The publicly televised trials have not had the impact on public opinion we expected. Far from helping the process of reconciliation, many would argue that ICTY has been a major source of 'fuel' for nationalism and political destabilization in this region over the past decade. One of the major reasons for this gap between expectation and reality is the absence of any serious Western review or criticism of its work and corresponding 'course corrections'.
>
> The reasons include the reluctance of Western political leaders to criticize an international institution they set up and whose leadership they appointed; the wide-spread belief that prosecuting war criminals responsible for the bloody years of violence in the Balkans is one of the most noble efforts to come out of that time (and consequently deserves unreserved support); and a general reluctance to be seen as 'interfering' in the work of an independent judiciary.[31]

There is some merit to this. One has to recognize that especially at the end of its mandate the ICTY judges have accumulated an enormous degree of power. They adjudicate and legislate, but they can also engage in fact-finding, initiate contempt proceedings, and have increased their supervisory powers over the prosecutor. This last point in particular raises pertinent questions, because under the current regime the issuance of indictments is made subject to the approval of the judges.[32] Interestingly, this usurpation of the prosecutorial prerogative by the judiciary is the result of the completion strategy imposed by the UN Security

[31] W Montgomery, 'Carla Departs…Finally', 6 January 2008, available at <http://www.b92.net/eng/insight/opinions.php?nav_id=46724>.

[32] See Rule 28 (A): 'On receipt of an indictment for review from the Prosecutor, the Registrar shall consult with the President. The President shall refer the matter to the Bureau which shall determine whether the indictment, *prima facie*, concentrates on one or more of the most senior leaders suspected of being most responsible for crimes within the jurisdiction of the Tribunal. If the Bureau determines that the indictment meets this standard, the President shall designate one of the permanent Trial Chamber Judges for the review under Rule 47. If the Bureau determines that the indictment does not meet this standard, the President shall return the indictment to the Registrar to communicate this finding to the Prosecutor.'

Council on the ICTY.[33] One witnesses here, as a result of examining one single rule, a chain of 'independence' problems, namely the Security Council interfering with the operation of the ICTY, resulting in the ICTY judges interfering with the powers of the prosecutor.

The lack of supervision of judges may be seen as safeguarding judicial independence, in the sense that we indeed should be critical of states and others interfering in an unorganized and often politically motivated fashion with the functioning of the ICTY and other international criminal tribunals. But full independence, lacking checks and balances, is an undesirable and dangerous prospect for international criminal justice. This is especially the case when that system has as yet proved incapable of developing internal checks and balances and, as is the case with the ICTY, has had the legislative function, to a significant degree, usurped by the judiciary.

The absence of supervision, indispensable for proper or balanced independence, in the legislative and adjudicative functions of judges is most felt in the area of human rights. It would be naive to think that the ICTY would be immune from human rights violations, for the simple reason that it is ultimately a human rights court. Where and whenever criminal proceedings are conducted, human rights are by definition at stake and even the most developed and fair national systems have had their occasional condemnation from human rights courts.[34] One must acknowledge on that basis that at least a fraction of ICTY law and practice must be in violation of human rights law. This is the inevitable result of a lack of critical distance in relation to cases that generate great societal unrest or concern. For some time now, the present author has therefore advocated a mechanism of supervision, where the law and practice of the ICTY and other international criminal courts is subjected to scrutiny.[35] This mechanism can be found in the existing supervisory organs in human rights law or it can be created as a new organ for this particular task. If nothing along these lines is done, it is predicted that increasingly accused persons before the international criminal tribunals will find their way to domestic courts in the Netherlands asking, on the basis of applicable case law from the European Court of Human Rights, for the national courts to put an end to or provide

[33] See UN SC Resolutions 1503 and 1534 (2004). The operative paragraph of the latter reads as follows: '*Calls on* each Tribunal, in reviewing and confirming any new indictments, to ensure that any such indictments concentrate on the most senior leaders suspected of being most responsible for crimes within the jurisdiction of the relevant Tribunal as set out in resolution 1503 (2003)...'.

[34] The Netherlands, for example, has a tradition of difficulty in ensuring the accused's right to question prosecution witnesses. It has resulted in established violations of Art 6 in, among other cases: *Kostovski v The Netherlands* (App No 11454/85) ECHR 20 November 1989 and *Van Mechelen v The Netherlands* (App No 55/1996/674/861–864) ECHR 30 October 1997.

[35] See G Sluiter, *Het internationaal strafprocesrecht—De geboorte van een rechtsgebied (The Law of International Criminal Procedure—The Birth of a Field of Law)* (Amsterdam: Vossiuspers UvA, 2007) 19–21.

a remedy for human rights violations which have occurred, or are ongoing, on the host state's territory.[36]

The aforementioned absence of external supervision is exacerbated by the absence of checks and balances within the ICTY system. It leaves us with extremely powerful judges. In other words, we put an enormous degree of faith in them for making and applying the law. This is disconcerting even with the most qualified judges. This is without mentioning the problems surrounding the selection of judges, a process which is, as we know, highly politicized.

V. An Unfortunate Procedural Creation: The Law regarding Detention on Remand

In light of the above concerns, one may be tempted to ask as a matter of principle whether the procedural lawmaking power of judges has proved to be problematic in practice. Of course, the proof of the pudding is always in the eating and failing a considerable number of instances of 'bad law' one may be content with the situation as it is, and perhaps even advocate it as a model for other courts. A thorough and detailed analysis of all rules and amendments would clearly exceed the scope of this contribution. This section will therefore confine itself to what may be regarded as one unfortunate example of legislative activity which aptly illustrates some of the concerns expressed above.

The example concerns the manner in which the ICTY judges have handled the law regarding detention on remand. One can think of various reasons why accused before international tribunals should remain detained on remand, but it is fundamentally wrong to regard pre-trial detention as a rule instead of an exception. Even in the most serious cases and in the most complex circumstances the burden of proof should lie with the prosecutor to satisfy the judges that (a) there is sufficient evidence justifying detention, and (b) detention is necessary on the basis of a restricted number of grounds. Detention as a rule rather than exception

[36] On the basis of the following cases, a (residual) responsibility exists for state parties to the ECHR when international organizations commit human rights violations on their territory. *Waite and Kennedy v Germany* and *Beer en Regan v Germany* (App Nos 26083/94 and 28934/95) ECHR 18 February 1999, para 67: 'The Court is of the opinion that where States establish international organisations in order to pursue or strengthen their cooperation in certain fields of activities, and where they attribute to these organisations certain competences and accord them immunities, there may be implications as to the protection of fundamental rights. It would be incompatible with the purpose and object of the Convention, however, if the Contracting States were thereby absolved from their responsibility under the Convention in relation to the field of activity covered by such attribution.' Also *Matthews v UK* (App No 24833/94) ECHR 18 February 1999, para 32: 'The Court observes that acts of the EC as such cannot be challenged before the Court because the EC is not a Contracting Party. The Convention does not exclude the transfer of competences to international organisations provided that Convention rights continue to be "secured". Member States' responsibility therefore continues even after such a transfer.'

poses a legal problem in light of international human rights standards, which require the reverse.[37] From the case law of the European Court of Human Rights it follows that a person charged with an offence must always be released pending trial unless the state can show that there are relevant and sufficient reasons to justify continued detention.[38] The European Court has identified in its case law the following reasons for continued detention: the risk that the accused will fail to appear for trial; the risk that the accused would take action to prejudice the administration of justice, or commit further offences, or cause public disorder; and the risk that release may give rise, by reason of the particular gravity of the accusations and public reaction to them, to a social disturbance.[39] The burden of proving the presence of these circumstances rests in all cases with the state, and under no circumstances can the continuation of detention be used to anticipate a custodial sentence.[40] In addition to the ECHR law, one should mention Article 9(3) of the ICCPR, according to which it shall not be the general rule that persons awaiting trial shall be detained in custody.[41] Viewing detention on remand as exceptional is, of course, closely related to the presumption of innocence fundamental to criminal proceedings.

In light of these unequivocal standards, the initial version of Rule 65, common to the ICTY and the ICTR, and the existing case law on provisional release, is astonishing. The incipient language of Rule 65 reads as follows:

> (A) Once detained, an accused may not be released except upon an order of a Trial Chamber.
> (B) Release may be ordered by a Trial Chamber only in exceptional circumstances, after hearing the host country and only if it is satisfied that the accused will appear for trial and, if released, will not pose a danger to any victim, witness or other person.
> (C) The Trial Chamber may impose such conditions upon the release of the accused as it may determine appropriate, including the execution of a bail bond and the observance of such conditions as are necessary to ensure his presence for trial and the protection of others.
> (D) If necessary, the Trial Chamber may issue a warrant of arrest to secure the presence of an accused who has been released or is for any other reason at liberty.

Subparagraph (B) of this rule raises two fundamental problems. Most significant is the reference to the exceptional nature of liberty prior to conviction. This cannot be viewed otherwise than as a flagrant violation of international human rights law.[42] The unfairness ensuing from this proposition lies to a large degree in

[37] eg ICCPR, Art 9(3).
[38] *Smirnova v Russia* (Apps No 46133/99; 48183/99) ECHR 24 July 2003, para 59.
[39] cf *Letellier v France* (App No 12369/86) ECHR 26 June 1991, para 35. [40] cf ibid.
[41] On Art 9, see 'General Comment 08 (16) of the Human Rights Committee', UN Doc A/37/40 (1982) Annex V, 95–6: 'Pre-trial detention should be an exception and as short as possible.'
[42] See H Friman, 'Commentary' in A Klip and G Sluiter (eds), *Annotated Leading Cases, vol. IX* (Antwerp: Intersentia, 2006) 347; DJ Rearick, 'Innocent until Alleged Guilty: Provisional Release at ICTR' (2003) 44 Harv ILJ 591.

the shifting of the burden of proof. It follows from this rule that the accused carries the burden of satisfying the Chamber that he or she will appear for trial and will not pose a danger to victims and witnesses.

The uncritical application of Rule 65(B) in the initial case law is striking. For example, in the *Blaškić* case the Trial Chamber held that:

> ... both the letter of this text and the spirit of the Statute of the International Tribunal require that the legal principle is detention of the accused and that release is the exception; that, in fact, the gravity of the crimes being prosecuted by the International Tribunal leaves no place for another interpretation even if it is based on the general principles of law governing the applicable provisions in respect of national laws which in principle may not be transposed to international criminal law.[43]

Subparagraph (B) is also problematic from a different perspective. One may read into the conditions for provisional release (assurance of re-appearance for trial and non-interference with witnesses), *a contrario*, grounds justifying continued detention. Yet, this certainly does not correspond to domestic practice, where additional and alternative grounds may be found.[44] Furthermore, the ICC Statute also contains an additional ground in Article 58(1)(b)(iii), which addresses arrest for the purpose of preventing the continued commission of the crime.[45]

In this light, the formulation of Rule 65 is too modest, a fact which presumably justified its amendment in November 1999. As the grounds for detention were limited to the circumstances to which it referred, one might safely claim, based on routine tribunal practice, that release is granted only in exceptional circumstances. However, the result might have been entirely different if other grounds for detention had been admitted in Rule 65. Taking into consideration domestic practice, the prosecutor would not have much difficulty in proving that provisionally releasing a person indicted for genocide or war crimes would create a serious risk of social disturbance in the societies concerned.[46] This

[43] *Prosecutor v Blaškić* (Order Denying a Motion for Provisional Release) IT-95-14-T (20 December 1996).

[44] eg risk of social disturbance in the Netherlands (Dutch Code of Criminal Procedure, art 67a); in France: prevention of a fraudulent conspiracy between a person under judicial examination and his or her accomplices, protection of a person under judicial examination, putting an end to an offence and preventing its renewal, putting an end to an exceptional and persistent disruption of public order caused by the seriousness of the offence (French Code of Criminal Procedure, art 144); in Germany: suspicion of having committed certain offences (German Code of Criminal Procedure, §§ 112 and 112a).

[45] Rome Statute of the International Criminal Court (1998) UN Doc A/CONF.183/9, entered into force 1 July 2002, 2187 UNTS 90.

[46] eg in the Netherlands the risk of social disturbance is deemed inherent in the provisional release of a person suspected of a crime punishable by 12 or more years of imprisonment. Regarding such offences, (continued) detention is generally imposed as a rule on that ground. Note that this practice may seem to be at odds with the position of the European Court of Human Rights in *Letellier v France* (n 39 above): the protection of public order ground is only relevant and sufficient to justify detention if 'based on facts capable of showing that the accused's release would actually prejudice public order', and as long as the latter 'remains actually threatened' (ibid para 51).

particular ground has met with the approval of the European Court of Human Rights in *Letellier v France*.[47] Whereas this could make the line between the criteria set out in Rule 65 and those affirmed by national practices rather fine, the drafters of the Rules could have avoided confusion and criticism by adopting a rule underscoring the exceptional nature of detention and prescribing the variety of grounds for detention. This would both ensure the conformity of Rule 65 with widely accepted human rights standards and legitimize, from that very perspective, continued provisional detention in the majority of cases before the Tribunals.

However, another rather unfortunate approach has been followed, which has done damage in two ways. First, the old version of Rule 65 has been criticized from a human rights angle, something which can be said to have negatively affected the Tribunals' image and reputation. Secondly, the rule change undeniably has had the result of unequal procedural treatment of various defendants, ie defendants after the amendment of the Rule enjoyed the benefits arising from shifting of the burden of proof justifying continued detention to the prosecutor, in contrast to the defendants who had previously been denied provisional release in comparable situations.

The conclusion is that the ICTY has been incapable of adequately dealing with such a vital issue as deprivation of liberty. The judges have adopted a rule and applied it for a considerable length of time in a manner which was in direct violation of international human rights law.

VI. Conclusion: Lessons Learned

The role of judges in procedural lawmaking at the ICTY has received only scant attention. It was taken for granted, regarded as an inevitable consequence of a new system that had to be flexible and easily adjustable. However, compared to other international criminal tribunals—the *ad hoc* post-Second World War international military tribunals and the permanent ICC—the judges of the ICTY and the ICTR have been endowed with the most far-reaching procedural lawmaking powers.

The ICTY judges have been very active in this role. To their credit, one must acknowledge that they have always sought to improve the system and intended to avoid unpleasant surprises in the procedure. Situations that occur at the ICC within the context of the inflexible Statute and Rules of Procedure and Evidence—such as the problems occasioned by the conflicting norms of Articles 54(3)(e) and 67(2) of the ICC Statute—have never arisen to a similar degree at the ICTY.

[47] ibid.

But this is not to say that the lawmaking role of the judges is not subject to criticism. With reason, one must be extremely suspicious about the accumulation of such significant powers within one body, namely, the judiciary. This is especially the case when the rule-making process is non-transparent and when there is no external supervision of the role judges perform within the ICTY. Indeed, there is a problem from the perspective of the accused's right to an independent tribunal and from the perspective of the importance of separation of powers and checks and balances for the proper administration of justice. This seems not just to be a theoretical issue: in their lawmaking the judges have given birth to bad rules, like that regarding detention on remand. This could have been prevented, or the negative consequences mitigated, by a restriction in lawmaking powers and a mechanism of external supervision.

It is therefore concluded that neither the ICC nor the ICTY provide for a useful procedural lawmaking model. The ICC is too rigid and the ICTY is too flexible. The latter vests the judiciary with powers not envisaged by the separation of powers, and without appropriate checks and balances. Furthermore, in order to minimize the vulnerability of the judges in their dual role as lawmakers and adjudicators, the lawmaking process would benefit from independent input. For example, while the judges would still formally adopt the amendments to the Rules of Procedure and Evidence, an independent commission could play a role in developing the substance of the rules and amendments. One could also envisage the stronger input of participants, prosecution, and defence, in order to achieve more balanced results, which might count on more support.[48]

As to the interpretation and application of amended rules, each system of law, especially one in which the judges combine the legislative and judicial function, benefits from regular scrutiny from a human rights supervisory organ. It gives the system an important degree of legitimacy and eventually will result in better procedural rules.

[48] cf the Extraordinary Chambers in the Courts of Cambodia (ECCC), Internal Rule 3 which allows requests for amendments to be made by a Judge, a Co-Investigating Judge, a Co-Prosecutor, the Head of the Defence Support Section, the Head of the Victims Unit, and the Director or Deputy Director of the Office of Administration. However, they cannot participate in the adoption process. At the ICTY, only a Judge, the Prosecutor, and the Registrar can, pursuant to Rule 6, propose amendments.

14

Trying Cases at the International Criminal Tribunals in the Absence of the Accused?

Håkan Friman

I. Introduction

International criminal law and international criminal procedures are at the crossroads of international law and criminal law, or between international lawyers and criminal lawyers. Two different legal traditions exist with conflicting expectations as to what the law and the role of judges should be.

This plays out in different ways. First, the procedural law of international tribunals is normally provided rather rudimentarily in the constituting Statutes, as adopted by states (or the United Nations Security Council), and it is left to the judges to establish more detailed procedural rules, either in a separate legal instrument or in practice.[1] Although it may be debatable whether it should be considered a substantive or a procedural issue, the conditions for exercising jurisdiction are a matter that is always set forth in the constituent instrument of an international court. This practice was followed with respect to the International Criminal Tribunal for the former Yugoslavia (ICTY) and the International Criminal Tribunal for Rwanda (ICTR),[2] but not for the International Criminal Court (ICC),[3] which has prompted some critical comments.[4] Hence, the judges of the ICTY and ICTR are required to act as formal lawmakers when it comes to procedural law. This is a feature that, generally, international lawyers should

[1] eg the International Court of Justice: see the ICJ Statute, Arts 30 and 48; and the International Tribunal for the Law of the Sea (ITLOS): see the ITLOS Statute, Arts 16 and 27. See also C Brown, *A Common Law of International Adjudication* (Oxford: OUP, 2007) 38–40 and the contribution by Göran Sluiter (Ch 13 above).

[2] ICTY Statute, adopted by UNSC Res 827 (1993), and ICTR Statute, adopted by UNSC Res 955 (1994); both later amended by other UNSC Resolutions.

[3] The Rome Statute of the International Criminal Court (ICC Statute), 2187 UNTS 3, UN Doc A/Conf183/9. See also the Rules of Procedure and Evidence, negotiated and adopted by states.

[4] eg D Hunt, 'The International Criminal Court: High Hopes, "Creative Ambiguity" and an Unfortunate Mistrust in International Judges' (2004) 2 JICJ 56.

be more comfortable with than criminal lawyers, although national traditions in this respect differ (as is further discussed below).[5]

Secondly, there is always the question of how much statutory law is required. The principle of legality requires that the law is clear, accessible, and predictable. These features are particularly pronounced when it comes to criminal law and criminal procedures. However, the law may be expressed in different forms: in statutory law, as adopted by the constitutionally competent body, or in case law, as established by the courts of law. Here national legal traditions depart fundamentally. The civil law tradition rests solidly upon statutory law adopted by the national parliament, while the common law tradition, on the contrary, is traditionally based on the jurisprudence established by the courts. Hence, it may be that the dividing line is not to be drawn between international lawyers—accustomed as they are to regard, *inter alia*, 'customary international law' as binding law—and criminal lawyers, but rather between criminal lawyers from different national legal traditions. Indeed, some international lawyers have expressed the view that the rather detailed ICC Statute represents an 'excess of codification', which was due to the influence of criminal lawyers and their view of the principle of legality.[6]

But a new court does not have any directly relevant earlier jurisprudence to rely upon. Because of the development of human rights and due process standards, moreover, the ICTY and ICTR did not have much assistance from the Nuremberg and Tokyo precedents with respect to procedural law. Against this background, written law was the natural option in order to satisfy the interest of legal certainty.

Thirdly, international instruments which are negotiated and adopted by states reflect a very high degree of political compromise, arguably more so than equivalent domestic pieces of legislation. This may be reflected in less than clear drafting in order to make the provisions acceptable to everyone involved, sometimes labelled as 'constructive ambiguity'.[7] In turn, the application of the law may require rather far-reaching use of different tools for legal interpretation, which may be considered as the judges actually making the law.

Fourthly, more likely than not, international procedural law will suffer from *lacunae* that may have to be overcome by the court in the case at hand. Two fundamentally different approaches are possible: the point of departure may be either that whatever is not explicitly forbidden is allowed or, on the contrary, that whatever is not explicitly allowed should be considered forbidden. Again,

[5] Generally too, this lawmaking power, unaccompanied by review mechanisms or sufficient safeguards, has its critics: eg M Swart, 'Ad Hoc Rules for Ad Hoc Tribunals? The Rule-Making Power of the Judges of the ICTY and ICTR' (2002) 18 *South African Journal of Human Rights* 570.

[6] eg A Pellet, 'Applicable Law' in A Cassese *et al* (eds), *The Rome Statute of the International Criminal Court: A Commentary, Vol. 1* (Oxford: OUP, 2002) 1057.

[7] See C Kress, 'The Procedural Law of the International Criminal Court in Outline: Anatomy of a Unique Compromise' (2003) 1 JICJ 603.

domestic legal traditions, and thus the distribution of competences between the legislative and judicial powers, are likely to influence the point of view taken. National statutes or jurisprudence on criminal procedures, on the other hand, are developed over a much longer period of time during which coherence and consistency have been shaped.

As already noted, the judges of the ICTY and the ICTR were tasked with creating criminal procedures for the respective Tribunals and the question arises how they have performed this legislative role. Using the issue of trials *in absentia*, and a substitute for such procedures, as the example, this chapter will argue that the judges have taken this role seriously and responsibly by avoiding very controversial mechanisms, although strong merits could be identified, and by striving for solutions as widely acceptable as possible.

II. Trials *in Absentia* and Substitute Proceedings

A. For and against trials *in absentia*

Someone accused of a crime should not be able to flee justice and the possibility to do so harms not only the case at hand, but also the credibility of the criminal justice system as such. In practice, however, there will always be such opportunities, not least due to the imperfection of international cooperation in this field. By accepting trials *in absentia*, statutes of limitation for prosecution may be overcome (if shorter than the limitation for execution of the sentence) and evidence may be obtained and preserved.[8] Victims who give evidence are also given an opportunity to make their statements in court, with whatever rehabilitating effect this may have, in spite of the disappearance of the accused.

Nonetheless, the drawbacks are obvious. Presence, or at least some form of participation, is often necessary for conducting a proper defence; legal counsel without contact with and instructions from the accused cannot be expected to fully do this.[9] A general concern is also that trials *in absentia* may be open to abuse.[10] It is not just defence interests which are a motivation for the presence of the accused in the proceedings. Such presence will also assist the court in arriving at correct conclusions concerning the matter before it; it allows the court a first hand impression of the accused and provides an opportunity to verify the accuracy of his or her statements and compare them with those of others. Moreover, the reappearance of the accused may require a complete rehearing of the case

[8] *Colozza v Italy* (App No 89) ECHR 12 February 1985, para 29.

[9] That was explicitly recognized in the Nuremberg Judgment concerning the defence of Martin Bormann, who was tried in his absence: *Nazi Conspiracy and Aggression: Opinion and Judgment* (US Government Printing Office, 1947) 48.

[10] eg A Cassese, *International Criminal Law* (Oxford: OUP, 2nd edn, 2008) 389.

(see below) and custodial or other penalties imposed cannot be enforced as long as the convicted person is absent.

It may be argued, however, that trials *in absentia* are not intrinsically unfair as long as the accused has all the necessary guarantees to be able to exercise the right to be present and to intervene at trial.[11] Instead, this should be considered a policy choice which concerns the general objectives of international criminal justice rather than the rights of the accused. Indeed there are some proponents for the ICTY trying war criminals *in absentia*.[12]

B. A controversial matter

As a starting point, one may note that the Charter of the International Military Tribunal at Nuremberg permitted trials *in absentia*, if this was deemed to be in the interests of justice, and the Tribunal made use of this procedural device.[13] This was a source of criticism.[14] However, the subsequent procedures in the occupied zones under Control Council Law No 10 did not permit such trials, with the exception of temporary absence or absence with the permission of the Tribunal.[15] The Statute of the International Military Tribunal for the Far East at Tokyo (IMTFE) did not contain a provision allowing for trials *in absentia*, but nor did it explicitly recognize the right of the accused to be present at trial.[16] War crimes trials *in absentia* had been held on earlier occasions, for example by France and Belgium after the First World War.[17]

[11] See S Zappalà, *Human Rights in International Criminal Proceedings* (Oxford: OUP, 2003) 125–6.

[12] eg R Wedgwood, 'War Crimes: Bosnia and Beyond—War Crimes in the Former Yugoslavia—Comments on the International War Crimes Tribunal' (1994) 34 Va JIL 267; A Pellet, 'Le Tribunal criminel pour l'ex-Yougoslavie. Poudre aux yeux ou avancée decisive?' (1994) 98 *Revue générale de droit international public* 7, 48; H Schwartz, 'Trials *in Absentia*' (1996) 4 *Human Rights Brief* 18; and H Schwarz and L Cutler, 'Try Them *in Absentia*', *International Herald Tribune*, 29 August 1996.

[13] See Art 12 of the Charter of the International Military Tribunal for the Trial of the Major War Criminals, appended to the Agreement for the Prosecution and Punishment of Major War Criminals of the European Axis, London 8 August 1945, as amended by Protocol to Agreement and Charter, 6 October 1945, 85 UNTS 251, 59 stat 1544. The accused, Martin Bormann, was tried and convicted *in absentia*, but since he remained at large the sentence (death penalty) was never enforced. Generally, see W Schabas, '*In Absentia* Proceedings Before International Criminal Courts' in G Sluiter and S Vasiliev (eds), *International Criminal Procedure: Towards a Coherent Body of Law* (London: Cameron May, 2009) 327–71.

[14] eg T Taylor, *The Anatomy of the Nuremberg Trials: A Personal Memoir* (New York: Alfred A Knopf, 1992) 630.

[15] See Military Government Ordinance No 7 of 18 October 1946 ('Organization and Power of Certain Military Tribunals'), Art IV(d).

[16] See the Charter of the International Military Tribunal for the Far East, 19 January 1946, TIAS No 1589, Art 9.

[17] See A Kramer, 'The First Wave of International War Crimes Trials: Istanbul and Leipzig' (2006) 14 *European Review* 441, 449.

There are many examples underlining that trials *in absentia* are controversial and that various legal systems, and states, view them very differently. As will be discussed further below, international human rights bodies and courts have also been asked to assess whether trials *in absentia* are compatible with international fair trial norms.

Strongly held opinions on the matter of *in abstentia* trials have been expressed in the sphere of international criminal cooperation, which is unsurprising since this is a field in which national differences are typically exposed and must be managed. For example, cooperation in the form of extradition has been denied in several cases with reference, at least in part, to the fact that the underlying judgment was issued after proceedings where the accused was not present.[18] Indeed, reference to trials *in absentia* as a mandatory or discretionary ground for refusal is common in international instruments on inter-state cooperation.[19]

The approach to trials *in absentia* in inter-state international criminal cooperation has not been consistent. In light of human rights developments and in the general interest of enhancing criminal cooperation, moreover, an absolute and non-nuanced approach appears unsatisfactory. Hence, within the European Union a framework decision on decisions rendered in the absence of the person concerned at trial has recently been adopted by the Council of Ministers.[20] It has yet to be implemented in the Member States but will, once in place, provide a more uniform and cooperation-oriented scheme concerning judgments rendered after trials *in absentia*. While not outlawing trials *in absentia*, nor trying properly to define the concept, the framework decision requires certain minimum rights for the convicted person and creates a similar scheme for the various forms of criminal cooperation when trials *in absentia* may be an issue, ie amendments to five other framework decisions on the European Arrest Warrant, as well as recognition and enforcement of custodial or non-custodial penalties, financial penalties, or confiscation orders.[21]

[18] eg J Dugard and C Van den Wyngaert, 'Reconciling Extradition with Human Rights' (1998) 92 AJIL 187, 203.

[19] eg the Second Additional Protocol to the European Convention on Extradition, ETS 98, Art 3; and the (UN) Model Treaty on Extradition, UNGA Res 45/116 (Annex) Art 3(g).

[20] Council Framework Decision of 26 February 2009 amending Framework Decisions 2002/584/JHA, 2005/214/JHA, 2006/783/JHA, 2008/909/JHA, and 2008/947/JHA, thereby enhancing the procedural rights of persons and fostering the application of the principle of mutual recognition to decisions rendered in the absence of the person concerned at the trial (2009/299/JHA, [2009] OJ L81/24–36). Italy has made a special Declaration postponing the implementation of the Framework Decision ([2009] OJ L97/26).

[21] Council Framework Decision of 13 June 2002 on the European arrest warrant and the surrender procedures between Member States (2002/584/JHA, [2002] OJ L190/1–20); Council Framework Decision of 27 November 2008 on the application of the principle of mutual recognition to judgments in criminal matters imposing custodial sentences or measures involving deprivation of liberty for the purpose of their enforcement in the European Union (2008/909/JHA, [2008] OJ L327/27–46); Council Framework Decision of 27 November 2008 on the application of the principle of mutual recognition to judgments and probation decisions with a view to the supervision of probation measures and alternative sanctions (2008/947/JHA, [2008] OJ L337/102–22);

The discontent from some quarters concerning trials *in absentia* has not been confined to the field of international legal cooperation. This was also a factor, for example, when the jurisdictional reach and practice of the Belgian laws on war crimes and other international crimes came under scrutiny—and strong international pressure for change—some years ago.[22] The Belgian example involved a combination of a far-reaching criminal jurisdiction and procedural features which included the possibility of rendering a verdict without having secured the presence of the accused. The controversy also arose when the issue of trials *in absentia* was brought up and debated with respect to the ICC.[23]

C. The law of the ICTY and the ICTR

(1) *Rules of procedure and evidence*

As in all other international tribunals, with the exception of the ICC, the judges of the ICTY and the ICTR were explicitly entrusted with the development and adoption of more detailed procedural rules for the Tribunals.[24] Generally, such rulemaking has often been exercised to expand procedural powers appreciably[25] and the ICTY and ICTR are no exception.[26] In the case of the ICTY and the ICTR, different reasons for the delegation of this responsibility to the judges have been advanced.[27] The Statute was drafted under time constraints and states and others providing input to the process largely ignored procedural matters. Criminal procedures are also highly technical and controversial in the sense that they vary considerably in different legal systems. In addition, an intention was to draw upon the expertise and practical experience of the judges to be elected, something that the Security Council itself did not possess.

Council Framework Decision of 24 February 2005 on the application of the principle of mutual recognition to financial penalties (2005/214/JHA, [2005] OJ L76/16–30); Council Framework Decision of 6 October 2006 on the application of the principle of mutual recognition to confiscation orders (2006/783/JHA, [2006] OJ L328/59–78).

[22] See eg L Reydams, 'Prosecuting Crimes Under International Law on the Basis of Universal Jurisdiction: The Experience of Belgium' in H Fischer *et al* (eds), *International and National Prosecution of Crimes Under International Law: Current Developments* (Berlin: Berlin Verlag, 2001) 799–816.

[23] See H Friman, 'Rights of Persons Suspected or Accused of a Crime' in RS Lee (ed), *The International Criminal Court—Issues, Negotiations, Results* (The Hague: Kluwer, 1999) 247–62, and Schabas (n 13 above) 359–66.

[24] The ICTY Statute, Art 15 and the ICTR Statute, Art 14. Cf the ICC Statute, Arts 51–2 whereby the states retain the power to adopt the Rules of Procedure and Evidence and leave the responsibility for the development of so-called Regulations of the Court to the judges. Cf also the Nuremberg Tribunal Statute (n 13 above) Art 14(e), which entrusted the four Chief Prosecutors with the drafting of the rules of procedure and the judges of the Tribunal with the power to adopt them.

[25] See Brown (n 1 above) 39.

[26] See eg G Lombardi, 'Legitimacy and the Expanding Power of the ICTY' (2003) 37 *New England Law Review* 887.

[27] See V Morris and M Scharf, *An Insider's Guide to the International Criminal Tribunal for the Former Yugoslavia, Vol I* (New York: Transnational, 1995) 176.

The judges of the ICTY went about this matter with great energy but with little guidance or precedent, starting at the very first plenary meeting in November 1993.[28] A guiding principle was to adopt only measures on which there was broad agreement, ie generally agreed, recognized concepts, and it was deemed important to develop precise and detailed written rules for the principal aspects of the proceedings.[29] The first Rules of Procedure and Evidence were adopted at the second plenary session in February 1994, but they have since been amended numerous times.[30]

It was noted that the procedures were largely adversarial in nature, although with some important deviations, and the intention was to create a purpose-made set of rules, taking into account the special circumstances of the armed conflict at hand and the ICTY's almost complete dependence on state cooperation.[31] The Tribunal was also very much aware of the fact that the accused, and their home states, were likely to be trying to evade international justice and that it would therefore need tools to deal with such matters to the extent permitted by the Statute. The considerations concerning trials *in absentia* should be understood against this background.

The legislative power of the judges in the field of criminal procedures was very broad, but not without certain limitations, such as the requirement that they must be consistent with principles of justice and international law, as guiding principles of the United Nations, and with the Statute.[32] Reportedly the judges also had different principled views on how to approach the exercise—some favoured a more innovative, teleological approach, whereas others preferred a more cautious, strictly constructionalist, or positivist approach—and a balance had to be struck.[33]

The ICTR Rules of Procedure and Evidence were created under quite different circumstances. The ICTR Statute directed the judges to adopt the ICTY Rules of Procedure and Evidence, but allowed them to make 'such changes as they deem necessary'.[34] The main reasons behind this choice were to ensure consistency and to allow the expeditious adoption of the ICTR Rules.[35]

[28] See the 'First Annual Report of the International Tribunal for the Prosecution of Persons Responsible for Serious Violations of International Humanitarian Law in the Territory of the Former Yugoslavia', UN Doc A/49/342-S/1994/1007, paras 52–7.

[29] ibid paras 53 and 57.

[30] On 10 December 2009, the 44th revised version of the ICTY Rules of Procedure and Evidence was adopted (UN Doc IT/32/Rev.44).

[31] ICTY 'First Annual Report' (n 28 above) paras 71–5 and 84–9.

[32] Morris and Scharf (n 27 above) 178–9, also mention, *inter alia*, constraining factors such as not creating new substantive law or imposing new obligations on states, and upholding the independence of the Office of the Prosecutor.

[33] See ICTY 'First Annual Report' (n 28 above) para 53. See also Morris and Scharf (n 27 above) ibid.

[34] ICTR Statute, Art 14.

[35] See V Morris and M Scharf, *The International Criminal Tribunal for Rwanda, Vol 1* (New York: Transnational, 1998) 413.

(2) *Trials* in absentia

The Statutes of the ICTY and ICTR do provide, in line with the International Covenant on Civil and Political Rights (ICCPR), that the accused shall be entitled to be tried 'in his presence'.[36] They do not, however, explicitly prohibit trials *in absentia*, although some argue that such a prohibition follows implicitly from the right to be present and other provisions, in particular the provision of the ICTY Statute which provides for the presence of an accused before the trial date may be set and the trial may commence.[37] The Secretary-General, in his report to the Security Council on the establishment of the ICTY, was of the opinion that a trial 'should not commence until the accused is physically present before the International Criminal Tribunal' and referred to the 'widespread perception' that trials *in absentia* would be incompatible with Article 14 of the ICCPR.[38] This conclusion was reached after the main objectives for such trials—public condemnation or moral sanction and preservation of evidence for future use—had been taken into account.[39] The conclusions of the Secretary-General, as expressed in the report, followed a proposal by France to allow for trials *in absentia*, and opposing views from a number of other states, and as a result the idea was discarded on both legal and political grounds, but primarily the latter.[40]

Against this background of the dependence on state cooperation and the inherent difficulties of actually getting hold of the suspects or accused in practice, the judges of the ICTY were seriously considering allowing trials *in absentia*. The First Annual Report states that 'a provision for trials by default, coupled always with the necessary protections as to due process and a right of review, has a certain attraction'.[41] But for a 'number of reasons', not further elaborated upon, the Tribunal decided not to take this course.[42]

Since there are no public minutes available from these sessions we cannot know for sure how the discussion went or what these reasons were. But there are some accounts of a more anecdotal nature. The question of trials *in absentia* was one of the most important issues when the first Rules of Procedure and Evidence were developed,[43] and according to Judge Gabrielle Kirk McDonald 'one of the most contentious issues'.[44]

[36] ICTY Statute, Art 21(4)(d); and ICTR Statute, Art 20(4)(d).

[37] ICTY Statute, Art 20. See eg S Murphy, 'Progress and Jurisprudence of the International Criminal Tribunal for the Former Yugoslavia' (1999) 93 AJIL 57, 75; and Morris and Scharf (n 35 above) 503.

[38] 'Report of the Secretary-General Pursuant to Paragraph 2 of Security Council's Resolution 808 (1993)', UN Doc S/25704 (1993), para 101.

[39] Morris and Scharf (n 27 above) 215.

[40] See D Shraga and R Zacklin, 'The International Criminal Tribunal for the Former Yugoslavia' (1994) 5 EJIL 360, 376–7.

[41] ICTY 'First Annual Report' (n 28 above) para 90.

[42] ibid.

[43] Morris and Scharf (n 27 above) 180.

[44] G Kirk McDonald, 'Trial Procedures and Practices' in G Kirk McDonald and O Swaak-Goldman (eds), *The Law and Enforcement of International Offences—The Experiences of International and National Courts, Vol. 1* (The Hague: Kluwer, 2000) 554.

Some judges clearly favoured trials *in absentia* and considered this method to be compatible with the ICTY Statute as well as being appropriate.[45] A proposal to provide for such trials in the Rules of Procedure and Evidence was also submitted by France.[46] But others were against this proposal, although not all would exclude trials in the absence of the accused altogether. For example, Judge Kirk McDonald has recalled that she opposed any trial in the absence of the accused, except if he had absconded after submitting himself to the jurisdiction of the Tribunal, and instead proposed a procedure for preservation of evidence in case the accused failed to appear;[47] a precursor to the later compromise on Rule 61 proceedings (see below). But the opponents won the day. Judge Cassese, the first President of the ICTY, has explained that important factors were the primarily adversarial nature of the procedures in combination with 'the unique features of international criminal proceedings'.[48] In particular, the search for and collection of evidence is typically very difficult in international criminal investigations, especially for the defence. As a result, the presence of the accused is crucial to the fairness of the proceedings in order to ensure that instructions can be given to the defence counsel; to promote the effective cross-examination of witnesses; and to provide the accused with the possibility to give evidence at trial if he or she so chooses.

Nevertheless, the prevailing view appears to have been that trials *in absentia* were inappropriate rather than prohibited as such. This view was also explicitly expressed by the ICTY Appeals Chamber in the *Blaškić* case.[49] The Chamber held, *inter alia*, that even if the accused has clearly waived his right to be present at trial, it would be extremely difficult, or even impossible, for the Tribunal to determine the innocence or guilt of that accused.[50] Hence, trials *in absentia* were an option to be considered, which appears to have been discarded for reasons of appropriateness rather than reasons of principle. This said, it probably cannot be ruled out that the ICTY would allow a trial to continue if the accused absconded after it had commenced.[51] As already mentioned, Judge Kirk McDonald was indeed prepared to allow trials *in absentia* under the limited circumstances in which this is normally permissible in common law jurisdictions.

The first Prosecutor, Richard Goldstone, also argued in terms of inappropriateness in his opening statement of the first Rule 61 proceedings, when stating:

> I would submit that other convincing reasons could also have been found to justify the decision not to make provision for trials *in absentia*. Such trials tend not to satisfy calls for

[45] Concerning the arguments for the conclusion that such a trial could and should be introduced, see Morris and Scharf (n 35 above) 503–4.

[46] ibid. See also Pellet (n 12 above) 48.

[47] Kirk McDonald (n 44 above) 555. See also G Kirk McDonald 'Problems, Obstacles and Achievements of the ICTY' (2004) 2 JICJ 558, 561.

[48] Cassese (n 10 above) 392–3.

[49] *Prosecutor v Blaškić* (Appeal Chamber Decision on the Request of the Republic of Croatia for Review of the Decision of Trial Chamber II of 18 July 1997) IT-95-14A (29 October 1997) para 59. See also Zappalà (n 11 above) 126–7.

[50] See *Blaškić* (n 49 above) ibid.

[51] Cassese (n 10 above) 393–4.

justice and create an impression of being 'show trials'. The evidence is untested and any conviction and sentence that may follow are empty shells and would be so perceived. If the person 'convicted' is later arrested and brought for trial the earlier proceedings would have to be disregarded and a trial would begin *de novo*.[52]

Subsequently, the ICTY judges were confronted by an expert group proposal to consider trials *in absentia* under certain circumstances, as a measure to expedite proceedings.[53] However, the judges declined and reportedly concluded that the retrial that would be required once an accused was apprehended would, in fact, tend to increase the workload of the Tribunal.[54]

In case of misconduct, both the ICTY and the ICTR Trial Chambers may order the removal of the accused from the courtroom and continue the proceedings in his or her absence.[55] In practice, moreover, trial proceedings before both the ICTY and the ICTR have been conducted in the absence of the accused when he has boycotted the proceedings or has been unable to take part due to physical or mental ill-health.[56] Allowing an unfit accused to stand trial, even if present in the courtroom, has been equated to allowing trials *in absentia*: the rule that such trials are not permitted 'would appear to be devoid of any substance if it related to the mere physical presence of the accused in court'.[57]

One may note that the ICC Statute, adopted in 1998, explicitly rules out trials *in absentia*, but allows for the removal of a disruptive accused from the trial and provides for the possibility of a hearing to confirm the charges in the absence of the accused.[58] The Special Court for Sierra Leone, which uses the ICTR Rules as its point of departure, has opted to prohibit trials *in absentia* but with two exceptions: if the accused has made his initial appearance before the Court and either refuses to appear at trial or absconds.[59] The Special Court, faced with

[52] *Prosecutor v Nikolić* (Trial Chamber Transcript) IT-94-2-R61 (9 October 1995) 54.

[53] 'Report of the Expert Group' (mandated by the UN General Assembly) UN Doc A/54/634 (22 November 1999) 25.

[54] See D Mundis, 'Improving the Operation and Functioning of the International Criminal Tribunals' (2000) 94 AJIL 759, 760–2.

[55] ICTY, Rule 80(B) and ICTR Rules of Procedure and Evidence, respectively. See further the contribution by Gillian Higgins (Ch 11 above).

[56] eg the accused, Jean-Bosco Barayagwiza, refused to participate in his trial before the ICTR: see W Schabas, *The UN International Criminal Tribunals—The Former Yugoslavia, Rwanda and Sierra Leone* (Cambridge: CUP, 2006) 421 (with references) Barayagwiza's claim that he was illegally convicted after being tried '*in absentia*' has been rejected both on appeal (*Prosecutor v Nahimana et al* (Appeals Chamber Judgment) ICTR-99-52-A (28 November 2007)) and after a motion for review (*Barayagwiza v Prosecutor* (Appeals Chamber Decision on Jean-Bosco Barayagwiza's Motion for Review and/or Reconsideration of the Appeal Judgment of 28 November 2007) ICTR-99-52A-R (22 June 2009)).

[57] *Prosecutor v Strugar* (Trial Chamber Decision Re the Defence Motion to Terminate Proceedings) IT-01-42 (26 May 2004) para 32.

[58] The ICC Statute, Arts 61(2) and 63. On confirmation hearings in the absence of the accused, see also the ICC Rules of Procedure and Evidence, Rules 123–6.

[59] Special Court for Sierra Leone Rules of Procedure and Evidence, Rule 60.

boycotting accused, has also allowed the trial to proceed without the accused being present.[60]

Among hybrid national-international criminal tribunals ('internationalized criminal courts'), different solutions have been chosen. The Special Panels for Serious Crimes in East Timor,[61] as established by the then United Nations administration, and the Extraordinary Chambers in the Courts of Cambodia,[62] established by an agreement with the United Nations, have excluded trials *in absentia*. The Special Tribunal for Lebanon, on the contrary, may allow trial *in absentia*, drawing on the ordinary Lebanese law of criminal procedure.[63]

(3) Rule 61 proceedings

Although trials *in absentia* were ruled out, the judges of both the ICTY and the ICTR decided to introduce special proceedings when arrest warrants, issued upon the confirmation of the indictment by a single judge, could not be executed—so-called Rule 61 proceedings.[64] Rule 61 was introduced in the very first version of the ICTY Rules of Procedure and Evidence.[65] The Rule was amended at the fifth plenary session in January 1995 to provide for examination of witnesses, and further amended at subsequent sessions.[66] It was also included in the original ICTR Rules and was likewise subject to later amendments.[67]

The primary aim of the rule was to address the non-cooperation of some states and it would serve as a method of triggering the reporting to the Security Council of a state's non-compliance with the obligation to cooperate, although other purposes have also been advanced.[68] There were clearly more strategic or political rationales behind Rule 61 as well. Among those were the need to show action and potency in spite of non-cooperation by states; to underline that the absence of the accused was due to the failure of states and not of the Tribunal; to propel the

[60] eg *Prosecutor v Gbao* (Trial Chamber Ruling on the Issue of the Refusal of the Third Accused, Augustine Gbao, to Attend Hearing of the Special Court for Sierra Leone on 7 July 2004 and Succeeding Days) SCSL-04-15 (12 June 2004) para 8.

[61] Art 5 of UNTAET Regulation 2000/03, as amended by Regulation 2001/25.

[62] Rule 81 of the ECCC Internal Rules (rev 2) of 5 September 2008.

[63] The Statute of the Special Tribunal for Lebanon, Art 22; and the Rules of Procedure and Evidence, Rules 106–9. See also C Aptel, 'Some Innovations in the Statute of the Special Tribunal for Lebanon' (2007) 5 JICJ 1107, 1121–2; and P Gaeta 'To Be (Present) or Not To Be (Present)' (2007) 5 JICJ 1165.

[64] The ICTY Rules of Procedure and Evidence, Rule 61; and the ICTR Rules of Procedure and Evidence, Rule 61.

[65] ICTY Rules of Procedure and Evidence, original version (Doc IT/32) adopted on 11 February 1994.

[66] For the history of the ICTY and ICTR Rule 61, see JRWD Jones and S Powles, *International Criminal Practice* (Oxford: OUP, 2003) 567–8. See also 'Second Annual Report of the International Tribunal for the Prosecution of Persons Responsible for Serious Violations of International Humanitarian Law in the Territory of the Former Yugoslavia', UN Doc A/50/365-S/1995/728, para 24.

[67] ICTR Rules of Procedure and Evidence, original version adopted on 29 June 1995.

[68] eg Kirk McDonald (n 47 above) 561–2. See also Zappalà (n 11 above) 127–8.

Security Council to act; and to justify the Tribunal's existence.[69] Moreover, it has been argued that the proceedings also gave some solace to victims, by providing an opportunity to testify, and permitted the Tribunal to publicize its work and make its existence known.[70]

Rule 61 proceedings are held in the absence of the accused and may result in the Trial Chamber finding that 'there are reasonable grounds for believing that the accused has committed all or any of the crimes charged in the indictment', and in the issuance of an international arrest warrant addressed to all states. In addition, the Trial Chamber may order provisional measures to freeze the assets of the accused, without prejudice to the rights of third parties. Another result may be the certification of a state's refusal to cooperate with the Tribunal and the subsequent notice of this determination to the Security Council.

The formal requirements for these proceedings are that the initial arrest warrant has not been executed within a reasonable time, that all reasonable steps to secure the arrest have been taken, and that the whereabouts of the fugitive are unknown. The hearing is held in open court, at which the prosecution presents its evidence and witnesses may be examined. Hence, the proceedings allow for hearing live testimony of witnesses, something which has happened in all ICTY Rule 61 hearings. However, the proceedings do not result in a verdict where guilt or innocence is determined in accordance with the standard of proof for a conviction.

In practice, Rule 61 proceedings were conducted by the ICTY in only a few cases in 1995 and 1996, at a time when very few accused had been arrested and surrendered to the Tribunal.[71] All but one of the accused who were dealt with in this way have subsequently been surrendered to the ICTY and have thereafter been proceeded against like all other accused, including with regard to amendments to indictments. The cases against three of the accused have subsequently resulted in Trial Chamber or Appeals Chamber judgments; in one case (against three accused) the Trial Chamber judgment is currently on appeal. The case against Karadžić has since reached the trial stage. With the second Chief

[69] M Thieroff and E Amley Jr, 'Proceeding to Justice and Accountability in the Balkans: The International Criminal Tribunal for the Former Yugoslavia and Rule 61' (1998) 23 Yale JIL 231, 239–45; and R Kerr, *The International Criminal Tribunal for the Former Yugoslavia: An Exercise in Law, Politics, and Diplomacy* (Oxford: OUP, 2004) 102.

[70] eg *Prosecutor v Karadžić and Mladić* (Trial Chamber Review of the indictment pursuant to Rule 61 of the Rules of Procedure and Evidence) IT-95-5-R61 (11 July 1996) para 3. For a more sceptical view, see eg Thieroff and Amley (n 69 above) 247–50; and S Furuya, 'Rule 61 Procedure in the International Criminal Tribunal for the Former Yugoslavia: A Lesson for the ICC' (1999) 12 LJIL 635, 643–4.

[71] *Prosecutor v Nikolić* (Trial Chamber Review of the indictment pursuant to Rule 61 of the Rules of Procedure and Evidence) IT-94-2-R61 (20 October 1995); *Prosecutor v Martić* (Trial Chamber Decision) IT-95-11 (8 March 1996); *Prosecutor v Mrkšić, Radić & Šljivančanin* (Trial Chamber Decision) IT-95-13 (3 April 1996); *Karadžić and Mladić* (Trial Chamber Review) (n 70 above); *Prosecutor v Rajić* (Trial Chamber Review of the indictments pursuant to Rule 61 of the Rules of Procedure and Evidence) IT-95-12 (13 September 1996). See also F Patel King and A-M La Rosa, 'The Jurisprudence of the Yugoslavia Tribunal: 1994–1996' (1997) 8 EJIL 123.

Prosecutor, Louise Arbour, strongly opposed to this procedure, there were no further Rule 61 hearings after 1996 and a new strategy, indictments issued under seal, was applied instead.[72] She considered the proceedings detrimental to the work of the Prosecutor since they revealed much of the evidence before the apprehension of the accused and were a waste of valuable time and resources.[73] The ICTR has never conducted any Rule 61 proceedings, which is most likely due to the fact that, at an early stage, this Tribunal had a large number of indicted accused in its custody.

The Rule 61 proceedings have not been free from criticism. In fact, only one side of the coin, the prosecution case, is presented in these proceedings. Hence, misgivings have been expressed with respect to the fairness of the proceedings and also to certain claimed purposes behind the procedure.[74] One notable example is the criticism of the view that they may contribute to the establishment of a 'permanent judicial record for all time'.[75] The potential precedental effect of the factual and legal findings in the Rule 61 ruling has also been questioned.[76] But although some of these rulings have indeed been referred to as authoritative,[77] it is reassuring to note that the Trial Chamber judgment in *Mrkšić et al* moves away from the legal findings in the Rule 61 decision (by another Chamber) in the same case.[78]

In addition to their absence, Rule 61 does not allow the accused to be represented by defence counsel in the proceedings, a feature that has been criticized and which does not apply to similar proceedings before the ICC.[79] One reason that has been advanced for this choice is that participation of counsel would make the process too similar to a trial *in absentia*.[80] Another source of criticism has been the non-disclosure of written evidence used in the proceedings.[81] It has

[72] See L Arbour, 'The Crucial Years' (2004) 2 JICJ 396, 398–9.

[73] See ibid. See also Kerr (n 69 above) 100.

[74] eg Thieroff and Amley (n 69 above) 247–50, on what is labelled 'The Truth Commission Analogy'.

[75] cf ICTY Prosecutor Goldstone's opening statement at the first Rule 61 hearing: see *Prosecutor v Nikolić* (Trial Chamber Transcript) IT-94-2-R61 (9 October 1995) 59.

[76] eg Furuya (n 70 above) 645–7 and 649–57: Patel King and La Rosa (n 71 above) 142.

[77] eg *Prosecutor v Tadić* (Trial Chamber Opinion and Judgment) IT-94-1-T (7 May 1997) para 643; *Prosecutor v Galić* (Trial Chamber Judgment and Opinion) IT-98-29-T (5 December 2003) para 57, fn 101; or by indirect reference to the Trial Chamber's findings, *Prosecutor v Galić* (Appeals Chamber Judgment) IT-98-29-A (30 November 2006) para 132.

[78] *Prosecutor v Mrkšić, Radić and Šljivančanin* (Trial Chamber Judgment) IT-95-13/1-T (25 September 2007) paras 448–56.

[79] eg Jones and Powles (n 66 above) 570 (with further references to ICTY decisions). See also A Klip, 'Witnesses before the International Criminal Tribunal for the Former Yugoslavia' (1996) 67 *Revue internationale de droit pénal* 267; Furuya (n 70 above) 666; Kerr (n 69 above) 101. Cf the ICC Statute, Art 61(2). In case a trial *in absentia* is allowed at the Special Court for Sierra Leone, the accused may also be represented by counsel: SCSL Rules of Procedure and Evidence, Rule 60(B).

[80] See A Quintal, 'Rule 61: The "Voice of the Victims" Screams Out for Justice' (1998) 36 Col JTL 723, 757.

[81] eg F Patel King, 'Public Disclosure in Rule 61 Proceedings before the International Criminal Tribunal for the Former Yugoslavia' (1997) 29 *NYU Journal of International Law and Politics* 523.

also been argued that counsel for the prosecution may be given 'a false sense of security and confidence in the quality of their case' since unopposed and unchallenged evidence looks better than it is.[82]

Some observers have concluded that the ICTY Rule 61 hearings were held 'as sort of trials *in absentia*, to redress the imbalance created by so many indictees remaining at large'.[83] This is particularly evident when compared to the Rwanda situation, where the suspected *génocidaires* had lost the conflict and thus were more likely to be surrendered to the Tribunal. And the proceedings do undoubtedly have certain trial-like features, such as live witness testimony. But the ICTY Trial Chambers have been cautious to note that the procedures did not constitute a trial *in absentia*.[84] One judge went further in his separate opinion to one of the decisions and categorized Rule 61 as 'basically an apology for this Tribunal's helplessness in not being able to effectively carry out its duties', and a second-best method 'to inform the world, through open hearings, of the terrible crimes with which the accused is charged and the evidence against the accused that would support his conviction at trial'.[85]

The solution has often been referred to as 'innovative', 'imaginative', or 'unique'.[86] Nonetheless, the Rule 61 proceedings are not entirely novel when compared to national procedures, and it has been noted that they are 'somewhat akin' to so-called committal proceedings (transfer of a case from one court to another for trial) that exist, *inter alia*, in England and Wales.[87] It has also been observed that there are procedural similarities with federal grand jury hearings under United States law, but that the two procedures diverge on the philosophy of purpose: while the grand jury is a proactive mechanism to prevent government overreaching and false claims, Rule 61 proceedings are meant to publicize the alleged acts of the accused and prompt all nations to find and arrest him or her.[88]

D. Approaches in national law

In some states the right of the accused to be present at trial is set forth in the constitution. In an extensive survey of national constitutions, Cherif Bassiouni

[82] Arbour (n 72 above) 399.

[83] See Jones and Powles (n 66 above) 569; Thieroff and Amley (n 69 above) 258–60.

[84] eg *Rajić* (Trial Chamber Review) (n 71 above) para 3; *Nikolić* (Trial Chamber Review) (n 71 above) para 3.

[85] *Rajić* (Trial Chamber Review—Separate Opinion by Judge Sidhwa) (n 71 above) para 7.

[86] eg Thieroff and Amley (n 69 above) 274; Furuya (n 70 above) 637; and Cassese (n 10 above) 393.

[87] *Rajić* (Trial Chamber Review—Separate Opinion by Judge Sidhwa) (n 71 above) para 9. See also Jones and Powles (n 66 above) 569–70.

[88] See B Hildreth, 'Hunting the Hunters: The United Nations Unleashes Its Latest Weapon in the Fight Against Fugitive War Crimes Suspects—Rule 61' (1998) 6 *Tulane Journal of International and Comparative Law* 499, 516.

has identified 25 constitutions which enshrine this as a fundamental right, although some of them also acknowledge certain exceptions.[89]

There is clearly a division between the two traditional models for criminal trials—the adversarial model and the inquisitorial model—with respect to the views concerning trials *in absentia*.[90] One explanation offered relates to the overall purpose of the trial: to punish the offender or to ascertain the truth.[91] However, both models should be considered as truth seeking, as well as efficiency seeking, and it is difficult to conclude that one is more inclined towards punishment than the other. Hence, other explanations should be explored. The most obvious one is that the adversarial model presupposes the participation of both adversaries, each gathering evidence and presenting its case to the court.[92] The inquisitorial model, on the other hand, has an investigating judge or the prosecutor who conducts the investigation and collects evidence also to the benefit of the defendant, which means the disadvantage of the accused's absence can be said to be less pronounced.

This is too simple an explanation.[93] Traditionally, trials *in absentia* were banned in common law, but over time many national jurisdictions have allowed certain exceptions. Today English law accepts that a trial may continue, and even commence in some circumstances, in the absence of the accused, if he or she has waived the right to be present,[94] while Scottish law prohibits trials (on indictment) in the absence of the defendant.[95] In the United States, trials may proceed if the accused has absconded voluntarily[96] or when he or she acts disruptively.[97] A similar jurisprudence has been developed in Australia.[98]

[89] M Cherif Bassiouni, 'Human Rights in the Context of Criminal Justice: Identifying International Procedural Protections and Equivalent Protections in National Constitutions' (1993) 3 Duke JICL 235, 279–80.

[90] Of the 25 national constitutions identified by Bassiouni (ibid), almost all belonged to states with common law systems; the states were: Albania, Antigua and Barbuda, Bahamas, Barbados, Belize, Botswana, Dominica, Equatorial Guinea, Fiji, Gambia, Grenada, Guyana, Kenya, Kiribati, Malta, Mauritius, Nauru, Papua New Guinea, St Christopher-Nevis, Solomon Islands, Swaziland, Tuvalu, Uganda, Zambia, and Zimbabwe.

[91] See Zappalà (n 11 above) 128.

[92] eg Cassese (n 10 above) 389.

[93] See also Council of Europe, *Judgments* in Absentia, European Committee on Crime Problems (CDPC), Committee of Experts on the Operation of European Conventions in the Penal Field (PC-OC), Secretariat Memorandum prepared by the Directorate of Legal Affairs, 3 March 1998 (doc PC-OC(98)7) 2.

[94] See eg the House of Lords in *R v Jones (Anthony William)* [2002] UKHL 5, [2002] 2 WLR 524 (HL). See also PW Ferguson, 'Trial in Absence and Waiver of Human Rights' (July 2002) *Criminal Law Review* 554–65.

[95] With the exception of unruly defendants: see Criminal Procedure (Scotland) Act 1995, s 153(1).

[96] eg *Diaz v United States* 223 US 442 (1912); and *Kirk v Dutton* (1994) WL 561146 (6th Cir) 11 Oct 1994, cert denied, 514 US 1129 (1995).

[97] eg *Illinois v Allen* 397 US 337 (1970). On US law in this respect, see also D Brown, 'The International Criminal Court and Trial *in Absentia*' (1999) 24 *Brooklyn Journal of International Law* 763.

[98] eg *R v McHardie and Danielson* (1983) 2 NSWLR 733.

Among civil law jurisdictions, one may note that French law allows a trial to result in a verdict and sentence if the defendant, with knowledge of the summons, does not appear without having a valid excuse or after expressing the wish to be judged in his or her absence.[99] In such cases, however, the process is still considered adversarial (*contradictoire*) and the judgment will not be set aside automatically on request, as in the case of a proper conviction by default, the latter applying when the trial is held and judgment rendered without it having been established that the defendant knew of the summons.[100] The scope for trials *in absentia* under Italian criminal procedures is far-reaching and the mechanism is often relied upon in practice. This is reflected in the number of Italian cases on this matter before the European Court of Human Rights and the fact that Italy was the country employing the special rule on delayed implementation of the EU Framework decision on trials *in absentia*.[101] Spanish law, on the other hand, prohibits trials *in absentia*, except for certain strict exceptions.[102]

In German law, the principle is that the main hearing may not commence without the defendant being present, but the trial may continue if he or she has voluntarily waived the right to be present.[103] Trials *in absentia* were also permitted under the law of the former Yugoslavia where the accused had fled or concealed himself in order to avoid prosecution, and there were 'particularly important reasons for trial *in absentia*'.[104]

In some jurisdictions, trials in the absence of the accused are allowed primarily with respect to less serious and less complex offences. Swedish law, for example, permits trials *in absentia* if the matter nonetheless 'can be satisfactorily investigated' and there is no ground to impose a longer custodial sentence than three months, although a longer sentence may be imposed if the defendant has absconded or suffers from a serious mental disturbance.[105] Hence, while it is true that many civil law jurisdictions are more inclined to accept more far-reaching trials *in absentia* than is normally the case in common law jurisdictions, there are notable differences within the 'legal families' due to other influences and considerations. Moreover, states belonging to the different legal traditions and with varying views of such trials have adhered to international human rights instruments setting forth the accused's right of presence at trial.[106] Consequently, they have all considered their own system to be compatible with this right. Hence,

[99] French Code of Criminal Procedure (*Code de procédure pénale*), arts 410–11.

[100] ibid arts 412 and 487. See also arts 489, 494, and 494–1 on repeated absence.

[101] See n 20 above.

[102] Spanish Code of Criminal Procedure (*Ley de enjuiciamiento criminal*), arts 786 and 841.

[103] German Code of Criminal Procedure (*Strafprozessordnung, StPO*), § 230–9.

[104] Federal Republic of Yugoslavia Code of Criminal Procedure, art 300. Similarly, the 2006 Criminal Procedural Code of the Republic of Serbia, art 328 provides for such trials: 'if he is at large or is otherwise not accessible to government authorities, provided that particularly important reasons exist to try him *in absentia*' (unofficial translation).

[105] Swedish Code of Judicial Procedure (*rättegångsbalken*) Ch 44, s 15.

[106] See section E herein.

a comparative legal analysis would not resolve the issue when the judges of the ICTY and the ICTR were seeking to determine the most appropriate approach to be taken.

E. Approaches by international human rights bodies

Article 14(3)(d) of the ICCPR provides that: '[e]veryone charged with a criminal offence shall have the right... to be tried in his presence'.[107] The Human Rights Committee has been required to determine whether trials *in absentia* are compatible with the right of the accused to appear at trial. Of course, well aware of the different domestic views and approaches, the Committee has found that such trials may be acceptable under certain circumstances 'in the interest of the proper administration of justice'.[108] The reasons for the absence are of importance and a trial *in absentia* is permissible, for example, 'when the accused person, although informed of the proceedings sufficiently in advance, declines to exercise his right to be present'.[109] But even if the person was not summoned in a timely manner and informed of the proceedings against him, and thus the right to be present at trial was violated, the violation may be remedied if the accused is entitled to a retrial in his presence.[110] After being present at the trial, the subsequent sentencing *in absentia* has not been considered a violation of the accused's right to be present.[111]

The European Convention on Human Rights (ECHR),[112] in contrast, does not explicitly set forth the right to be present at one's trial. Based on an overall assessment of the object and purpose of the fair trial guarantees in Article 6 of the ECHR, however, the European Court of Human Rights has concluded that a person charged with a criminal offence has the right to be present at trial.[113] Moreover, the right to 'effective participation' in a criminal trial includes not only presence but also the ability 'to hear and follow the proceedings'.[114] This, however, has not led the Court to the conclusion that trials *in absentia* are incompatible with the Convention *per se* the Convention is not to be interpreted 'in a way which would entirely overthrow the traditions of national legislation'.[115]

Instead, the European Court of Human Rights has focused on establishing conditions under which trials *in absentia* are considered compatible with the fair

[107] International Covenant on Civil and Political Rights (16 December 1966) 999 UNTS 171.
[108] eg *Mbenge v Zaire* (decision 25 March 1983; UN Doc CCPR/C/18/D/16/1977) para 14.1.
[109] ibid.
[110] *Maleki v Italy* (decision 15 July 1999; UN Doc CCPR/C/60/D/699/1996) para 9.5.
[111] *Weiss v Austria* (decision 3 April 2003; UN Doc CCPR/C/77/D/1086/2002) para 9.2.
[112] Convention for the Protection of Human Rights and Fundamental Freedoms of 4 November 1950, European Treaty Series (ETS) No 5.
[113] First established in *Colozza v Italy* (n 8 above) para 27, and later upheld in, *inter alia*, *Monnell and Morris v United Kingdom* (App No 115) ECHR 2 March 1987, para 56.
[114] *Stanford v United Kingdom* (App No 282-A) ECHR 23 February 1994, para 26.
[115] S Trechsel, *Human Rights in Criminal Proceedings* (Oxford: OUP, 2005) 254.

trial rights of the ECHR. This approach is in line with a Resolution adopted by the Committee of Ministers of the Council of Europe which sets forth criteria for proceedings held *in absentia*.[116] The possibility of a retrial, ie a fresh determination of the merits of the charge, both in law and in fact, is considered fundamentally important.[117] The right to be present, either during the original proceedings or in a retrial, is considered an essential element of fair trial rights.[118] Often a short time limit applies from the formal notification of the judgment on a trial *in absentia*, but this has been accepted and a failure to make use of the possibility to obtain a retrial may be considered as a waiver, although a waiver must be established in an unequivocal manner and be attended by certain safeguards.[119] But even without a possibility of a retrial, the Court has accepted trials *in absentia* if the absence of the accused is his or her deliberate decision.[120]

Consequently, the notification of, or attempts to notify, the accused not only of the charges but also the coming trial (or possibility to obtain a retrial) is of decisive importance. The European Court of Human Rights has furthermore held that it is the state, not the person concerned, that must demonstrate that he or she was aware of the date of the trial.[121] However, it is thereafter for the authorities to assess whether the accused showed good cause for his or her absence or any circumstances warranting the finding that the absence was for reasons beyond his or her control.[122] Moreover, the Court has concluded that a person charged with a criminal offence has a right, albeit not absolute, to be effectively defended by a lawyer and that he or she does not lose the benefit of this right merely on account of not being present at the trial.[123]

In conclusion, both the Human Rights Committee and the European Court of Human Rights have accepted trials *in absentia* as compatible with the fundamental right of the accused to be present at trial, but only if certain procedural safeguards are observed. These safeguards could surely have been met had the judges of the ICTY and the ICTR decided to allow such trials.

III. Evaluation of ICTY and ICTR Practice

Legislation is not a simple matter. It is one thing to reach a reasonable solution in the case at hand but quite another to establish rules that will stand the test of time and provide acceptable results although the circumstances may vary. The

[116] Resolution 75(11) on the criteria governing proceedings held in the absence of the accused, adopted by the Committee of Ministers on 21 May 1975.

[117] eg *Colozza v Italy* (n 8 above) para 29.

[118] eg *Stoichkov v Bulgaria* [2005] ECHR 9808/02 (24 March 2005) para 56.

[119] eg *Colozza v Italy* (n 8 above) para 28; *Poitrimol v France* (App No 277-A) ECHR 23 November 1993, para 31.

[120] eg *Poitrimol v France* (n 119 above) para 30.

[121] eg *FCB v Italy* (App No 208-B) ECHR 28 August 1991, para 35.

[122] eg *Medenica v Switzerland* (App No 20491/92) ECHR 2001-VI 14 June 2001, para 57.

[123] eg *Sejdovic v Italy* (App No 56581/00) ECHR 1 March 2006, para 91.

judges of the ICTY and ICTR were faced with this challenge when establishing the Rules of Procedure and Evidence. In addition, they had to find solutions that were acceptable to all of them—a situation similar to that faced by the states negotiating the ICC Statute—and to observers from across the globe in order to safeguard the legitimacy of the Tribunals as proper criminal courts.

Both Tribunals have refrained from introducing trials *in absentia* as a means to raise the stakes for fugitive offenders, put pressure on states to cooperate, and the Security Council to react to non-cooperation, and to show that they are not paper tigers. Antonio Cassese has convincingly argued that the ICTY judges were not prevented by law from allowing trials *in absentia* but that, even so, it was reasonable to decline this tool due to the fact that the 'combination of the demands and implications of the adversarial system with the unique features of international criminal proceedings' may make the presence of the defendant at trial, before it commences, indispensable.[124] In particular, the search for and collection of evidence may be very difficult in international trials, since the court is often far away from the crime scene, witnesses may reside in many countries, there is no investigating judge to assist, the defence has a limited investigative capacity, and there is a long time lapse between the event and the court proceedings. Hence, there was a conscious choice to avoid resorting to a rather extreme and controversial procedural solution, and in the words of a later ICTY President, Theodor Meron, 'thus risking the tribunal's credibility, its most precious asset'.[125]

Instead the Tribunals, in practice only the ICTY, resorted to the compromise solution: the Rule 61 proceedings. They represent a compromise in many different ways, and certainly lend themselves to criticisms, and, indeed, most commentators have been critical.[126] Many argue that the Rule 61 proceedings are in fact a version of trials *in absentia*, although without a verdict and sentence, and so in spite of the Trial Chambers being careful to stress that this is not the case, they at least share many features with such trials.[127] Others have held that the creation of a 'public record', the fact-finding function, makes the process much akin to a truth commission, rather than that of a criminal court.[128] In addition, and as mentioned above, some procedural features of the Rule 61 proceedings—such as the one-sidedness of the evidence, the non-participation of defence counsel, and the disclosure regime—may be criticized.

Some proponents of ICTY trials *in absentia*, especially France, were disappointed with this compromise, claiming that the Rule 61 proceedings were a legal aberration and a substitute that satisfied no one.[129] Others came to the conclusion

[124] Cassese (n 10 above) 392–3.

[125] T Meron, 'Answering for War Crimes: Lessons from the Balkans' (1997) 76 *Foreign Affairs* 2, 4.

[126] See eg Pellet (n 12 above); Schabas (n 13 above); Thieroff and Amley (n 69 above); Furuya (n 70 above); Klip (n 79 above); and Patel King (n 81 above).

[127] eg Schabas (n 13 above) 351–3.

[128] eg Quintal (n 80 above) 750–6.

[129] eg H Ascensio and A Pellet, 'L'activité du Tribunal pénal international pour l'ex-Yougoslavie (1993–1995)' (1995) *Annuaire français de droit international* 101, 110; and Pellet (n 12 above) 48.

that they still turned out to be useful; the proceedings maintained and even intensified the pressure on the accused, pending political developments allowing for their arrest.[130]

Moreover, even some of the harshest critics of the rationales (and politics) behind the Rule 61 proceedings, and the procedural solutions, acknowledge that this procedural device should not be considered as a failure.[131] It was an attempt to meet the need to put pressure on uncooperative states, while at the same time ensuring the legality (and more general legal acceptance) of the solution. It was crafted as a compromise between a common law view disfavouring trials *in absentia* (ending in a judgment and sentence) and a civil law view which considers such trials essential for the proper functioning of the Tribunals. Leaving aside some of the procedural features, much of the criticism has targeted the Rule 61 proceedings when seen as an end in themselves. Although various statements by the ICTY, including some from judges and prosecutors, indicate that that was the case, a better understanding of this procedural mechanism is to consider it, arguably, a means for bringing about arrests and subsequent full-blown trials. However, such statements, most likely aimed at making the procedure more attractive, may instead have done the rule a disfavour.

With the benefit of hindsight, one may conclude that other procedural vehicles proved more successful for securing arrests, in particular the use of sealed indictments. But the mere fact that the rule existed, and was employed, exposed the ICTY's determination to pursue its indictments and to agitate for action by those who could and should assist, underpinned by public and live evidence. Hence, Rule 61 should be understood and assessed in systemic and political terms, rather than in legal terms. This is clearly a task for a legislator, but not necessarily one that sits comfortably with the role of a judge.

IV. Conclusion

In line with the tradition of international courts in general, the procedures of the ICTY and ICTR were essentially left to the judges to decide. Regardless of whether one considers this a cause for concern, the approach appears difficult to avoid in practice; even the criminal procedures of the ICC, where the negotiating states really tried to provide a comprehensive codification, leave much room for judicial interpretation and lawmaking. State-drafted procedures will inevitably include compromises, which in part are the result of preferences stemming from the different domestic legal traditions.

[130] eg P Tavernier, 'The Experience of the International Criminal Tribunals for the Former Yugoslavia and for Rwanda' (November 1997) 321 IRRC 605.

[131] eg Thieroff and Amley (n 69 above) 274.

Nonetheless, an international criminal court requires clear, predictable, fair, and effective procedures. Against the limited directions given in the Statutes, and the fact that the judges have also had to bridge the different legal traditions, the judges of the ICTY and ICTR have arguably taken a serious and responsible approach to the creation of procedural rules for the Tribunals. The approach to trials *in absentia* and the so-called Rule 61 proceedings may serve as an example.

The survey above shows that trials *in absentia* exist domestically and it is clear that they may serve a purpose for a tribunal which is completely dependent on the cooperation of others for the arrest and surrender of suspected or accused persons. However, such trials are controversial and domestic practices differ fundamentally. The judges of the Tribunals refrained, on balance, from introducing this procedural mechanism. Instead, the proceedings conducted 'in lieu' of trials *in absentia*—the Rule 61 proceedings—represent an attempt to find a compromise between the different legal traditions and approaches to such trials. Although these proceedings give rise to questions concerning their purpose and procedural efficiency, this compromise is arguably a reasonable one. Moreover, and confirming this conclusion, the compromise solution adopted for the ICC is very similar to the Rule 61 proceedings.

In conclusion, the judges of international criminal courts will, in practice, always be tasked with a degree of procedural lawmaking, either through an extensive scope for interpretation of given rules or by explicit powers. Whether one is comfortable with this or not depends, at least in part, on one's own domestic legal inheritance. Regardless of this, however, the examples in this chapter affirm that the judges of the ICTY and ICTR have made serious efforts to find broadly acceptable solutions, something that is generally a difficult exercise with respect to criminal procedures.

15

The Judicial Role in the Definition and Implementation of the Completion Strategies of the International Criminal Tribunals

Fidelma Donlon

I. Introduction

As the International Criminal Tribunals for the former Yugoslavia and Rwanda approach the end-date of their judicial operations, the discourse regarding their legacies is gaining momentum. It is unquestionable that the judges of the *ad hoc* Tribunals have shaped a corpus of international law which will provide guidance to the International Criminal Court, existing and future hybrid institutions, as well as national courts. Shortly after the International Criminal Tribunal for the former Yugoslavia (ICTY) was created the judges drafted a set of international criminal procedural rules in the form of the Rules of Procedure and Evidence.[1] The first version of the Rules of Procedure and Evidence of the International Criminal Tribunal for Rwanda (ICTR) was essentially copied from the ICTY Rules. Subsequently, the judges of the *ad hoc* Tribunals have frequently amended the rules of the respective institutions to best cater for the unique demands of international criminal trials. Accordingly, it is no surprise that the jurisprudential

[1] See Statute of the International Tribunal for the Prosecution of Persons Responsible for Serious Violations of International Humanitarian Law Committed in the Territory of the Former Yugoslavia since 1991, UN Doc S/25704 (1993) Annex, 36; and UN Doc S/RES/827 (1993). See also Statute of the International Tribunal for Rwanda: UN Doc S/RES/955 (1994) Annex, 3. The ICTY Statute, Art 15 and the ICTR Statute, Art 14 provide that the judges of the Tribunals shall adopt rules of procedure and evidence for the conduct of pre-trial proceedings, trials and appeals, the admission of evidence, the protection of victims and witnesses, and other appropriate matters. The ICTY and the ICTR Rules of Procedure and Evidence (RPE), Rule 6(A) provides that the Rules may be amended if agreed to by not less than ten permanent judges at a plenary meeting or in accordance with RPE Rule 6(B) an amendment may otherwise be adopted if it is unanimously approved by the permanent judges. For further discussion relating to the development of the Rules of Procedure and Evidence, see the contributions of Göran Sluiter and Håkan Friman (Chs 13 and 14 above).

legacy of the Tribunals, together with the essential contribution made by the judges in terms of defining the Tribunals' criminal procedures during the set-up years, is widely focused upon by practitioners and academics.[2]

Much less analysed, however, is the instrumental and intriguing role played by the judges in relation to the closure of the ICTY and the ICTR. In fact, the comprehensive completion strategy designed to conclude the Tribunals' mandates can in many ways be attributed to the ICTY judges. In addition, as the procedural lawmakers of the Tribunals, the judges have not only defined the regulations required for the conduct of fair criminal trials, by amending Rule 11*bis* of the Rules of Procedure and Evidence the judges have created one of the most critical legal mechanisms required to implement the completion strategy. They have empowered the Tribunals to refer the cases of intermediate and lower-level accused to the authorities of a willing and adequately prepared state for trial.

Unlike the International Criminal Court, the ICTY and the ICTR were not intended to be permanent institutions; hence, the courts must complete their missions at some point in the future. The ICTY has jurisdiction over crimes committed 'between 1 January 1991 and a date to be determined by the Security Council upon the restoration of peace' in the former Yugoslavia.[3] The temporal jurisdiction of the ICTR is more specific and it is not linked to the restoration of peace in the African Great Lakes region. Instead the Rwanda Tribunal is competent to deal with offences committed between 1 January and 31 December 1994.[4] Yet, as one eminent academic has pointedly observed: 'It would seem that *ad hoc* tribunals are almost by definition confronted with the difficulty of knowing when to stop.'[5] Nevertheless, the first detailed plan to end the mission of the ICTY originated from within the Tribunal and was presented to the Security Council by the former President, Judge Claude Jorda. Defining the completion strategy and winding-down of the judicial operations of the Tribunals is an arduous task. After all, as Judge David Hunt once remarked, the ICTY 'will not be judged by the number of convictions which it enters, or by the speed with which it concludes the Completion Strategy which the Security Council has endorsed, but by the fairness of its trials'.[6] In August 2003, the timeline to end the temporal

[2] For an in-depth study of the jurisprudential legacy of the Tribunals, see W Schabas, *The UN International Criminal Tribunals— The Former Yugoslavia, Rwanda and Sierra Leone* (Cambridge: CUP, 2006); A Zahar and G Sluiter, *International Criminal Law: A Critical Introduction* (Oxford: OUP, 2008); A Cassese, *International Criminal Law* (Oxford: OUP, 2003).

[3] UN Doc S/RES/827 (1993) para 2.

[4] UN Doc S/RES/955 (1994) para 1 and ICTR Statute, Art 1.

[5] Schabas (n 2 above) 40.

[6] *Prosecutor v Milošević* (Dissenting Opinion of Judge David Hunt on Admissibility of Evidence-In-Chief in the form of Written Statements) IT-02-54-AR73.4 (21 October 2003; Majority Decision given 30 September 2003) paras 20–22. In his dissent Judge Hunt sternly criticized his fellow Appeals Chamber judges in relation to their interpretation of Rule 92*bis*. He stated that the majority Appeals Chamber decision drove a 'horse and cart' through the previous interpretation of Rule 92*bis* regulating the admission of written statements in lieu of oral testimony, which resulted in a violation of the rights of the accused. Judge Hunt opined that the only reasonable explanation

jurisdiction of the Tribunals was included for the first time in a Security Council resolution. Resolution 1503 called upon the Yugoslavia and Rwanda Tribunals to complete all investigations by the end of 2004, all first instance trials by the end of 2008, and all work in 2010.[7] To achieve these timelines, the Tribunals were directed by the Council to concentrate on the prosecution and trial of the most senior leaders most responsible for crimes within their jurisdiction and to refer cases involving those who did not bear this level of responsibility to national jurisdictions.

The central theme examined in this chapter is the distinct and dynamic part played by the Tribunals' judges, in particular the ICTY judges, in the development and implementation of the completion strategies. Section I will analyse the genesis and evolution of the strategies to identify the contribution made by the judges to the formulation of the policy required to end the missions of the *ad hoc* Tribunals. The chapter will further explore the various measures taken by the Security Council to expedite the winding-down process of the Tribunals' operations, in particular, the directives to concentrate prosecution and trials on the most senior leaders and refer intermediate and lower-rank accused to national courts for trial. The Security Council did not amend the Tribunals' Statutes to create a statutory limitation on the level of accused to be prosecuted or to legislate for the formal referral process. Thus, section II will explore the idea that, although the *political* driving force behind the completion strategies was and still remains the Security Council, the *policy* driving force and the key procedural legislator underpinning the strategies are the judges of the *ad hoc* Tribunals. This notion will be considered via a detailed examination of the purpose and intent of the procedural law created by the judges to regulate the far-reaching referral process. In this respect, Rule 11*bis* of the ICTY and ICTR Rules will be extensively examined. The discussion will then move on to consider, in section III, the steps taken by the ICTY judges to define the Tribunal's prosecutorial policy at two key moments in the history of the institution. The disparity of opinion between the judges of the Yugoslavia and Rwanda Tribunals in relation to the extent to which they were prepared to amend the Rules of procedure and Evidence to ensure the application of the seniority criterion by the prosecutor will also be addressed. The amendment of the ICTY's Rule 28(A) will be discussed in this regard. Finally,

for this appeared to be a desire to assist the prosecution in bringing the completion strategy to a rapid conclusion. However, in his separate opinion, Judge Shahabuddeen noted that it was not surprising that the completion strategy had not been mentioned in the majority decision. He noted that it had not been referred to in the decision as it had nothing to do with the matter. Judge Shahabuddeen remarked that the reasoning set out in the majority decision left no room for a judicial finding that the completion strategy had been taken into account. See *Prosecutor v Milošević* (Separate Opinion of Judge Shahabuddeen Appended to Appeals Chamber's Decision dated 30 September 2003 on Admissibility of Evidence-In-Chief in the form of Written Statements) IT-02-54-AR73.4 (31 October 2003) para 21.

[7] UN Doc S/RES 1503 (2003) preamble.

the chapter will briefly survey the completion strategies as a catalyst for judicial reform in Bosnia and Rwanda.

II. The Origins and Evolution of the Completion Strategies: The Judges' Contribution

As early as 1998, officials and member states of the Security Council voiced their unease regarding the slowness of the ICTY and ICTR proceedings; the associated length of detention of accused; the rising budgets of the Tribunals; and the time that would be required to finally complete their mandates.[8] The former United Nations legal adviser, Ralph Zacklin, later remarked: 'The *ad hoc* Tribunals have been too costly, too inefficient and too ineffective. As mechanisms for dealing with justice in post-conflict societies, they exemplify an approach that is no longer politically or financially viable.'[9] But the most contentious question was why, after almost seven years of operations and expenditures totaling US$400 million, only 15 trials had been completed by the *ad hoc* Tribunals.[10] Thus, in 1998, the General Assembly, following the advice of the Fifth Committee responsible for the financing of the Tribunals, requested the Secretary-General to carry out a review of their functioning and operations.[11] In 2000, the Expert Group appointed by the Secretary-General to evaluate the effective work of the institutions noted in their final report that, although trials could be made more efficient, until the 'winding-down process' started, the financial resources required to fund the Tribunals could not be reduced.[12]

The judges of the Yugoslavia Tribunal were also tackling the question of winding-down judicial operations at that time. Shortly after he was elected President of the ICTY, one of the most influential figures involved in the evolution of the completion strategy, Judge Claude Jorda, observed that the ICTY was 'at a turning point in its history'.[13] Noting the very high costs associated with international justice and the Tribunal's obligation to the international community, Judge Jorda identified setting a time frame for the completion of the ICTY's mission as one of his primary objectives. The President also indicated that to expedite proceedings

[8] See generally, D Raab, 'Evaluating the ICTY and its Completion Strategy Efforts to Achieve Accountability for War Crimes and their Tribunals' (2005) 3 JICJ 82–102. See also C Aptel, 'Closing the UN International Criminal Tribunal for Rwanda: Completion Strategy and Residual Issues' (2008) 14 *New England Journal of International and Comparative Law* 169, 170–1.

[9] See R Zacklin, 'The Failings of *Ad hoc* International Tribunals' (2004) 2 JICJ 541, 545.

[10] See 'Report of the Expert Group to Conduct a Review of the Effective Operation and Functioning of the International Tribunal for the Former Yugoslavia and the International Criminal Tribunal for Rwanda', UN Doc S/2000/597 (2000) para 35.

[11] UN Doc A/RES/53/212 (1999) para 5.

[12] See 'Report of the Expert Group' (n 10 above) para 262.

[13] ICTY Press Release, 'Statement by Judge Claude Jorda, President of the International Criminal Tribunal for the Former Yugoslavia', CC/P.I.S/466-E (27 January 2000).

and improve pre-trial case management in the future, 'maximum use needs to be made of [the] Rules of Procedure and Evidence'.[14] Subsequently, the judges undertook an analysis of all possible measures available to the Tribunal to enable it to manage its overburdened workload efficiently. The efforts of the ICTY judges culminated in the presentation of a report by President Jorda to the Security Council in 2000 which indicated that the Tribunal would not be able to complete judicial activities before 2016, unless certain measures were approved by the Council.[15] Three measures were proposed by the judges to accelerate the completion of trials. The first measure involved conferring on senior legal officers the authority to take certain decisions regarding the conduct of pre-trial proceedings (setting deadlines, hearing witnesses by deposition, etc).[16] Secondly, the creation of a pool of *ad litem* judges to increase trial capacity was suggested.[17] Finally, it was proposed that the Appeals Chamber would be enlarged.

Another measure and a flavour of, in this author's opinion, the most far-reaching component of the ICTY completion strategy—the transfer of cases to the Balkan states as a means to reduce the Tribunal's caseload—was suggested to the Security Council for the first time in the report. Drawing on what they referred to as the Nuremberg model, the judges discussed the possibility of the ICTY concentrating 'on a restricted number of high-ranking leaders' and transferring 'lower ranking criminals' to the Balkan states.[18] This measure was no doubt rooted in the growing consensus among the judges of the *ad hoc* Tribunals that, in spite of the importance of creating an international jurisprudence and of victims seeing the trial of perpetrators, 'the major objectives of the Security Council are in large part not fulfilled if only low-level figures rather than the civilian, military and paramilitary leaders who were allegedly responsible for the atrocities are brought before the Tribunals for trial'.[19] Although the transfer of cases from the ICTY to national authorities would have undoubtedly reduced the Tribunal's caseload and thus the time needed to complete its mission, due to the volatile political climate in the Balkans and security concerns for witnesses, victims, and accused, the ICTY judges did not support this measure in 2000.[20]

Nevertheless, the Security Council responded positively to the other measures suggested by the judges by adopting Resolution 1329. To enable the Tribunals to expedite the conclusion of their work at the earliest time, the Council amended the ICTY Statute to establish a pool of *ad litem* judges.[21] In addition, the Statutes

[14] ibid.

[15] See 'Report of the International Tribunal for the Prosecution of Persons Responsible for Serious Violations of International Humanitarian Law Committed in the Territory of the Former Yugoslavia since 1991', UN Doc S/2000/865 (2000) para 35.

[16] ibid para 97.

[17] ibid paras 106–127.

[18] ibid paras 56–7.

[19] See 'Report of the Expert Group' (n 10 above) para 96.

[20] See 'Report of the International Tribunal' (n 15 above) paras 53–4.

[21] UN Doc S/RES 1329 (2000) paras 1 and 4.

of the ICTY and ICTR were amended to enlarge the Appeals Chambers.[22] Interestingly, in Resolution 1329 although the Council took note of the Tribunals' position that senior leaders should be tried before them rather than minor actors, it did not go so far as to direct the *ad hoc* Tribunals to concentrate indictments on this category of offender and transfer other cases to national courts.[23] Instead, the Council recalled the concurrent jurisdiction exercised by the Tribunals with national courts and noted ICTY Rule 11*bis* which at that time authorized a Trial Chamber to suspend an indictment to allow a national court to process a case.[24]

The concept of completing the work of the *ad hoc* Tribunals appears to have gained some traction with the ICTR judges in 2001. The former President of the Rwanda Tribunal, Judge Erik Møse, has reported that when the judges of the two Tribunals met in Dublin there appeared to be broad consensus that it was time to contemplate the life span of the two institutions possibly by 'reviewing the prosecutorial policy or setting a target date for the filing of the last indictment'.[25] In a subsequent address to the Security Council, President Jorda reiterated the judges' view that the ICTY should focus more on cases involving high-ranking military and political officials.[26] Under certain conditions, cases involving lower-level perpetrators could be transferred to the Balkan states. An indication of the willingness of the ICTY judges to use their authority as the Tribunal's procedural lawmakers to create a legal mechanism for the transfer of cases can be deduced from the remarks made to the Council. At that time, Judge Jorda stated that the judges would consider what amendments to the rules would be required to redefine the relationship between the ICTY and national courts.[27] Yet Prosecutor Del Ponte appeared less adamant that the seniority criterion should be applied to the selection of suspects for investigation and trial. She warned the Council to avoid 'the trap of separating the accused into big fish and small fish'.[28] Quite rightly, the Prosecutor explained that many accused played a role somewhere in between these two extremes—as key organizers and motivators at the district or local level. For example, although ICTR investigations concentrated on senior officials in the command structures of the government, military, media, clergy, and the business world, the Prosecutor argued that lower-level perpetrators also justified her attention.[29] From the perspective of victims, she opined it was the direct perpetrators who brought their world to an end rather than the remote figures who planned the genocide.[30] Linking prosecutions with efforts to maintain peace, she noted: 'Unless these local leaders are brought to justice . . . the ordinary

[22] ibid paras 1–3. Initially the ICTY and the ICTR had two distinct Appeals Chambers but with the same judges serving in both. With the adoption of Resolution 1329 two additional judges were provided for the ICTR Appeals Chamber.

[23] UN Doc S/RES 1329 (2000) preamble.

[24] ibid.

[25] See E Møse, 'The ICTR'S Completion Strategy—Challenges and Possible Solutions' (2008) 6 JICJ 667, 667.

[26] UN Doc S/PV.4429 (2001) 5.

[27] ibid.

[28] ibid 9.

[29] ibid 10.

[30] ibid.

population will not come to terms with the past, and the process of reconciliation and building a stable peace will suffer accordingly.'[31]

Despite the concerns expressed by the Prosecutor, less than a year later and for the first time, the three organs of the ICTY jointly agreed to the application of the seniority criterion in the selection and trial of cases.[32] Paradoxically, as the ICTY reached its highest point of judicial activity, pressure from the Security Council to set an end date for operations was most acutely felt by the Tribunal.[33] Responding to the Council's demands, in June 2002, President Jorda presented a report to the Security Council, jointly prepared by the President, the Prosecutor, and the Registrar. In essence, this report is the comprehensive ICTY completion strategy. Broadly, it outlines structural and operational reforms to expedite proceedings. More critically, it proposes the referral of certain cases to national courts to enable the Tribunal to direct activities 'in a manner more in line with the spirit of the mission it received from the Security Council... to give priority to the prosecution of the most serious crimes which directly threaten international peace and security'.[34] Thus, in the completion strategy, the ICTY advocated that the correct approach to be taken by the Tribunal was to prosecute the 'main political and military figures', leaving the trial of their subordinates to the national courts.[35] The three organs of the ICTY jointly presented a two-pronged process of 'concentration' and 'referral' as the mechanism for the ICTY to complete investigations around 2004 and first instance trials around 2008. The concentration prong involved the Tribunal focusing on the prosecution and trial of the highest-ranking political and military leaders. The referral prong involved the transfer of intermediate and lower-level accused to national courts which could process cases effectively by adhering to the internationally recognized standards of human rights and due process. The strategy also hinted at the level of responsibility of the accused to be transferred. It suggested that perpetrators who held a position of command at an intermediate level between the major leaders indicted and tried by the ICTY and the low-ranking subordinates indicted and tried by the national courts pursuant to the Rome Agreement of 18 February 1996, should be transferred.[36]

As previously noted, the completion strategy also demonstrates the readiness of the ICTY judges to act as legislators regarding the procedures required

[31] ibid 9.

[32] As a follow-up to the presentation of the reform programme in 2001 by President Jorda, in January 2002 the President, the Prosecutor, and the Registrar set up a working group to consider the problems involved in setting up a case referral process: see UN Doc S/2002/985 (2002) para 19.

[33] UN Doc S/2002/678 (2002) para 1.

[34] 'Report on the Judicial Status of the International Criminal Tribunal for the Former Yugoslavia and the Prospects for Referring Certain Cases to National Courts', UN Doc S/2002/678 (2002) para 2. In essence, this document is the ICTY Completion Strategy.

[35] ibid para 36.

[36] ibid. See also *Rome Agreement*, signed by Presidents Izetbegovic, Tudjman, and Milošević (18 February 1996).

to implement the referral process. The Tribunal sought the endorsement of the Security Council to transfer mid-level accused to the War Crimes Chamber in the Court of Bosnia and Herzegovina for trial and declared that, if the Security Council endorsed the plan, the judges would proceed to adopt the necessary amendments to the Rules of Procedure and Evidence.[37] On 23 July 2002, the ICTY completion strategy and the broad timelines for conclusion of its activities were endorsed by Presidential Statement.[38] The Security Council followed up with Resolution 1503 which describes a completion plan composed of 'three interlocking components'.[39] The first component, the completion timelines, directs the Tribunals to complete investigations by the end of 2004, all first instance trial activities by the end of 2008, and all work in 2010.[40] The second component, the application of the seniority criterion by the Tribunals, directs the courts to concentrate on the prosecution and trial of the most senior leaders suspected of being most responsible for the crimes within their jurisdiction. The third component, the referral of cases to national courts, authorizes the ICTY and the ICTR to refer cases of those who do not bear the same level of responsibility as senior leaders to competent national jurisdictions. Although the ICTY judges played an instrumental role in the evolution of the strategy, at least one judge highlighted that the strategy should not impact the conduct of proceedings. In the *Nyiramasuhuko* case, Judge Hunt cautioned that the endorsement by the Security Council 'in the strongest terms' of the completion strategy in Resolution 1503 should not be interpreted as an encouragement by the Council to the ICTY or the ICTR to 'conduct its trials so that they would be other than fair trials'.[41]

[37] In December 2004, the laws required to create the Chamber were adopted by the Bosnian parliament. The laws created 'Section I for War Crimes of the Criminal and Appellate Divisions of the Court of Bosnia and Herzegovina'; the 'Special Department for War Crimes' in the Prosecutor's Office of Bosnia and Herzegovina; and the international Registry for Section I for War Crimes of the Criminal and Appellate Divisions of the Court of Bosnia and Herzegovina and the Special Department for War Crimes in the Prosecutor's Office of Bosnia and Herzegovina. The 'War Crimes Chamber' is hereinafter the term used to describe the hybrid components of the various Bosnian institutions.

[38] UN Doc S/PRST/2002/21.

[39] The term 'three interlocking components' is used by L Johnson, 'Closing an International Criminal Tribunal While Maintaining International Human Rights Standards and Excluding Impunity' (2005) 99 AJIL 158, 159, to describe the strategy as formulated by the Council in UN Doc S/RES 1503 (2003) preamble.

[40] For a proposed lesson to be extracted from the framework of the completion strategy, see D Tolbert, 'The Ends of International Justice: Closing International Tribunals' (2007) 2 *International Justice Tribune Series—2007 Year of Assessment* 11, 14. Tolbert argues that, while there is value in setting target dates, as they help to concentrate minds, it is critical that they are recognized as target dates and not deadlines for completion. He remarks that predicting future trial schedules is much more of an art than a science. For tribunals which have completion strategies in the future it should be borne in mind that the strategies should not create arguments for the opponents of international justice as has inadvertently been done by the *ad hoc* completion strategies.

[41] *Prosecutor v Nyiramasuhuko* (Decision in the Matter of Proceedings Under Rule 15*bis* (D), Dissenting Opinion of Judge David Hunt) ICTR-97-21-T (24 September 2003) para 17. See also *Milošević* (Hunt Dissenting Opinion) (n 6 above) paras 20–22.

The ICTR did not present a comprehensive completion strategy until 2003.[42] Arguably, the Rwanda Tribunal was slower to accept the strategy underpinned by the concentration of trials on the most senior leaders. In part this may be because the ICTR felt its work already concentrated on trying many of the senior figures who orchestrated the genocide.[43] This was a valid argument, since by 2000, the detainees in the custody of the ICTR included one former Prime Minister, ten former Cabinet Ministers, six other senior political appointees, four senior military officers, three former provincial governors, and five mayors of provincial capitals.[44] However, the reticence of the ICTR to present a comprehensive plan did not go unnoticed by the Council. Rather than wait for the ICTR to present a report, in Resolution 1503 the Security Council urged the ICTR 'to formalize a detailed strategy, modeled on the ICTY Completion Strategy to transfer cases involving intermediate- and lower-rank accused to competent national jurisidctions... including Rwanda' to facilitate the completion of its work in 2010.[45] In effect, this was a direction from the Council to the ICTR to apply the seniority criterion and meet the completion timelines by referring cases to national courts. In 2003, the first comprehensive ICTR completion strategy was forthcoming under the leadership of President Erik Møse.[46]

The evolution of the completion strategies illustrates that, unlike the ICTY, the ICTR was more reactive than proactive in relation to defining and presenting a comprehensive plan to the Security Council.[47] From 2000, the ICTY judges were instrumental in shaping the policy and legal framework required to put into practice a strategy underpinned by the referral of intermediate- and lower-level perpetrators to national courts. At that time the ICTY judges first discussed the advantages and disadvantages of transferring cases to the Balkan states but stopped short of recommending this procedure to the Council as a way to reduce the Tribunal's workload. Yet due to positive political development in the Balkans and increased cooperation between the ICTY and the Office of the High Representative to Bosnia and Herzegovina the judges revisited the policy of case referral. Ultimately, the completion strategy as described in Resolution 1503 originated at the ICTY and was largely conceived by the Tribunal's judges. As has been pointed out above, it appears that the ICTR completion strategy was forthcoming due to the pressure exerted by the Security Council, in particular the

[42] UN Doc S/2003/946.

[43] See the comment of the ICTR in relation to the recommendation of the experts that leaders should be tried rather than minor perpetrators in the 'Report of the Expert Group' (n 10 above) 140. As a comment on the recommendation the ICTR noted: 'This re-statement of the obvious objective of the Security Council is of relevance to the proceedings before the ICTY and not ICTR, as the detainees in Arusha are alleged to be civilian and military leaders.'

[44] See Møse (n 25 above) 668.

[45] UN Doc S/RES/1503 (2003) preamble.

[46] UN Doc S/2003/946, the first comprehensive ICTR completion strategy.

[47] See comments of J Fomete, 'Countdown to 2010: A Critical Overview of the Completion Strategy of the International Criminal Tribunal for Rwanda (ICTR)' in E Decaux, A Dieng, and M Sow (eds), *From Human Rights to International Criminal Law: Studies in Honour of an African Jurist, the Late Judge Laity Kama* (The Hague: Martinus Nijhoff, 2007) 361.

direction given in Resolution 1503. The Council urged the ICTR to formulate a plan, modelled on the ICTY completion strategy in order to complete all first instance trials by the end of 2008, and all of its work in 2010.

III. Rule 11*bis*: The Far-reaching Case Referral Mechanism Created by the Judges

A. The purpose and intent of the Rule 11*bis* referral mechanism

An integral component of the *ad hoc* Tribunals' completion strategies is the referral of intermediate- and lower-level accused to national courts for trial. In 2000, the Expert Group evaluating the effective functioning of the Tribunals identified the ICTY's Rule 11*bis* as the possible procedural mechanism to manage 'second-tier perpetrators' as the Prosecutor focused on 'leadership cases'.[48] Entitled, 'Suspension of Indictment in case of Proceedings before National Courts', the original rule authorized a Trial Chamber to suspend an indictment against an accused in anticipation of proceedings before the national court of a state in which the accused was arrested, if that state was prepared to prosecute the case.[49]

There was, however, no parallel provision in the ICTR Rules. The experts recommended that the Rwanda Tribunal include in its Rules of Procedure a provision similar to the ICTY Rule 11*bis*.[50] Interestingly, in 2000 the ICTR remarked that the need for such a rule had not been demonstrated to the Tribunal.[51] In fact, the amendment was proposed at the sixth plenary but was not adopted by the judges. But perhaps the need for a regulation similar to the ICTY Rule 11*bis* in the ICTR Rules had in fact been demonstrated two years earlier in the *Ntuyahaga* case. In 1998, the ICTR charged Bernard Ntuyahaga with a single count of crimes against humanity for the murder of the former Prime Minister of Rwanda and ten Belgian peacekeepers. The other three counts in the indictment charged the accused with genocide and violations of common Article 3 to the Geneva Conventions and Additional Protocol II. They were not confirmed by the reviewing judge. Consequently, pursuant to Rule 51, the prosecutor sought to withdraw the indictment, declaring that a single count relating to murder would not serve her objective of 'exposing the totality of crimes committed in Rwanda in 1994'.[52] The prosecutor argued that the withdrawal of the indictment would promote the exercise of concurrent jurisdiction by facilitating the prosecution of

[48] 'Report of the Expert Group' (n 10 above) para 101.

[49] See ICTY RPE IT.32. Rev.12 (1997), Rule 11*bis*(A) and (B).

[50] See Report of the Expert Group (n 10 above) para 16.

[51] ibid Annex 1 'Comments of the International Tribunal for the Former Yugoslavia, and the International Criminal Tribunal for Rwanda, observations of the Prosecutor and comments of the Secretary-General, where relevant', para 74.

[52] UN Doc S/1999/943 (1999) para 35.

the accused by national courts.[53] With this in mind she requested the transfer of Ntuyahaga to the government of the United Republic of Tanzania. In addition, the Belgian government requested the ICTR to hand over the accused for trial before their courts. The Belgian government went so far as to submit that the ICTR's Rules of Procedure should be modified to include a provision similar to the ICTY Rule 11*bis*.[54] However, the judges noted that Rule 11*bis* was limited to the state in which the accused was arrested and was not applicable in the *Ntuyahaga* case, since it was not clear whether the arresting state, Tanzania, was prepared to try the accused. Granting the prosecutor leave to withdraw the indictment, the Chamber declared that neither the ICTR Statute nor the Rules of Procedure and Evidence empowered the Tribunal to refer proceedings to any national jurisdiction.[55] Thus the ICTR did not have the jurisdiction to order the release of Ntuyahaga into the custody of a given state.[56] Considering that Belgium was willing and adequately prepared to take the case but the ICTR did not have the required procedural mechanism to transfer the accused to that state, it seems surprising that the Tribunal remarked in 2000 that the need for a regulation similar to the ICTY Rule 11*bis* had not been demonstrated. Surely the need for a referral procedure had already been evidenced by the *Ntuyahaga* case. If anything, the case showed the need for a wider procedural regime which would have facilitated the referral of accused to jurisdictions other than arresting states.

Nonetheless, in 2002 the ICTR Rules of Procedure and Evidence were amended to include a more comprehensive Rule 11*bis* regulating the suspension of an indictment which was inspired by the principle of universal jurisdiction.[57] Although pursuant to the ICTY rule the Yugoslavia tribunal was empowered to transfer a case to the arresting state, for the first time the new ICTR rule authorized the court to transfer accused to a jurisdiction other than the state in which the accused was arrested—to the authorities of the 'receiving State'.[58] The ICTR judges adopted the new Rule 11*bis* to enable the ICTR to focus on a limited

[53] *Prosecutor v Ntuyahaga* (Trial Chamber Decision on the Prosecutor's Motion to Withdraw the Indictment) ICTR-98-40-T (18 March 1999) para 1(i).

[54] The Trial Chamber noted that even if the ICTR Rules contained a provision similar to the ICTY Rule 11*bis* the provision would not be applicable in the *Ntuyahaga* case since the ICTR was not aware whether the arresting state, the United Republic of Tanzania, would be willing to continue the proceedings in their courts. ICTY Rule 11*bis* was limited to cooperation with the state in which the accused was arrested.

[55] *Ntuyahaga* (Trial Chamber Decision) (n 53 above) para 1.

[56] ibid para 3.

[57] For information in relation to the ICTR 12th Plenary Session, 5–6 July 2002, at which the judges adopted the ICTR RPE, Rule 11*bis*, see ICTR Press Briefing, ICTR/INFO-9-13-22.EN (8 July 2002). For a discussion in relation to the ICTR applicable law prior to the adoption of the ICTR RPE, Rule 11*bis*, see *Ntuyahaga* (Trial Chamber Decision) (n 53 above). The ICTR RPE, Rule11*bis* entitled 'Referral of the Indictment to another Court' was introduced less than two years later at the 14th Plenary Session, 23–24 April 2004.

[58] ICTR RPE (2002), Rule 11*bis* A(ii).

number of important cases to push forward with its completion strategy and finish first instance trials by 2008.[59]

But with the formal implementation of referring cases involving intermediate- and lower-level accused to national courts forthcoming, the ICTY judges debated the Tribunal's power to do so. They were concerned that the Statute contained some ambiguities in this respect. In fact, at the extraordinary plenary session of 23 April 2002, the judges suggested that the Security Council amend the Statute to empower the ICTY to refer cases.[60] Although Article 29 of the Statute imposed on all United Nations member states a general obligation to cooperate with the ICTY, it was not without question whether this provision could be interpreted as permitting the Tribunal to compel national courts to try referred persons for all charges in the indictments issued by the Prosecutor. Nor were the judges convinced that the principle of concurrent jurisdiction and the primacy of the ICTY could be interpreted as sanctioning the far-reaching referral process required to facilitate the completion strategy and the winding-down of the ICTY mission by 2010.[61]

To implement the completion strategy referral process, the ICTY advocated that the scope of application of the existing Rule11*bis* governing the suspension of an indictment needed to be expanded.[62] The original ICTY rule provided that an indictment could be suspended only if the state in which the accused was arrested had jurisdiction. The ICTY contemplated broadening the jurisdictions to which it could refer a case to beyond just the arresting state. The Tribunal maintained that it should be authorized to refer cases to states where the crimes were perpetrated.[63] The inclusion of states with territorial jurisdiction over the crimes was a strategic move by the ICTY for a number of reasons. First, as noted in 2001 by President Jorda, the judicial systems of the states of the former Yugoslavia would have to be 'reconstructed on democratic foundations' before any cases could be transferred.[64] Considering the urgent need to refer cases to meet the completion timelines, there was not sufficient time to wait for the reform of those judicial sectors. Instead, the Tribunal supported the creation of the hybrid War Crimes Chamber in the Court of Bosnia and Herzegovina. The ICTY intended to refer most of its cases involving intermediate-level accused to the Bosnian Court. Yet a number of the accused which the Tribunal wanted to transfer were Serbs with both Bosnian and Serbian citizenship. Before their transfer to the ICTY, rather than surrendering to the Bosnian authorities, some of the accused had surrendered to the authorities of Serbia and Montenegro. Without amending Rule 11*bis* to include states with territorial jurisdiction there was, thus, a possibility that those accused would have to be transferred back to Serbia and Montenegro rather than to the War Crimes Chamber in the Court of Bosnia and Herzegovina.

59 See ICTR Press Briefing (n 57 above).

60 See 'Report on Judicial Status' (n 34 above) para 37.

61 ibid.

62 ibid para 35.

63 ibid para 38.

64 UN Doc S/PV.4429 (2001) 5.

Secondly, getting witnesses to testify in trials, be they in Bosnia and Herzegovina or Serbia and Montenegro, was a thorny issue. Many witnesses believed that Serbia was a safe refuge for Bosnian war criminals. Ultimately, the chances of convincing Bosnian prosecution witnesses to travel to Belgrade to testify in trials were slim. It was widely considered that witnesses would be more willing to testify in a Bosnian court if appropriate support and security services were provided for them. The War Crimes Chamber planned to provide the services. Therefore, to ensure the possible referral of cases to the Bosnian War Crimes Chamber, Rule 11*bis* had to be amended to include states of territorial jurisdiction.

Moreover, the referral of the indictment's supporting material to national courts gave rise to concerns. It was likely that some of the victims' and witnesses' statements in the files were covered by protective measures. To ensure the continued security of victims and witnesses, the ICTY advised amendment of Rule 11*bis* to empower the Tribunal to order national courts to uphold its protective measures.[65]

Rule 11*bis* governing the suspension of an indictment did not specify the appropriate level of responsibility for an accused to be tried in a national court. In its completion strategy report, the ICTY noted that, since the war in the former Yugoslavia involved states, autonomous entities, and paramilitary groups carrying out widespread offences, it was difficult to pinpoint precisely which accused should be referred.[66] Nevertheless, the Tribunal maintained that for reasons of transparency vis-à-vis the international community and the states of the former Yugoslavia, Rule 11*bis* should be amended to incorporate two criteria to be assessed when deciding on a referral. The position of the accused and the gravity of the crimes charged were the suggested criteria. The judges noted that it would be for the competent Trial Chamber 'to access and set out *in concreto* the main points of those criteria', at a later stage.[67]

Another major concern, regarding the referral of cases to national courts, related to the characterization and confirmation of the charges contained in the international indictment. Although the ICTY was prepared to refer cases to states in the former Yugoslavia, some trepidation remained regarding the ability of national courts to ensure the accused would be tried for all of the crimes in the Tribunals' indictments. This concern was bolstered by the text of the original Rule 11*bis* governing the suspension of an indictment. It prescribed that, if a case was transferred to a national court, the indictment issued by the Tribunal would be suspended pending the start of proceedings. This, in the opinion of the ICTY, gave too much latitude to national courts to drop or change the charges against an accused. Focused on creating a robust referral mechanism, the ICTY intended to guarantee that an accused, referred to a national jurisdiction pursuant to Rule 11*bis*, would answer for all the crimes as characterized and confirmed

[65] 'Report on Judicial Status' (n 34 above) para 41. [66] ibid para 42. [67] ibid.

in the Tribunal's indictment.[68] The position taken by the Tribunal regarding the characterization and confirmation of charges in their indictments is hardly surprising. To reduce its caseload and meet the 2010 completion timeline, the ICTY planned to refer a number of cases to national courts. Naturally, the Tribunal wanted to alleviate any risk of the international crimes in its indictments being characterized as ordinary crimes in a national indictment. Such a situation would result in the ICTY invoking its primacy and requesting the deferral of the case back to its jurisdiction. This would defeat the purpose of case referral resulting once again in an increase in the Tribunal's caseload.

Finally, it was suggested in the report that the competent Trial Chamber should be authorized to decide *ex officio* to refer a case after giving the prosecutor and, if applicable, the accused the opportunity to be heard.[69] Interestingly, not unlike the objections raised by the Prosecutor in 2004 about the amendment of Rule 28(A), which will be discussed later in this chapter, the Prosecutor did not agree to a Trial Chamber being authorized to act *ex officio*. She maintained that this would infringe on her statutory powers. The ICTY indicated that if the Security Council approved the proposals, whether the Statute was amended or not, Rule 11*bis* would be amended by the judges to reflect their suggestions. Subsequently, the Security Council Presidential Statement endorsed the intention of the ICTY to amend its Rules of Procedure and Evidence to facilitate the referral of cases to national jurisdictions.[70]

B. ICTY and ICTR Rule 11*bis*

The general principle of the *ad hoc* Tribunals' primacy over national courts is declared in the ICTY and ICTR Statutes.[71] As the Security Council intended when it adopted the Statutes, the details of how the Tribunals assert their primacy are defined by the judges and set out in the Rules of Procedure and Evidence.[72] Part II of the Rules, entitled 'Primacy of the Tribunal', sets out the circumstances under which the *ad hoc* Tribunals may assert their primacy.[73] Moreover, in the event of corresponding or competing prosecutions in national courts, the mechanism for the deferral of cases to the Tribunals' jurisdiction is also expounded in the rules. As Jann Kleffner has remarked, prior to the adoption of the Tribunals' completion strategies, the Rules of Procedure and Evidence displayed a preoccupation with deciding how the ICTY and the ICTR could assume jurisdiction over cases.[74] Following the endorsement of the completion strategies, the Tribunals'

[68] ibid para 40. [69] ibid para 43. [70] UN Doc S/PRST/2002/21.

[71] ICTY Statute, Art 9; ICTR Statute, Art 8.

[72] See 'Report of the Secretary-General pursuant to Paragraph 2 of Security Council Resolution 808', UN Doc S/25705 (1993) para 65.

[73] ICTY RPE Rule 7*bis*–Rule 13; ICTR RPE Rule 8–Rule 13.

[74] J Kleffner, *Complementarity in the Rome Statute and National Criminal Jurisdictions* (Oxford: OUP, 2008) 68.

judges transformed the rules by incorporating the mechanism and procedures needed to refer cases to domestic courts for trial.

The power of the ICTY to refer its cases to national jurisdictions has been challenged on the grounds that Rule 11*bis* lacks a legal basis in the Statute and in any implied or inherent powers that the Tribunal may have.[75] In the *Stanković* case the Appeals Chamber rejected that argument for two main reasons. First, the judges explained that, even though there is no explicit statutory provision regulating the referral of cases to national jurisdictions, in accordance with the ICTY's concurrent relationship with national courts as foreseen under Article 9 of the Statute the transfer of accused to domestic jurisdictions could be contemplated.[76] Secondly, the Appeals Chamber highlighted that in various resolutions the Security Council had confirmed the legal authority of the ICTY to refer cases and implicitly recognized the authority of the ICTY judges to amend the Rules of Procedure and Evidence to do so.[77] But there was a procedural gap in the applicable law of the Tribunals: the Rules of Procedure and Evidence did not specify how and according to what criteria the Tribunals could refer cases, in which indictments had been confirmed, to national courts for trial. Pursuant to the Statutes of the *ad hoc* Tribunals, the judges are empowered to adopt rules of procedure 'for the conduct of the pre-trial phase of proceedings, trials and appeals, the admission of evidence, the protection of victims and witnesses and other appropriate matters'.[78] In Resolutions 1503 and 1534 the Security Council recognized the Tribunals' implicit statutory authority to refer cases to national courts and directed the ICTY and the ICTR to refer intermediate- and lower-rank accused to domestic jurisdictions. Thus it was entirely appropriate for the Tribunals' judges to amend Rule 11*bis* to define the procedural law required to support the referral process implied under Article 9 of the Statutes.

At an extraordinary plenary, held in September 2002, the ICTY judges revised Rule 11*bis* entitling it, 'Referral of the Indictment to Another Court'.[79] In 2004, the ICTR judges revised the rule governing suspension of an indictment to adopt the corresponding Rule 11*bis* regulating the referral of an indictment to national courts.[80]

The current text of Rule 11*bis* is not identical in the Rules of Procedure and Evidence of the two *ad hoc* Tribunals. Nevertheless, the case referral mechanism

[75] *Prosecutor v Stanković* (Appellant's Brief) IT-96-23/2-AR11*bis*.1 (1 July 2005) para 5.

[76] *Prosecutor v Stanković* (Decision on Rule 11*bis* Referral) IT-96-23/2-AR11*bis*.1 (1 September 2005) para 14.

[77] ibid paras 15–17. See also UN Doc S/RES 1503 (2003); UN Doc S/RES 1534 (2004).

[78] ICTY Statute, Art 15; ICTR Statute, Art 14.

[79] Ninth Annual Report of the ICTY, UN Doc S/2002/985 (2002) para 42.

[80] ICTR Press Briefing (n 57 above). In July 2002, the ICTR judges introduced Rule 11*bis* governing suspension of indictments and authorizing a Trial Chamber to transfer a case to a competent national jurisdiction. According to the ICTR, the purpose of the new rule was to enable the Rwanda Tribunal to concentrate on a limited number of cases to meet the timelines in the completion strategy.

created by the rules is practically the same. Rule 11*bis* (A) provides that, after an indictment has been confirmed and before the start of trial, whether or not the accused is in the custody of the Tribunal, a request for referral can be heard. ICTY Rule 11*bis* (A) authorizes the President to appoint three permanent judges to the Referral Bench, which will determine whether to refer a case or not. The situation is slightly different at the ICTR, as the President designates cases to different Trial Chambers. The creation of the permanent ICTY Referral Bench was a very positive development. As the referral hearings increased, the three permanent judges became increasingly familiar with the national courts and laws of the referral states. The judges could effectively analyse objections raised by both the prosecution and defence in this respect as many of the objections raised in the various cases were the same. Overall, the ICTY Rule 11*bis* jurisprudence is comprehensive and consistent. The same situation does not necessarily prevail in the ICTR. Rather than creating a permanent Referral Bench, the President designates referral cases to various Trial Chambers. In a number of ICTR cases rejecting referral motions, the grounds for refusal varied between the Chambers.[81] As a general comment and from the perspective of building a national judicial system sufficiently robust to meet the standards required by the *ad hoc* Tribunals to refer a case, the lack of clarity from the ICTR, when stipulating the problems preventing the referral of cases, does not help a state like Rwanda, which is willing to accept cases, to remedy those problems.

A broader issue to be explored is whether the management of the Tribunals' referral process is in fact an appropriate judicial function. The decision to refer accused to national courts for trial is a judicial one in cases where indictments exist, whereas the decision to refer other non-indicted cases to national authorities rests exclusively with the Prosecutor. It is therefore interesting to consider whether the Tribunals could have created an alternative transfer regime for indicted cases without involving the judges in the procedure? For example, could the referral of indicted cases to national jurisdictions be managed in the same way as the transfer of the so-called 'Category 2 cases', which are handed over by the ICTY and the ICTR Office of the Prosecutor to national authorities without any judicial supervision at all?[82] The Rule 11*bis* procedures are applicable to cases in which indictments have been confirmed.[83] Therefore, the Tribunals were satisfied that sufficient evidence existed to provide reasonable grounds for believing that the persons charged in the indictments had committed crimes within their jurisdiction.[84] On the other hand, the Category 2 cases do not involve indicted

[81] See W Schabas, 'Transfer and Extradition of Genocide Suspects to Rwanda', presentation at Redress conference 'The Extradition of Rwandese Genocide Suspects to Rwanda: Issues and Challenges' (1 July 2008).

[82] UN Doc S/2005/782 (2005) para 40. The ICTR Prosecutor indicated that according to the 2004 Completion Strategy he intended to transfer files involving 32 individuals to national jurisdictions for trial.

[83] See ICTY RPE Rule 11*bis*(A); ICTR RPE Rule 11*bis*(A).

[84] See ICTY RPE Rule 47(B); ICTR RPE Rule 47(B). The Rule provides that, if the prosecutor is satisfied in the course of an investigation that there is sufficient evidence to provide reasonable

persons. The ICTY files are best described as collections of materials from the Prosecutor's investigations which never actually reached the indictment phase.[85] The ICTR files are composed of some investigations which are ready for trial and some dossiers requiring further investigation by domestic authorities.[86] There is a critical distinction between the two types of case. The Rule 11*bis* cases have reached the pre-trial stage of proceedings before the Tribunals and involve persons who have been publicly indicted.[87] On the contrary, the Category B cases are at various stages of investigation and the Prosecutor has not issued indictments. The distinction justifies the application of different case referral regimes and necessitates the transfer of indicted persons to domestic authorities by judicial decision.

It is paramount that the rights of persons indicted by the Yugoslavia and Rwanda Tribunals be respected in the course of referral proceedings and also by national courts after a transfer has been ordered. In this regard the Tribunals' judges play a critical role: they are required to adjudicate questions relating to the fairness of the transfer and/or issues that might prejudice the rights of the accused.[88] Rule 11*bis* permits the referral of cases to the state in whose territory the crime was committed; the state in which the accused was arrested; or any state having jurisdiction and willing and adequately prepared to accept such a case.[89] Thus, for example, in situations where there are concurrent jurisdictions among states based on the territoriality and nationality principles, the Tribunals' judges are required to resolve conflicts of competing claims for jurisdiction. Moreover, to safeguard the rights of the accused, many of whom have spent years in the Tribunals' custody awaiting trial, it is correct that the accused are given the opportunity to raise objections before the judges regarding their referral to a national court for trial. For example, in *Mejakić et al* the accused submitted

grounds for believing that a suspect has committed a crime, an indictment shall be prepared and submitted for confirmation to a judge.

85 UN Doc S/2007/663 (2007) para 15. See also D Tolbert and A Kontic, 'The ICTY: Transitional Justice, the Transfer of Cases to National Courts, and Lessons for the ICC' in C Stahn and G Sluiter (eds), *The Emerging Practice of the International Criminal Court* (Leiden: Martinus Nijhoff, 2009) 157.

86 UN Doc S/2005/782 (2005) para 40.

87 The submission and confirmation of indictments is governed by ICTY RPE, Rule 47 and ICTR RPE, Rule 47 under Part Five of the Rules of Procedure and Evidence entitled 'Pre-Trial Proceedings'.

88 The judges' role is not vital in the transfer of Category 2 cases. No individuals are indicted and awaiting trial before the Tribunals in these cases, therefore there are no accused to contest the fairness of the case transfer. In addition, after the Category 2 file is transferred to the national authorities there is no guarantee that indictments will be issued or who they may be issued against.

89 ICTY RPE, Rule 11*bis* (A)(i), (ii), (iii); ICTR RPE, Rule 11*bis* (A)(i), (ii), (iii). The inclusion of the third category of state, a country with jurisdiction and the capacity to try the accused, was considered necessary due to the inability of some courts in the territorial states to guarantee the protection of internationally recognized fair trial rights. See comments of S Williams, 'The Completion Strategy of the ICTY and the ICTR in International Criminal Justice: A Critical Analysis of Institutions and Procedure' in M Bohlander (ed), *International Criminal Justice: A Critical Analysis of Institutions and Procedures* (London: Cameron May, 2007) 153.

that, based on their citizenship, the appropriate state for the case to be referred to was Serbia and Montenegro.[90] Due to the territoriality principle, the Prosecutor and Bosnia and Herzegovina argued that the state of referral should be Bosnia.[91] Serbia and Montenegro submitted that it was willing and adequately prepared to accept the case.[92] The ICTY Appeals Chamber explained:

> ...where there are concurrent jurisdictions under Rule 11*bis* (A)(i)–(iii) of the Rules, discretion is vested in the Referral Bench to choose without establishing among these three options and without requiring the Referral Bench to be bound by any party's submission that one of the alternative jurisdictions is allegedly the most appropriate. A decision of the Referral Bench on the question as to which State a case should be referred (vertical level, ie between the International Tribunal and individual States) must be based on the facts and circumstances of each individual case in light of each of the prerequisites set out in Rule 11*bis* (A) of the Rules.[93]

In *Mejakić et al* the Referral Bench transferred the case to the Bosnian authorities: the judges determined that Bosnia and Herzegovina had 'a significantly greater nexus' with the accused and the offences they allegedly committed than Serbia and Montenegro.[94]

Judge Mohamed Shahabuddeen has observed that it would be inappropriate for judges to prioritize the completion strategy above the rights of the accused in proceedings before the Appeals Chambers.[95] It would be equally wrong for the Tribunals to prioritize the referral of cases to national courts without first exploring whether referral states could guarantee the protection of internationally recognized human rights standards. In this regard, the Tribunals' judges play an essential role in the referral process. In accordance with Rule 11*bis*, before ordering the referral of a case, the judges must be satisfied that the accused will receive a fair trial in the national court and that the death penalty will not be imposed or carried out.[96] This provision contains the explicit condition that the ICTY and the ICTR may only refer accused persons to national courts that will ensure the application of international fair trial standards. Thus it is not only the fairness of the referral process that the Tribunals' judges safeguard, they also play a critical role in protecting the rights of witnesses and accused before and after a case is transferred to a domestic jurisdiction. For example, as suggested by the ICTY in the completion strategy report, Rule 11*bis* (D)(ii) provides that the Referral Bench may order that protective measures for certain witnesses or

[90] *Prosecutor v Mejakić et al* (Decision on Prosecutor's Motion for Referral of Case Pursuant to Rule 11*bis*) IT-02-65-PT (20 July 2005) para 34.

[91] ibid para 33.

[92] ibid para 36.

[93] *Prosecutor v Mejakić et al* (Decision on Joint Defence Appeal Against Decision on Referral under Rule 11*bis*) IT-02-65-PT (7 April 2006) para 44. See also *Prosecutor v Janković* (Decision on Rule 11*bis* Referral) IT-96-23/2-AR11*bis*.2 (15 November 2005) para 33.

[94] *Mejakić* (Decision on Rule 11*bis* Referral) (n 90 above) paras 41–2.

[95] See *Milošević* (Shahabuddeen Separate Opinion) (n 6 above) para 21.

[96] ICTY RPE, Rule 11*bis* (B); ICTR RPE, Rule 11*bis* (C).

victims remain in force after a referral.[97] Moreover, to determine the capability of a state to hold fair trials, it is established in Rule 11*bis* case law that the judges must consider whether the principles enshrined in the Statutes will be protected by the national court.[98] The Statutes prescribe basic fair trial principles which reflect the standards enshrined in the International Covenant on Civil and Political Rights.[99] Thus in Rule 11*bis* proceedings the judges have considered the capacity of national courts to ensure that the accused will have a fair and public hearing; will be presumed innocent until proven guilty; will be informed promptly and in detail of the charges in a language understood by the accused; will be tried without undue delay; will have legal assistance; and will be entitled to cross-examine witnesses and to communicate with counsel of his or her own choosing.[100] Interestingly, in this respect, during Rule 11*bis* hearings, the judges of the *ad hoc* Tribunals act more like members of an international human rights body than an international criminal court, as they are required to consider and assess the capacity of states to adhere to human rights norms. This is an entirely appropriate judicial function: it would be outrageous if the Tribunals transferred indicted persons to jurisdictions that did not respect the international standards which the accused would be afforded if their trials proceeded before the ICTY or the ICTR.

In some regards, the judges' determination of a state's capacity to deliver fair trials conducted during Rule 11*bis* referral proceedings is not unlike the judges' assessment of the ability of a state to diligently prosecute a case during deferral proceedings. In fact, after a case is referred to a national court for trial, Rule 11*bis* creates a system to ensure that the case is diligently prosecuted and the accused receives a fair trial in the state concerned. According to this system the judges ensure that the trial of referred cases proceeds before national courts in a way that is acceptable to the Tribunals.[101] Pursuant to Rule 11*bis* (D)(iv), the prosecutor is authorized to send observers to monitor the proceedings in the national courts.[102] At any time before the accused is found guilty or acquitted by a national court, the judges may revoke the referral order, invoke primacy, and request the deferral of the case within the terms of Rule 10. Although Rule 11*bis* does spell out the criteria which judges must be satisfied exist in a state before they can refer a case, no criteria are specified in the rule for revocation of an order. Instead Rule 11*bis* (F) prescribes that deferral of a case will be requested within the terms of Rule 10.[103] Rule 10 stipulates that a Trial Chamber may issue a formal request for deferral on any of the grounds specified in Rule 9.

[97] ICTY RPE Rule 11*bis* (D)(ii); ICTR RPE Rule 11*bis* (D)(ii).

[98] *Prosecutor v Hategekimana* (Decision on the Prosecution's Appeal Against Decision on Referral Under Rule 11*bis*) ICTR-00-55B-R11bis (4 December 2008) para 4.

[99] ICTY Statute, Art 21; ICTR Statute, Art 21.

[100] ibid.

[101] See comments of Williams (n 89 above) 202.

[102] ICTY RPE Rule 11*bis* (D)(iv); ICTR RPE Rule 11*bis* (D)(iv).

[103] ICTY RPE Rule 11*bis* (F); ICTR RPE Rule 11*bis* (F).

Three broad grounds for deferral of a case to the competence of the ICTY are listed in Rule 9.[104] First, the Prosecutor may request deferral if the crimes being charged under national law are characterized as ordinary crimes. Secondly, a case may be deferred if the proceedings lack impartiality or independence, or are designed to shield the accused from international criminal responsibility, or the case is not diligently prosecuted. The third ground for deferral is if the case involves significant factual or legal questions which may have implications for prosecutions before the Tribunal. To a large extent, the first ground for deferral—the characterization of international crimes as ordinary crimes—is not particularly relevant in cases transferred under Rule 11*bis*. This is due to the fact that the Tribunals made it clear to potential referral states that their courts would have to respect the charges contained in the international indictment before any case would be referred. Consequently, the Bosnian law regulating the transfer of cases from the ICTY provides that if the Tribunal transfers a case with a confirmed indictment to Bosnia, the national prosecutor shall initiate criminal prosecution according to the facts and charges in the ICTY indictment.[105] The national prosecutor may add charges to the indictment but may not drop charges from the ICTY indictment.[106] The Tribunal's indictment is adapted to make it compliant with national laws and will only be accepted if the War Crimes Chamber is satisfied that the ICTY indictment has been adequately adapted.[107] Likewise, the Rwandan Organic Law on the transfer of cases from the ICTR also states that the ICTR indictment shall be adapted to ensure compliance with national law and shall be subsequently accepted by the High Court.[108] The third ground for deferral under Rule 9 does not assume much relevance in referral cases either. Most probably, if a case involved significant factual or legal questions which have implications for other prosecutions before the *ad hoc* Tribunals, the Prosecutor would not request the referral of that case in the first place.

[104] ICTY RPE, Rule 9. The grounds listed for a request for a deferral in the ICTR RPE, Rule 9 differ. The ICTR rule stipulates that a deferral request may be made by the Prosecutor if the proceedings in any state are the subject of an investigation by the Prosecutor; or should be the subject of an investigation by the Prosecutor due to the seriousness of the offences, the status of the accused, or the general importance of the legal questions involved in the case. For a decision on deferral under ICTR Rule 11*bis* (F), see *Prosecutor v Bagaragaza* (Decision on Prosecutor's Extremely Urgent Motion for Revocation of the Referral to the Kingdom of the Netherlands Pursuant to Rule 11*bis* (F) and (G)) ICTR-2005-86-11*bis* (17 August 2007).

[105] See 'Law on the Transfer of Cases from the ICTY to the Prosecutor's Office of BiH and the Use of Evidence collected by ICTY in Proceedings before the Courts in BiH', art 2(1), *Official Gazette of Bosnia and Herzegovina* No 76/06.

[106] ibid art 2(2).

[107] ibid art 2(1).

[108] Organic Law No 11/2007 Concerning Transfer of Cases to the Republic of Rwanda from the International Criminal Tribunal for Rwanda and From other States, art 3–art 4, *Official Gazette of the Republic of Rwanda*, Year 46 (19 March 2007). In April 2009, Rwanda adopted amendments to the Organic Law.

The key concern for the Tribunals after a case has been referred under Rule 11*bis* is that the accused will receive a fair trial and the case will be diligently prosecuted by the national authorities. Thus the second ground for deferral under Rule 9 relating to proceedings lacking impartiality is significant. This opinion is supported by the decision of the Appeals Chamber in the *Janković* case. According to the Chamber, 'Rules 11*bis* (D)(iv) and 11*bis* (F) serve as precautions against a failure to diligently prosecute a referred case or conduct a fair trial'.[109] Interestingly, the first Rule 11*bis* order to be revoked, resulting in the deferral of the case back to the ICTR, was not the result of an unfair trial or suspicious prosecution. Rather, in *Bagaragaza*, the decision to refer the case to the Kingdom of the Netherlands was predicated on the Trial Chamber's belief that the Dutch courts were competent to prosecute the accused. It later transpired, however, that the Dutch authorities did not have jurisdiction to prosecute the case.[110] The referral order was, thus, revoked, and the authorities in the Netherlands were requested to defer to the competence of the ICTR, in accordance with Article 28 of the Statute and Rule 10 of the Rules of Procedure and Evidence.

As a result of the completion strategies, the Security Council has prescribed general prosecutorial guidelines for the ICTY and the ICTR. The Council has not become involved in the specific details of individual cases. Rather, it has urged the Tribunals in reviewing indictments to ensure that they concentrate on the most senior leaders. The implications of referring indicted persons from the Tribunals back to national courts for trial are serious. To a large extent the criteria applied by the Prosecutors to select the suspects who fall into the category of most senior leader are vague.[111] But, from the perspective of national trials, it is essential that victims and witnesses, who will be required to testify in those trials, understand why persons who were originally indicted by the ICTY and the ICTR will not be tried at the international level. Furthermore, to protect the credibility of the Tribunals and the referral process it is even more important that the decisions related to the selection of the indicted persons to be transferred to domestic jurisdictions are transparent. As a consequence of the judges' involvement in Rule 11*bis* proceedings, the legitimacy of the case referral process has been strengthened. For example, unlike the ICTR rule, ICTY Rule 11*bis* (C) stipulates additional criteria for the Referral Bench to contemplate before deciding to refer a case.[112] As suggested by the ICTY in the 2002

[109] *Prosecutor v Ademi and Norac* (Decision for Referral to the Authorities of the Republic of Croatia Pursuant to Rule 11*bis*) IT-04-78-PT (14 September 2005) para 57.

[110] *Bagaragaza* (Decision on Referral Motion) (n 104 above).

[111] GA Knoops, 'Challenging the Legitimacy of Initiating Contemporary International Criminal Proceedings: Rethinking Prosecutorial Discretionary Powers from a Legal, Ethical and Political Perspective' (2004) 15 *Criminal Law Forum* 365, 370–90.

[112] Although the ICTR judges are not directed under Rule 11*bis* to assess the level of responsibility of the accused and the gravity of crimes charged when deciding to refer an accused, the criteria have already been applied by the ICTR Prosecutor to assist him with the selection of accused suitable for transfer. Moreover, the decision of an ICTR Trial Chamber to refer a case to the authorities

completion strategy report, the judges must consider the gravity of the crimes charged and the level of responsibility of the accused when deciding whether to refer a case or not. This gives effect to the policy of the Security Council as directed in Resolution 1534 that the efforts of the Tribunal should focus on the trial of the most senior leaders suspected of being most responsible for crimes within the Tribunal's jurisdiction. The ICTY rule has also opened the door for the judges to determine the suitability of the accused selected by the Prosecutor for referral to domestic jurisdictions. In the course of the Rule 11*bis* proceedings the judges of the Yugoslavia Tribunal have developed transparent principles for the assessment of the gravity of crimes charged and the level of responsibility of the accused. The principles were applied by the judges to each indicted person on a case-by-case basis with the result that the referral judgments clearly explain why certain accused were selected for trial by national courts and why others were appropriate for trial at the international level. Thus the judges have made a significant contribution to the understanding of how persons indicted by the ICTY were selected for transfer to national courts for trial. This challenges the perception that the referral process is simply a means to dispose of all cases back-logged in the Tribunals to other courts. Instead, the judges' application of clear selection principles based on the gravity of crimes and the level of responsibility of the accused supports the notion that, to facilitate the completion strategies, the Tribunals have implemented a legitimate prosecution strategy, underpinned by a division of labour based on the seniority of accused, between international and national courts. In this respect, the contribution of the Tribunals' judges to the legacy of the ICTY and the ICTR is vital.

IV. ICTY Rule 28(A): A New Oversight Role for the Judges of the Yugoslavia Tribunal

When creating the ICTY and the ICTR the Security Council did not impose a statutory limitation on the seniority of the accused to be tried by the Tribunals. Instead, Article 1 of the ICTY Statute declares that the Tribunal is empowered to try the perpetrators of 'serious' violations of international humanitarian law.[113] Likewise, the ICTR was created to prosecute persons responsible for genocide

of a state is discretionary. In this respect, see *Prosecutor v Munyakazi* (Decision on the Prosecution's Appeal Against Decision on Referral Under Rule 11*bis*) ICTR-97-36-R11*bis* (8 October 2008) para 5; *Hategekimana* (Decision on Prosecution's Appeal) (n 98 above) para 5. Thus, although under ICTR Rule 11*bis* the judges are not specifically directed to consider gravity and the level of responsibility of an accused, the judges will consider the purpose and intent of the rule when deciding referral motions. Thus, if the Prosecutor filed a request to refer the case of a most senior leader most responsible for the Rwandan genocide to a national court, it is most likely the judges would exercise their discretion and reject the request.

113 UN Doc S/RES 827 (1993).

and other 'serious' violations of international humanitarian law.[114] Thus the statutory emphasis was placed on the gravity of the crimes committed in the respective conflicts rather than on the level of responsibility of the perpetrators.[115] Nevertheless, prior to the implementation of the completion strategies, the *ad hoc* Tribunals could try all serious violations of international humanitarian law, regardless of the level of responsibility of the suspects, be they a Head of State or an opportunistic thug. Obviously, this meant the scope of perpetrators to indict was vast. Hence the ICTY and the ICTR Prosecutors are by necessity required to develop strategies to target perpetrators and crimes in a manner which allows them to manage the resources available to them in a way that will best serve the Tribunals' mandates.[116] It is well established in the case law of the Tribunals that the Prosecutor has broad discretionary power in the choice of the perpetrators for investigation. As the Appeals Chamber explained in the *Akayesu* case:

> Investigation and prosecution of persons responsible for serious violations within the jurisdiction of the Tribunal fall to the Prosecutor and... it is her responsibility to 'assess the information received or obtained and decide whether there is sufficient basis to proceed'. In many criminal justice systems, the entity responsible for prosecutions has finite financial and human resources and cannot realistically be expected to prosecute every offender which may fall within the strict terms of its jurisdictions. It must of necessity make decisions as to the nature of the crimes and the offenders to be prosecuted.[117]

Yet in spite of the well-recognized discretionary power of the ICTY Prosecutor, at two critical moments in the history of the institution, the Tribunal's judges have played a definitive role in defining the prosecution parameters. This point is illustrated by the actions of the judges during the creation phase of the ICTY following the announcement of the 'pyramidal prosecution strategy'. It is further demonstrated by the amendment of Rule 28(A) by the ICTY judges as a response to the Security Council's adoption of Resolution 1534 during the completion phase of the Tribunal.

In 1995 the ICTY's Chief of Investigations revealed that a 'pyramidal prosecution strategy' would be employed by the Office of the Prosecutor.[118] Following this strategy, the prosecution would initially target lower-level suspects, and then progressively move upwards to political and military leaders.[119] But the ICTY judges did not agree that targeting lower-level offenders first was the correct strategy to be adopted. The judges believed that the role of the Tribunal was

[114] See UN Doc S/RES 955 (1994) and ICTR Statute, Art 1.

[115] See generally JH Ralston and S Finnin, 'Investigating International Crimes: A Review of International Law Enforcement Strategies Expediency v Effectiveness' in DA Blumenthal and TLH McCormack (eds), *The Legacy of Nuremberg: Civilising Influence or Institutionalised Vengeance?* (Leiden/Boston: Martinus Nijhoff, 2008) 50–7.

[116] See generally Ralston and Finnin (ibid) 49.

[117] *Prosecutor v Akayesu* (Appeals Chamber Judgment) ICTR-96-4-A (1 June 2001) paras 94–6.

[118] A Cassese, 'The ICTY: A Living and Vital Reality' (2004) 2 JICJ 585, 586.

[119] ibid.

immediately to target the military and political leaders or high-ranking commanders, based on the notion of command responsibility as per Article 7(3) of the Statute.[120] Consequently, the judges decided to meddle in prosecutorial policy, acting 'as a collective body, and with a view to having a say in the future direction and the overall role of the tribunal'.[121] They wanted to discount, as much as possible, minor perpetrators. In a letter to the Prosecutor the ICTY President recalled the Nuremberg Charter's explicit reference to the mandate of the International Military Tribunal to try 'major' war criminals. Judge Cassese argued that the premise of the ICTY Statute was the same—it insisted on the need to prosecute persons responsible for 'serious' violations. Quite rightly, the President noted that 'an international court cannot go after all those who have committed atrocities'.[122] Referring to the limited financial and human resources and the need to rely on state cooperation, the President opined that the ICTY must 'concentrate on the leaders or at least on those who planned and ordered atrocities, including the top brass of the states and other parties involved in the conflict'.[123]

Following an intervention of this nature by the judges, it is hardly shocking that the former ICTY Prosecutor, Richard Goldstone, subsequently remarked that his relationship with the judges, especially in the early days, was complicated. Maintaining that they were hugely frustrated by a lack of judicial work, he has remarked that there was a 'determined attempt by the judges to become involved in the work and policies of the Office of the Prosecutor'.[124] But it appears that the judges' opinion in relation to the ICTY's prosecution policy was very persuasive, to the extent that, in February 1995, the Prosecutor undertook to 'issue appropriate indictments at the earliest possible time'.[125] The indictments subsequently issued were against two of the most senior political and military Bosnian Serb leaders, Radovan Karadžić and Ratko Mladić. Nevertheless, a large number of relatively minor figures were also indicted around that time.[126] The ICTR prosecution strategy was not questioned by the ICTR judges during the

120 ICTY Statute, Art 7(3) states: 'The fact that any of the acts... was committed by a subordinate does not relieve his superior of criminal responsibility if he knew or had reason to know that the subordinate was about to commit such acts or had done so and the superior failed to take the necessary and reasonable measures to prevent such acts or to punish the perpetrators thereof.'

121 Cassese (n 118 above) 586.

122 ibid 587.

123 ibid.

124 R Goldstone, 'A View from the Prosecution' (2004) 2 JICJ 380, 381.

125 ICTY Press Release, 'The Judges of the Tribunal for the former Yugoslavia express their concern regarding their programme of judicial work for 1995', CC/PIO/003-E (1 February 1995).

126 For an analysis of a suggested internal coordination mechanism in the ICTY, see PM Wald, 'ICTY Judicial Proceedings: An Appraisal from Within' (2004) 2 JICJ 466, 469. Commenting on the creation of a Coordinating Council in 2000 which was designed as a forum for the three ICTY organs to discuss common problems, Judge Patricia Wald has remarked that the expansion of the Council concept to encompass discussion of the Prosecutor's priorities and the judges' concerns would have been useful. Discussion in relation to concluded cases could have been used to identify both good and bad practices. Judge Wald observed: 'While the Prosecutor is still the ultimate decision-maker on whom and when to prosecute, she too might profit from discussion of her overall strategy and priorities. This could be particularly true in the scale-down era, in which the ICTY now finds itself attempting to meet an exit goal within a finite number of years.'

creation phase. From the outset, Prosecutor Goldstone defined the policy based on the level of responsibility of the accused rather than the gravity of the crimes they allegedly committed. He stated that due to the limited financial and human resources available to his office there was 'no choice but to concentrate . . . efforts on individuals who had been in positions of responsibility'.[127] The primary ICTR targets were the political, military, and administrative leadership of Rwanda at the time of the genocide. They were the individuals who planned and supervised the genocide.[128]

In 1995, by letter and public statement, the ICTY judges tried to ensure that the Tribunal's strategy would be focused on the senior leaders who planned the conflict. In 2004, as part of the completion strategy, the judges went further than public statements. They used their authority as the Tribunal's procedural lawmakers to ensure that the Prosecutor would adhere to the seniority guidelines given by the Security Council. In fact, by amending Rule 28(A), the judges introduced for the first time into the ICTY procedural regime some judicial oversight regarding the level of responsibility of the suspects to be indicted. As has been discussed above, as a means to push forward the completion strategies and reduce case backlogs, the goal of the judges of the *ad hoc* Tribunals and the Security Council was to narrow the personal jurisdiction of the Tribunals to the highest-ranking offenders. The Council, however, did not amend the Statutes to achieve this goal. Rather, with the adoption of various resolutions, the Council provided new guidelines to the Tribunals to apply the seniority criterion. Resolution 1503 called on the ICTY and the ICTR to complete all work in 2010 by focusing trials on the 'most senior leaders suspected of being most responsible' for the crimes within the jurisdiction of the Tribunals. Pursuant to Article 18(4) of the ICTY Statute if the Prosecutor determines that a *prima facie* case exists, an indictment shall be prepared and submitted to a judge for confirmation. Commenting on the authority of a confirming judge to dismiss an indictment, Judge Patricia Wald stated in her partial dissenting opinion in the *Jelisić* case:

> The trial Judges are not given any power to reject the indictment because they do not think it is a wise use of the Tribunal's resources or for any other reason other than the lack of a *prima facie* case. Nowhere in the Statute is any Chamber of the ICTY given authority

[127] UN Doc S/1996/778 (1996) para 42.

[128] HB Jallow, 'Prosecutorial Discretion and International Criminal Justice' (2005) 3 JICJ 145, 151. By 1996, the ICTR had indicted 21. It appears from the indictments that Goldstone was moving forward according to the strategy of prosecuting persons most responsible for the genocide at both the national and district level. Only a number of the accused initially indicted were senior political and military figures at the time of the genocide. They included Theoneste Bagosora, who was effectively in control of military and political affairs in Rwanda during the genocide; André Ntagerura, the Minister of Transport and Communications; and Anatole Nsengiyumva, the Chief of Intelligence of the Rwandan Army. All other accused were mid-level leaders, including Jean-Paul Akayesu, the *bourgmestre* of the Taba commune, and Ferdinand Nahimana, the director of the Radio Television Libre des Mille Collines.

to dismiss an indictment or any count therein because it disagrees with the wisdom of the Prosecutor's decision to bring the case.[129]

Thus, in 2003, it was the Prosecutor's prerogative to select the persons to be indicted and the judges had no authority to determine whether the subjects of any new indictments satisfied the seniority standard set by the Security Council in Resolution 1503. As noted by the former ICTY President, Judge Theodor Meron, the application of the seniority criterion spelled out in Resolution 1503 in the indictment process was a 'matter clearly between the Council and the Prosecutor'.[130] If sufficient evidence was presented to make a *prima facie* case, then the indictment had to be confirmed by a judge regardless of the seniority of the accused.[131]

Yet, despite the directions given by the Council, it appears that at least one organ of the *ad hoc* Tribunals was initially slow to push forward with implementation of the completion timelines. In January 2004, the UN Internal Oversight Office presented its review of the work of the ICTY and the ICTR Office of the Prosecutor. The report concluded that 'overall, there was insufficient information to confirm the Tribunals' contention…that the Office of the Prosecutor investigation and prosecution mandates would be completed by 2004 and 2008 respectively'.[132] The Oversight Office put forward detailed recommendations to ensure future transparency in presenting information on the completion strategy to the Security Council and to ensure progress towards ending the activities of the Tribunals.[133] Further concerns were generated in 2003 by the ICTY President's reports that the Prosecutor intended to submit 14 additional indictments for confirmation. This would cause a two-year slippage in the completion timelines previously adopted.[134] Determined to push the Tribunals to stick to the completion timelines set out in Resolution 1503, the Council responded to reports of tardiness by adopting Resolution 1534 which contained two further key directives to the *ad hoc* Tribunals. First, the Prosecutors were called upon to review their caseloads to determine which cases should be transferred to competent national jurisdictions.[135] Secondly, to ensure application of the seniority criterion, the Council called on each Tribunal 'in reviewing and confirming

[129] *Prosecutor v Jelisić* (Appeals Chamber Judgment, Partial Dissenting Opinion of Judge Wald) IT-95-10-A (5 July 2001) para 4. See also ICTY Statute, Art 19(1) entitled 'Review of the Indictment', which provides: 'The judge of the Trial Chamber to whom the indictment has been transmitted shall review it. If satisfied that a *prima facie* case has been established by the Prosecutor, he shall confirm the indictment. If not so satisfied, the indictment shall be dismissed.'

[130] UN Doc S/PV 4838 (2003) 6.

[131] See ICTY Statute, Art 19(1) (n 129 above). The original Rule 28(A) provided that, on receipt of an indictment for review from the Prosecutor, the Registrar shall consult with the President who shall designate one of the permanent Trial Chamber Judges for the review.

[132] 'Report of the Office of Internal Oversight Services on the review of the Office of the Prosecutor at the International Criminal Tribunals for Rwanda and for the former Yugoslavia', UN Doc A/58/677 (2004) summary, para 3.

[133] ibid para 39.

[134] UN Doc S/PV 4838 (2003) 5.

[135] UN Doc S/RES/1534 (2004) para 4.

any new indictments, to ensure that any such indictments concentrate on the most senior leaders suspected of being most responsible for crimes' within the Tribunals' jurisdiction.[136] Under ICTY Rule 47 indictments are reviewed by a judge who shall examine each of the counts charged and determine whether a case exists against the suspect. By calling on the ICTY and the ICTR to ensure that the criterion would be applied during the 'review' and 'confirmation' stage of the indictment process, the Council must have envisaged some form of future judicial supervision of new indictments to ensure that only the most senior leaders proceeded to trial.[137] The Security Council further called on each Tribunal to take all possible measures to complete investigations by the end of 2004 and all work in 2010 and urged the institutions 'to plan and act accordingly'.[138]

Less than two weeks later the ICTY judges transformed the situation pertaining to the involvement of judges in the indictment process. In a response to the call of the Security Council in Resolution 1534 to ensure that new indictments meet the seniority threshold, the ICTY judges amended Rule 28(A) at an Extraordinary Plenary held on 6 April 2004.[139] The amended rule empowers the judges through the Bureau[140] to decide 'whether the indictment, *prima facie*, concentrates on one or more of the most senior leaders suspected of being most responsible for crimes within the jurisdiction of the Tribunal'.[141] By adopting this amendment the judges have created a new procedure which subjects the discretion of the ICTY Prosecutor to judicial supervision. If the Bureau is satisfied that the suspect meets the seniority standard, the indictment shall be submitted to a reviewing judge. However, if the judges' Bureau decides that the standard is not satisfied, the indictment shall be returned to the Prosecutor. Therefore, in accordance with the procedure defined in Rule 28(A) the judges' Bureau ultimately decides whether a person indicted by the Prosecutor is one of the most senior leaders responsible for the crimes committed in the former Yugoslavia and thus whether the indictment will be submitted for confirmation.

Regarding the amendment of Rule 28(A), many commentators agree that there is nothing inherently wrong with the notion of judges participating in decisions related to who should be prosecuted, as is the procedure in many civil law jurisdictions and the International Criminal Court.[142] But there are divergent views in relation to whether or not the independence of the ICTY Prosecutor was encroached upon by the adoption of the new procedure. Arguing that the scope of the amended rule may be *ultra vires*, Daryl Mundis has stated that deciding who

[136] ibid para 5. [137] Raab (n 8 above) 87. [138] UN Doc S/RES 1534 (2004) para 3.

[139] ICTY Press Release, 'Judges Amend Rule 28 at Extraordinary Plenary', JL/P.I.S/837e.

[140] ICTY RPE, Rule 23(A) states that the Bureau shall be composed of the President, the Vice-President, and the Presiding Judges of the Trial Chambers. [141] ICTY RPE, Rule 28(A).

[142] Pursuant to inquisitorial procedures typically instructing magistrates to prepare cases by collecting evidence of both guilt and innocence. In common law jurisdictions the authorities responsible for prosecution generally prepare cases. For the admissibility of cases before the ICC, see Rome Statute of the International Criminal Court, UN Doc A/CONF.183.9 (the 'Rome Statute') Art 17.

to prosecute, by Statute, is a duty arguably placed exclusively within the authority of the Prosecutor.[143] According to Larry Johnson, Rule 28(A) does not violate the Statute; in his opinion, it is 'part and parcel of the completion strategy and a response to the invitation issued by the Security Council in Resolution 1534'.[144] He argues that, just as a reviewing judge, pursuant to Article 19 of the Statute, examines an indictment to decide if a *prima facie* case has been established by the Prosecutor, pursuant to Rule 28(A), the Bureau reviews the indictment to decide if, *prima facie*, it meets the seniority threshold set down by the Security Council. The critical point is that in both instances the Prosecutor has previously assessed a given case and independently decided to indict a suspect.

As specified in the Secretary-General's report on the establishment of the ICTY and pursuant to Article 16(2) of the ICTY Statute, the independent Prosecutor is responsible for the conduct of all investigations and prosecutions and 'shall not seek or receive instructions from any Government or from any other source'.[145] As noted by Johnson, despite the amendment of Rule 28(A) the judges do not intervene in the Prosecutor's decision-making process in relation to which suspects to indict. The Prosecutor acts independently without receiving instructions from any source. Thus, in this regard Rule 28(A) as amended does not limit the discretionary power of the ICTY Prosecutor to open investigations and/or indict suspects. One observer has remarked that '[s]etting the parameters of prosecutorial policy, as opposed to implementing it, is a legislative function'.[146] Since 2000, the Security Council has given guidelines in relation to the appropriate ICTY prosecutorial policy to be applied during the winding-down process and the judges have amended the Rules of Procedure and Evidence accordingly. But with Rule 28(A) the judges have created a procedure to safeguard the most senior leader prosecution policy—it is effectively an indictment filter mechanism to ensure the seniority standard is satisfied in the indictments submitted by the Prosecutor.[147] Arguably, this procedure is a check on the ICTY Prosecutor's discretion, as it is the judges' Bureau that ultimately decides if a suspect falls within the parameters of the senior leader policy. It appears that the Prosecutor has adhered to the seniority criterion and, since the adoption of Resolution 1534, has not indicted any intermediate- or lower-level accused. In the history of the Tribunal, and considering the pressure exerted on the ICTY to commence trials in the early years of its operations, it is interesting to pose the question whether, if Rule 28(A) as amended had existed in 1995, Duško Tadić would have been tried in Germany rather than before the Yugoslavia Tribunal.[148]

143 DA Mundis, 'The Judicial Effects of the "Completion Strategies" on the *Ad hoc* International Criminal Tribunals' (2005) 99 AJIL 142, 148.

144 Johnson (n 39 above) 165–6.

145 See 'Report of the Secretary-General' (n 72 above) paras 85–9.

146 Raab (n 8 above) 99.

147 Johnson (n 39 above) 168.

148 *Prosecutor v Tadić* (Amended Indictment) IT-94-1-I (14 December 1995).

Finally, the disparity of opinion between the judges of the *ad hoc* Tribunals in relation to the possible amendment of the ICTR Rule 28(A) is evidenced by the position taken by the ICTR judges. Reportedly, the judges of the Rwanda Tribunal did not amend the rule as they maintained that judicial scrutiny of the application of the seniority criterion in the indictment process violated the Statute by limiting the independence of the Prosecutor.[149] In her report to the Security Council in 2004, Prosecutor Del Ponte objected to the action taken by the ICTY judges. She stated her opinion that the Rule 28(A) amendment 'was contrary to the Statute and unnecessary in light of the independence given to [the Prosecutor] under the Statute'.[150] However, the members of the Council took no action in relation to the concerns raised by the Prosecutor.[151]

V. Conclusion

By ordering the referral of a case under Rule 11*bis*, the *ad hoc* Tribunals do not relinquish their primacy over national courts. The concurrent jurisdictional relationship between the international tribunals and national courts, enshrined in the Statutes of the Tribunals, is not changed by Rule 11*bis*. What has changed, however, is the policy of the Security Council and the Tribunals for the former Yugoslavia and Rwanda towards invoking their primacy. The revision of Rule 11*bis* by the judges of the *ad hoc* Tribunals, to create a more far-reaching mechanism for the transfer of cases than was previously possible under the rule governing the suspension of an indictment, signalled a new era in the history of the courts. As one principal commentator has put it: 'Within less than a decade, the emphasis was upon sending cases back to national courts, not withdrawing them in favour of the international tribunals.'[152] During the opening era of the ICTY and the ICTR, the Tribunals used their deferral power to transfer cases from national courts to their jurisdiction, to enable them to commence operations. Now in the closing epoch, due to the active role played by the judges as both policy and lawmakers, the Tribunals are empowered to refer cases to national courts, to enable them to end their judicial operations.

In conclusion, the judges' revision of Rule 11*bis* has created a new complementary relationship between international and national jurisdictions underpinned by the distribution of cases and information.[153] This represents a significant stage

[149] Mundis (n 143 above) 148.

[150] UN Doc S/2004/420, 'Enclosure II Assessment of Carla Del Ponte, Prosecutor of the International Criminal Tribunal for the Former Yugoslavia, provided to the Security Council pursuant to paragraph 6 of Security Council resolution 1534', para 41. See also ICTY Weekly Press Briefing, 28 April 2004.

[151] See Johnson (n 39 above) 156.

[152] Schabas (n 2 above) 383.

[153] For an analysis of the new relationship, see M El Zeidy, 'From Primacy to Complementarity and Backwards: (Re)-Visiting Rule 11*bis* of the *ad hoc* Tribunals' (2008) 57 ICLQ 403. El Zeidy posits that the amendment of Rule 11*bis* reflects a new angle in the understanding of primacy and

in the evolution of the ICTY and the ICTR, a phase marked by a legitimate concurrent approach to the prosecution of perpetrators by both the international tribunals and national courts. In many ways, the completion strategies have also acted as a catalyst for judicial reform efforts in Bosnia and Rwanda. As early as 2002, the ICTY advised the Security Council that the creation of the hybrid War Crimes Chamber was a prerequisite to the transfer of intermediate-level accused to Bosnia.[154] The following year, the Office of the High Representative and the ICTY negotiated and signed their Joint Conclusions providing for the establishment of the Chamber.[155] Subsequently, the Office of the High Representative established and co-chaired an Inter-Agency Implementation Task Force, in cooperation with staff from the ICTY and the Bosnian Ministry of Justice, to coordinate the establishment of the Chamber.[156] In fact many governments supported the Chamber in order to advance the completion strategy.[157] The War Crimes Chamber was inaugurated in 2005; since that time the Tribunal has transferred six cases involving ten accused to the institution.[158] In addition to the trials of the accused transferred from the ICTY, in 2008, the Chamber was running trials against approximately fifty other suspects.[159]

Sadly, Rwanda has not received the same level of assistance from the international community to build its national judicial capacity to the standard required by the ICTR for the transfer of cases.[160] If a hybrid chamber similar to the

complementarity: the rule creates a system of complementarity but does not rule out the tribunal's primacy.

[154] 'Report on Judicial Status' (n 34 above) para 85.

[155] The Office of the High Representative to Bosnia and Herzegovina (OHR) was created under Annex 10 of the Dayton Peace Agreement. It is an international organization which is responsible for the implementation of the civilian aspects of the Peace Agreement. See also: 'Joint Conclusions of the ICTY and the Office of the High Representative regarding the domestic prosecution of war crimes in Bosnia and Herzegovina', The Hague, 21 February 2003, on file with the author. See also: ICTY Press Release, 'OHR-ICTY Working Group on Development of BiH Capacity for War-Crimes Trials Successfully Completed', OHR/P.I.S/731e.

[156] For details and an analysis of the establishment of the War Crimes Chamber, see F Donlon, 'Rule of Law: From the International Criminal Tribunal for the Former Yugoslavia to the War Crimes Chamber of Bosnia and Herzegovina', in DF Haynes (ed), *Deconstructing the Reconstruction: Human Rights and Rule of Law in Postwar Bosnia and Herzegovina* (Aldershot: Ashgate, 2008).

[157] ibid. At the first international fund-raising conference for the Chamber, donors pledged a total of €18.7m.

[158] *Prosecutor v Stanković* (Decision on Rule 11*bis* Referral) IT-96-23/2-AR11*bis*.1 (1 September 2005); *Prosecutor v Ljubičić* (Decision on Appeal Against Decision on Referral Under Rule 11*bis*) IT-00-41-AR11*bis* (4 July 2006); *Janković* (Decision on Rule 11*bis* Referral) (n 93 above); *Prosecutor v Rašević and Todović* (Decision on Savo Todović's Appeal Against Decisions on Referral Under Rule 11*bis*) IT-97-25/1-AR11*bis*.2 (4 September 2006); *Mejakić* (Decision on Joint Defence Appeal) (n 93 above); *Trbić* (Decision on Referral of Case Under Rule 11*bis* with Confidential Annex) IT-05-88/1-PT (27 April 2007).

[159] For War Crimes Chamber statistics, see '2008 Annual Report of the Registry for Section I and II of the Court of Bosnia and Herzegovina'. For a critical assessment of the work of the War Crimes Chamber, see *Narrowing the Impunity Gap: Trials before Bosnia's War Crimes Chamber* (Human Rights Watch, February 2007).

[160] To date the ICTR has denied the transfer of five accused to Rwanda for trial: see *Munyakazi* (Decision on Prosecution's Appeal) (n 112 above); *Prosecutor v Kanyarukiga* (Decision on the Prosecution's Appeal Against Decision on Referral Under Rule 11*bis*) ICTR-2002-78-R11*bis*

Bosnian model had been established in Rwanda, most probably, the ICTR would have, by now, successfully transferred accused under Rule 11*bis* to the country for trial. Nevertheless, the cooperation between the ICTR and the Rwandan authorities in relation to the future referral of cases is strong. In 2008, the ICTR Prosecutor, at the request of the national prosecution service in Rwanda, engaged in training seminars for national prosecutors and investigators on best practices in the investigation and prosecution of international crimes and evidence management.[161] In addition, the Rwandan Organic Law on the transfer of cases from the ICTR has been amended to allay the concerns expressed by the ICTR in relation to trials before a single judge and the willingness of defence witnesses to testify in Rwanda.[162] The Prosecutor General of Rwanda has informed the Security Council that '[a]t this crucial juncture, Rwanda still believes that the major interest, shared with the Security Council, is to find an amicable conclusion of the *ad hoc* mandate of the Tribunal'.[163]

The former President of the Yugoslavia Tribunal, Judge Fausto Pocar, has questioned whether, by building its legacy in the Balkan region through partnership and cooperation, the ICTY is implementing a 'continuation' rather than a completion strategy.[164] It appears the Rwandan government also has a similar vision of the ICTR's legacy—it is hoping for a legacy that complements ongoing judicial reform efforts in the country and one that supports the growth of national institutions.[165] In this respect, in particular by designing and adopting Rule 11*bis* to regulate the case referral process, the judges of the *ad hoc* Tribunals have not only contributed to the legacy of the ICTY and the ICTR, they have also contributed to the future of international criminal justice by a creating a robust procedural regime which shows how complementarity can work in practice.

(30 October 2008); *Hategekimana* (Decision on Prosecution's Appeal) (n 98 above); *Prosecutor v Kayishema* (Decision on the Proseuctor's Request for Referral of Case to the Republic of Rwanda) ICTR-01-67-R11*bis* (16 December 2008); *Prosecutor v Gatete* (Decision on the Prosecutor's Request for Referral to the Republic of Rwanda) ICTR-2000-61-R11*bis* (17 November 2008). One reason for the rejection of the Prosecutor's requests for referral was an inconsistency between two Organic Laws which resulted in the concern that life imprisonment could amount to life imprisonment 'in isolation'. Other reasons included the unwillingness of defence witnesses to travel to Rwanda for trial, thus jeopardizing the accused's right to a fair trial and trial by a single judge.

[161] UN Doc S/PV.5904 (2008) 11.

[162] In April 2009, Rwanda adopted the Organic Law amending the Law on the transfer of cases to the Republic of Rwanda from the ICTR and from other states, *Official Gazette of the Republic of Rwanda*, Year 46 (19 March 2007). According to the amended law, the President of the High Court may now appoint a bench of three judges for trials rather than a single judge trial. Additionally, if a witness cannot appear for the defence, the law provides that the witness may testify abroad before a national or a foreign judge.

[163] UN Doc S/PV.5904 (2008) 29.

[164] F Pocar, 'Completion or Continuation Strategy? Appraising Problems and Possible Developments in Building the Legacy of the ICTY' (2008) 6 JICJ 655, 656.

[165] See the comments of the Prosecutor General of Rwanda, Mr Ngoga, in UN Doc S/PV.5904 (2008) 29.

Index